PILGRIM JOURNEY

John Henry Newman 1801–1845

VINCENT FERRER BLEHL, S. J.

BURNS & OATES

London and New York

BURNS & OATES
A Continuum imprint
The Tower Building
11 York Road, London SE1 7NX

ISBN 0 86012 3 111

First published 2001

Typeset by CentraServe Ltd, Saffron Walden, Essex
Printed and bound in Great Britain by
Biddles, Guildford and King's Lynn

THE PILGRIM

There stray'd a while, amid the woods of Dart,
    One who could love them, but who durst not love.
A vow had bound him, ne'er to give his heart
    To streamlet bright, nor soft secluded grove.
    'Twas a hard humbling task, onwards to move
His easy-captured eyes from each fair spot,
    With unattach'd and lonely step to rove
O'er happy meads, which soon its print forgot:-
Yet kept he safe his pledge, prizing his **pilgrim-lot.**

(*VV*, 61)

'For years I must have had something of an habitual
notion, though it was latent, and had never led me to
distrust my own convictions that my mind had not
found its ultimate rest, and that in some sense or
other I was on a **journey.**'

(*Apo.*, 119)

Contents

Acknowledgements

In March 1957 I arrived at the Birmingham Oratory to assist Fr Stephen Dessain in setting up the project of publishing the *Letters and Diaries* of Newman, of which I edited two volumes. Since then I have been involved in Newman research which I pursued mostly at the Oratory archives where I experienced the well-known hospitality of the Oratorian Fathers, a tradition going back to Newman.

In 1980 I relinquished my position as Professor and Chairman of the English Department of Fordham University, New York, to become Chairman of the Historical Commission whose task was to investigate Newman's life, virtues and reputation for sanctity. This work was completed in 1986, when I was appointed Postulator of the Cause for Newman's canonization with the commission to draw up the case for Newman's sanctity. During all this time I was provided with room and board at the Birmingham Oratory. On matters pertaining to the Cause I continue to work in close co-operation with Fr Gregory Winterton, who has done so much to promote it. I take this opportunity once again of expressing my appreciation of their kindness and for permission to publish in their entirety for the first time Newman's prayers composed as an Anglican, as well as excerpts from unpublished letters of Newman and of his correspondents.

In researching and writing this book I have profited from regular discussion with two close friends and colleagues: Gerard Tracey, Archivist and present editor of the *Letters and Diaries*, and Günter Biemer, the distinguished German Newman scholar and Director of the Internationale Deutsche Newman Gesellschaft. The former also provided me with materials from Newman's contemporaries, and checked unpublished letters for accuracy, so that I did not have to rely only on typed copies which were also made available to me.

I wish to thank St Bede's Publications (Petersham, Mass.) for permission to use a few paragraphs from my book *The White Stone*. Finally I owe a special debt of gratitude to Anne Schwarz for her patient typing of the manuscript.

Abbreviations

Apo.	*Apologia pro Vita Sua*
Ari.	*The Arians of the Fourth Century*
Ath. I, II	*Select Treatises of St. Athanasius*, 2 vols.
AW	*John Henry Newman: Autobiographical Writings*, ed. Henry Tristram; London and New York 1956
BOA	Birmingham Oratory Archives
CS	*Catholic Sermons of Cardinal Newman*, ed. at the Birmingham Oratory, London 1957
DA	*Discussions and Arguments on Various Subjects*
Dev.	*An Essay on the Development of Christian Doctrine*
Diff. I, II	*Certain Difficulties felt by Anglicans in Catholic Teaching*, 2 vols.
Ess. I, II	*Essays Critical and Historical*, 2 vols.
FL	Ed. Dorothea Mozley, *Newman Family Letters*, London 1962
GA	*An Essay in Aid of a Grammar of Assent*
HS I, II, III	*Historical Sketches*, 3 vols.
Idea	*The Idea of a University*
Jfc.	*Lectures on the Doctrine of Justification*
KC	*Correspondence of John Henry Newman with John Keble and Others*, 1839–45, ed. at the Birmingham Oratory, 1917

LD	*The Letters and Diaries of John Henry Newman*, ed. Charles Stephen Dessain *et al.*, vols. I–VIII, Oxford 1978–99, XI–XXII, London 1961–72, XXIII–XXXI, Oxford 1973–7
LG	*Loss and Gain: The Story of a Convert*
Med.	*Meditations and Devotions of the Late Cardinal Newman*
Mix.	*Discourses addressed to Mixed Congregations*
Moz. I, II	*Letters and Correspondence of John Henry Newman during his Life in the English Church*, ed. Anne Mozley, 2 vols., London 1891
OS	*Sermons preached on Various Occasions*
PPS	*Parochial and Plain Sermons*, 8 vols.
Prepos.	*Lectures on the Present Position of Catholics in England*
SD	*Sermons bearing on Subjects of the Day*
SE	*Stray Essays on Controversial Subjects, variously illustrated*, Private 1890
Ser. I	*John Henry Newman Sermons 1824–1843*, vol. I, ed. Placid Murray, OSB, Oxford 1991
Ser. II	*John Henry Newman Sermons 1824–1843*, vol. II, ed. Vincent Ferrer Blehl, S. J., Oxford 1993
SN	*Sermon Notes of John Henry Cardinal Newman, 1845–1876*, ed. Fathers of the Birmingham Oratory, London 1913
US	*Fifteen Sermons preached before the University of Oxford*
VM I, II	*The Via Media*, 2 vols.
VRS	*Verses on Religious Subjects*
VV	*Verses on Various Occasions*
Ward I, II	Wilfrid Ward, *The Life of John Henry Cardinal Newman*, 2 vols. London 1912
W. G. Ward	Wilfrid Ward, *William George Ward and the Oxford Movement*, Second edition, London 1890

Introduction

The present biography explores Newman's growth in holiness and Truth, i.e., religious Truth, and the mutual influence of one upon the other. It was the quest for these two goals which gave meaning and direction to his life as an Anglican. The former is the more difficult to explore, since it involves not only a study of his words and actions but of his inner life and motivation, which are often hidden. Yet materials for such a task exist, though hitherto not fully exploited. For example, Newman said that he could bear an examination in the writings of Thomas Scott. What precisely and in detail was there in these writings that so formed him that he could say that to their author he almost owed his soul. So also Newman's *Verses on Various Occasions*, though rarely rising to the level of poetry, are rich in insights into his interior life especially during the Mediterranean voyage. From 1816 to 1837 he composed prayers which are not only put into their proper context but published for the first time in their entirety. So, too, Newman's sermons often shed light on his own interior life because he not only practised what he preached but preached what he practised. Moreover there are at times oblique references to personal spiritual experiences in his sermons, and these are ferreted out.

It may be questioned how can one discern and trace growth in holiness when it is primarily a spiritual process? Here Newman himself is of help. In an important sermon, 'Sudden Conversions', he likened growth in holiness to the 'slow, gradual and continual' growth of plants. One day 'they grow more than another, they make a shoot or at least we are attracted to their growth on that day by some accidental circumstances, and it remained on our memory'. (*PPS* VIII, 15, 225–6)

In relinquishing Evangelicalism he revised his view of conversion, which he claimed was not a one-time affair, as the Evangelicals believed, but rather a series of calls by God to an individual at various times in his life under the guidance of divine Providence, to which he responds in faith. It is possible therefore to discern and map out these various conversions or stages of spiritual development, as will be shown in detail.

In 1874 Newman noted in his private journal that his habit was not to write or publish 'without a call. What I have written has been for the most part . . . works done in some office I held or engagement I had made – all my Sermons are such, my Lectures on the Prophetical Office, on Justification, my Essays in the British Critic and translation of St Athanasius.' In light of this I have considered his writings not only in themselves but also in relation to his spiritual life which was a reciprocal one. For example, Newman maintained that he adopted the *Via Media* from the Anglican divines, not on the basis of private judgement, but because he felt it a *duty* imposed by conscience. Conversely the study of the Monophysite controversy which destroyed his view of the *Via Media* prompted him to enter on a stricter life of prayer and asceticism.

Though Newman maintained 'that a man's life lies in his letters', surely not there alone. I have relied not only on his letters but also on a judicious choice of the other half of his correspondence both published and unpublished. I have also quoted from Newman's contemporaries with excerpts, a number of which have been hitherto unused. Though quite familiar with the many books on the Oxford Movement and recent attempts, not entirely successful, to reinterpret it, in fact involving certain historical distortions, I have concentrated on the essentials without repeating endless details, and have highlighted the spiritual, ascetical and religious impact of Newman on it, since this seems to have been lost sight of in concentrating on the theological controversies.

Newman's life as an Anglican was not only a journey into holiness and Truth, it was also a journey of self-discovery. I have not tried to cover up or hide his defects: for example, his cocksuredness up to 1839 and his rudeness in letters to Roman Catholics. In time he became aware that actions spring from multiple motives, some perhaps hidden from consciousness. Towards the end of his journey, after a prolonged period of self-examination, he became convinced he was not under a delusion, he was not acting out of *ressentiment*, that he was speculatively certain that the Roman Catholic Church was indeed the true Church of Christ, and that he had a call in conscience to join it. Only one who had grown in deep self-knowledge could have written the honest and penetrating analysis of his state of soul which he composed before his ordination in Rome. (*AW*, 239–42, 245–8)

I hope I have laid to rest the view that Newman became a recluse at Littlemore, out of touch with what was going on, withdrawn, almost completely shut up within himself – words used to describe him there. So, too, I have tried to correct misunderstandings of him after Tract 90. In the *Apologia* Newman remarked that 'from the end of 1841, I was on my deathbed, as regards my membership with the Anglican Church'. Some critics and biographers have viewed the life of Newman after Tract 90 from this perspective. But this is like telling in advance the ending of a story, thereby robbing the prior narrative of events of its drama and suspense. Because he was becoming more and more convinced that the Church of England was in schism and the Church of Rome the true Church, it did not follow in his mind that he should or would leave the Church of England, and this for a variety of reasons, as will be seen. Moreover, Newman again and again affirmed he did not know where Providence was leading him and the Movement as well. That is why he could truthfully say in the *Apologia* that only gradually did he become aware of being on his death-bed as regards the Anglican Church, and though he intended 'gradually to fall back into Lay Communion', he 'never contemplated leaving the Church of England'. It was probably only at the beginning of 1845 that he did so.

It could be that some readers may be put off by the account of Newman's spiritual life as presented in Chapters 2 and 3, but it must be borne in mind that this is partly owing to the tone and language of his private journals, which were not meant for publication. Moreover, Newman was still a novice in the spiritual life, and few mature members of religious congregations would like their youthful journals revealed to the world. Nevertheless without such a detailed treatment of his inner life the continuity and change involved in his growth in holiness would not be seen in their proper perspective. Would the *Parochial and Plain Sermons* be so rich in realizations of the Christian mysteries, full of psychological insights, and abounding in quotations from Scripture, if Newman had not trained himself from his youthful years in rigorous self-examination, meditation and assiduous study of the whole of the Scriptures?

That John Henry Newman is a classic spiritual writer is commonly acknowledged. His spiritual doctrine, however, is contained mostly in sermons, and some commentators thought that it is not a distinctive spirituality. Although elements of it had been recognized, I attempted in *The White Stone: the Spiritual Theology of John Henry Newman* (Petersham, Mass., St Bede's Publications 1994) to present for the first time a comprehensive synthesis of his unique spirituality. I hope that the present biography will serve as a complement to that earlier work.

NOTE

Newman's punctuation, capitalization, grammar and spelling (even when obsolete) have been retained in all quotations from the writings, published and unpublished. Diamond brackets are used to indicate alternative words written by him above a word or words.

CHAPTER ONE

Early Years

John Henry Newman was born in Old Broad Street, London, 21 February 1801. The site is now marked by a blue plaque on the Visitors' entrance to the London Stock Exchange. He was the eldest of six children born to John Newman and Jemima Fourdrinier, who had been married on 24 September 1799 in St Mary's, Lambeth, London. He was baptized, 9 April 1801, in the church of St Benet Fink, no longer in existence. His brothers and sisters, to whom he became greatly attached, were Charles (b. 16 June 1802), Harriett (b. 10 December 1803), Francis (b. 27 June 1805), Jemima (b. 19 May 1808), and Mary (b. 9 November 1809). Their father, a son of a Cambridge man, whose forebears can be traced back at least to the seventeenth-century, was a partner in a small banking firm. Their mother was the daughter of a paper manufacturer of Huguenot ancestry who came to England on the Revocation of the Edict of Nantes. The Newmans were sufficiently well off financially to afford a town and country house, the former at 17 Southampton Street (now Southampton Place) near Bloomsbury, to which the family moved before the birth of Charles.

Newman's childhood was a happy one and all his life he remembered the house at Ham in great detail, so much so that he said he could pass an examination in it. He loved it, and by chance many years later he found his mother '(who was very reserved in her feelings) had as great a love of it. She seemed so surprised.' When, at school, he dreamed of heaven, it was of Ham. He remembered clearly the different trees in the garden and he recalled, 'the mower's scythe, cutting the lawn, used to sound so sweetly as I lay in a crib'. In 1840 he said he could hardly think of it 'without tears'. (*LD* XV, 396–7; *LD* VII, 340)

Although it is often said that he was raised in an Evangelical household, this is not true, as his brother Francis testified. Moreover, his parents loved to go to concerts, theatre and dances, all of which were frowned upon by Evangelicals. His parents were ordinary members of the Church, neither high nor low. They went to church on Sunday and participated in evening prayers. Of the latter the only ones he remembered later were two hymns by Isaac Watts which formed part of them. The first began:

AN EVENING SONG

And now another day is gone,
I'll sing my Maker's praise,
My comforts ev'ry hour make known
His providence and grace.

But how my childhood runs to waste!
My sins, how great their sum!
Lord, give me pardon for the past,
His providence and grace.

I lay my body down to sleep,
Let angels guard my head,
And through the hours of darkness keep
Their watch around my bed.

With cheerful heart I close mine eyes,
Since Thou wilt not remove;
And in the morning let me rise
Rejoicing in Thy love.

The other was a Sunday hymn, but Newman remembered only the lines in it, 'I have been there and fain would go 'Tis like a little heaven below.' (*AW*, 150) The hymn begins:

O Lord, how delightful 'tis to see
A whole assembly worship Thee,
At once they sing, at once they pray,
They hear of heaven, and learn the way.

I have been there, and still would go;
'tis like a little heaven below;
not all my pleasures, nor my play
should tempt me to forget this day,

Oh, write it on my memory, Lord,
the texts and doctrines of thy Word,
that I may break thy laws no more,
but serve thee better than before!

With thoughts of Christ, and things divine,
fill up this foolish heart of mine;
that, hoping pardon through his blood,
I may lie down, and wake with God.

It might seem extravagant to begin an account of Newman's spiritual life with his childhood imagination of the invisible world, had he not himself thought it significant enough to begin the account of his religious opinions with it 'as having a bearing on my later convictions'. He quotes from his own recollections when he was grown up. 'I used to wish the Arabian Tales were true: my imagination ran on unknown influences, on magical powers, and talismans . . . I thought life might be a dream, or I an angel, and all this world a deception, my fellow-angels by a playful device concealing themselves from me, and deceiving me with the semblance of a material world.' Nor was this entirely erased, for when he was fifteen years old, 'Reading in the Spring of 1816 a sentence from [Dr Watts'] "Remnants of Time," entitled "the Saints unknown to the world", to the effect that "there is nothing in their figure or countenance to distinguish them," &c.,&c., I supposed he spoke of Angels who lived in the world, as it were disguised.' (*Apo.*, 2)

Nor can these opinions be summarily dismissed as owing to childish or boyish credulity fading away in the light of mature reflection, for there is the astonishing sermon preached on the Feast of the Holy Innocents in 1833, 'The Mind of Little Children'. (*PPS* II, 6) In it he speaks of the child as having come 'out of the hands of God, with all lessons and thoughts of Heaven freshly marked upon him', or in the words of Wordsworth, 'trailing clouds of glory'. True he has the stain of sin and though it is washed away, there remains in him a root of evil. But this we know full well – we know it from our own recollection of ourselves, and our experience of children – that there is in the infant soul, in the first years of its regenerate state, a discernment of the unseen world in the things that are seen, a realization of what is Sovereign and Adorable, and an incredulity and ignorance about what is transient and changeable, which mark it as the fit emblem of the matured Christian, when weaned from things temporal, and living in the intimate conviction of the Divine Presence.

Newman precludes any possible misinterpretation that he is affirming that a child has formed principles, habits of obedience, true discrimination between the visible and the unseen, 'such as God promises to reward for Christ's sake, in those who come to years of discretion.' Evil there is in him, but 'he has this one great gift, that he seems to have lately come from God's presence, and not to understand the language of this visible scene, or how it is a temptation, how it is a veil interposing itself between the soul and God'. Newman goes on to assert 'the distinctness' with which conscience tells the child the difference between right and wrong.

Newman was brought up with a love of the Bible, taught by his mother but especially by his grandmother and aunt. ' "And Jacob said, It is enough – Joseph my son is yet alive, I will go and see him before I die." They are the words which made the first impression on my mind of any in the Bible, before I was six years old, perhaps a good deal earlier.' (*LD* XIII, 267) His knowledge and love of it would grow stronger and stronger with the years. From it he learned the doctrine of God's providence which he later said was nearly the only doctrine held with a real assent by the multitudes who were raised on Bible religion. (*GA*, 57) There is in the *Grammar of Assent* an important passage, generally considered to be autobiographical, in which he uses the example of a child of five or six years who comes to the age of reason and 'who is safe from influences destructive of his religious instincts'. It is used to show how it is possible to have not just a notional but a real apprehension of the existence of God and His providence, so that 'he has that within him which actually vibrates, responds and gives a deep meaning to the lessons of his first teachers about the will and the providence of God'. (*GA*, 115)

> Supposing he has offended his parents, he will all alone and without effort, as if it were the most natural of acts, place himself in the presence of God, and beg of Him to set him right with them. Let us consider how much is contained in this simple act. First, it involves the impression on his mind of an unseen Being with whom he is in immediate relation, and that relation so familiar that he can address Him whenever he himself chooses; next, of One whose goodwill towards him he is assured of, and can take for granted – nay, who loves him better, and is nearer to him, than his parents; further, of one who can hear him, wherever he happens to be, and who can read his thoughts, for his prayer need not be vocal; lastly, of One who can effect

a critical change in the state of feeling of others towards him. That is, we shall not be wrong in holding that this child has in his mind the image of an Invisible Being, who exercises a particular providence among us, who is present every where, who is heart-reading, heart-changing, ever-accessible, open to impetration. . . . (*GA*, 112–3)

It should be noted that the image Newman speaks of need not be a visual one; in fact, it may be interpreted as auditory since he often speaks of conscience as the 'voice of God' in the soul. That this was based upon his personal experience as a child is confirmed by his statement in 1843, 'God put it into my heart, when 5 or 6 years old, to ask *what* and *why* I was.' (*AW*, 223) Newman goes on to show how this image also contains an apprehension of God as a Lawgiver who commands one to do the right and avoid what is evil.

Finding God in conscience, and the realization of God's personal providence became fundamental principles of Newman's life and spirituality, and, moreover, they shed light on what he meant when he said that his first conversion was a 'returning to, a renewing of, principles, under the power of the Holy Spirit, which I had *already* felt, and in a measure acted on, when young'. (*AW*, 172)

At the age of seven Newman was sent to a private school run by Dr Nicholas, a kind and friendly man, for whom Newman conceived an affectionate attachment. For his part the head said 'no boy had run through the school, from the bottom to the top, so rapidly as John Newman'. (*AW*, 29) On 25 May 1810 he was studying Ovid and Greek; by November 19 he did his first lesson in Virgil; on 11 February 1811 he composed his first Latin verses; 25 May 1812 he began Homer; 26 January 1813 Mr Mullins, the curate of St James, Piccadilly, presented him with a Greek New Testament. (*LD* I, 6–13)

In January 1810 the boy began to keep a diary, which he continued most of his life. From the entries and his letters home it is evident he had the normal boy's appetite for greengages, oranges, sugar candies, tarts and almond cakes, and he looked forward to 'mince pies, Turkies, and the other good things of Christmas'. His father gave him a violin and he took lessons. He used to call Beethoven 'the Dutchman' (to plague my Music Master) because he was 'Van' Beethoven. Later he would call him 'a gigantic nightingale'. He did not engage much in sports, but though he did not swim, he used to dive, to ride, and to walk long distances – exercises he kept up, on and off, for a good deal of his life. He also took dancing lessons.

He was not isolated from his fellow students; in fact, he started a Spy Club, of which he was the Master. There is a cartoon done by 'our enemy' in which he is in command of the group. He wrote the *Spy* and the *Anti-Spy*, against each other, modelled on the *Spectator*. He also wrote the *Beholder*, which ran through forty numbers. He composed Latin verses and wrote a letter to Harriett in verse:

> Tell Jemima.
> Once upon a time; a
> Letter came from her pen
> And I did not answer it then:
> Therefore tell her I'm her debtor
> Of a long agreeable letter:
> Of pleasant school and different places.
> I'll inform her how the case is:
> Pray do send me then a letter, a
> Nice epistle: Yours et cetera
> John H Newman (*LD* I, 16–7)

Newman appended a note to this in which he thinks he took the last rhyme 'cetera' from Thomas Moore's *The Twopenny Post Bag* (1813). He never wrote without an eye to style and there are examples of his writing in that of Addison and Gibbon. He was a pretty good imitator, and this went on until he discovered his own style in writing sermons. Many a writer before him learned his craft from first imitating someone else.[1]

Newman acted in several of Terence's comedies, in one of which, *Eunuchus*, he took the part of a woman. Later he would coach the students at the Oratory School in acting, though he expurgated the text. Before leaving Ealing he already began to help with the education of his sisters, a process which continued not only at Trinity but later as well. Harriett was the oldest and closest in age, and once he told her that she was the one who understood him the most, but it was to Jemima that he later turned for sympathy and understanding in his anguish about leaving the Church of England. Mary was the darling of them all. John felt her loveliness was 'unearthly'. Although as an elder brother he occasionally tried to boss them, this was taken in good spirit.

Newman left no record of his religious life at Ealing except for his first conversion which took place the last six months before he left. There is a Book of Common Prayer in the possession of Dorothea Mozley, with a

note on the inside cover: 'My mother promised to give me a Prayer Book
– I was impatient she did not do so at once – and without leave, in an
impatient headstrong mood, went and bought this for her – which she,
though she must have felt it, without saying a word, gave me. J H N'.
The date of the gift was 30 January 1815. (*LD* I, 14, n. 4) He later
recalled that in the same year he thought he would like to be virtuous but
not religious. 'I did not see the *meaning* of loving God.' He contended
against his tutor, Mr Mayers, in favour of Pope's *Essay on Man*. 'What, I
said, can be more free from objection than it? does it not expressly
inculcate, ' "Virtue alone is happiness below" '? (*AW*, 169)

At this time Newman began to read sceptical works such as Paine's
Tracts against the Old Testament and Hume's *Essays*, which apparently
he enjoyed. He read some verses of Voltaire denying the immortality of
the soul, and said something like this to himself, 'How dreadful, but how
plausible.' In addition to this sceptical attitude of mind, he seems to have
fallen into serious sin, so much so that later he confessed to John Keble,
that at that time he was 'living a life of sin, with a very dark conscience
and a very profane spirit'. In his journal he described himself at that time
as 'more like a devil than a wicked boy'. It does not seem that these can
be dismissed as pious exaggerations common to saints and holy persons.
For example, in *Meditations and Devotions* he confesses to having lifted
up his hand against the face of Christ: 'Turn back in memory, and
recollect the time, the day, the hour, when by wilful mortal sin, by
scoffing at sacred things, or by profaneness, or by dark hatred of this thy
Brother, or by acts of impurity, or by deliberate rejection of God's voice,
or in any other devilish way known to thee, thou has struck The All-holy
One.'

It is difficult to see how this confession would apply to Newman at any
time after his first conversion. The use of the term 'devilish', moreover,
tends to confirm the previous reference to his earlier life. But there is
confirmation also in some of his verses on his Guardian Angel: 'And
when, ere boyhood yet was gone, / My rebel spirit fell, / Oh! thou didst
see, and shudder too, / Yet bear each deed of hell.' He was, if not in a
state of unbelief, at least in one of scepticism. In a letter to Sr Mary
Imelda Poole in 1856 he wrote, 'I was at Bridgewater [*sic*], forty years ago
next July an ungodly, unbelieving boy of 15.'

On several occasions Newman describes a boy who had hitherto,
despite transgressions, respected the authority of conscience, but upon
emerging into youth deliberately sins and falls from religious practice into
unbelief or scepticism. The gradual transgression of the first command-

ment of the Law, he continues, 'is generally attended by a transgression of the fifth'. In this passage and in a similar one, he describes how this leads to a loss of enjoyment of one's home and family circle: 'His curiosity now takes a new turn; he listens to views and discussions which are inconsistent with the sanctity of religious faith. . . . As time goes on, however, living with companions who have no fixed principles . . . or worse, hearing or reading what is directly against religion, at length, without being conscious of it, he admits a sceptical influence upon his mind . . . he does not recognize it . . . till some day suddenly, from some accident, the fact breaks upon him, and he sees clearly that he is an unbeliever himself.

Another indication that this is autobiographical is his affirmation that such an experience leads to a loss of enjoyment of one's home and family circle. In the verses 'Mortal Sin' he writes that 'I sought awhile / The scenes I prized before; / But parent's praise and sister's smile / Stirred my cold heart no more.' Several other sets of verses, 'The Stains of Sin', 'The Wounds of Sin', and 'The Scars of Sin'; make reference to this youthful encounter with sin.

FIRST CONVERSION

In March 1816 Newman's father's bank stopped payment in the aftermath of the end of the Napoleonic wars. All payments were made by the end of the month, but the bank did not reopen, causing a problem for him and the family. The house at Southampton Street was let, and in the autumn the family settled in Alton, where Mr Newman tried unsuccessfully to manage a brewery. It must have been a terrible blow to him and his wife. Arrangements were made for John to stay at Ealing for the summer. He fell ill, the first of three illnesses which were accompanied by profound spiritual experiences. 'The first keen, terrible one, when I was a boy of 15, and it made me a Christian – with experiences before and after, awful and known only to God.' (*AW*, 150) This is another indication that Newman did not consider himself a Christian at the time. The dates of his conversion Newman listed as 1 August to 21 December when he left school.

Fortunately Mr Mayers, a young master at the school, won the boy's confidence and he became his spiritual guide. He had gone through a conversion and was now an Evangelical. Newman later remarked that 'it was a time of reflection, and when the influence of Mr Mayers would have room to act upon me. Also, I was terrified at the heavy hand of God which came down upon me.' (*AW*, 150) Fr Dessain thought that this referred to the family reverses and his own illness, but there is no way of knowing for sure. The experiences before and after the illness 'being known only to God' can only be conjectured. If one recollects that he had been 'living a life of sin, with a very dark conscience', perhaps his description of the feelings that accompany a sinful conscience may shed some light on it.

In the *Grammar of Assent* Newman enumerates, for example, 'various perturbations of mind which are characteristic of a bad conscience, and may be considerable, – self-reproach, poignant shame, haunting remorse, chill dismay at the prospect of the future'. (*GA*, 108) In a sermon he affirms 'conscience is severe, and even stern. It does not speak of forgiveness, but of punishment; it does not tell him how he is to get better. It suggests to him a future judgment; it does not tell him how he can avoid it. Moreover it does not tell him how he is to get better . . . he feels himself in bondage to a tyranny which, alas! he loves too well, even while he hates it.' (*OS*, 67) In the light of these terrifying experiences one can understand and appreciate Newman's gratitude for his conversion:

O who can tell the number and the heinousness of my sins! who can show forth worthily the innumerable mercies of God or the benefits He continues to shower upon me, while I remained nevertheless in hardened obstinancy, till at last, O incomprehensible goodness! He deigned to turn me from the error of my ways, to open my eyes and to guide me into the right path, to give me His Holy Spirit, and to make me fall down before Him. (Appendix of Prayers)

Even more important than Mr Mayers' teaching were the authors he put in the boy's hands. The most influential of these was Thomas Scott of Aston Sandford, the grandfather of Sir George Scott, the architect. Thomas Scott was 'the writer who made a deeper impression on my mind than any other, and to whom (humanly speaking) I almost owe my soul', Newman wrote in the *Apologia*. In a letter to Lord Lifford, Newman wrote, 'In Scott's works I could bear to stand an examination. From the age of 15, when first I knew them, I was attracted by the earnestness and manliness and independence of his character; he seemed to me one who was willing to stand on God's side against the world, and I have never lost this impression of him.' (12 September 1837, *LD* VI, 129) Besides his unworldliness Newman admired his opposition to Antinominianism, and the practical character of his writings. *The Force of Truth*, the history of Scott's conversion, deeply impressed Newman. 'He followed truth wherever it led him, beginning with Unitarianism, and ending in a zealous faith in the Holy Trinity. It was he who planted deep in my mind that fundamental truth of religion.' (*Apo.*, 5)

Two other works fed Newman's inchoate spiritual life: William Law's *Serious Call to a Devout and Holy Life* (1729) and Philip Doddridge's *Rise and Progress of Religion in the Soul*. William Law (1665–1761) was a Nonjuror and defender of Christianity against eighteenth-century rationalism. His book influenced, among others, Dr Johnson, Edward Gibbon, Thomas Scott. Theologically opposed to Calvinism, it nevertheless impressed upon Newman 'the main Catholic doctrine of the warfare between the city of God and the powers of darkness'. (*Apo.*, 6) The other work by Doddridge (1702–51) Newman later gave to several of the parishioners he visited in St Clement's parish. (*LD* I, 196, 234, 252) In a subsequent passage in the *Apologia* Newman affirmed that 'from the age of fifteen, dogma has been the fundamental principle of my religion'. Spirituality without a foundation in dogma was henceforth incomprehensible to him. 'I cannot enter into the idea of any other sort of religion; religion, as a mere sentiment, is to me a dream and a mockery. As well can there be filial love without the fact of a father, as devotion without the fact of a Supreme Being.' (*Apo.*, 49) Newman later gave a fuller explanation of this fundamental principle when exploring the question of the development of doctrine. (*Dev.*, 346–52)[2]

From Scott, Newman learned the two great obstacles to spiritual growth are sin and worldliness. Indeed the two are related. 'What is more productive of immorality and mischief among mankind? Does not an inordinate pursuit of worldly objects occasion a vast proportion of the crime and miseries that fill the earth?' Only the doctrine of the cross 'can break the fatal association in his [the believer's] mind between the idea of happiness and that of worldly prosperity'. The Christian is represented in the Scriptures 'as a soldier, engaged in an arduous warfare with potent enemies,' with an evil world, which is Satan's grand engine in all his stratagems and assaults'. He uses the things of the world to seduce men to evil conduct, but also and more commonly 'into an inexpedient or excessive use or pursuit of worldly things'.[3]

The practical character of Scott's teaching is especially revealed in two chapters – 18 and 19 – 'On the Dispositions and Character peculiar to the true Believer'. They sum up much of what was mentioned in the previous chapters. In the true believer the truths of revelation are not mere *notions* in the mind, but embraced with a living faith: which has a transforming efficacy upon the heart. Newman's distinction between notional and real knowledge and assent, as well as his insistence on obedience as the correlative of faith, have their seeds in Scott.

The first disposition Scott lays down is humility, the sensibility of one's own weakness and a comparison of oneself to Christ, a realization of the necessity of depending on God. He is conscious 'that he has no power in himself either to resist temptations, endure tribulations, face dangers, or perform duties; and that he can only "be strong in the Lord, and in the power of his might" (2 Cor. 12. 9, 10; Eph. 6. 10; Phil. 4. 13)'. The second disposition laid down by Scott is submission to God's will and authority of God, deeming his service perfect freedom, and especially 'habitual *submission* to his providence', with the recognition that 'every affliction is medicinal to the soul, and conducive to its sanctification'. He learns patience and even joy in suffering. Thirdly, the fear of God, that is, 'reverential fear of the divine majesty, authority, holiness, and glory' which 'produces solemn awe, humble adoration, serious recollection, and jealous circumspection; which induces a man to act habitually as in the presence of the all-seeing and heart-searching God, and influences him to universal conscientiousness, even in his most secret actions, and in respect of his inmost thoughts . . .' This 'fear of God' is the effect of grace, and it grows in harmony with holy love.

The fourth disposition of the true Christian is love of God. 'The truths of the gospel, when received by living faith, are wonderfully suited to excite and increase admiring love of the divine perfections, as displayed in all the works of God; but especially in that of redemption by Jesus Christ.' The soul begins to thirst for God and experiences 'lively gratitude for mercies inestimable . . . and unmerited'. There will be a particular regard to the person of Christ, 'as one with the Father and the divine Spirit, and the equal object of all love, confidence, honour, gratitude, and adoration. . . . This love of Christ is the grand constraining principle of all evangelical obedience.'

The fifth characteristic of the true believer is spiritual mindedness, i.e., 'he is disposed to seek his happiness in spiritual things, because he is capable of relishing and delighting in them'.

In chapter 19, a continuation of the same subject, Scott lists certain other characteristics of the true believer: 1) Indifference to the world, and the things of the world; 2) love of neighbour as oneself; 3) certain moral traits such as honesty, truthfulness or what can be summed up in living a blameless life; 4) a disposition 'to love mercy', to be kind and liberal in doing good; and 5) 'to do good to all, and harm to none, to suffer long, to forbear, forgive, and pursue peace with all.'

Obviously the acquisition of all these dispositions is a matter of time and growth, but there was plenty to feed the mind and will of one who now resolved to live a spiritual life. In the *Apologia* he summed it up by saying, 'I deeply felt his influence; and for years I used almost as proverbs what I considered to be the scope and issue of his doctrine, "Holiness before peace", and "Growth the only evidence of life".' (*Apo.*, 5)

Besides Scott, Newman also read William Romaine, another Evangelical author, from whom he learned the doctrine of election to eternal glory, a doctrine which he now took up, but which faded away with time, because it was not a genuine certitude, as he later explained in terms of the *Grammar of Assent*. For the moment, however, it tended to confirm him in his early mistrust of the reality of material phenomena, 'making me rest,' he said, 'in the thought of two and two only absolute and luminously self-evident beings, myself and my Creator'.[4] This is one of those frequently quoted passages of the *Apologia*. From it some commentators and indeed some of his opponents during his lifetime concluded that he was anti-social, a recluse, autocentric. Long before the publication of the *Apologia* in 1864, he had used the same words in a sermon, 'The Immortality of the Soul', preached in 1833. Writing to Maria Giberne he quoted this as an example of 'catachresis', a rhetorical term for a monstrous metaphor, e.g., 'darkness visible'. The context of the sermon makes it clear that it does not isolate one from the love of relatives and friends. There are passages in the sermon, e.g., 'Our first life is in ourselves; our second in our friends', to say nothing of the sermon, 'Love of Relatives and Friends'; which preclude such interpretations, but it seems that this is one of the myths about Newman that does not die. ('Present Blessings', *PPS* V, 19, 279; 'Love of Relations and Friends'. *PPS* II, 5, 51–60)

What other effects were there of Newman's conversion? He became certain of God's existence, 'as cutting at the root of doubt, providing a chain between God and the soul . . . I know I am right. How do you know it? I know I know. How? I know etc.' Newman gives a reference to the *Grammar of Assent*, p. 195–7, ed. 4. There he defines certitude as 'the perception of a truth with the perception that this is a truth . . . as expressed in the phrase, "I know, that I know, etc." Certitude is a reflex conviction and 'religion demands more than an assent to its truth; it requires a certitude'. The scepticism or disbelief into which he had fallen was eradicated and wiped out. Moreover, the experience touched his affections, in fact, his entire being: 'Thou didst change my heart, and in part my whole mental complexion at that time.' Hence he insisted that his conversion was not merely a 'reforming', 'I know and am sure that before I was blind, but now I see.' Later he would also recognize it as a great act of God's providence. (*AW*, 165, 268)

There were two other works which Newman read in the autumn of 1816 'each contrary to each, and planting in me the seeds of an intellectual inconsistency which disabled me for a long course of years'. The first was Joseph Milner's *History of the Church of Christ* (1794), which introduced him to the world of the Fathers and 'the religion of the primitive Christians'. He later told Henry Wilberforce, 'It is 30 years this month [September 1846] . . . since God made me religious, and St Ambrose in Milner's history was one of the first objects of my veneration.' (*LD* XI, 252, *Apo.*, 4 and 7) This interest developed in time when he was able to explore them in depth. At the moment he was 'enamoured of the long extracts from St Augustine, St Ambrose, and the other Fathers' he found there. This love of the Fathers was unfortunately counterbalanced by the influence of Thomas Newton, author of *Dissertation on the Prophecies* (1754), who convinced him that the Pope was the Antichrist. 'My imagination,' he wrote, 'was stained by the effects of this doctrine up to 1843; it had been obliterated from my reason and judgment at an earlier date.' (*Apo.*, 6–7)

At this time, too, Newman had what he called 'an anticipation', which he reluctantly mentioned in the *Apologia*, that it would be God's will that he lead a single life. This anticipation remained almost unbroken until 1829, after which there was no break at all. It was connected in his mind, he said, with the conviction that a single life would be required by whatever he chose to do in his life. In a draft version of the passage in the *Apologia*, he was more specific regarding this vocation: 'This imagination . . . was not founded on the Catholic belief of the moral superiority of the single life over the married, which I did not hold till many years afterwards when I was taught it by Hurrell Froude. It arose from my feeling of separation from the visible world, and it was connected with a notion that my mission in life would require such a sacrifice as it involved. When I was first on the Oriel foundation, it was associated in my mind with Missionary employment, or with duties in Oxford.'[5]

He distrusted self, fearing lest he fall into sin, but confident in God's help. Before leaving Ealing for Alton, he weighed within himself how he should act with his parents and handle himself when invited to dances, theatres and other entertainments, not that he considered these sinful in themselves but that they would be a temptation to him, and so he prayed, 'Give me strength. . . . Above all keep me from preferring gatherings, dances and pleasures to my God. . . . Further, guard me against the temptations of the flesh.' He resolved to present his scruples to his parents, if urged to do so, but with humility and a readiness to act against his own judgement, if commanded to do so. At the same time he would not judge others. (*AW*, 153) The prayers Newman composed the following year all reveal great gratitude to God, and distrust of self.

Newman later came to realize that his conversion was not an Evangelical one. Though 'he had indeed been converted by it [Evangelical teaching] to a spiritual life . . . he had not been converted in that special way which it laid down as imperative, but so plainly against rule, as to make it very doubtful in the eyes of normal Evangelicals whether he had really been converted at all'. A number of Evangelicals did not hesitate to write and tell him so, especially after the publication of the *Apologia*. His conversion was not sudden and his feelings were not *violent*. (*AW*, 79–80) But of the fact that he was converted he remained more certain than that he had hands and feet.

As a result of his readings and spiritual experience Newman mapped out a programme for growth in sanctity. It consisted in daily reading of the Scriptures, prayer, self-examination, and later devout and frequent reception of the Eucharist. He resolved to be detached from the world.

It would take years before Newman put into theological perspective the significance of this conversion experience, but in addition to the effects mentioned he was to become, to use a phrase frequently employed by the writers he read and one used by himself in his early sermons, 'a religious inquirer' as well as a pursuer of holiness, for the two were intimately linked. The first stirrings of theological inquiry can be observed in a letter to Mr Mayers thanking him for the gift of Beveridge's *Private Thoughts*.[6] In the letter Newman complains that there is a passage which he does not completely understand, and that even before he had read it, he had debated within himself 'how it could be that baptized infants, dying in infancy, could be saved, unless the Spirit of God was given them; which seems to contradict the opinion that *baptism* is not accompanied by the Holy Ghost'. (*LD* I, 32–3) The doctrine of the need for universal conscious conversion with the concomitant denial of what was called 'baptismal regeneration' had practically become the touchstone of Evangelical orthodoxy. Mr Mayers' explanation evidently satisfied Newman at the time, though later he would come to accept baptismal regeneration.

Beveridge's work is not mentioned in the *Apologia*, as Newman later explained in a note inside his copy, 'because I am speaking there (i.e., in the *Apologia*) of the formation of my doctrinal opinions, and I do not think that they were influenced by it. I had fully and eagerly taken up Calvinism into my religion before it came into my hands. But no book was more dear to me, or exercised a more powerful influence over my devotion and my habitual thoughts. In my private memoranda I even wrote in its style.'[7] Joseph Bacchus called the work 'a solid treatise on the duties of a Christian life. It is severe in its tone, and makes no appeal to the imagination or to the emotions . . . It speaks much for the maturity of Newman's religious life when he was only sixteen, that such a book should have captivated him.' (*KC*; 117)

Even when he had given up moderate Calvinism, Newman did not hesitate to give this work to his cousin Harriot Fourdrinier, writing 'This work is not always scriptural in the exposition of *doctrine*, but its simple, pure, and instructive piety outweighs all incidental indiscretion which occur in some of its statements of scriptural truth.' (*LD* II, 87) In his review of Dr Wiseman's *Lectures on the Catholic Church*, Newman called Beveridge 'truly in every sense of the word, one of the lights of our Church', and defended him against the assertion that he held the ultra-Protestant view of Scripture as the only rule of faith.[8] In his eighties when he recovered the copy with the letter he had sent, Newman wrote to Spencer Northcote, who retrieved it, 'Beveridge's book is a very impressive one with very little Protestantism in it.'

Everything that Newman wrote in praise of Scott in his *Apologia* could be equally affirmed about Beveridge's work. It is eminently practical. After an introductory chapter summarizing the articles of Christian faith, Part One is divided into resolutions varying from three to seven with regard to conversation, thoughts, affections, works, actions, relation with others and one's talents. Part Two treats such topics as religious education and formation especially of children, knowledge of God and the mystery of the Trinity, worldly riches and their danger, self-denial, striving to enter by the narrow gate, imitation of Christ, our call and election, and it ends with Christ's second coming. Any one at all familiar with Newman's *Parochial and Plain Sermons* will recognize at once that Newman covers the same ground. The particular emphases of the first three volumes centre on the Christian's endeavours, his duties, self-denial, the danger of riches and worldliness, the necessity of entering by the narrow gate – themes with which he was completely familiar from having meditated on Beveridge's work.

Both Beveridge and Scott emphasize that the true Christian must struggle to overcome the evil tendencies in his nature and consequently the Christian life is one of warfare. Both authors, following St Paul, call such a Christian 'Christ's soldier', and the use of this term in Newman's journal undoubtedly stems from his acquaintance with these two authors who provided him with a solid education in traditional spirituality. Beveridge seems to have impressed on him the doctrine of the corruption of human nature, for he quotes him in one of his earliest sermons, No. 19 (*Ser.* I, 302–14), on this subject. He re-preached this sermon seven times, the last on 21 December 1841, each time quoting Beveridge on the sinfulness of all that one does.

> Take e.g. the words of the excellent Bishop Beveridge. 'I do not only (he says) betray the inbred venom of my heart by poisoning my common actions but even my most religious performances also, with sin. I cannot pray, but I sin – nay I cannot hear or preach a sermon, but I sin – I cannot give an alms or receive the Sacrament but I sin – nay I cannot so much as confess my sins, but my very confessions are still aggravations of them. My repentance needs to be repented of – my tears want washing – and the very washing of my tears needs still to be washed over again with the blood of my Redeemer.'

The reflections or sermonettes of spring 1817 (after May) were probably written, Newman recorded later, in the same style as Beveridge, and these he mercifully consigned to the fire in 1874. Newman's early journals are composed in a repelling style, which he recognized to be such, and explained as follows, 'I seldom wrote without an eye to style, and since my taste was bad, my style was bad ... Also my Evangelical tone contributed to its bad taste.' Why then did he not destroy them too? He answered, 'I am loth to destroy altogether the record of God's mercies to me, of the wonderful things he has done to my soul and of my early moral and spiritual history.' And for these they are most valuable, no matter what the style. He also wanted to give Ambrose St John, who was intended to be his biographer, what he called 'elbow room' in his knowledge. A vainer man would have acted otherwise. (*AW*, 149, 154)

CHAPTER TWO

Snapdragon and Glittering Prizes

Newman was entered in Trinity College on 14 December 1816, but he did not take up residence until the following June. The first part of 1817 he spent at home in Alton. His eyes would not permit his reading much, 'but from 18 March he read steadily for about six hours a day, taking Sundays off, till he went up for his first full term in October 1817, when the rate increases to an average of nine or ten hours a day, till 25 May 1818, shortly after gaining the Trinity scholarship'. The works he studied were:

Sophocles, the whole; Herodotus; Xenophon, *Anabasis*; Cicero; *De Officiis, De Senectute, De Amicitia*; Ovid, a small amount; Juvenal, four satires; nearly the whole of Horace; Tacitus, *Agricola, Germania*, and some of the *Annals*; the whole of Virgil; five plays of Terence. He read some New Testament in Greek and a little of the Septuagint. There were also Greek Exercises, Latin Exercises (sentences), Latin composition, Latin Verses; and learning by heart from various books including the popular schoolbooks of Richard Valpy (1754–1836); and he spent a short time on *Logicae Artis Rudimenta*. In Mathematics it was Euclid till he went up to Trinity, then Trigonometry, Algebra and Mechanics were added.

Newman also recorded some walks, sometimes with his parents, sisters, or grandmother; and fairly often, when at home, '*sorores audivi*,' for one or two hours at a time; and occasionally he read to his sisters. He also recorded occasional half-hours of violin practice. (*LD* I, 31, n. 1)

Newman's inclination for hard work was probably confirmed by his reading of Scott's *Essays*, one of which was devoted to the necessity of developing the talents given one by God. This is not contradicted by his later statement that Evangelicalism was not congenial to his mind because of 'his love of hard secular work and his literary tastes, in which an Evangelical proper has no sympathy', because there he is speaking of it as a system and not referring to individuals – a distinction he made in his letter to Lord Lifford already referred to. (*LD* VI, 129) Moreover according to Fr Dessain, Newman cancelled this passage in his Autobiographical Memoir.[1]

In April and November 1817 Newman composed two sets of prayers. They seem to be spontaneous outpourings of praise and love of God for temporal and spiritual blessings as well as petitions for further graces and blessings. They provide an insight into his devotional life, as it was nourished by Beveridge's *Private Thoughts*. They are designed for morning and evening recitation. Both sets contain prayers of gratitude for his conversion. These and all subsequent prayers are given in Appendix One.

A TEST OF PRINCIPLE

Newman came into residence in June 1817 when most were leaving for the Long Vacation. He occupied another man's room for three weeks. 'There I spent a solitary three weeks, no one being up but two or three men waiting for little-go examination.' It was from here that he saw the snapdragon growing against the wall separating Trinity from Balliol, and which, in a poignant passage in the *Apologia*, he wrote 'I had for years taken it as the emblem of my own perpetual residence even unto death in my University.' (*LD* XXV 106: *Apo.*, 237) Soon, however, he struck up a friendship with John Bowden, three years his senior. Thereafter they studied together, took recreation together, and became known as 'inseparables'. It was a friendship that lasted to Bowden's death in 1844.

Newman tells in his 'Autobiographical Memoir' how impatient he was to be directed in his reading, and that he went to the President of Trinity, Mr Lee, who kindly told him he left such matters to be answered by the tutors. Nevertheless he could not get any information, and the evening before departing for home, he saw one of the tutors in top-boots on horseback on his way into the country. 'Thinking it his last chance, he dashed into the road, and abruptly accosting him, asked him what books he should read during the Vacation.' The tutor kindly referred him to one of his colleagues still in College who gave him the answer to all his difficulties. (*AW*, 33)

In the autumn when the term began Newman faced the first test of his principles. Wine parties at which the participants got drunk were common, and someone as studious as Newman was fair game. He accepted an invitation to one of these parties at which they tried to get him drunk.

This he resisted, and after downing three glasses, he refused any more and left. This, however, was not the end. Ten days later, they burst into his room, locked the door and tried to bully him. Newman ordered them to leave the room. As Newman relates it in his journal, 'One of them said he would knock me down, if I were not too contemptible a fellow'. A parenthesis is revealing, in which Newman notes that he was 6 feet 3 or 4 inches high, and stout in proportion. He later came back and apologized. Newman told him to forget it; the other shook hands and went. This was a display of the same courage with which he attempted as a boy of fifteen to row around the Isle of Wight in an open boat in July 'in the midst of a persevering drizzle and a dangerous sea', and later firmly to rebuke 'a drunken butcher by St Mary's who suddenly poured out to a companion a torrent of execration and blasphemy'.[2]

A few days previously, Newman had taken Communion for the first time in the Anglican Church on 17 November. On the same day he wrote down a long series of prayers, or perhaps the date indicates that he completed them on this day. The first four prayers are devoted to asking God's grace to offer thanksgiving for many graces and temporal blessings. In the fifth prayer he asks, 'Let me attend and apply to my studies, but let me have thy glory in view as the end of all my pursuits.' He extends his intercessory prayers beyond family, relations and friends to 'all mankind', including Jews, Muslims, pagans, heretics and schismatics. This list grew longer and longer in subsequent intercessory prayers. Prayers IX and X are a tissue of Scripture texts particularly from the psalms, which reveal how much the Scriptures had become a part of his inner life. The piling of text upon text displays Newman's Evangelical emotions. Later, when his father issued a stern warning about such emotion, he mentioned explicitly this trait. 'It is proper to quote scripture, but you poured out texts in such quantities.' (*AW*, 179) The only portion Newman later transcribed is No. IV which certainly came from the heart, for it expresses his gratitude to God for the graces of his conversion. The later text reads:

> Lord, I praise Thee for calling me to the light of Thy Gospel – for my birth in a country where Thy true religion is found, and for Thy goodness in enlightening my soul with the knowledge of Thy truth, that, whereas I was proud, selfrighteous, impure, abominable, Thou was pleased to turn me from such a state of darkness and irreligion, by a mercy which is too wonderful for me, and make me fall down humbled and abased before Thy footstool. O let me so run the race

that is set before me that I may lay hold of everlasting life, and especially let me make Thee, O Holy Jesus, my pattern in my pilgrimage here, that Thou mayst be the portion of my soul to all eternity.

He ends this set of prayers with a scriptural quotation which became a favourite one. 'Whom have I in heaven but thee, And whom on earth that I desire besides thee? My flesh and my heart faileth, but God is the strength of my heart and my portion forever!'

Two or three years younger than the ordinary undergraduate, Newman astonished his tutors with his knowledge especially in mathematics. Mr Short, his tutor, urged him to stand for the Scholarship which for the first time was opened to outsiders. If a Trinity man won against outside competition it would be an honour for the College and boost its standing. Newman had not intended to try that year but at the urging of his tutor he decided to do so. Once decided, he was sanguine he would succeed, but now he was fearful that his heart was 'too much set upon it'. Accordingly he prayed for spiritual indifference:

Let me not rely too much upon getting the scholarship – let me not be lead [*sic*] away from Thee by the hopes of it. So let me order my spirit, that, if I get it not, I may not be disappointed, but may praise and bless Thy name, as knowing better than myself what is good for me. O Lord God of hosts, grant it not to me, if it is likely to be a snare to me, to turn me away from Thee. May I so dispose myself that I may praise Thy name, whether I receive it or not.

On 18 May 1818 he was elected Scholar of Trinity. He attributed his success to God. 'I prayed, and he was pleased to hear my petition, and yesterday, out of his infinite kindness He gave me the scholarship', he wrote in his journal the following day. (*AW*, 157–8) He then jotted down a prayer of praise:

O praised be the Lord God of Israel who only doth wondrous things! Give me grace, make me holy, for Thou alone canst. Save me and bring me to those realms where Thou shinest in unclouded majesty, and make me praise Thee (then) to all eternity. (*AW*, 158)

He described the examination and its sequel in a letter to his mother on 25 May 1818: 'They first made us do some verses – then some Latin translation – then a Latin theme – then a chorus of Euripides – then an English theme – then some Plato, then some Lucretius, then some Xenophon, then some Livy. Most of the Latin and Greek we had to construe off to them. What is more distressing than suspense?'

The following part of the letter reveals Newman's shyness, bouts of which he continued to experience all his life.

First, as I was going out, before I had changed my gown, one of the candidates met me, and wanted to know if it was decided. What was I to say? 'It was': 'And who had got it?' 'O, an in-college man,' and I hurried away as fast as I could. On returning with my newly earned gown I met the whole set going to their respective homes. I did not know what to do. I held my eyes down. By this I am a scholar for nine years at £60 a year. (*LD* I, 52–3)

At that time £60 was quite a sum, more than Newman later earned as curate of St. Mary's. His feelings of anxiety, yet of hope, he described in still another letter to his mother:

I am sure I felt the tortures of suspense so much, that I wished and wished I had never attempted it. The idea of 'turpis repulsa' haunted me. I was not very well. My head ached continually. I tried to keep myself as cool as possible, but I could not help being sanguine. I constantly reverted to it in my thoughts, in spite of my endeavours to the contrary. Very few men thought I should get it, and my *reason* thought the same. Even he with whom I am most intimate [Bowden] thought my case desperate and betted against me. My age was such a stumbling block. [i.e. *I* could stand again, others could not.] But I, when I heard the voice of the dean summoning me before the Electors, seemed to myself to feel no surprise. I am told I turned pale. (*LD* I, 53)

Shortly afterwards Newman passed his responsions or what was popularly called 'the little go', which was not so demanding as the scholarship examination. During the Long Vacation of 1818 Newman said he was 'idle', meaning by that he did not read in preparation for his final examination, though he was occupied with Gibbon and Locke. For the former he conceived great admiration, especially after a second perusal the following summer. To Bowden he wrote that with all his faults 'few can be put in comparison with him; and sometimes, when I reflect on his happy choice of expressions, his vigorous compression of ideas, and the life and significance of his every word, I am prompted indignantly to exclaim that no style is left for the historians of an after day'. (October 1819, *LD* I, 67)

During this time Newman did not neglect his prayer life. There is a long prayer or really a series of prayers, since there is no central theme developed in them, but a tissue of texts or ideas from Scripture especially the psalms and sentiments which he acquired from his Evangelical reading. It is headed 'Evening Prayer. September 20th 1818 – J. H. Newman.' He never transcribed anything from it. [See Appendix]

AN INTERLUDE

Upon return to Oxford for Michaelmas term, he like many an undergraduate was not content merely to study for examinations, but, as he later put it, he began 'to dabble in matters foreign to academical objects'. (*AW*, 40) He and Bowden decided to start a periodical called *The Undergraduate* in imitation of Addison's *Spectator*. As a preparation for it they composed a tale in verse called *St Bartholomew's Eve*. Newman later described it as follows:

> His and Bowden's poem was a romance founded on the Massacre of St. Bartholomew. The subject was the issue of the unfortunate union of a Protestant gentleman and a Catholic lady, ending in the tragical death of both, through the machinations of a cruel fanatical priest, whose inappropriate name was Clement. Mr Bowden did the historical and picturesque portions, Mr Newman the theological. There were no love scenes, nor could there be, for, as it turned out to the monk's surprise, the parties had been, some time before the action, husband and wife by a clandestine marriage, known, however, to the father of the lady.' (*AW*, 40–2)

Stylistically the poem has few merits, but it contains a passage written by Newman which reveals one of the poles in his personality which was kept in dynamic tension with its opposite. Namely, love of solitude with love of people and society. The passage was incorporated into a poem 'Winter Eclogue IV', which Newman sent to his sister Harriett (*LD* I, 58–60). There are a number of verbal revisions which he made in publishing it under the title 'Solitude', the first set of verses in *Verses on Various Occasions*. The latter version is given here.

SOLITUDE

There is in stillness oft a magic power
To calm the breast, when struggling passions lower;
Touch'd by its influence, in the soul arise
Diviner feelings, kindred with the skies.
By this the Arab's kindling thoughts expand,
When circling skies inclose the desert sand;
For this the hermit seeks the thickest grove,
To catch th'inspiring glow of heavenly love.
It is not solely in the freedom given
To purify and fix the heart on heaven;
There is a Spirit singing aye in air,
That lifts us high above all mortal care.
No mortal measure swells that mystic sound,
No mortal minstrel breathes such tones around, –
The Angels' hymn, – the sovereign harmony
That guides the rolling orbs along the sky, –
And hence perchance the tales of saints who view'd
And heard Angelic choirs in solitude.
By most unheard, – because the earthly din
Of toil or mirth has charms their ears to win.
Alas for man! he knows not of the bliss,
The heaven that brightens such a life as this.
Oxford   *Michaelmas Term, 1818.*

In these periods of solitude, often when he walked alone, Newman meditated and prayed.

St. Bartholomew's Eve was an introduction to the larger and more ambitious project of a periodical modelled on Addison's *Spectator*. Six numbers were printed before it was abandoned because the name of its author got out. It reveals the feeling that Oxford education, if it is to be a bona fide education must be enlarged beyond the academic routine. In one essay not published Newman proposed the creation of a debating society (this was before the present Oxford Union was begun), which would meet in the music room every two weeks to debate questions covering 'the whole range of history, poetry and the fine arts, indeed nothing would be excluded but the politics of the last 100 years'. Such a society would be 'a school for the future senator or lawyer, it would enlarge and refine the mind, it would be a most agreeable relaxation after the toils of the day'. (*LD* I, 63)

Newman remained always reticent about his interior life, and if it were not for his journals and poems, one would have little knowledge of it at all. The poem 'My Birthday' reveals that his fundamental and habitual attitude of praise and gratitude had undergone no change. 'It is my Birthday; – and I fain would try, / Albeit in rude, in heartfelt strains to praise / My God, for He hath shielded wondrously / From harm and envious error all my ways, / And purged my misty sight, and fixed on heaven / my gaze.' He will not celebrate it in that 'mood, in which the insensate crowd / Of wealthy folly hail their natal day, – / With riot throng, and feast, and greetings loud, / Chasing all thoughts of God and heaven away.'

> No! give to me, Great Lord, the constant soul,
>   Nor fooled by pleasure nor enslaved by care;
> Each rebel-passion (for Thou canst) control,
>   And make me know the tempter's every snare.
>   What, though alone my sober hours I wear,
> No friend in view, and sadness o'er my mind
>   Throws her dark veil? – Thou but accord this prayer,
> And I will bless Thee for my birth, and find
> That stillness breathes sweet tones, and solitude is kind.
>
> Each coming year, O grant it to refine
>   All purer motions of this anxious breast;
> Kindle the steadfast flame of love divine,
>   And comfort me with holier thoughts possest;
>   Till this worn body slowly sink to rest,
> This feeble spirit to the sky aspire, –
>   As some long-prisoned dove toward her nest –
> There to receive the gracious full-toned lyre,
> Bowed low before the Throne 'mid the bright seraph choir.
>
>   (*VV* 5–8)

There is an entry in his journal which reveals his romanticism and looks forward to the famous passage on music in the Oxford University sermon 'The Theory of Developments in Religious Doctrine'. (*US* 346)

'1819. March 21. Sunday evening. Bells pealing. The pleasure of hearing them. It leads the mind to a longing after some thing. I know not what . . . What does it do? We have a kind of longing after something dear to us, soothing. Such is my feeling at this minute, as I hear them'. (*AW*, 160–1) And the beginning of that marvellous empathy to enter into others' sorrows is apparent in a letter to his mother, 4 June 1819, when his friend Bowden lost his sister:

> . . . Such a variety of circumstances flash on my memory, and all that I have heard Bowden say they used to do, and their different amusements together, and the different memorials there are of her, that I know not how to reflect upon it; I shrink from it; and if *I* so feel it, what must be their feelings who have lost a daughter and a sister. (*LD* I, 65)

Later the loss of his own sister and of Hurrell Froude would increase and deepen this sense of empathy for others.

The Dean, Kinsey, took him to Professor Buckland's lectures on geology, at the time 'a new and interesting science'. Newman enjoyed them, though he did not understand all of them 'from not knowing the principles of the science'. (*LD* I, 65) He also attended lectures on mineralogy, as well as history lectures because he heard that the names were given to the Prime Minister. Indeed he was half conscious, or later became conscious that 'some mental and moral change' was taking place within him. 'Not liking to go into the Church' he began to think of a career in law, it was what his father had hoped for him, and he was enrolled in or entered at Lincoln's Inn on 19 November 1819.

NO HONOURS

In the summer of 1819 he read history: Herodotus, Thucydides, and Gibbon, and upon returning to Oxford for the next term he applied himself ten to eleven hours each day in reading. By Christmas time he was beginning to get anxious and to wish the coming year in which he would take his final examinations were over. The following summer he spent at Trinity which was deserted for the Long Vacation. He did not mind the solitude, because the goal seemed now in sight, but the prospect looked alternately dark and bright, but 'when I try to divest my mind of flurried fear,' he wrote to his mother, 'I think I may say I have advanced much more and much more quickly and easily than I had expected'. (*LD* I, 81) And to his brother Frank, he reveals his closeness to God:

> Here at Oxford I am most comfortable. The quiet and stillness of every thing around me tends to calm and lull those emotions, which the near prospect of my grand examination and a heart too solicitous about fame and too fearful of failure are continually striving to excite. I read very much certainly, but I may say (I trust), without deceiving myself or losing sight of my unnumbered transgressions, that God sanctifies my studies by breathing into me all the while thoughts of Him, and enables me to praise Him with joyful lips, when I rise and when I lie down, and when I wake in the night.

As to the event of the examination, he tells Frank,

> It is in the Lord's hands; let Him do as it seemeth to Him good. It is my daily, and (hope) heartfelt prayer, that I may not get any honours here, if they are to be the least cause of sin to me. As the time approaches, and I have laboured more at my books, the trial is greater. May God give me strength still to say, 'Let me get no honours, if they are to be the slightest cause of sin to me.' And do you, my dear Francis, pray for me in the same way. (*LD* I, 82–3)

Though he tried to keep cool, he found it difficult. Why? First, he felt it a duty 'to take no thought for the morrow': He could not think much of the schools without '*wishing* much to distinguish myself in them – that much wishing would make me discontented if I did not succeed; therefore it would be coveting, for *then* we covet when we desire a thing so earnestly as to be dissatisfied if we fail in getting it. *I* am labouring at the means, but the *success* of those means is not in my hands; I am doing *my* part, but *God* chooseth the eve [ent] and I know he will choose for the best.' He asks his sister therefore not to wish that he gains honours, but to obtain what is best for him. 'For then, whether I succeed or fail, I shall have the comfort of feeling assured that I have obtained *real* advantage and not apparent.' He then quoted from Samuel Johnson's *Vanity of Human Wishes*,

> Still raise for good the supplicating voice,
> But leave to Heav'n the measure and the *choice*.
>
> (*LD* I, 85)

This remained a fundamental principle of Newman's prayer life. Fr Neville, his literary executor, testified in his notes that Newman never began a work of consequence without having made it the subject of prayer, novenas, masses and litanies. Because he left the event to prayer, he was consequently able to accept much that must have been trying to him with 'a remarkable equanimity, from his consciousness that he and others had to the best of their ability left such things in God's hands in prayer'. Neville further remarks that people sometimes mistakingly said he accepted something without concern, whereas really it was that though pained, sometimes most deeply pained and wounded, he had the consolation of being able to take whatever it was that had turned up, as the very thing he had looked for [wanted], namely God's answer to his prayers. No one attains to such a state of equanimity without long practice, and, it may be said, Newman began here at Oxford.

When Newman thought of the examination he seemed caught in a dilemma. On the one hand it was his duty to do as well as he could; secondly, if he did not he would disappoint the hopes of his fellow students and tutors, and family, but on the other hand, if he did succeed, perhaps he would fall into sin. On 17 September 1820 he read over his memorandum of 19 May 1818 when he gained the scholarship. He is troubled, not that gaining the scholarship was a sin, as one commentator erroneously asserted, but that having gained it, he grew 'cold, remiss and ungrateful. Could I be so lowly and resigned beforehand, so thankful on succeeding, and yet in a few short weeks become so vain, so puffed up, so proud, so quarrelsome, so very wicked?' So again he prays: 'Lord, give me content and confidence in Thee, and, above all, grant me not my heart's desire by any means, if the price be transgression in consequence'. (*AW*, 158–9) With ruthless self-analysis he wondered if in so praying he was being hypocritical, as he mentioned in a letter, about 12 September, to Walter Mayers: 'I often find that I am acting the part of a very hypocrite; I am buoyed up with the secret idea, that by thus leaving the event in the hands of God, when I pray, He may be induced, as a reward for so proper a spirit, to grant me my desire. Thus my prayer is a mockery.' (*LD* I, 87) The trial was increased when he discovered, as he mentions in another letter to Walter Mayers, he was not properly prepared:

And I have not been advised, or have been advised wrongly, what books to read. I have fagged at books which will be of no service to me, and this to such an extent that I think six months of very hard reading has been thrown away. And what I have read besides, I have

read so irregularly and out of place that my mind is a labyrinth more
than any thing else. So much for human means – as to the probable
will of God, no one can imagine the sins into which I fell after I got
the Scholarship. The recollection of my ingratitude, this is which lies
heavy on my heart, and unnerves my arm in the day of battle.

However, since your letter, I have besought Him to calm my mind:
to keep me from thinking of the morrow: to give me resignation to a
merciful chastisement, and humility in an O how unmerited success.
(*LD* I, 89)

By 8 November, he thought his success 'very, very precarious'. (*LD* I,
92) All this of course took its toll on his nervous and sensitive nature.
Called up a day sooner than he expected, he lost his head, utterly broke
down, and after vain attempts for several days had to retire, only making
sure first of his B.A. degree. When the class list came out, his name did
not appear at all on the Mathematical side of the Paper, and in Classics it
was found in the lower division of the second class of honours, which at
that time went by the contemptuous title of 'under-the-line', there being
as yet no third and fourth classes. (*AW*, 47: 39–40)

Further light is shed in a letter written at the time. 'When I got into
the schools I was so nervous, I could not answer half a dozen questions.
The nervousness, I may add the illness, continued whenever I approached
the schools, and, after a week's procrastinated efforts, I have this morning
retired from the contest.' (*LD* I, 95) A further detail is given in another
letter, 'I will grant I was unwell, low-spirited, and very imperfect in my
books: yet, when in the schools, so great a depression came on me, that I
could do nothing, I was nervous in the extreme, a thing I never before
experienced, and did not expect – my memory was gone, my mind
altogether confused.' (*LD* I, 99)

His first thought was the disappointment he may have given to his
father and mother. As he wrote to his father on 1 December, 'And most
willingly would I consent to a hundred times the sadness that now
overwhelms me, if so doing would save my mother and you from feeling
vexation.' Already he is feeling that he had been relieved of a load.
Knowing what his feelings must be, his mother wrote at once to console
him, saying that the only thing that troubled them was that he himself
was troubled. He replied immediately:

I am ashamed to think that anything I have said should have led you
to suppose that I am at all pained on my own account. . . . I am

perfectly convinced that there are few men in the college who do not feel for me more than I feel for myself. I wish to repeat and convince you that I really am not at all sad now, and my only sorrow, I will not say it was slight, arose from the pain I expected to give you and my Father. . . . I have never looked up to success as such a god, or bowed myself so low before the idol of fame, as to have the serenity of my mind disturbed by gaining or losing the prize. I am sure success could not have made me happier than I am at present. . . . Very much I *have* gone through, but the clouds are passed away . . . (3 December 1820, *LD* I, 95–6)

Louis Bouyer commented on this correspondence as follows:

The self-control of which these letters give evidence is the more remarkable seeing that that sensitive nature of his could never before have been so painfully and deeply stirred. Not every young man of nineteen would recover such complete serenity of mind within a week of sustaining so rude a shock. The feat implies an extraordinary degree of self-control, a singular power of self-detachment, very remarkable in one who has so often been portrayed as an example of morbid sensibility and incurable egoism.[3]

To this I would add that Newman had had his prayers answered in the way God wished it. For he writes to Walter Mayers, January 1826:

There is a great difference between believing a thing to be good, and feeling it; now I am thankful to say, I am not only enabled to believe failure to be best for me, but God has given me to see and know it. . . . I think I can see clearly that honour and fame are not desirable. God is leading me through life in the way best adapted for His glory and my own salvation. I trust I may always have the same content and indifference to the world, which is at present the *prevailing* principle in my heart – yet I have great fears of backsliding.' (*LD* I, 99)

Newman here strikes a note that will be heard again and again: trust in God's Providence when one cannot see where he is leading one, but his share of disappointment, as his subsequent life bears witness, was not at an end.

Newman became happy that he did fail. Apropos of his writing for the Latin prize a year later, he wrote to Harriett, 'I could enlarge and tell a long story and show many reasons why I so happily failed in the schools, and point out how that disappointment was at once a chastisement for former offences, and a kind preventive of future.' It also brought with it a measure of self-knowledge. 'Now I am conscious that, among *many* other diseases of the mind, I am very vain, and the least success is apt to alter me, – witness my getting the Trinity Scholarship.' In the light of this his prayer was 'I trust I ask sincerely, Give me nothing which will in any way delay me in my Christian course.' (*LD* I, 118) That course was pointed in the direction of Christian perfection, and he now entered one of the 'strictest' periods of his life as an Anglican.

CHAPTER THREE

Inner Warfare: Conquering Self

On 12 February 1821 Newman returned to Oxford, as his scholarship had not yet expired. He began attending Buckland's lectures on mineralogy, which he summarized in substance for his sisters. He composed a piece of music which he sent to them. He also attended in the next term Buckland's lectures on geology, which he did not summarize. The science he felt was in its infancy and hence had no regular system, 'but they open an amazing field to imagination and poetry'. He still belonged to the Music Club and consistently attended the public concerts. The year 1821 Newman set down as the date 'when he was more devoted to the evangelical creed and more strict in his religious duties than at any previous time'. (*AW*, 80) He spent the summer drawing up a long document (90 pages) summarizing his Evangelical beliefs. When he came to write about conversion, however, he had to go by the books, as his own conversion was not the same. Sheridan, who explored Newman's views on justification, summarizes these beliefs as follows:

All the main points of Evangelicalism are there: the cardinal principle of justification by faith and faith alone, with the consequent disparaging remarks about baptismal regeneration; the dim view of human nature as corrupted by original sin ('man does *only* evil continually', and even of the justified man it is said that 'his understanding is still darkened and his heart polluted'); the insistence upon complete gratuity of election; the predestination of individuals to salvation; the doctrine of final perseverance, which, while not explicitly stated, is supposed in the last part; a certain vindictive quality in God's justice, which demands that redemption be not merely a question of Christ's obedience, but of punishment as well.[1]

Newman's preoccupation with theological matters manifested itself even in his dreams. He records on 1 June 1821: 'About a week ago I dreamed a spirit came to me, and discoursed about the other world. . . .

Among other things it said that it was absolutely impossible for the reason of man to understand the mystery (I think) of the Holy Trinity, and in vain to argue about it; but every thing in another world was so *very, very plain*, that there was not the slightest difficulty about it. I cannot put into any sufficiently strong form of words the ideas which were conveyed to me. I thought I instantly fell on my knees, overcome with gratitude to God.' (*AW*, 166–7) Subsequent entries for this year reveal a similar preoccupation.

The Evangelicals placed special emphasis on reading Scripture. The second essay of Scott's *Essays on the Most important Subjects in Religion*, is entitled 'On the importance of revealed truth; the duty of reading the Scriptures, and the manner in which it should be performed.' Scott recommends that one read the whole of Scripture and that one search the Scriptures *daily*; read them 'with the express purpose of appropriating the information communicated by it from God to man', use helps in searching the Scriptures but not to depend on them, and lastly to chart one's course from it. On this last point he expands as follows:

We should accompany our reading with impartial self-examination, both in respect of our knowledge, judgment, dispositions, affections, motives, words, and actions, in every particular, at present and in times past; that we learn the state and wants of our souls: and with self-application . . . that, beseeching the Lord to pardon what is past, and to help us for the future, we may without delay or reserve, begin to practice what we know, waiting for further light in such matters as still continue doubtful or obscure to us . . . the scriptures thus studied are, 'able to make us wise unto salvation, by faith in Jesus Christ.'

There are entries in the journal which show that Newman followed these recommendations. At one time he was reading the Scriptures together with Francis using Scott's Commentary, to which sessions he invited Charles, who was pleased. (10 August and 1 September 1822, *AW*, 174–5) In August 1822 he gave the first hour of the day to reading the Bible. In Autumn 1823 he began to memorize portions, even whole books, of the Bible, finished the Epistle to the Ephesians and chapters of Isaiah. (*AW*, 187, 194–5) Entries in Book I of Newman's journals from April 1821 to 2 February 1823 show how often his reading the Scriptures raised theological questions in his mind. Indeed the roots of his theology lay in his spiritual life. Both books of his journal constitute a testimony to his putting into practice the last recommendation of Scott. Some of these self-examinations were made in preparation for receiving the Eucharist.

During 1821 Newman's devotion to the Holy Eucharist was intense. On 4 August he wrote in his private journal: 'I have this week been preparing myself for the Sacrament, which, God willing, I hope to take with my brother Francis once a fortnight during the Long Vacation. These are my answers to Doddridge's Questions in his *Rise and Progress*.'[2] To help with his personal examination of conscience he bought, as he notes on 18 August, a copy of Haweis's *Spiritual Communicant*. There are further entries on 23 October and 1 December. His mother being informed of the intentions of John and Francis to take the sacrament once a fortnight, 'seemed to think I began to be righteous overmuch, and was verging upon enthusiasm. I was also leading Francis with me.' (*AW*, 175) In fact Francis was a stronger Evangelical than John. As to the implied reference to Evangelicals, it is an established fact that the practice of Holy Communion was restored to the place of honour in which it was once held, not by the High Church, but by the Evangelicals. Wesley and the Oxford Methodists restored the practice of weekly Communion.

Sheridan affirms that 'following Beveridge, Doddridge, and Scott, he regarded the reception of Holy Communion as the supreme act of renewal of his personal covenant with Christ', and that 'this was why he has such an intense aversion to the college Gaudy during his early days at Trinity: he regarded it as a wholesale profanation of the Lord's Supper'.[3]

The journals reveal how faithfully Newman examined his behaviour and his intense efforts to live a Christian life of perfection. He records his sins and defects, e.g., impure thoughts, pride, vanity, ambitiousness, anger (especially against his brother Frank), contentiousness and ill-temper. John had received his father's consent that Frank come up to Oxford in the autumn of 1821, his expenses being paid by John whose earnings would come from private tutoring. They took up lodgings together at Seale's Coffee House, where Bowden used to lodge. Francis apparently irritated him, for he frequently mentions his ill-temper toward him. One entry, 31 December 1822, reads:

> 'Ah', I answered (my mother), 'I have felt while with Francis at Oxford, a spirit of desperate ill temper and sullen anger rush on me, so that I was ready to reply and act in the most cruel manner to intentions of the greatest kindness and affection. So violent has this sometimes proved, that I have quite trembled from head to foot, and thought I should fall down under excess of agitation.' (*AW*, 188–9)

Francis was apparently unaware of this or had forgotten it, for John when examining himself for secret hidden faults before becoming a Catholic in 1845 wrote Frank and asked forgiveness for his cruelty toward him, Frank replied that he could not remember any.

The grace to perform self-examination became the subject of his prayers: 'O God, grant me to grow in grace daily, and continually to examine myself, that I may always know how my accounts stand, whenever called upon to reckon for my stewardship.' (1 September 1821, *AW*, 175) He developed this thought briefly in one of his earliest sermons, No. 19, 'Corruption of Human Nature'. 'If the sins of one day be so numerous, what must be the sins of the week? and then what of the year? and what lastly in the day of doom the dreadful sum of all the sins of our whole life, those which we ourselves know and those we do not remember and those which we never knew to be sins! What too the fearful weight of punishment before *His* judgment seat who weighs all actions and has the Keys of hell and death.' (*Ser.* I, 306)

Though as a Catholic he relinquished the doctrine of the corruption of human nature, he nevertheless retained this vivid sense that the longer one lived the more sins one commits and is therefore accountable for at the Last Judgment. In *Meditations and Devotions* he reflects: 'All my sins, offences, and negligences, not of one day only, but of all days, are in Thy book. . . . As the spendthrift is overwhelmed by a continually greater weight of debt, so am I exposed continually to a greater and greater score of punishments catalogued against me. . . . I shall have put upon me the punishment of ten thousands sins – I shall for this purpose be sent to Purgatory – how long will it last? . . . Not til I have paid the last farthing.' (*Med.* 345)

The young Newman records when he fails in the practice of self-examination, e.g., the entry for 23 October 1821; 'it is now eight weeks since I partook of the Lord's Supper, and I ought to have cast up my accounts before this.' (*AW*, 177), or the entry for 1 December 1821: 'Tomorrow I am to take the Sacrament. It will be five weeks since I last examined my self.' (*AW*, 178) At the beginning of 1822 he reviews the past year in general terms. On the credit side he lists having more time for religious exercises than when he was 'a fagging drudge,' and Easter or Act Term he devoted nearly entirely to religion. (23 January 1822, *AW*, 181)

DIFFICULTIES IN THE PRACTICE OF PRAYER

Entries in his private journal reveal that prayer, in which he felt 'deficient', was a central preoccupation in his spiritual life. (4 August 1821, *AW*, 174) Hence he was able to record not long after, 'I trust I have prayed more frequently . . . and have felt the peace and love of God diffused on my heart. I have interceded more frequently for others.' (1 September 1821, *AW*, 175) Intercessory prayer became one of the key elements in his prayer life. On 1 June 1822 he resolves to read 'the form of social prayer with Francis three times a week'. (*AW*, 186)[4] The journal likewise indicates that like anyone who attempts to pray regularly he experienced periods of dryness and distraction. Thus he records: 'I can read religious books, the most spiritual, with great pleasure, and, when so engaged feel myself warmed to prayer and thanksgiving; but let the appointed hour of devotion arrive, and I am cold and dead. My head is full of God during the day, and particularly of the salvation of others, and I can offer up heartfelt prayers in my solitary walk, but this dreadful listlessness comes on me morning after morning and evening after evening.' (13 May 1821, *AW*, 165–6) He mentions distractions in prayer in an entry for 1 December 1821; 'My mind wanders so in prayer, it is quite shocking.' (*AW*, 178) Part of the problem may have been owing to the Evangelical emphasis on 'heart' and 'feelings,' for when he gave up Evangelicalism he affirmed that 'its emotional and feverish devotion and its tumultuous experiences were foreign to his nature, which indeed was ever conspicuously faulty in the opposite direction, as being in a way incapable, as if physically, of enthusiasm, however legitimate and guarded'. (*AW*, 82) When he does experience these feelings he is happy, e.g., 'I felt at one time today more ardent affection towards my dear Saviour than I recollect feeling before, and a more eager desire to depart and be with Christ which is far better.' (10 October 1821, *AW*, 177)

Like any person trying to advance in the spiritual life he at times feels he is making no progress at all. 'As to ill temper, hastiness of spirit, cruelty, harshness of speech, I have not advanced an inch. I pray against it every morning, and when I am entering into it, but my hard heart will have its own way.' (23 November 1821, *AW*, 177) On the other hand, he does record progress, e.g., 'I trust that, though still very defective, I have not been so cruel to Francis since June 2, when I took the Sacrament.' (30 June 1822, *AW*, 186) and 'I am glad to say that in my solitary walks, that is, my daily, I have had nearly always my mind disposed for secret prayers, and have generally made use of that interval from study, or a good part of it, in interceding for all friends, and for all mankind.' (15 September, *AW*, 187) Again he records: 'I trust my heart is purer than it was; this year I certainly have not been attacked, as before, by my besetting sin [unspecified] – particularly the last half – yet I am not what I ought to be.' (21 February 1824, *AW*, 196)

Preaching played an important role in Evangelicalism, and so it is not surprising to find that Newman noted in his journal when he heard a good sermon. 'Today and last Sunday I heard Dr Pearson at St James's Chapel. Ever since there was an idea of our coming out of town, I have prayed God that, when absent from home, we might have faithful preachers of His word, wherever we went. And see how graciously he has answered my prayer.' (23 September 1821, *AW*, 176) These sermons certainly had their effect, for he mentions taking up the suggestion of Mr Grant in his sermon at Kentish Town Chapel, to 'mark the days or seasons of mercy, and commemorate them in succeeding years by some act of charity – Ebenezer'. He designated the following days: '1. My birthday February 21, 1801. 2. The day of my baptism, April 9, 1801. 3. The first or last days of my conversion, Aug. 1 and December 21, 1816. 4. The day I matriculated at Oxford, December 14, 1816. 5. The day I got the Trinity Scholarship, May 18, 1818. 6. The day I got my Testamur and lost my class, November 27, 1820. 7. The day when our prospects so changed, November 3, 1821.' (*AW*, 179, 181)[5]

THEOLOGY OF HOLINESS (1822–3)

After drawing up a summary of his Evangelical beliefs in 1821, Newman continued to theologize, and when he was striving for control over himself and to progress in spiritual matters, he composed a ten-page document which he later dated as 1822 or 1823. In it he explores the nature of essential holiness. Sheridan compares this with the treatment of holiness given in the 'Collection of Scripture Passages' of 1821, and remarks that whereas the latter 'contains a lengthy *description* of conversion, this document is really Newman's *theology* of conversion worked out in systematic fashion'.[6]

Since holiness is necessary for salvation and not natural to man, it must be implanted in him by God. Hence Scripture teaches the necessity of conversion, or 'a radical change of heart and sentiments taking place in every one who would be saved'. How is this effected? 'The agent is God through the instrumentality of His Spirit. The means is the Word of God and Instruction. The principle and root of it in our souls is faith. The process is one of humiliation and hearty repentance and turning to God, on the knowledge of our sin and conviction of our misery.' The first alteration of sentiment is instantaneous, but the 'revolution of sentiment' normally takes time; it is a progress. Newman then goes on to explore the relation between this conversion and baptism, and concludes that baptism is an 'accidental adjunct' of regeneration, it is not a common accompaniment, nor is it an indispensable condition.[7]

'Holiness is not regeneration but the term to which regeneration tends.' In what does it consist? Newman asks; does holiness consist 'in the performance of good actions, in being just, charitable, temperate? or in certain religious exercises, in attending the ordinances of grace, in frequenting God's house and table? or in both -- or is it something beyond them?' He does not give a strict definition but makes several points: 1) holiness is not mere good living, though it includes this; 2) it arises from a conviction of the importance of eternal things, i.e., a recognition that living in and for the world is not primary, that living for God is; 3) this does not arise from nature, but is implanted by God through the Holy Spirit; 4) it is the knowledge and will to obey God's law in all things as this will is actualized, through God's grace in the course of time. This process continues through one's entire lifetime; 5) it is not necessarily connected with baptism, otherwise how explain that many Christians appear unholy and unspiritual, though they were baptized?[8]

In this treatment of holiness Newman appeals to experience: first that man by nature is not holy, that even in the just, those who are made righteous with the righteousness of Christ imputed to them, sin remains. Like St Paul, he discovers within him 'a law, that, when I would do good, evil is present within me'. Man remains sinful by nature, even after justification, as experience testifies. So, also, that baptism is not essential to the process of conversion may be deduced from the experience of nominal Christians. There is no recognition at this stage of his theological development of grace raising one to a higher level of being. Regeneration is 'delivery from the bondage of sin', and is needed to heal the wounds of sin. Experience will later militate against his Evangelical beliefs when he sees that Calvinism will not work in a parish.[9]

Newman's Evangelicalism, at least as it influenced his actions, was a trial to his father. On Sunday, 30 September 1821, John was suddenly called downstairs to give his opinion whether he thought it was a sin to write a letter on a Sunday. He found that his brother Frank had refused to copy one. Apparently John sided with Frank, and 'A scene ensued more painful than any I have experienced.' He records however the following day, 'My Father was reconciled to us today. When I think of the utter persuasion he must entertain of the justice of his views of our apparent disobedience, the seeming folly of our opinions, and the way in which he is harassed by worldly cares, I think his forgiveness of us an example of very striking candour, forbearance, and generosity.' (*AW*, 176)

This, however, was not the end. On 6 January 1822 after church his father spoke to him as follows:

> I fear you are becoming etc. . . . Take care . . . You are encouraging a nervousness and morbid sensibility, and irritability, which may be very serious. I know what it is myself, perfectly well. I know it is a disease of mind . . . Depend upon it, no one's principles can be established at twenty. Your opinions in two or three years will certainly, *certainly* change . . . Take care, I repeat. You are on dangerous ground. The temper you are encouraging may lead to something alarming. Weak minds are carried into superstition, and strong ones into infidelity . . . Do nothing ultra. Many men say and do things, when young, which they would fain retract when older, and for shame they cannot. (*AW*, 179)

John's reaction is interesting. Never for a moment does he question his own judgement or admit that he might be wrong, though ironically a year and a half later he poses the question, 'Why may not females employ themselves in needle work on the sabbath? . . . Is it in itself wrong? (3 August 1823, *AW*, 171) This confidence would be shaken when later as a curate at St Clement's he began to relinquish Evangelicalism. In his 'Autobiographical Memoir,' he repeats the words of his father, and adds, 'yet very few years passed. before, against his confident expectations, his Father's words about him came true'. (*AW*, 82)

Several letters reveal the firmness of his trust in divine Providence. On the impending bankruptcy of his father, he writes to his mother that all families have their sorrows and troubles, and how fortunate that theirs is from without rather than within. 'We are not disunited by internal variance.' This distress heightens all affection and love. As to the trial itself, he quotes St Paul, 'All things work together for good to those who love God.' (Rom. 8:28). 'I am firmly and rootedly persuaded of this.' (*LD* I, 113) His father must have been touched by this, for he writes:

I trust when this dreadful Storm is over under Providence that my Mind will be settled and calm enough to consider well which my state of agitation has hitherto disabled me from the advantages which you so feelingly and with such good practical sense describe. To me none of the least are the Blessings of having such Children so deeply endowed with the best of Principles both as to religion and high honor and I am proud to say of not contemptible abilities Amongst *them* let *this* be a consolation to *you* that as the Eldest you have by example as well as by precept and instruction so greatly contributed to the Moral Beauty as well as to the cultivation and enlargement of their Minds . . .

   God bless you my dear John and with Love to Francis I am . . . (*LD* I, 114)

In a preachy letter to his aunt, which he justifies by saying that affliction allows one to talk on religious topics without offence, John developed this theme at great length. However distasteful it may sound to modern ears, it is perhaps the most Evangelical letter he ever wrote, not only by reason of its content, but by the approach to the subject, the vocabulary, the stock phrases, and especially by its emotional language, the language of enthusiasm.

Thank God, the severe dispensation, which has visited us, has as yet no terrors for me – God grant I may continue in the same state of mind – I really quite hail it and rejoice in it; for I think it is very likely to be productive of great good to all of us. Surely it is a mark, a striking mark, of the divine care and protection; for He seems to be withdrawing from us all those 'things of the earth' on which we might be tempted to 'set our affections', in order that we may look upwards, and 'lay up treasure in Heaven', and sit loose to all earthly objects, and seek all our joys and pleasures from holiness and the love of God. I am convinced that nothing can be a greater snare and evil to a person than unalloyed prosperity. I cannot say how I should behave were the offer of possessing them made to me, but in my present state of mind there is nothing I would rather deprecate than wealth, or fame, or great influence. Every reflection suggests more strongly and more strongly the conclusion of the Apostle – 'having food and raiment let us be therewith content' – a conclusion infinitely more cheering than a dry submission or a cold acquiesence in what is deemed unavoidable; for it is attended by a conviction that God gives us that which is best for us

to have. To those who are conscious that they long to love God and to
be perfectly holy, every dispensation of Providence, which the dull
world is accustomed to regard as unfortunate, gives rise to the most
fervent gratitude; and they exult in undergoing trials and passing
through the flames of calamity, for they trust and expect to come forth
purified and refined, with the dross of human corruption purged away.
It is thus, through God's grace, that I feel with respect to our present
circumstances; they may be painful, they may be grievous; but I exult
and triumph, and my heart beats high at the thought that God is
cutting away all ties which might bind me to the world and preparing
me for the Kingdom of which perfect holiness is the characteristic
glory. – When I add to this reflection, the delightful thought that those
I love most may be undergoing the same blessed discipline and
preparation as myself, how can I but rejoice with joy unspeakable at
the event that has taken place?

Newman was well aware of its Evangelical tone, for he concludes this
sermonette with the admission, 'this may be called enthusiasm, but it is
an enthusiasm which I wish never to lose; it is a feeling which I am
persuaded is alone powerful to support under suffering, and which I pray
God all who smile at, may soon themselves experience'. (*LD* I, 115–6)

No wonder his father was concerned about his son's Evangelicalism. If
Newman at this point could foresee the many failures, disappointments,
misunderstandings, slanders, he would have to sustain, would he have
shown the same enthusiasm? The question, however, is unreal. At this
stage Newman is like the Apostles, James and John, who, when asked by
Christ, 'Are you able to drink the cup that I am baptized with?' replied,
'We are able.' Many would be the opportunities of showing trust in divine
Providence. He well understood the hopes and desires of young people,
but he told them in a sermon he would later preach at St Mary's,
'Whether they will be fulfilled or not, is in God's hand. He may be
pleased to grant the desires of your heart; if so, thank Him for His Mercy;
only be sure, that all will be for your highest good.' (*PPS* I, 26, 349)

Meanwhile Newman was to realize two desires of his heart. On 11
January 1822 his father told him he should make up his mind what he
wanted to be. 'So I chose; and determined on the Church. Thank God,
this is what I have prayed for.' The following day he returned to Oxford.
His father's last words were, 'do not show any ultraism in any thing'. By
this time he had decided to stand for the Oriel Fellowship; in a few
months he would be selected a Fellow of Oriel. (*AW*, 180)

CHAPTER FOUR

Turning Point

Newman did not accept his failure to take honours as a measure of his intellectual abilities; so in a way it is not surprising that he decided to try for the prestigious Oriel Fellowship, 'the great object of the ambition of half the Bachelors of Oxford'. (*LD* I, 137) For one thing the choice did not depend upon how a man did in his public examinations, but his powers to think and to judge. So much was this so that Oriel had been severely criticized for having passed over in the previous year a first class man in favour of two candidates who had only second class honours. The *Edinburgh Review*, moreover, attacked the impartiality of the examiners. This did not disturb Newman since he did not think he would succeed on the first attempt, but it would be a good preparation for a subsequent try or at least for some other fellowship.

No sooner did he think of standing than he experienced an inner spiritual conflict and struggle:

> How active still are the evil passions of vain glory, ambition etc in my soul! After my failure last November, I thought that they never would be unruly again, for I felt so resigned through God's grace that it seemed as if the honours of the world has no longer any charm in themselves to tempt me with. Alas! no sooner is any mention made of my standing for a fellowship, than every mound and barrier seems swept away, and the tides of passion spread and overflow and deluge me in every direction, and without thy help, O Lord, what will be the end of this? (*AW*, 177)

Two weeks later he records in his diary: 'How desirous I am of worldly honour! There is every reason for thinking I shall not succeed in my object, and I seem to see it would not be good for me – but my evil heart boils over with vain-glorious anticipations of success.' (*AW*, 178)

The conflict continued in the following months as his journal records:

Hope will arise, do what I will; but it is instantly beaten down by some very weighty reflections. 1. I am not humble or spiritual enough to bear success yet. 2. It will make me too independent in money matters – at present God is trying me, and feeding me by the ravens [I Kings 17:6]. I have need of a severe discipline in this respect. Independence would make me secure. 3. Provision seems to be made for me for some time. Last 5th of January I wrote to my Aunt, and said, 'I deprecate that day in which God gives me any repute, or approach to wealth.' Alas, how I am changed! I am perpetually praying to get into Oriel, and to obtain the prize for my Essay. O Lord, dispose of me as will best promote Thy glory – and, after that, as will best advance my sanctification – but give me resignation and contentment. O Lord Jesus, in all thy dispositions concerning me, to rise or fall, give me that heavenly peace which passeth understanding. (5 February 1822, *AW*, 182–3)

To pay for Francis's education he would have to have more pupils. For a while his father was not going to send Francis back after his first term, but reversed his decision. Newman wrote in his diary upon getting another pupil: 'Three things I have been praying for lately, and all three Thou hast granted me – that I might be in the Church, that Francis might come to Oxford, and that I might have another pupil.' (*AW*, 182)

While preparing for the Oriel competition, one of those emotional entanglements occurred, not unknown among loving persons, each of whom are more concerned for the other than for themselves. It began when John's mother wrote him a beautiful letter congratulating him on his 21st birthday:

I cannot let this 21st anniversary of your birthday pass, without a line of congratulation from me . . . As my words flow from the heart of a Mother, I know they will meet a kind reception. I thank God, it is a day of rejoicing to us all; to your Father and me, that it has given us a Son who has uniformly persevered in improving the talents given him, and in forming his character both morally and religiously to virtue. And now we have no more the dear child, we may boast instead, a companion, counsellor and friend. To your dear brothers and sisters it has given a second father, to whom they are much indebted for the improvement and cultivation of their minds; and, proud and happy am I to say, you are worthy of each other. To yourself, my dear, it is a day

of thankfulness and rejoicing, that you have been guided and protect[ed] in this good path to fulfil all these duties so satisfactorily to
your nearest and dearest connections, and likewise to form other
friendships, which promise to be permanently valuable, and that you
are placed in the situation that seems most suited to your abilities and
character. These and innumerable other blessings we have all of us to
be grateful for, and I rely with humble but perfect confidence in that
Almighty Power who has hitherto preserved you, that He will diffuse
His blessings on your future years (*LD* I, 122)

In writing to thank her, John mused about his feelings on becoming a
man and the personal responsibility this would entail. 'I seem now more
left to myself, and, when I reflect upon my own weaknesses, I have cause
to shudder.' As the transcription of the letter (the only extant copy)
breaks off at this point, there is no way of knowing what more he said, if
any in explanation of this remark. He continued the letter, begging his
father and mother not to think that he had a chance of succeeding in the
Oriel examination, as something in her and his father's letter seemed to
indicate. The greatest pain he suffered in not taking Honours in the
Schools was the disappointment he felt he had given to them.

Mrs Newman replied saying that she and his father were anxious that
he was depressed, not getting enough relaxation, not taking care of his
health. She likewise assured him that 'nothing but your own over-anxiety
can make you suppose we glance a thought at Oriel. If it had not been
from fear of improperly discouraging you, I should have repeatedly said I
thought it unlikely you should *ever* succeed among so many candidates.'
She went on to administer a bit of motherly correction.

To show you I do not think you *too old* for a Mother's correction and
advice, I shall not hesitate to tell you I see one great fault in your
character, which alarms me very much, as I observe it increases upon
you seriously; and, as all virtues may degenerate into vices, it is every
one's duty to have a strict guard over themselves to avoid extremes.
Your fault is want of self confidence, and a dissatisfaction with yourself,
that you cannot exceed the bounds of human nature. Else, why should
you, who *at least* equal in talents, prudence, and acquirements most
young men of your age, allow yourself to be so desponding as to think
you need to 'shudder at your own weakness' . . . If I have from anxiety
thought your letter more serious than you intended, forgive me. (*LD* I,
123–4)

This set off alarm bells in John's head and he hastened to write listing all the wine and music parties he was attending. He got the Proctor [Mr Kinsey] to write his father to testify to his good health, which he did, as did his brother Frank. He then got to the heart of the matter. He assured his mother that the sentiments and opinions he expressed in his letter were not new, but 'exactly the same for these five years ... If they had made me melancholy, morose, austere, distant, reserved, sullen, then indeed they might with justice be the subject of anxiety: but if ... I am always cheerful, if at home I am always ready and eager to join in any merriment, ... then my principles ... cannot be accused of bad practical effects. Take me when I am most foolish at home ... stop me short, and ask me *then* ... whether my opinions are less gloomy, no, I think I should seriously return the same answer that I 'shudder at myself.' (*LD* I, 124–5)

This does not, however, clear up the meaning of what he meant by shuddering at himself. In his journal for the 21st, he writes, 'Have I grown in grace this year past? ... how very proud and bitter I am in spirit! how unforgiving – how unclean – how timid – how lukewarm in prayer. It is dreadful to go through the list ...' (*AW*, 183) It is probable that he is thinking of all his failures to correct his faults. It must also be recalled that according to his Calvinistic belief in the corruption of human nature, all feeling and desires that arose spontaneously within him were not tendencies to sin, as in the traditional Catholic view, but actual sins. Also it is not an uncommon mistake for persons not well advanced in spiritual matters to think they can conquer all impulses directly by will power.[1]

Why did Newman do so brilliantly in this examination when he did so poorly in the other? There was the absence of fear of disappointing his parents, there was the knowledge that he could try again, if not successful. Just before taking the examination for his degree he discovered that not having had proper guidance he had wasted so much time in reading what was useless for it. But now he was better prepared. Since the main thing seemed to be Latin composition, he began to learn, not only how to write Latin compositions, but the principles behind the study. Previously he had thought that Latinity consisted in using good phrases. He now came to realize that he should have started with the whole rather than with the parts, and that 'good Latinity lies in structure; that every word of a sentence may be Latin, yet the whole sentence remain English: and that dictionaries do not teach composition'.[2] The occasion of this discovery was a work of Edward Copleston, *Praelectiones Academicae*, a series of lectures delivered terminally while he was Professor at Oxford, from 1802 until 1812. Two years later Newman actually drew out these principles in a paper called, 'Hints on Latin composition', but at the moment he was actually applying them. For exercise he decided to contend for the Latin prize, which he did not succeed in winning, but in the course of doing this work with the aid of the *Praelectiones*, he grasped the 'idea' of Latin composition, and progressed more rapidly thereafter.

Consequently he was able to write to his father, 'I assure you that they know very little of me and judge very superficially of me, who think I do not put a value on myself *relatively* to others. I think (since I am forced to speak boastfully) few have attained the facility of comprehension which I have arrived at, from the regularity and constancy of my reading, and the laborious and nerve-bracing and fancy-repressing study of Mathematics, which has been my principle subject.' (*LD* I, 122–5) Newman comments on the change of feeling from when he went into the examination for his degree: 'As, when I was going up for my Degree Examination, every day made my hopes fainter, so now they seem to swell and ripen, as the time approaches.' (18 March 1822, *AW*, 184)

The examination must have been a gruelling experience, lasting as it did five days, and the first two days, eight or nine hours. The examiners were kind, and a lunch was served at one o'clock consisting of sandwiches, fruit, cake, jellies, and wine, and there was a blazing fire. He was stiff from sitting nearly nine hours on rather hard benches. By Tuesday 'I was very, very nervous, and I prayed earnestly for strength, and God gave it to me most wonderfully'. (*AW*, 185) Impressed by Newman's performance three of the electors went to Trinity to enquire about his character. So excited was his tutor, Mr Short, that he could not help sending for Newman whom he encouraged to continue and fortified him with a dinner of lamb cutlets and fried parsley, a bodily refreshment, Newman later recorded, 'which had some share in the re-assurance with which Short's words inspired him'. (*AW*, 62) On Wednesday and Thursday several times he 'comforted' himself with a motto in Oriel Hall, '*Pie repone te.*'

On Friday 12 April Newman was elected Fellow of Oriel, a day which he felt 'to be the turning point of his life, and of all days the most memorable'. It was a day he always kept in remembrance. When the Provost's butler arrived to convey the news, Newman was playing the violin. The butler in what was probably a usual speech said 'he had, he feared, disagreeable news to announce, viz. that Mr Newman was elected Fellow of Oriel, and that his immediate presence was required there'. As Newman himself narrates in the third person, 'The person addressed, thinking that such language savoured of impertinent familiarity, merely answered "Very well" and went on fiddling. This led the man to ask whether perhaps he had not mistaken the rooms and gone to the wrong person, to which Mr Newman replied that [it] was all right.' No sooner did the man leave than Newman threw down the violin and 'dashed down stairs with all speed to Oriel College. And he recollected after fifty years the eloquent faces and eager bows of the tradesmen and others whom he met on his way, who had heard the news, and well understood why he was crossing from St Mary's to the lane opposite at so extraordinary a pace.' (*AW*, 62) He proceeded to the tower to receive the congratulations of the assembled Fellows. 'I could bear the presence of Copleston, and many other of the lights of Oriel; but when Keble advanced to take my hand, I quite shrank and could have nearly sunk into the floor, ashamed at so great an honour.' The excitement at Trinity was intense, and students rushed in all directions to Trinity to men they knew, to congratulate them on the success of their College. The bells were set ringing from three different towers, which Newman had to pay for. (*LD* I, 139; *AW*, 63)

Newman took his seat in the chapel at Oriel and dined in the Common Room. He sat next to Keble 'and, as I have heard him represented, he is more like an undergraduate than the first man in Oxford – so perfectly unassuming and unaffected in his manner'. (*LD* I, 131) How Newman looked upon his success from a spiritual point of view may be gathered from a letter to his aunt whom he was trying to console in her money troubles.

A month ago, every thing was uncertain and dark as to my future prospects. I seemed to have no hopes in the University, I had few friends, no reputation, no provision for the morrow. I was sensible that every thing I eat, even, I had no idea how it was to be paid for – I knew that every day was adding to what was owing and I saw no quarter from which relief could come; as to getting a fellowship this year, when I examined it seriously and rationally, there seemed no chance. I had completely failed in the schools, I was looked down upon and despised by those who heard I was a competitor for the Oriel Election. I had not been attending either to classics or mathematics the last year – the other candidates were men who had taken high honours and come *fresh* from the schools and scholastic reading. Yet by that Heavenly Arm before which the most difficult things are as nothing, I was in an instant secured in comfort and tranquility. He rolled away every barrier, He dispelled every cloud; in the morning every thing was uncertain, and by noon everything was sure and settled. Now this was in no respects done by my own strength. . . . it was God and God alone who accomplished it . . . it was the work of Providence. And before it took place, I was by God's grace fully persuaded that He *would* save me and preserve me; I did not indeed anticipate so early and complete a deliverance, and I thought I should have need of long patience, but I was convinced that God would watch over me. . . . (*LD* I, 138)

The University was astonished at Newman's success, as he told his father. 'Kinsey's joy is very great. Ogle says nothing has given him so much satisfaction, since he came into his present situation, whether since he took his first class, since he became M.D. since he undertook the Tutorship of Trinity, or since he married Mrs Ogle seems uncertain.' (*LD* I, 135) F. R. Thresher, a fellow student at Ealing with Newman, predicted great things for him. 'Behold you (to take a peep into futurity) in Holy Orders, taking pupils in College, and having a Curacy within a short distance, then Public Tutor, Vicar of ——, Provost, Regius Professor of Divinity, Bishop of ——, Archbishop of Canterbury. Or shall we say thus, — student-at-law, Barrister, Lord Chancellor, or at least Lord Chief Justice of the King's Bench. Which of these ladders is it your intention to climb? You now have it in your power to decide.' (*LD* I, 137)

Meanwhile, his continued self-scrutiny and dissatisfaction with his efforts at self-control went on: On Sunday, 2 June, he records:

Weeks go on, and I am not a bit better, or rather I am worse; and this morning I have to take the Sacrament. O good God, I am unmerciful, hard hearted, unforgiving, pitiless . . . I pray and bless Thee that this temptation, into which I have been gradually sinking this last half year, is not one of painful and perplexing doubts and fits of unbelief. I praise and bless Thee that it is not a fiery attack from my besetting sin. What will become of me? I am rolling down a precipice, and there is no arm in the universe that can save me but that of Jesus.

. . . 1st I will read the form of social prayer with Francis three times a week, by God's grace. 2nd I will try to repress every injurious word, though I think I am in the right. 3rd I will study my Bible at least an hour a day. 4th I will strive to drive away every wandering thought during my prayers. (*AW*, 186)

At the end of the month he writes 'I have been miserably beset (with bad thoughts) this last week. I trust that, though still very defective, I have not been so cruel to Francis since June 2, when I took the Sacrament.' And on 15 July he records: 'I give an hour a day to the Apocalypse. My idea is to interpret its symbols etc by other Scriptures, and *then* to compare it with actual events. I find it most delightful.' (*AW*, 186–7)

VARIOUS TASKS

Newman spent the Long Vacation at Oxford, getting up lectures in Latin and Greek for his pupil. In his journal for 19 July he confesses: 'I have shown petulance and ill nature towards my pupil. I find it very irksome to be so tied down as I am. I am too very solitary.' He then composed a rather Evangelical prayer, 'Pound me, Lord, into small bits grind me down, anything for a meek and quiet spirit.' (*AW*, 187) He is grateful that he gets on better with his pupil, 'not but that I am conscious of very great perverseness and ill humour in heart, but I have seldom shown it in my words'. But on 15 September, 'Since I wrote last, I have sometimes shown a most ungovernable spirit towards my pupil; still however, on the whole, I think, thank God, I am, meeker than I was; at least I do not show it so much.' On 3 August 1856 Newman added a note here which is crossed out in pencil: 'how I longed for it to be over! My pupil was a little wretch, aged 17'. (*AW*, 187) On 11 October he writes to Harriett that he is liberated, 'Liber sum – [my pupil having gone] and I have been humming, whistling, and laughing out loud to myself all day. I can hardly keep from jumping about.' (*LD* I, 154) No doubt the reception of £90 from his pupil contributed to his elation.

During these early days after he was elected a Fellow, it was his custom to take a daily walk alone. Once he ran into Copleston, then Provost, with one of the other Fellows. 'he turned round, and with the kind courteousness which sat so well on him, made me a bow and said, "Numquam minus solus, quam cum solus,"' (Never less alone than when alone.) This Newman mentioned in the *Apologia*. Only in his journal does he reveal that he was accustomed to spend all or a good part of the time in prayer, 'interceding for all friends, and for all mankind'. (*Apo.*, 15–16; *AW*, 187)

The summer was not entirely taken up with his pupil. He assisted Richard Whately in an article on Logic for the *Encyclopaedia Metropolitana*, which later became the basis for his well-known book *Elements of Logic*. Upon becoming a Fellow, Newman could not be drawn out in conversation by reason of his shyness, awe of his colleagues, and 'that real isolation of thought and spiritual solitariness, which was the result of his Calvinistic beliefs'. Some of the leading Fellows decided to put him in the hands of Richard Whately, who rode and walked with Newman and drew him out. It was not long before he could report to them they had made no mistake in choosing him, 'he was the clearest-headed man he knew'. (*AW*, 65–6)

Newman also composed a letter on 22 September 1822 to the *Christian Observer*, an Evangelical periodical, in which he offered advice to religious students not to leave their prayers to the last minute before retiring lest they be too exhausted and drowsy to make them properly. He warned against the danger of regular attendance at chapel making one's prayer 'formal and heartless'. This was a standard Evangelical theme, as also his suggestion that on Sunday the student should not substitute mere theological for devotional studies. What his father had said about a previous letter to the *Christian Observer* would apply even more to this. 'That letter was more like the composition of an old man, than of a youth just entering life with energy and aspiration.' (*LD* I, 150–4)[3]

He managed to get Francis entered in Worcester, but he would not be able to come into residence right away but would have to continue his studies at home which John mapped out for him. He assured his father to have no anxiety about his taking care of Francis financially, 'Every thing will, I see it will, be very right, if only you will let me manage.' And he did for that year, though later he was to have some financial troubles again. By February he had four pupils and would get more.

On 2 February, as Probationary Fellow he pronounced his Oration in Latin in Oriel Hall. In re-reading it for the first time in 1874, he noted: 'I read this now for the first time this 51 years with sad tenderness, as if I loved and pitied the poor boy so ignorant of the future, who then wrote and delivered it before the Provost and Fellows, now almost all dead, but to whom I then looked up with great reverence and loving pride. JHN. July 30, 1874.' (*LD* I, 157) On his birthday, he wrote in his journal:

First, let me notice the most wonderful and most parental manner in which the Lord has supported Francis and myself in temporal things. Michaelmas year we began with hardly any thing . . . I had indeed one pupil, but there did not seem any possibility of my having more. However, by God's grace, I was enabled to trust in Him, and I entertained . . . no apprehension of want or difficulty. How He has answered that trust! . . . I have been enabled nearly entirely to support

Francis . . . to enter him at Worcester . . . and it seems as if I should have the requisite sum to pay for him, when he comes to reside. (*AW*, 189)

He goes on to note that 'two great courses of sin' stained the past year, 'ill temper and self conceit'. He mentions the comment of the Provost on his Oriel oration, that it was 'spirited'. 'Well, I have been brooding on this, and repeating the composition again and again to myself. Wherever I go, I think people are looking at me and thinking of me . . . Again, I am a great liar, a mean liar . . . from pride, lest I should confess myself wrong.'

On 4 April he was admitted actual Fellow of Oriel, and prayed, 'Gracious God, let me in this so favoured station, in which Thy Mercy has lodged me, do every thing for Thy glory.' (*AW*, 190) The same day Pusey was elected Fellow of Oriel, and the two shortly afterwards formed a close friendship. One of the less pleasing traits of the Evangelicals, as Newman later came to realize, was the presumptuousness, because one is elected, to judge of the spiritual state of others. They attempted to measure the divine gift in each by its sensible effects, and accounted none to be Christians but those they supposed they could ascertain to be such, 'by their profession, language and carriage'. This was precisely what Newman attempted to do in his early contacts with Pusey, and he later recorded that his remarks about Pusey in his journal commenced 'in a high patronizing tone', and he proceeds to quote from his journal to illustrate it.

April 4, 1823 he writes, speaking of the election of Fellows, 'I thank God that two men have succeeded this morning,' (E. B. Pusey and W. R. Churton) 'who, I trust, are favorably disposed to religion, or at least moral and thinking, not worldly and careless men'; and he goes on to pray that they may be brought 'into the true Church' . . . By May 2 Newman has advanced further in his good opinion of him. He writes, 'I have had several conversations with Pusey on religion, since I last mentioned him. Thank God, how can I doubt his seriousness.' His very eagerness to talk of the Scriptures seems to prove it. . . . And on May 17 he remarks 'That Pusey is Thine, O Lord, how can I doubt? his deep views of the Pastoral Office, his high ideas of the spiritual rest of the Sabbath, his devotional spirit, his love of the Scriptures, his firmness and zeal, all testify to the operation of the Holy Ghost; yet I fear he is prejudiced against Thy children. Let me never be eager to convert him to a *party* or to a form of *opinion.* Lead us *both* on in the way of Thy commandments. What am I that I should be so blest in my near associates!' (*AW*, 75)

On 10 May Newman began to read the Life of Henry Martyn[4] whose sanctity he found 'inspiring', and to whom he paid tribute in one of his first sermons, No. 12 (*Ser.* II, 266). Martyn after receiving the highest honour, Senior Wrangler, at Cambridge in January 1801, became a missionary. After a long talk on a walk with Pusey in the autumn Newman began to pray that, though he lacked the necessary qualifications, God would make him a missionary, thinking it 'the highest privilege from God I can possess'. (*AW*, 191, 194) During the autumn Newman was memorizing whole books of Scripture, a practice he recommended to his sister Harriett. 'The benefit seems to me incalculable. It imbues the mind with good and holy thoughts. It is a resource in solitude, on a journey, and in the sleepless night. . . . And let me press most earnestly upon you and my other dear sisters, as well as on myself, the frequent exhortations in Scripture to prayer. If you three, and Francis, and myself join in incessant supplications for all who are dear to us, what may not be expected!' (13 October 1823, *LD*, I, 167) Meanwhile he was working very hard and by Christmas was in money straits because he had not yet been paid by his students, which forced him to trust 'not in myself'. He prays, 'I am fully confident Thou wilt relieve me – how mercifully I have been delivered hitherto!' (19 December 1823; 9 February 1824, *AW*, 195–6) Upon entering his room he found a letter containing £35.

Dr Charles Lloyd, Canon of Christ Church, upon becoming Regius Professor of Divinity, began lectures to which four Fellows from Oriel and four from Christ Church, were invited. Newman attended them during the years 1823 and 1824. These were run in a catechetical fashion. Lloyd was more interested in apologetics than in the contents of faith, making light of the internal evidence for Christianity in comparison of its external proofs; hence his liking for exegetical criticism, historical research, and controversy, than for dogma and philosophy. He belonged to the high-and-dry school, though far larger in his views. Newman shared an attachment to him and respected him, though he did not exercise the intellectual influence on him that Whately did. To the latter he was grateful for having taught him how to think, and from him he learned 'one momentous truth of Revelation, . . . the idea of the Christian Church, as a divine appointment, and as a substantive visible body, independent of the State, and endowed with rights, prerogatives, and powers of its own'. (*AW*, 69–71)

Lloyd asked Newman to compose a work for him for the use of students in divinity, containing various things found only in Latin, 'as respecting the Talmuds, the Septuagint version etc etc . . .' so Newman began to read the Homilies, Apocrypha, and Mant's Prayer book, and to search the Bible, with reference to the question of Regeneration. (13 March 1824, *AW*, 197) Nothing apparently came of this, but it would not be long before Newman would be deeply involved in the latter question.

CHAPTER FIVE

Responsibility for Souls

After an unsuccessful attempt at fasting, Newman began to do so, apparently for the first time on 17 and 24 March, and it seemed to him later to have been in preparation for his coming ordination. On 1 May at Pusey's suggestion, seconded by Tyler, Hawkins, Jelf, and Ottley, he accepted the curacy of St Clement's parish of about 1500 parishioners and ever growing larger. Newman wrote in his journal, 'St Clement's Church is to be rebuilt – but, before beginning the subscriptions, it is proposed, Gutch the Rector being incapacitated through age, to provide a Curate, who shall be a kind of guarantee to the subscribers that every exertion will be made, when the Church is built, to recover the parish from meeting houses, and on the other hand alehouses, into which they have been driven for want of convenient Sunday worship.' Having made the decision, he was somewhat aghast at 'the arduousness' of the under-taking, and felt tempted to draw back, but, no matter how unpalatable to some twentieth century spiritual tastes, he took courage in reminding himself, 'I am Christ's soldier.' Earlier he had prayed to be such, by now he was convinced he was. But still in consulting biblical texts on the ministry and the meaning of the ordination vows, every text 'came home to me with tenfold force'. This is but another instance of Newman's imaginative ability 'to realize' spiritual truths. For some time he had been thinking of joining the Bible Society, and now judging it better to do so before engaging in the work he was undertaking he went and subscribed to it. (*AW*, 199)

Newman wrote to his father that he was convinced 'it is necessary to get used to parochial duty early, and that a Fellow of a College after twenty years residence in Oxford feels very awkward among poor and ignorant people'. At the end of the month Newman completed a hastily commissioned article on Cicero for the *Encyclopaedia Metro-politana*, and on 13 June he was ordained deacon in Christ Church. Newman was somewhat overwhelmed by this total commitment to the Lord.

It is over. I am thine, O Lord; I seem quite dizzy, and cannot altogether believe and understand it. At first, after the hands were laid on me, my heart shuddered within me; the words 'for ever' are so terrible. It was hardly a godly feeling which made me feel melancholy at the idea of giving up all for God. At times indeed my heart burnt within me, particularly during the singing of the Veni Creator. Yet, Lord, I ask not for comfort in comparison of sanctification ... I feel as a man thrown suddenly into deep water. (*AW*, 200)

The following day he prayed with Francis but was overcome with emotion. ' "For ever", words never to be recalled. I have the responsibility of souls on me to the day of my death.' It was a responsibility he would never lose sight of.

Only in the light of this total commitment can one understand the enormous energy and zeal with which he undertook his work, visiting all the parishioners in their homes. His father advised against visiting the poor, but he went ahead anyway. He was proud to report to his father that the poor did not react to this invasion of 'an Englishman's castle' as galling to their feelings:

In all places I have been received with civility, in most with cheerful-ness and a kind of glad surprise, and in many with quite a cordiality and warmth of feeling. One person says, 'Aye, I was sure that one time or other we should have a proper minister – , another that 'she had understood from such a one that a nice young gentleman was come to the parish – ' a third 'begged I would do him the favour to call on him, whenever it was convenient to me' (this general invitation has been by no means uncommon) Another, speaking of the parish she came from said, 'the old man preached very good doctrine but he did not come to visit people at their houses as the new one did.' Singularly enough, I had written down as a memorandum a day or two before I received your letter, 'I am more convinced than ever of the necessity of frequently visiting the poorer classes – they seem so gratified at it, and praise it.' (*LD* I, 184)

He told the dissenters he made no distinction between them and regular churchgoers; 'I count you all my flock, and shall be most happy to do you a service out of Church, if I cannot within it.' He took care always to speak kindly of Mr Hinton, the Dissenting Minister, for, as he told his father, 'there is too much irreligion in the place for me to be so mad as to drive away so active an ally as Mr Hinton seems to be'. (*LD* I, 184)

VISITING THE SICK

He confided to Pusey that, 'the most pleasant part of my duties is visiting the sick . . . my visits quite hallow the day to me, as if every day were Sunday'. (*LD* I, 191) He transcribed into a thick copy-book his diary notes on sick people, whom he saw regularly, bringing some of them wine and medicines. But he was mostly interested in their spiritual state which he viewed according to Evangelical teaching. Since all have to undergo a conscious change of heart, he tried to bring this about. An entry in the appendix to his diary illustrates this:

an old man – afflicted with cancer in the throat etc. etc. had been opulent as a farmer – very bad character – seemed to wish to RELY ON CHRIST, without change of heart – gradually became unwilling to see me – whenever well enough, went to public house – I behaved imprudently in wishing him to '*love*' an enemy – he *perhaps* mistaking the meaning of the word *love* – still more imprudently, in immediately introducing the subject into the prayer that followed – he would not allow me to finish the prayer, saying he was ill – would not see me. But I *afterwards* found my pressing him to go to church had offended him also – said I did him no good, and perhaps had better not come. He one day was softened but relapsed. After some time he again seemed to wish to see me. I could not get him to say more than that he was conscious he was a sinner and relied on Christ. When I prest him with texts about newness of heart, he spoke slightingly of Scripture – I warned him against the suggestions of Satan. . . . Some time after, happening to call on him, I found him very different – in tears etc. etc. With great earnestness he begged me to pray for him, said he feared he had driven matters too late, begged me to call constantly on him etc. His poor frame was horribly emaciated – he begged me to pray too for his release. – After some days he was brought into great comfort and peace, expressing at the same time the utmost abhorrence of his sins – he grew weaker and weaker and at length departed (as I trust) in the Lord. Amen. His whole illness lasted about a year – and his agonies (according to the Physician who attended him) were indeed extraordi-

nary. The whole of this time God seemed to have been drawing him
and at last he owned it and felt it. (*LD* I, 177–8)

Miss Edgington and her parents were the first 'evidently superior
persons' he got to know in St Clement's. She had burst a blood vessel. In
visiting her, which he continued to do, he found her well-disposed. 'Her
case,' he wrote in the appendix to his diary 'is very painful – it is like a
sword going thro' my heart. – Her mother has since told me she said that
when I entered her room she thought of Jesus Christ in the picture. I
should not have put this down did not St Paul say to the Gal. "Ye
received me as Jesus Christ" – and tho' ministers now are immeasurably
below St Paul, yet Christ is infinitely above Paul as well as us. – I am
indeed a sinner.' The parents had lost another daughter and now were
left childless. (*LD* I, 187, 232)

Newman however was idealistic and inexperienced, for he added in his
diary that he could not understand the grounds of Miss E's dislike of a
Mrs Bradley, who came once or twice to visit her until her mother
discouraged further visits. To the young Newman at the time, Mrs
Bradley 'seems to have a remarkably active spirit of religion, (visiting
many persons in the parish,) and withal most pleasingly modest in her air
and deportment'. Many years later he met her in Littlemore and left a
note dated 'April 15. 1840.' 'She has a nasty smooth unnatural manner,
and I cannot conceive how I could have been taking in [*sic*] by her. But I
took things then on faith – i.e. I had faith that God's presence ever was,
where people spoke in a certain way. I viewed things through the
imagination in a remarkable degree.' (*LD* I, 232, and n. 3)

The case which he set down as having affected him the most was that
of a young widow by the name of Mrs Flynn who burst a blood vessel.
After attending her for three weeks or a month she showed various
manifestations of a converted life, such as reading the Scriptures constantly and taking the sacrament which she had never done before.

She thanked me, and said that by reading the Scriptures to her, I had
enlightened her much. The day she died, she said, on my asking her
about her feeling peace etc, 'Yes, I do, I do – very much (and then
seeming to allude to my having *repeated* often on different visits that
she must trust in Christ as she had not explicitly said so) 'you do not
think, Sir, I trust to myself do you? I trust entirely to Christ – I know
I am a great sinner – we are all sinners – but I trust to be saved thro'
Christ – 'or words to this effect – I saw her three times this day – and

she was very impatient for my coming asking 20 times whether the hour was come – and she had her senses and peace to the last. No case had affected me like this. (*LD* I, 196)

Initial rebuff did not deter him from continuing to visit a sick person such as Mrs Pattenson. He did not realize at first how ill she was. He was unable to go for ten days and she sent begging him to come. He read the Scriptures to her and prayed, 'She [was] *much* comforted, *particularly* with prayers. Her eyes looked at me with such a meaning, I felt a thrill I cannot describe – it was like the gate of heaven.' When he returned that evening as he had promised, she had already died. (*LD* I, 199)

Newman's perseverance was admirable, e.g. in visiting Miss Hale, a young woman with cancer of the throat, whose state he judged 'unsatisfactory'. He was able however to persuade her mother to go regularly morning and evening to church. His first visit was on 31 December 1824, but the diary records regular visits until just before he left St. Clement's with no indication of success. (*LD* I, 205, 278)

In addition to caring for the sick and the dying, he had to collect money for the new church. He had made a second visitation of the parish to collect subscriptions but they totalled only £420. 2s. 6d., including the £10 10s. he himself donated. Newman was very busy during November and December with meetings. At one of these a committee was set up, and Newman composed a letter to be used in the fundraising. Copleston, the Provost, was 'kind enough to *correct* and *rewrite* it', he told Jemima. A draft of the reported meeting is extant in Copleston's handwriting, and in examining it years later in 1874 he wrote, 'it was one of the instances characteristic of Copleston, that he thus helped a young inexperienced man in a difficulty arising out of his being in a new situation'. (*LD* I, 202 and 203, n. 1) The drive was successful and brought in over the £5,000 that was required.

From the beginning Newman felt the necessity of catechizing the children, but there were no adequate facilities, so he began a private subscription to pay for the cost of building a gallery in the church for which Pusey donated a stove. So in February 1825 he was able to start classes which were held morning and afternoon.

PRIVATE PRAYERS

From the beginning of his ministry Newman organized a series of prayers
for various intentions. He did so by dividing them up for each day of the
week. The first set comprised a series of references to readings and
prayers in Scripture and the Book of Common Prayer. When he later
transcribed from the collection, he copied only the general intentions
listed for each day as follows:

Sunday   intercession for the extension of Christ's kingdom.
Monday   prayer for faith, holiness etc.
Tuesday   prayers for good works, usefulness etc.
Wednesday   intercession for Christ's Church, particularly for his
                ministers.
Thursday   prayers for heavenly wisdom.
Friday   for deliverance from sin, for pardon and peace,
Saturday   for strength and ready help.

As usual his prayers were for supernatural graces and not for material
blessings.

The next set of prayers Newman afterwards dated as composed
between June and September 1824. They represent a great expansion of
the previous set, and for each day of the week he placed the intentions
under three general headings: 'Pray for', 'Pray against', 'intercede for'.
The first category is mostly for supernatural graces and virtues both
theological and moral. The list is quite impressive, including as it does,
fervour in prayer, faith, trust in God and hope, realization of the unseen
world . . ., love of God, humility, meekness, patience, forgiveness of
injuries, preferring others to himself, kindness and charity to all men,
purity, temperance, self-denial, truthfulness, wisdom and knowledge,
discernment of spirits, zeal, unweariedness, undauntedness, perseverance,
working for God's glory, regarding himself as a mere instrument, for
success in preaching, visiting the sick, teaching, and catechizing.

The second group contains mostly petitions to avoid those sins and
faults that are contrary to these graces and virtues, e.g. pride, arrogance,
vanity and self-conceit, anger, harsh words, lying, insincerity, lukewarmness – all faults which he had mentioned in his examinations of
conscience.

Newman's intercessory prayer has broadened in extent and is both general and specific. He prays for the universal church of Christ, for the Church of England, for nominal Christians, for heretics, schismatics, papists, Jews, Mohammedans, heathen, missionaries and missionary societies, for England, dominions, all nations and peoples. More specifically, he intercedes for Oriel and Trinity Colleges, the two universities, for parents and family individually, for friends who are named. The following have specific reference to his work in the parish: his flock at St Clement's, dissenters, rector, churchwardens and other offices, the young and the old, women labouring with child, rich and poor, for blessings on his work, that the church may soon be rebuilt and well, for unity, and growth in godliness.

NO CORDIALS

When Newman began to preach, his parishioners complained they could not hear him. This he remedied by taking some wine beforehand. His first sermons he sent to his mother and sisters, telling the former, 'I am aware they contain truths, which are unpalatable to the generality of mankind – but the doctrine of Christ crucified is the only spring of real virtue and piety, and the only foundation of peace and comfort.' (*LD* I, 181) The Evangelicals considered the atonement as the key doctrine of Christianity and the means of conversion, and to this he was referring.

His mother sent him some texts which she hoped he would preach on. He doubted he could do so right away. 'My parish (I fear) wants to be taught the very principles of Christian doctrine – it has not *got so far* as to abuse them ... I shall certainly *always* strive in every pulpit *so* to preach the Christian doctrine, as at the same time to warn people that it is quite idle to pretend to faith and holiness, unless they show forth their inward principles by a pure, disinterested, upright line of conduct.' (*LD* I, 188–9) Perhaps this was the reason he decided to add another sermon each Sunday for the afternoon service. When one considers the length of these sermons, all written out by hand, it is understandable that he found the composition exhausting and after only two weeks was beginning to run out of ideas. Writing the sermons forced him to think and already he records, 'the question of regeneration perplexes me very much'. It would continue to do so.

Not long after he began to preach he mentions in his journal 'Those who make comfort the great subject of their preaching seem to mistake the end of their ministry. *Holiness* is the great end. There must be a struggle and a trial here. Comfort is a cordial, but no one drinks cordials from morning to night. (*AW*, 172) The themes of these sermons were more or less those of the moderate Evangelicals he had read: the call to holiness; the necessity of living a Christian life; the opposition to formalism and apathy in religion; the exhortation to study and meditate on the Scriptures; the importance of 'realizing' the truths of Scripture; the stress on man's sinfulness and the need of repentance; conversion and unworldliness; and the recommendation of frequent reception of the Eucharist.

Pusey told Newman that Lloyd had been informed by a friend on good authority that the parishioners liked him very much but that he 'damned them too much'. Newman commented, 'Being conscious as having said little *on the whole* of future punishments (so Lloyd took it), I was at first perplexed – afterwards I thought it must mean I dwelt much on the corruption of the heart – and that explained it.' (*LD* I, 203, n. 2) Indeed Newman wrote two sermons on this subject, Nos. 19 and 21, of which the former alone is extant. It is Calvinistic in tone, and though subsequently preached again on a number of occasions, cannot be reconciled with his views on original sin as expressed in *Lectures on Justification*. It seems to consider sin what Catholic theologians called *concupiscence* or the tendency to sin which remains as a result of original sin. There are also a number of sermons treating of different types of sin, of which the most successful is No. 101. 'Sins against Conscience'. The fact that he preached it again on eleven occasions shows the importance he attached to it. It enunciates the principle that one must follow conscience in order to attain to truth. The close connection between holiness and the attainment of truth will become evident in Newman's life itself. (*Ser.* II, 304–15)

In the beginning Newman relied on standard Evangelical commentaries by Joseph Trapp, Daniel Whitby, Philip Doddridge, Zachary Pierce, Thomas Scott, Charles Simeon and George Stanhope (see *Ser.* II, 221, n. 2 and 227, n. 2.) From Charles Simeon's *Helps to Composition, or, Six Hundred Skeleton Sermons*, 5 Vols., he learned the technique of dividing his sermons into generally three headings, though sometimes as many as four or five. Only in 1831 did he relinquish this mechanical form of structure. So also for many of the sermons on biblical theology he used commentaries. Gradually however he began to strike out on his own. A good example of this is Sermon No. 87, 'Difference between Grace and Blessing', in which, though he admits the terms are sometimes used interchangeably, he refers blessing to the natural gifts of God and grace to the supernatural ones. Most of the sermons preached at St Clement's are concerned with the 'practical' details of Christian life, especially with the long course of sixteen sermons on the Parables of the Gospel. What astonishes is the ability he developed to illustrate any assertion of truth by references that range over the entire canon of Scripture. Newman began to attract gownsmen from the colleges to the church services, but this he deemed an occasion of vanity of mind. (*AW*, 204) More and more parishioners began to come to church, and whether this was owing to his preaching or visiting them in their homes is not clear, but it was probably a combination of both.

NEW RESPONSIBILITIES

On Sunday morning, 26 September 1824, Newman arrived in London by night coach because his father was ill. His father knew him, tried to put out his hand and said 'God bless you'. He asked him to read chapter 33 of Isaiah. John also read James 1, Isaiah 54, and Luke 3, all in one way or another dealing with hope in and prayer for salvation. On Tuesday evening he and Charles sat up until 4 a.m., his mother, Francis and Harriett, all night. On Wednesday his last words were to Mrs Newman, 'God bless you, thank my God, thank my God' and lastly 'my dear'. On Wednesday toward evening they all joined together in prayer, and Mr Newman drew his last breath at 9.45. In his journal Newman wrote, 'On Thursday he looked beautiful, such calmness, sweetness, composure, and majesty were in this countenance. Can a man be a materialist who sees a dead body? I had never seen one before.' (*AW*, 202–3)

There were differences between father and son, but there does not seem to be any evidence that this destroyed their mutual love and respect for each other, though at times after his death John had guilt feelings. 'I have sometimes thought with much bitterness that I might have softened his afflictions much by kind attentions which I neglected. I was cold, stiff, reserved. I know I hurt him much . . . When . . . he noticed to me his pain that . . . I hardly said a word. Why could I not have said how much I owed to him, his kindness in sending me to Oxford etc. etc. It is over, irrevocable. O for a moment to ask his forgiveness . . .' It is difficult to evaluate this because Newman cut out what would have shown what the occasion was. (*AW*, 208)

At this time his mother said to him that she hoped to live to see him married, but '*I* think' he wrote in his journal, 'I shall either die within a College walls, or a missionary in a foreign land.' (*AW*, 203) Shortly after ordination on 3 July Newman had called at the Church Missionary House to enquire about the qualifications of a missionary, and they said 'weakness of voice, shortness of sight, want of eloquence, are not sufficient impediments. Indeed the Stations most deficiently filled are such as, requiring scholastic attainments, do not require bodily vigour.' (*AW*, 201) This must have encouraged him, but now with the death of his father, such a vocation seemed ruled out, as the care of his mother and the family fell upon his shoulders.

Although Francis's expenses remained a burden until after John became a tutor, his brother Charles remained one for all his life both to John and to the other members of the family. Intellectually gifted, nevertheless he lacked common sense. Attracted toward socialism he felt that the employer and employee were equal. This cost him his job at the Bank of England which Bowden's father had obtained for him. Wandering from job to job and from place to place he at length came to the conclusion that he had been so disadvantaged in life that he had 'claim in justice' to be supported by his family, 'just as if he were a cripple or bedridden'. (*LD* I, 182) In August 1823 on a walk in London they had a long argument on religion, in which Charles objected to some of the teachings of the Bible. John argued that before judging Scripture doctrines, it was incumbent on every one 'to read the Bible constantly and attentively, to pray for grace to understand it incessantly, and to strive to live up to the dictates of conscience and what the mind acknowledges to be right'. (*AW*, 192–3)

On 23 February 1825 Charles wrote that he had come to the judgement 'entirely against Christianity', and that Robert Owen, the socialist, 'for practical motives to action . . . beats St Paul hollow'. The correspondence which carried on for months and according to Harriett made John ill, filled eight exercise books, when copied out. In these letters John enunciated a fundamental principle of his religious thought, that right moral dispositions are essential for a correct evaluation of the evidence for Christianity. The intellect by itself cannot reach conviction. Newman's terminology is still Evangelical: 'I consider the rejection of Christianity to arise from a fault of the *heart*, not of the *intellect* . . . not from mere error of reasoning, but either from pride or from sensuality.' It is necessary to distinguish the *contents* of revelation from its *evidences*. Charles was rejecting the '*credentials* of Christianity' because he disliked the *contents*. 'Had you felt not only the desirableness of religious truth, but also our inability to attain it of ourselves, you would not have been seduced into your present opinions. Nor, till you have recourse to the Author of Nature himself for direction, humbly, sincerely, perseveringly; can you expect to possess real knowledge and true peace.' Here in kernel is the argument that Newman developed most fully in the *Grammar of Assent*. This correspondence likewise demonstrates Newman's ability already to handle controversy. (*LD* I, 219, 228)

In his annual self-examination on his birthday, 21 February 1825, he expressed gratitude for the love of his mother and sisters, that the church subscription 'flourishes greatly', and the prospects for the Sunday School are hopeful. He is also grateful that God has supported him and Francis for the last three years, and that he was able to borrow money to pay off outstanding debts including the account at Lincoln's Inn. As far as his spiritual development is concerned, he sees an improvement. Though his parish occupies a good deal of time which leaves little opportunity for study of the Scriptures, still they come before him in composing sermons, and 'I am constantly praying in my walks, business etc., yet I am by no means satisfied with myself. Of late too I have neglected stated self examination.' Though not having so much opportunity of displaying pride, he feels himself still very proud, but not so ill tempered as he was; he seems more pure in heart with no grievous attacks, only one or two momentary temptations from which he was able to turn away. (*AW*, 204–5)

Though he had become Junior Treasurer of Oriel on 16 October 1824, it may seem strange that Newman added to his burdens by accepting the offer of Richard Whately to become Vice-Principal of St Alban's Hall. Though there were not more than a dozen undergraduate students residing there, it had a reputation for the poor quality of its students, and he would have to be Dean, Tutor, and Bursar as well as conducting chapel services. The reason for his acceptance he set down in his journal, 'I have all along thought it was more my duty to engage in College offices than in parochial duty. On this principle I have acted.' (26 March 1825, *AW*, 205) His mother wrote to Harriett, 'Were it anyone but John I should fear it would be too much for his *head* or his *heart* at so early an age; but in him I have the comforting anticipation that he will use his power for the benefit of those who entrust him with it; that he will not be high-minded; that he will be sedulous to avail himself of his talents and authority, to correct and improve a Hall . . .' (*LD* I, 222, n. 1) One of his first acts of authority was to discharge James the butler. At the same time he had a dispute with the singers in the church who left, and Newman got the entire congregation to sing *en masse*. (*LD* I, 231, 233)

CHAPTER SIX

The Search for Truth Begins in Earnest

During the Term he sometimes neglected morning prayer 'either from forgetfulness or excess of work'. (*AW*, 206) Having to put the accounts in order at St Alban's and help clean up the place took so much time that his duties as Junior Treasurer at Oriel carried over into the Long Vacation. Meanwhile his grandmother died on 23 May. He called her his 'earliest benefactor'. On 29 May he was ordained priest in Christ Church. He recorded that his feelings were different from what he had felt when he was ordained deacon a year before.

> I hope I was not exactly uncharitable then; still I certainly thought that there might be some among them who were coming to the Bishop . . . without the Spirit of God. But when I looked round today, I could hope and trust that none were altogether destitute of divine influence . . . Then, I thought there were many in the visible Church of Christ, who had never been visited by the Holy Ghost; now, I think there are none but probably, nay almost certainly, have been visited by Him (*AW*, 206)

The reason for the difference was the change that took place which led to his relinquishing Evangelical principles. The catalyst of this change was Edward Hawkins to whom he paid tribute in his Autobiographical Memoir, 'Hawkins bore a very high character, . . . he had an abiding sense of duty . . . He was clear headed and independent in his opinions, candid in argument, tolerant of the views of others, honest as a religious inquirer . . . a good parish priest, and preached with earnestness.' At the time he never drank wine on the grounds of health and predicted he would never live beyond forty. In fact at the time Newman wrote the above he had already reached the age of eighty-five years. (*AW*, 77)

In the summer of 1824, the Fellows being away, Newman and he dined together, took an evening walk and had tea. Newman in his parochial difficulties found him 'a kind and able adviser.' Hawkins criticized Newman's first written sermon, 'Man goeth forth to his labour . . .' on the grounds of an implied denial of baptismal rebirth or regeneration. It divided Christians into two rigid classes, one all light, the other all darkness, whereas 'Men are not either saints or sinners; but they are not so good as they should be, and better than they might be . . . Preachers should follow the example of St Paul; *he* did not divide his brethren into two, the converted and unconverted, but he addressed them all as "in Christ" . . . and this, while he was rebuking them for irregularities and scandals which had occurred among them.' (*AW*, 77) Hawkins gave him a copy of John Bird Sumner's *Apostolic Preaching*, from which he had derived this view. This book, Newman said, more than anything else succeeded in rooting out his Evangelical principles, though his parochial experience confirmed what Hawkins had predicted to him. Calvinism 'would not work in a parish; that it was unreal'. (*AW*, 79, 206) Moreover the necessity of composing sermons obliged him to systematize his views, and he began to realize that he had taken almost on trust from Scott and other Evangelical commentators many doctrines which he could not find confirmed by Scripture, e.g., the predestination of individuals. (*AW*, 204)

This change, however, did not come about quickly or easily; in fact, it was at times agonizing, as his journals show. Reading Sumner, for example, he remarks, 'I am always slow in deciding a question; last night I was so distressed and low about it, that a slight roughness from someone nearly brought me to tears, and the thought even struck me I must leave the Church. I have been praying about it before I rose this morning, and I do not know what will be the end of it. I think I really desire the truth, and would embrace it wherever I found it.' Again a week later, 'took tea with Mr Shepherd. He and Mrs S. seem to wish me to be more calvinistic. What shall I do? I really *desire* the truth.' (24 August and 3 September 1824, *AW*, 202)

In December he notes that he is lodging in the same house as Pusey, and they have had many conversations on the subject of religion, 'I arguing for imputed righteousness, he against it, I inclining to separate regeneration from baptism, he doubting its separation'. (*AW*, 203) On 13 January 1825 he records, 'I think, I am not certain, I must give up the doctrine of imputed righteousness and that of regeneration as apart from baptism.' (*AW*, 203) On 21 February he notes that on several questions connected with regeneration, 'though I have thought much, and (I hope) prayed much, yet I hardly dare say confidently that my change of opinion has brought me nearer to the truth'. And finally, a year later, on 21 February 1826, he writes, 'I am almost convinced against predestination and election in the Calvinistic sense, that is, I see no proof of them in Scripture. Pusey accused me the other day of becoming more High Church. I have doubts about the propriety of the Bible Society.' (*AW*, 208)

There was another principle which Newman learned from Hawkins which likewise had an effect upon his thinking, and that was the role of tradition. He has explained this in the *Apologia*:

> He lays down a proposition, self-evident as soon as stated, to those who have at all examined the structure of Scripture, viz. that the sacred text was never intended to teach doctrine, but only to prove it, and that, if we would learn doctrine, we must have recourse to the formularies of the Church; for instance to the Catechism, and to the Creeds. He considers, that, after learning from them the doctrines of Christianity, the inquirer must verify them by Scripture. (*Apo.*, 9)

One of the facts of that tradition was the constant and universal acceptance of the baptism of infants. If a conscious conversion is necessary for justification, how explain this practice?

A third influence on Newman's re-examination of the question of baptismal regeneration was that of Joseph Butler's *The Analogy of Religion Natural and Revealed to the Constitution and Course of Nature*, of 1736, which Newman began to read on 25 June 1825, and continued to read four months later. Setting aside for the moment one of Butler's principles, 'probability is the guide of life', since it was important only later in his thinking and writing on faith, let us look at the other principle, 'the very idea of an analogy between the separate works of God leads to the conclusion that the system which is of less importance is economically or sacramentally connected with the more momentous system . . .' He goes on to affirm, 'and of this conclusion the theory, to which I was inclined as a boy, viz. the unreality of material phenomena, is a ultimate resolution'. (*Apo.*, 10) This is not the only example of Newman finding in an author what he already held in germ. This sacramental principle he would find reinforced by Keble's *Christian Year* in 1827, and of course explicitly and definitely found in the writings of the Alexandrian Fathers of the Church. In mentioning Keble, Newman defines the 'Sacramental system' as 'the doctrine that material phenomena are both the types and the instruments of real things unseen'. (*Apo.*, 18) The operative word here is *instrument* lest one think that Newman meant that one escaped into some Platonic world leaving visible realities behind. Its implication for understanding the visible nature of the Church is revealed in a number of sermons preached in the second half of 1825, 'Our admittance into the church our title to the Holy Spirit', No. 118; 'On the communion of Saints', No. 120 and 'The use of the Visible church'. No. 121. Hence Newman's remark in the *Apologia* with regard to Butler's work, 'Its inculcation of a visible Church, the oracle of truth and a pattern of sanctity, of the duties of external religion, and of the historical character of Revelation, are characteristics of this great work which strike the reader at once.' (*Apo.*, 10)

These sermons teach that in baptism the Holy Spirit is given *generally* to all the visible Church, i.e., to all who are called Christians. Even sinners have this privilege, the promise of the Holy Spirit to sanctify them, which remains all their life. The Holy Spirit is given not only to individuals but also to the universal Church which is not restricted to this or that country but embraces all who are baptized. Though he retains the distinction between invisible church (the only one the Evangelicals looked upon as the real Church) and the visible Church, the visible Church is the ordinary means of instruction in God's revelation. It would take some time before Newman accepted baptismal regeneration, and for years 'certain shreds and tatters' of Evangelical doctrine hung about his preaching. This was particularly true with regard to a series of sermons preached at St Mary's in 1829 on the Epistle to the Romans, and more precisely in his Evangelical understanding of such terms as 'justification', 'faith', and 'justification by faith alone'. Evangelicals separated 'justification,' an instantaneous act, from regeneration, or sanctification, which was progressive. Justification, for example, remains extrinsic or imputed. God declares man justified and treats him as such, though intrinsically he remains a sinner. Not until later, in the mid-1830s, did Newman come to accept a justification that is intrinsic, identified with regeneration, produced by the Holy Spirit, not from without, but dwelling in the soul, a holiness first imparted in baptism but capable of development over a lifetime. Moreover, he did not separate himself from such Evangelical groups as the missionary and Bible societies until 1830, thinking that by remaining he could reform them.

Newman later looked upon his transition from Evangelicalism as an illustration of the difference between genuine and apparent certitudes as he explained it in the *Grammar of Assent*. In that work he affirms that religion is a collection of beliefs, some certain, others only of opinion.

Applying this to his own case he wrote that in his early beliefs there were four doctrines which he held as certain: those of the Holy Trinity, of the Incarnation, of Predestination and the Lutheran 'apprehension of Christ', or 'justification by faith alone'. The first three, 'which are doctrines of the Catholic Religion, and, as being such, are true', did not fade away, whereas the fourth, as not being true did. 'Having this confused idea of Christian doctrine and of his own apprehension of it, and considering the evangelical teaching true, because there were great truths in it, he had felt and often spoken very positively as to his certainty of its truth and the impossibility of his changing his mind about it'. (*AW*, 80–1)

Newman also asserted later that certain peculiarities of Evangelicalism were never congenial to his nature from the very start, though he imagined he held them. 'Its emotional and feverish devotion and its tumultuous experiences were foreign to his nature, which indeed was ever conspicuously faulty in the opposite direction, as being in a way incapable, as if physically, of enthusiasm, however legitimate and guarded.' (*AW*, 82) This should not be interpreted to mean that Newman thought himself incapable of powerful emotions. Indeed his emotions were both strong and deep. What he meant was that he could not artificially stimulate or excite emotions instead of his feelings and affections being the appropriate response to religious objects as these were 'realized' by the religious imagination.

WORK WHILE IT IS DAY

Newman contracted for two articles for the *Encyclopaedia Metropolitana*, which were combined as 'The Life of Apollonius Tyanaeus; with a comparison of the miracles of Scripture and those related elsewhere, as regards their respective object, nature, and evidence,' and though he started to read in the Spring of 1825, he was unable to get to writing it until the Long Vacation. During that time his mother and sisters came and stayed until the end of September in Whately's house at St Alban's. On 7 August Newman administered the Sacrament for the first time (deacons were not allowed to celebrate it) and his sisters Jemima and Mary partook it for the first time. It was an occasion of great joy for both of them and for him, and he writes in his journal later, 'O how I love them. So much I love them, that I cannot help thinking Thou wilt either take them hence, or take me from them, because I am too set on them. It is a shocking thought.' (*AW*, 207) In two years' time Mary would be dead.

Nor was the expression of his affections confined to his private journal. He was concerned always about writing to them, and the poems he composed for their birthdays, light in spirit and tone, convey his feelings. In an affectionate letter to his aunt he expresses his thanks to her and her mother for their religious guidance:

That we are living together in peace and harmony and affection, and that we have (as I trust we have) the fear of God before our eyes, is under God owing to my dear Grandmother and yourself. – I in particular have cause to bless God for giving me such valuable and kind relatives. If I have been called of God to serve Him in His ministry, and if I am in any measure enabled by Him to fulfil my calling, it is to you two I must especially point as the instruments in His Providence in having from my youth turned my thoughts towards religion. (*LD* I, 251)

At this time Newman was beginning to struggle with writing and rewriting his work on miracles. S. L. Pope wrote in reply to an apparently hastily written note from Newman, 'I am extremely sorry to discover that, owing no doubt to the multiplicity of business in your hands you are in a complete nervous fever. You certainly overwork yourself, and your Epistle informed me without your mentioning it that you were in very low spirits. Come down and pay me your promised visit – country air, novelty, superb scenery, and relaxation from intense and overwhelming study.' (*LD* I, 256–7) That relaxation he could not take until the end of September when he stayed a fortnight with Bowden in Southampton. From there he writes to his mother, 'I have *tried* to write, for I have little or no time, from a different reason indeed from my want of time at Oxford – for here it has been drives, sailings, music etc. . . . The weather indeed has been beautiful . . . we have been round the Needles, made an excursion to Carisbroke – dined with Mr Ward. We breakfasted also with Judge Bailey. We have had music almost every evening. Bowden, you know, plays the bass. I saw Kinsey at Mr Ward's.' But even in vacation Newman could not overcome the compulsion to work, for he continues, 'I have not been idle. I am reading Davison on Primitive Sacrifice; and have written much on other subjects, and thought about some Sermons.' (*LD* I, 261–2)

Though Newman had a natural drive to work, it seems also to have been intensified by his supernatural motivation, for he writes in his diary in his annual review the following 21 February, 'Life seems passing away,

and what is done? Teach me, Lord, the value of time, and let me not
have lived in vain'. And he returns to this topic again before the end of
his entry. 'I trust I am more careful of my time than I was. My very
much business has made me hoard it as a miser. I have (I hope) more
serious views of the nothingness of the world. I have a great dread of
having lived in vain, and life is wearing on.' (*AW*, 207–8) This anxiety
occurs again and again in his lifetime. In a letter to his aunt before he
undertakes the tutorship at Oriel, he writes, 'I feel I have a great
responsibility laid upon my shoulders, and hope I shall be directed and
strengthened to make use of the talents put into my hands.' It always
seemed to me that it was Scott's Essay on the Improvements of one's
Talents which was behind Newman's drive to make use of his abilities,
but it could have been the general Calvinistic work ethic as well.

The excursion plus Dr Bailey's prescription for bark taken for three
weeks have 'made me so strong,' he writes to his mother, 'that parish,
Hall, College, and Encyclopaedia go on together in perfect harmony'.
This is the last extant letter from 14 November to the end of January,
during which time Newman worked diligently at all these tasks as the
diaries indicate. Nevertheless they took their toll, for a later entry in the
diary for 14 January reads, '*it was now first that I felt what in the event
became a chronic indigestion, from which I have never recovered. I overworked
myself at this time.*' (*LD* I, 272) On 27 January 1826 Newman declined
Smedley's proposal that he do an article on the Fathers of the Church of
the second century because he did not feel he could accomplish it in the
required time of one year. He made a counter-proposal to do a paper on
the Fathers of the Church of the second and third centuries, which he
could do in two years. Though Smedley did not accept, this was not the
end of the project nor of his intention to study the Fathers.

It was not until 24 March that he was able to ship off the first part of
his article on miracles, and by this time he had decided to resign from St
Clement's with a view to becoming tutor at Oriel. How cautious Newman
had now become in his thinking may be seen in a letter to Harriett who
expressed pleasure with the sermons he had sent home. 'Do not be run
away with by any opinions of mine. I have seen cause to change my mind
in some respects, and I may change again. I see I know very little about
any thing, though I often think I know a great deal.' (*LD* I, 280) On 31
March, Hurrell Froude was elected Fellow of Oriel with Robert Wilberforce, an event of great significance for Newman's subsequent intellectual
and spiritual development.

On 23 April Newman preached his last sermon as a curate of St Clement's (he preached several times later). In his sermon he expressed sorrow if he had inadvertently hurt any one in any way. Wherever God would lead him, he would not forget his ordination vow which binds him to complete dedication to the cause of Christ and His Church.

> . . . for this at least I can thank God that from the first I have looked upon myself solely as an instrument in His hand, and have looked up to Him for all the blessing and all the grace by which any good could be effected. For I have felt and feel now that it is only as He makes use of me that I can be useful – only as I put myself entirely into His hands that I can promote His glory, and that to attempt any [even] the slightest work in my own strength is an absurdity too great for words to express. He has been pleased to bring me into His ministry and to lay the weight of an high office upon me – and wherever His good providence may lead me I trust I shall never forget that I am dedicated and made over entirely to Him as the minister of Christ, and that the grand and blessed object of my life must be to promote the interest of His cause, and to serve His church, and contribute to the strength of His Kingdom, and make use of all my powers of mind and body, external and acquired, to bring sinners to Him, and to help in purifying a corrupt world – In this good work I willingly would be spent; and I pray God to give me grace to keep me from falling, and ever true to that vow by which I have bound myself to Him that I may at length finish my course with joy and the ministry which I have received of the Lord Jesus to testify the gospel of the grace of God Acts 20 (end lesson for the day – a reference to St Paul's farewell to the elders at Ephesus)

It would be difficult to find a more explicit and forceful statement of Newman's dedication to the ministry.

On 29 April he sent off a package containing his essay on miracles to Smedley, and immediately wrote to his mother from whom he had just received letters. 'The first minute, after having rid myself of it, I dedicate to you. I have felt much that my engagements of late drove me from you, hindered my conversing with you, making me an exile, I may say, from those I so much love. But this life is no time for enjoyment, but for labour, and I have especially deferred ease and quiet for a future life in devoting myself to the immediate service of God.' He looks forward to spending some time with them in the summer, and ends by saying, 'May God bless us all . . . and give us grace to thank Him that we love each other so much, and are so well fitted to be each other's company.' (*LD* I, 283)

Though exhausted from all his labours and under a doctor's care, this did not stop Newman from planning to read all the Fathers of the Church. In answer to Harriett's request that he give her 'something to do', he suggested, 'Compare St Paul's speeches in the Acts with any of his Epistles, with a view of finding if they have any common features. Make a summary of the doctrines conveyed in Christ's teaching, and then set down over against them what St Paul added to them, what St Peter, what St James, what St John – and whether St Paul differs from the other three in any points whether of silence or omission, or whether they all have peculiar doctrines etc. etc.' There is no extant reply to Mary's letter in which she confesses she now knows why she finds it hard to write because she is ashamed of what she writes, but now that she has confessed it, she finds it easier. (*LD* I, 283, 286, n. 2)

Just before Frank took a double first in his degree examinations, June 1826, John wrote a humorous letter to his mother how she should treat him when he came home.

I hereby send you a young person from Oxford, to whom I hope you will be kind for my sake. – his stay will be short, so I trust the favor I ask will not be too great. – You must indulge him in some things poor young gentleman – he has got some odd ideas in his head of his having been lately examined, of his having been thanked for the manner in which he acquitted himself, particularly in the mathematical school – and of a general belief in Oxford that his name will appear in both first classes – you must not thwart him in these fancies, but appear to take no notice of them, and gently divert his attention to other subjects. – He is a great talker; be sure you do not let him talk. poor young fellow – he is particularly apt to talk when persons are in the room – you have better therefore keep him as much to himself as possible – He behaves particularly ill in the company of ladies, chattering at a great rate, young man, and especially when I or other discreet person is not by; perhaps then you had better keep him in the back building – or send him up into the study, for he will be remarkably sedate among the children there.

He can mend shoes, string pianos, cut out skreens, and go on errands – the last is his forte – employ him in errands while he is with you and the time will pass pleasantly enough. – I forgot to say that he could sharpen knives. – He is very docile, while kindly treated, and quite harmless. – Do not frighten him – and believe me

With love to all, Yours most dut. J H N –

P. S. I thought it best to caution you – keep your eye upon him. – He is to eat no breakfast or dinner while with you. Deluge him with gruel, of which he is fond. (*LD* I, 290–1)

After receiving the news about Frank's success, Mrs Newman wrote to John, 'It is very delightful about Frank. I am more thankful on your account than on his. He is a piece of adament. You are such a sensitive being.' (*LD* I, 291, n. 1)

Not having St Clement's to take care of, Newman took over duty from Samuel Rickards at his parish in Ulcombe, near Maidstone, Harriett acting as his housekeeper. He found it a 'charming spot' and wrote 'we have been so delighted with the variety of views as to feel the want of words to express our admiration'. (*LD* I; 294) Unable to stay 'idle' he studied Hebrew, getting through Genesis. He complained to Jemima that Harriett does not let him read her letters, but just conveys the news. 'Now it is not so much for the *matter* of letters I like to read them, as from their being written by those I love.' (*LD* I, 297) On 21 September he left Ulcombe, going through Brighton to Worthing to Bowden's family. He went to the coast especially for bathing, which he found restorative of health, and then gathered information on houses in Brighton which he recommended to his mother rather than Worthing. When he returned to Oxford, he 'felt as if I could have rooted up St Mary's spire and kicked down the Radcliffe'.

He told Richards that 'my spirits most happily rise at the prospect of danger, trial, or any call upon me for unusual exertion'. (*LD* I, 304) The challenge would come in the form of the Gentlemen-Commoners.

CHAPTER SEVEN

Behind the Veil:
An Invisible World

Newman did not consider the office of tutor a mere secular occupation but a pastoral one and hence a particular means of fulfilling his ordination vow. In his journal he wrote 'May I engage in them / the duties of a tutor / . . . remembering I am a minister of God, and have a commission to preach the gospel . . . and that I shall have to answer for the opportunities given me of benefitting those who are under my care.' (*AW*, 209) In this he was supported to a certain extent by the Laudian statutes which considered a tutor 'a moral and religious guardian of the youths committed to him'. Oxford was not the secular university it is today, but was still looked upon as a religious educational institution and a preserve of the Church of England. Moreover Newman felt he had the example of Origen who exercised it as a pastoral one, and 'had by means of the classics effected the conversion of Gregory, the Apostle of Pontus, and of Athenodorus his brother'. (*AW*, 91)

Towards the end of a sermon he preached on Easter Sunday morning, 15 April 1827, in the College chapel, he remarked, 'So much do institutions such as ours bear . . . the appearance <character> of mere seats of learning . . . that those who do not know us well, may think our spiritual office lost in our literary occupations. . . . – I intreat you to account otherwise . . . believe that we consider our offices in this place, not of this world, but as important stations in the church of Christ to which we have been called by Christ Himself – Account of us as thinking much and deeply of your eternal interests . . . as intent upon doing you good in the silent opportunities of private intercourse.' (*Ser.* I, 340–1)

Newman began by setting himself against the Gentleman-Commoners, 'young men of birth, wealth or prospects', whom he thought were 'the scandal and the ruin of the place'. According to his own account 'he behaved towards them with a haughtiness which incurred their bitter resentment'. He was particularly opposed to young men being compelled, or even allowed as a matter of course to go 'terminally' to Communion, and was shocked at the reception he received when he complained of it 'as a profanation of a sacred rite'. This was the same reason why he was disturbed by the Gaudy at Trinity. When he asked Copleston, the Provost, if it was obligatory for students to communicate, he replied, 'That question never, I believe, enters into their heads, and I beg you will not put it into them.' And when he complained that a number of students got intoxicated at a champagne breakfast, after Communion, he was told, 'I don't believe it, and, if it is true, I don't want to know it.'

In disgust Newman, hating 'the martinet manner then in fashion with College Tutors', cultivated relations of friendship with his own students, who in turn began to realize his genuine interest and concern for them, and responded with affection and hard work. (*AW*, 89–90) Most tutors were content to lecture. If one of their students wanted to study for honours he would have to engage a private tutor whether his own or another at his own expense. From the beginning Newman did not follow this, as one of his first pupils testified. Thomas Mozley wrote to his mother in June 1826: 'Newman – my new tutor – has been very attentive and obliging, and has given me abundance of good advice. He has requested me to consider carefully what information and instruction I require for my course of reading, and also to determine what books to take up, and he will have a little conversation with me before the vacation.' (*LD* I, 290, n. 1)

Newman's kindness was combined with a certain strictness and his manner was such as no one would take liberties with him. William Lockhart later affirmed that 'Newman could do more by a few words than any one living. "What did he say to you?" was asked of one who had been called up by Newman for some more or less serious matter. "I don't know," said the other, "but he looked at me." Punctuality was one demand not only on students but also on servants. The story is told of a man who came late to a lecture, arriving at 12.15 p.m., well after the lecture had begun. '"You are *very* late, Mr So-and-so," was the lecturer's gentle reproof. "I didn't hear the clock strike, sir," the man replied. "and I am sure, Mr So-and-so," Newman quietly retorted, "the clock struck – as many as it ever could."' Newman's popularity with students soon spread.

The interest felt by Newman for his pupils and by his pupils for him was contagious, for young men are certain to find out quickly who really cares for them and has interests in common with them. There were plenty of college tutors in those days whose relation to the undergraduates about them was simply official and nominal. Newman stood in the place of a father, or an elder and affectionate brother. There were indeed intractable subjects at Oriel as there are everywhere, but some of those very men became in after years repentant and ardent admirers. This was a source of temptation to conceit and vanity. 'My pupils have, or I take care to fancy they have, a high opinion of me', he writes in his journal. (*AW*, 210) It is also an indication of the joy he took in his work.

On 12 February 1827 Newman completed a paper of 60 quarto pages, 'Remarks on Infant Baptism 1827,' on the first page of which he noted: 'This was written for my Sisters against my brother Frank.' The documentation was taken from William Wall's *History of Infant Baptism*, but the argumentation was Newman's own, namely, that infant baptism has been the practice of the Church since the first ages after the Apostles to the present day. 'Infant Baptism is a duty obligatory upon us, *unless* it is proved from Scripture either directly or indirectly to be forbidden to us.' That there is no such proof from Scripture Newman attempted to prove in the second part. The objection of the Evangelicals that the conduct of most Christians proves they have not been improved by Baptism is groundless, 'Only God, who searches the heart can answer that question.'

The importance Newman attached to this document may be gathered from the fact that he took out precious time from his work as a tutor to compose it, though today the accompanying letter is perhaps more valuable as indication that he had shed the cocksuredness with which he earlier held to his Evangelical convictions. Instead there is a tentativeness and a humility. It also reveals how much he now depends on divine enlightenment in answer to prayer.

> My present attempt to explain the grounds upon which infant-baptism seems to me a duty binding on all Christians, is not offered to your attention, my dear Sisters, without my feeling deeply the weakness and fallibility of my own reason, and my consequent need of a Heavenly Guide to direct me into the truth. I have, while considering my subject, continually prayed God for wisdom and a sound judgment – I pray the same now most heartily on putting pen to paper – and, with His grace, will not cease to do so till I have finished what I propose. (*LD* II, 4–5)

His letters during the following months show him in good spirits and filled with gossip about what was going on in the college and in the university. Thoughts of a missionary vocation seem to have faded away, replaced by those relating to his academic career. On his birthday, 21 February, he writes in his journal,

> I am becoming somewhat worldly; thoughts about livings, the Provost-ship, promotions etc come before my mind. I am remiss in private prayer, and reading the Scriptures. I *do* struggle against this, but *how* difficult it is! At home at Christmas I was very self willed, harsh, proud, ill tempered.
>
> I am not aware of any Christian grace I have grown in, except it be that I have a conviction of the value of time, and the necessity of working while it is yet day . . .
>
> My present duties I see; what I shall be, I know not. This, thank God, I have, viz a recklessness of tomorrow, an utter thoughtlessness how I am to live and to be supported years hence. (*AW*, 210)

In the *Apologia* he attributes this falling back to the fact that he was drifting in the direction of liberalism, beginning to prefer intellectual excellence to moral. He began to think of the Trinity in a way that tended toward Arianism, without recognizing it, e.g., in a sermon preached on the mediatorial Kingdom of Christ, 15 April 1827. He criticized the Athanasian Creed as 'unnecessarily scientific,' he admitted to a certain disdain for antiquity, exhibited 'in some flippant language against the Fathers,' in his articles on miracles. He rejected a number of miracles as being incompatible with God's wisdom (*Apo.*, 13–14) All these seemed to indicate a misuse of reasoning on matters that transcend reason, which was the essence of liberalism.

Newman spent July in Brighton where he met Miss Giberne for the first time. She would become a lifelong friend. Her sister had married Mr Mayers and Francis who visited him at Over Worton fell in love with Maria, but she had given her heart to a young officer, Robert Murcott, who had gone to India and intended to return and marry her. Maria played the harp and could sketch and paint. Not intellectual but rather romantic in her feelings, she was none the less intelligent, with common sense, and later did Newman a great service in collecting the witnesses for the Achilli trial. She was prepared to dislike him having heard that he was a 'stiff Churchman'.

From 2 August to 19 September Newman took over the duty of the Revd. E. G. Marsh at Hampstead, where he also tutored G. P. Golightly, who was later to be his bugbear and persecutor, and Henry Wilberforce, who was to become a lifelong friend. Newman described Henry as 'small and timid, shrinking from notice, with a bright face and intelligent eyes'. Newman took to him at once, as Henry did to him. He soon became a great favourite with Newman's sisters. Overly concerned about preparing for his first stint as public examiner, Newman read on an average of seven or eight hours a day, despite the vermin with which the house was rife. When he wrote to Marsh about it, he 'a most meek, gentle, amiable man', wrote back 'that it was one of the trials of this life and so must be borne'. (*LD* XXIII, 38)

While at Hampstead Newman and his sister Harriett visited John Cazenove, on whom Newman made a deep impression, for forty years later he wrote to Newman, 'I call to mind with thankfulness the many delightful hours that my Wife and myself have passed in your society and that of your late excellent Sister. Our humble hospitality to you was indeed a very poor return for the enjoyment you afforded us. We always looked forward to having you with us, as constituting one of the greatest pleasures of our existence, and our own experience could testify to the influence you possessed over those with whom you came in contact.' (*LD* XXIII, 59, n. 1) Newman for his part never forgot Cazenove's kindness to him.

With Mary and his mother he visited Samuel Rickards at Ulcombe. While there he composed 'the Snapdragon, a Riddle' for Mrs Rickard's flower album. In a letter to Harriett she wrote, 'And now here is John come to keep me company, or rather to be plagued by the children. I wish you only could see him with both on his lap in the great armchair pulling off and then putting on his glasses. They are quite overjoyed to see him.' (*LD* II, 28) This was a trick he regularly employed to amuse the children of his friends. Moving on to the Wilberforces he met the Emancipator, the father of Robert and Henry, who impressed him deeply by his 'unaffected humility and simplicity'. (*LD* II, 25–30, 34–5)

At this time his aunt was in serious financial trouble, news of which Mrs Newman communicated to John, who gave her advice how to handle it, but the large sum of money that had to be raised distressed him. His mother wrote to Harriett, 'I have had various communications with dear John Henry: he is, as usual, my guardian angel.' (*LD* II, 36) The exams began, and they 'at once excited and fatigued me . . . My dreams were full of the Schools and of examinations. To complete it, the news came of the promotion of the Provost to a Bishoprick, and we had the prospect of an immediate vacancy in the headship of Oriel. This completed my incapacity.' While examining in the schools he found his memory gone and had to leave in the middle of the day. He was leeched on the temples and went off with Robert Wilberforce for Highwood, where he was treated by Dr Babington who became his regular doctor until his death in 1856. (*AW*, 212–13)

A DEATH IN THE FAMILY

In his Evangelical fervour Newman had boasted to his aunt that he rejoiced in affliction as coming from God, and now God put him to the test. On 5 January 1828 his beloved sister Mary died suddenly at the age of nineteen. She was gifted, Newman wrote of her to Robert Wilberforce, 'with that singular sweetness and affectionateness of temper that she lived in an ideal world of happiness, the very sight of which made others happy . . . For myself indeed, I have for years been so affected with her unclouded cheerfulness and extreme guilelessness of heart that I have become impressed with the conviction that she would not live long, and have almost anticipated her death.' But just as this anticipation prepared him providentially for the event, now it made him think there were more trials in store, that might be inflicted on him. Indeed there were to be, but he makes a statement that is not easy to interpret: 'More trials have I had and have, than most men.' Was this a passing feeling of self-pity occasioned by the event or was it a solid conviction? It is difficult to say. Given his isolation from others, from which he was only now beginning to emerge, would such a comparative judgement have a basis in fact? Be that as it may, he was determined to accept such trials with what can only be looked upon as *supernatural*, not natural joy. (*LD* II, 50)

Upon being told of imminent death Mary said 'she could not help wishing to live, both to be with us, and in order that she might have time to grow more like her Savior and more meet for heaven – but that she felt that to depart and be with Him was far better'.

This was a great comfort to John. Newman was fond of Keble's *Christian Year*, so much so that he once thought one of the verses his own. He later revealed to Keble on Easter Eve 1843 that his 'Poem on this day was so great and true a comfort to me years ago in that very severe trial, the loss of a dear Sister. Between her death and funeral that Poem was ever in my mind' (15 April 1843) The poem begins:

> At length the worst is o'er, and Thou art laid
>   Deep in Thy darksome bed;

> All still and cold beneath yon dreary stone
>   Thy sacred form is gone;
> . . . .
> Thou sleep'st a silent corpse, in funeral
>   fetters wound.
>
> Sleep'st Thou indeed? or is Thy spirit fled,
>   At large among the dead?

The poem ends:

> Prisoner of Hope thou art – look and sing
>   in hope of promis'd spring.
> As in the pit his father's darling lay*
>   Beside the desert way,
> And knew not how, but knew his God would save
>   Even from that living grave,
> So buried with our Lord, we'll close our eyes
>   To the decaying world, till Angels bid us rise.

(*Gen. 37, 24. They took him and cast him into a pit, and the pit was empty, there was no water in it). So comforted was he that he wrote after Keble's name, 'Barnabas the Son of Consolation', a reference to Acts 4, 36, on which Keble also wrote a poem.

The pain of loss remained a long time, in fact it may have been a wound that never healed, for in his old age he could not think of her without tears coming to his eyes. The spiritual effects were great: in addition to strengthening his belief in God's providence, he became intensely aware of the transitoriness of life, a sense heightened shortly afterwards by the death of Mr Mayers. As he assured his widow, 'We think we see things and we see them not – they do not exist, they die on all sides, things dearest and pleasantest and most beloved. But in heaven we shall all meet and it will be *no* dream.' (*LD* II, 58)

The greatest spiritual effect, however, seems to have been an enlivened sense of an invisible world hidden behind the veil of this world, but more real than this world. Four months after her death he writes to Jemima that when riding with companions in the countryside, 'Dear Mary seems embodied in every tree and hid behind every hill. What a veil and curtain this world of sense is! beautiful but still a veil.' Nature from now on speaks to him of this world behind the visible, in which Mary dwells and with whom he can have contact. Writing the following November to Harriett of a solitary ride in the country he says, 'A solemn voice seems to chant from every thing. I know whose voice it is – it is her dear voice.' (*LD* II, 69, 108)

From the beginning he was determined to store up memories of her, even asking Jemima to write down all the details about her she could remember, the more minute the better. He told her he found it distressing to talk about her in the third person, to allude to her as out of the way, and only to converse about her. (*LD* II, 61, 62) This sensation he made use of later in a sermon, 'The Lapse of Time.' Speaking of the death of dear ones he writes: 'They have been followed by the vehement grief of tears, and the long sorrow of aching hearts; but they make no return, they answer not; they do not even satisfy our wish to know that they sorrow for us as we for them. We talk about them henceforth as if they were persons we do not know; we talk about them as third persons; whereas they used to be always with us, and every other thought which was within us was shared by them.' (*PPS* VII, 1, 4)

The thought of Mary should be a joy and a help. Her image is associated 'with all pleasant thoughts and bright / With youth and loveliness.' Hence she is

> Joy of sad hearts, and light of downcast eyes!
>> Dearest thou art enshrined
> In all thy fragrance in our memories;
>> For we must ever find
>>> Bare thought of thee
> Freshen this weary life, while weary life shall be.
>
> (*VV*, 28)

Memory plays a significant role in Newman's spirituality, as witnessed by various sermons, such as 'A Particular Providence as Revealed in the Gospel', (*PPS* II, 9), 'Christ Manifested in Remembrance', (*PPS* IV; 17), 'Remembrance Of Past Mercies', (*PPS* V, 6), 'Life, the Season of Repentance', (*PPS* VI, 2), and others. In another poem Newman draws a lengthy picture of what Mary was like, but concludes joining her memory and her presence in the invisible world.

> Such was she then; and such she is,
>> Shrined in each mourner's breast;
> Such shall she be, and more than this,
>> In promised glory blest;

When in due lines her Saviour dear
        His scatter'd saints shall range,
And knit in love souls parted here,
        Where cloud is none, nor change.
                                                (*VV*, 32)

Finally in a poem written on the second anniversary of her death, 'Epiphany-Eve', he sees the meaning of her death as drawing those she left behind into the invisible world where she dwells.

Loveliest, meekest, blithest, kindest!
Lead! we seek the home thou findest!
Tho' thy name to us most dear,
Go! we would not have thee here.
Lead, a guiding beacon bright
To travellers on the Eve of Light.
Welcome aye thy Star before us,
Bring it grief or gladness o'er us.
                                                (*VV*, 54)

The theme of living in the invisible world will grow more and more frequent, but it seems to have been given an impetus by reason of this experience. Out of it came many wonderful sermons on the invisible world, which made it a real world for his auditors. It is important to keep in mind that Newman is talking not only of memory or having a mental image of someone who has died and resides in the invisible world, but that one lives in that *presence*. The distinction has been analysed by Gabriel Marcel, the French Catholic existentialist. As a result of this experience Newman began to set himself against rising in the Church, worldly ambition was effectively obliterated, and intellectual pursuits subordinated to the pursuit of holiness.

PRIVATE PRAYERS AND GRATITUDE

During 1828 he composed some morning and evening prayers. The morning prayer is a long one of thanksgiving for all the blessings he has received and which he enumerates from the time of his birth 'from kind and anxious parents' to his ministry in which he has had opportunities to do good to others. He thanks God too for his afflictions: 'I praise and magnify Thy name for every affliction Thou has put or now layest upon me, and I acknowledge thankfully that hitherto all has worked for good.' The prayer ends with an acknowledgement of his unworthiness for all God's goodness to him.

The evening prayer is a confession and review of all his sins, sins he had already listed in his private journal when he made his examinations of conscience. It shows that Newman had not in any way lost a keen sense of his sinfulness, and the necessity of pleading for mercy and forgiveness. He ends with a plea: 'Give me eyes to see what is right and a heart to follow it, and strength to perform it; and grant that I may in all things press forward in the work of sanctification, and ever do Thy will, and at length through Thy mercy attain to the glories of Thy everlasting Kingdom through Jesus Christ our Lord.' (Appendix)

In addition to this morning prayer of thanksgiving thoughts of gratitude crop up here and there during the years following Mary's death, and these not merely for good things but for suffering as well. In the verses, 'A Thanksgiving', dated 20 October 1829, which bears the sub-title 'Thou in faithfulness hast afflicted me,' he thanks God not only for 'Blessings of friends, which to my door / Unask'd, unhoped, have come; / And choicer still, a countless store / Of eager smiles at home,'

> Yet Lord, in memory's fondest place
> I shrine those seasons sad,
> When, looking up, I saw Thy face
> In kind austereness clad.
>
> Sweet was the chastisement severe,
> And sweet its memory now.
>
> Yes! let the fragrant scars abide,
> Love-tokens in Thy stead,
> Faint shadows of the spear-pierced side
> And thorn-encompass'd head
>
> (*VV*, 46)

Writing to his mother on 16 July 1830 he remarks, 'I have so much daily to be grateful for, that I am sometimes overpowered with surprise. I quite reproach myself; I have so many enjoyments. . . . I seem so selfish. I believe my first wish on earth is for your happiness and comfort, my dear Mother, though I do not show it near so much as I ought and desire. It hurts me so that we should be so little together this vacation,' to which his mother replied, that the idea of his selfishness made her smile. 'You know, like yourself, I am no flatterer; but I know . . . to value the many, many blessings I have always possessed. . . . For yourself, you were the silent pride of my early life, and I now look to you as the comfort and guide of my age.' (*LD* II, 251–2)

NEW FRIENDS: KEBLE AND FROUDE

In the election of a new Provost to replace Copleston, who was made a bishop, the choice came to lie between Keble and Hawkins. Newman supported Hawkins because he knew him better than Keble and thought him more practical and better able to bring about needed reforms in both the College and University. He made Jenkyns laugh by saying, 'You know we are not electing an Angel, but a Provost. If we were electing an Angel, I should, of course vote for Keble, but the case is different.' (*LD* II, 45, n. 1) Actually, as he was to find out, Keble and he were closer underneath, especially in their view of the tutorship. On becoming Provost, Hawkins resigned St Mary's and Newman was installed in his place. It was the beginning of a new stage in his life. Summarizing in the *Apologia* the change that took place in him from 1826 to 1828, he affirms that up till 1826, 'to no one in Oxford . . . did I open my heart fully and familiarly,' but he changed when he became tutor, wrote some essays that were well-received, preached his first university sermon, became in 1827 a public examiner in the schools, and vicar of St Mary's in 1828. 'It was to me like the feeling of spring weather after winter; and, if I may so speak, I came out of my shell, and remained out of it till 1841.' (*Apo.*, 15–16)

Though Newman does not attribute the change to his gradual rejection of Evangelicalism, there does seem to have been some connection. The Evangelicals thought it necessary to examine oneself to see if one were in a spiritual state, whether one were spiritually minded. The system consequently led to continual self-contemplation and introspection in all departments of conduct. This, he felt, brought about a subtle, habitual self-esteem, which in turn led one to prefer one's own views to those of others and 'a secret, if not avowed persuasion that he is in a different state from the generality of those around him'. (*PPS* II, 15, 163–74) In his journals, as has been seen, Newman recorded vain thoughts of his superiority of intellect, and that he looked down on others, and in his relations with Pusey he tried to find out whether 'he belonged to Christ'.

It is interesting that the last entry in his private journal is dated 21 February, 1828.

The letters and diaries for 1828 show that Newman had indeed emerged from his shell. There are frequent contacts with students and colleagues, walking and riding together or dining. In fact he started a dining club, the first members of which were Froude, Robert Wilberforce, himself, Branston, Rickards and Round but expanded to include thirteen or so others. (*LD* II, 67, 143) A letter to Robert Wilberforce shows how he was able to open up himself to his friends.

> I have made up my mind not to go to Froude's. . . . I am not yet in a state to visit any where – One thought alone has occupied my mind these 6 months – never ½ an hour together out of it, I think. And at times in the day it almost overpowers me. – Nothing but being at home can make me recover myself. I cannot reconcile my imagination to the *fact* – and when I am from home this irrational incredulity, this involuntary scepticism gains its hold upon me, and makes me seem to myself in a dream. At home . . . I can grapple with it more. . . . I really think I feel God most good and am quite and wholly convinced and satisfied His will is right, wise and merciful. (*LD* II, 82)

Newman went on to say that 'It will be effort enough to go to Keble, which yet I wish so much.' He did go to Keble but only for two days, noting in his diary later, '*this was the first symptom of our growing intimacy*'. In the *Apologia* he attributed it to Hurrell Froude, who said, 'Do you know the story of the murderer who has done one good thing in his life? Well; if I was ever asked what good deed I had ever done, I should say that I had brought Keble and Newman to understand each other.' (*LD* II, 88; *Apo.*, 18)

Newman later confessed to Keble that God 'repeatedly and variously chastised me and at last to wean me from the world He took from me a dear sister – and just at the same time, He gave me kind friends to teach me His ways more perfectly.' These friends were of course Keble and Froude. Though there is sufficient evidence to show that Newman had changed spiritually as a result of his sister's death, it is not so easy to establish what Newman meant when he said that God had sent him Keble and Froude 'to teach me His ways more perfectly'. In the seeming absence of such evidence one can only conjecture how that came about, and it seems probable that it was more by way of example than by actual verbal instruction. We have seen how Newman tried to cope with feelings of intellectual superiority and lack of modesty. Keble and Froude (who learned from Keble) disliked any display of knowledge, nor did they pride themselves on their knowledge. Keble was quite humble and content to live the life of a country pastor with great devotion to his parishioners. Was it Keble's example that made Newman think of being a country pastor? Keble's and Froude's influence seems to have been intangible. Perhaps Sheridan summed this up best when he wrote:

> To a man like Newman, hesitating a few years before between Evangelicalism and its alternative, the High Church party, the choice seemed to be between the 'spiritual' and the 'material', between a religion of intense interior conviction (though basically unstable, because it was both sentimental and irrational) and one which had preserved all the outward forms, but from whose body the spirit had long since departed. The persons of Froude and Keble showed him that the disjunction was not inevitable, that it was possible to be High Church and still be both profoundly and authentically religious.[1]

In the spring of 1829 Peel, the representative of the university in Parliament, reversed his opinion and declared himself in favour of Catholic Emancipation, which the government, headed by the Duke of Wellington, wanted to pass in order to stave off a civil war in Ireland. He felt obliged to resign, but he then offered himself for re-election, so if he were successful, Oxford would be committed to Catholic Emancipation. The Provost, without consulting the Common Room, as was usual in such a question of policy, went to London and threw the weight of the college in favour of Peel and the government, and when he returned and found the Fellows opposed he treated them with contempt.

Newman and his friends started a campaign against re-electing Peel. Newman was not against Catholic Emancipation as such; this was not the issue. He saw in Peel's move 'one of the signs of the Times, of the incroachments of philosophism and indifferentism on the Church'. (*LD* II, 120) Newman was jubilant when the campaign was successful. 'We have achieved a glorious Victory,' he wrote to his mother. 'It is the first public event I have been concerned in, and I thank God from my heart both for my cause and its success. We have proved the independence of the Church and of Oxford', and to his sister Jemima he wrote, 'In these perilous times the influence of the Church depends on its Character. It is not once in a Century that Oxford and the Church are in opposition to Government. I would not have lost this opportunity of showing our independence for the world. I look upon that opportunity as providential and intended (probably) to bear upon times to come and events as yet undisclosed' – an utterance that was prophetic. (*LD* II, 125, 128) For Hawkins the defeat of Peel must have been a bitter pill indeed and increased his estrangement from the Fellows. 'He put an end to all frank and easy intercourse between himself and us.' (*LD* II, 248)

Whately took his 'humourous revenge' by inviting the least intellectual men in Oxford to dinner, 'men most fond of port,' 'made me one of this party; placed me between Provost This and Principal That, and then asked me if I was proud of my friends.' Newman's comment was that Whately saw more clearly than he that Newman was separating himself from Whately's own friends 'for good and all'. (*Apo.*, 15) Though Newman continued to walk on occasions with Whately and the latter offered him the Vice-Principalship of St Alban's once again, the intimacy between them was broken.

A FIRM DECISION

In February Newman made a firm resolution to live a celibate life. He recorded that he had learned from Froude to view celibacy as a higher state of life, but there is no reason to believe that this determined his own choice. Nor was he against clergymen marrying. In fact he thought it better if country clergymen did marry. 'The celibate is a high state of life, to which the multitude of men cannot aspire – I do not say that they who adopt it are necessarily better than others, though the noblest *ethos*[2] is situated in that state.' He thought the condition of the Church was such as to need men freed from marital commitments to dedicate themselves single-heartedly and totally to the work of the Church. He hoped that some of his friends and pupils would adopt it. (*LD* III, 23, 43, 67, 70)

One can only conjecture why he made a definite commitment at this particular time. The successful campaign against the re-election of Peel as representative from Oxford gave him an insight into the condition of the Church and the difficult times it would probably have to face. 'All parties seem to acknowledge,' he writes to his mother, 'that the stream of opinion is setting against the Church. I do believe it will ultimately be separated from the State, and at this prospect I look with apprehension.' Moreover, he continues, 'the talent of the day is against the Church. The Church party, (visibly at least . . .) is poor in mental endowments. It has not activity, shrewdness, dexterity, eloquence, practical powers. On what then does it depend? on prejudice and bigotry.' (*LD* II, 129–30) At this time too he writes to Jemima, 'I am more than ever imprest too with the importance of staying in Oxford many years – "I am rooted etc" – nay feel more strongly than ever the necessity of there being men in the Church, like the R Catholic friars, free from all obstacles to their devoting themselves to its defence. This has been shown me, among other things, by the instances in my own knowledge of the exertions made by government in behalf of Mr Peel.' (*LD* II, 133)

The reference, 'I am rooted etc' is to his verses on the Snapdragon growing in the wall opposite his freshman rooms in Trinity, which, he later wrote, he took as 'the emblem of my own perpetual residence even unto death in my University.' (*Apo.*, 237) In these verses which bear the sub-title 'A Riddle' one can perhaps also see Newman's view of holiness of life:

> Humble – I can bear to dwell
> Near the pale recluse's cell,
> And I spread my crimson bloom,
> Mingled with the cloister's gloom
> ─ ─ ─ ─ ─ ─ ─ ─
> So for me alone remains
> Lowly thought and cheerful pains.
> ─ ─ ─ ─ ─ ─ ─ ─
> Mine, the Unseen to display
> In the crowded public way,
> Where life's busy arts combine
> To shut out the Hand Divine.
>
> Ah! no more a scentless flower,
> By approving Heaven's high power,
> Suddenly my leaves exhale
> Fragrance of the Syrian gale.
> Ah! 'tis timely comfort given
> By the answering breath of Heaven!
> May it be! then well might I
> In College cloister live and die.
>
> (VV, 21–3)

This same thought of the hiddenness yet radiance of inner holiness is developed in another poem of this period, September 1829. 'The Hidden Ones.'

Hid are the saints of God;–
Uncertified by high angelic sign;

– – – – – – – –

Christ rears His throne within the secret heart.
From the haughty world apart.

– – – – – – – –

Yet not all – hid from those
who watch to see; – 'neath their dull guise of earth,
Bright bursting gleams unwittingly disclose
Their heaven-wrought birth.

(VV, 42–3)

CROSSING SWORDS WITH CHARLES AND DIFFERING WITH FRANK

In August 1830 Newman composed a long letter to his brother Charles which covered twenty-four folio pages in draft. In it he reviewed the controversy he had been having since 1825. It is important as showing John Henry as exercising great controversial skills, especially with one who would not stick to the questions at issue but brought in all sorts of extraneous matter. The main points of the discussion are maintained: the necessity of moral disposition to examine the question of revelation, especially 'the duty of prayers for divine guidance' in judging the *evidences* for it and not its *contents*. These evidences cannot be demonstrated but allow a cumulation of probabilities sufficient for certitude, which remained basically Newman's position thereafter.

The entire question surfaces again in October of the same year when he devoted three sermons to 'Truth hidden when not sought after', (*PPS* VIII, no. 13): 'The Self-Wise Enquirer', (*PPS* I, no. 17); 'Obedience to God the way to Faith in Christ', (*PPS* VIII, no. 14). In the first he makes the point stressed in an earlier letter to Charles that 'those who reject Christianity wilfully, are such as do not love moral and religious truth'. The reason for the diversity of religious opinion is that men don't make the effort to seek Truth and to pray for it. 'To seek and gain religious truth is a long and systematic work.' Moreover, truth must be sought through obedience. A person who follows conscience even when that conscience is in error, will be led along the path to Truth, for his opinions will not be the result 'of mere chance reasoning or fancy, but of an improved heart'. In describing the contest to Jemima he uses metaphors of combat, such as a boy's wrestling match and 'choosing my weapons'. In years to come there would be plenty of duels; now he was perfecting his skills. In the third sermon Newman demonstrates how this is a scriptural truth, and he cites St Paul, who followed his conscience even though in error, and when he was arrested by the heavenly vision he at once 'obeyed'. 'He was not sinning *against light*, but *in* darkness.' (*PPS* VIII, p. 210)

There is a portion of Newman's draft that he did not include in his letter. According to his memorandum it deals with the chief points that Charles overlooked, 'that revelation is *universal* – and that its obscurity is intended as a trial'. The only difference between us and the heathen nations is that '*we* have a written, *they* an unwritten memorial of it'. Hence Islamism and polytheism in their different forms contain revelations from God. 'I do not say they *are* revelations, but they *embody* revealed truths with more or less clearness and fulness.' (*LD* II, 281) This is important as explaining Newman's later statement that portions of the teaching of the Alexandrian Fathers 'came like music to my inward ear, as if the response to ideas, which, with little external to encourage them, I had cherished for so long'. Commentators have generally and rightly applied this to the sacramental principle, but it rightly applies also to the doctrine of 'economies', which will be discussed again.[3]

In June 1826, John Henry was proud of his brother Frank when he took a double first, and he wrote an affectionate set of verses for his twenty-first birthday, which occurred later in that month.

> Dear Frank, this morn has usher'd in
>   The manhood of thy days:
> A boy no more, thou must begin
>   To choose thy future ways:
> To brace thy arm, and nerve thy heart,
>   For maintenance of a noble part.
>   ++++++
> Dear Frank, we both are summon'd now
>   As champions of the Lord:-
> Enroll'd am I, and shortly thou
>   Must buckle on the sword:
> A high employ, nor lightly given,
> To serve as messengers of heaven!
>   ++++++
> O! may we follow undismay'd
>   Where'er our God shall call!

And may His Spirit's present aid
  Uphold us lest we fall!
Till in the end of days we stand,
As victors in a deathless land.

(*VV*, pp. 12–15)

It was however, not long, before, far from their being comrades in arms, a distance arose between them. In February 1827 John Henry, alarmed at Frank's influence on his sisters and mother concerning baptism, drew up a long treatise on infant baptism, as has been seen.

In 1830 he took the opportunity afforded him by a letter from Frank to voice some of his sentiments about the Evangelicals: 'I give no credit to *words*. . . . My ground of sure hope as to another's spiritual state is the sight of a consistent *life*. . . . Multitudes in the so-called religious world. . . . think they know things because they can say them, and understand because they have heard them – or, account themselves Christians because they use Scripture phrases – or, to believe in Christ with the heart and to be changed in their moral nature because they assent fully to certain doctrines (not hard to admit as intellectual truths without any moral preparation) that we can do nothing of ourselves, have no merit, or are saved by faith: – or (again) imagine they have habits or a character when they have only feelings.' (*LD* II, 183) Here in germ is the theme developed at length in the sermon 'Unreal Words'. (*PPS* V, 3)

In 1827 Frank, while a tutor in a family in Ireland, met John Nelson Darby, who later founded the Darbyites, a branch of the Plymouth Brethren, and decided to become a missionary in Persia. In May 1830, without consulting John, Frank simply announced the fact of his going abroad which would leave the burden of taking care of his mother, sisters, and a bankrupt aunt to John, not that John would not have told him it would be a privilege to do so. But John was clearly annoyed and in a postscript to a letter of 27 May 1830 to Jemima added, 'Frank has offered Froude some of his books as not needing them any more. *He has made no such offer to me. One would think I had a prior claim.*' (*LD* II, 227) Charles, who lost his job in the bank, came frequently to visit his mother and sisters. In a letter to John his mother wrote, 'He is as earnest in Mr Owen's plan as Frank can be in his "just cause", yet it is very striking how similarly self-willed they each are. They each consider they *alone* see things rightly.' (*LD* II, 263) Frank left in September for Persia. The expedition proved a disaster, the women in the group never coming back alive.

Since his mother wished to leave Brighton and move closer to John, the latter acceded to her wishes and set her up in a house at Rose Hill, Iffley. Later they would move to another house there called Rose Bank. With his love of details he superintended the entire operation. At least once a week or more he walked over to see her, sometimes by himself or with someone like Froude, dining and/or sleeping there. Frederic Rogers, one of Newman's brightest pupils, lodged in Iffley in 1832 and at times visited Rose Hill for music sessions with Newman and his sisters.

CHAPTER EIGHT

Loss and Gain

REFORMING THE TUTORIAL SYSTEM

Though Keble and Froude shared Newman's view of the tutorship as a pastoral office they were reluctant, 'by reason of that almost fastidious modesty and shrinking from the very shadow of pomposity, which was the characteristic of both Keble and Froude, they were in a later year as well as now, indisposed to commit themselves in words to a theory of a Tutor's office, which nevertheless they religiously acted on'. (*AW*, 91) Newman on the contrary was accustomed to formulate any clear view he had of a matter and, being a man of action by temperament, was impatient to enforce it.

At the beginning of 1829 with the support of Robert Wilberforce and Hurrell Froude, fellow tutors, Newman introduced a modification in the tutorial system that gave them greater contact and influence with their own pupils and obviated the necessity of hiring private tutors. Dornford, the Dean and Senior Tutor, allowed this on a trial basis, though Newman later admitted that 'it is impossible to deny that it would have been better to have mentioned the new plan of Lecturing to the Provost in the first instance – yet, it did not strike Dornford to do so, as is plain from his letter of Dec 26/28'. (*LD* II, 250, n. 1) When Hawkins found out about it, in due time he ordered them to return to the old system. In the quarrel between the tutors and the Provost there was first a difference in educational principle, the tutors favouring personal influence over system, while the Provost maintained that they were 'sacrificing the many to the few, and governing, not by intelligible rules and their impartial application, but by a system, if it was so to be called, of mere personal influence and favoritism'. (*AW*, 92)

There were many other factors involved, not least of which was the conviction that the office of tutor was a pastoral one and that if this obligation of their ministry could not be fulfilled in the tutorship, they could have no more to do with it. Newman thought the Provost did not realize the strength and depth of this principle and attributed his conduct to irritation and ill health, and that it would pass away. Moreover, the Provost, in the eyes of the tutors, did not live up to their expectations. While he was a 'Tribune of the people' before he became Provost and called for reform, now he reversed his view and declared all was well, 'They accused him . . . of assuming state and pomp, and of separating himself from his own Fellows, as if his membership in the Hebdomadal Board was a closer tie than his membership with his College, and moreover, of courting the society and countenance of men of rank and name, whether in the world, or in the state, or the Church.' (*AW*, 97)

After consulting with the former Provost, Copleston, who supported him, Hawkins ordered the tutors to return to the old system: if they did not, he would no longer assign them pupils. This was unacceptable to Newman. Consequently, though a compromise was abstractly possible, 'there was a ever-widening theological antagonism between the two parties, and an impatience on the side of Newman, and an unsympathetic severity on the part of Dr Hawkins, who, with admirable command of temper and composure of manner, refused to retire one hair's breadth from the position he had taken up, with a stern obstinancy which made any accomodation impossible'. (*AW*, 102)

It is remarkable that Newman never lost his affection for Hawkins. Until he left Oxford there was between them 'a state of constant bickerings – of coldness, dryness, and donnishness on his part, and of provoking insubordination and petulance on mine. We differed in our views materially, and he, always mounting his high horse, irritated me and made me recoil from him. In my innermost heart I have always loved, as well as respected him'. (*LD* II, 202) When Burgon's article on Provost Hawkins appeared in the *Quarterly Review*, Bloxam wrote: 'Of course there is no mention of his taking every opportunity of snubbing Newman, even in the most trifling matters. These will never come out – but I knew it at the time.'[1] In his private Journal Newman recorded on 25 June 1869 that from 1830 to 1843 Hawkins was 'my great trial'. (*AW*, 267) Newman's ability to retain affection for those who helped him, even when they were no longer friends, was true not only of Hawkins but Whately and others as well. Unlike Pusey, Newman never wished the election undone, and he came to see his removal from the tutorship an act of Divine Providence. 'I voted . . . for Hawkins from my great affection for, and admiration of him. I have never ceased to love him to this day.' (Newman to Pusey, 29 June 1882, *LD* XXX, 107; *AW*, 96)

Newman was now free to concentrate on the Fathers. 'Though I liked ecclesiastical history, and had begun reading it in 1828 ... yet I doubt whether I should have *written* on such subjects. Thus the Movement would not have begun, I think but for the act of Hawkins, as I, on leaving the Tuition took to the Arians, so Hurrell took to St Thomas à Beckett.' (*LD* XXII, 218, cf., *AW*, 96)

But this is to jump ahead. Before that decision was made there was a period in which Newman seemed somewhat at sea. In the course of a sermon, 'The Early Years of David', preached on 23 May 1830, he remarked in passing, 'How difficult is it for such as know they have gifts suitable to the Church's need to refrain themselves, till God makes a way for their use.' (*PPS* III, 4, 53) At first he thought of taking up the study of analytical mathematics, and he began to pursue it. In July he rode down to Brighton. On route his horse fell, he rolled over a heap of stones, and cut his nose with his spectacles, the practical effect of which was that he thereafter did not ride with his spectacles on, but a letter written to Rickards is revealing:

I will but say it is now many years that a conviction has been growing upon me (say since I was elected here) that men did not stay at Oxford as they ought – and that it was my duty to have no plans ulterior to a College residence. To be sure, as I past through a 100 miles of country just now in my way to and from Brighton, the fascination of a country life nearly overset me – and always does. It will indeed be a grevious temptation, should a living ever be offered me, when now even a curacy has inexpressible charms – and I will not so far commit myself as to say it must be wrong to take one under all circumstances. (*LD* II, 254–5)

Rickards replied that he would like to see him employed almost exclusively in parish matters at St Mary's and little more, and 'especially in preaching', that he would make a name for himself. (*LD* II, 256) Is it to this that Newman is referring jocosely in his letter to Froude, 'I think of setting up for a great man – it is the only way to be thought so. I have ever been too candid, and have in my time got into all sorts of scrapes. I shall learn wisdom rapidly now. – Besides, men must have *their run*, if they are worth any thing'. Newman's notation on this remark is, 'how strange I should say so then, – when the very words, about my officious candour and my scrapes of *after* years are continually in my thoughts now!' (*LD* II, 258–9, and n. 1)

Newman wanted to have a curate for Littlemore, to enable him to concentrate on St Mary's, and asked Blencowe, a new Fellow at Oriel, who declined it. Newman, disapproving of the mode in which he did so, told Froude that he was going to write to Blencowe 'but am desponding. All my plans fail. When did I ever succeed in any exertion for others? I do not say this in complaint; but really doubting whether I ought to meddle.' Newman annotated this letter thirty years later, 'It is remarkable to me to find myself making the very complaints then, thirty years ago, which are ever rising up in my mind *now*.' He refers to his sermon on 'Jeremiah, A Lesson for the Disappointed', preached on 12 September 1830. (*LD* II, 289, and n. 1) In it he summed up Jeremiah's ministry in four words, 'good hope, labour, disappointment.' When Jeremiah's hopes were destroyed, he became resigned, which seems to be what Newman did at the time. 'To expect great effects from our exertions for religious objects is natural indeed . . . but it arises from inexperience of the kind of work we have to do, – to change the heart and will of man. It is a far nobler frame of mind, to labour, not with the hope of seeing the fruit of our labour, but for conscience' sake, as a matter of duty; and again, in faith, trusting good *will* be done, though we see it not.' (*PPS* VIII, 9, 127, 129)

There are also subtle indications that he was disappointed at not being able to bring about needed reforms in the Church Missionary and Bible Societies. On 9 March the previous year Newman had been elected secretary of the Oxford branch of the Church Missionary Society. In February 1830 he privately printed a pamphlet, *Suggestions in behalf of the Church Missionary Society*, whose purpose was to enlarge the number of subscribers to the Society and 'to direct and strengthen the influence of the University and thereby of the Anglican hierarchy, upon it'. It was not well received by the Evangelicals, and on 8 March he was replaced as secretary by an extreme Evangelical. Not long after, he resigned from the Bible Society, having come to the conclusion that the society 'recognizes no *Church principles* . . . IT MAKES CHURCHMEN LIBERALS . . . it makes them feel a wish to conciliate Dissenters at the expence of truth. . . . but then I thought that by joining it *you removed* them . . . whereas now from experience I think different – I think *a man is himself drawn over to them.*' (*LD* II, 265)

But the greatest disappointment, though he does not say so, must have been the failure to reform the tutorial system and having to give up the tutorship. 'My heart was wrapped up in that kind of life.' (*LD* XXII, 218) That avenue of influence was now closed to him, and he was becoming more and more convinced that personal influence was the means of 'propagating the Truth', as he named the University sermon he would later preach. At this point however he expressed it thus:

> Men live after their death – or, still more, they live not in their writings or their chronicled history but in that 'unwritten memory' exhibited in a school of pupils who trace their moral parentage to them. As moral truth is discovered, not by reasoning, but [by] habituation, so it is recommended not by books but by oral instruction. Socrates wrote nothing – authorship is the second-best way. (*LD* II, 255)

A few months later he preached the sermon, 'The World's Benefactors', in which he stated:

> Those men are not necessarily the most useful men in their generation, nor the most favoured by God, who make the most noise in the world, and who seem to be principals in the great changes and events recorded in history. . . . On the whole, if we would trace truly the hand of God in human affairs . . . we must . . . turn our eyes to private life, watching . . . for the true signs of God's presence, the grace of personal holiness manifested in His elect; which . . . are mighty through God, and have influence upon the course of His Providence, and bring about great events in the world at large, when the wisdom and strength of the natural man are of no avail.
>
> Whether in the area of temporal benefits or that of morals and religion the great benefactors of the Church are unknown.
>
> Who taught the Doctors and Saints of the Church? . . . Did Almighty Wisdom . . . not subject them to instructors unknown to fame, wiser perhaps than themselves? . . . Why indeed should we shrink from this gracious law of God's present providence in our own case? . . . His marvellous providence worked beneath a veil, . . . 'and to see Him who is the Truth and the Life, we must stoop underneath it, and so in our turn hide ourselves from the world. . . . Hid are the saints of God; and if they are known to men, it is accidentally, in their temporal office, as holding some high earthly station, or effecting some mere civil work, not as saints. St Peter has a place in history, far more as a chief instrument of a strange revolution in human affairs, than in his true character, as a self-denying follower of his Lord, to whom truths were revealed which flesh and blood could not discern. (*PPS* II, 1, 1, 4–10)

By the beginning of 1831 Newman had become reconciled to no longer being a tutor. 'Much as I have lamented my separation from the College, and earnestly as I have desired to prevent it, nothing on earth (I think) would now make me return. My health seems to be so cogent a reason, and providentially so *clear* an one, pointing out what I ought to do. . . . I am satisfied the Provost acts on his conscience, and with great pain to himself. – tho' I altogether disapprove his principles and question his judgment.' (*LD* II, 307) Newman's present problem was to decide what work he would undertake. His continued concern about the country and the Church was heightened by the Whigs coming to power and the introduction of the Reform Bill on 1 March, though he felt his inability to do anything about it. (*LD* II, 317) As he later remarked in the *Apologia*, 'The vital question was, how were we to keep the Church from being liberalised? there was such apathy on the subject in some quarters, such imbecile alarm in others . . .' (*Apo.*, 30)

Newman did not hope for much from the Evangelicals, of whom he thought little as a class. 'I thought they played into the hands of the Liberals.' (*Apo.*, 31) As he wrote to Golightly,

'There is your Record [Evangelical paper] whiggified. So it will ever be. The children of evangelical parents, if they see the world, will generally turn liberals; on the same principles as the sons of Rome turn infidels. . . . The Propheticals . . . look like a hopeful progeny from the Evangelicals. I wish they would discard some of their notions and they would have my sanction. I do not despair, if there were a general break-up, of their becoming better Churchmen. – About Calvinism I do not care in the abstract. Persons for me may out calvin Calvin, so that they avoid two practical errors – 1. *judging their neighbours* – and thinking because a Higher Power has (according to their creed) divided the world into two, that they can divide it also. 2. Putting forth Christian motives etc. solely, always, and to all men – which leads ultimately to no men feeling them. . . . I would have Christ set forth *from the first* as the object of our worship. (*LD* II, 308)

Newman later developed these ideas in a correspondence with Samuel Wilberforce and James Stephen in the early part of 1835 after the publication of his first volume of *Parochial Sermons* and in the final chapter of his *Lectures on Justification*. Meanwhile he continued to preach not against any individual Evangelical but Evangelicalism as a system, though not by name. When he decided to write on the Councils, Pusey encouraged him by saying, 'I hope, it and indeed your whole undertaking will be of use to the Church as well as to individuals in it, by shewing that she is awake.' (*LD* II, 320)

LABOURING ON *THE ARIANS OF THE FOURTH CENTURY*

In March 1831 Hugh James Rose and Lyall, editors of the new Theological Library, asked Newman to write a history of the Councils. Newman had been thinking of writing a study of the Thirty-Nine Articles, and Rose, a Cambridge man and editor of the *British Magazine*, thought a history of the Councils would be an appropriate introduction. He began work in June, but interrupted it to take a vacation with Froude in Devonshire. They left Cowes by boat, 'It was a delightful night and the sea beautiful', he wrote to his mother. He and Froude decided to sleep on deck. In consequence Froude caught a cold, which turned into the epidemic influenza and was the beginning of his long and fatal illness.

In Dartington the beauty of the place flooded Newman's senses:

What strikes me most is the strange richness of every thing. The rocks blush into every variety of colour – the trees and fields are emeralds, and the cottages are rubies. A beetle I picked up at Torquay was as green and gold as the stone it lay on, and a squirrel which ran up a tree here just now was not a pale reddish brown, to which I am accustomed, but a bright brown red. Nay, my very hands and fingers look rosy, like Homer's Aurora, and I have been gazing on them with astonishment. . . . The exuberance of the grass and the foliage is oppressive, as if one had not room to breathe, though this is a fancy – the depths of the valleys and the steepness of the slopes increase the illusion. . . . The scents are extremely fine, so very delicate, yet so powerful, and the colours of the flowers as if they were all shot with white. The sweet peas especially have the complexion of a beautiful face – they trail up the wall, mixed with myrtles, as creepers. As to the sunset, the Dartmoor heights look purple, and the sky close upon them a clear orange. When I turn back to think of Southampton water and the Isle of Wight, they seem by contrast to be drawn in india-ink or pencil.

Though he was not especially in a poetic mood, the following lines came into his head, which he entitled, 'The Pilgrim'.

THE PILGRIM

For an Album
There stray'd awhile, amid the woods of Dart,
   One who could love them, but who durst not
   love.
A vow had bound him, ne'er to give his heart
   To streamlet bright, or soft secluded grove.
'Twas a hard humbling task, onwards to move
His easy-captured eyes from each fair spot,
   With unattach'd and lonely step to rove
O'er happy meads, which soon its print forgot:-
Yet kept he safe his pledge, prizing his pilgrim-lot.
                         (*VV*, 61)

While in Dartington he preached the sermon, 'Scripture a Record of Human Sorrow.' (*PPS* I, sermon 25) The purpose of this record, he said, is 'to save us pain, by preventing us from enjoying the world unreservedly; that we may use not abusing it'. Nor does this view make one gloomy. The true Christian rejoices in those earthly things which give joy, but in such a way as not to care for them when they go. For no blessings does he care much, except those which are immortal, knowing that he shall receive all such again in the world to come.' (*PPS* I, 25, 332–3) When the sermon was published, Hurrell Froude commented on it: 'I can see the train of thought that suggested it . . . and since then, I never have been well – and then came my poor sister's business – who by the by is now at Madeira for the same cause as I am here.' Newman explained about his sister, 'He did not like the match; her husband had *every high qualification* of this world, but Hurrell did not like his religious tone, as Whiggish.' (*LD* V, 19, and n. 3)

Newman later recalled this visit and the sense of foreboding it induced, which led to his composing the sermon: 'I saw a number of young girls collected together, blooming and in high spirits – "And all went merry as a bell – " And I sadly thought what changes were in store, and what hard trial and discipline was inevitable. I cannot trace their history – but Phyllis and Mary Froude married and died quickly – Hurrell died. One, if not two of the young Champernownes died. My sermon was dictated by the sight and the foreboding. At that very visit Hurrell caught and had his influenza upon him, which led him by slow steps to the grave.' (*LD* V, 19, n. 2)

Working hard at the Fathers he nevertheless found time to give lectures at Littlemore from October to January. On 24 October his pupils made him a present of 36 volumes of the Fathers – among which were the works of 'Austin, Athanasius, Cyril Alexandrinus, Epiphanus, Gregory Nyssen, Origen, Basil, Ambrose, and Irenaeus'. In 1827 Pusey had purchased volumes of the Fathers in Germany and sent them to Newman. So 'altogether now I am set up in the Patristical line – should I be blessed with health and ability to make use of them'. (*LD* II, 369) Of the historians he read he conceived a low opinion, and so he began to see how the Fathers could shed light on the subject of the Councils.

Meanwhile Whately was made Archbishop of Dublin, and again offered Newman the Vice-Principalship of St Alban's Hall, which he declined, but thought Whately might offer him something in Dublin. This he would also have to refuse, but the offer never materialized. It seems he should stay in Oxford where he could make a contribution as a theologian, for theology, he felt, was badly neglected there. This determination is reflected in the ordination sermon he preached on 18 December 1831, 'On the ministerial Order, as an existing divine institution', in which he affirmed that the Church from its earliest days had always opposed error and sought 'to promote Truth and Holiness'. It was the special duty of a minister in the Church, therefore, to have 'a systematic view of Truth' and to hold theologically correct views, so as to guide others. (No. 323) Moreover, 'if times are troublous', he wrote to Harriett, 'Oxford will want hot headed men, and such I mean to be, and I am in my place.' (*LD* II, 367)

LIKE MUSIC TO MY INWARD EAR

As Newman wrote in what has now become a famous passage in the *Apologia*:

> What principally attracted me in the ante-Nicene period was the great Church of Alexandria, the historical centre of teaching in those times. Of Rome for some centuries comparatively little is known. The battle of Arianism was first fought in Alexandria; Athanasius, the champion of the truth, was Bishop of Alexandria; and in his writings he refers to

the great religious names of an earlier date, to Origen, Dionysius, and others, who were the glory of its see, or of its school. The broad philosophy of Clement and Origen carried me away; the philosophy, not the theological doctrine; and I have drawn out some features of it in my volume, with the zeal and freshness, but with the partiality, of a neophyte. Some portions of their teaching, magnificent in themselves, came like music to my inward ear, as if the response to ideas, which, with little external to encourage them, I had cherished so long. These were based on the mystical or sacramental principle, and spoke of the various Economies or Dispensations of the External. I understood these passages to mean that the exterior world, physical and historical, was but the manifestation to our senses of realities greater than itself. Nature was a parable: Scripture was an allegory: pagan literature, philosophy, and mythology, properly understood, were but a preparation for the Gospel. The Greek poets and sages were in a certain sense prophets; for 'thoughts beyond their thought to those high bards were given'. There had been a directly divine dispensation granted to the Jews; but there had been in some sense a dispensation carried on in favour of the Gentiles. He who had taken the seed of Jacob for His elect people had not therefore cast the rest of mankind out of His sight. In the fulness of time both Judaism and Paganism had come to nought; the outward framework, which concealed yet suggested the Living Truth, had never been intended to last, and it was dissolving under the beams of the Sun of Justice which shone behind it and through it. The process of change had been slow; it had been done not rashly, but by rule and measure, 'at sundry times and in divers manners', first one disclosure and then another, till the whole evangelical doctrine was brought into full manifestation. And thus room was made for the anticipation of further and deeper disclosures, of truths still under the veil of the letter, and in their season to be revealed. The visible world still remains without its divine interpretation; Holy Church in her sacraments and her hierarchical appointments, will remain, even to the end of the world, after all but a symbol of those heavenly facts which fill eternity. Her mysteries are but the expressions in human language of truths to which the human mind is unequal. It is evident how much there was in all this in correspondence with the thoughts which had attracted me when I was young, and with the doctrine which I have already associated with the Analogy and the Christian Year. (*Apo.*, 26–7)

Herein are the seeds of his later view of the development of doctrine. The practice of the *disciplina arcani* (the discipline of the secret) was an application of the same principle of 'economy', whereby the Christian teacher only gradually initiated the catechumen into the mysteries of faith. Modern scholars believe that the *disciplina arcani* lasted only a brief time and not so long as Newman asserted, but the principle of economy henceforth became fundamental in Newman's thought. He applied it to the use of language to express Truth (i.e. an accommodation), particularly Christian mysteries. As a Catholic, in the Preface to the third edition of the *Via Media*, he would apply it to the harmonization of the different functions of the Church. It gave rise to the Tractarian practice of 'reserve'. Newman's enemies accused him of having 'economized' as an Anglican: that is, while outwardly professing Anglicanism, he secretly intended to lead men to Rome.[2]

The sacramental principle Newman saw as flowing from the dogma of the Incarnation, for the latter 'establishes in the very idea of Christianity the sacramental principle as its characteristic'. So while as an Evangelical he looked upon the Atonement as the central truth of Christianity, he now looked upon the Incarnation as such. (*Dev.*, 324–5) A full understanding of the principle involves an understanding of the meaning of the word 'world'. The latter refers not merely to the world of nature, but more often to the actions of men in society both in the past and in the present. All these have their own reality in themselves but at the same time subserve a hidden and invisible world which is their basis. (*Ess.* II, 192)

The sacramental principle is at the root of many of Newman's sermons, as well as of his own religious life. The latter is not something totally distinct from his daily life and activity. It is what gives it its religious meaning. Two sermons in particular (not to mention those on the invisible world) will elucidate these remarks. In the sermon 'Doing Glory to God in Pursuits of the world' he affirms that the true Christian 'will see Christ as revealed to his soul amid the ordinary actions of the day, as by a sort of sacrament. Thus he will take his worldly business as a gift from Him, and will love it as such.' (*PPS* VIII, sermon 11)

How one consecrates one's activities to God he explained in an earlier sermon called 'Mental Prayer'. What he calls 'mental prayer', is a state or habit which consists in the continuous activity of prayer. The life imparted in baptism opens the eyes of the mind, 'so that we begin to see God in all things by faith, and hold continuous intercourse with Him by prayer', and this leads eventually 'to the perfection of Divine obedience'. What is faith, he asks, 'but the looking to God and thinking of Him continually, holding habitual fellowship with Him, that is, speaking to Him in our hearts all through the day, praying without ceasing'? From Newman's description of this type of prayer, it is evident that it is not at all times expressed in words. It is, for example, 'doing all things to God's glory: that is, so placing God's presence and will before us, and so consistently acting with a reference to Him, that all we do becomes one body and course of obedience, witnessing without ceasing to Him who made us, and whose servants we are'. It is, in short, 'living in God's sight'. (*PPS* VII, 15)

So although prayers at set times and with set forms are necessary as well, as Newman preached in his next sermon, 'Times and Forms of Private Prayer', still these prayers do not completely fulfil the Pauline injunction 'to pray always', as mental prayer does. The prayer Newman calls 'mental' was known to the Fathers, especially St Augustine and St John Chrysostom, but the classic phrase to describe it is St Ignatius Loyola's 'contemplation in action'.[3] Hence Newman's enormous activity especially during the Oxford Movement was not a distraction from his private prayer but its complement and expression. (*PPS* VI, 16)

In the *Arians* Newman contrasted the Alexandrian Fathers' reverence for revelation with the logical disputatiousness of the Aristotelian schools of Antioch, conducted by the Sophists. Arius was trained in the techniques which, Newman said, were more suited to detect error than to establish truth. Moreover, the continued employment of reason in secular objects generated a spirit of intellectual questioning which, when employed on objects that transcend reason, namely, the truths of revelation, led to heresy. Here was a parallel with the liberalising spirit of the Oriel noetics who, as Mark Pattison said in his *Memoirs*, called everything into question, appealing to first principles and disallowing authority as a judge in intellectual matters. Newman would be forced to clarify what was and what was not 'rationalism' in dealing with religious truth. This he did in Tract 73, 'On the Introduction of Rationalistic Principles into Religion'.[4]

Newman did not think dogmatic formulations were desirable in themselves, for 'freedom from symbols and articles is abstractly the highest state of Christian communion, and the peculiar privilege of the primitive Church'. (*Ari.*, 36–8, 133–5) On the other hand Newman defended the expression of dogma, not merely as necessary to refute heresy, but also because it 'directly assists the acts of religious worship and obedience'.

(*Ari.*, 145–6) The statements in the Athanasian Creed, for example, are not cold bare formal propositions and abstractions conveying mere notions to the intellect. They are 'hymns of praise and thanksgiving; they give glory to God as revealed in the Gospel, just as David's Psalms magnify His Attributes as displayed in nature, His wonderful works in the creation of the world, and His mercies towards the house of Israel'. Hence, they are especially suited to divine worship inasmuch as they kindle religious affections.' (*PPS* II, 3, 27–9; *GA*, 133; *Diff.* II, 86)

The influence of the Fathers is especially evident in the enlargement and deepening of his Christology. It seems too that it was under the inspiration of the Fathers that Newman came explicitly to hold the indwelling of the Holy Spirit. The sermons on this occur after he had read Athanasius especially.[5] The principle of personal influence Newman seems to have developed in more explicit terms after reading the Fathers, for he beheld it exemplified in St Athanasius whom he explicitly mentions in the University Sermon, 'Personal Influence the Means of Propagating the Truth', (22 January 1832) as having impressed his image on the Church for ages to come. 'Such men . . . light their beacons on the heights. Each receives and transmits the sacred flame, trimming it in rivalry of his predecessor.' (*US*, 5, 91–6)

Though Newman sometimes acknowledged a direct influence of the Fathers, e.g., for the sermon on the angels, 'The Powers of Nature', (*PPS* II, 29; *Apo.*, 28) still it was not so much this or that idea he took up but rather a vision of the Church, a vision that would guide him through the years of the Movement and eventually lead him into the Catholic Church. With the 'divided and threatened' Establishment, he compared the 'fresh and vigorous Power' of the Church of the Fathers:

> In her triumphant zeal on behalf of that Primeval Mystery, to which I had had so great a devotion from my youth, I recognized the movement of my Spiritual Mother. 'Incessu patuit Dea'. The self-conquest of her Ascetics, the patience of her Martyrs, the irresistible determination of her Bishops, the joyous swing of her advance, both exalted and abashed me. I said to myself, 'Look on this picture and on that'; I felt affection for my own Church, but not tenderness; I felt dismay at her prospects, anger and scorn at her do-nothing perplexity. I thought that if Liberalism once got a footing within her, it was sure of victory in the event. I saw that Reformation principles were powerless to rescue her. As to leaving her, the thought never crossed my imagination; still I ever kept before me that there was something greater than the Estab-

lished Church, and that that was the Church Catholic and Apostolic,
set up from the beginning, of which she was but the local presence and
organ. She was nothing, unless she was this. (*Apo.*, 31–2)

Rushing to finish the *Arians* on time, he overworked and experienced
fits of dizziness, which made him lie down. Whenever thereafter he
experienced the same phenomen he recalled this prime example and
compared all other instances to it. Newman went off for a brief visit to
Rickards who had left Ulcombe for Stowlangtoft. He passed by Cambridge on 16 July where he failed to find Rose, to whom he wanted to
deliver the second third of his MS., but Rose was away. Newman was
startled at the beauty and atmosphere of the place. 'I cannot believe that
King's College is not far grander than any thing with us', he wrote to his
mother. (*LD* III, 66–7)

In Oxford that summer there was a threat of cholera, but not in his
parish or in Littlemore, otherwise he would not have left, though later he
was accused of doing so. The correspondence gives the lie to the
accusation. He and his mother had laid plans the previous winter to help
in the event of an outbreak. She was to secure a cottage in Littlemore and
set it up as a hospital. The possibility of his catching the cholera made
him think of death, but 'there is on one's own mind the strong impression
. . . that one is destined for some work, which is yet undone in my case.
Surely my time is not yet come.' (*LD* III, 72) When Froude left Oxford
on 31 July they parted 'as if perhaps we might not see each other again.
With reference to the memory of that parting, when I shook hands with
him and looked into his face with great affection, I afterwards wrote the
stanza, "And when thine eye surveys, With fond adoring gaze, And
yearning heart thy friend, Love to its grave doth tend,"' This was the last
verse of 'Reverses', written on 30 January 1833, *VV* 125–6, (*LD* II, 92,
n. 1)

Newman returned to Oxford from Rickards and the following week he
went to Brighton to complete arrangements for getting rid of his mother's
house and then to Tunbridge Wells to visit Woodgate. While with the
latter he composed and preached two important sermons, the passage of
the Reform Bill in June being both an irritant and a stimulus: 'Knowledge
of God's will without Obedience', and 'the Religion of the Day'.[6] In them
he attacked the religion of Civilization, which was a substitute for
authentic Christianity. The latter sermon especially is a devastating
analysis of the religious attitudes which were sapping the spiritual strength
of the Church. In place of the full harmony of the Christian religion with

its delicate balance of opposites, such as love and fear, it seizes upon the brighter aspects of religion and substitutes an outward show of respectability for the inward monitor of conscience, which it reduces to a moral sense, or the sense of the beautiful. 'Religion is pleasant and easy; benevolence its chief virtue; intolerance, bigotry, excess of zeal, are the first sins. Austerity is an absurdity.' Such a religion takes a colouring from Christianity but it is such as the refined intellect of any age might erect. It is neither hot not cold. Newman concluded 'Here I will not shrink from uttering my firm conviction that it would be a gain to this country were it vastly more supersticious, more bigoted, more gloomy, more fierce in its religion than at present it shows itself to be. Not, of course, that I think the tempers of mind herein implied desirable, which would be an evident absurdity; but I think them infinitely more desirable and more promising than . . . a cold, self-sufficient, self-wise tranquillity.' (*PPS* I, 14, 320–1)

SERMONS AT ST MARY'S (1828–32)

Newman saw preaching as only a partial fulfilment of his duty as a pastor. Teach he must, but preaching by the very limitations of a sermon (no matter how lengthy by present day standards) was limited in effect. Sermons were too short 'to embrace the peculiarities of doctrine, and necessarily too general in exhortation to apply to the variety of character and individual circumstances of those to whom they were addressed'. They must be supplemented by catechesis. In the first anniversary sermon at St Mary's he deplores the fact that there are no regular catechitical classes for the children, even though he catechized them for confirmation.[7]

A partial way of overcoming the intrinsic limitations of a sermon was to give courses. This he had done at St Clement's and he continued to do so at St Mary's at least for the first few years. Some of these are short, others longer. There is a course on the two sacraments of Baptism and the Eucharist, for these two were the only ones recognized as such in the Church of England, since it was asserted these alone were instituted by Christ. They were numbered 167–172. Of these, the first is not extant, 168 'Infant Baptism', was published in *PPS* VII, 16, and the rest in *Sermons 1824–43*, I.

A second group of sermons consisted of fourteen on St Paul's Epistle to the Romans, which Newman delivered on Sunday afternoons from 25 January to 28 June 1829 with an interruption during Lent. At this time

Newman still adhered to the Evangelical distinction between justification which is external and a one-time affair and sanctification which is a long term process. Faith alone justifies, but works of obedience are required even by the just. Newman tries to reconcile these two doctrines. Though he had already begun to read the Fathers of the Church, he did so, by his own admission, 'on Protestant principles of division, and hunted for Protestant doctrines and usages in them. My headings ran, "Justification by faith only", "sanctification" and the like.' (*Diff.* I, 371) Since some of the sermons were repeated in revised form, it is possible to trace the development of his doctrine until its final acceptance in *Lectures on Justification* of the indwelling of the Holy Spirit who both justifies and sanctifies internally in baptism. These are now published in *Sermons 1824–1843*, II.

A third group of sermons was devoted to the history of the Jewish people. He gave four different courses on Jewish history from Abraham to the prophets inclusive, totalling twenty-five sermons in all. These were preached from 12 July 1829 to September 1830. He attempted especially to show how God's providence over his chosen people continued despite their sins and attempts to thwart His plan of salvation. These sermons are notable for some wonderful moral portraits of the chief figures of Jewish history: Abraham, Moses, Saul, David, Solomon, Jeroboam. Though some of these figures are not patterns for Christians to follow, 'yet the chief of them are specimens of especial faith and sanctity, and are set before us with the evident intention of exciting and guiding us in our religious course'. Newman himself published some of these and the rest are now published in Volume II of *Sermons 1824–1843*.

A fourth group dealt with the Liturgy. These were composed against the background of the Church Missionary Society which he felt disarranged the parochial system, gave prominence to preaching over public worship and other religious ordinances, and 'make the people the basis and moving principle of her constitution'. In sermons 213 and 214, 'On the duty of public Worship', and 'On Preaching', he affirmed that preaching is subordinate to public worship, which is the purpose of gathering together in church. In speaking of the Liturgy he refers not only to celebrations or services but to the administration of the sacraments and ordinances or rites, in brief, all contained in the Book of Common Prayer. He also gave a course on the Liturgy from 31 January to 4 April 1830, in which he showed how the Liturgy preached doctrine and also helps to form the Christian character, e.g., to faith, love, reverence and self-denial.

In March 1830 Newman instituted Saints' Days services, which he thought useful because 'it in some degree keeps up the memory of the Saints and so of old times and because it gives me an opportunity of knowing the more religious part of my Congregation – for such, as a whole, I conceive these Saints-Day worshippers to be'. (*LD* II, 201–2) The Saints were those mentioned in Scripture. The sermons preached at these services tell us little about the saints themselves, even allowing for the fact that there is relatively little known about them. They are used by Newman as a means to develop a moral or spiritual truth or even to inculcate a dogmatic one. For example, St John provides an occasion to preach on the love of relatives and friends, St Thomas, for a sermon on faith. Some of these sermons were published in Volume II of *PPS*, the rest will appear in Volume III of *Sermons 1824–1843*. 'The special benefit to be derived from the observance of Saints' Days', he said in a sermon preached on All Saints Day, 1831, 'lies in their setting before the mind the pattern of excellence for us to follow.' In so doing the Church follows the example of Scripture which portrays for us the lives of those men who were God's special instruments, the chief of them, specimens of 'faith and sanctity', to guide us in our spiritual course. (*PPS* II, 32, 393–4, 399) Newman composed 54 new sermons in 1830, and 45 in 1831. In each of these years he wrote a greater number than in any other while he was Vicar of St Mary's. When he came to publish his sermons, he chose more from 1831 than from any other year.

During the years 1830–2 he also delivered eight University Sermons, which are more lectures than sermons. Some of these are as important as containing the foundational principles he was developing for a philosophy of religion which he continues to explore in subsequent University Sermons and eventually in the *Grammar of Assent*.

In sermon 2, 'The Influence of Natural and Revealed Religion', he outlines the path by which conscience leads to the truths of natural religion.

Conscience is the essential principle and sanction of Religion in the mind. Conscience implies a relation between the soul and a something exterior, and that, moreover, superior to itself; a relation to an excellence which it does not possess, and to a tribunal over which it has no power. And since the more closely this inward monitor is respected and followed, the clearer, the more exalted, and the more varied its dictates become, and the standard of excellence is ever outstripping, while it guides, our obedience, a moral conviction is thus at length obtained of the unapproachable nature as well as the supreme authoriy of That, whatever it is, which is the object of the mind's contemplation. Here, then, at once, we have the elements of a religious system; for what is Religion but the system of relations existing between us and a Supreme Power, claiming our habitual obedience. (*US*, 2, 18–19)

Not only is conscience the sanction of Natural Religion, 'it is, when improved, the rule of morals also'. 'But here is a difference; it is, as such, essentially religious, but in Morals it is not necessarily a guide, only in proportion as it happens to be refined and strengthened in individuals.' (*US*, 2, 18–20) There is a distinction between the religious and moral aspect of the indivisible act of conscience, as he later explained in the *Grammar of Assent*. (*GA*, 105ff.)

In sermon 3, 'Evangelical Sanctity the Completion of Natural Virtue', he rejects what he would later call 'The Religion of Civilization', as neither Christian morality, though it may look like it, nor a part of natural religion but a product of the cultivated intellect and stemming from the advancement of civilization. (*US*, 3, 40–1; cf., *Idea*, Disc. 8; *GA*, 396, and n. 3) By comparison he describes the 'special elevation' and 'exalted ideal' of authentic Christian holiness.

In sermon 4, 'The Usurpation of Reason', he condemns an illegitimate use of Reason, namely, arguing in the subject matter of religion from secular principles and without a sufficient knowledge of its subject matter. Such principles are utilitarian, political, Epicurean, or forensic. Certain moral and religious dispositions are essential to reason correctly in the matter of religion.

In sermon 6, 'On Justice, as a Principle of Divine Governnance', he disputes the emphasis placed on God's benevolence to the neglect of His justice, whether in current philosophy, or doctrinally in Socinianism or Theophilanthropism. Guilt, sorrow for sin, fear of punishment are rejected as superstitions, but they are fundamental feelings that constitute Natural Religion. Nor are those feelings entirely wiped out by the gospel. These assertions are more fully developed in the *Grammar of Assent*.

Two other University Sermons are important as cnunciating the principle of personal influence and the fundamental importance of Christian holiness. In sermon 5, 'Personal Influence, the means of propagating the Truth', after outlining the problems involved in the transmission of religious Truth, Newman affirms that the latter 'has been upheld in the world not as a system, not by books, not by argument, nor by temporal power, but by the personal influence of such men . . . who are at once the teachers and the patterns of it'. He proceeds to speak of the 'moral power which a single individual, trained to practise what he teaches, may acquire in his own circle, in the course of years'. After speaking of the attraction exerted by unconscious holiness especially on those 'who have already, in a measure, disciplined their hearts after the law of holiness', he concludes that 'such considerations lead us to be satisfied with the humblest and most obscure lot; by showing us, not only that we may be the instruments of much good in it, but that (strictly speaking) we could scarcely in any situation be direct instruments of good to any besides those who person- ally know us, who ever must form a small circle'. It seems that Newman at this point of time assigned to himself an obscure role, and resigned himself to the fact that, if he was to have any influence, it would be by reason of holiness of life. The principle of personal influence would guide him in his efforts for the Oxford Movement.

In sermon 7, 'The contest between Faith and Sight', after having illustrated the often confusing and unsettling effect the world has upon the young when they come in contact with it, affirms that the power of the world or worldliness lies mainly in assailing the imagination, so that the vision of Christianity seems unreal, its teaching impracticable, its preachers irrational and puerile. He finds encouragement, however, in thinking how much may be done 'in way of protest and teaching, by the mere example of those who endeavour to serve God faithfully . . . By the counter-assertions of a strict life and a resolute profession of the truth, we may retort upon the imaginations of men, that religious obedience is not impracticable, and that Scripture has its persuasives.' The testimony of a martyr or of a confessor 'breaks in upon that security and seclusion in which men of the world would fain retire from the thought of religion'. Holiness, Newman asserts once again, is the best weapon with which to challenge the world.

CHAPTER NINE

A Long Day's Journey into Light

On 9 September Hurrell Froude invited Newman to accompany him and his father Archdeacon Froude to the Mediterranean, an invitation which after an initial hesitation he accepted. Exhausted from work on the *Arians* he was forced to be idle, which he always found hard. 'The violin has been my only care.' He kept in contact with his friends and former pupils. To Henry Wilberforce, who apparently could not make up his mind what he wanted to do in life, Newman suggested writing for the *British Magazine* of which Rose was the editor. '. . . suppose you were to give a sketch of the life of Loyola and the philosophic peculiarities of his rise – or of St Francis. I am much set on understanding *the mode* in which the Monastic orders rose, in order to see whether one could not in all simplicity and godly sincerity found such a society, if times got bad.' (*LD* III, 107)

At this time there is the first indication of a tension between himself and Harriett. It seems that he wrote her a letter in which he complained of her not having unreserved confidence in him. In her reply she pointed out the causes. 'And first, is your own manner, which I am sure you must know is sometimes very trying to me, and which I cannot always understand. . . . Another difficulty I have felt in speaking to you freely, is the great difference I see in our opinions on many points; so that you would be so far from sympathizing with my impressions.' She added a third cause, that she did not like all of his friends. In a subsequent letter she wrote, 'There are only three of them of whom I have spoken sharply, apparently without assigning reasons; only one against whom I have any thing like a serious charge. . . . It grieves me very much that you should have the idea that I have sometimes received your confidence coldly. . . . I only notice it to tell you how highly and warmly I have ever prized your kind and often unbounded confidence. . . . I do not think your advice to me "cold". Do not regret, dear John, having disturbed me . . . I am quite content that you should speak of low spirits and want of health as the cause – that is all I wished. . . . I hope there is no need for me to say that in whatever way it is I have at any time vexed you, I grieve for it extremely.' (*LD* III, 107–8) At the time of Mary's death he had told Harriett that she was the one to whom he felt closest, and so he would obviously be sensitive to her reactions. At times in his life Newman was in need of sympathy, but whether this was one such occasion, is difficult to establish.

It was in the course of this correspondence that Newman learned that on the advice of Lyall, co-editor of the Theological Library, Rose decided not to publish the *Arians* as part of the Library, because it was more a history of the Arians than of the Councils, but also, as Lyall wrote to Newman, it used the anti-Protestant and 'Romanist' idea of a secret tradition and endorsed Clement's view of a revelation to the pagans. The rejection was a keen disappointment to Newman, who never forgot it. In listing one of the reasons why he did not want to stop the Lives of the English Saints was that it seemed unfair to disappoint those who had already written theirs. 'I know myself when I was much younger, how very annoying such a disappointment is; the more so, because it cannot be, or is not, hinted at.' (To Hope, 6 November 1843, *KC*, 284) Nevertheless both Rose and Lyall agreed that the work should be published and were confident that Rivington would publish it. This the firm did, but it was delayed until the following autumn.

On 8 December Newman and the Froudes left Falmouth on board the packet *Hermes*. On 11 December he saw 'the high mountains of Spain, the first foreign land I ever saw'. On 13 December he caught sight of the Portuguese coast, 'the first foreign soil I have come near', and 15–17 stopped in Gibraltar, 'the first foreign land I ever put foot on'. (*LD* II, 129, 137, 146) He found the place 'wonderful', and wrote to Harriett, 'I never felt any pleasure or danger from the common routine of pleasures, which most people desire and suffer from – balls, or pleasure parties, or sights – but I think it does require strength of mind to keep the thoughts *were* <wh!!> they should be while the varieties of strange sights, political moral and physical, are passed before the eyes.' (*LD* III, 146) It is indicative of what tight control Newman had learned to exercise over his thoughts.

Stopping in Malta he spent a wretched Christmas in quarantine, 'deprived of the comfort and order of an Established Church', listening to the beautiful bells. 'A Christmas without Christ,' he called it in a set of verses that attest his sense of loneliness:

> I hear the tuneful bells around,
> The blessèd towers I see;

A stranger on a foreign ground,
They peal a fast for me.
                              (*VV*, 98)

From 28 December to 8 January they visited Corfu, with stops at
Zante and Patras. 10 January to 7 February they spent in Malta, twelve
days of the stay in quarantine. This was followed by five nights in Sicily,
with a trip to Egesta and a fortnight in Naples with visits to Herculaneum,
Pompeii, Salerno, Paestum, and Amalfi. On 2 March Newman and the
Froudes arrived in Rome. Newman had a sharp eye for detail and a keen
interest in all he saw and the people with whom he came in contact. He
had also more than the usual power of introspection. In letters to his
mother and sisters he shows his literary ability to communicate his
impressions and observations as well as his emotional reactions. If it were
not for the verses included in his letters, they would be of no more
interest than the travel narratives of many a voyager of the last century.
The verses, however, are significant in revealing the spiritual purification
and development he underwent which gave meaning to the entire journey,
ending in a conviction that God had a work for him to do in England.

THE VERSES

Before leaving England Newman had proposed to Rose that he and
others have two pages in each number of the *British Magazine*, of which
Rose was editor, for four brief verses, 'each bringing out forcibly *one*
idea'. The purpose would be to convey 'certain truths and facts, moral,
ecclesiastical and religious, simply and forcibly, with greater freedom,
and clearness than in the Christian Year. . . . It might be called Lyra
Apostolica.' (*LD* III, 119–20) Newman composed many of these verses
on board ship and during his journeys before reaching Rome and then
again on the journey back to England. They touch on a variety of topics,
some deeply personal. As always he is conscious of his past sins, as in
'Wanderings' which has reference to his sinful life before his first conversion (*VV*, 75), and the need of forgiveness ('Absolution', *VV*, 83),
and to accept suffering as a penance ('Penance', *VV*, 95). Unlike David
to whom God offered a choice, he asks God to, 'choose Thyself the
woe'. ('Judgment', *VV*, 112) In accordance with his habitual conviction
he is confident that truth will be proclaimed by the few, the holy, the
Saints whom God raises up, 'Rear'd on lone heights, and rare,/ His

Saints their watch-flame bear,' ('The Course of Truth', *VV*, 97) He must be patient and seek

> With thoughts in prayer and watchful eyes,
> My seasons sent for thee to speak,
> And use them as they rise.
>   ('A Word in season,' *VV*, 87)

Off the coast of Zante, one of the Ionian Isles, he is reminded of the Greek Fathers, who had occupied his thoughts when writing the *Arians*, and he composed verses in their honor:

> *The Greek Fathers*
> Let heathen sing thy heathen praise,
> Fall'n Greece! the thought of holier days
>   In my sad heart abides;
> For sons of thine in Truth's first hour
> Were tongues and weapons of His power
> Born of the Spirit's fiery shower,
>   Our fathers and our guides.
>
> All thine is Clement's varied page;
> And Dionysius, ruler sage,
>   In days of doubt and pain;
> And Origen with eagle eye;
> And saintly Basil's purpose high
> To smite imperial heresy,
>   And cleanse the Altar's stain.
>
> From thee the glorious preacher came,
> With soul of zeal and lips of flame,
>   A court's stern martyr-guest;
> And thine, O inexhaustive race!
> Was Nazianzen's heaven-taught grace;
> And royal-hearted Athanase,
>   With Paul's own mantle blest.
>   (*VV*, 102–3)

Of the biblical saints St Paul was closest to his heart as, of the Fathers, was Athanasius.

Coming into sight of Ithaca, he was enchanted by the view. 'Ithaca was the first poetical place I ever heard of, being used to learn Pope's Odyssey by heart as a child.' He could hardly describe his feelings, which were not caused by any classical association, 'but by the thought that I now saw before me in real shape those places which has been the earliest vision of my childhood'. He gazed upon the isle for a quarter of an hour, and 'thought of Ham and of all the various glimpses, which memory barely retains and which fly from me when I pursue them, of that earliest time of life when one seems almost to realize the . . . remnant of a pre-existent state. Oh how I longed to touch the land and satisfy myself it was not a mere vision.' He thinks by association of Moses gazing on the promised land.

> Blest scene! thrice-welcome after toil –
>   If no deceit I view;
> Oh might my lips but press the soil
>   And prove the vision true!
>   (*LD* III, 172–3, 254, *VV*, 106–7)

Like many a traveller he found travel an effort at times. Though he enjoyed the sights, at the same time he wished he were back in his rooms at Oriel and he shies away from social contacts. He tries to unravel the reasons for this. Is it owing to past disappointments or because like many a shy person he is sensitive to slights? Or is it owing to fatigue and overwork?

> whether or not my mind has been strained and wearied with the necessity of constant activity, I know not – or whether or not having had many disappointments, or suffered much from the rudeness and slights of persons I have been cast with, I shrink involuntarily from the contact of the world – and whether or not, natural disposition assists this feeling, and a perception (almost morbid) of my deficiencies and absurdities, any how neither the kindest attentions nor the most sublime sights have over me influence enough to draw me out of way, and deliberately as I have set about my present wanderings, yet I heartily wish they were over . . . and had much rather *have* seen them than *see* them, tho' the while I am extremely astonished and almost enchanted at seeing them. (*LD* III, 177–8)

Perhaps it was in the same mood he composed the lines of the verses 'Melchizedek':

> Thrice blest are they who feel their loneliness;
>> To whom nor voice of friends nor pleasant scene
>> Brings aught on which their saddened heart can lean.
> Yea, the rich earth, garbed in her daintiest dress
> Of light and joy, doth but the more oppress,
>> Claiming responsive smiles and raptures high;
>> Till, sick at heart, beyond the veil they fly,
> Seeking His Presence, who alone can bless.
>
> (*VV*, 108, *LD* III, 183)

By the time he reached Malta, he longed for the fifteen days of peace in the Lazzaretto.

Harriett responded to these remarks, 'I hope the fortnight of repose in the Lazaret will quite set you up for your tour. I quite understand all your feelings, and your wish of finding yourself in Oriel. . . . Yet I wish I could say any thing to persuade you not to think of your "deficiencies" and "absurdities – " which I well know exist only in your own mind.' (*LD* III, 186)

Having caught a bad cough he decided to stay indoors at Valletta but urged the Froudes to go sightseeing in the morning and to dine out at night without him. Fortunately he felt neither lonely nor depressed. 'Thank God, my spirits have not failed me once – they used when I was solitary – vid verses on my birthday [*VV*, 5–8], but I am more callous now. Last night . . . I was much comforted by thinking over Psalm 121 which had been in the service of the day, which was sung at St Mary's before I left and which I had not thought of since.'[1] (*LD* III, 209) Unable to be idle he wrote more verses and read a novel. The five sonnets devoted to the Patriarchs were finished, '*being as a whole* the best thing I have done perhaps in a rhyming way'. (*LD* III, 206) He also took fifteen lessons in conversational Italian. From Rome he later wrote to Thomas Mozley, 'I had learned the grammar and structure of the language some years ago, and could read it pretty well. . . . Italian is a very easy language – were I to be here a few months, and threw myself into native society, I should easily master it.' (*LD* III, 209–11, 243)

The party moved on to Sicily, 'to which (in spite of dirt and other inconveniences) I feel drawn as by a loadstone', he wrote to Harriett (*LD* III, 213). Palermo he called 'the filthiest, yet the noblest city, I have seen. – O the miserable creatures we saw in Sicily – I never knew what human suffering was before – children and youths . . . with features sunk and contracted with perpetual dirt, as if it was their only food.' At Calatafimi, he found the children who belonged to the inn, slept in holes in the wall of the inn, 'which smelt (not like a dog kennel) but like a wildbeast's cage, almost overpowering us in our room upstairs. I had no sleep all night from insects of prey – but this was a little evil.' The Church was in a deplorable state, stripped of its temporalities. (*LD* III, 223–4, 245) Nevertheless what he saw of Sicily, he wrote to Henry Wilberforce, 'makes me quite burn to see more of it.' (*LD* III, 223–4, 245)

Impressed as he was with Messina and Palermo, the highlight was the visit to Egesta, which he described with rapturous delight to Jemima and to Henry Wilberforce: 'wonderful place, piercing the heart with a strange painful pleasure!'

> What a ride we had from Palermo to Egesta! no words will convey the impression of it – The distance to Calatafimi is about 43 miles, and then you go on mules to the temple, 43 miles. The road lies amid the wildest scenery conceivable, intermixed with exuberantly fruitful plains, stocked full of olives, oranges, lemons, vines, locust trees etc. and brimming full of corn. The temple lies at the extremity of a long and rich valley, in the midst of desolation. It is built on a steep circular hill, with rocks about, and on the adjacent heights the ruins of the two towns of Egesta – itself being the only living thing (so to say) among the scattered masses. A miserable shepherd's hut with ragged dogs is situated close on the temple, making a circuit of mud and filth on one side of it – besides this, there are no signs of man or beast except a strange Sicilian bull among the ruins. The hills are all very steep, and mount Eryx just shows itself in the distance. It is a most magnificent site for a town which adds to the contrast of actual loneliness. And something of awe besides comes over the mind at the thought how the old Elymi ever thought of pitching their tents in so wild a place. (*LD* III, 245)

After Sicily there was a fortnight's stay in Naples, which he found 'a wretched' 'a vile place,' with trips to Herculaneum, Pompeii, Salerno, Paestum, and Amalfi. These visits elicited varying degrees of pleasure. Pompeii at first aroused no great interest, though the poor weather may have dampened it.

> I did not go to it with expectations. It was neither the theme of Homer, nor the tomb of Virgil – I had seen ruins enough already to bring before me past times – all the curiosities of this very place . . . are

brought together in the Museum at Naples – And what past age did it carry one back to? one of the most profligate and abandoned in history. . . . There is scarce ground for doubting that the fire from Vesuvius was as strictly judicial as that which overwhelmed the cities of the plain. (*LD* III, 253)

Yet in three weeks' time strange 'relentings' came over him and 'I almost yearn in my mind over this guilty place, with which I would fain persuade myself I have no sympathy.' His explanation was 'that the human heart will in spite of itself claim kindred with every thing human – and in the blackest deformity pities its brethren – enters into their feelings and experiences what bad tendencies they have developed – and imagines their present fearful remorse – according to the old saying, "Homo sum, humani nihil etc." And, if we feel this in the worst places, what is felt on the other hand in brighter scenes? where the historical deeds are more comfortable, or the scenery itself is fine.?' (*LD* III, 254) One such scene was Messina. He composed verses which are introduced by the same quotation from Terence '*Homo sum; humani nil à me alienum puto*' ('I am a man; I count nothing human indifferent to me.'):

> Why, wedded to the Lord, still yearns my heart
>   Towards these scenes of ancient heathen fame?
>   Yet legend hoar, and voice of bard that came
> Fixing my restless youth with its sweet art,
> And shades of power, and those who bore a part
>   In the mad deeds that set the world on flame,
>   So fret my memory here, – ah! is it blame? –
> That from my eyes the tear is fain to start.
> Nay, from no fount impure these drops arise;
> 'Tis but that sympathy with Adam's race
> Which in each brother's history reads it's own.
> So let the cliffs and seas of this fair place
> Be named man's tomb and splendid record-stone,
> High hope, pride-stain'd, the course without the prize.
>
> (*VV*, 129)

It was with this kind of sympathy that he later credited St Paul.[2]

Of the sixty-one verses he had written by 20 March, only five had been written since Malta. 'My muse is run dry', he told Jemima. (*LD* III, 265) These verses are really mini-meditations; they rarely, if ever, rise to the level of poetry. For Newman the idea was primary. Their significance lies in revealing how his thoughts were constantly centered on religious subjects.

ROME: HOW SHALL I NAME THEE?

Newman arrived in Rome on 2 March and spent six delightful weeks there. He could not but be impressed by the size and magnificence of its treasures, but his Protestant prejudices caused him to have mixed religious feelings. On the one hand, it was 'the place of martyrdom and burial of Apostles and Saints . . . the city to which England owes the blessing of the gospel – But then on the other hand the superstitions; – or rather, what is far worse, the solemn reception of them as an essential part of Christianity – but then again the extreme beauty and costliness of the Churches – and then on the contrary the knowledge that the most famous was built (in part) by the sale of indulgences – Really this is a cruel place. – There is more and more to be seen and thought of, daily – it is a mine of all sorts of excellences, but the very highest.' (*LD* III, 240–1; cf. 232, 260–2)

   Newman began to read over and reflect on the prophecies about Rome in the Book of Revelation and propounded his view in a long letter to Pusey. He enquired into the history of Gregorian chant. 'I feel very much my want of knowledge on the subject – for tho' I am very fond of music, I am very unlearned in it, having had little opportunity to become acquainted with it as a language.' (*LD* III, 255) He saw the Pope pontificate in the Church of Santa Maria sopra Minerva, not liking his being borne aloft or the children kissing his foot, 'and yet as I looked on, and saw all Christian acts performing the Holy Sacrament offered up, and the blessing given, and recollected I was in church, I could only say in very perplexity my own words, "How shall I name thee, Light of the wide west, or heinous error-seat?" – and felt the force of the parable of the tares – who can separate the light from the darkness but the Creator Word who prophesied their union? And so I am forced to leave the matter, not at all seeing my way out of it. – How shall I name thee?' (*LD* III, 268) This was a reference to the verses he composed and sent to Jemima, 5 March, upon his arrival in Rome. (*LD* III, 232)

> Far sadder musing on the traveller <pilgrim> falls
>   At sight of thee, O Rome,

Than when he views the rough sea-beaten walls
   Of Greece, thought's early home;
For thou wert of the guilty <hateful> four, whose doom
   Burdened the prophet's scroll;
But Greece was clean, till in her evening's gloom
Her name and sword a Macedonian stole.

And next a mingled throng besets the breast
   Of bitter thoughts and sweet;
How shall I call thee, Light of the wide West,
   Or heinous error-seat?
O Mother erst, close following Jesus' feet!
   Do not thy titles glow
Mid those stern judgment fires, which shall complete
Crime's weary <rebel>course and heavenawarded woe?

On 6 April Froude and he called on Dr Wiseman, then rector of the English College, and had a long talk with him among other things about the prospect of reunion. They discovered to their dismay 'that not one step could be gained without swallowing the Council of Trent as a whole . . .' 'that the doctrine of the infallibility of the Church made the acts of each successive Council obligatory for ever'. So Froude wrote to Christie. He continued saying Newman 'declares that ever since I heard this I have become a staunch Protestant, which is a most base calumny on his part, though I own it has altogether changed my notions of the Roman Catholics, and made me wish for the total overthrow of their system. I think that the only *topos* now is "the ancient Church of England", and as an explanation of what one means, "Charles the First and the Nonjurors."'[3] Newman however was much more anti-Roman than Froude (*Apo.*, 24–5) He too wrote to Christie, 'As to my view of the Romanist system, it remains, I believe, unchanged. A union with Rome, while it is what it is, is impossible; it is a dream. As to the individual members of the cruel church, who can but love and feel for them?' (*LD* III, 277) And to Henry Jenkyns, Fellow of Oriel, Newman wrote, 'I do not like to talk of the lamentable mixture of truth with error which Romanism exhibits – the corruption of the highest and noblest views and principles, far higher than we Protestants have, with malignant poisons – as Solomon says. Dead flies cause the precious ointment to stink.' (*LD* III, 280)

In February Newman heard of the Church Temporalities Bill (eventually passed in July 1833) which proposed abolishing ten sees of the

Established Church in Ireland, and he was indignant at the encroachment of the state on the Church. He and Froude also became aware in March that Thomas Arnold, headmaster of Rugby, in his book *Principles of Church Reform*, called for religious comprehensiveness to prevent the 'calamity' of disestablishment. 'If I understand it right,' Newman wrote R. F. Wilson, 'all sects (the Church inclusive) are to hold their meetings in the Parish Church – though not at the same hour. . . . He excludes Quakers and Roman Catholics.' With biting irony and sarcasm Newman proposed an amendment.

> 'pass an Act to oblige some persuasions to *change* the Sunday – if you have two Sundays in the week, it is plain you could easily accommodate any probable number of sects. And in this way you would get over Whately's objection against the Evangelical (or other) party – make *them* keep Sunday on Saturday. Nor would this interfere with the Jews' worship (which of course is to be in the [[Parish]] Church). . . . Luckily the Mohammedan holiday is already on a Friday. (*LD* III, 258)

He feared that the Church in England might well be disestablished. 'I sincerely trust our Clergy may quit them like men – if some of the Bishops would but give the signal.' (*LD* III, 247) The time was coming when 'every one must choose his side'. His spirits about the future prospect of the Church were lifted when he heard that Keble 'at length is roused, and (*if* once up) he will prove a second St Ambrose – others too are moving'. (*LD* III, 264) Getting ready for the battle, he sent off two numbers of the *Lyra Apostolica* to Rose for inclusion in the May and June issues of the *British Magazine*. He requested that Rose put a line of notice before every number of the 'Lyra' to signify that 'The Editor is not responsible for the opinions contained in it.' This, he felt, would give liberty to speak freely. (*LD* III, 247, 249, 251) Borrowing a copy of Homer's *Iliad* from Bunsen, the Prussian ambassador to the Vatican, Froude chose as a motto for the *Lyra* 'the words in which Achilles, on returning to battle, says, "You shall know the difference, now that I am back again."' (*Apo.*, 34) But before the battle would begin, Newman was to undergo a spiritual purification and preparation.

On 9 April the Froudes left Rome for Civitavecchia to take a steamer to Marseilles and then travel through France to England. Left alone by himself for the first time in a foreign land, he wandered about in sadness, recognizing that Rome, not as a place, but as 'the scene of sacred history, has a part of my heart, and in going away I was tearing it as if in twain'.

He went back again to visit the Church of Sta Maria in Cosmedin which Dionysius founded AD 260 and where St Augustine was said to have studied rhetoric. 'I mounted the height where St Peter was martyred, and for a last time wandered through the vast space of his wonderful Basilica and surveyed his place of burial, and then prepared for my departure.' (*LD* III, 282) He was taking back with him an increased love of what he would come to call 'the Church Catholic and Apostolic, set up from the Beginning,' of which the Established Church 'was but the local presence and the organ.' (*Apo.*, 31–2)

In Naples he prepared for his Sicilian expedition by hiring a servant, buying pots and pans and various necessities, the price of which he carefully calculated. While waiting for the boat he took a trip to Vesuvius, 'an expedition which has introduced me to the most wonderful sight I have seen abroad . . . and in which I have undergone more labour and *active* pain . . . I ever recollect my having!' The party descended into the crater and he came home with blistered hands and feet from the warm ash. (*LD* III, 284–5) On 21 April he arrived at Messina. The following day he set out from Messina in an irritated mood and feeling the loss of a companion: 'a tour is of all other times that in which you make friends of acquaintances – familiarity ensues and character is drawn out, as it never otherwise is'. The following day they approached Taormina, where he climbed up to the theatre and saw a view 'a nearer approach to seeing Eden, than anything I had conceived possible'. (*LD* III, 302–3)

The trip to and from Syracuse was rigorous, Newman having nothing to eat for twenty-four hours, but in accordance with his general view he stored up experiences spiritual as well as sensible to be enjoyed more in memory than in the experience itself, but also to strengthen him 'amid coming pains and fears', in the manner of St Paul:

TAORMINA

"And Jacob went on his way, and the Angels of God met him."

Say, hast thou track'd a traveller's round,
    Nor visions met thee there,
Thou couldst but marvel to have found
    This blighted world so fair?

And feel an awe within thee rise,
    That sinful man should see

Glories far worthier Seraph's eyes
Than to be shared by thee?

Store them in heart! thou shalt not faint
'Mid coming pains and fears,
As the third heaven once nerved a Saint
For fourteen trial-years.
Magnisi. April 26, 1833. (*VV*, 135)

IN THE SHADOW OF DEATH

On 30 April he had experienced some feverishness which went away and the following day he set off again, getting to Leonforte on 3 May where he fell ill of a fever, probably typhoid. Here he underwent the third spiritual experience associated with an illness. He felt he was given over to the devil. Lying in bed the first day he felt that God was fighting against him, and this He had been doing ever since he left Rome, and the reason was self-will. Yet he kept saying to himself, 'I have not sinned against light.' He thought he had shown self-will in returning to Sicily against the judgement of the Froudes and also the Wilberforces at Naples. At one point however, he had 'a most consoling overpowering thought of God's electing love, and seemed to feel I was His'. These feelings, though heightened by delirium, 'still are from God in the way of Providence'.

The next day the feelings of self-reproach increased. He thought he had been disrespectful and insulting to the Provost, his superior, in the matter of the tutorship and he examined himself to see if he had any feelings of resentment against him when taking the Sacrament. He repented and resolved to do penance by not preaching at St Mary's or anywhere for a length of time 'as a penitent unworthy to show myself'. He recalled that his last act before leaving Oxford was to preach a University sermon on the character of Saul against self-will, so that he seemed to have been predicting his own condemnation. 'I seemed to see more and more my utter hollowness.' He thought he had been developing Keble's convictions rather than his own, 'as a pane of glass, which transmits heat being cold itself'.

Newman's humility was not a false humility but an honest evaluation of himself. This will be seen in even greater degree in the self-examination he made in his retreat before ordination to the priesthood in 1846. At this point however he sets down:

I have a vivid perception of the consequences of certain admitted principles, have a considerable intellectual capacity of drawing them out, have the refinement to admire them, and a rhetorical or histrionic power to represent them; and, having no great (i.e. no vivid) love of this world, whether riches, honors, or any thing else, and some firmness and natural dignity of character, take the profession of them upon me, as I might sing a tune which I liked – loving the Truth, but not possessing it – for I believe myself at heart to be nearly hollow i.e. with little love, little self-denial. I believe I have some faith, that is all – and as to my sins, they need my possessing no little amount of faith to set against them and gain their remission.

Gennaro, his servant, thought him dying, and Newman gave him a direction to write to, if he did, but 'I said "I do not think I shall" – "I have not sinned against light" or "God has still work for me to do." I think the latter.' (*AW*, 124–7)

Newman then thought he 'would try to obey God's will as far as I could, and, with a dreamy confused notion, which the fever (I suppose) occasioned, thought that in setting off the fourth day from Leonforte, I was *walking* as long as I could in the way of God's commandments, and putting myself in *the way* of His mercy, as if He would meet me. (Isa. 26. 8)'. (*LD* IV, 8, *AW*, 121 ff.) After walking seven miles, he collapsed. Gennaro got him into a hut where a nearby doctor came to examine him. After resting for several hours he was placed on a mule and journeyed four miles up a steep hill to Castro Giovanni, where he had lodgings in a house of a man of some property. For three weeks he received great personal care on the part of his host and medical care from a doctor. He was bled and fed medicines, but the cure was worse than the disease. He was overcome with weakness so that he could not raise his hand to his head. Gennaro slept in the same room, as he could not bear to be alone. The nights were long and delirious. After eleven days the crisis passed and as he got better he longed for the daylight, and when the light came through the shutters he soliloquized, 'O sweet light, God's best gift etc.'

A number of questions arise in interpreting this experience and the document he subsequently drew up which describes it in detail. Did Newman repent of having resigned the tutorship? The answer Newman himself gave in a letter to Henry Wilberforce, in which he remarks, 'tho' I could not (and do not) at all repent the doing so, yet I began to understand that the *manner* was hasty and impatient'. He also thought he might have profaned the Sacrament, 'the Lord's Supper', in having cherished some resentment against the Provost for putting him out of the tutorship, but this impression faded away. What did not fade away and was the core of the experience – the realization that, despite all his efforts he was really seeking his own will, and for this reason God was fighting against him. Hence the true object of his repentance was self-will.

Newman's repentance therefore had a real object, not an imagined one, but its significance is liable to be missed if one does not recall what he meant by true repentance as he explained in a sermon, 'Christian Repentance', preached on 20 November 1831. In it he affirms:

The most noble repentance (if a fallen being can be noble in his fall), the most decorous conduct in a conscious sinner, is an *unconditional surrender* of himself to God – not a bargaining about terms, not a scheming (so to call it) to be received back again, but an instant *surrender* of himself in the first instance. (*PPS* III, 5, 96)

It is this unconditional surrender to God's will that he mentions in the verses, 'Lead Kindly Light'. Such repentance, however, is not a single act nor an initial one. 'The truest kind of repentance as little comes at first, as perfect conformity to any other part of God's law. It is gained by long practice – it will come at length. . . . It is, indeed, easy enough to have good words put into our mouths, and our feelings aroused, and to profess the union of utter-abandonment and enlightened sense of sin; but to claim is not really to possess these excellent tempers. Really to gain these is a work of time.' (98) From the time of his first conversion Newman was trying to acquire this type of repentance which is sometimes referred to as compunction or habitual repentance, the most recent attempt being revealed in the verses already mentioned. 'Wanderings', 'Judgment', 'Absolution', 'Memory'. That Newman had acquired it may be judged from the promptness with which he repents and resolves to do penance.

Newman accused himself of being 'hollow'. What did he mean by that? He used the word twice. The second time, he adds, 'i.e., with little love, little self denial'. For Newman truth had to be realized, that is, not only grasped as a reality, which is what he means by realization, but put into action. The latest instance of this affirmation was in a letter written from Rome, in which he says, 'Doubtless no religious emotion is worth a straw, or rather it is pernicious, if it does not lead to *practice*. Good thoughts are only good so far as they are taken as means to an exact *obedience* or at least this is the chief part of their goodness.' (*LD* III, 292)

The first use of the word 'hollow' seems to be explained by what follows, and that is 'insincere'. Not that he does not hold these convictions but they are not original with him, but come from Keble, though he puts them forth as his own. Earlier he had used the word 'hollow' to mean 'insincere'. It could be argued, however, that the simile, 'a pane of glass, which transmits heat being cold itself', fits better with the later interpretation he gives, 'with little love'. In 1839 he would preach a sermon, 'Love, the One Thing needful', in which he asserts '. . . serious men. . . feel that though they are, to a certain point, keeping God's commandments, yet love is not proportionate, does not keep pace, with their obedience; that obedience springs from some source short of love. This they perceive; they feel themselves to be hollow; a fair outside, without a spirit within it.' (*PPS* V, 23, 331)

Lastly, and perhaps most important of all, is the interpretation of Newman's assertion, 'And at one time I had a most consoling overpowering thought of God's electing love, and seemed to feel I was His.' Was this a mystical experience, i.e., the action of God which is 'not merely a silent working of grace,' but an action of which he was 'sensibly and consciously aware'? It certainly seems to be the latter, and one indication is the inability to put it into words, which is commonly the experience of the mystics. He writes to Wilberforce, 'not that I can describe the feeling in words'. Newman took it as 'an instance of God's mercy to me'.

For some time prior to his illness a feeling or intuition began to take shape in his mind that God had some work for him to do in England. He alludes to this in a letter to Christie, which he mentions in the account of his illness.

> I trust I shall be conducted back safely, to be made use of. I do not mind saying this, for I do not think I am actuated by ambitious views, though, power, when possessed or in prospect, is a snare. At present to me it is neither in possession or prospect. . . . At present I can truly say that I would take the lot of retirement, were the choice offered to me, provided I saw others maintaining instead of me those views which seem to me of supreme and exclusive importance.' (*LD* III, 278; *AW*, 121, 136)

When departing from Wiseman in Rome, the latter expressed the wish he might visit Rome a second time, but Newman said, 'with great gravity, "We have a work to do in England."' (*Apo.*, 34) During his illness Newman had a confident feeling he would not die, 'and gave as a reason . . . that "I thought God had some work for me" – these I believe were exactly my words. And when, after the fever, I was on the road to Palermo, so weak I could not walk by myself, I sat on the bed in the morning May 26 or May 27 profusely weeping, and only able to say that I could not help thinking God has something for me to do at home. This I repeated to my servant to whom the words were unintelligible of course.' (*AW*, 122, 136) So what was an intuition seems to have turned into a conviction and explains his impatience to get home quickly. It was also the reason why he thought that he had been given over into the hands of the devil, 'I could almost think that the devil saw I am to be a means of usefulness, and tried to destroy me.' (*AW*, 121–2; cf. *KC*, 315–6)

In examining the Sicilian experience one thinks of the struggles of the hermits in the desert or of the purifications undergone by the saints before they became docile instruments in the hands of God. Certain it is that Newman penetrated into the deep recesses of his soul and found the stumbling block to the realization of his aspirations to serve God in the Church. Even though he sincerely desired to be an instrument in the hands of God, still given his activist temperament and his firm conviction of personal influence as the means of propagating the Truth, the danger was that he could become the instrument not of God's will but of his own. It would be a subtle temptation. It seems only now was God ready to loosen the reins and let him go, chastened and submissive, protected from self-love and self will, and on his guard against the temptations that normally come with power, success, and fame.

Newman looked upon the experience as a turning point in his life as an Anglican priest and saw in it 'a strange Providence'. It looked not only to the future but to the past. It was the culmination of a purification and spiritual development which had been taking place since the time he failed to reform the Bible and Church Missionary Societies and especially the tutorial system. At that time he composed the sermon on Jeremiah, and its lessons were never forgotten. 'Give not over your attempts to serve God, though you see nothing come of them. Watch and pray, and obey your conscience, though you cannot perceive your own progress in holiness.' Newman later said that this sermon 'was in my mind *all through* the movement'. (*LD* XXIV, 272–3) The hours spent in meditation on the Scriptures, in composing his sermons and in reading of the great saints of the early Church had taught him more fully the ways of God.

A TEST OF PATIENCE

Upon his recovery Newman had to walk with a stick even when he got to Palermo. The day before he left for Palermo his impatience to get home began and lasted the rest of his stay abroad. He was expecting to sail almost daily, and was 'homesick and much disappointed' at the delay of almost three weeks. But he recovered his health rapidly, and composed a fair number of verses for the *Lyra*. All during his stay abroad his thoughts were filled with thoughts of home. He was constantly waiting for letters and was disappointed when after three months' waiting he received only two. For the last two months the thought of home had brought tears to his eyes, as often as it occurred. (*LD* III, 310) Sometimes he would enter a church and rest until his sadness and impatience passed.

THE GOOD SAMARITAN

O that thy creed were sound!
   For thou dost soothe the heart, Thou
      Church of Rome,
   By thy unwearied watch and varied round
Of service, in thy Saviour's holy home.
   I cannot walk the city's sultry streets,
   But the wide porch invites to still retreats,
Where passion's thirst is calmed, and care's
      unthankful gloom.

   There, on a foreign shore,
The home-sick solitary finds a friend:
   Thoughts, prison'd long for lack of speech,
      outpour
Their tears; and doubts in resignation end.
   I almost fainted from the long delay,
   That tangles me within this languid bay,
When comes a foe, my wounds with oil and
      wine to tend.

                 (*VV*, 153)

In Palermo he learned from 'Galignani' that Rogers was elected Fellow of Oriel, and he wrote to congratulate him and tell of his illness in

Leonforte and the rapidity of his recovery. On the twelfth day after the crisis 'I began a journey of three days to Palermo going one day sixty-two miles; and here, where I have been these ten days, I have surprised everyone by my improvement.' He ended by saying how '*very* homesick' he was. (*LD* III, 312–5)

Gennaro was to return to his wife and family in Naples. He had been in charge of all Newman's belongings including money and nothing was lost. 'He was humanly speaking the preserver of my life, I think. . . . He nursed me as a child. An English servant never would do what he did.' He wanted Newman's old blue cloak, but Newman was too attached to it by reason of its associations. 'It had nursed me all through my illness; had even been put on my bed, put on me when I rose to have my bed made etc. I had nearly lost it at Corfu – it was stolen by a soldier but recovered.' So he gave Gennaro £10, a considerable sum in those days, in addition to his wages. As he made the last entry in the account of illness in Sicily, 25 March 1840, at Littlemore, the cloak was still with him and on some cold nights used on his bed. (*AW*, 138)

Newman continued to write verses during the time he was waiting for a boat. These verses show the Christian warrior getting ready to do battle, but recognizing that God alone gives the victory, and his work may never be completed.

> One only, of God's messengers to man,
> Finish'd the work of grace, which He began . . .
> List Christian warrior! thou, whose soul is fain
> To rid thy Mother of her present chain; –
> Christ will avenge his Bride yea, even now
>   Begins the work, and thou
> Shalt spend in it thy strength, but, ere He save,
>   Thy lot shall be the grave.
>   (*VV*, 139–40)

As so often, St Paul is his example, when he thinks it might be best to plant flowers in the Lord's garden 'in meekness and in love/ And waiting for the blissful realms above', he is reminded that

> Runs not the Word of Truth through every land,
> A sword to sever, and a fire to burn?
>   If blessèd Paul had stay'd
>   In cot or learned shade,

With the priest's white attire,
  And the Saints' tuneful choir,
Men had not gnash'd their teeth, not risen to slay,
But thou hadst been a heathen in thy day.

(VV, 141–2)

Sailing from Palermo on an orange boat bound for Marseilles, on 13 June, St Paul is ever in Newman's mind. In his impatience he wonders if St Paul when imprisoned suffered from the cessation of his labours, and concludes with a plea that the Lord 'create with zeal a patient heart'. (*VV*, 165) They are becalmed in the Straits of Bonifacio, but he is consoled by a vision of a figure and a voice speaks, 'St Paul is at thy side.' (*LD* III, 307, *VV*, 168)

It is in this spirit of humble unconditional surrender to God's will that he composed at sea the verses 'Pillar of the Cloud'; but popularly known as 'Lead Kindly Light'.

I was not ever thus, nor pray'd that Thou
  shouldst lead me on.
I loved to choose and see my path, but now
  Lead Thou me on.
I loved the garish day, and spite of fears,
Pride ruled my will: remember not past years.

(VV, 156–7)

From now on Newman is fearful of self-will. Though he will become the *de facto* leader of the Oxford Movement, he never sought it nor to exercise power. When unable, by reason of circumstances, to rein in his disciples, a friend wrote quoting his verses written in Palermo on St Gregory Nazianzen, 'Thou couldst a people raise, but couldst not rule.' (*Apo.*, 59) The remainder of the verses referring to Gregory's retirement from the patriarchal throne seem prophetic of Newman's resignation from the Movement and his retirement to Littlemore to live a life of monastic asceticism.

Thou couldst a people raise, but couldst not rule: –
  So, gentle one,
Heaven set thee free, – for, ere thy years were full,
  Thy work was done;
According thee the lot thou lovedst best,

> To muse upon the past, – to serve, yet be at rest.'
>> (*VV*, 152)

Already he was beginning to see the trial in Sicily in the perspective of personal providence. As in former days in his life, ''twas trial did convey ... To my tormented soul such larger grace.'

> So now, whene'er, in journeying on, I feel
> The shadow of the Providential Hand,
> Deep breathless stirrings shoot across my breast,
> Searching to know what He will now reveal,
> ... what stricter rule command,
> And girding me to work His full behest.
>> ('Providences'; in *LA*, 'Semita Justorum',
>> in *VV*, 187, 'When I look back')

Like that of St Paul at the time of God's revelation to him the change was not a radical change of principle, but his energies were channelled in a different direction and purified, or, as he said of himself, I was 'in all things the same, except that a new object was given me'. ('Sudden Conversions,' *PPS* VIII, 15, 227–8; *Apo.*, 36)

All during his passage to Marseilles, he was writing verses, in general of superior quality than his earlier ones, preparing himself for the battle against infidelity. He must not be afraid to claim powers he dreads or be deterred by misunderstanding of his motives, 'But with pure thoughts look up to God, and keep/ Our secret in our heart.' ('Pusillanimity,' *VV*, 176) Though the gospel creed is 'a sword of strife,' 'Meek hands alone may rear: / And ever Zeal begins its life / In silent thought and fear.' ('Zeal and Meekness;' *VV*, 170) Time spent in prayer is not wasted ('The Church in Prayer,' *VV*, 173–4). God grants prayers, 'but in his Love / Makes times and ways His own.' ('James and John,' *VV*, 177–8). In all trials his consolation must be to remember Christ's words. ''Tis I; be not afraid,' ('Consolation,' *VV*, 183–4) Despite the desolation 'on a voyage, when calms prevail, / And prison thee upon the sea,/ He walks the wave, He wings the sail,/ The shore is gain'd, and thou art free.' ('Desolation,' *VV*, 63–4)

He arrived in Marseilles on 27 June, and left the next day for Lyons. Upon arrival in Lyons he was forced to rest a day, as his ankles were swollen. He felt as though 'some unseen power, good or bad, was resisting my return ... God is giving me a severe lesson of patience,' he writes to his mother, 'and I trust I am not altogether wasting the discipline. It is His will'. (*LD* III, 310)

On 8 July he crossed the Channel from Dieppe, reached London at night, and returned to Oxford the following evening. His brother Frank had arrived back from Persia a few hours before.

CHAPTER TEN

Setting Sail

A few days after Newman's return to England Keble preached his Assize Sermon in the university; it was published under the title 'National Apostasy'. 'I have ever considered and kept the day,' Newman wrote in the *Apologia*, 'as the start of the religious movement of 1833.' The situation that evoked it was the planned suppression of ten Irish episcopal sees; the bill was passed in August. Would the government stop here or go on to impose doctrinal changes in the liturgy, or even to disestablish the Church entirely. The latter might not be a bad thing, but people must be prepared for it. That there was need of reform seemed obvious, what form should this take?

Newman confronted these possibilities in accordance with his fundamental principles. The first principle was that of personal influence. How he wished that 'we had one Athanasius, or Basil, we could bear with 20 Eusebiuses'. In the absence of such, one had to make the best of a difficult situation and do what one personally could do. He began therefore by publishing the *Tracts for the Times*, and distributed them as widely as possible. The first Tract issued an appeal for his fellow clergymen to choose sides in the coming conflict. The Church has an intrinsic authority, independent of the state, based upon the bishops as successors of the apostles and therefore with internal powers and spiritual resources. 'Should the Government and the country so far forget their GOD as to cast off the Church, to deprive it of its temporal honours and substance, *on what* will you rest its claim of respect and attention which you make upon your flocks? Hitherto you have been upheld by your birth and education, your wealth, your connexions; should these secular advantages cease, on what must CHRIST'S ministers depend?' He replied, 'I fear we have neglected the real ground on which our authority is built – OUR APOSTOLICAL DESCENT.' He went on to wish the bishops 'the spoiling of their goods and martyrdom', and he urged his fellow presbyters 'Exult our holy Fathers the Bishops, as the Representatives of the Apostles and the Angels of the Churches.'

The bishops did not know what quite to make of this. How many believed in their apostolic descent? It was not a view universally held in the Church. Newman wrote in the *Apologia* that he learned the doctrine from William James, a Fellow of Oriel, though being an Evangelical at the time was 'somewhat impatient of the subject'. Later in a letter to Keble, 23 November 1844, he wrote he was first introduced to it by Hurrell Froude in 1829 (after James on 'Episcopacy' in 1823). (*Apo.*, 10; *KC*, 351) There was not in the Church of England a universally accepted comprehensive, systematic, authoritative body of doctrine to which one could appeal in justification of the doctrine of apostolic succession or other doctrines. A great latitude of opinion on matters of doctrine was tolerated. Newman faced this difficulty and tried to remedy it, as will be seen, by constructing the *Via Media* in his work *The Prophetical Office of the Church*.

The third Tract on 'Alterations in the Liturgy' disapproved of changes in the Book of Common Prayer in response to objections of the liberals and the Evangelicals. The former wanted to do away with the references to hell, the imprecatory psalms and damnatory clauses of the Athanasian Creed. The latter did not like the reference to regeneration in the baptismal service, and the presumption in the burial service that the dead person was saved.

Before the end of the year, twenty tracts were published, mostly by Newman who continued to write about apostolic succession as the basis of episcopal authority, and also about the visible Church. Keble, Bowden, Harrison and Pusey also wrote some, the latter, No. 18, 'Thoughts on the Benefits of Fasting enjoined by our Church'. The Tracts set up the authority of the bishops and that of the Liturgy or Book of Common Prayer as the means of overpowering an Erastian state. (See *Diff.* I, 126ff) Newman's strategy was to get the Tracts distributed in various parts of the country and to contact as many persons as possible to share in the work. At one point he himself rode about the countryside distributing them to various rectories.

The Tracts soon ran into opposition from Mr Palmer, who was the 'organ and representative' of the high and dry establishment whose '*beau ideal* in ecclesiastical action was a board of safe, sound, sensible men.' (*Apo.*, 40) He had many connections in London and was in favour of a large or overall committee or association. In a frank letter to him Newman listed his reasons for not wanting such a committee: 1) the absence of episcopal sanction, an objection Newman had levelled against the Church Missionary Society; 2) it will excite jealousy, 'whereas no one can

complain of *individual* exertion'; 3) one will have to bring persons who
don't agree with us, whereas 'we feel our opinions are *true*; we are sure
that, few tho' we be, we shall be able to propagate them by the force of
the truth'; 4) there is a growing feeling that 'Societies are bad things,'
that people with low views get the upper hand in them, whereas
'individuals, who are seen and heard, who act and suffer, are the
instruments of Providence in all great successes'; lastly, to form an
association one has to have a definite object. We are not ready for that,
but 'defend the doctrine and discipline of the Church' is vague enough, –
vague for this reason, 'we are on the defensive, and not knowing *where*
and *how* we shall be attacked, we cannot say how we are to act'. (*LD* IV,
68) This letter illustrates what Dalgairns later told Newman, who criticized a proposal of the London Oratorians, that he saw every aspect and
conceivable difficulty of any proposal.

Palmer wanted Newman to stop the publication of the Tracts, which
Newman apparently did momentarily, but he wrote to Froude, who had
left Oxford for home and was about to go to Barbados for his health, 'I
want advice sadly . . . I am half out of spirits – but how one outgrows
tenderness! Several years back, to have known that ½ or all Oxford shook
their heads at what I was doing, (e.g. about the Church Missionary
Society) would have hurt me much – but somehow now I manage to
exist. Do give me some advice and encouragement.' As a result of his
experience in Sicily, he was on his guard, 'I so fear I may be self willed
in this matter of the Tracts – pray do advise me according to your light.'
(*LD* IV, 100–1) Both Keble and Froude 'advocated their continuance
strongly, and were angry with me for consenting to stop them.' (*Apo.*, 43)

Samuel Rickards and Perceval likewise disapproved of the Tracts. To
both, Newman defended them. To the latter Newman wrote:

> As to the Tracts . . . every one has his own taste. You object to some
> things, another to others. If we altered to please every one, the effect
> would be spoiled. They were not intended as symbols *é cathedrâ*, but
> as the expression of individual minds; and individuals, feeling strongly,
> while on the other hand, they are incidentally faulty in mode or
> language, are still peculiarly effective. No great work was done by a
> system; whereas systems rise out of individual exertions. Luther was
> an individual. The very faults of an individual excite attention; he
> loses, but his cause (if good and he powerful-minded) gains. This is
> the way of things; we promote truth by a self-sacrifice. (*Apo.*, 41–2)

Given Newman's sensitive nature, it required self-discipline to stick to his principles, as is clear from a letter he wrote to Miss Giberne thanking her for her encouragement:

A person like myself hears of nothing but his failures or what others consider such . . . and one's best friends act as one's best friends ought, tell one of all one's mistakes and absurdities. I know it is a good thing thus to be dealt with. . . . All things one tries to do, *must* be mixed with great imperfection – and it is part of one's trial to be obliged to attempt things which involve incidental error, and give cause for blame. This is all very humbling, particularly when a person has foretold to himself his own difficulties and scrapes. . . . But it is a good discipline and I will gladly accept it. (*LD* IV, 147)

The second personal action Newman took was to comb the Fathers of the Church for light and guidance. He began to publish a series of sketches in the *British Magazine*, 'Letters on the Church of the Fathers', and continued them until May 1837. The purpose of these was 'to introduce the religious sentiments, views, and customs of the first ages into the modern Church of England'. (*Apo.*, 73) Two papers dealt with St Ambrose. The lesson to be learned from him is that in the event the State casts off the Church, 'we must *look to the people*'. Newman treated the subject with great tact and rhetorical skill. He was careful to mention the many fruits which the Church has derived from the state and not to say that he was advocating such a separation on the part of the state. To have asserted such would have alienated many readers. He himself thought such a separation would be good for the spiritual life of the Church, but at the same time he believed it wrong actively to agitate for such a separation as it would be sinful to oppose legitimate authority which had set up the union.

In the *Apologia* Newman affirmed that he 'wished to make a strong pull in union with all who were opposed to the principles of liberalism, whoever they might be', and hence his third action was to compose a series of letters that were published in the Evangelical newspaper *The Record*. 'The heading given them was, "Church Reform". The first was on the revival of Church Discipline; the second, on its Scripture proof; the third, on the application of the doctrine; the fourth was an answer to objections; the fifth was on the benefits of discipline.' (*Apo.*, 42) The sixth was not published, for which the Editor apologized but added his

serious regrets at the theological views of the *Tracts*. On 2 December
they printed extracts from the *Tracts*, but in the next issue, 5 December
they added: 'With such sentiments as those contained in the extracts
given in our last paper, we can have no fellowship.' In the same issue
the *Record* attacked the Tracts and derided the doctrine of Apostolic
Succession as a foundation on which to rest the safety of the Church.
Newman apparently did not expect this rebuff on the part of the *Record*.
In a private letter to the Editor he gave numerous points on which the
writers of the *Tracts* and the *Record* agreed, but he ended up defiantly,
'I believe they [the authors of the *Tracts*] do not fear you, as being
confident that the cause of truth and of primitive Christianity will prevail; though they would be much concerned of course to find themselves
opposed by men for whom they have the respect they feel for the
Conductors of the Record. *Is not Gamaliel's advice in point*, Acts V, 38.
39? – ' (*LD* IV, 130–1 and notes.)

In the *Apologia* Newman commented on these various actions: 'Acts of
the officious character, which I have been describing, were uncongenial to
my natural temper, to the genius of the Movement, and to the historical
mode of its success: – they were the fruit of that exhuberent and joyous
energy with which I had returned from abroad, and which I never had
before or since.' James Mozley wrote to his sister Anne, 'Newman is
becoming perfectly ferocious in the cause. "We'll do them". he says, at
least twenty times a day – meaning the present race of aristocrats and the
Liberal oppressors of the Church in general.' Newman's health was
restored; in fact it came back with such a rebound that friends at Oxford,
seeing him, did not well know that it was he, and hesitated before they
spoke to him. Moreover, he had the consciousness that he was employed
in that work

> which I had been dreaming about, and which I felt to be so momentous
> and inspiring. I had a supreme confidence in our cause; we were
> upholding that primitive Christianity which was delivered for all time
> by the early teachers of the Church, and which was registered and
> attested in the Anglican formularies and by the Anglican divines. That
> ancient religion had well nigh faded away out of the land, and it must
> be restored. It would be in fact a second Reformation; – a better
> reformation, for it would be a return not to the sixteenth century, but
> to the seventeenth. No time was to be lost, for the Whigs had come to
> do their worst and the rescue might come too late. . . . I felt as on
> board a vessel, which first gets under weigh, and then the deck is

cleared out, and the luggage and live stock stowed away into their proper receptacles. (*Apo.*, 43–4)

It was also the zeal of St Paul.

Zeal, however, should be combined with prudence and good judgement. So Tyler, the former Dean of Oriel, advised Newman. Newman had sent him, as editor of S.P.C.K., some sermons which Tyler wanted altered before publishing. This Newman was willing to do, but Tyler sent them back, 'in the most ludicrous hypocritical way imaginable'. Newman wrote Froude. 'He gives *no reason* for not taking my Sermons,' but appended a postscript 'I hear strange things at Oxford. I hope our friends there may have as much judgment as they have integrity and zeal. Salvam fac Ecclesiam tuam, Domine, Amen.' Newman, who could not stand humbug, put on his boxing gloves, which was probably why Rogers plucked the reply of 12 December 1833.

As you say, the Church is in a perilous state, and we have all of us need of great prudence. The great difficulty is to combine judgment and zeal, or rather to be sure that zeal is not mere party feeling, and judgment mere cowardice – for I suppose, where zeal is real, a person has too deep a sense of hazard and responsibility of acting, to be otherwise than very cautious and deliberate. Yet, it is quite true, as you observe, that persons whose zeal one cannot in charity doubt, yet are destitute of judgment. As to ourselves in Oxford, I have great reliance on the air of the place – and, since we always have shown prudence, ... it is to be hoped we shall still. But after all, individuals are but creatures of the times – and if any party in Oxford, and myself as one of them are carried on to a resistance of civil tyranny, we shall be merely the instruments and in our place the organs of the deep though silent Church feeling through the country. It is plain we can do nothing of ourselves. (*LD* IV, 100, 139, 271)

In commenting on this letter of 7 August 1860, Newman wrote: 'Poor dear Tyler, I cannot deny, had the principle of humbug in him – but this letter shows me how very brusque and fierce I must have been just then. Can one begin a movement in cold blood?' (*LD* IV, 100, 139, n. 1)

Nevertheless, Newman urged prudence in the instructions he drew up for his associates how they should conduct themselves in their endeavour 'to rouse the clergy to inculcate the Apostolic Succession and to defend the Liturgy'.

Beware of any intemperance of language. You may mention *facts* illustrative of the present tyranny exercised over the Church, as much as you please, according to your discretion. If men are afraid of Apostolic ground, then be cautious of saying much about it – if desirous, then recommend prudence and silence upon it at present . . . Recollect that we are *supporting* the Bishops – enlarge on the unfairness of leaving them to bear the brunt of the battle. (*LD* IV, 78–9)

This is an example of the use of the principle of reserve from the beginning of the Movement.

Although Newman disagreed with Palmer about the wisdom of forming a national association, he nevertheless helped with an address signed by 7000 clergy which was presented to the Archbishop of Canterbury, on 6 February 1834, in what Newman considered a watered-down fashion. It was, however, serviceable in strengthening the Archbishop against his opponents and in bringing out the Church 'as a body and power distinct from the State.' (*LD* IV, 121) He published 'Home Thoughts From Abroad', in the *British Magazine*, starting in January 1834. Newman had written it quite hastily in the previous August and sent it to Froude for criticism. The first part was a description of the various sites, which they had visited in Rome, but then Newman launched into an attack on the Romanists, as possessed of the evil genius of pagan Rome. Nevertheless 'the Christian pilgrim may traverse it, and diligently trace out, and piously venerate, the footsteps of apostles, bishops, and martyrs': But, as Froude remarked, 'all that is very well, and one hopes one has heard the end of name-calling when all [at] once you relapse into your protestantism and deal in what I take leave to call slang'. Froude did not approve of this 'second and most superfluous hit at the poor Romanists'. (*LD* IV, 37)

The fourth and perhaps the most significant personal action Newman took was the publication of the first volume of *Parochial Sermons* which appeared in March and was well received. The publication of this and subsequent volumes and reprints was instrumental not only in spreading and advancing the movement but they have proved of permanent value as classics of Christian spirituality. Richard Church pointed out the special role these sermons played in the Movement.

the Tracts were not the most powerful instruments in drawing sympathy to the movement. . . . without those sermons the movement might never have gone on, certainly would never have been what it was. . . . While men were reading and talking about the Tracts, they were hearing the sermons; and in the sermons they heard the living meaning, and reason, and bearing of the Tracts, their ethical affinities, their moral standard. The sermons created a moral atmosphere, in which men judged the questions in debate.[1]

The first volumes were directed not only against the lukewarm religion of the day, as he described it in sermon 24 of the first volume, 'the Religion of the Day', but also against Evangelicalism, as will be seen in the correspondence with Samuel Wilberforce and James Stephen. Newman was not the only one to recognize and condemn the worldliness of so many of the clergy and laity alike. Thomas William Allies was tormented by the condition of his parishioners in his country parish in Launton, Oxfordshire, to which he was exiled by Bishop Blomfield because of his outspoken support of the Movement. 'The thoroughly puritanised state of our population, the want of reverence in our churches, the absence of prayer, the atmosphere of unbelief, the rarity of Eucharistic celebrations, the want of discipline in our clergy, the contempt, or rather the complete ignoring of the priestly office and of confession . . . in short our having "in practice become . . . heathenised . . . infected with indifference. . . ." '[2]

Newman's sermons therefore fulfilled the object he called for in the first Tract, when he said:

> How can we 'hold fast the form of sound words', and 'keep that which is committed to our trust', if our influence is to depend simply on our popularity? Is it not our very office to *oppose* the world? Can we then allow ourselves to *court* it? to preach smooth things and prophesy deceits? to make the way of life easy to the rich and indolent and to bribe the humbler classes by excitements and strong intoxicating doctrine? [a reference to Evangelical Preaching] Surely it must not be so.

The Movement therefore was more than an attempt to defend the Church from the incursions of the state; it was a call for a stricter and deeper spiritual life. As Dean Church testified, 'the movement, whatever else it was, or whatever else it became, was in its first stages a movement for deeper religion, for a more real and earnest self-discipline, for a loftier morality, for more genuine self-devotion to serious life, than had ever been seen in Oxford'.[3]

THE FIGHT AGAINST LIBERALISM

In March 1834 a bill was introduced into Parliament to abolish religious tests in the universities. At Oxford in accordance with the statutes all students at the time of matriculation and again when presenting themselves for degree were obliged to subscribe to the Thirty-Nine Articles. At Cambridge no religious test was required at matriculation but before taking his degree a student had either to declare himself a member of the Church of England or to subscribe to the three articles of the Canons of 1604. This of course precluded Dissenters from taking degrees in the universities. On 17 March Newman wrote a letter to Hugh James Rose, as Editor of the *British Magazine*, against opening the universities to Dissenters. Will Dissenters be exempt from attending compulsory chapel services, Newman asked, or will they be forced against their consciences to attend 'upon forms which they disown? Is it allowable to recognize a kind of hypocrisy?' Briefly stated Newman's argument was that 'One cannot conduct a religious body on two different principles.' (*LD* IV, 208–12) It must be recalled that Oxford was not run on the secularist principles of the modern university. It was a religious institution of education; its university and college officials were in orders; its students came mostly from Anglican homes. Newman became involved in the agitation in Oxford, though he did not engage in the pamphlet warfare that ensued.

On 21 April he wrote to John Bowden, 'We have had a splendid meeting to-day of Professors, Deans and Tutors this morning – and have subscribed a manifesto by way of "protest" against certain prospective aggressions of the Legislature. I trust that in a day or two we shall bring out a document signed by *all* or nearly all the Tutors in the place, and most of the Professors.' (*LD* IV, 237) He also sent two letters to the *Standard* newspaper explaining Oxford's position, 'to admit dissenters among us would be in fact to repeal our entire *corpus statutorum*' which he explained in detail. Newman was both encouraged and 'quite astounded' by the support of Edward Burton, Regius Professor of Divinity and patristic scholar and William Sewell, Fellow of Exeter, both of whom put out pamphlets in opposition to the admission of Dissenters. Sewell's 'exposition of right principle', Newman wrote to Froude, 'has quite astounded me.' He would have to be accepted as 'a fellow labourer.' (*LD* IV, 268–9)

The result of these efforts was that the ministry withdrew a number of bills they were proposing for Church reform, but Newman was fearful that 'in the Vacation they will meditate evil and take their ground,' whereas the Oxonians 'are in danger of getting *callous* to the notion of Dissenters' coming here etc. – so that for what we know a bill might be passed next year with little opposition. At present men are *sore*; therefore, having established a raw, our game is to keep it from healing.' He came to the conclusion that, as far as he and Froude were concerned, 'other persons can do the day's work as well or better than we can; our business being only to give them a shove now and then'. He therefore set about to work during the interval on collating manuscripts of Dionysius for an edition. (*LD* IV, 268–79) He wrote to Benjamin Harrison in Paris to collate for him some manuscripts involving Dionysius. Because Kaye, Bishop of Lincoln, criticized the historical account of the *disciplina arcani* in the *Arians*, which was published the previous November, he was contemplating publishing a series of dissertations in a second volume, 'on the *disciplina arcani* – ' 'on the primitive Church's notion of the external world etc.' (*LD* IV, 268–79) On 1 August the House of Lords rejected the bill to admit Dissenters to the university, but this was not the end of the battle.

On 1 July Newman received a request at 7:30 in the morning that two people be married at 9 o'clock. He knew the father of the bride, Mr Jubber, and had tried to persuade him to have the daughter baptized which he had refused. As there was no time to consult the bishop, Newman expressed as kindly as he could that he could not marry his daughter since she was not baptized. In a distorted form this got into the papers and caused a row. He composed a letter to the bishop which he first sent to Keble and Pusey, both of whom approved but suggested alterations. This encouraged Newman, who wrote to his mother that he felt one man against the many, and 'no one apparently to encourage me; and so many black or averted faces, that, unless from my youth up I had been schooled to fall back upon myself, I should have been quite out of heart.' He added a delightful detail, 'I went and sat twenty minutes with Mrs Small [[the old dame school mistress at Littlemore]] by way of consolation'. (*LD* IV, 288–96) Newman would not have felt at ease with his conscience if he had done the marriage, and in retrospect, he told Henry Wilberforce, 'I trust it will do something towards establishing the following two principles – that baptism is of importance, and that the Church is above Law.' (*LD* IV, 312) Nevertheless, he resolved in the future not to refuse without consulting the bishop who would undoubtedly say, 'marry', as there was no legal right to refuse.

As a result of his opposition to the admission of Dissenters to the university and his refusal to marry Miss Jubber, Newman was regarded as an intolerant bigot by the liberals.

PASTORAL CONCERNS

Newman never forgot amid all this activity that he was first and foremost a pastor of souls. He continued to visit the sick, baptize and marry his parishioners both at St Mary's and at Littlemore. He was anxious to begin a weekly celebration of the Eucharist at St Mary's, but because of difficulties thought it better to start with Saints' Days. In April he initiated an evening service on Wednesdays followed by a 'lecture (ex tempore) on the Creed. . . . Next year I may take some lives of the saints, e.g. Hooker, Ridley, Bull, etc. – and in time no one can tell what will come of it.' What did become of it was his lectures which formed the bases of *The Prophetical Office of the Church* and the *Lectures on Justification*.

On 30 June Newman began a daily service in St Mary's, the timing partially owing to the fact that Oriel chapel was closed during the Long Vacation and Hawkins refused Newman's request that it be kept open. (*LD* IV, 287–9) This was part of his programme to restore practices of the Book of Common Prayer which had fallen into disuse. On 2 November 1834 in a sermon on 'The Daily Services' he explained his reasons:

> I have now said enough to let you into the reasons why I lately began Daily Service in this Church. I felt that we were very unlike the early Christians, if we went on without it; and that it was my business to give you an opportunity of observing it, else I was keeping a privilege from you.

If asked why he did so at this time, he replied that the state of public affairs was so threatening, that he could not bear to wait any longer. He determined to offer to God the Daily Service by himself,

> in order that all might have the opportunity of coming before Him who would come; to offer it, not waiting for a congregation, but independently of all men, as our Church sanctions; to set the example, and to save you the need of waiting for one another; and at least to give myself, with the early Christians, and St Peter on the house-top,

the benefit, if not of social, at least of private prayer, as becomes the Christian priesthood. (*PPS* III, 21, 310–12)

Newman was particularly attached to his parishioners in Littlemore and he engaged the help of his mother and sisters in the work of the parish. His brother Frank lectured him on worldliness in keeping them in a life-style that was not necessary, especially in providing them with a manservant. John was irritated and wrote him,

They are the instruments of temporal good to 200 people at Littlemore – they teach the children, set an example to the Parents. . . .
   True, they might give up housekeeping, and live in lodgings as somewhat cheaper, but then where would be the kitchen for Littlemore, with broth and messes? where the rice and tapioca from a housekeeper's closet? in a word, they enable me to spend a large sum upon the poor which I could not spend satisfactorily myself. [[How can I manage a parish without women?]] they take all my trouble upon themselves. What could I do better with the money? Give it to some Religious Society, to be spent by strangers in whom I had not reason to feel confidence? I suppose my money goes further, than yours in journeying to Persia. (*LD* IV, 329–30)

On 20 September 1834 Newman stopped at Alton *en route* to visit friends in the south and was overwhelmed with conflicting emotions which he described in detail to his mother in a letter. He felt 'it was as fearful as if I was standing on the grave of someone I knew, and saw him gradually recover life and rise again'. He remembered especially the first evening of his return from Oxford in 1818, after gaining the scholarship at Trinity and his father saying, 'What a happy meeting this!'

Often and often such sayings of his come into my mind, and almost overpower me; for I consider he did so much for me at a painful sacrifice to himself – and was so generous and kind; so that whatever I am enabled to do for you and my sisters I feel to be merely and entirely a debt on my part, a debt which he calls me to fulfil. (*LD* IV, 331–2)

Mrs Newman answered, 'Your recollection of your dear Father's "greeting" cheers me greatly. I have always a nervous dread lest you all can recall him only in pain and sorrow. . . . I often reflect with heartfelt delight and gratitude on the prospect of your labours being valuable to

future generations. But you must not spend yourself too much.' (*LD* IV,
331–2)

At this time Newman was concerned about the serious illness of
Bowden's sister and its effect upon his mother who had already lost a
daughter. They were constantly in his prayers and upon reception of the
news of her death in December, he wrote:

> Thank you for your account, which is very consoling: and that not
> merely for the time. Such seasons remain and expand upon the
> memory, and are afterwards quite fragrant, a foretaste of what shall be.
> It has been my privilege to think of your now happy sister, morning
> and evening, up to this day. What a blessed thing it is to have died, if
> prepared. Who knows what is in store for him in that last cup? (*LD*
> IV, 336, 351, 379)

THE *VIA MEDIA*

John Bowden, whom Newman called the 'Apostolicorum principes,'
warned in a letter of 14 July that Newman and the Oxford Tracts 'will be
one day charged with rank Popery', and suggested that a Tract be put out
refuting the charge. (*LD* IV, 304) Newman promptly took the hint and
produced two Tracts: *Via Media I & II*. In them he described the view
of the apostolicals or Tractarians as that of the Church itself, a middle
way between Romanism and popular Protestantism. In them he made
several important distinctions: a) that 'our Articles are not *a body of
divinity*, but in great measure only protests against certain errors of a
certain period of the Church. . . . There are many other doctrines [besides
the inspiration of Scripture] unmentioned in the Articles, only because
they were not then disputed by either party. . . . The Liturgy, as coming
down from the Apostles, is the depository of their complete teaching;
while the Articles are polemical, and except as they embody the creeds,
are mainly protests against certain definite errors.' Nevertheless the
Articles would remain the sticking point all during the Movement. (*VM*
II, 32–3)

In the second Tract Newman explained that the Reformation was one
in 'matters of *faith*', namely against the Popish doctrine of purgatory and
pardons, and the adding to the number of sacraments. He describes
Protestantism as 'the religion of so-called freedom and independence, as
hating superstition, suspicious of forms, jealous of priestcraft, advocating

heart-worship; characteristics, which admit of a good or bad interpretation, but which, understood as they are instanced in the majority of
persons who are zealous for what is called Protestant doctrine, are (I
maintain) very inconsistent with the Liturgy of our Church'. (*VV* II,
41–2) He contrasted the modern Protestant meaning of faith and that of
the Catechism, where 'the prominent notion is that of its object, the
believing "all the Articles of the Christian faith", whereas the prominent
notion conveyed by Protestants is to regard 'its properties, whether
spiritual or not, warm, heart-felt, vital'. He likewise quotes from the
Order for the Visitation, which the Protestant would omit as formal and
would add words about the atonement and original sin. (*VM* II, 43)

In this tract Newman also sets down the principle of development:

as time goes on, fresh and fresh articles of faith are necessary to secure
the Church's purity, according to the rise of successive heresies and
errors. These articles were all hidden, as it were, in the Church's
bosom from the first, and brought out into form according to the
occasion. Such was the Nicene explanation against Arius; the English
articles against Popery; and such are those now called for in this Age
of schism, to meet the new heresy, which denies the holy Catholic
Church – the heresy of Hoadley, and others like him. (*VV* II, 40)

'Corruptions are pouring in, which, sooner or later, will need a SECOND
REFORMATION.' (*VM* II, 48)

Bowden was not alone in wanting to forestall the charge of Popery
against the Tracts; Benjamin Harrison in Paris suggested that Newman
accept the invitation of the Abbé Jager to discuss the Tracts in controversy, so that 'at least your Protestant friends will see that there is a slight
difference between us and Popery'. Newman accepted the challenge and
it forced him to read up 'the Romish question' in the Anglican divines
such as Laud, Stillingfleet, and others. (*LD* IV, 360) Newman thought
that the long reply of the Abbé to his letter was 'so weak that so far it is
no fun', a judgement with which Hurrell Froude did not entirely agree.
The Abbé could not find in Scripture or in antiquity Newman's distinction between fundamental and non-fundamental articles of faith, and he
pointed out a number of inconsistencies in Newman's views.[4]

On 1 August 1834 the House of Lords had rejected the bill to admit
Dissenters into the university, but in the middle of the month R. D.
Hampden published a pamphlet, *Observations on Religious Dissent*, which
called for the abolition of all religious tests. Renn Dickson Hampden was

a Fellow of Oriel, a Noetic, and a personal friend of Whately and of Arnold. He was also Principal of St Mary's Hall, which gave him a place on the Hebdomadal Board. A second edition, revised, 'with particular reference to the use of religious tests in the university', appeared in November, a copy of which he sent to Newman. The pamphlet reiterated the principle laid down in his Bampton Lectures of 1832, namely that creeds, theological statements, systems of doctrine could not be identified with Christianity itself, 'with the simple religion of Jesus Christ, as received into the heart and influencing conduct'. In his thank-you letter Newman expressed his opposition to the principles contained in the pamphlet, 'tending as they do in my opinion altogether to make shipwreck of Christian faith'. He also expressed his regrets that its publication was the first step, as indeed it proved to be, 'towards interrupting that peace and mutual good understanding which has prevailed so long in this place, and which if once seriously disturbed will be succeeded by dissensions the more intractable because justified in the minds of those who resist innovation by a feeling of imperative duty'. Newman annotated this letter with the remark, 'This letter was the beginning of hostilities in the University.' (*LD* IV, 371 and notes)

Apparently it was being said that Newman was cutting his friends because of divergence of views. At this time Newman received a letter from Whately in which he said it was openly reported when he had visited Oriel the previous spring 'you absented yourself from Chapel on purpose to avoid receiving the Communion along with me; and that you yourself declared this to be the case.' Although Whately was in Dublin, he kept in close contact with his friends in Oxford, liberals like himself. In reply Newman denied the charge, saying the reason for his absence from College Chapel on that Sunday was that he held the service at St Mary's and that he had not known until later after the service that Whately was at Oriel. While expressing gratitude to Whately for all he had done for him, he nevertheless took the occasion to express 'the mixed and very painful feelings, which the late history of the Irish Church has raised in me'. This was a reference to Whately's support of the Whig Government in its suppression of the Irish sees. He then proceeded in accord with 'the dictates of duty and gratitude' to register his persuasion 'that the perilous measures in which your Grace has acquiesced are the legitimate offspring of those principles . . . which bear upon the fundamentals of all argument and investigation and affect almost every doctrine and every maxim on which our faith or our conduct depend'. (*LD* IV, 348–49)

Whately replied quoting a letter of eight years previous and he asked why Newman had not frankly had it out with him, as he had always shown himself open to honest debate. Newman replied 'Tho' I never concealed my opinion from you, I have never been forward', out of reticence to remonstrate with one who had shown him so much kindness and to debate with an archbishop. It was a question of opportunity, but even when they were on close terms, he never concealed his differences of opinion which have become clearer with time, namely, his objection to those opinions called 'Liberal,' e.g., 'the under valuing of antiquity, and resting on one's own reasonings, judgments, definitions etc rather than authority and precedent'. The suppression of the Irish sees brought the danger of such opinions before his mind. (*LD*, 357–9)

Newman was often frank in expressing his differences with others. This was part and parcel of his sincerity and honesty and he found it hard to understand criticism of himself as being disingenuous, intriguing or Jesuitical. He also recognized that at times it got him into scrapes. Nevertheless he was able to work and cooperate with others who did not share his opinions, since they agreed in substance and their difference was not one of first principles. Such was his relation with Hugh James Rose. One recalls the memorable words with which he concluded one of his Oxford University sermons. 'Half the controversies in the world are verbal ones; and could they be brought to a plain issue, they would be brought to a prompt termination. Parties engaged in them would then perceive, either that in substance they agreed together, or that their difference was one of first principles. . . . When men understand what each other mean, they see, for the most part, that controversy is either superfluous or hopeless.' (*US*, 200–1)[5]

An account of Newman's daily routine at this time is given by John Dennis Haycroft who was a servant in Oriel College and became scout or personal servant to Newman for seven years before he retired to Littlemore. One of his duties was to deliver MSS and proofs of the *Tracts for the Times* to the printers.

Haycroft used to say that Dr. Newman was of a cheery disposition, but somewhat particular in having things done punctually at the minute ordered. In those days, according to Haycroft's account, Dr. Newman often rose as early as 4 a.m., but hot water was not required before 7 a.m.[6] At 8 a.m. he went to St Mary's, then breakfast, followed by visit to the common-room, then work again until luncheon, which his servant often prepared early and placed in the window-sill, ready for use when required, Dr. Newman then helping himself. The afternoon was generally devoted to walking. . . . Tea was often made by Dr. Newman himself in his room about 5 p.m. Dinner and common-room would occupy the early hours of the evening, after which there would be more writing. If papers and proofs were ready by 11 p.m. Haycroft would see to their despatch, but if it was much later before they were finished, Dr. Newman would go out again himself.[7]

Amid all his work and study it is interesting to know that Dr. Newman found time to set simple papers on religious subjects – chiefly Old Testament – for young Haycroft to work out, and they were afterwards corrected by Dr. Newman.

And so, in the words of George Denison, Fellow and tutor of Oriel, 'the Catholic Revival set forth, and moved slowly, but steadily upon its way'.[8]

CHAPTER ELEVEN

An Undivided Heart

In January 1835 Newman journeyed to London because of a recurrence of a symptom of his illness in Sicily. He stayed at Bowden's house and met Manning for the first time with whom shortly after he had a long talk. He also met Rose, Westmacott, Boone, Editor of the *British Critic*, Wood, Le Bas, Hale, Worsley, Major Muirs, Rose's brother-in-law, Cooper, Harrison, H. Thornton, Gladstone, Cripps, Rogers of Balliol, and he left his card at other houses. Samuel Woods, who was a former pupil, became an ardent supporter of the Tractarian Movement and a very close friend. According to Frederick Rogers, in a letter to Newman on 13 January, 'You seem, from Harrison's account, to have made a great impression on Lebas by the Oxford Tracts. The prevailing feeling which they raised in him was a feeling of the degeneracy of the present times.' (*LD* V, 6, n. 2) Newman reviewed his *Life of Archbishop Laud* in the *British Critic* XVIII (April 1836).

Newman was encouraged by evidence of the principles of the movement taking hold in various parts of the country. In writing to thank Rickards for his 'handsome contribution' towards expenses, he remarked;

I trust the stimulus we have been able to give to Churchmen has been like the application of volatile salts to a person fainting, pungent but restorative. High and true principle there is all through the Church, I fully believe, and this supported and consecrated by our great writers of the seventeenth century; but from long quiet we were going to sleep. Not a month passes without our hearing of something gratifying in one part of the kingdom or another. I am quite surprised when I think how things have worked together, and this is in minute ways which none knows but myself. If it be not presumptuous, I should say the hand of God was in it. . . . Nothing is so consoling as to see the indestructibility of good principles; again and again they spring up, and in the least expected quarters. Ken and his party were scarcely disappearing when

Butler was raised up to carry on the spiritual succession even from among the Dissenters. (*LD* V, 26–7)[1]

It is not surprising therefore that Newman began to look upon the Movement not so much as a reformation, as a restoration. In March 1835 he published a pamphlet, 'The Restoration of Suffragan Bishops', in which he proposed that since dioceses had grown too large especially in industrial areas, the number of bishops be increased so they could take better care of the faithful. The bishop, he asserted, is 'the guardian of soundness and unity of doctrine' and should live among his people. Newman appealed to the principle of personal influence in concluding 'the appointment of Suffragans being a visible display and concentration of ecclesiastical power, and the substitution of the definiteness and persuasiveness of personal agency for the blind movements of a system'. (*VV* II, 89) Newman had the satisfaction of having a number of notes expressing approval of the pamphlet, 'and from persons I scarcely expected to like it; among others, Hale, Spry, Archdeacon Goddard, Joshua Watson etc.' (*LD* V, 58)

Newman's criticism of Evangelical preaching and the presentation of his own position and practice by comparison with it are clearly set forth in a correspondence with Samuel Wilberforce and James Stephen, the Colonial Under-Secretary and prominent member of the Clapham set. The former took exception to the first volume of Newman's sermons as deliberately suppressing 'the doctrine of spiritual influences', and the latter dismissed them as 'harsh and repulsive'. Newman admitted that his sermons were concerned not with influencing or converting (which Evangelical sermons were concerned with) but with the means of sanctification, which he felt Evangelical sermons were deficient in. 'We want the claims of duty and the details of obedience set before us strongly.' On the other hand, there is 'nothing definite or tangible in the teaching of the peculiars – all sermons are the same'. Newman then gave an amusing parody of a typical Evangelical paraphrase of Scripture:

Let not a widow be taken into the number under three score years old, having been the wife of one man, well reported of good works (not done in her own strength, but through the grace of the Holy Spirit) if she have brought up children (as real spiritual sons of God, having the renewal of which baptism is the outward sign) if she have lodged strangers, if she have washed the saint's feet (not as if the outward work was any thing, unless there is a real change of heart within,) if she have relieved the afflicted, (not trusting to her own doings, however charitable and useful, but renouncing her own righteousness for the pure and perfect etc) if she have diligently followed every good work (which are the fruits of a spiritual faith, which accepts the proferred redemption etc.) (*LD* V, 22)

Moreover, he objected to the Evangelical reiteration of consecrated phrases, such as 'Christ's righteousness, or blood, or our spiritual renovation', without conveying to their hearers 'the depth of meaning and extent of truths which alone adequately answer to those phrases', nor showing the difficulty of sanctification. (*LD* V, 47)

Newman denied that he wished to separate himself from the Peculiars, for he looked 'most hopefully towards numbers of them. They are a very heterogeneous party, but contain some of the highest and noblest elements of the Christian character among them.' 'Against the *spirit* of their school certainly I have spoken strongly and . . . I believe that spirit tends to liberalism and Socinianism.' Moreover he does not believe that preaching is the means of converting. Sermons in themselves are very limited in their effect and should be supplemented by catechetics. Sermons are subordinate to the sacraments and the Liturgy. 'The Church with the sacraments etc. and the life of good men seem to me the great persuasives of the Gospel, as being visible witnesses and substitutes for Him who is Persuasion itself.' (*LD* V, 32) Unfortunately 'Popery is the terror spread around our covenanted possession', which scares us 'from enjoying it to the full'. In conclusion Newman expressed his persuasion that 'the only way to arrest fanaticism, check profaneness, and take away the persuasiveness and influence of Popery, is to recur to this primitive Catholicism on which happily our Services are based'. (*LD* V, 47)

In March the Earl of Radnor reopened in Parliament the question of the admission of Dissenters into the universities, and a pamphlet war ensued. Oxford rallied and calling up clerical MA's from outside voted down by a vote of 459 to 57 in Convocation the proposal of substituting a declaration for subscription to the Thirty-nine articles at the time of matriculation. The proposed declaration read, 'I A. B. declare that I do, so far as my knowledge extends, assent to the Doctrines of the United Church of England and Ireland as set forth in her Thirty-nine Articles; that I will conform to her Liturgy and Discipline; and that I am ready and willing to be instructed in her Articles of Religion, as required by the Statutes of this University.' Froude arrived from Barbados in time to join in the enthusiasm. Anne Mozley, who saw him alight from the carriage and being greeted by his friends, described him as 'terribly thin – his countenance dark and wasted, but with a brilliancy of expression and grace of outline which justified all that his friends had said of him. He was in the Theatre the next day, entering into all the enthusiasm of the scenes, and shouting *Non placet* with all his friends about him. While he lived at all he must *live* his life.' (*Moz.* II, 106, n. 1) On 4 June Froude left Oxford never to return.

Neither Froude nor Newman were enthusiastic about the Thirty-nine Articles. Froude wrote to Newman, on 17 November 1833, 'I could be content to throw overboard the Articles keeping the Creeds', (*LD* IV, 112) and on 8 April 1834 he confided 'I have got over my scruple about the Articles – from considering the preface to them in which it is said that we are to understand them in their grammatical sense, which I interpret into a permission to think nothing of the opinion of their framers.' (*LD* IV, 254) Froude appealed to the writings of antiquity to interpret the Thirty-nine Articles, for he writes to Newman that the Franciscan (Froude called him a Jesuit) Francis Santa Clara Davenport showed them to be 'patient if not ambitious of a Catholic meaning' and apparently Laud did not think the interpretation over-strained. (4 March 1835, *LD* V, 68) This view anticipated that of Newman in *Tract 90*.[2]

Newman for his part thought the Articles 'accidentally countenance a vile Protestantism', and their framing was 'a great mistake'. Why then did he oppose dropping them? Newman felt that the abolition of the tests was the first step along the road to liberalism in Oxford and therefore had to be resisted. 'The advantage of subscription (to my mind) is its witnessing to the principle that religion is to be approached with a submission of the understanding. . . . the great lesson of the Gospel is faith, an obeying prior to reason, and proving its reasonableness by making experiment of it – a casting of the heart and mind into the system, and investigating the truth by practice.' (*LD* V, 196)

When Hampden learned that Newman was the editor of one of the pamphlets and major author with Henry Wilberforce of one: 'The Foundation of the Faith assailed in Oxford' (Newman having authorized the publisher to give his name upon enquiry), he fired a letter to Newman in which he claimed the latter was 'guilty' of 'dissimulation', 'falsehood, and dark malignity', the latter quality arising from a 'fanatical persecuting spirit'. As Newman reported to Bowden, 'he affirms that I should have been afraid so to have acted except under shelter of my "sacred profession" which means, as Froude says, that he, to *prove himself a Christian*, would have fought a duel with me, but for my being in orders. This is ingenious.' (*LD* V, 83–4, 93) Newman answered the charge of 'dissimulation', Hampden obtained the name from the publisher without difficulty. As to concealing his name in the background, he quoted his letter to Hampden in November upon reception of his pamphlet. Newman went on to answer the other charges but made the point that he recognizes 'as conceivable the existence of motives for approving or disapproving the conduct of another, distinct from those of a personal nature'. Unlike the behaviour of many of his adversaries Newman adhered to the principle of not attacking the person or imputing motives to another in controversy but to disagree with his opinions. Newman, even in his private letters, observed this rule, though he could not resist a humorous comment upon the behaviour of another, but this was rare, as with Eden when he was finally made a tutor:

> Eden is at last made Tutor – having sighed and panted for it as much as any lover for a smile from the fair object. At length he whispered to me the blissful intelligence that the Provost had signified a wish to talk on College matters with him in a few days. Meanwhile the Provost's affections lay in a different direction, or at least not on him, for he [[the Provost]] mistook a civil cardleaving of Mozley's, for a softening of purpose – and promptly paid him a second visit – but in vain. So all went right – and two days since E. [[Eden]] communicated to me the fact, or rather 'begged to introduce me to the New Tutor of Oriel', [[meaning himself.]] as if it had been 'Mrs Eden'. He has been talking on the subject incessantly ever since – before Norris [[NB. the Common Room man]] etc – nay I doubt not he has told every parishioner whose house he has entered since the event. (*LD* V, 190)

Lord Radnor's bill was thrown out in July 1835, and subscription to the Thirty-nine Articles at matriculation remained in force at Oxford until 1854. The fight against liberalism however was far from being over.

In January 1836 while in London Newman heard that Pusey, Keble, Hampden and himself were names put forward for the Professorship of Divinity at Oxford. In February, however, it was announced that Hampden was appointed. Newman who had no desire for the position was nevertheless appalled by the appointment, and sat up all night composing 'Elucidations of Dr. Hampden's Theological Statements', and left a copy at his door. Hampden asked Newman to retract the statement that he does not hold the truths of the Trinity and the Incarnation as '*revealed*': 'It is one thing to speak of truths themselves and another to speak of *modes of statement* or the *phraseology* in which the truths are expressed.' In a polite reply Newman said he had no doubt that Hampden believed the Trinity and the Incarnation, but he had spoken of him only as an author, '*and as such*, you seem to lie open to my remark, for since you state in your pamphlet that an Unitarian holds "the *whole* revelation" *as holding* "the basis of divine facts" you surely do deny that "the truths of the Trinity and Incarnation" are "revealed".' (*LD* V, 235–6)

A committee at Corpus Christi College adopted a report drawn up by Pusey which denounced 'the philosophy of Rationalism', and accompanied it with a declaration, 10 March, which deplored that the office of the King's Professor of Divinity in this university be entrusted to one, 'whose Publications abound with contradictions to the doctrinal truths which he is pledged to maintain, and with assertions of principles which necessarily tend to subvert not only the authority of the Church, but the whole fabric and reality of Christian truth'. The declaration abstained from 'imputing to the Author a personal disbelief of those doctrines which have been so seriously endangered by his Publications'. (*LD* V, 264–65) Thus, as Newman told Hampden, 'The first duty of all of us seems to be the defence of divine Truth', and the distinction Pusey and Newman made between Hampden's personal beliefs and his writing absolves them from the charge superficially made that they were acting 'uncharitably'.

In the midst of the row, an article, though not signed by Thomas Arnold, the famed Headmaster of Rugby, appeared in the *Edinburgh Review*, called 'The Oxford Malignants'. It was both a defence of Hampden and an attack on the Movement, affirming that the 'assault on Hampden was the outcome of "moral wickedness" and of "mingled fraud, and baseness, and cruelty, of fanatical persecution".' For such persecution 'the plea of conscience is not admissible; it can only be a conscience so blinded by wilful neglect of the highest truth, or so corrupted by the habitual indulgence of evil passions, that it rather aggravates than excuses the guilt of those whom it misleads'. Thus Arnold took his revenge by letting out his personal feelings against Newman for his remarks in Rome about him.

When Arnold heard that Newman in Rome had said, 'But is Arnold a Christian?' he wrote through Grant who had been present when the remark was made that Newman should write or print 'that in his view I do not understand what Christianity is. . . . But let him not use language which from its necessary ambiguity had all the ill effects of falsehood, not without some portion of its guilt.' (*LD* IV, 108) Newman did not apologize, as the remark was made in private and neither he nor his hearers were impugning Arnold's personal faith, but criticizing the unorthodoxy of his opinions on the interpretation of Scripture. Arnold was not convinced and thought Newman a bigot who used words ambiguously. Arnold adopted the principle of 'free inquiry' into Scripture and was tolerant of different dogmatic beliefs, mainly because he emphasized the moral teaching of Scripture. Though Newman objected to Arnold's liberalism, nevertheless he had the highest respect for his moral teaching and for the moral influence he had on his pupils and disciples. He was as energetic as Newman in waging war against 'worldliness' which he called 'the circumambient poison'.

The Hebdomadal Board voted to lay a statute before Convocation to remove from Hampden 'the power of appointing Select Preachers and judging of heresy', but though 400 non-residents came up to Oxford to shout 'Placet', the motion was vetoed by the Proctors. The motion was taken by another Convocation in May which had new proctors. Thereafter both Newman and Pusey were to bear the brunt of attacks from the liberals.

Despite the attacks, Newman did not lose his sense of humour, as testified by the anecdote about a visiting American professor who was invited to dine at the height of the Hampden controversy which was never discussed at table because of differing views of the Fellows: 'The American, not understanding this, suddenly cried out: "Well, Mr. Newman, what about this Hampden controversy?" Newman with the promptness of action that matched the quickness of his brain, at once seized a spoon, and taking a potato from the dish, said: "A hot potato".'[3]

In the summer of 1835 Newman was engaged in editing the fragments of St. Dionysius, Bishop of Alexandria in the middle of the third century, which led to his reading widely in the Fathers. 'But I have far greater objects in view', he told his Aunt. We can expect a spread of scepticism. 'The most religiously-minded men are ready to give up important doctrinal truths because they do not *understand their value*. . . . Thus, e.g., Sabellianism has been spreading of late years, chiefly because people have said "What is the harm of Sabellianism?[4] It is a mere name," etc. . . . Well what is the consequence? We just now have a most serious and impressive warning if we choose to avail ourselves of it. Poor Blanco White has turned Socinian, and written a book glorying in it.' Newman then quoted from the preface to 'Observations on Heresy and Orthodoxy,' in which Blanco White writes 'I have for some time been a *Sabellian*, but the veil is now removed from my eyes, for I find *Sabellianism is but* Unitarianism in disguise.' Newman went on to deplore the ignorance of the clergy on the subject and the lack of theological education. 'In my present line of reading, then, I am doing what I can to remedy this defect in myself, and (if so be) in some others. And it is a very joyful thought which comes to me with a great force of confidence to believe that, in so doing, I am one out of the instrument to which our gracious Lord is employing with a purpose of good towards us [*sic*].' (*LD* V, 120–1) As a result, Pusey and he decided to start a Theological Society, which began on 12 November 1835 at Pusey's, he giving the first paper which was followed by a paper by Newman 'On the Rule of Faith' on 20 November. It was not long before Newman reported to Froude, 'The Heads of Houses are much annoyed at our Theological [Society] – and I have had cold looks even from Wynter, Burton, Jenkyns, and Bridges'. When Hampden was appointed Regius Professor of Divinity Newman wrote to Bowden, 'What a luck thing it is just set up! my final scope in devising it was to restrain the vagaries of H. and such as he – but I little thought it would be so soon needed.' (*LD* V, 191, 237)

FORGIVE AND FORGET

This summer of 1835 a misunderstanding between Newman and Henry Wilberforce was set aside and the two remained close friends until the latter's death in 1873 when Newman preached at his funeral. In the early days of January 1834, although Henry met Newman in Oxford, he was afraid to tell him he was getting married. He asked Harriett to do so, but she did not. The bride to be was Mary Sargent, sister of Sophia who was engaged to George Dudley Ryder and of Caroline, the wife of Henry Manning. As Henry was Newman's protégé, so Ryder was Froude's and Froude was particularly annoyed at Ryder's decision to marry because he had made public pretensions to embracing the high ideal of celibacy. Newman mentioned in a letter to Keble that Froude 'wished to break with R. which must not be, I think'. (*LD* IV, 20)

Ryder must have informed Newman of his engagement and Newman must have replied, for there is a letter of Ryder which states, 'Of course I had not known you and Froude as long as I have, without being generally acquainted with your opinions on the subject. You object to me that I am too young to marry . . . Then you object to me that my conduct has been vacillating and undecided . . . Then, you ask me to consider whether I am not sinking into a mere conservative etc. I trust not.' (*LD* IV, 57)

Newman continued to correspond with Ryder after his marriage and became godfather to one of his children. (*LD* VI, 5–6)

In a letter of 1 December 1833 Rogers told R. F. Wilson,

> Ryder's marriage has annoyed Newman a little and Froude very exceedingly – Froude says that Ryder has taken him into [*sic*] think him a better kind of fellow, than to marry, and that R himself when he broke the matter evidently felt that he owed F an apology, and accordingly has almost (Wilberforce says quite) cut him. Poor H. W. himself complains bitterly of the ill-treatment R. has met with from N and F. / and / purposes to be gradually weaning himself from Newman's friendship, because he knows (he says) that when he marries he will be cut out, in common with Ryder – and consequently – being determined on that step, wishes to prepare himself for the consequences. (*LD* IV, 127)

According to Newman's diaries Henry was in Oxford from 17 to 31 December. By his own admission Henry had seen Eden the day he left, and 'I told him I was going to get married, because he asked roundly about my plans . . . He said something as if he thought it a secret, and I immediately said, "No I don't care who knows it, as I go away tonight . . ., only I did not wish it to be known as long as I was at Oxford." If E. says I made a confidant of him, he says what is absolutely untrue. I fully believed you had heard all about it from your sister, before I had that conversation with him.' So Henry to Newman, 19 February 1835, a year later. (*LD* V, 30)

Hearing from John Frederic Christie that Henry had fixed a date for his marriage, Newman composed a letter to Henry, which prudently he did not send, as it is a tangle of emotions, and Newman had long since learned to keep a tight control over his feelings and the expression of his affections. Self-control was a fundamental principle of the spiritual life, which he later tried to teach Miss Holmes.

> My poor dear foolish Henry,
>
> Dear, for auld lang syne – foolish, for being suspicious of me – poor, because I suppose you have been pained at your own suspicions. Why have you left it first to a casual word of yours, next to a letter of Christie's to acquaint me that the time is fixed for your changing your state and commencing to be a citizen of the world that now is? Was

not this very gross 'pusillanimity' on your part? for I will not fancy
there was any more pugnacious feeling mixed in the procedure. Yet it
shows almost a want of kindness towards me. What have I done, (state
any grounds,) to justify it? I really believe that, when you search your
heart, you will not find that your unwillingness proceeds from any
thing I can have done or said, however easy it is by word of mouth to
make vehement and voluble speeches. When have I ever questioned
the propriety of your marrying, or dared to interfere with your
Christian liberty? As exceptio probat regulam, it may be as well to
remind you that the single thing I said was I thought you would do
better to wait awhile – not that I did more than state my opinion when
asked. But you surely are inconsiderate – you ask me to give my heart,
when you give yours to another – and because I will not promise to do
so, then you augur all sorts of illtreatment towards you from me. –
Now I do not like to speak of myself, but in selfdefence I must say, it
is a little hard for a friend to separate himself from familiarity with me
(which he has a perfect right, and perhaps lies under a duty to do,) and
then to say, 'Love me as closely, give me your familiar heart as you
did, though I have parted with mine.' Be quite sure that I shall be free
to love you, far more than you will me – but I cannot, as a prudent
man, so forget what is due to my own comfort and independence as
not to look to my own resources, make my own mind my wife, and
anticipate and provide against that loss of friends which the fashion of
the age makes inevitable. This is all I have done and said with respect
to you – I have done it towards all my friends, as expecting they will
part from me, except to one, who is at Barbadoes. I dare not even
towards my sisters indulge affection without restraint. Now is it not
hard, when I a poor individual see what the chance is of my being left
alone, and prepare for it, that then I should be said to be the breaker
of friendships? it is the story of the lamb and the wolf; unless indeed
you think I do not feel at times much the despondency of solitariness
– (if I had had no experience of it this last year,) and why may I not
arm myself against what is inevitable? why must I give my heart to
those who will not (naturally, it would be a bad bargain for them,) take
charge of it? God grant all this discipline will make me give my heart
more to Him – but it is hard to be accused of inflicting it on others.

You are ever in my prayers, and will not cease to be – and I trust
you will never forget your present principles, nor the sentiment of
Keble's in which you seemed fully to acquiesce, that 'celibacy and

marriage were accidents, and did not alter by one jot or tittle a true Christian's mode of acting.'

My dear H. – you really have hurt me – You have *made* a *difficulty* in the very beginning of our separation. You should have reflected that to remove it, you would not only have to justify it to yourself but to explain it to me.

Ever Yrs affectionately John H Newman

P. S. At first I intended not to write, lest I should say what would seem unkind. But that itself seemed unkind – so I changed my mind. This is not the first letter I have written; I plucked it. Now, if you write and explain, please do not expect another letter from me at once – (*LD* IV, 169–70)

Newman understood quite clearly that the meaning of celibacy was giving one's total affection to Christ and Him alone 'with an undivided heart'. This did not mean it could be done without the mediation and love of other human beings. In fact he preached that the best way to learn to love all men was to begin with one's relatives and friends and then extend that love to others. The mediation which is excluded by virginity entails exclusively the type of mediation which is lived in conjugal love and which is marked by the unitive relations between two persons who mutually give themselves to one another in bonds of love. Such a union is sacrificed and the benefits of lifelong companionship are renounced 'for the sake of the Kingdom'.

In Newman's case this sacrifice took two forms, one was the exclusion of sympathy that only a wife could supply, the need for which he periodically experienced. This in turn entailed a certain amount of loneliness. Coping with this loneliness was part of his growth in holiness, a purification of selfish desires for sympathy, so that he could devote himself more fully and completely to the work of the Church. He would lose Froude, the only other person so close to him not only in fraternal affection but in sharing an ideal of total dedication to Christ by means of celibacy and to the needs of the Church at a time when it seemed in grave crisis and peril. With the death of his mother and the marriage of his sisters in 1836 he had no home but Oriel, but he came to recognize that his loneliness was intended by God to free him for greater service.

Anne Mozley pointed out that Newman expected great things from his young friends. 'The "heroic" was a sort of natural element with him – his

presence inspired a sense of greatness of companionship with him.' (*Moz.*
II, 225–6) Perhaps this explains his disappointment when some of them
did not reach the level of his ideals.

Newman did not believe the rumours about Henry's intended marriage
and told everyone not to believe them, an action which must have made
him look pretty foolish. He writes to Christie, 'Your news about H.W. is
most extremely probable – in every way, except one; that, tho' he has
been staying here with me till just now, he said not a word about it –
which is so unnatural that I cannot believe it is true – and so shall tell
every one. . . . And if there is a report (as there is) that he told other
people, I am still more incredulous – for *that* report must be false, and so
throws discredit on yours.' He said the same to Rogers, telling him not to
believe 'a silly report that is in circulation', and that 'he was spreading his
incredulity'. (*LD* IV, 175) Meanwhile Rogers had a reply from Henry
about his enquiry. 'I have no wish to deny the report in question. Indeed,
though I did not tell Neander / Newman / (as who would?), yet I did
tell his sister and gave her leave to tell him . . . Whether Neander will cut
me I don't know. . . . It is, I am sure, very *foolish* of Newman on mere
principles of calculation if he gives up all his friends on their marriage;
for how can he expect men (however well inclined) to do much in our
cause without co-operation? I suppose, however, he will cut me. I cannot
help it.' (*LD* IV, 176)

Contrary to Henry's expectations Newman did not cut him. On 16
January he received in Derby, where he was staying, a letter from Henry
which he answered at great length the following day. (*LD* IV, 177) Rogers
wrote on 20 January to Newman in reply to his. 'I must say, you do not
show your judgment. How can you possibly suppose, that after your way
of treating perditum illum H.W. you would be his first confidant? The
fact obviously is, that he came to Oxford with the intention of breaking
the matter to you; but, when he came near, and saw how fierce you
looked, his heart failed him, and he retreated *unsuccessful.* And now at this
moment he is hesitating about the best way of breaking it, and hoping
that some one else will save him the pain etc. etc.' He went on to quote
another reliable source, so he could not join Newman in his disbelief. (*LD*
IV, 176)

On 10 February Newman wrote to Henry, 'I shall be truly glad to see
you at the Installation [of the Duke of Wellington as Chancellor], and will
keep a bed room in College for you. I suppose you would not get a garret
even, under 10 guineas in the Town. If the worst comes to the worst, you
can have my library, or bath room.' (*LD* IV, 191) In a letter of 6 April he

offered Henry the curacy of Littlemore with the opportunity of the pulpit of St Mary's, as Isaac Williams was planning to resign because of ill health. In the event Williams did not resign, and Newman wrote saying he was sorry 'if I have unsettled you even for an hour . . . All I can say is, that my very writing . . . at least shows the desire I had still to be near you, as heretofore.' (*LD* IV, 233, 236)

Henry for his part was still fearful of losing Newman's friendship, as is evident from a paragraph in a letter of 27 May 1834 which he wrote in response to one of Newman's, dealing with the danger of his sister-in-law Mrs William Wilberforce's becoming a Catholic.

> I have loved you like a brother; and my saddest feelings have been often in thinking that, when in the events of life I am separated far from you, you will perhaps disapprove or misunderstand my conduct, and will cease to feel towards me, as you have done . . . and therefore every such mark of continued kind feeling warms my heart. . . . though I fear lest the breach of friendship should be on your side, I am afraid of the cause, which may produce it, only from my own. I am full of fear lest *I* should [be untrue to myself] one day; and also I have, I will confess, some dread, lest you should think me to have done so, even when it is not the case. Only, if you do, pray let me know openly what you do feel, and let me speak for myself. (*LD* IV, 258)

Henry came for the installation of the Duke on 10 June and stayed at Rose Hill. (*LD* IV, 266–7)

In a letter to Newman on 1 August Henry mentioned his marriage, but Newman did not allude to it in any of his letters, and the number of them fell off. This put ideas in Henry's head that Newman was either cutting him or was displeased with something he had done. As Rogers acted as a go-between and the correspondence between them is not extant, it is difficult to sort out entirely. Henry, feeling out of touch as he was living in a small village, wrote on 9 January asking for news. Newman was in London and did not return to Oxford until 27 January, and he seems not to have answered the letter. Henry wrote to Newman for his birthday in February 1835,

> I think, hardly a day . . . since I saw you, in which I have not thought with grateful affection of your kindness to me, and the benefits which I hope I have received from it.
>
> Now this is really after all the best answer I can make to the charges

which Roger's letter some time ago contained; for surely I could not intentionally do any thing to hurt your feelings. Now I really cannot bear again to enter into a long explanation of the circumstances. I tried to do so viva voce at Oxford, and you would not hear me; but now Rogers writes me word, after 14 months, that you wish me to explain my conduct. 1. in having said 'in Christ Church' that you had behaved ill to Ryder for being married and for intending it.

Henry denied he ever said Newman was unkind to Ryder, though he thought and still thought such was the case. As to making Eden a confidant, he gave the explanation already mentioned. (*LD* V, 30)

Newman hastily composed a reply which he did not send. In the meanwhile Rogers received a letter from Henry which he showed to Newman and prompted him to draft two more letters which he likewise did not send. All cover the same points, namely that he harbours no unChristian feelings toward Henry. He had only asked through Rogers that if it was in Henry's power to 'set right misunderstandings about me which you have given rise to, But, if you say you cannot, I am content. . . . . Except asking you this kindness; I do not know what I have done to make you think I am acting unchristianly. . . . Perhaps, however it was my not writing to you, which has made you think I had wrong feelings about you.' This he was the more sorry for, because he has no time for any but business letters, and even Froude has complained bitterly of his silence. He assured Henry 'that for all your imagination may do to make you think me estranged from you, I shall ever be found (please God) in all trying times, as before, Your affectionate friend . . . .' (*LD* V, 33–5)

It is too bad Newman did not send it, but perhaps he felt that, since Henry could not rectify the injury, it was best to let the matter drop and go on as usual with his business letters to him. Perhaps, too, he felt, as he later said, that explanations feed further misunderstandings, and so the matter rested, until 8 June, when Newman addressed not 'My dear Henry', as usual, but 'My dear H.W.'

June 8, 1835

I am surprised and hurt at the inconsiderateness which has led you, in spite of the unkindness I experienced last year from you and my Sister, to make me the channel of messages to her and her to me, as if to force upon me the recollection of what I fain would forget. I think this indelicate, to say the least, and accordingly I have not read her letter. Had I been you or she, I should (I think) at once have been frank and wiped out the offence by owning and regretting it. As it is, it remains for me to beg, that I may be suffered to have nothing to do with your intimacy [[with her?]] this I do, both to show to you my feeling about the matter, and to relieve for myself feelings, which, if pent up within me, may do me harm. So, for three years from the date of the offence, I shall bind myself to a definite line of conduct as regards you, which I the less mind doing because, for what I know, it may inconvenience myself. . . . etc etc.

Henry's unsuspecting action apparently touched a nerve. In a memorandum of 27 August 1860 Newman wrote, 'If I am asked, on looking back, what the origin of this misunderstanding with H.W. was, I say it was the feeling etc. of my poor sister H., now dead, about it. She triumphed in her heart over me, that H.W. married, *as I knew she did*.' (*LD* IV, 170) Henry did not answer this for several weeks (his wife was coming near to term), but when he did, the reply was pretty frank and he delivered a lecture to Newman on Christian behaviour. First, he never knew or suspected hitherto that Newman complained of his conduct in connection with his sister nor of hers. He observed that this was one out of several instances 'of the practical evil which springs from your habit of refusing either to state what the conduct you complain of is – or to hear any explanation of it. . . . But when I tried to explain what I had done and why, you refused to hear a word and as it now appears I was altogether ignorant of a large part of your ground of complaint and thus from mere ignorance as to what your feelings were was led again to wound them.'

As to the second subject, the resolution (whose nature was not clearly stated) to be observed for three years, this did not seem to Henry compatible with our Blessed Lord's teaching but was transferring Newman's stern and rigid demeanour towards those who oppose good principles 'to those who have behaved with *personal unkindness to yourself*' and he should be aware of this dangerous tendency observable by others beside Henry himself. He trusted from what Newman said that his feelings of affection towards him still obtained and he could still call himself Newman's friend. For his part there was no disposition to draw back. 'Your friendship is for many causes most valuable to me and endeared by so many ties that the thought of losing it is insupportable.

None beyond my nearest relations are so much loved by me as you are.'
Henry then announced the birth of a son, and asked for Newman's
prayers. (*LD* V, 107–8)

In his reply, which he later said was more gently worded than the
extant draft, he said that Henry's advice was as applicable to the present
case as Newman's direction would be on the topic of making steam vessels
or railroads. Nevertheless, 'owing to my Sister's distress. I said I should
tell you that I should entirely forego the protest I had intended – (indeed
if I can but once get you both to understand how much I have felt your
unkindness, not yours the most, I have my end – but the worst has been
I could get neither of you to understand I was in earnest,) not however
withdrawing one jot (of course) my expressed sense of it, but wishing to
be released from the necessity of thinking or hearing of the subject any
more. . . . The true Christian way is to forgive and forget, not to prove
yourself right. . . . As you must know, whenever we have been together
since that time [Christmas 1834], especially in June 1834 my manner
towards you has been what it was before – and my feelings have been the
same. You have not allowed me to rest, but in one way or other (if I must
say it) forced upon me your lightness of feeling on the subject – and then
gone on to accuse me with bearing it in mind, in neglecting to write to
you etc. which was a fancy. . . . We have made mutual accusations – do
let us forget them.' (*LD* V, 108–9)

Henry replied that the letter 'gave me so much sorrow that it brought
tears into my eyes at seeing that I had given you pain. To speak plainly I
am sure that I do not quite understand you as neither I am certain do you
me and added to this you have heard reports of sayings attributed to me
which I unhesitatingly repeat are false. But not withstanding all this your
letter was so kind and affectionate that it almost overpowered me. Never
could your past kindness fade from my recollection. . . .' (*LD* V, 109–10)

It might be appropriate to quote here what Newman wrote on 25
March 1840 when he was finishing his account of his illness in Sicily:

The thought keeps pressing on me, while I write this, what am I
writing it for? For myself, I may look at it once or twice in my whole
life, and what sympathy is there in *my* looking at it? Whom have I,
whom can I have, who would take interest in it? I was going to say, I
only have found one who even took that sort of affectionate interest in
me to be pleased with such details – and that is H. Wilberforce and
what shall I ever see of him? This is the sort of interest which a wife
takes and none but she – it is a woman's interest – and that interest, so

be it, shall never be taken in me. Never, so be it, will I be other than God has found me. All my habits for years, my tendencies, are towards celibacy. I could not take that interest in this world which marriage requires. I am too disgusted with this world – And, above all, call it what one will, I have a repugnance to a clergyman's marrying. I do not say it is not lawful – I cannot deny the right – but, whether a prejudice or not, it shocks me. And therefore I willingly give up the possession of that sympathy, which I feel is not, cannot be, granted to me. Yet, not the less do I feel the need of it. (*AW*, 137–8)

CHAPTER TWELVE

A Lost Comrade

Newman was happy to have Froude back in England from his long stay in Barbados, for he had missed him very much. Writing to him in January 1835 from London, Newman remarked, 'I could say much, were it of use, of my own solitariness, now you are away. Not that I would under value that great blessing, which is what I do not deserve, of so many friends about me . . . yet after all, as is obvious, no one can enter into one's mind except a person who has lived with one – and I seem to write things to no purpose as wanting your imprimatur. This happens in ten thousand ways.' Probably Newman was thinking of Froude when in a sermon he explained the meaning of 'watching'.

> Do you know what it is to have a friend in a distant country, to expect news of him, and to wonder from day to day what he is now doing, and whether he is well? Do you know what it is so to live upon a person who is present with you, that your eyes follow his, that you read his soul, that you see all its changes in his countenance, that you anticipate his wishes, that you smile in his smile, and are sad in his sadness, and are downcast when he is vexed, and rejoice in his successes? To watch for Christ is a feeling such as these; as far as feelings of this world are fit to shadow out those of another. (*PPS* IV, 22, 323)

Close friendship did not mean agreement on all ideas. Froude was far less anti-Roman than Newman and disapproved of the harsh language he used against the Church of Rome. In a letter of 28 December 1834, Froude wrote, 'When I get your letter I expect a rowing for my Roman Catholic sentiments. Really I hate the Reformation and the Reformers more and more . . . I have a theory about the beast and the woman / in Revelation / too, which conflicts with yours.' (*LD* V, 12, incorrectly dated) When this letter was printed in Froude's *Remains* it caused an enormous stir. In a letter of 30 January 1835 Froude also objected to

Tract 27, a reprint of Bishop Cosin's tract on Transubstantiation: 'Surely no member of the Church of England is in danger of overrating the miracle of the Eucharist. Besides the tract is in some places quite rationalist.'[1] Froude then quoted Pascal which implied Transubstantiation. Newman commented on this remark. 'Froude would not believe that I was in earnest, *as I was*, in shrinking from the views he boldly followed out. I *was* against transubstantiation.' Froude continued, 'I shall never call the holy Eucharist "the Lord's supper", nor God's Priests "ministers of the word", or the altar "the Lord's table" – etc, etc, innocent as such phrases are in them-selves, they have been dirtied – a fact you seem oblivious of on many occasions. Nor shall I ever abuse the Roman Catholics as a church for anything except excommunicating us. If they would give up this I think they are indefinitely the purest Church of the two. So much for fault finding.' (*LD* V, 18–19) Froude made two suggestions, one for a series of the 'Apostolic Divines in the Church of England', a suggestion Newman took up in the Catena Patrum; and secondly, taking up 'the Jansenist saints – Francis de Sales, the Nuns of Port Royal – Pascal etc. . . . Must it not be owned that the Church of England Saints, however good in essentials, are with a few rare exceptions deficient in the austere beauty of the Catholic *ethos*? / Keble / will be severe on me for this.' Newman does not seem to have read Post-reformation Roman Catholic saints, except the controver-sialists, until much later.

In other ways as well, Froude seems to have anticipated Newman in his thinking, though it is not easy to tell whether Newman took the views from him. For example, James Mozley remarked in 1832, 'The aristocracy of the country at present are the chief objects of his [Froude's] vitupera-tion . . . and thinks that the Church will eventually depend for its support, as it always did in its most influential times, on the very poorest classes.' It was at the end of 1833 that Newman proposed this in his sketch of St Ambrose. Also Froude writes, 'I think of putting the view forward [about new monasteries], under the title of a Project for Reviving Religion in Great Towns, certainly colleges of unmarried priests (who might of course retire to a Living, if they could or liked) would be the cheapest possible way of providing effectively for the Spiritual wants of a large population.' (*LD* IV, 38) In 'Home Thoughts from Abroad,' Newman writes, 'Great towns will never be evangelized merely by the parochial system . . . They are beyond the sphere of the parish priest, burdened as he is with the endearments and anxieties of a family, and the secular restraints and engagements of the Establishment. The unstable multitude cannot be influenced and ruled except . . . by the sight of disinterested and self-denying love and elevated firmness. . . . I think that Religious Institutions, over and above their intrinsic recommendation, are the legitimate instruments of working upon a populace . . .' (Title changed to 'How to Accomplish it', *DA*, 42)

Newman, however, was anxious to discuss with Froude his proposed reply to Abbé Jager. Froude took the Abbé's side in criticizing Newman's distinction between fundamentals and non-fundamentals. Though they dialogued by letter, Newman wrote Froude, 'I must, so be it, come down to you before Vacation ends, to get some light struck out by collision.' Newman spent 15 September to 11 October 1835 at Dartington.

As a result of his discussions with Froude, Newman dropped the distinction between fundamentals and non-fundamentals and substituted a less rigid and more flexible distinction between episcopal and prophetical tradition. By the episcopal tradition he meant the transmission of the doctrines of the creeds through apostolical succession, received and handed on, that is, from bishop to bishop. The prophetic tradition on the other hand was the presentation of these doctrines through preachers, theologians, catechists, and teachers. Though based on Scripture and tradition it proceeded to systematize, interpret and to apply them to a given time. As a result it could become obsolete or even corrupt. 'Whereas the other form was like the hard, bony structure of the body, the second is like the flesh that clothes it. The former guarantees what is static and gives firmness and certainty; the latter guarantees what is dynamic and assures growth. The former is essentially unchanging and unadulterated, the latter is exposed to corruption.'[2] This distinction Newman used in opposition to Hampden's view of tradition in an article entitled 'The Brothers' Controversy – apostolical tradition' in the *British Magazine* for July 1836 and of course more importantly in the *Prophetical Office of the Church*.[3]

While visiting Froude Newman read to him the sermons he had selected for a third volume of *Parochial Sermons*. He also composed three sermons and a work on Romanism, presumably what became *Tract 71*, 'On the Controversy with the Romanists.' While at Dartington he wrote to Bowden saying that since Rivington did not want the Tracts any more, he proposed to put out only a few the following year on Romanism, which would be a series like the 'Records of the Church'. 'First we shall have inquirers turning Papists, if we do not draw lines between ourselves and Popery. Next it will do us good, if we show we do differ from the Papists. Thirdly it is availing ourselves of a popular cry – this is what first got us on two years since (viz., when there was a cry against dissent) and we shall miss our opportunity if we do not do the like now as regards Popery. Fourthly it will be anticipating other parties by giving our own views of Romanism – and fifthly it is a very effectual though unsuspicious way of dealing a back-handed blow at ultra-protestantism.' (*LD* V, 150)

Perhaps the most important work Newman composed during his three and a half week stay at Dartington was *Tract 73*, 'On the introduction of rationalistic principles into religion', 56pp. (*Ess*, I, 30–99) As examples of this tendency Newman chose two works, Jacob Abbott's *The Corner-stone; or a familiar illustration of the principles of Christian Truth*, London 1834, and Thomas Erskine's *Remarks on the Internal Evidence for the Truth of Revealed Religion*, 6th ed., Edinburgh, 1823. The reason for his choices, as he later revealed, was 'my deep and increasing apprehension, that the religious philosophy, on which they are based, was making its way into Oxford, and through Oxford among the clergy, and by the writings of Dr. Whately, Dr. Hampden's Bampton Lectures and Mr Blanco White's (then) recent publications.' (*Ess*. I, 101) In Abbott's emphasis on Christ's humanity, and in seeing him primarily as a moral exemplar Newman detected a tendency that was 'antidogmatic, substituting for faith in mysteries the acceptance of a "manifestation" of divine attributes which was level to the reason'. (*LD* XXX, 168–9) Specifically he blamed Erskine for treating the Atonement, as a manifestation to our reason of God's justice instead of reverencing it as a mystery. (*Ess* I, 30–48) He later explained this in detail in a letter to Henry Wilberforce on 11 August 1836. 'Erskine seems to think the Atonement a *manifestation to our reason* of God's *justice*. I reply – no – not to our *reason* – if it is revealed to all that God's justice is satisfied in the Death of Christ – this is addressed to our *faith* – it is a *mystery*.' (*LD* V, 336–7)

What is of lasting value in the Tract, however, is its analysis of what is and what is not rationalism in religion.

> Rationalism is a certain abuse of Reason; that is, a use of it for purposes for which it never was intended, and is unfitted. To rationalize in matters of Revelation is to make our reason the standard and measure of the doctrines revealed; to stipulate that those doctrines should be such as to carry with them their own justification; to reject them, if they come in collision with our existing opinions or habits of thought, or are with difficulty harmonized with our existing stock of knowledge. And thus a rationalistic spirit is the antagonist of Faith; for Faith is, in its very nature, the acceptance of what our reason cannot reach, simply and absolutely upon testimony. (*Ess*. I, 31)

Not all reasoning with regard to revealed religion is rationalistic. For example,

> it is not Rationalism to set about to ascertain, by the exercise of reason, what things are obtainable by reason, and what are not . . . nor to determine what proofs are necessary for the acceptance of a Revelation, if it be given . . . nor, after recognizing it as divine, to investigate the meaning of its declarations, and to interpret its language; nor to use its doctrines, as far as they can be fairly used, in inquiring into its divinity; nor to compare and connect them with our previous knowledge, with a view of making them parts of a whole; nor to bring them into dependence on each other, to trace their mutual relations, and to pursue them to their legitimate issues.

The rationalist, however, makes himself his own centre, not his Maker. Truth, consequently, is not something objective; and religion is something subjective. 'by objective truth' is meant 'the Religious system considered as existing in itself, external to this or that particular mind', to believe in it 'is to throw ourselves forward upon that which we have but partially mastered or made subjective'. Objective religion contains mysteries, because 'no revelation can be complete and systematic, from the weakness of the human intellect; *so far as* is not such, it is mysterious'.

The rationalist rejects mystery on the basis that 'I cannot believe anything which I do not understand'. (*Ess.* I, 40) In the *Grammar of Assent* Newman later showed how it is possible to give an assent to what one does not fully understand. 'Revelation is religious doctrine viewed on its illuminated side; a Mystery is the selfsame doctrine viewed on the side unilluminated.'

On his return to Oxford Newman wrote Froude that Keble had married on 10 October, the day before he left Froude, 'and told no one; he only informed Oriel he was resigning his fellowship'. Keble was 43 and he took the living in Hursley. Isaac Williams in his *Autobiography* stated that Newman always felt annoyance at Keble's marriage.[4] Newman told Froude that he was getting Rogers, Mozley or Williams to visit him at Christmas, 'but if no one comes, I will come myself, which would be too great a pleasure'. (*LD* V, 154) Froude replied, 'Don't let them go back from their intentions. . . . your own offer of coming down again is a piece of benevolence I hardly know how to thank you for. If you could do it without waste of time, you might certainly do good here, which is a sop to my conscience in indulging the wish.' In the event Rogers came. As in previous letters Froude wrote, 'Before I finish I must enter another protest against your cursing and swearing at the end of the first via media as you do – What good can it do? and I call it uncharitable to an excess. How mistaken we may ourselves be on many points that are only gradually opening on us. Surely one should reserve 'blasphemous' 'impious' etc for denial of the Articles of Faith –' (*LD* V, 156) Newman withdrew the passage several years before he published his retractations of anti catholic statements (*VM* II, 431–2) Newman justified himself by saying that he was following the Divines of the English Church.

Newman was distressed to learn that for two years his brother Frank denied the personality of the Holy Spirit and the duty of praying to Christ. He wrote to Frank in November to warn him that his views would lead him to unbelief. 'That wretched nay (I may say) cursed Protestant principle, (not a principle in which our Church has any share, but the low arrogant cruel ultra-Protestant principle) – your last letter showed me you had so far imbibed as to be in great peril. . . . On what ground of reason or Scripture do you say that every one may gain the true doctrines of the gospel for himself from the Bible?. . . . Till you give it up, till you see that the unanimous witness of the whole Church . . . is as much the voice of God . . . as Scripture itself, there is no hope for a clearheaded man like you.' (*LD* V, 167) He added that, much as he would not meet Frank 'in a familiar way or sit at table' with him, he would receive him if he came to see him or wished to write. 'My *ground* of my separating from Frank,' he later said, 'was that he was *originating* schism, when he returned from Persia – that he was a *teacher* of a *new* sect. This he gave over about 1838 – and then I at once changed my mind and went to see him.' (*LD* V, 315, n. 1)

The battlelines were being drawn, as Newman realized when he went to London in January 1836, where he met many persons and 'formed some not improfitable [*sic*] alliances', for example, with Joshua Watson who had a stake in the *British Critic*, and William Dodsworth, minister at Margaret Street Chapel, who had a proposal to organize a series of Spring Lectures from Oxford, Cambridge and the Country Divines. To Thomas Mozley, Newman wrote, 'the Peculiars [Evangelicals] are mustering and marshalling tremendous force. . . . what think you their having offered to collect for the Bishop of London £150,000 for building Churches in London, if they may themselves present to them? – Our persecution is on the eve of beginning. The first stroke will have fallen, if Hampden or such "forerunner of Antichrist" (for it does not now do to mince matters) be placed in the Divinity Chair.' To Pusey who was depressed at the prospects of things, he wrote it is better to see things as they are. 'The mass of those called High Church have had no principles. . . . they go by expedience. . . . Is it not very clear that the English Church subsists *in the State*, and has no internal consistency (in matter of fact, I do not say in theory) to keep it together? is bound into one by the impositions of articles and the inducements of State protection, not by *ethos* and a common faith?' Newman then indicated the direction in which at least his efforts from now on should go, 'Let us preach and teach, and develop our views into system, and in all likelihood we may be instruments in the preservation of the Church.' (*LD* V, 210, 213–15)

On 28 January 1836 the third volume of *Parochial Sermons* appeared. Newman had told Henry Wilberforce that Boone had put in the *British Critic* 'an extremely kind article on the 2 volumes . . . and I wish to make hay while the sun is fair. Persons do not get notions [[men do not gain ideas]], only words, from one or two volumes – as Froude says, there is nothing like *rubbing in* one's views – so this new volume will have nothing very new in it, only repetition, enforcement, application, etc.' (*LD* V, 149) This would be especially true of such sermons as, 'Faith and Obedience', 'The Contest between Truth and Falsehood in the Church', 'The Church Visible and Invisible', 'The Gift of the Spirit', 'Regenerating Baptism', 'Infant Baptism', 'The Daily Service', 'Religious Worship a Remedy for Excitements'. Newman was happy to receive the favourable remarks of Samuel Rickards about it, 'as I intended it to be milder and more affectionate than the others, i.e. I selected my severe ones for the first and my gentler ones for this. Else I should have been taken for an Evangelical (so called) by the Evangelicals, or rather 'a promising < an interesting > man', whom they had not to learn from, but could look down upon benignantly. I know their way: they *would* not have understand [*sic*] that my *system* (i.e. the Catholic) was not theirs, and was one and consistent with itself – but would have dropped what they did not like, and have incorporated the mangled fragments they chose to admit in their own hodge-podge.' (*LD* V, 247) In the first edition of the 3rd Volume Newman inserted an Advertisement which read:

As to the resemblance of the author's opinions to Romanism, – if Popery be a perversion or corruption of the Truth, as we believe, it must, by the very force of the terms, be like that Truth which it counterfeits; and therefore the fact of a resemblance, as far as it exists, is no proof of any essential approximation in his opinions to Popery. Rather, it would be a serious argument against their primitive character, if to superficial observers they bore no likeness to it. Ultra-Protestant-ism could never have been corrupted into Popery.

The reviewer in the *British Critic* quoted this and proceeded to point out certain sermons in which some persons would discover 'a fearful resemblance to Romanism', e.g. 'Faith and Obedience'. He discussed several other sermons which he praised: sermon 8, 'Contracted Views in Religion', and sermon 12, 'The Humiliation of the Eternal Son', in which Newman comments on the prevalent theology of recent centuries which has 'well nigh ceased to regard Christ, after the pattern of the Nicene Creed as God', and that 'the religious world little thinks whither its opinions are leading; and will not discover that it is adoring a mere abstract name or a vague creation of the mind for the Ever-living Son, till the defection of its members from the faith startle it, and teach it that the so-called religion of the heart, without orthodoxy of doctrine, is but the warmth of a corpse, real for a time, but sure to fail, ' – an obvious reference to the Evangelicals'. After commenting on several other ser-mons, the reviewer concluded, 'We have sufficiently shown that, in our judgment, the charge of a propensity to Romanism, with which Mr. Newman has been assailed, is nothing more or less than the result of a chimerical and panic terror.'

The review was published in April 1836 and illustrates the defensive position of the Tractarians, but Newman realized that something more positive and systematic was needed and this he attempted to provide in his *Lectures on the Prophetical Office of the Church*.

Newman's concern for the spiritual welfare of the Church can be overlooked in concentrating on the ecclesiological debate. Thus the second instalment of 'Home Thoughts Abroad' is used, as Newman himself did in the *Apologia*, to illustrate how he viewed the controversy between Rome and the Anglican Church. The controversy, he affirmed, turned on antiquity versus catholicity. The Roman Church criticized the Anglican as lacking the note of catholicity, i.e., universality, since it is cut off from the Universal Church, while the Anglican accuses the Roman of having corrupted the doctrine of antiquity by adding to the original faith. (*Apo.*, 110–11) But there is much more in the article. Newman criticized the present state of the Church for the worldliness of its clergy and its failure to provide for the spiritual needs of its members. Illustrative of this is the fact that when a person in a family takes a religious turn, the natural impulse is to join the Wesleyans or the Dissenters. 'The more religious minds demand some stricter religion than that of the generality of men; if you do not gratify this desire religiously and soberly, they will gratify it themselves at the expense of unity.' Among the recommendations he made for the purification and development of the spiritual life of the Church were preaching about and the administration of the sacraments and ordinances, observation of fast days and daily services, religious education of women and the creation of religious orders. (*DA*, 37–41)

> On his birthday, 21 February 1836, always a day of self-examination and spiritual reflection, Newman wrote Jemima:
>
> Thanks too, and thank also my Mother and Harriett for their congratulations upon this day. They will be deserved, if God gives me the grace to fulfil the purposes for which He has led me on hitherto in a wonderful way. I think I am conscious to myself that, whatever are my faults, I wish to live and die to His glory – to surrender wholly to Him as His instrument to whatever work and at whatever personal sacrifice – though I cannot duly realize my own words when I say so.
>
> He is teaching me, it would seem, to depend on Him only – for . . . I am soon to lose dear Froude – which, looking forward to the next 25 years of my life, and its probable occupations, is the greatest loss I could have. (*LD* V, 240–1)

It was on this day or the following Sunday that he preached the sermon, 'Ventures of Faith', the only Anglican sermon to have been published separately because he was requested to do so. In the sermon he pointed out the sacrifices that the apostles made for the faith, and stated 'We know what it is to have a stake in any venture of this world. We venture our property in plans which promise a return. . . . What have we ventured for Christ?' Richard Church, an undergraduate, heard this sermon and determined on the ministry. Two years later he was elected Fellow of Oriel and became one of the increasing number of Newman's young loyal and devoted disciples. Newman in these years at times mentioned that he did not see the outcome of his efforts nor the end of the Movement. He seems to have been referring to himself in one place in the sermon when he remarked, 'the circumstances of the times cause men at certain seasons to take this path or that, for religion's sake. They know not whither they are being carried; they see not the end of their course; they know no more than this, that it is right to do what they are now doing; and they hear a whisper within them which assures them . . . that whatever their present conduct involves in time to come, they shall, through God's grace, be equal to it.' (*PPS* IV, sermon 20)

Froude died on 28 February 1836. Though not a total surprise, it was a strong blow. Tom Mozley in a letter to his sister Maria tells how Newman received the news. 'He opened the letter in my room, and could only put it into my hand, with no remark. He afterwards, Henry Wilberforce told me, lamented with tears (not a common thing for him) that he could not see Froude just to tell him how much he felt that he had owed to him in the clearing and strengthening of his views.' (*Moz.* II, 172) Writing to his close boyhood friend, Bowden, he said

I can never have a greater loss, looking on for the whole of my life – for he was to me, and he was likely to be ever, in the same degree of continual familiarity which I enjoyed with yourself in our Undergraduate days; so much so that I was from time to time confusing him with you and only calling him by his right name and recollecting what belonged to him, and what to you, by an act of memory. . . . I never on the whole fell in with so gifted a person – in variety and perfection of gifts I think he far exceeded even Keble.

His reaction was similar to what he experienced at the death of his sister Mary. 'Yet every thing was so bright and beautiful about him, that to think of him must always be a comfort. The sad feeling I have is, that one cannot retain on one's memory, all one wishes to keep there and that as year passes after year, the image of him will be fainter and fainter.' (*LD* V, 249)

Newman was disturbed that people did not consider his pain as that which 'belongs to the loss of relatives'. The loss was the same as that of his sister Mary, for he mentions to Harriett the grace he is now receiving – the same which he experienced at Mary's death. 'I am learning more than hitherto to live in the presence of the dead – this is a gain which strange faces cannot take away.' (*LD* V, 311–13) The following year he inscribed a large number of prayers composed in Latin, one of which is for his sister Mary and his 'brother in the Lord' Richard Froude (see Appendix of Prayers). Thereafter they were associated in his mind, in his prayers and with the graces given to him. It seems to these latter he is referring in the sermon 'Divine calls,' when he suggests

Perhaps it may be the loss of some dear friend or relative through which the call comes to us; which shows us the vanity of things below, and prompts us to make God our sole stay. We through grace do so in a way we never did before; and in the course of years, when we look back on our life, we find that sad event has brought us into a new state of faith and judgment, and that we are as though other men from what we were. We thought, before it took place, that we were serving God, and so we were in a measure; but we find that, whatever our present infirmities may be, and however far we be still from the highest state of illumination, then at least we were serving the world under the show and the belief of serving God. (*PPS* VIII, 1, 28)

With the death of Froude and other events which came on top of it, Newman indeed entered into a higher state of union with God.

Given the nature of their relationship it is understandable that Froude's loss carried with it a special poignancy, for, as he wrote to Samuel Rickards, 'no one is there else in the whole world but he whom I could look forward to as a contabernalis for my whole life'. (*LD* V, 247) In the manner of Elisha he told Keble, 'I do earnestly trust it will be granted to me, who have most claim on it, so to say, to receive his mantle – most claim, as having most need – and you, as his teacher, neither requiring it, nor naturally being heir to it – but I would fain be his heir.' (*LD* V, 253)

In some ways Newman and Froude were alike. Dean Church remarked that loose reasoners 'unexpectedly found themselves led on blindfold, with the utmost gravity, into traps and absurdities by the wiles of his mischievous dialectic'. Newman writes in the *Apologia* about his own behaviour 'I was not unwilling to draw an opponent on step by step, by virtue of his own opinions, to the brink of some intellectual absurdity, and to leave him to get back as he could. . . . I used irony in conversation, when matter-of-fact-men would not see what I meant.' (*Apo.*, 45) Thomas Mozley noting it in Froude's writing commented, 'Unpleasant as irony may sometimes be, there need not go with it, and in this instance there did not go with it the smallest real asperity of temper.'[5] The irony stemmed from a distaste, in Newman's case, and in that of Froude, an implacable hatred of sham and pretences. Dean Church also commented on another similarity between them. 'In Froude he found a man who . . . as quick-sighted, as courageous, and as alive to great thoughts and new hopes as himself. Very different in many ways, they were in this alike, that the commonplace notions of religion and the Church were utterly unsatisfactory to them, and that each had the capacity for affectionate and whole-hearted friendship.' Both had powerful intellects and the capacity for rigorous thinking. They were like comrades in arms, 'each mind caught fire from the other, till the high enthusiasm of the one was quenched in an early death.'[6]

Newman was not exaggerating when in the *Apologia* he described Froude as 'a man of the highest gifts, – so truly many-sided. . . . a man of high genius, brimful and overflowing with ideas and views, in him original. . . . an intellect as critical and logical as it was speculative and bold'. Though his purpose in the *Apologia* was to speak of his religious and theological opinions he could not resist paying tribute to Froude's 'gentleness and tenderness of nature, the playfulness, the free elastic force and graceful versatility of mind, and the patient winning considerateness in discussion, which endeared him to those to whom he opened his heart'. (*Apo.*, 23–24) Newman particularly admired him for having 'a severe idea of the intrinsic excellence of Virginity; and he considered the Blessed Virgin its great Pattern. He delighted in thinking of the Saints; he had a vivid appreciation of the idea of sanctity; its possibility and its heights. . . . He embraced the principle of penance and mortification. He had a deep devotion to the Real Presence, in which he had a firm faith . . . .' Froude had introduced Newman to a religious ethos which was hitherto unknown to him.

In commenting upon Froude's influence on Newman commentators have relied on the *Apologia*, but there Newman is recording only the effect on his theological opinions which he acknowledged as follows: 'He taught me to look with admiration towards the Church of Rome, and in the same degree to dislike the Reformation. He fixed deep in me the idea of devotion to the Blessed Virgin, and he led me gradually to believe in the Real Presence.' In his letters, however, he acknowledged much more. To Bowden he wrote, 'I cannot describe what I owe to him as regards the intellectual principles [i.e. philosophy] of religion and morals.' (*LD* V, 249) Shortly before he had written to Froude, 'since I am conscious I have got all my best things from Keble and you, I feel ever something of an awkward guilt when I am lauded for my discoveries. . . . You and Keble are the philosophers and I the rhetorician.' (*LD* V, 224–5)

Newman was not alone in speaking of the beauty and attractiveness of Froude's personality. Frederick Oakeley, who was a college contemporary and enjoyed constant contact and familiar acquaintance with him, commented that despite Froude's invective against the aristocracy, he himself was a perfect gentleman.

To a form of singular elegance, and a countenance of that peculiar and highest kind of beauty which flows from purity of heart and mind, he added manners the most refined and engaging. That air of sunny cheerfulness which is best expressed by the French word *riant* never forsook him at the time when I knew him best, and diffused itself, as is its wont, over every circle in which he moved. I have seen him in spheres so different as the common-rooms of Oxford and the after-dinner company of the high aristocratic society of the West of England; and I well remember how he mingled even with the last in a way so easy yet so dignified as at once to conciliate its sympathies and direct its tone. . . . Popular among his companions from his skill in all athletic exercises, as well as for his humility, forbearance, and indominable good temper, he had the rare gift of changing the course of dangerous conversation without uncouth abruptness or unbecoming dictation.[7]

Beneath the surface, however, was a streak of melancholy, which may account for his low spirits in Barbados, 'the blue devils' which depressed him and were perhaps owing to his struggle with tuberculosis; a struggle that ended only with his untimely death.[8]

CHAPTER THIRTEEN

The Emerging Leader

March 1836 marks the beginning of a new stage in Newman's personal life both spiritual and social as well as in the direction of the movement. In a memorandum Newman noted 'March 1836 is a cardinal point of time. It gathers about it, more or less closely, the following events' which he described as 'a new scene gradually opened'. (*LD* V, 246–7)

1. Froude's death
2. My mother's death and my Sister's marriage
3. My knowing and using the Breviary
4. First connexion with the *British Critic*
5. The Tracts become treatises
6. Start of the Library of the Fathers
7. Theological Society
8. My writing against the Church of Rome
9. Littlemore Chapel

Upon Froude's death his father asked Newman to accept some book from Hurrell's library as a memento. He chose Butler's *Analogy*, but it was already promised to someone else. Rogers suggested that Newman take Froude's Breviary. He did so and began to recite it daily and to spend three or four hours in prayer. Despite his many occupations at this time when the Hampden controversy was at its height, Newman managed to compose Tract 75, 148 pages, 'On the Roman Breviary as embodying the substance of the devotional services of the Church Catholic' which was published on 24 June. A second edition was expanded to 207 pages.

In it he affirmed that the recitation of the Breviary was an excellent form of private devotion and would impress persons with a truer sense of the excellence of the psalms. He also thought it would be a way of reappropriating to the Anglican Church a Catholic practice which had fallen by default to the Roman Catholics. In accordance with Anglican principles he criticized invocation to Mary and the saints and all offices and antiphons in honour of our Lady. The excessive number of hagio-graphical lessons, the failure to include the whole compass of the Bible in the Scripture readings for a year, and the interruptions of the scripture readings by many saints days were also objected to. Though Newman's account of the development of the Breviary was based on reputable authorities, one modern liturgist has affirmed that some of his statements would have to be qualified in light of more recent scholarship, e.g., 'the origin of Terce, Sext and None are now ascribed not to the supposed times of Jewish prayer but to the Roman divisions of the day.[1]

Newman's mother wrote him a letter on 12 April, the anniversary of his becoming a Fellow of Oriel, which was probably her last letter to him. It contained a prophecy: 'I know you must feel your position one of great responsibility, as many influential members of future times will most likely have their characters and religious opinions formed and confirmed by you. Happy am I to think that you know yourself insufficient to such important duties and that you seek guidance and aid where alone it can be given perfect and sure.' But she was disturbed by the suspicions cast upon his views as 'favouring Catholicism'. (*LD* V, 276)

In April, amid the Hampden controversy, Jemima was married to John Mozley, who was chosen to succeed his father in the family printing business. Jemima moved to Derby and Anne stayed to keep Harriett company. Within three weeks Mrs. Newman collapsed and died on 17 May. John and Harriett were with her. J. B. Mozley wrote in one of his letters, that 'up to the time of the funeral Newman was dreadfully dejected, his whole countenance perfectly clouded with grief, and only at intervals breaking out into any thing like cheerful conversation'. (*Moz.* II, 195)

Anne Mozley relates how at the funeral service Newman kept kneeling at the altar when all was over, lost in prayer and memory, till at length Mr Isaac Williams, who had officiated, touched his shoulder to recall him to the necessity of joining the mourning train in the return to the desolate home. She also quotes from one of her letters that 'when we came back from the funeral the sun was in the house again; of course it did not bring back the change; but as if Mr. Newman thought that grief had reigned long enough, he seemed by a sort of resolute effort to throw it from him, and resume his usual manner'. He remained as a member of the family party for a few days, and joined in the long walks which were taken to Shotover and Bagley Wood where the scenery reminded him of Sicily and he spoke of his illness there. (*Moz.* II, 196)

Jemima's marriage and his mother's death relieved him of the task of caring for their welfare. A year earlier, when in debt, he prayed 'that God would either give me the means of doing what I wished towards you all,' he wrote to Jemima, 'or remove the necessity'. It now seemed 'just as if I had been praying for the death of her, whom I have always looked forward to as living for many years'. (*LD* V, 322) Concerning his relations with his mother, which he felt slightly strained of late, he told Jemima he was distressed that the pressure of work hindered his being more often with his mother lately, but also by the difference in their religious views. She thought she differed from him and that he was surrounded by admirers and had his own way, whereas 'I, who am conscious to myself I never thought any thing more precious than her sympathy and praise, had none of it'. This made him realize that he had taken a false step in wishing her to be at Oxford. Though he never regretted the step for the good she did in Littlemore and for Jemima's happy marriage, still he suffered by it.

> I know in my own heart how much I ever loved her, and I know too how much she loved me. – and often, when I had no means of showing it, I was quite overpowered from the feeling of her kindness. I have some sort of dread and distress, which I cannot describe, of being the object of attention. . . . I recollect about two years ago, after I had fainted away, my Mother most kindly stooping down to take up my feet and put them on the sofa. I started up – I could not endure it. I saw she was hurt, yet I did not know how to put things right. I felt it something quite shocking that any one, above all she, should so minister to me. Nay, when I seemed rude, it often rose from feelings very different from what appeared. (*LD* V, 314)

This is another instance of Newman's sensitivity to the feelings of others.

Reflecting on this many years later he described the tension that was created by their close proximity. When they lived in Brighton, he went to see them for weeks together, removed at distance from his work in Oxford, but when they came to the place of his occupation the distance seemed one of mind:

> And, when they, in their kindness, tried . . . to overcome what to them was an invisible obstacle, then I got worried . . . by their affectionateness.
>
> Moreover . . . they did not like some of my greatest friends. And

again, from the first they did not like the distinctive principles of the Oxford Movement; and, the more it developed, the wider did their difference from me in respect to it grow.

And then again, there was the different position in which they stood from mine, and the different judgment they formed, as regards each of my brothers.

These differences, though they tried to hide them and make the best of them made me very sore. (*LD* V, 313–5)

When Harriett moved to Derby, she and Jemima were concerned about John's being lonely, but he wrote to Harriett, 'Thank God, my spirits have not sunk, nor will they, I trust. I have been full of work, and that keeps me generally free from any dejection. . . . I am speaking of dejection from solitude; I never feel so near heaven as then. . . . It is a better thing to be pursuing what seems God's call, than to be looking after one's own comfort.' (*LD* V, 311–12) To Jemima he wrote more precisely, 'I am not more lonely than I have been a long while. God intends me to be lonely. He has so framed my mind that I am in a great measure beyond the sympathies of other people, and thrown me upon Himself. . . . God, I trust, will support me in following whither He leads.' (*LD* V, 313)

A FRIENDLY DIALOGUE WITH HUGH JAMES ROSE

In 1836 the Movement entered into a new phase. Pusey's work on baptism, a lengthy treatise, became part of the Tracts. The latter in turn were no longer short works of more or less ten pages designed to stir up, but became treatises. Not only did the Evangelicals step up their attacks on the Tractarians as introducing Popery into the Church, but High Church and Establishment clergy became suspicious of the direction in which the Movement was going, prompted by fears that it would lead to Romanism. A good indicator of this was Hugh James Rose, who gave expression to this fear in a cordial correspondence with Pusey and Newman at the end of April and during May. Rose acknowledging the lack of a substantive school of Divinity applauded the efforts of the Oxonians to proclaim the old truths, nevertheless the clergy need guidance in the study of antiquity, and should be taught through the writings of the great Lights of the Church, rather than to look for supplements and corrections of its defects.

Newman replied that the Anglican system is in matter of fact incomplete and that there are hiatuses which were never filled up and it did no good to try and conceal or ignore them. Rose in his reply felt that it was a duty to keep things as they were and he feared that by acknowledging that our system is imperfect we should be taking away the only *authority* which the mass of Churchmen have, and lead to perplexity in some, and rash theorizing in others. Newman replied that they were trying to meet the latter difficulty in *Tract 71*, pp. 34, 35, just published and had begun to meet it in the Catena Patrum No. 74. Newman adds that 'should we ultimately draw up a system of divinity from our Divines, surely we shall be free of the charge of unsettling'. As to *why* these additional things at all, this is a day of scrutiny and controversy and it is good to be open and frank. 'Really I do think the Revolution Protestantism is too cold, too tame, too Socinian-like to reach the affections of the people – we must invest the Church with its treasures, and make communion with it a privilege as well as a duty. . . . Again it strikes me, if we *are* reviving things, why not, while we are about it, raise them a peg or two higher, if the position gained be truer and securer?' (*LD* V, 291–2, 294–5) 'We think ourselves perfection and look down on the Romanists. Now *supposing* a man thinks that, greatly as the Romanists have sinned, we have sinned too, supposing he has suspicions that perchance judgments are upon the Anglican Church in consequence, he cannot allow himself to proclaim the existing system of things to be perfect.'

Rose in his reply became more explicit. 'The impression which they would produce on my mind, *if I did not know you*, . . . is nearly this. "The *hearts* and *affections* of these writers are not with us. Their *judgment*, arising from deep learning, thought and piety, is *against* Rome decidedly; they think that she has much which we want."' He also wondered what Newman wanted done now.

Newman replied with a distinction between the 'Church of England' and the 'Anglican Church'.

> You have spoken the truth, not that I would go and tell every one at Charing Cross. I do *not* love 'the Church of England – ' The Anglican Church, the old Church of 1200 or 1600 years, the Church of the builders of our Cathedrals, the Church again of Andrewes, Laud, Hammond, Ken, and Butler, (so far forth as they agree together, and are lights shining in a dark place) . . . I love indeed, and the later not a whit less fervently than the earlier . . . I do not like the Church of the Reformation. . . . In like manner I love our Church as a portion and a realizing of the Church Catholic among us – but this leads me to

mourn over our separation from the Latins and Greeks. . . . I cannot love the 'Church of England' commonly so designated – its very title is an offence . . . for it implies that it holds, not of the Church Catholic but of the State.

Surely it is a matter of fact, the 'Church of England' has never been one reality, except *as* an Establishment. Viewed *internally*, it is the battle field of two opposite principles; Socinianism and Catholicism – Socinianism fighting for the most part by Puritanism its unconscious ally. What is *meant* when I am asked whether I love the 'Church of England?' Even granting there *was* a deliverance at the Reformation, I cannot be more than thankful for it, I cannot rejoice and exult, when it is coupled with the introduction of doctrinal licentiousness, . . . Popish Liturgy, Calvinist Articles and Arminian Clergy; is it not this *in substance* the witness of every external impartial spectator? Is not the highest *praise* given to the Establishment, that it admits a variety of opinions? . . . As to the Articles, luckily they are none of them positively Calvinistic, luckily what is wanting in one is supplied in another – but taking separate articles there are grave omissions, which it is a mercy have been elsewhere set right. . . . They are a 'port' in distress . . . How can I love them for their own sake, or their framers!

Newman on the other hand deplored the giving up practically to the Church of Rome 'what we might have kept – so much that was high, elevating, and captivating. . . . My heart is *with* Rome, *but not as Rome*, but as, and so far, as she is the faithful retainer of what we have practically thrown away.' One such would be claiming the Breviary as ours, showing historically that the addresses to the Virgin are modern interpolations. A selection from the Breviary would show how much is in the book of Psalms, of which the bulk of people have no knowledge. Also prayers for the dead, could be recovered without the Roman corruptions like purgatory.

In answer to Rose's affirmation that it was necessary to try to love in order to love, he like Froude and Keble were 'bigotted' to the Church of England, e.g. Keble's *Christian Year* and my sermons which 'teem with the spirit of high Establishmentism'. They have had other principles which have occasioned a change since, but 'I cannot accuse myself of not beginning, as all ought to begin, with reverence and enthusiasm towards the system I found myself in'.

Newman concluded the letter with a judgement that the alterations in the Eucharistic Service were a *sin* in our forefathers, which he bears resignedly as one would 'the loss of a limb'. The omission of the prayers to the Holy Ghost and the commemoration of the dead are 'defects in doctrine', and speaking confidentially he revealed that he silently makes an offering and prays for the dead in Christ.

Rose in a friendly reply said, 'I think we now understand one another pretty well. – I would only say that some of the points of which you complain, seem to me either susceptible of easy remedy or hardly to require any.' As to an amended Breviary he saw no objection to one by Newman, Williams or Keble, but he did not think that the Church could do it, but thought there would be no objection if were set forth by authority for voluntary use of Christians. He concluded, 'Ever, my dear Newman, most truly, heartily, and with sincere regard and attachment, yours, H. J. Rose.[2]

Two recent events helped stimulate Newman to take up the question of Romanism. James Tyler wrote Newman an account of his attendance at a lecture of two hours by Wiseman on the real principles of 'Popery', which was well attended.

> The points he was labouring to prove from the Scriptures themselves from the earliest traditions, from the course of history, and the reason of the thing itself . . . was the necessity and existence of an infallible Church . . . that this infallible Church must be in Communion with the see of Rome. All this he said he would prove by evidence. . . . But the proof of proofs . . . he was enabled to give by a celebrated Protestant Divine. . . . Mr Newman who in a work on Arianism proved, that not by the Scriptures, but by oral instruction was it the practice of the Church to train the Catechumens for the mysteries of the Gospel. etc.

He then asked, 'When did the Church first swerve from the Faith?' There were two extreme answers, one said that it was from the Council of Nicaea; 'at the other extreme was the dictum of the same Protestant Divine, that it was not till the Council of Trent. This same Mr Newman proves all I want.' (*LD* V, 252) It is hard to believe that Newman did not have this lecture in mind, especially the remarks on infallibility, when he gave his lectures on Romanism in Adam de Brome chapel starting on 16 May. The other event was the anonymous publication by Dr Dickinson, a chaplain to Archbishop Whately, 'A pastoral epistle from his holiness the Pope to some members of the University of Oxford, faithfully translated from the original Latin,' whose object was to attack the Tracts as popish. (*LD* V, 270, n. 4)

There is an amusing account of the antics of William George Ward and his friend Stanley who as undergraduates attended Newman's lectures on Romanism in Adam de Brome chapel in St Mary's in May and June 1836. According to the Dean of Norwich in a letter to Ward's son, Wilfrid, they sat full in front of Newman's desk.

> Your good father was the most demonstrative of men – wholly incapable of suppressing any strong emotion which for the time got possession of him; and as these lectures awakened in him the strongest emotions both of admiration for their power, and (at that time) indignant repudiation of their conclusions, he put the preacher somewhat out of countenance by his steadfast gaze, his play of feature as some particular passage stirred him, his nudges of Stanley, and whispered 'asides' to him ('What would Arnold say to that.' etc. etc.) Your father's manner and gestures were so pronounced that no one in the congregation could help noticing them; and it was well known also that the criticisms, which the demonstrations gave expression to, were at that time unfriendly. Mr. Newman, however, proved equal to the occasion, and at the lecture immediately succeeding one at which Ward had been specially demonstrative, we found the benches of the congregation turned side-ways (as in college chapels) so that he and Stanley could not, without turning their heads askew, look the preacher in the face.[3]

At first Newman was not sure he wanted to take the time and trouble to revise the lectures for publication, but in the event he did.

In the spring of 1835 Newman had decided to build a church at Littlemore, and in May offered Golightly, his former pupil, the curacy. Golightly however was cautious and warned Newman that he might later not like the tone of his sermons and offered to show some to Newman. Newman did not accept the offer, which he later admitted 'was imprudent'. Golightly went ahead and bought himself a house in Oxford. During the year Golightly began to declaim against Newman's patronage of Clement of Alexandria, his incaution, his strange sayings so very unsatisfactory – such a pity as hurting Newman's influence, etc. So Newman told Froude (*LD* V, 185). Golightly preached a sermon in January so unlike Pusey's on the same day that people thought he was preaching against Pusey. Then he went around speaking against Pusey's view on post-baptismal sin. Pusey criticized two passages in Golightly's sermon on baptism and Golightly thought this was the reason for his chief offence in Newman's eyes. Newman wrote Golightly that 'having the fullest confidence in the soundness of your formal doctrine, I am no longer certain that you will consistently maintain it in your preaching. To speak openly, I do not see now, how I can take an *irrevocable* step about Littlemore – any step which puts that part of my Parish once and for ever beyond my own superintendance.' It was this sense of responsibility that guided Newman's hesitation. '. . . a charge has been committed to me – I cannot consistently make it over to another, without having the responsibility before God of what he does, if I do it with my eyes open'. (*LD* V, 297, and n. 1; 307) Golightly withdrew in June 1836 on the issue of lack of confidence, but as Newman later wrote, 'he never got over it. We were never friends again.' In fact, Golightly became his enemy.[4]

William Tuckwell, Oxford's well-known surgeon who lived in Iffley, remembers when the Littlemore church was going up and he 'met Newman almost daily striding along the Oxford Road, with large head, prominent nose, tortoise shell spectacles, emaciated but ruddy face, spare figure whose leanness was exaggerated by the close-fitting tail-coat then worn'.[5] When they began to dig they found 22 skeletons laid East and West. 'Dr Ingram of Trinity has now discovered that in all probability there was actually a Church on about the same spot on which we have built.' (*LD* V, 366–7)

The chapel was dedicated on 22 September, fourteen months after Mrs Newman had laid the first stone. The day was fine, and a group of friends from various places were present including Tom Mozley and his sister, Henry Wilberforce and his wife, Rogers, Robert Williams who came from Dorsetshire for the purpose, and Isaac Williams, Newman's curate. 'The Bishop read the Consecration portion of the service – the Archdeacon the Gospel – I the Epistle – Williams the morning prayers – I preached. The Chapel was as full as it could hold – we had two Baptisms afterwards.' There was a profusion of flowers in bunches all about the chapel. Newman gave the children buns. The bishop liked the sermon and asked later to read it. (*LD* V, 366)

The anniversary of the dedication was kept as a sacred memory by Newman and J. R. Bloxam. The latter had just come into residence as Fellow of Magdalen College and two days before the dedication walked to Littlemore, found the door of the chapel open, and went in. As he in 1886 reminded Newman, 'You were alone placing the stone cross over the Altar. Turning round, and seeing a stranger, you asked me, if I thought it threw a sufficient shadow.' Shortly afterwards Bloxam offered his services as a curate, but Newman told him Isaac Williams had already been chosen. Bloxam became curate in the following year.[6]

As Harriett moved up to Derby in June, Newman was now free to devote all his energies to the Movement. The letters reveal him as emerging gradually as its *de facto* leader. He was extremely busy, reading over Froude's papers which his father had given him, getting Keble to publish some of his sermons, arranging for the publication of the *Lyra Apostolica* in book form, revising and re-writing his lectures on Romanism. In September, Pusey and he agreed to edit a library of the Fathers of the Church, and Newman contacted various possible translators. At times he seems impatient of delays, as with Keble and Henry Wilberforce, both of whom were known to their friends as procrastinators. Hence Newman's pressure on both. As far back as the previous April he had reminded Keble of his promise of a volume of sermons. '*We are raising a demand for a certain article – and we must furnish a supply*. Men are curious after Apostological principles, and we must not let the season slip. The seizing opportunities is the beginning, middle, and end of success – or rather, to put it higher, is *the* way in which we cooperate with the providential course of things.' One gets the impression, however, that Newman expected, or at least thought, his friends could keep as many irons in the fire or balls in the air or work at the pace he could. For, he went on to say, 'We expect too your papers [[letters]] on Sacramentals, which will be most useful here. . . . Also, will you be ready to talk to Pusey about your version of the Psalms? I have a plan too . . . for Williams, you and I to publish some day an Anglican breviary – and in order to raise a feeling towards it, shall bring out in July a Tract containing specimens.' (*LD* V, 279) Keble brought some of his sermons with him when he came to Oxford in June. Newman returned them in July and asked about Keble's parish sermons which would be more popular. 'It seems to me a great object, as Sir Walter Scott beat bad novels out of the field, in like manner to beat out bad sermons by supplying a *more* real style of sermon. The tone would in time be raised. When people have once got hold of sermons with matter, nature, and reality in them, they would loathe the flummery which is popular.' (*LD* V, 327) Rogers offered to help with putting together the *Lyra*, which Newman accepted. Through Henry he got Samuel Wilberforce to review the work in the *British Critic*. Meanwhile he had finished a review of Wiseman's lectures, which was published in the *British Critic* XX (1836) 373–403).

In July, Harriett had become engaged to Tom Mozley. Newman gave her £30, an amount which he wished he had been able to give Jemima, and asked Tom to accept the silver and furniture from Rose Bank. He also secured a college living at Cholderton for him. He was disturbed, however, when he heard they were planning their marriage for September, which he thought too soon after their mother's death, but when they disagreed, he accepted and attended the wedding in Derby on 22 September. As usual he could not stand to be idle, so he brought along Froude's papers and Keble's sermons to look over. But it was not all work, for he engaged in music making as well.

In 1836 Newman told Miss Giberne that he considered Pusey a saint, who unconsciously showed . . . 'entire and absolute surrender of himself in thought word and deed to God's will – and, this being so, I shall battle for him whenever his treatise [on Baptism] is attacked, and by whomsoever'. (*LD* V, 281) The occasion to fulfil this resolution came in the form of a vicious attack on it in the Evangelical *Christian Observer*. It asserted that the treatise was based upon 'the authority of the darkest ages of Popery. . . . The learned Professor ought to lecture at Maynooth, or the Vatican, and not in the chair of Oxford.' It asked, 'will an approver of the Oxford Tracts answer it in print?' Newman took up the challenge and composed two letters which were printed in the magazine in February, March, April, and May 1837, but accompanied by extensive editorial commentary. Newman felt that he did not have a level playing field, and his friends advised him to stop any further debate in their pages lest his fierce language repel moderate Evangelicals. Newman therefore conceived the idea of publishing 'what will be almost a book on Justification, and perhaps allude in the Preface to the Christian Observer.' Newman later observed that 'As my Lectures on the Prophetical Office of the Church, rose out of my correspondence with Abbé Jager, so those on Justification rose out of my controversy with the Christian Observer.' (*LD* VI, 53, and n. 2)

Meanwhile, back in December he encouraged Maria Giberne's plan to write children's books inculcating apostolical principles. 'Your plan is the very thing I have been wishing, and casting about in every direction how it might be done. I am sure we shall do nothing till we get some ladies to set to work to poison the rising generation.' (*LD* V, 384) Harriett, too, would take up the challenge.

In 1837 the Tracts which had not been selling well took a turn for the better, owing to the change initiated with Pusey's Tract on baptism. The earlier Tracts suddenly began to sell, and Rivington undertook reprints and doubled the number of all future editions. 'Apostolicity is growing so fast in Oxford that I trust it is not too fast', Newman wrote to Henry Wilberforce. 'At Exeter right opinions are strong. At Magdalen, Trinity, University and Oriel nucleuses are forming. Marriott goes the whole hog – Browell is much stronger – Christ Church alone is immobile.' Six months later he wrote again, 'There are still more movements among us here – I mean yearnings and advances towards Catholicism in unlikely quarters.' (*LD* VI, 42, 126)

On 6 February Newman began his weekly soirées, which continued until the affair of *Tract 90*. They were not intended to indoctrinate students in apostolical principles. James Mozley described one of the parties which had just begun. 'Last night went off very well – about eight or nine men. Conversation flowing continuously, and every one at his ease. Newman can manage a thing of this kind better than Pusey . . . We talked on a variety of subjects.' Another undergraduate reported, that Newman 'talks to me of every sort of subject except what is called Tractarianism, and that he has never mentioned.' (*LD* VI, 21, n. 4)

James Anthony Froude recollected,

With us undergraduates Newman . . . spoke . . . about subjects of the day, of literature, of public persons and incidents, of everything which was generally interesting. He seemed always to be better informed on common topics of conversation than any one else who was present. He was never condescending with us, never didactic or authoritative; but what he said carried conviction along with it. When we were wrong we knew why we were wrong, and excused our mistakes to ourselves while he set us right. Perhaps his supreme merit as a talker was that he never tried to be witty or to say striking things. Ironical he could be, but not ill-natured. Not a malicious anecdote was ever heard from him. Prosy he could not be. He was lightness itself – the lightness of elastic strength – and he was interesting because he never talked for talking's sake, but because he had something to say.

The graduates and young fellows, however, he did try to influence, and it was for these apparently that he started the weekly early Eucharist Service in St Mary's on 9 April. He was pleased with the attendance. 'Last Sunday,' he wrote to Harriett, 'I had thirty six communicants. In the course of four Sundays the Alms have amounted to between £19 and £20. I divide them between the Diocesan Fund for increasing small livings and the new London Clergy Aid Society.' (*LD* VI, 65) J. M. Capes later wrote, 'Week after week, and year after year, in sunshine and in storm, a body of men availed themselves of the weekly Communions, which could be found there alone in all Oxford, while the occasional princely gifts to the purposes of the church, which were given at their offertory, attested to the superiority to the mammon-worship of their country.'[7] Newman later recalled these weekly services in his Lectures on Anglican Difficulties, 'Can I wipe out from my memory, or wish to wipe out, those happy Sunday mornings, light or dark, year after year, when I celebrated your communion-rite, in my own church of St Mary's; and in the pleasantness and joy of it heard nothing of the strife of tongues which surrounded its walls?' (*Diff.* I, 81–2)

On 11 March 1837 Newman's Lectures on the Prophetical Office of the Church was published. Although it was in part an answer to his critics that he was propagating Romanism, this was not its formal purpose. As he mentioned in his introduction, 'it is proposed . . . to offer helps towards the formation of a recognized Anglican theology in one of its departments. . . . We have a vast inheritance, but no inventory of our treasures. . . . it remains for us to catalogue, sort, distribute, select, harmonize, and complete.' The Anglican Divines of the seventeenth century were primarily apologists, not systematic theologians. They were mainly interested in refuting opponents. Newman was attempting to provide an integral system with the help of the Anglican Divines. He later explained to Mrs William Froude, 3 April 1844, 'It was my great aim to build up the English system into something like consistency, to develop its idea, to get rid of anomalies, and to harmonize precedents and documents, I thought, and still think, its theory a great one.' He told Jemima that the lectures constituted 'no advance on any thing I have said – but a systematizing, consolidating, supplying premises etc.'. Why do this? He answered in the Introduction, Christians 'have a demand on their teachers for the meaning of the article in the Apostles' Creed, which binds them to faith in "the Holy Catholic Church". Indirectly one comes into collision with the theology of Rome. The Anglican theory is presented as a 'Via Media' between the corrupt Roman system, which appeals to its own infallibility and that of Protestantism which appeals to private judgement. 'Popular Protestantism,' he employed in his introduction 'to designate that generalized idea of religion, now in repute, which sees all differences of faith and principle between Protestants as minor matters, as if the larger denominations among us agreed with us in essentials, and differed only in the accidents of form, ritual, government, or usage.'

There was another reason why Newman published the work, which he

mentioned in the *Apologia*. 'I felt . . . that there was an intellectual
cowardice in not finding a basis in reason for my belief, and a moral
cowardice in not avowing that basis. . . . Alas! it was my portion for whole
years to remain without any satisfactory basis for my religious profession,
in a state of moral sickness neither able to acquiesce in Anglicanism, nor
able to go to Rome. But I bore it, till in course of time my way was made
clear to me.' (*Apo.*, 66) Before then he was determined by preaching and
influencing others to help bring about 'a living Church, made of flesh and
blood, with voice, complexion, and motion and action, and a will of its
own', even if the work would not be accomplished in his days. (*Apo.*, 72)

Newman recognized the chief objection to the theory, namely that
'viewed as an integral system, has never had existence except on paper; it
is known, not positively but negatively, in its differences from the rival
creeds, not in its own properties'. He agreed that 'it still remains to be
tried whether what is called Anglo-Catholicism, the religion of Andrewes,
Laud, Hammond, Butler, and Wilson, is capable of being professed, acted
on, and maintained on a large sphere of action and through a sufficient
period, or whether it be a mere modification or transition-state whether
of Romanism or of popular Protestantism, according as we view it'. But
he was confident that it could be put into practice because 'Truth has the
gift of overcoming the human heart, whether by persuasion or by
compulsion, whether by inward acceptance or by external constraint; and
if what we preach be truth, it must be natural, it must be seasonable, it
must be popular, it will make itself popular. . . . As time goes on, and its
sway extends, those who thought its voice strange and harsh at first, will
wonder how they could ever so have deemed of sounds so musical and
thrilling.'

Newman had been apprehensive about the reception it would receive.
'I cannot conceal from myself that it is neither more nor less than hitting
Protestantism a hard blow in the face.' (*LD* VI, 8) If it was such to
Protestantism, it was likewise to Rome. Two different elements must be
distinguished, as Newman himself did in the Preface to the third edition,
the rhetorical and the argumentative. Of the former he gives plenty of
examples, but the most serious of them occurs at the beginning of the
third lecture, in which derangement or a worse calamity is attributed to
the Roman Church. This passage he included in the list of retractations
which he published in 1843. (See *VM* II, 431)

> In truth she is a Church beside herself; abounding in noble gifts and
> rightful titles, but unable to use them religiously; crafty, obstinate,

wilful, malicious, cruel, unnatural, as madmen are. Or rather, she may be said to resemble a demoniac; possessed with principles, thoughts, and tendencies not her own; in outward form and in natural powers what God has made her, but ruled within by an inexorable spirit, who is sovereign in his management over her, and most subtle and most successful in the use of her gifts. Thus she is her real self only in name; and, till God vouchsafe to restore her, we must treat her as if she were that evil one which governs her. And, in saying this, I must not be supposed to deny that there is any real excellence in Romanism even as it is, or that any really excellent men are its adherents.

Newman said at the beginning of the Retractations he was dealing only with the rhetorical declamations, not with arguments he used and which at this time he still held. As far as the arguments used against Rome these he reduced to two: 'one is the contrast which modern Catholicism is said to present with the religion of the primitive Church, in teaching, conduct, worship, and polity' and until this difficulty was solved he could not enter the Catholic Church. This he did in an *Essay on the Development of Christian Doctrine*. The other was what seemed at first sight a difference between its formal teaching and its popular manifestation. In these lectures and afterwards Newman is referring not to its formal teaching but to the popular manifestations, e.g., devotions to Our Lady, etc.

Newman was pleased, perhaps even flattered, by what Dr Routh said in accepting the request that Newman dedicate his work to him. Dr Martin Joseph Routh, President of Magdalen College and erudite scholar and theologian, had spent two hours with Newman discussing his *Arians*, and had voted for him to be Professor of Moral Philosophy. Newman reported to Rogers that Routh 'said he had allowed very few dedications to him, and mentioned particularly the case of one person who wished to dedicate, and he advised him to address some one who could be a better patron, which the man did; but, said he, "I will not say so to Mr Newman, as I am sure he is not looking to get on in life."' (*LD* VI, 7) Routh had a high respect and personal regard for Newman, calling him 'vir valde perspicax et eruditus.' Bloxam writes that 'Up to 1845 when Newman declined the appointment, he always sent me over to Littlemore to ask Newman to be examiner for the Johnson scholarship. On the last occasion, Newman wrote to decline in the following words:-

I wish I could convey to you how much I felt the great kindness of your message to me by Mr. Bloxam. It seems almost intrusion and impertinence to express to you my gratitude, yet I cannot help it. You are the only person in station in Oxford, who has shown me any countenance for a long course of years; and, much as I knew your kindness, I did not expect it now.'[8]

Newman was also pleased with the reaction to the work. 'It only shows how deep the absurd notion was in men's minds that I was a Papist; and now they are agreeably surprised. . . . Any one who knew any thing of theology would not have confounded me with the Papists,' he wrote to Jemima, and again shortly after: 'Not only have I the most astonishing proofs from very unlikely persons *in Oxford* of the approximation or adhesion to us in consequence of my last book on Romanism – (which have been very gratifying and comfortable indeed, but do not go to prove to the satisfaction of the London people, that Popery is not in Oxford) but I hear the same thing kind of thing from *London* people also.' He admitted, however, that 'in some important points our Anglican *ethos* differs from Popery, in others it is like it – and on the whole far more like it than like Protestantism.' (*LD* VI, 61; 71)

CHAPTER FOURTEEN

Spiritual Growth

The death of his mother and the marriage of his sisters not only freed Newman to devote himself completely to the Movement; they occasioned a reassessment and reorganization of his spiritual life. Reading Froude's papers, especially his journal, seems to have had a decided effect on him. It is clear that now Newman graduated to a higher level of spirituality which is manifested in his prayer life, his asceticism, and his concern for others.

PRAYER

The death of Froude and of his mother introduced Newman into a renewed dwelling in the invisible world. This was aided by his daily reading of the Breviary, which must have taken three to four hours. On 11 February 1837 he started to note by letters in his diary if he had omitted any of the Hours, e.g., 'no M.L. or P. of B.' (No Matins, Lauds or Prime of Breviary). In Oriel Newman lived in two rooms. From his bedroom he could go through a passage into a gallery of the chapel. Here he used to say his prayers.

Two letters to Henry Wilberforce, 25 March and 9 May 1837, shed light on his own practice of prayer, though they were in answer to enquiries from a lady to Henry, whose appetite for prayer and devotions had been stimulated by Newman's sermons. As to the length of prayers Newman answered, 'if we are to give hours to prayer during the day', this is impossible, he believed, without forms, and so he recommended the Breviary devotions, which, he said, 'take up from 3 to 4 hours a day', presumably in a slow recital. 'They are very unexciting, grave, and simple. They are for the whole year, varying day by day more or less. This again I like much; it keeps up attention and rouses the imagination towards the course of the Christian year, without exciting it. . . . Another peculiarity of the Breviary is that the bulk and stress of the Service is in the morning

– viz. when our time is more our own and our mind most fresh. To leave the body of our prayers for night, is like putting off religion to a deathbed.'

The psalms, he felt, should be 'the basis of all devotion. . . . This is one great excellence of the Psalms – as being not *continual addresses* to Almighty God, (which require a great effort and stretch of mind) but meditations on His attributes etc. mutual exhortations, interspersed with some more like prayers.' Newman liked the shortness of the prayers in the Breviary Service. After pointing to other features and excellences of the Hours, he summed up by saying, 'Let the devotions of each day consist of a certain number of Psalms, with Hymns, Collects and Sentences – and let a certain portion of Scripture be read each day.' He concluded by recommending the Litanies in Jeremy Taylor's *Golden Grove* and the intercessions in Bishop Andrewes' *Private Devotions.*[1] (*LD* VI, 46–9)

In the second letter to Wilberforce, he recommended *A Collection of Private Devotions: in the practice of the Ancient Church, called the Hours of Prayer*, compiled by Bishop John Cosin and first published in 1627, and shortly to be reprinted. 'These are but *daily* devotions, I think – not weekly or yearly. Yet they are excellent in themselves, and useful as a beginning.' Disinclination to devotion, he thought, should not be yielded to, and not a reason for discontinuing it, unless proceeding from bodily indisposition. He thought two things contribute to attention in prayer,

> first to put a certain *space* of time to prayer . . . so that if we have done sooner through involuntary hurrying, to remain fixed on our knees to the end of it – or to proceed to other prayers. Next to observe as nearly as possible the right hour. This does not apply so much to devotions *thro'* the day, which are shorter; but *longer* devotions are, I think difficult to attend to, engage in etc. when out of their due season. – All this shows the morning to be the right time for them, for then we can command our time.' (*LD* VI, 65–7)

In all this Newman did not rule out 'the piety and duty of spontaneous ejaculations'.

Henry Wilberforce also told Newman of another lady who turned from Evangelicalism after reading Newman's sermons: 'One only regrets,' she said, 'that he can never know the sort of gratitude felt toward him by many of whom he knows nothing – but perhaps one day he will know it.' For the rest of life Newman would receive letters expressing similar acknowledgments of his spiritual influence. Newman was touched and hoped for her prayers:

> Such things do not seem to comfort or cheer me; I feel so conscious I am like the pane of glass (to use the common simile) which transmits heat yet is cold. I dare say I *am* doing good – but I have no consciousness that I retain any portion of it myself – or that I am more of an instrument of God than Solomon, or Jehu might be. But if I think I am getting persons to pray for me in my life and in death, yea after death I gain something I can take hold of. Also when I hear such things as you have said, one is insensibly drawn in affection towards the unknown friend – and that of course is also a great comfort. (*LD* VI, 57)

The importance and value Newman attached to such intercessory prayer may be gathered from the sermon on 'Intercession' preached in February 1835. Basing his teaching on St Paul's epistles and the Acts of the Apostles, Newman concluded that, 'intercession is the characteristic of Christian worship, the privilege of the heavenly adoption, the exercise of the perfect and spiritual mind'. It is especially the prerogative and privilege of the obedient and the holy. Behind Newman's concept of intercessory prayer is the theology of the Holy Spirit, who unites the baptized not only with Christ, but with each other. Under the inspiration of the Holy Spirit, the Christian is made over into the image of Christ, so that as Christ intercedes above, the Christian intercedes here below. In the contest between good and evil the Christian by reason of his intercessory power plays a role, and hence is involved in the eternal destiny of individual persons. The special role he assigns to intercession is perhaps the distinctive characteristic of his teaching on prayer. (*PPS* III, sermon 24)

The teaching of this sermon Newman put into practice, for in 1835, 1836, and 1837 he composed a number of private prayers, with lists of names of persons to be prayed for. One set of prayers, beginning, 'For the Church Catholic', which Newman later dated in pencil as 1835, was expanded twice, the first expansion probably in 1836. It is interesting that these prayers include prayers for the dead. Shortly after Froude's death Newman remarked in a letter to Robert Wilberforce that praying for the dead 'is so very natural, so soothing, that if there is no command against it, we have (it would seem) a call to do it. And it is so great a gift, if so to *be able* to benefit the dead, that I sometimes am quite frightened at the thought how great a talent our Church is hiding in a napkin', (*LD* V, 260) In a correspondence with George Stanley Faber in 1838, Newman defended the practice as an ordinance and therefore need not be found in Scripture. (*LD* VI, 231)

In the prayers Newman composed in 1835 it is also interesting that he mentions the names of roughly 45 persons, whereas the lists in the following years were expanded to include hundreds of names. Newman's admiration for the collects in the Breviary, because of their brevity apparently, prompted him to imitate them in the twenty-two prayers he composed in excellent ecclesiastical Latin and dated 10 July 1837. These prayers can be divided roughly into four divisions: first for the Church in general, then for the Church in the Diocese of Oxford, followed by prayers for the University and colleges and those connected with them, and finally for his relatives and friends, living and dead. [see Appendix]

Breviary hymns

Hymns were an integral part of the Roman Breviary, and in Tract 75 Newman had included fifteen translations he made of them. He seems to have been enamoured of the Latin hymns and in 1838 he published two collections of them. *Hymni Ecclesiae e Breviariis Romano, Sarisburiensi, Eboracensi et aliunde* and *Hymni Ecclesiae e Breviario Parisiense.* The preface to the latter, written in English, is important as revealing Newman's comparison between psalms, which constitute the bulk of the Office, and the hymns.

> The Psalms. . . . are longer and freer than Prayers; and . . . are less a direct address to the Throne of Grace than a sort of intercourse., first with oneself, then with one's brethren, then with Saints and Angels, nay, even the world and all creatures. They consist mainly of the praises of God; and the very nature of praise involves a certain abstinence from intimate approaches to Him, and the introduction of other beings into our thoughts through whom our offering may come round to Him. . . . the Songs or Canticles of the Church, which are also inspired . . . are a kind of Psalms written for particular occasions, chiefly of thanksgiving. Such are the two Songs of Moses, the Song of Hannah, those in Isaiah, the Song of Hezekiah, of Habakkuk, of the Three Children, of Zacharias, of the Blessed Virgin, and of Simeon; most of which are in the Breviary, and the last four are retained in our own Reformed Prayer Book.
> Hymns, however, being of the nature of praises, cannot be altogether

brought down to that grave and severe character which, as being direct addresses to God, they seem to require, and this is their peculiar difficulty. To praise God specially for Redemption, to contemplate the mysteries of the Divine Nature, to enlarge upon the details of the Economy of Grace, and yet not to offend, to invoke with awe, to express affection with a pure heart, to be subdued and sober while we rejoice, and to make professions without display, and all this not under the veil of figurative language, as in the Psalms, but plainly, and (as it were) abruptly, surely requires to have had one's lips touched with a 'coal from the Altar', to have caught from heaven that 'new song' 'which no man could learn; but the hundred and forty and four thousand which were redeemed from the earth', the virgin followers of the Lamb.[2]

The spirit in which these words were written is another example, as are so many of his sermons, of the truth of Bishop Clifford's remark in his funeral sermon that Newman 'had from his childhood a great idea of the majesty and greatness of God'.

During this year Newman translated many hymns for Williams' and Wood's proposed English translation of the Roman Breviary. Altogether Newman translated forty-seven of the Latin Office hymns, ten of which have only recently been published.

On 18 June 1837 Newman preached at Cholderton one of his most unforgettable sermons, 'The Invisible World', and repeated it again at Boscombe the following Sunday. In it he attempted the difficult task of trying to make the invisible world as real to faith as the external world is to the senses. In the following years Newman gave the impression in his sermons that he himself dwelt in this world. For example Principal Shairp wrote, 'The look and bearing of the preacher were as of one who dwelt apart, who, though he knew his age well, did not live in it. From his seclusion of study, and abstinence, and prayer, from habitual dwelling in the unseen, he seemed to come forth that one day of the week to speak to others of the things he had seen and known.' And Lockhart who was affected by the sermons wrote 'I could never have believed beforehand, that it was possible that a few words, read very quietly from a manuscript, without any rhetorical effort, could have so penetrated our souls. I do not see how this could have been, unless he who spoke was himself a *seer*, who saw God, and the things of God, and spoke that which he had seen, in the keen, bright intuition of faith.'[3]

FASTING

The development of Newman's prayer life was matched by an increase in his ascetical practices, especially fasting. On 30 January 1837 he began to record secretly in his diary his fasting and how much on a particular day. This was about ten days before the beginning of Lent on 8 February. During Lent he regularly fasted on Wednesday and Friday. Thereafter he fasted on the Ember Days. When Newman received Froude's journal from his father in late August 1837, the existence of which he had not known before, giving an account of Froude's fastings, he wrote to Rogers, 'These new papers have quite made my head whirl, and have put things in a new light.' Keble also 'was extremely surprised on reading his Journal, to find that he had been so long and so strict in the duty of Fasting. I had not an idea of it . . . for years after the date of that journal'. (*LD* VI, 120, 136, n. 2. See also *Remains*, I, p. 69)

Prior to 1837 Newman had problems fasting mainly owing to indigestion stemming from his overactivity in the last year at St Clement's, as he explained to Pusey when the latter showed him his Tract on Fasting.

> I have tried every mode of fasting hitherto, yet in no case without producing symptoms which medical men tell me I must guard against. . . . I have sometimes omitted breakfast, sometimes dinner, sometimes dined at one o'clock sparingly as a last meal, but it is all the same. . . . On the other hand I confess at present a greater cross in its way could hardly be put on me than this inability. . . . So I take it as intended as a safeguard against spiritual pride, without of course giving up the attempt of observing the spirit of fasting in lesser matters, or the hope of being sooner or later enabled.
>
> At present I almost resolve to set days apart for prayer and confession, and let fasting take its chance as it may.
>
> I would not have a person so rigid in keeping fast, as to refuse the wish of a friend to whom it may be a kindness to join him for some particular reason at a meal. (3 July 1835, *LD* V, 91–92)

Whether reading the record of Froude's fasting had anything to do with it or not, certain it is that Newman began at this time to fast almost every Friday and sometimes on Wednesday as well. He usually included the details, whether breakfast, lunch or dinner. During Passion Week in 1838 he fasted every day. Omitting Friday during the 1st Easter Week, he resumed his Friday fasting and also fasted on Rogation and Ember Days. On Friday, June 22, when he was finishing his pamphlet in answer to Faussett, he did not fast but made up for it the following day. For the rest of 1838 he fasted regularly on Fridays.

One can obtain an insight into Newman's motives for fasting from a sermon he preached on the first Sunday of Lent 1838, 'Fasting a Source of Trial'. (*PPS* VI, 1) Fasting must be motivated by love of Christ and the desire to imitate him. 'If we fast, without uniting ourselves in heart to Christ, imitating Him, and praying that He would make our fasting His own, would associate it with His own, and communicate to it the virtue of His own, so that we may be in Him, and He in us; we fast as Jews, not as Christians.' Secondly, as Christ's fasting was a prelude to His temptations, we may expect that such will be the case in that of the Christian, for weakness of body and therefore of self-command opens one to temptations to irritability, sloth, and other weaknesses which it is hard to throw off. Nevertheless, it is always a spiritual benefit eventually, and often 'a sensible' benefit at the time.

Newman thought that one of the chief sources of worldliness in clergy and laity alike was the love of comfort and hence an obstacle to the development of a vital spiritual life. He told Pusey he thought a good deal could be said 'on the danger of what is an Englishman's boast *comforts*. E.g. in Oxford, you ring the bell, have every thing done and [*sic*] you wish in a moment. You ride in from the country, go in to the Common Room, wine and biscuits are brought you at once. . . . we have no *wants* – we have everything our own way.' (*LD* V, 92) As the principles of the Movement took hold in Oxford, others felt the same way. Isaac Williams, for example, writes:

Expensive parties, too, still continued, especially among the Heads of Houses, who used to eat and drink very freely, and therefore with them our principles made us very unpopular. . . . . Fridays in Lent were still the chief days for party-giving with the heads of houses, but the younger members of the university were much changed; many did not dine in Hall on Fridays – I had my self never done so, ever since I was elected fellow – and much less wine was drunk in common room except by the seniors.[4]

Newman thought many of the clergy lived too comfortable a life. On 8 June 1837 he recorded in his diary that he went with Keble and his wife and Isaac Williams to Bisley, where Keble's brother Tom had taken the poor and neglected living there. Though Newman does not mention it, the bishop was there for confirmations and according to Isaac Williams Newman expressed to him his disgust at so luxurious a dinner prepared for a bishop. 'It would be better at such a time, he said, that a bishop should only ask for a little dry bread and salt and water.' Williams' conclusion puts it rather mildly, 'These things, and the great annoyance he always felt at John Keble's marriage, indicated feelings not at all in unison with the established state of things in the Church of England.'[5]

On 13 November 1839 Pusey preached a sermon, in which he spoke of the increase in luxury among the undergraduates of late years, but 'he took occasion to say that those *in station* [meaning the heads of houses] might do well to live more simply than they did'. According to J. B. Mozley 'he dropped his voice at this part, which had the effect of course of giving increased solemnity to the admonition; for there was breathless silence in the church at the time. Pusey however meant the undergraduates not to hear, as he told Newman in utmost simplicity after. It was to have been a sort of aside from the preacher in the pulpit to the Vice-Chancellor over the way. The Master of Balliol was seen to march out afterwards with every air of offended dignity.' (*LD* VII, 186, n. 3) The sermon lasted two hours, but one undergraduate, Frederick Temple, wrote to his mother he could have listened more than one hour longer. Just before the following Lent Pusey preached in the University Church a sermon in which he 'strongly recommended that we should abstain from giving parties or joining in convivialities, but rather try if possible to fix our minds on the coming Fast day, the great Day of Atonement in the Christian Church'. As a result young Temple decided to get over all his parties before Lent.[6] None of this of course went well with the Heads of Houses.

COMFORTING OTHERS IN SORROW

Just as the loss of his sister Mary increased his sympathy for others similarly afflicted, the death of Froude seems to have sharpened his empathy for others. After hearing from Rogers that his sister's condition seemed beyond hope, Newman wrote, 1 June 1837:

Your letter of this morning made me very sad indeed. . . . If it turns out as you forbode, it is only a fresh instance of what I suppose one must make up one's mind to think, and what is consoling to think, that those who are early taken away are the fittest to be taken, and that it is a privilege so to be taken, and they are in their proper place when taken. Surely God would not separate from us such, except it were best both for them and for us, and that those who are taken away are such as are most acceptable to Him seems proved by what we see; for scarcely do you hear of some especial instance of religious excellence, but you have also cause of apprehension how long such a one is to continue here.

Such indeed was Newman's premonition of his sister Mary. He continued:

The more we live in the world that is not seen, the more shall we feel that the removal of friends into the unseen world is a bringing them near to us, not a separation. I really do not think this fancifulness. I think it is attainable – just as our Saviour's going brought Him nearer, though invisibly, in the Spirit. (*LD* VI; 75–6)

In the following year, 6 May 1838, Newman developed at length this notion of Christ's invisible presence in a sermon, 'The Invisible Presence of Christ in the Church'. 'We have lost the sensible and conscious perception of Him; we cannot look on Him, hear Him, converse with Him, follow Him from place to place, but we enjoy the spiritual, immaterial, inward, mental, real sight and possession of Him; a possession more real and more present than that which the Apostles had in the days of His flesh, *because* it is spiritual, *because* it is invisible.' (*PPS* VI, sermon 10, p. 121)

Rogers' father was deeply moved by this letter and one from Pusey in a similar vein. 'I never saw him so affected in speaking of any thing. He could hardly speak of them – and he is not apt to lose command of himself in that way.' (*LD* VI, 98) His daughter died on 22 September, the anniversary of the consecration of Littlemore church. Newman liked such coincidences. (*LD* VI, 143–4)

In a letter to Manning who was shortly to lose his wife, Newman developed another thought which he would mention again and again in his letters of condolences to friends all through the rest of his life: such sorrows are a sign of God's love.

Oriel College, July 14/1837

My dear Manning,

You and yours have been much in my thoughts lately, and I have been continually doing that which you ask of me. It has truly grieved me to hear of the severe trial you are under, though really such trials are our portion. I think one may say it without exaggeration, but they who seek God do (as it were) come for afflictions. It is the way He shews His love, and to keep from doing so is His exception. I suppose we may consider His words to the Sons of Zebedee addressed to us. It often strikes me so when I am partaking the Holy Communion that I am but drinking in (perchance) temporal sorrow, according to His usual Providence. Hence St. Peter tells us not to think affliction a strange thing. Let this then, my dear Manning, be your comfort, – You are called to trouble as we all are, and the severer the more God loves you. He may mercifully consider your present distress and suspense sufficient for His inscrutable purposes – if so it will come to an end with nothing more. But anyhow be sure He does not willingly afflict us, nor will put a single grain's weight more of suffering than it is meet and good for you to bear – and be sure too that with your suffering your support will grow, and that if in His great wisdom and love He take away the desire of your eyes, it will only be to bring her really nearer to you. For those we love are not nearest to us when in the flesh, but they come into our very hearts as being spiritual beings, when they are removed from us. Alas! it is hard to persuade oneself this, when we have the presence and are without experience of the absence of those we love: yet the absence is often more than the presence, even were this all, that our treasure being removed hence, leads us to think more of Heaven and less of earth.

Manning wrote on 21 July that suspense was no longer a trial. 'If you could know how much comfort your letter gave me . . . .' Newman wrote again, 23 July,

I thank you for your welcome tho' sad letter – when I read it, it quite affected me, yet I cannot say why, and it seems almost taking a liberty to say that it did. We must take these things as they are sent; only be sure that you will never pass happier days in your whole life, than this awful and still time, before you lose what is so dear to you. You will feel it to be so in memory, so make much of it, and thank God. We do not feel His Hand while it is still upon us, but afterwards.

Have you not felt this is the case in the Church Services?[7] These days will make your future life only happier, that is in real happiness, tho' it is so difficult to understand at the time. Everything is good and acceptable, which tends to bring us into the calm expectant state of indifference to the world, which is the perfection of earthly comfort. The thought of the dead is more to us than the sight of the living, tho' it seems a paradox to say so. I mean it has a happiness peculiar to itself, unlike and higher than any other. Do you not recollect the touching words 'Heu quanto minus est cum caeteris versari quam tui meminisse'.

I am writing what I know would be quite unworthy your reading were it not that I may thereby shew that I really feel for you – that I trust you do believe. I put up prayers in the Church as you desired, and will continue. Marriott who is here desires his kindest thoughts.

Manning wrote on 25 July, the day after his wife's death: 'Many and heartfelt thanks for your kind letter of this morning. I hardly know what has drawn me so closely, and in one way suddenly to your sympathy, but I feel something in the way you deal with my sorrows, particularly soothing and strengthening' (*LD* VI, 102, n. 1.)

One observes in Newman's letters from 1836 on an ever-increasing number of persons for whose health and welfare he was concerned. Newman's empathy is most clearly seen in letters to friends, and two more instances should be noticed: the illness of Bowden and the death of Mrs Pusey. To Bowden, his oldest friend from Oxford days, Newman wrote on 21 February 1939, the birthday they both shared, 'It is a day which among its other thoughts must ever bring before me the image of one of the kindest, most generous, and most sweet-minded persons I ever have been allowed to know. . . . You are ever in my thoughts. It is now near 22 years that I have had the great privilege of knowing you. I could go on thus indulging my own feeling for a long while – but I must take care not to tire you,' (*LD* VII, 39)

In May, Pusey's wife was given up. Pusey asked Newman if he would walk with him between 6 and 7 a.m., before Maria's day began. Newman of course acquiesced. Pusey thought the impending death was a punishment for his sins, a view from which Newman tried gently to dissuade him. (*LD* VII, 78, nn. 2 and 3) On Trinity Sunday, Mrs Pusey died. Newman sent a brief note, in which he said, 'This is a day especially sacred to peace – the day of the Eternal Trinity, who were all blessed from eternity in themselves, and in the thought of whom the mind sees the end of its labours, the end of its birth, temptations, struggles, and sacrifices, its daily dyings and resurrection.' (*LD* VII, 84). This was a brief summary of his concluding remarks in the sermon he had preached that day, 'Peace in Believing'.

> After the fever of life; after wearinesses and sicknesses; fightings and despondings, languor and fretfulness; struggling and failing, struggling and succeeding; . . . at length comes death, at length the White Throne of God, at length the Beatific Vision. After restlessness comes rest, peace, joy; our eternal portion, if we be worthy; – the sight of the Blessed Three . . . in light unapproachable, in glory without spot or blemish; in power without 'variableness, or shadow of turning.' (*PPS* VI, 369–70)

On the same day Newman went to see Pusey, and the latter wrote to Keble, 'God has been very merciful to me in this dispensation, and carried me on, step by step, in a way I dared not hope. He sent Newman to me (whom I saw at my mother's wish against my inclination) in the first hour of sorrow; and it was like the visit of an angel.' On 27 May Newman wrote to Bowden, 'It is now 21 years since Pusey became attached to his late wife; when he was a boy. For 10 years after he was kept in suspence; and 11 years ago he married her. Thus she has been the one object on earth in which his thoughts have centered for the greater part of his life. I trust and earnestly hope he will be supported under this heavy blow. He has not realized till lately, that he was to lose her.' (*LD* VII, 84) Pusey himself wrote on 16 July, 'God bless and reward you for all your love and tender kindness. . . . Your first visit . . . was to me like that of an Angel sent from God: I shrunk from it beforehand, or from seeing any human face, and so I trust I may the more hope it was God's doing. . . . I pray that He may make you what, as you say, there are so few of, a "great saint".' (*LD* VII, 83, n. 2) Newman walked with Pusey almost every day in June until Pusey left Oxford.

These letters of sympathy, which continued all through his life and have been anthologized, are a compelling testimony to his widespread love and affection for others.[8] Persons who got to know Newman recognized this wonderful power of empathy. John Branston, who was a student at Oriel when Newman was a Probationary Fellow and then Fellow of Exeter 1824–30, wrote to Newman 10 April 1844 upon the loss of his wife. He asked him to write 'what you think I need in a state of desolation and bereavement'. He did so, he affirmed, because 'when I lived at Oxford for a short time, I think [I] received more spiritual good from your conversation than you thought of, and since that time I have from your published works gained very great instruction comfort and support'.

Others who knew Newman not personally but from his sermons felt this as well. There is an extant letter with the name erased, written on 27 February 1845, which reads in part, 'I cannot conclude without begging to be allowed to express my deep and heartfelt gratitude to you for the comfort, consolation, and hope I have derived from your Sermons. They have solved for me many difficulties, cheered me in despondency, strengthened me against temptation, and fixed more firmly in my mind those everlasting truths, so necessary to be felt by all, and especially by such, as I am, young, ardent, and daily exposed to the trials peculiar to youth and a sanguine temperament.'

From 1837 on there is an ever-increasing number of letters to relatives, friends and strangers who consulted him on religious matters, whether scriptural, dogmatic, spiritual or historical. One of these was Catherine Holsworth, a highly intelligent woman, who began corresponding with Newman in 1838 (*LD* VI, 197–8). In 1839 she married Hurrell Froude's brother William, continued to consult Newman and became a confidant and lifelong friend. She, Miss Giberne, and Miss Holmes looked to Newman for spiritual counsel and guidance. Responding to persons who wrote to him for help in their religious problems became a hidden and silent apostolate that continued all through his lifetime.

FORGIVENESS OF SIN

One religious difficulty which continued to surface was the forgiveness of post-baptismal sin. Henry Wilberforce and Miss Giberne consulted Newman about it in the spring of 1836 (*LD* V, 286, 296). Pusey had raised the issue in his Tract on Baptism, and in the Prophetical Office of the Church Newman expressed his uncertainty. 'We do not know how far sins committed after Baptism are forgiven. . . . . Nor do we know when it is that forgiveness is formally conveyed to individual Christians who have lapsed into sin, whether it is in this life, or upon death, or during the intermediate state, or at the day of judgment.' (*VM* I, 94) Newman was well aware of the Roman Catholic doctrine which he then explained. Roman Catholics divide sin into mortal and venial, the former 'throw the soul out of a state of grace, and deserve eternal punishment, such as murder, adultery, or blasphemy. Venial sins deserve a punishment short of eternal, a punishment that is, in time, or before the day of judgment. . . . Upon repentance the eternal punishment is forgiven, and that through the Sacrament of Penance, and then the temporal punishment alone remains.' This punishment is expiated by voluntary or imposed penance in this life and if not entirely expiated, it is so in Purgatory. (*VM* I, 95–7)

Anglicans did not recognize Penance as a Sacrament, holding that only two were established by Christ: Baptism and the Holy Eucharist. On the other hand, the Book of Common Prayer approved confessional absolution in certain circumstances. e.g., in the alternate exhortation for the Communion Service which urged any one troubled before taking communion. This was not generally observed in Newman's day. In the Visitation of the Sick the minister was directed to urge the person to confession of sin and then to absolve according to the formula laid down. It was this formula Newman used when he heard a confession upon request on 18 March 1838.

As to the punishment due to sin, Newman not holding Purgatory, was forced to hold that all punishment due to sin is suffered in this life, or at least this seems to be, but one can never be sure, since when he speaks of the forgiveness of sins, he does not always say whether he is speaking of the sin itself, of its punishment, or of both. At times it seems he is speaking of both. In one sermon he argues, 'God has not absolutely forgiven the sin past; here is proof He has not, – He is punishing it.' (*PPS* IV, 8, 125)

Newman devoted a number of sermons to the treatment of sin, punishment, and repentance, some preached in 1836, but the majority in 1837, 1838, and 1839. He published some of these in Volume IV of the *Parochial Sermons* at the end of 1838. Newman intended this to be his best volume, and indeed it contains some of his finest sermons, e.g., 'The Strictness of the Law of Christ', 'Obedience without Love as instanced in the Character of Balaam', 'The Invisible World', 'The Greatness and Littleness of Human Life', 'The Ventures of Faith', 'Christ Hidden from the World'. It was the only volume he attempted as a Catholic to republish with corrections.

Newman, however, meant it not only to be his best, but to be a source of comfort for those who were striving to live a good life but wondered about their sins. 'I mean the whole to be on that one subject, how mercy and judgment can be reconciled.' The entire volume, he said, turns on sermons 7, 'Chastisement amid Mercy', and 8, 'Peace and Joy amid

Chastisement'. (*LD* VII, 25) Indeed the reaction was what Newman intended. Manning wrote from Rome that he was comforted by the sermon, 'The Church a Home for the Lonely'; Hook from Leeds expressed 'a thousand thanks for the 14th Sermon ['Greatness and Littleness of Life']. A. J. Christie was particularly struck by sermons 7 and 3, 'Chastisement amid Mercy', and 'Moral Consequences of Single Sins', and wrote, 'I have always rather wondered myself to hear the Romish doctrine of Purgatory called so uncomfortable whereas were it *true*, there is *something* in it that would answer to a sort of need we may well feel of punishment. This will explain what I mean when I call the first of these Sermons [i.e. 7] an especially comforting – supplying this need without involving the horrors of the Roman Creed.' And Pusey sent Newman a letter that was written to Hook, 'as an instance in which a sermon of yours had been of great comfort; he sent it in reference to what he had once said to you about the supposed want of comfort in Catholic views, which you published your 4th volume to remove.' (*LD* VII, 29, 54, 25, n. 5, 374, n. 4)

Nevertheless Newman had to explain a number of distinctions to Miss Holmes, who referred to one of these sermons.

> I do not wish to speak positively on a subject like Absolution . . . though it be the instrument of the forgiveness of sins, God does not forgive them absolutely and entirely in it, as He does in Baptism. The only question is, in *what sense* He forgives them in it, *how far* He forgives them.
>
> Sin has two out of many consequences – it throws us out of God's favour, and it incurs a punishment. These are not identical. God often punishes those whom He loves, and then we call the punishment chastisement. I suppose our Church holds that absolution restores the soul to God's *favour*, but it pronounces nothing about the *punishment*. Now in the sermon you refer to, I speak . . . of the *penal* consequence of sin, with the distinct allowance or assumption that it is forgiven so far that the person committing it is in God's *favour* or in a state of grace.

Despite the sermons in Vol. IV, which gave comfort, apparently Newman thought further elucidation of post-baptismal sin was necessary or desirable, for in 1839 he preached two sermons which he published in Vol. V. In the first, 'Transgressions and Infirmities', he distinguishes between the two, the former being deliberate or voluntary, the latter due to lack of full consent or involuntary. He gives a partial list of the former, namely habits of vice as such, e.g., fornication, adulteries, homosexuality, idolatry, covetousness, all violent breaches of the law of charity such as thievery, extortion, murder, all profaneness, heresy and false worship; hardness of heart, going against light. All these throw a man out of the state of grace, i.e. of God's favour. Though all these sins are voluntary, Newman seems at one point to admit the possibility that a voluntary sin can be slight. (*PPS* V, 14, 205) The lesson Newman draws is that one should not let sin remain upon one since it can lead to further transgressions, but as time goes on one should grow freer from infirmities. On the other hand, should one fall, one can recover, 'but not without much pain, with fear and trembling'. (p. 206) The quotation from St Paul occurs frequently in Newman's sermons. Newman's doctrine of sin partly accounts for the criticism raised against them as being severe or gloomy.

In the second sermon, 'Signs of Infirmity', Newman gives various examples of infirmities which lead to transgressions, if not checked: (1) the remains of Original sin, such as involuntary movements of pride, profaneness, unbelief, deceit, selfishness, greediness, etc.; (2) those which stem from former habits of sin, though now long abandoned; sins arising from want of self-command, for example, anger, sloth, cowardice; (3) sins which result from sudden temptation when one is taken unaware . . . All these are due to a lack of full consent on the part of the sinner or are involuntary. Newman however does not distinguish clearly between the tendency to sin, as a consequence of original sin or what is traditionally called 'concupiscence' and sins which follow from it. At times it seems that concupiscence is sin. (*PPS* V, 9, 120 and V, 7, 90) Because of this, Newman as a Catholic would not allow sermon 9 to be included in Copeland's selection because of the assertion on p. 120, 'The body of death which infects us, . . . sins because it *is* sin,' though he thought it otherwise a good sermon. (*LD* XXVIII, 250)

Newman concludes the sermon with words of comfort for those who despond because of their infirmities; 'Even to know only thus much, that infirmities are no necessary mark of reprobation, that God's elect have infirmities, and that our own sins may possibly be no more than infirmities, this surely, by itself, is a consolation.' Moreover, 'to reflect that . . . He has given us a care for our souls, an anxiety to secure our salvation; a desire to be more strict and conscientious, more simple in faith, more full of love than we are, all this will tend to soothe and encourage us, when the sense of our infirmities makes us afraid.' That Newman included himself in these remarks is clear from what he adds,

'And if further, God seems to be making us His instruments for any purpose of His, for teaching, warning, guiding, or comforting others, resisting error, spreading the knowledge of the truth, or edifying His Church, this too will create in us the belief, not that God is certainly pleased with us . . . but that He has not utterly forsaken us, and knows us by name, and desires our salvation.' (*PPS* V, 15, 219–20)

While sins of infirmity are blotted out by a life of faith, and forgiveness by the presence of the Holy Spirit, transgressions on the other hand, since they drive out the Holy Spirit, can only be pardoned after a long course of continued acts of repentance. Since one can never be sure when this takes place, one has to live in fear and trembling, and practice continual repentance, prayer, penance, and patience. In an age which was trying to multiply comforts and to rid life of daily inconveniences and discomforts, Newman urged penance especially during Lent. 'Give back some of God's gifts to God, that you may safely enjoy the rest. Fast, or watch, or abound in alms, or be instant in prayer, or deny yourselves society, or pleasant books, or easy clothing, or take on some irksome task or employment.' He further recommended that those who have sinned grievously should practice habitual repentance, and 'to look on all pain and sorrow . . . as a *punishment* for what they once were; and to take it patiently on that account, nay, joyfully, as giving them a hope that God *is* punishing them here instead of hereafter'. (*PPS* VI, 2, 24–5)[9]

As a result of the preaching of Newman, Pusey and others, multitudes all over the country adopted a stricter rule of life. 'They have subjected their wills, they have chastened their hearts, they have subdued their affections, they have submitted their reason. Devotions, communions, fastings, privations, almsgiving, pious munificence, self-denying occupations, have marked the spread of the principles in question.' In attending the ordinances of the Church 'they became more strong in obedience and dutifulness, had more power over their passions and more love towards God and man'. So Newman wrote in *Difficulties Felt by Anglicans*. (*Diff.* I, 70–1)

As time went on, however, it seems that this penitential aspect of the Movement had been forgotten. For in 1917 Fr Bacchus felt it necessary to remind his readers of it. He underlined 'penitential' in Newman's statement, 'Men want an outlet for their devotional and penitential feelings,' and remarked, 'the reader should note these words, for it is so often ignored, that the Tractarian movement was a call to repentance, and that its spirit was a penitential one based upon a keen realisation of the fearful character of post-baptismal sins. . . . Works of penance were repugnant to the Calvinistic system, they were an integral part of that of the Tractarians.' (*KC*, 172–3)

Despite Newman's efforts to comfort people with regard to their sins, especially those of infirmity, the need for confession began to manifest itself to clergy and laity alike. The former saw the need of it as a pastoral tool. To Keble who consulted him about it, Newman wrote, 'Confession is the life of the Parochial charge; without it all is hollow, and yet I do not see my way to say that I should not do more harm than good by more than the most distant mention of it. Reading the first Exhortation at the Communion is the only thing I do of a direct kind. I hope that that is of a nature to startle those who listen, though not enough perhaps to persuade them' (*Moz.* II, 405) Newman felt all would be in a better state if confession was practised, but it ought to be a belief of the Church, not a private opinion, in order 'to secure us with any tolerable certainty, from wavering of mind, and confession turning out a misery instead of a comfort'. Yet he felt 'we are not a real genuine Church, a Church all glorious within, till we return to this primitive and scriptural practice'. (*LD* VII, 466) Thomas Allies met Henry Wilberforce for the first time at the consecration of St Saviour's in Leeds, and Henry said to him, 'I am fairly beat, done in my parish., I feel we can do nothing in the Church of England without confession, but how we are to get it, I see not.'

While these and other Tractarian clergy regarded confession as necessary for the spiritual direction of their parishioners, non-clerical Tractarians looked to it for peace of soul. This was owing partially to what was considered the severity of Pusey's doctrine on post-baptismal sin, as enunciated in his Tract on Baptism. Fanny, bride-to-be of William Alexander, the future Archbishop of Armagh, and her friends were enthusiastic adherents of the Movement who placed the *Tracts for the Times* between the leaves of the Bible which they read together and to whom 'Newman's name was scarcely below St Paul's'. Fanny consulted Henry Phillpotts, the Bishop of Exeter, about habitual confession. He replied that while the Church does not absolutely forbid it, it discourages it, 'in as much as she does not even contemplate the practice – except in two cases', which he then mentioned from the Book of Common Prayer, and concluded that 'it is likely to prove a grievous error if that which should be the occasional and exceptional expedient, be made the rule of life'.[10]

CHAPTER FIFTEEN

Theologian and Editor

Having decided to publish his lectures on justification, Newman was faced with the task of revising them, which proved a formidable one. Before the work was published Newman described for Jemima the strenuous effort he put into it:

> My book on Justification has taken an incredible time. I am quite worn out with correcting. I do really think that every correction I make is for the better. . . . I write – I write again – I write a third time, in the course of six months – then I take the third – I literally fill the paper with corrections so that another person could not read it – I then write it out fair for the printer – I put it by – I take it up – I begin to correct again – it will not do – alterations multiply – pages are re-written – little lines sneak in and crawl about – the whole page is disfigured – I write again. I cannot count how many times this process goes on. (*LD* VI, 192–3)

Part of his problem lay in the originality of the work. As he explained to Bowden, 'It is the first voyage I have yet made proprio marte, with sun, stars, compass and a sounding line, but with very insufficient charts. It is a terra incognita in our Church, and I am so afraid, not of saying things wrong so much, as queer and crotchety – and of misunderstanding other writers for really the Lutherans etc. as divines are so shallow and inconsequent, that I can hardly believe my own impressions about them. (*LD* VI, 188–9)

The work was directed against the Lutheran dictum 'that justification by faith alone was the cardinal doctrine of Christianity'. That doctrine, he asserted, was 'a paradox in Luther's mouth, a truism in Melancthon's. I thought that the Anglican Church followed Melancthon, and that in consequence between Rome and Anglicanism, between high Church and low Church, there was no real intellectual difference on the point'. (*Apo.*, 72) Again it was an attempt to build up a system of Anglican theology, which might 'tend to inform, persuade, and absorb into itself religious minds, which hitherto have fancied, that, on the peculiar Protestant questions, they were seriously opposed to each other'. (p.vii) It likewise showed that the traditional Lutheran doctrine imprisoned men in their own feelings, leading to subjectivism and self-contemplation.

Newman, as has been seen, distinguished justification from sanctification. He now set himself the task to show how they were combined. Justification by faith and sanctification by good works or obedience are not inconsistent with each other. Justification by faith alone is an erroneous view of Christian doctrine, and justification by obedience, a defective one. Justification is the application of Christ's merits through the instrument of baptism, as affirmed by one of the thirty-nine Articles. Seeking to establish a via media, he criticized what he thought was the defective Roman formula of 'inherent righteousness', and substituted a more comprehensive definition, '. . . we are justified by grace, given through Sacraments, impenetrated by faith, manifested in works'. Justification, he argues from Scripture and St. Augustine, 'consists in our being grafted into the Body of Christ or made His members, in God dwelling in us and our dwelling in God, and that the Holy Ghost is the gracious Agent in this wonderful work'. (*Jfc.*, 202) One of the most penetrating and appealing chapters in the book is Lecture IX. 'Righteousness the Fruit of our Lord's Resurrection', in which he shows how our justification is communicated by the risen Christ through the mission of His Holy Spirit. It is only in the twentieth century that Catholic theologians have rediscovered this momentous connection.

The final chapter of the work is an argument, at greater length and detail, of a letter he had written to Lord Lifford, 12 September 1837, in response to the latter's criticism of Newman's sermon *PPS* II, 15, 'Self-Contemplation.' Lord Lifford cited Scott and Simeon as examples to disprove Newman's assertions about the Evangelicals. Newman in his reply affirmed that he was not speaking of individuals nor of the old school but of the tendency of the modern school. (*LD* VI, 128–33) Newman's point is that these have introduced a system of doctrine 'in which faith or spiritual-mindedness is contemplated and rested on as the *end* of religion instead of Christ.' Stress is placed on the act of believing rather than 'on the Object of belief, on the comfort and persuasiveness of the doctrine rather than the doctrine itself'. Dwelling on faith and spiritual-mindedness as ends obscures the view of Christ. 'They are led to enlarge upon the signs of conversion, the variations of their feelings, their aspirations and longings, and to tell all this to others.' (*Jfc.*, 324–6, 336) True faith, however, rests in its object.

> And this being the difference between true faith and self-contempla-
> tion, no wonder that where the thought of self obscures the thought of
> God, prayer and praise languish, and only preaching flourishes. Divine
> worship is simply contemplating our Maker, Redeemer, Sanctifier, and
> Judge . . . The Ancients worshipped; they went out of their own minds
> into the Infinite Temple which was around them. They saw Christ in
> the Gospels, in the Creed, in the Sacraments and other Rites; in the
> visible structure and ornaments of His House, in the Altar, and in the
> Cross . . . They gave Him their voices, their bodies, and their time,
> gave up their rest by night, and their leisure by day, all that could
> evidence the offering of their hearts to Him. (*Jfc.*, 337–8)

The work is the most original he had so far produced, and reveals him as a masterful theologian. Döllinger called it 'the greatest masterpiece in theology that England produced in a hundred years'. Not only did it uncover the weakness of the Lutheran dictum of Justification by faith alone, which the Evangelicals had adopted, the last chapter is a devastating exposure of the shallowness and unreality of the standard current Evangelical mode of preaching. Moreover the entire book combined the precision of abstraction with the warmth and 'cor ad cor loquitur' of the best of Newman's sermons. As Bremond remarked so aptly, it 'treats doctrine not as abstract theory, but as the expression of a living reality in which the Christian soul finds its spiritual sustenance'.[1] That reality is Christ. 'True faith is what may be called colourless, like air or water; it is but the medium through which the soul sees Christ, and the soul as little rests upon it or contemplates it, as the eye can see the air'. (*Jfc.*, p. 336) It shows Newman as the forerunner of 20th century attempts to reunite dogmatic and spiritual theology.

The book does not seem to have stirred up much controversy. George Stanley Faber, who had published in the year before *The Primitive Doctrine of Justification* wrote a friendly letter in which he mentioned his reservations, later discussed in the appendices to the second edition of 1839. Le Bas in an article in the *British Critic* in July thought the book difficult reading and remarked 'And, once or twice, his imagination seems to have seduced him a little way into the realms of shadowy and mystical fancies'. Newman called it 'an unfavourable and very puzzleheaded critique'. But he told Jemima he was on the whole 'at ease' about them. '. . . At first I thought I should be very obscure – but am satisfied from what people say that I am not, except so far as the subject obliges me.' He compared the difficulties of Faber and Le Bas with 'how simple the subject appears to those who take it up for the first time. A lady wrote me word the other day, whom I had damped before the book came out with the warning that it would be an abstruse subject, that she had not found any difficulty in the subject from beginning to end, not denying of course that it requires attention – and she is far too clever a person and clearheaded to think she understands what she does not. It is curious to see how warmly women take up the whole Catholic system and how intelligently, when they do.' (*LD* VI, 253–4)

FROUDE'S *REMAINS*

A month after Hurrell Froude's death on 28 February 1836, the Froude family sent Newman a collection of his papers, which consisted of sermons, Becket papers, an essay on rationalism and various other articles. These were put at the disposal of Newman and Keble to publish if they so wished. The papers were circulated among friends and their opinion solicited. Newman was hesitant about publication, but the others were in favour, and Newman acquiesced, stating his reasons to Keble,

> These Thoughts will show people what is the real use of such memoranda, . . . not to ascertain our spiritual state in God's sight, but by way of improving ourselves, discovering our faults etc.
>   They show *how* a person may indulge *metaphysical* speculations to the utmost extent and yet be *practical*. . . .
>   They present a remarkable instance of the temptation to rationalism, self-speculation etc. subdued. . . . We see his mind only breaking out into more original and beautiful discoveries, from that very repression which seemed at first to be the utter prohibition of his powers. . . . His profound Church views, as brought out in the Becket Papers, have sometimes seemed to me as a sort of gracious reward for his denying himself that vulgar originality which is rationalistic.

Before all was settled, Isaac Williams suggested that a selection of Froude's correspondence be included. Newman agreed and told Keble that among other things they contained 'the first hints of principles etc.

which I and others have pursued and of which he ought to have the credit. . . . We have often said the movement, if any thing comes of it, must be *enthusiastic* – now here is a character fitted above all others to kindle enthusiasm – should we not show what he was in himself?' (*LD* VI, 86–7) He gave further reasons in a letter to Rogers.

1. to show his mind, his unaffectedness, playfulness, brilliancy, . . . implying, not expressing, sacred thoughts; his utter hatred of pretence and humbug. . . . 3. To show the history of the formation of his opinions. . . . 4. To show how deliberately and dispassionately he formed his opinions; they were not taken up as mere fancies. . . . Here his change from Tory to Apostolical is curious. 5. To show the interesting *growth* of his mind, . . . his remarkable struggle against the lassitude of disease, his working to the *last*. . . . 6. For the intrinsic merit of his remarks.

Rogers agreed but pointed out the possibility that the letters could give the impression that the Tractarians were 'plotters'.

On 25 August Newman received from Archdeacon Froude, Hurrell's Private Journal of 1826–27, of which Newman had previously been unaware. It recorded details of his fasting, temptations, struggles to overcome self. Newman wrote to Rogers, 'These new papers have quite made my head whirl, and have put things quite in a new light.' (*LD* VI, 120) The more Newman read of them the more he was impressed. He began to think that 'a fresh instrument of influence is being opened to us in these Papers', as he wrote to Bowden. 'They do certainly portray a saint. They bring out, in the most natural way, an *ethos* as different from what is now set up as perfection as the East from the West.' But while 'all persons of unhacknied feelings and youthful minds must be taken by them – others will think them romantic, scrupulous, over refined etc., etc.'. (*LD* VI, 145) This apprehension remained even close to the time of their publication, for he writes to Bowden again, in January 1838, 'Froude's volumes will open upon me a flood of criticism, and from all quarters. It is just a case where no two persons have the same judgment about particulars.' (*LD* VI, 188)

When the first two volumes of Froude's *Remains* appeared in February 1838 Newman's fears were fulfilled; it was attacked from every quarter. Geoffrey Faussett, Margaret Professor of Divinity at Oxford, preached against them and the Tractarians on 20 May, but kept back the publication of it until shortly before people would come up to Oxford for Commemoration. In this way they would read the sermon and go away before Newman would have time to answer it. Newman, however, took precautionary action. He wrote and printed up the greater part of his answer before the sermon came out. When it did appear, he stayed up all night and finished his answer in the morning. Thus he was able to publish his own pamphlet shortly after Faussett's and before Commemoration. (*LD* VI, 258) Newman's reply was both an admirable defence of Froude and an excellent statement of Tractarian principles. Its tone was moderate, calm, in contrast to the virulent invective of Faussett's remarks, such as 'an increasing *aberration* from Protestant principles', 'a disposition to *overvalue* the importance of Apostolical tradition', of '*exaggerated* and *unscriptural* statements', of a '*tendency* to depreciate the principles of Protestantism', and to 'palliate' the 'errors of Popery', of a gradual and near *approximation* towards 'the Roman superstitions concerning the Lord's supper'. All of this, Newman replied, is a matter of private opinion. It is pure assertion without proof.

Newman here invoked without using the terminology his distinction between the episcopal and prophetic offices of the Church. The doctrines of the latter 'are distinct from the Church's own doctrines; they may be held or abandoned. . . . The English Church once considered persecution to be a duty; I am not here called on to give any opinion on the question; but certainly the affirmative side of it was not binding on everyone of her members. . . . I will not write in a hostile tone against any person or any work which does not, as I think, contradict the Articles or the Prayer Book.' Newman asked why this right of private judgement should be infringed and those who exercise it should be spoken of as if they were heretics.

Newman answered the charge that Froude had written in favour of Popery, and proved his anti-Roman sentiments from the *Remains* itself. He then proceeded to the complaint that the two volumes are promoting the revival of Popery. He replied by showing those doctrines have been taught in the Anglican Church by such divines as Hooker, Andrewes, Laud, Bramhall, Taylor, Thorndike, Bull, Ken, and others, and quotes at length from the writings of Bramhall dealing with the Real Presence, the Sacrifice of the Mass, Adoration *in* the Sacrament, Prayers for the Faithful Departed, the Invocation of Saints, and Monasteries.

Another question as to which there is a liberty of opinion is whether the Church of Rome is 'the mother of harlots' and the Pope, St. Paul's 'man of sin'. Newman had held this, but now he affirmed that he could not see how one holding apostolical succession could hold it. For if it were true, 'then the great Gregory, to whom we Saxons owe our conversion, was Antichrist, for in him and in his times were those tokens of apostasy fulfilled, and our Church and its Sees are in no small measure the very work of the "Man of sin"'. (*VM* II, 199–219)

Newman then proceeded to the main point of discussion, the Eucharist, the real presence of Christ in it, and the question how He is present. Before closing, Newman replied to Faussett's censure of Tractarian 'rigid mortifications and painful penances' and his complaint of their 'gloomy views' of sin after baptism. With dialectical skill mixed with irony he answered Faussett and backed up his assertions with quotations from the lives of Anglican divines.

I much regret that, while censuring 'rigid mortifications and painful penances,' you have not given us to understand whether you mean '*rigid* mortifications and *painful* penances' or 'mortifications and penances,' as such; whether you object to them in toto, or only in excess. I wish, when speaking of 'self-abasement' as Papistical, and of '*gloomy* views of sin after Baptism,' you had said what views of it are at once appropriate to backsliders and yet not gloomy; whether you consider repentance itself cheerful or gloomy; . . . whether every self-abasement savours of Popery, or what those are which do not so savour; whether any self-abasements are pleasant; . . . whether (to come to our Church's words and rules) to confess an '*intolerable* burden of sins' is 'gloomy,' whether it is pleasant to be '*tied and bound* with the chain of our sins,' or to be '*grieved* and *wearied* with their burden,' whether 'to bewail our own sinfulness' is a cheerful exercise; . . . whether 'days of fasting or abstinence' are pleasant or 'painful;' whether the 'godly discipline,' the restoration of which, as we yearly protest, is much to be wished, would not be 'rigid' and 'painful,' and likely to 'call us back at once to the darkest period of Roman superstition;' . . . Nor is this all; what the Church has enjoined, her most distinguished sons, of whatever school of thought, have practised. (*VM* II, 251–2)

Newman's zeal for the promotion of apostolical principles was founded on his desire for the spiritual renovation of the existing Church as he makes clear in his closing remarks,

Thousands of hungry souls in all classes of life stand around us; we do not give them what they want, the image of a true Christian people, living in that Apostolic awe and strictness which carries with it an

evidence that they are the Church of Christ. This is the way to
withstand and repel Roman Catholics; not by cries of alarm, and
rumours of plots, and dispute, and denunciation, but by living up to
the creeds, the services, the ordinances, the usages of our own Church
without fear of consequences, without fear of being called Papists; to
let matters take their course freely, and to trust to God's good
Providence for the issue. (*VM* II, 256)

Though major, it was not the only attack; another was launched by
Lord Morpeth in a debate in the House of Commons. As reported in the
Dublin Record, 'the Debate was rendered remarkable for bringing before
the notice of the country, through Lord Morpeth, a sect of damnable and
detestable heretics, of late sprung up at Oxford, – a sect which evidently
affects Popery and merits the heartiest condemnation of all true Christians'. (*LD* VI, 281–2) Gladstone however defended Newman and Pusey,
and characterized the assertion 'as a mere vulgar calumny'. (*LD* VI, 276,
n. 1.) If Newman saw saintliness in Froude's fastings and mortification,
James Stephen in the *Edinburgh Review* spoke with contempt of them.
And an article, 'Treason within the Church', accused the Tractarians of
'doing the work of the apostate church, and of her most subtle missionaries, the followers of Ignatius Loyola'. (*LD* VI, 266, n. 3, 282, n. 2.)

Of Newman's supporters Edward Churton was probably the most
distressed. He visited Newman in his rooms and let loose with a volley
against the *Remains*. He was so over-excited that Newman told Keble that
'it is difficult to put his protest into mere words'. (*LD* VI, 222) This was
in March. By September he had still not got over it. He wrote to
Newman: 'Your opponents will never find ground to stand upon, *unless
you are so kind as to give it to them* . . . you must perceive that, since the
appearance of Froude's *Remains*, your friends are perplexed, and some
who were neuters have declared against you . . . pray think of the peril of
new divisions and on points confessedly unnecessary'. (*LD* VI, 324, n. 4)
Newman replied, 'You are very kind to be so frank in the expression of
your opinion about me. . . . While we hold the same faith, I should be a
fool if I did not allow you to have your own opinion about matters which
are not of faith, about historical events and characters. . . . Still less have
I any right to complain of your censuring me in matters of conduct and
judgment, when I claim a right to censure our predecessors in the
Church. It would be very inconsistent.'

Newman further remarked that he was so constituted that he disliked
to keep things in. 'While the world thought, I liked Jewell etc or rather

while my friends thought it, I was uncomfortable. I am glad an opportunity has been given me to show them what I am. . . . I cannot help fancying that you were easier after speaking out in my room; give me credit for the same state of mind.' Newman had powerful emotions which he had brought under control. His further remarks manifest his character. '. . . if I did not try to rule myself, I could say violent things, and astonish you as much perhaps as you astonished me when I last saw you. . . . Is all the strong feeling, all the expression of it, to be on one side only? why should we not bear with each other, agreeing so clearly in main matters as we do . . . . . .' He went on to say that he still thought Keble and he had acted 'on the truest and wisest view of what is *expedient*. . . . the pain persons feel is not proof we are not right. Operations which save life are often painful.' (*LD* VI, 325) Churton replied that 'if the pain . . . were confined to persons opposed to your principles, I would allow the force of such an argument: but when you cannot but be aware that the pain is felt by those, who would give up everything but a good conscience to approve *every thing* you do, it seems to me quite inapplicable.' (*LD* VI, 334, n. 2) Newman acted according to his principles, for though he did not like the tone of Churton's article, 'Revival of Jesuitism', especially with regard to remarks about devotions to the Immaculate Conception and to the Sacred Heart, which he mentioned to Churton, he nevertheless published the article since it was mainly historical. Oakeley cited this article in criticizing Newman for using the paring knife too sparingly.

Another result of the publication of Froude's *Remains* was the Martyrs' Memorial put up in honour of Cranmer, Latimer and Ridley, who were burned in the reign of Queen Mary. Golightly spearheaded the drive. Pusey at first subscribed, but, since one of the aims was to put the Tractarians to the test, he was persuaded to withdraw, as his subscription might be interpreted as a division in the ranks.

If Froude's criticism of the Reformation and his sympathy for the Church of the Middle Ages disturbed and alienated some High Church and Establishment members, on the other hand, it helped William George Ward to become a member of the Movement. Ward had felt that Newman's lectures in 1836 did not go far enough in condemning the Reformation. Moreover Froude's open speech and direct intellect resembled Ward's. Wilfrid Ward has spelled out the attraction of the *Remains* for his father.

The boldness and completeness, the uncompromising tone of the *Remains* took hold of Mr. Ward's imagination. Authority in religion was the avowed principle. A clear, explicit rule of faith was thus substituted for perplexing and harassing speculation. There was no temporising, or stopping short. Mr. Ward's dislike of the current system was echoed in the plain statement which he was for ever quoting. 'At length (under Henry VIII) the Church of England fell. Will she ever rise again?'

Froude's writing, then, recommended itself to Mr. Ward. . . . Froude's picture of the mediaeval Church was that of an absolute, independent spiritual authority direct, uncompromising, explicit in its decrees, in contrast with the uncertain voice of the English Church with its hundred shades of opinions differing from and even opposed to each other. . . . The stand for moral goodness against vice and worldliness was witnessed in the highest and most ideal types of sanctity in Church history. . . . The doctrine of a supernatural world and supernatural influences was not minimised, . . . it was put forth in the fullest and most fearless manner. Angels and saints, as ministers of supernatural help, were recognised, and their various offices in aiding and protecting us and listening to our prayers on all occasions forced on the attention constantly, in the Catholic system. There was no mistiness or haze or hesitation. All was clear, complete, definite, carried out to its logical consequences.[2]

From 8 May to 7 August 1838 Newman delivered a series of lectures in the Adam de Brome chapel in St Mary's 'On the Scripture Proof of the Doctrines of the Church', which were published in September as *Tract 85*. They reveal Newman's mastery of the techniques of controversy and exude a quiet confidence reflective of his own confidence in the cause. The lectures are concerned with a difficulty which could be advanced against the system of theology which he had constructed in the lectures on Romanism and on justification, namely, that it is not contained in Scripture. Ultra-Protestants who deny a Church doctrine such as the apostolic succession 'because it is not clearly taught in Scripture,' are inconsistent since they accept 'the divinity of the Holy Ghost, which is nowhere literally stated in Scripture'. 'No system is on the surface of Scripture; none but has at times to account for the silence or the apparent opposition of Scripture as to particular portions of it.' (*DA*, 113, 126)

Newman concludes that there are three possibilities: either Christianity contains no definite message, creed, revelation, system: secondly, that 'though there is a true creed or system revealed, it is not revealed in Scripture, but must be learned collaterally from other sources,' or a *via media*, that is the Anglican position, the first alternative, that of Latitudi-narians, the second position, that of the Roman Catholics.

Newman then proceeds to argue against latitudinarianism or liberalism in religion and to affirm dogma as the fundamental principle of religion. (*DA*, 129; cf. *Apo.*, 48–9) Since the structure of Scripture is irregular and unmethodical, one must conclude that it contains no definite message or that it does, but the message is indirectly and covertly revealed, since it is under the surface. In these lectures Newman displays a masterful knowledge of Scripture and the difficulties of exegesis. He also employs a favourite technique of argument from analogy, to expose inconsistencies in his adversaries' positions.

A SHIFT IN THE WINDS

That his enemies attacked did not much bother Newman; it was to be expected and he often took these attacks in good humour, and even joked about them. But criticism from a bishop or more precisely his own bishop was another thing. And so the first real crisis and test of conscience came from his bishop. The Bishop of Oxford in his triennial Visitation Charge stated that as regards doctrine there were many truths enunciated in the Tracts which were valuable, but there were also words and expressions which could lead others into error and that he feared more for the disciples than the masters, and he cautioned the Tractarians 'lest in their efforts to re-establish unity, they unhappily create fresh schism; lest in their admiration of antiquity, they revert to practices which heretofore have ended in superstition'. (*LD* VI, 285–6)

Newman, who had an unusual high respect for authority particularly a bishop's ('a Bishop's lightest word ex cathedra is heavy'), was so upset that he wrote twice in one day to Keble for advice. He then wrote to Archdeacon Clerke, as a friend, not as officially connected with the bishop, saying he could not continue with the indefinite censure, that he would withdraw the Tracts, except those over which he had no control, and discontinue them. If, however, the archdeacon could learn what Tracts contained expressions the bishop referred to, he would withdraw those and continue the Tracts. As the archdeacon did not know, Newman then wrote to the bishop. The bishop replied that he in no way intended to censure the Tracts, that Newman had misunderstood what he said, that to withdraw the Tracts would do harm, regretted he had given Newman pain, and asked Newman to wait until the Charge was printed.

In the printed version the bishop added a footnote with reference to his remarks about the Tracts that it was not his intention to censure them. Newman appreciated the bishop's letter, but nevertheless felt the lack of encouragement except from Keble for which he thanked him. 'Your quotation from Virgil brought tears into my eyes – No one has encouraged me but you.' Keble had ended one of his letters with 'O passi graviora, dabit Deus his quoque finem,' (*Aeneid* I, 199) and added 'I will not change Virgil's plural, though you *say* you are absolutely alone.' (*LD* VI, 286–90, 294, 295–7, 309, and n. 3)

This incident raised in Newman's mind the question what call he had to do what he was doing. In writing to Keble for the first time Newman made an interesting revelation which would come up again shortly in connection within the ranks of the Apostolicals, likewise occasioned by the publication of the *Remains*. He confessed that 'nothing would be more pleasant to my feelings if it was right to do it, than to retire into myself and to set about reading without writing'. (*LD* VI, 287)

At this time two young laymen, Samuel Wood and Robert Williams, were translating the Breviary into English at their own expense, and Newman was translating some hymns for them. George Prevost sent Newman a peremptory and hasty note to inform him how distressed he and others, particularly Thomas Keble, were to hear of the translation and suggested that Newman ask the translators to suspend their work immediately. Newman corresponded with Keble who thought it unwise to proceed with the work at that time. After considering ways of editing the translation to make it more acceptable, Newman received word from the translators that they decided to save Newman trouble and anxiety by stopping the work, despite the pecuniary loss and disappointment.[3]

This however was but a further example of differences with Prevost, Thomas Keble and the country parsons. As Newman revealed in a letter to John Keble on 21 November, he learned indirectly from J. F. Christie that Tom Keble was one of those persons included in Newman's remark in his letter to Faussett as holding at once the apostolical succession, and that the Pope was Antichrist. Newman wrote to Thomas Keble expressing his 'sorrow for what was quite unintentional and to say that in truth he did not think he held the Pope to be *the* Antichrist'. He had already modified the passage in a second edition. Thomas Keble wrote to Newman enclosing what he called 'this impertinent message from Mr Burke, "You never give yourself time to cool – You cannot survey, from its proper point of sight, the work you have finished, before you decree its final execution – You never go into the country, soberly and dispassionately to observe the effect of your measures on their objects. You cannot etc. etc. etc." In good earnest I wish you would go to Hursley or any where else, to be a little while out of the way of your Faussetts, Shuttleworths, etc.' He also said he was sorry to hear Newman was proposing hastily to give up the Tracts. (*LD* VI, 309. n. 1) The tone of the letter hurt Newman, but he said nothing. He asked Tom Keble if at the anniversary of the dedication of Littlemore he could make a collection for the poor at Bisley, to which Keble assented and Newman sent down the money. At the same time Keble sent Newman a Tract which Newman thought was for publication, so he had it printed up and sent Keble ten proofs. In answer Keble said he was perplexed at his having acted so hastily.

It has been said that there are two types of leaders: one acts by dictates and the other operates by consensus and this latter Newman was. Consequently for the peace of all parties Newman wrote to John Keble putting himself entirely in his hands including his own opinions and their expression.

> First I put myself entirely into your hands. I will do whatever you suggest. I really do hope I have no wish but that of peace with all parties, and of satisfying you. If you tell me to make any submission to anyone, I will do it. . . . I wish parties would seriously ask themselves *what* they desire of me. Is it to stop writing? I will stop any thing you advise. Is it to show what I write to others before publishing? it is my rule. Pusey saw my letter to Faussett; Williams and others heard and recommended the publishing of my Lectures. Is it to stop my weekly parties or any thing else? I will gladly do so. Now this being under-stood, may I not fairly ask for some little confidence in me as to what, under these voluntary restrictions, I do? People really should put themselves into my place, and consider how the appearance of sus-picion, jealousy, and discontent is likely to affect one, who is most conscious that every thing that he does is imperfect, and therefore soon begins so to suspect every thing that he does as to have no heart and little power remaining to do any thing at all. (*LD* VI, 347)

Keble sent a kind reply, in the course of which he explained how the misunderstanding arose, for which he John was in part responsible, but went on to say about his brother: 'He does not, I think, sufficiently enter either into the difficulties of the position into which you have been called, or into the keenness of your feelings – (for you know, my dear N. you are a very sensitive person-). . . . I cannot bear you to regard him as unkind or unfriendly. . . . and although I can in some sort understand, how very painful, nay bitter at times must be the sensation, when you are blamed by those from whom you looked for support, I suppose it was a kind of thing on which you must have counted when you devoted yourself to this cause, and that as you did not begin for their approbation, neither will you leave off for their blame, except you really see reason to acquiesce in it.' (*LD* VI, 348)

In reply Newman said he did not write for the country clergy, but '*ought* one to speak, though one *may* be making way here /i.e. Oxford/, if it is at the expense of the country clergy. . . . I have *no call* – I am not in station. . . . When then a man like your brother *does* object, he has my own latent feelings on his side. . . . It is still a great question with me whether I should not be doing better by reading and preparing *for future* writing on the Fathers, than by offhand work; and with this view giving up the Tracts, the B.C. /British Critic/ and preaching at St. Mary's.' In a second letter he again repeated, 'To read and otherwise employ myself on the Fathers without venturing any thing of my own, is what would give me most peace of *conscience*. . . . My constant feeling when I write, is that I do not realize things, but am merely drawing out intellectual conclusions – which . . . is very uncomfortable.' Newman added a note to this in 1885 referring to his account of his illness in Sicily about being hollow. (*LD* VI, 350, 353)

Newman was hurt not so much by the criticisms but by the manner in which they were made, as seems clear from his statement to Keble, 'This I feel, that if I am met with loud remonstrances before gentle hints are tried, and suspicions before proof, I shall very soon be silenced, whether persons wish it or no.' (*LD* VI, 347) Keble tried to unravel the misunderstanding, by quoting from his brother's letter explaining how Prevost came to write such a hasty note, for which he, Tom, took responsibility and was sorry for. At this time Newman's *Tract 85* came out which contained passages which Tom Keble and others thought were hastily written and could be used against them. He thought it would be good if there were two people to read over any Tract before publication. Newman was willing to have two persons designated by Tom to do so. He also wrote a letter of apology to Prevost for any pain he had given him in his letter in which he criticized the peremptoriness of Prevost's letter. (*LD* VI, 356–8, 361)

The entire incident shows not only Newman's sensitivity to the opinions of others, but also sensitive conscience as to whether he was doing right or whether he was following self-will. It also showed, Isaac Williams to the contrary, Newman's meekness.

In between the two incidents of the bishop's Charge and the differences with T. Keble and Co., Newman celebrated the anniversary of the dedication of Littlemore church, which was always a joyous occasion for him. He preached the sermon, 'Remembrance of Past Mercies', (*PPS* V, 6) He sent the material to the publishers for his fourth volume of sermons and Rose, who announced his departure for Rome for the winter on account of his poor health, gratefully accepted Newman's offer to dedicate the volume to him, '. . . as a very great *honour* publicly – and privately a *very very* high gratification indeed. . . . May God bless you and prosper your labours in His cause.' Rose died in January and Newman wrote Jemima, 'Do you not think that many Newspapers and many Reviews and Magazines are necessary to outweigh the pleasure of this letter?' (*LD* VI, 327, n.3; *LD* VII, 11). Newman was anxious that Keble, whom he visited at Hursley from 22 to 26 October would review Manzoni's *I Promessi Sposi*, with which he was quite taken, but Keble declined for lack of practical knowledge of the R. C. system. (*LD* VI, 329 and n. 2)

Early in 1836 Newman came to an arrangement with the publisher of the *British Critic* to supply about a third of the articles for each issue. This was another outlet for Apostolical principles, but Newman became disillusioned with the policy of the editor, J. S. Boone, and disapproved of two articles that appeared, so he announced his intention to withdraw from the magazine. Boone resigned and Newman, much against his inclinations, agreed in January 1838 to take over as editor in July. He corresponded with many of his friends soliciting articles. Thus the *British Critic* became the organ of the Movement.

According to Frederick Oakeley the magazine exercised an extraordinary influence, and one of the chief reasons for its success was Newman as editor. 'If he had a fault as an editor, it was that he erred on the side of forbearance and largeness of spirit. He used the pruning-knife, if anything, too sparingly. . . . But, in general, the Review gained by these expansive principles of tolerance. . . . Light articles, which must always be an editor's great difficulty, are mingled in due proportion with the graver, and they are generally pervaded by a brilliant and accomplished tone of kindly wit.'[4] Newman himself published ten articles, most of which were later republished in *Essays Critical and Historical*.

In the summer Newman took a house for young writers in Aldate's opposite Christ Church. With the help of donations from his friends he agreed to supply rent, taxes, rates, and keep two servants beside buying furniture, kitchen utensils and other necessities, and to provide for the occupants their board, coals, candles, etc. These were James Mozley, Pattison, A. J. Christie, his brother C. H. Christie, F. M. R. Barker, and C. Seager. Though not the success Newman anticipated, three of them: Pattison, A. J. Christie, and Mozley obtained fellowships. (*LD* VI, 328 n. 1) Newman had initiated two new projects of translations, the translation of Fleury's *Ecclesiastical History*, which Rose had long pushed for, and that of St Thomas's *Catena Aurea. Commentary on the Four Gospels, collected out of the Works of the Fathers.* A. J. Christie began the revision of the former, and Pattison helped with the translation of the latter.

Before the end of the year two volumes of the Library of the Fathers appeared, and Newman helped R. W. Church with his translation of St Cyril's Catechetical Lectures.

CHAPTER SIXTEEN

Influence and Shock

That by 1839 Newman had become the leading figure at Oxford, certainly in the eyes of the undergraduates, is well-attested, even by those who outgrew his influence. For example, William Alexander, later Archbishop of Armagh, wrote, 'I had not been long a resident in Oxford before I was smitten with a great desire to see and hear one whose influence was upon every lip and not a few hearts in the University.'[1] Others like John Duke Coleridge, later Lord Chief Justice of England, never outgrew his influence. 'The genius, the penetration, the sanctity, pehaps, too, the *eironeia* of Newman drew him by an irresistible spell, and never relaxed their hold. . . . Through every modification and change of doctrine and faith, he loved and honoured the man, and believed that he was a teacher "sent from God." '[2]

Students used to point out Newman when they saw him in the streets. William Lockhart wrote years later:

I have a vivid remembrance of my first seeing John Henry Newman when I was quite a youth at Oxford. He was pointed out to me in the High Street. I should not have noticed him if his name had not been mentioned by my companion. He was walking fast, with a very peculiar gait, which was his own. It was like a man walking fast in slippers and not lifting his heel. It was not dignified; but you saw at a glance that he was a man intent on some thought, and earnest in pursuing some purpose, but who never gave a thought as to what impression he was making, or what people thought about him. When one came to know and study him, it was plain that his mind was so *objective* that his own subjectivity was well-nigh forgotten. Hence his simplicity, meekness, and humility; God, not self, was the centre of all his thoughts.[3]

Dean Lake summed up the evidence when he wrote, 'Much as Pusey and Keble might be respected, they were, especially to us undergraduates, nothing in comparison with Newman. . . . he was, in his love and fearless following of truth, and in the courage which his whole conduct exhibited, the one great man, the hero, of the movement.'[4] James Anthony Froude, despite his later rejection of apostolical principles, bore this out. 'Far different from Keble, my brother, from Dr. Pusey, from all the rest, was the chief of the Catholic revival – John Henry Newman. Compared with him, they were all but as ciphers, and he the indicating number.' Froude compared Newman to Julius Caesar both facially and in character and personality. 'Both were formed by nature to command others. . . . *Credo in Newmanum* was a common phrase at Oxford.'[5]

Oakeley pointed out that Pusey was far more dogmatical in the direction of consciences than Newman.

> He always seemed much surer of his ground; and, as positive teaching and authoritative direction were just what thoughtful Anglicans wanted, he was in great request as a spiritual guide. He even undertook, it was commonly said, people's conscientious burdens, and made himself responsible for the consequences. Mr. Newman, on the other hand, in the midst of his great influence, was diffident of himself and unwilling to give strong opinions. Yet it is remarkable that in actual hold upon others there was no comparison between the two. Dr. Pusey's power over consciences was limited by the degree of his disciples' obedience; Mr. Newman's penetrated and swayed them in spite both of themselves and of himself. He ruled them without aiming at rule, and they acted under his influence while scarcely conscious of it. His casual words were treasured up as oracles, his hints were improved into laws; his very looks and gestures were watched as a mirror of his thoughts; his latent feelings tenderly consulted, his wishes reverently anticipated, even his very peculiarities unconsciously copied. His personal influence in the Church of England was something to which experience suggests hardly a parallel.[6]

If the last sentence sounds exaggerated, it is supported by one of Principal Shairp which goes even further in affirming he was 'a man in many ways the most remarkable that England has seen during this century, perhaps the most remarkable whom the English Church has produced in any century'.[7]

What was it in Newman's character and personality that accounts for the great attraction he had for others? Principal Shairp attempted to explain it without denying that it was mysterious:

There was of course learning and refinement, there was genius, not indeed of a philosopher, but of a subtle and original thinker, an unequalled edge of dialectic, and these all glorified by the imagination of a poet. Then there was the utter unworldliness. . . . the tamelessness of soul, which was ready to essay the impossible.

It was this mysteriousness which, beyond all his gifts of head and heart, so strangely fascinated and overawed, – that something about him which made it impossible to reckon his course and take his bearings, – that soul-hunger and quenchless yearning which nothing short of the eternal could satisfy.[8] Isaac Williams could not fathom what went on inside Newman. Often after walking together, when leaving him, have I heard a deep secret sigh which I could not interpret. It seemed to speak of weariness of the world, and of aspirations for something he wished to do and had not yet done. Of the putting out of Church principles he often spoke as of an experiment which he did not know whether the Church of England would bear, and knew not what would be the issue.

The brightest times Williams looked back upon were the Sunday evenings when they dined together with a few friends,

because such repose and relaxation seemed to me to bring out the higher and better parts of Newman's character. I allow that something sarcastic and a freedom of remark would blend with such unbendings, but it was better out in playfulness than fermenting within. But at all times there was a charm about his society which was very taking and I do not wonder at those being carried away who had not been previously formed, like myself, in another, or at all events, an earlier school of faith.[9]

There seems common agreement that the sermons Newman preached at St Mary's were the chief influence on undergraduates. Newman was accustomed to enter (some said to glide into) St Mary's in a surplice, and when he reached the lectern in the middle aisle, to drop down upon his knees, and remain fixed in mental prayer for a few moments, and then to begin the evening service. Many have remarked on the power and beauty with which he read the lessons from Scripture. Lockhart, who was one of those who commented on his reading, remarked, 'some men, but very few like Newman, have the power of using words, as some extraordinary

violinists are said to have used their instruments, so as to draw forth
sounds that would have seemed beyond the reach of earthly music.'[10]
Henry Wilberforce after many years had a vivid recollection of the scene
he described.

> The great church, the congregation which barely filled it, all breathless
> with expectant attention. The gaslight, just at the left hand of the
> pulpit, lowered that the preacher might not be dazzled; themselves
> perhaps standing in the half-darkness under the gallery, and then the
> pause before those words in the 'Ventures of Faith' thrilled through
> them – 'They say unto Him we are able.'[11]

Newman would read a sentence of his sermon rapidly and then pause. He
would read the next sentence and pause again. His voice was extremely
clear and distinct, some said, 'monotonous.' But there was a feeling of
repressed emotion which seemed to gather force as he went on. There
were no gestures, no attempt at rhetorical effect. The preacher was
completely absorbed in the meaning of his text.

The influence of these sermons on undergraduates was immense. James
Anthony Froude described how 'Newman, taking some Scripture character for a text, spoke to us about ourselves, our temptations, our experiences. . . . He seemed to be addressing the most secret consciousness of
each of us, as the eyes of a portrait appear to look at every person in a
room.' He gives an example of Newman's power to effect a realization of
a spiritual truth:

> Newman had described closely some of the incidents of our Lord's
> Passion; he then paused. For a few moments there was a breathless
> silence. Then in a low, clear voice, of which the faintest vibration was
> audible in the farthest corner of St Mary's, he said, 'Now I bid you
> recollect that He to whom these things were done was Almighty God.'
> It was as if an electric stroke had gone through the church, as if every
> person present understood for the first time the meaning of what he
> had all his life been saying.[12]

Dean Lake wrote how much intellectual and religious pleasure many
enjoyed in attending St Mary's four o'clock service on Sunday, and
'although Tait made some very serious attempts to spoil our dinners by
altering the dinner hour, as a penalty, they were only received with
amusement and indifference.' Like Froude, Lake attests that 'the preacher

seemed to enter into the very minds of his hearers, and, as it were, to reveal them to themselves, and to tell them their very innermost thoughts.[13] Principal Shairp made the same point, 'He laid his finger – gently, yet how powerfully – on some inner place in the hearer's heart, and told him things about himself he had never known till then.'[14]

William Lockhart later wrote, 'he had the wondrous, supernatural power of raising the mind to God, and of rooting deeply in us a personal conviction of God, and a sense of its presence. He compelled us to an intuitive perception of moral obligation.'[15]

In addition to being the parish church, St Mary's was also the University Church. The University made use of it chiefly for the preaching of sermons on Sundays and Saints' Days. J. M. Capes later described the many shades of opinion that were put forth in the course of a year:

> In the morning (the period being that of which we are chiefly speaking) the Fathers are upheld, in the afternoon they are ridiculed; to-day baptismal regeneration is preached, next Sunday we are taught the Lutheran 'justification by faith only'; a 'select preacher' eulogises the *Tracts for the Times*, and is followed by a country parson, who broadly hints that Mr. Newman and Dr. Pusey are disguised Jesuits; and the 'Bampton Lecturer' for the year expounds some systematic view or crotchet of his own, which if not the most flagrantly heretical, is probably the most irresistibly somniferous of all the heretical and somniferous topics to which this celebrated pulpit gives birth.

Capes compares these sermons with those of Newman which followed on them. In addition to the townspeople

> scattered thickly throughout the church were seen a crowd of black-gowned listeners, young and middle-aged, and sometimes, though rarely, old, who thronged to hear the clear, even, earnest, and monotonous voice of one whose whole soul was in every word he uttered; and who, with whatever errors or gradual changes he displayed, was manifestly possessed with the ideas of God, of sin, of death, of judgment, and of eternity.[16]

Newman's influence spread far beyond Oxford owing to his writings but especially to his published sermons. At a time when the Church seemed internally divided and there were conflicting views of dogma and revelation, Newman's theological works provided a platform on which to stand. To many who deplored the low spiritual temperature of the Church, Newman's sermons helped people to grow spiritually. Both before and after his conversion he received letters of gratitude for his services to the Church and for the writer's own spiritual development. For example, H. L. K. Bruce, 15 October 1843, 'I cannot help testifying on this occasion my strong sense of the glorious services you have conferred on the Church – the greatest in my esteem since Bull and Waterland saved us from the curse of Arius and Socinus. For myself I owe to your labours that I have been sent in search of something better than the fantastic vagaries that this age considers theology.' An extant letter, 27 February 1845, with name erased, reads, 'I cannot conclude without begging to be allowed to express my deep and heartfelt gratitude to you for the comfort, consolation and hope I have derived from your sermons. They have solved for me many difficulties, cheered me in despondency, strengthened me against temptation, and fixed more firmly in my mind those everlasting truths, so necessary to be felt by all.' Just after his conversion a country gentleman, W. Sancroft Holmes, wrote on 25 November 1845, 'You are well known to me, as you are to thousands so to speak. I have lived on your writings; I have looked up to you as my spiritual Master.' But it was not only within the Church that Newman's sermons were read. Newman was highly regarded by many of the Dissenters and when his sermons were republished in 1868 they sold in large numbers among them. (*LD* XXIV, 177, n. 1)

Isaac Williams commented on the spread of the Movement as indicated by the number of visitors who came to Oxford from Ireland, Scotland, and especially from America. Among those who came from Ireland were James Todd, tutor at Trinity College, Dublin, who attacked the popular notion of the Pope as Antichrist; Lord Adare, M.P. for West Glamorgan, a member of a group of High Churchmen in Ireland who adopted Tractarian views; and Aubrey de Vere, who was at Trinity College and visited Newman in Oxford in 1838, and became a lifelong friend. He left a picture of Newman at this first encounter.

Early in the evening a singularly graceful figure in cap and gown glided into the room. The slight form and gracious address might have belonged to a youthful ascetic of the middle ages or a graceful and high-bred lady of our own days. He was pale and thin almost to emaciation, swift of pace, but, when not walking, intensely still, with a voice sweet and pathetic both, but so distinct that you could count each vowel and consonant in every word. When touching upon subjects which interested him much, he used gestures rapid and decisive, though not vehement; and while in the expression of thoughts on important subjects there was often a restrained ardour about him; yet, if individuals were in question, he spoke severely of none, however widely their opinions might differ from his. As we parted, I asked him why the cathedral bells rang so loud at so late an hour. 'Only some young men keeping themselves warm', he answered.[17]

Later de Vere used to visit Newman almost every summer in Birmingham and seems to have been the first to recognize the harmonious blend of seemingly opposite qualities in Newman's personality. Newman, he said, had 'a tenderness marked by a smile of magical sweetness that had nothing of softness.' He had an unusual combination of a logical mind and an intuitive and vivid imagination. He was a man of action and of contemplation, with an interest in earthly matters as well as in the supernatural world.[18] Paradoxically despite the complexity of Newman's personality, George Smythe, poet, friend of Faber, and parliamentarian, after meeting Newman in 1839, thought him 'more simple than any other man I ever met except the Duke of Wellington'.[19]

Of the Americans who visited Oxford, Williams mentioned a Dissenting preacher and D. D. with whom Newman and Pusey were particularly impressed. This was probably Leonard Woods, noted American scholar, theologian and Presbyterian, who visited Oxford from 18 to 28 October 1840. He had become the President of Bowdoin College in 1839. At the time of his death in 1879 Newman wrote of him, 'the impression he made upon me during the short period of our acquaintance was great . . . At Oxford we all thought that he would become either an Anglican or a Catholic. Isaac Williams also mentioned John Williams, an Episcopalian from Washington College, Hartford, Connecticut, who visited him at Bisley. Newman entertained him at Oxford in October 1840. He later became Bishop of the Diocese of Connecticut.

Prior to those mentioned by Williams, came John Henry Hopkins, first Protestant Episcopal Bishop of Vermont from 2 to 8 April 1839, and John Strachan, Bishop of Toronto, who visited in October 1839 while Newman was away, but who wrote on 23 May 1840, 'the sound principles which your writings and those of your friends are disseminating in England are rapidly gaining ground in the United States and this Province'. (*LD* VII, 59–60; 163–4, and n. 1)

In late 1838 William George Ward adopted Tractarian principles and was joined by Frederick Oakeley who from 1839 was minister of Margaret Street Chapel in London which became a centre for Tractarian worship. Oakeley later paid tribute to Newman's leadership in the following words:

> The spirit of Mr. Newman, its great chieftain, was diffused more or less through its whole range; and no one who associated with him during its progress can ever forget the cautious wisdom with which he proceeded in every step: repressing indiscreet zeal, sustaining the weak-minded, steadying the irresolute, softening the over-severe, and ever interposing the sage counsel and the charitable construction in aid of the erring judgment or in arrest of the hasty censure.[20]

He with Faber, Dalgairns, James Anthony Froude and John Brande Morris became what sometimes has been called the 'extreme' wing of the party. Meanwhile in London there were new accessions to the Movement. In 1837 James Hope and Edward Badeley, both London lawyers, became close friends of Newman, while Thomas Dyke Acland, M.P. for West Somerset, together with his friends S. F. Wood and Robert Williams, was at the centre of a group of London Tractarians. Nor did the Movement fail to penetrate Cambridge University. J. F. Russell, one of the leading members of the Camden Society, became one of the first Cambridge sympathisers with it. He with W. J. Irons visited Newman and Pusey in November 1837 and left a vivid account of it in a letter to a friend, a small portion of which is here transcribed:

> On Wednesday, after breakfast, Irons and I called on Newman. He was seated at a small desk in a comfortable room, stored with books. He is a dark, middle-aged, middle-sized man, with lanky black hair and large spectacles, thin, gentlemanly, and very insinuating. He received us with the greatest kindness, and said he had been invited to meet us at Pusey's, but had 'so grevious [*sic*] a cold' that he feared he could not come. Irons, however, overruled all objections, and when we left him he gave us to understand that we should meet him.

After narrating the dinner conversation, Russell described how Pusey's children ran into the room and one climbed on Newman's knee and hugged him, Newman then putting his spectacles on him, and next on his sister, and great was the merriment of the Puseyan progeny. 'Newman, it is said, hates ecclesiastical conversation. He writes so much that when in society he seems always inclined to talk on light, amusing subjects. He told them a story of an old woman who had a broomstick which would go to the well, draw water, and do many other things for her; how the old woman got tired of the broomstick, and wishing to destroy it broke it in twain, and how, to the old woman's great chagrin and disappointment, *two* live broomsticks grew from the broken parts of the old one!' (*LD* VI, 164–5)

SAILING ALONG

During the spring, Newman suffered from the perennial problem with his teeth. He added a note later to his entries in his diary about this affliction. '*From the time I was 16, my teeth were slowly decaying, with pain concomitant all along.*' (*LD* VII, 61, 70) Having written so much he also suffered from pains in his wrist. He writes to Jemima on 25 March, 'This is the tenth letter I have written today, and my hand is tired.' (*LD* VII, 55) In 1869 he once wrote twenty letters in one day, eighteen on another day. (*LD* XXIV, 389, 256) By 1839 Newman was accustomed to the opposition of the Peculiars and he laughed at the absurd stories told about himself and fellow Tractarians. Newman mentioned in a letter that the Master of University 'had been assured by a lady at Cheltenham that we offered sacrifices every morning. He explained it by morning prayers. No, she said, it was not that – she knew for certain we killed *something*, she did not know what – (qu. little children? or each other? or frogs and spiders? or what?)' (*LD* VII, 17) Perhaps the most famous story is the one about Pusey travelling in a coach and hearing a woman saying that she knew for a fact that Dr. Pusey sacrificed a lamb on Fridays. Pusey intervened and said, 'Madam, I am Dr. Pusey, and I assure you I do not know how to kill a lamb.'

The skies were still bright, the winds filling the sails. In 1838 the Tracts had sold out within six months, reports came in of the spread of Tractarian principles, e.g., from Hook of Leeds, who reported to New-man, 'Right principles are advancing here in an astonishing manner. I do not mean so much here in Leeds . . . but throughout the West Riding. . . . A thousand thanks for the 14th Sermon in your last Volume ['The Greatness and Littleness of Human Life']. Had you written nothing else I should love you for that.' (*LD* VII, 54) So, too, at Oxford, despite the opposition of the Heads of Houses. Newman wrote to Jemima, 'How long good opinions are to prosper here, I know not – but certainly they are growing most remarkably at present. At St John's the Common Room (of

10 fellows) has gradually come round – and this is pretty much the case
every where. A stranger the other day promised me £100 a year to give
away in theological scholarships etc.' (*LD* VII, 66)

H. A. Woodgate dedicated his Bampton Lectures to Newman, the text
of which was seconded by 'a council of men, including Bowden and
Johnson.' 'To/ the Reverend/ John Henry Newman, B.D./ Fellow of
Oriel College/ in token of long and intimate friendship,/ and as a tribute
of respect/ to the highest intellectual endowments,/ consecrated,/
throughout a life of consistent purity and holiness,/ to the cause of
Christ's Church,/ this volume is inscribed, by his sincere and affectionate
friend,/ H.A.W.' (*LD* VII, 77, n. 1)

Now that the spring issue of the *British Critic* was out, Newman felt he
had a breathing space, which he intended to use to bring out a second
edition of the *Arians*. Though he made notes for this, a second edition
was not published. 'In the course of my reading I intend to put notes to
our Translation of Theodoret's Heresies etc., to translate S. Cyril against
Nestorius, and to finish (if possible) my edition of S. Dionysius. These
luckily will lie in the way and hardly take me more time. Accordingly I
am missing my yearly lectures in Ad. de Br's Chapel this term – they
were to have been a continuation of Tract 85 [Lectures on the Scripture
Proof of the Doctrines of the Church. Part I, *DA*, 109–253] – and would
have taken me much thought and reading. The question of the Pope's
being Antichrist would have come in.' Notes for these lectures are extant
in the Appendix to his diary. (*LD* VII, 65–6, 483–8)

A monument to the memory of Newman's mother, executed by his old
Ealing classmate and friend, Westmacott, was put up in the Littlemore
chapel on 20 June. The inscription read:

> Sacred to the memory of Jemima Newman/ who laid the first stone of
> this chapel,/ 21st July 1835,/ and died before it was finished,/ 17th
> May 1836,/ in the 64th year of her age./
> Cast me not away in the time of age; forsake me not when
>   My strength faileth me.
> Until I have showed thy strength unto this generation,
>   and power to all them that are yet for to come.

The text was taken from the Visitation Service in the Book of Common
Prayer. Newman's mother had quoted parts of that psalm and applied it
to herself in a letter to him. (*LD* VII, 93, 127, and n. 2)

Editing the *British Critic* added to Newman's already busy life. Part of his problem as editor was the failure of some contributors to meet deadlines, which meant that Newman had to compose articles himself to fill up an issue. The bright side of this was that he himself composed a number of perceptive articles during 1839–41, which he later republished in *Essays Critical and Historical*. Some of these are of historical importance. In January 1839 he published an article on the Epistles of St Ignatius, in which he remarked with regard to the Fathers, especially the apostolical Fathers, 'if a man begins by summoning them before him, instead of betaking himself to them, – by seeking to make them evidence for modern dogmas, instead of throwing his mind upon their text, and drawing from them their own doctrines, – he will to a certainty miss their sense'. This was precisely the mistake Newman had made and admits once again having done so. (*Ess*. I, 228, 227) He would come to recognize that he made another mistake in relying on the Anglican Divines for statements from the Fathers with regard to the Roman Catholic Church. Moreover to interpret any Father aright one must have a knowledge of theology, particularly the theology of other Fathers of the Church. It was owing to this lack that Newman attributed Keble's inability to follow him in his later thinking. At this point, however, Newman shows the existence of 'dogmatic expressions' which form a perfect continuity with the fourth-century Fathers and which already exist in the writings of St. Ignatius.

It should likewise be noted that, in dealing with these various 'dogmatic expressions', Newman uses the argument from converging probabilities, a theory he would later develop in the *Grammar of Assent*. Passing from the form of St Ignatius's teaching on justification is the Catholic, not the Protestant, teaching that salvation is communicated to man, not merely by the atonement of Christ, but by the risen Christ, present to man in the sacraments. Since this is of capital importance in Newman's own spiritual theology with regard to sanctification it deserves to be quoted in full:

> It would seem then to be certain, that Ignatius considers our life and salvation to lie, not in the Atonement by itself, but in the Incarnation; but neither in the Incarnation nor Atonement as past events, but, as present facts, in an existing mode, in which our Saviour comes to us; or, to speak more plainly, in our Saviour Himself, who is God in our flesh which has been offered up on the Cross in sacrifice, which has died and has risen. The being made man, the being crucified in atonement, the being raised again, are the three past events to which the Eternal Son has vouchsafed to become to us what He is, a Saviour; and those who omit the Resurrection in their view of the divine

economy, are as really defective in faith as if they omitted the Crucifixion. On the Cross He paid the debt of the world, but as He could not have been crucified without first taking flesh, so again He could not, as it would seem, apply His atonement without first rising again. Accordingly, St Ignatius speaks of our being saved and living not simply in the Atonement, but, as the passages already quoted signify, in the flesh and blood of the risen Lord, first sacrificed for us, and then communicated to us. (*Ess.* I, 247–8)

At this time Newman had supreme confidence in his controversial status, and 'still growing success, in recommending it to others'. (*Apo.*, 93) In this feeling he composed and published in the *British Critic* an important article, 'The State of Religious Parties', later titled 'Prospects of the Anglican Church', in which he examined the reasons for the spread of Catholic principles. Even before men entered intellectually into their truth, 'there was a growing tendency toward the character of mind and feeling of which Catholic doctrines are the just expression'. Writers such as Walter Scott, Wordsworth and Coleridge indicate what was going on in men's minds, showing that the present state of affairs are 'the result of causes far deeper than political or other visible agencies, – the spiritual awakening of spiritual wants.' (*Ess.* I, 272)

To show the truth of this Newman referred to the different theological antecedents of those who were preaching the revived doctrines. This led him to acknowledge and lament the extravagances of some of their disciples and said the doctrines themselves should not be condemned because of these aberrations, and quoted from the preface of 'Plain Sermons' which tried to discourage such extravagances.

The future of the Anglican Church, as a new birth of ancient religion of Antiquity, he did not predict, but ventured to say that 'neither Puritanism nor Liberalism had any permanent inheritance within her.' As to the latter he thought the formularies of the Church would prevent it from making serious inroads upon the clergy, and it is 'too cold a principle to prevail with the multitude'. As to the former, Puritanism or Evangelicalism has no intellectual basis; no internal ties, no principle of unity, no theology. Its adherents are already separating from each other; 'they will melt away like a snow-drift'. The present situation will not continue:

In the present day mistiness is the mother of wisdom. A man who can set down a half a dozen general propositions, which escape from destroying one another only by being diluted into truisms, who can hold the balance between opposites so skilfully as to do without fulcrum or beam, who never enunciates a truth without guarding himself against being supposed to exclude the contradictory, who holds that Scripture is the only authority, yet that the Church is to be deferred to, that faith only justifies, yet that it does not justify without works, that grace does not depend on the sacraments, yet is not given without them, that bishops are a divine ordinance, yet those who have them not are in the same religious condition as those who have, – this is your safe man and the hope of the Church; this is what the Church is said to want, not party men, but sensible, temperate, sober, well-judging persons, to guide it through the channel of No-meaning, between the Scylla and Charybdis of Aye and No. (*Ess.* I, 302)

Men who read, however, will not be able to keep standing in that very attitude which is called 'sound Church-of-Englandism or orthodox Prot-estantism'. 'Premises imply conclusions; germs lead to developments; principles have issues; doctrines lead to action. . . . They may take one view or another . . . but it will be a consistent view. It may be Rationalism or Erastianism, or Popery, or Catholicity; but it will be real.' Newman ended with an appeal to the ultra-Protestants:

Surely it will be better for you . . . instead of reproaching them /the Tractarians/ with a storm, which is none of their raising, to thank them for making the best of a bad matter, or not the worst, if not the best. The current of the age cannot be stopped, but it may be directed; and it is better that it should find its way into the Anglican port, than that it should be propelled into Popery, or drifted upon unbelief. . . . Would you rather have your sons and daughters members of the Church of England or of the Church of Rome? (*Ess.* I, 305–7)

Little did Newman realize that all belief in a *Via Media* would soon vanish forever from his mind.

SPRINGING A LEAK

The Long Vacation started early and Newman was alone in the College except for the mice, 'which are at this moment making a sociable rustling among my papers and behind the arras', he wrote to Henry Wilberforce.

(*LD* VII, 106) He was devoting his time to reading up the Eutychian controversy in preparation for a Latin edition of Dionysius the Areopagite of Alexandria, which he had left off several years before. Eutyches, having been condemned by a synod for holding one nature in Christ, was acquitted by the General Council of Ephesus. At the insistence of Pope Leo the Council of Chalcedon (451) was called and it rejected both the Council of Ephesus and the doctrine of Eutyches, declaring Christ to be not only 'of' but 'in' two natures. As he later wrote to Mrs William Froude on 5 April,

> I found the Eastern Church under the superintendence (as I may call it) of Pope Leo. I found that *he* had made the Fathers of the Council to unsay their decree and pass another. . . . I found that Pope Leo based his authority upon St Peter. I found the Fathers of the Council crying out 'Peter hath spoken by the mouth of Leo', when they altered their decree.

The Churches of the East, resenting Western interference on the part of Leo, went into schism for thirty-five years, the Eutychians becoming the extreme party; the Monophysites, the moderate party.

At first the only things about the Council of Chalcedon that struck Newman, as he wrote to Rogers, were 'the great power of the Pope (as great as he claims now almost), and the marvellous interference of the civil power, as great almost as in our kings.' (*LD* VII, 105) But by the end of August he had become alarmed, for he saw an analogy between the situation of the fifth century and that of the Church of the *Via Media*. 'I saw my face in that mirror, and I was a Monophysite. The Church of the *Via Media* was in the position of the Oriental communion, Rome was, where she now is; and the Protestants were the Eutychians.' (*Apo.*, 114)

In *Difficulties of Anglicans* Newman explained, 'I thought I saw in the controversy . . . and in the Ecumenical Council connected with it, a clear interpretation of the present state of Christendom, and a key to the different parties and personages who have figured on the Catholic or the Protestant side at and since the era of the Reformation.' The Anglo-Catholics (subscribers to the *Via Media*), though moderates, could in theory, but not in practice, disassociate themselves from the Protestants, who were the extreme party, and both were in separation from Rome, which stood where it always was. (*Diff.* I, 373)

Friends who were more sympathetic to Rome than Newman put into his hands an article by Wiseman in the *Dublin Review* on the Anglican claims. It drew a parallel between the Donatists and the Anglicans. At first the article did not disturb Newman because he thought that an analogy was not exact, since the Donatist controversy took place in Africa, and was a dispute between altar and altar and not between Churches. But Robert Williams, whom Newman described in the *Apologia* as 'my friend, an anxiously religious man, now, as then, very dear to me, a Protestant still', pointed out the palmary words of St Augustine, which were contained in one of the extracts made in the Review, and which had escaped Newman's notice. 'Securus judicat orbis terrarum.' He kept repeating these words, which went beyond the Donatists and applied to the Monophysites as well. Wiseman translated it as 'Wherefore, the entire world judges with *security*, that they are not good, who separate themselves from the entire world, in whatever part of the entire world.' 'They gave a cogency to the Article, which had escaped me at first. They decided ecclesiastical questions on a simpler rule than that of Antiquity, nay, St Augustine was one of the prime oracles of Antiquity; here then Antiquity was deciding against itself.' (*Apo.*, 116–7)

A letter to Mrs. William Froude sheds a special light on this.

The fact, to which the Monophysite controversy had opened my eyes, that antagonists of Rome, and Churches in isolation, were always wrong in primitive times, and which I had felt to be a *presumption* against ourselves, this article went on to maintain as a *recognised principle and rule* in those same ages. It professed that the *fact* of isolation and opposition was *always taken* as a *sufficient* condemnation of bodies so circumstanced, and to that extent that the question was not asked *how did the quarrel arise?* which was right, and which wrong? who made the separation? but that the *fact* of separation was reckoned anciently as decisive against the body separated. This was argued chiefly from the language of St Augustine, as elicited in the Donatist controversy, and the same sort of *minute* parallel was drawn between the state of the Donatists and our own, which I had felt on reading the history of the Monophysites. (9 April 1844)

In the *Apologia* Newman describes the effect of these words upon him:

Who can account for the impressions which are made on him? For a mere sentence, the words of St. Augustine, struck me with a power which I never had felt from any words before. To take a familiar instance, they were like the 'Turn again Whittington' of the chime; or, to take a more serious one, they were like the 'Tolle, lege, – Tolle, lege,' of the child, which converted St. Augustine himself. 'Securus judicat orbis terrarum!' By those great words of the ancient Father, interpreting and summing up the long and varied course of ecclesiastical history, the theory of the *Via Media* was absolutely pulverized.[21]

I became excited at the view thus opened upon me. (*Apo.*, 117)

Newman mentioned his feelings to only two persons: Rogers and Henry Wilberforce. To the former he wrote on 22 September, regarding the article:

It does certainly come upon one that we are not at the bottom of things. At this moment we have sprung a leak, and the worst of it is that those sharp fellows, Ward, Stanley and Co will not let one go to sleep upon it. . . . How are we to keep hot heads from going over? Let alone ourselves. I think I shall get Keble to answer it. . . . And now, Carissime, good bye. It is no laughing matter. . . . I will not blink the question, so be it; but don't suppose I am a madcap to take up notions suddenly. Only there is an uncomfortable vista opened which was closed before. I am writing upon *first* feelings. (*LD* VII, 154–5)[22]

From 5 to 11 October Newman visited Henry Wilberforce at Bransgore, and to him he revealed his doubt. In 1869 Henry published an account of the meeting.

It was in the beginning of October, 1839, that he made the astounding confidence, mentioning the two subjects which had inspired the doubt, the position of St. Leo in the Monophysite controversy, and the principle, 'securus judicat orbis terrarum' in that of the Donatists. He added that he felt confident that when he returned to his rooms, and was able fully and calmly to consider the whole matter, he should see his way completely out of the difficulty. But, he said, I cannot conceal from myself, that for the first time since I began the study of theology, a vista has been opened before me, to the end of which I do not see. He was walking in the New Forest, and he borrowed the form of his expression from the surrounding scenery. His companion, upon whom such a fear came like a thunderstroke, expressed his hope that Mr Newman might die rather than take such a step. He replied, with deep earnestness, that he had thought if ever the time should come when he was in serious danger, of asking his friends to pray, that, if it was not indeed the will of God, he might be taken away before he did it. Of such a meanwhile he spoke only as a possibility in the future, by no means as of a thing that had already arrived. But he added, with especial reference to Dr Wiseman's article on the Donatists 'It is quite necessary that I should give a satisfactory answer to it, or I shall have the young men around me – such men,' he added, 'as [W. G.] Ward of Balliol – going over to Rome.'[23]

How did Newman react intellectually and spiritually to this experience? He recognized, as he said in the *Apologia*, that 'I had a good deal to learn on the question of the Churches, and perhaps some new light was coming upon me. He who has seen a ghost, cannot be as if he had never seen it. The heavens had opened and closed again. The thought for the moment had been, "The Church of Rome will be found right after all;" and then it had vanished. My old convictions remained as before.' (*Apo.*, 118) On 27 October he preached 'Divine Calls', a sermon commonly ignored by biographers and commentators, though Newman mentions it in the *Apologia* in this connection. In the sermon, he remarked, 'they who are living religiously have from time to time truths they did not know before, or had no need to consider, brought before them forcibly; truths which involve duties, which are in fact precepts, and claim obedience'. In this sermon, Newman affirms the close connection between the search for truth (i.e., religious truth) and holiness. Of the various modes of viewing truth,

> Only one is the truth and the perfect truth. . . . God knows which it is; and towards that one and only Truth He is leading us forward. He is leading forward His redeemed . . . to the one perfect knowledge and obedience to Christ; not, however, without their co-operation, but by means of calls which they are to obey, and which if they do not obey, they lose place, and fall behind in their heavenly course. He leads them forward. . . . We pass from one state of knowledge to another; we are introduced into a higher region from a lower, by listening to Christ's call and obeying it. (*PPS* VIII, 2, 27–8)

Newman however only quotes in the *Apologia* the ending of the sermon, which derides worldly success and fame in comparison of obedience to insight into truth. This, however, was not a new idea, for in the dialogue that takes place in 'Home Thoughts from Abroad', one of the disputants attacks the *Via Media* as a theory which was stuck once and for all with the Non-jurors, to which his opponent retorts, 'I see you are of those who think success and the applause of men everything, not bearing to consider, *first*, whether a view be true, and then to incur boldly the "reproach" of upholding it. Surely, the Truth has in no age been popular and those who preached it have been thought idiots, and died without visible fruit of their labours.' (*DA*, 20) Ironically the principle is now applied to relinquishing the *Via Media* and perhaps even to becoming Roman.

This principle seems to have been in his thoughts at this time, for the Sunday following the preaching of the sermon, 'Divine Calls', Newman preached an older sermon on 'The Vanity of Human Glory', and in a letter to be given to Williams, if Woods thought best, as will shortly be considered, Newman remarks that 'if at any future time, I have any view opened to me, I will try not to turn from it, but will pursue it, wherever it may lead. I am not aware of having any hindrance, whether from fear of clamour, or regard for consistency, or even love of friends, which would keep me from joining the Church of Rome, were I persuaded I ought to do so.' (*LD* VII, 180)

There is another important sermon preached on 10 November, No. 543, on inward holiness as a guide to test the holiness and truth of doctrines which may perplex a believer. It gives an insight into Newman's inner dispositions at this time: trust in God's personal Providence and a determination to live more strictly, as a means of obtaining God's guidance into Truth.

> To Him then let us commit ourselves in all perplexities. In all darkness He is our light – He will lead us forward in His own way. If we can say with sincerity about ourselves and brethren, that we verily do believe we and they are seeking holiness, seeking to be new creatures more and more day by day, seeking to live more and more strictly, why need we care? Why may we not cast all our care on Him who careth for us? (1 Pet. 5) – Why will we not repose ourselves in the thought that He who gave us, in such measure as we have it, an anointing of divine grace, will . . . cleanse our soiled sight and quicken our spiritual perceptions, and lead us into His perfect way in the day of His power. (*Ser.* I, 250)

Accordingly one of the first actions Newman took was to increase the severity of his customary fasting. Whereas the previous Lent he had fasted until 5 p.m., on the Ember Day, 21 September, he wrote in his journal, 'To my surprise I found that on Wednesday and yesterday

(Ember) I could fast till the evening without inconvenience. . . . I did not taste bread, biscuit, or any food whatever either day till 8 o'clock in the evening. . . . Gratias tibi Domine – whither art Thou leading me?' (*AW*, 216) Prayer and fasting would be the means by which he struggled toward the Truth, and which he would constantly recommend to persons attracted to Rome.

Although Newman says in the *Apologia* that the *Via Media* had come down under the blows of St Leo, he also asserts that 'it was not at all certain as yet, even that we had not the Note of Catholicity; but, if not this, we had others. My first business then, was to examine this question carefully, and see, whether a great deal could not be said after all for the Anglican Church, in spite of its acknowledged short-comings.' Accordingly upon his return from visiting Wilberforce, he set to work answering the argument of Wiseman, as he later told Mrs Froude.

It is my sincere belief and principle, that it is right to resist doubts and to put aside objections to the form of doctrine and the religious system in which we find ourselves. I think such resistance pleasing to God. If it is His will to lead us from them, if the doubt comes from Him, He will repeat the suggestion. He will call us again as He called Samuel; He will make our way clear to us. Fancies, excitements, feelings go and never return; truth comes again and is importunate. The system in which we have been placed is God's voice to us, till he supersede it. (9 April 1844)

The article appeared in the *British Critic* in January 1840 under the title, 'The Catholicity of the Anglican Church', and addresses the difficulty, 'the Church being "one body" how can we, estranged as we are from every part of it except our own dependencies, unrecognized and without intercommunion, maintain our right to be considered part of that body?' He replies, 'one point is acknowledged, one must be conceded, and one will be maintained, by all Anglo-Catholics; that the Church is One, is the point of *doctrine*; that we are estranged from the body of the Church, is the point of *fact*; and that we still have the means of grace among us, is our point of *controversy*.' (*Ess*. II, 16–17) In answer to the objection against the Anglican Church he affirmed that the separate portions of the Church need not be united together, for their essential completeness, except by the tie of descent from one original, i.e., by apostolic succession.

Newman then develops his view of unity. Bishops are the centre of unity. 'Each is the ultimate centre of unity and independent channel of grace; they are all equal, and schism consists in separating from them, or setting up against them in their particular place. Introducing one Church into the heart of another, or erecting altar against altar, is schism, in the ecclesiastical sense of the word, and forfeits the gifts of the Gospel, for it strikes at the principle of unity and touches the life of the Church. Such is the essence of unity, and the essence of schism: but an organized union of Churches, though proper and fitting, does not enter into the formal notion of a Church.' (*Ess.* II, 23–4) Granted that perfect intercommunion was the state of the Church of the Fathers, the question is whether it is an *essential* note, a *sine qua non* or 'that the essence of the Church does not rather lie in the possession of the Apostolic Succession.' (*Ess.* II, 39)

As to St. Augustine's saying with regard to the Donatists, 'securus judicat orbis terrarum,' it is hard to suppose that St. Augustine intended this 'as a theological verity equally sacred as an article in the Creed. . . . Not less unreasonable surely is it to make a saying of St. Augustine the turning point of our religion, and to dispense with all other truths in order to maintain this in the letter.' (*Ess.* II, 41–3) All rules have their exceptions. Newman cited a number of instances from patristic history, such as Melitius and Lucifer, Bishop of Cagliari in Sardinia, to show that despite their separation from Rome they were considered saints. There are moreover other notes of the Church, and one is *life*. Newman concludes that 'much as Roman Catholics may denounce us at present as schismatical, they could not resist us, if the Anglican communion had but that one Note of the Church upon it, to which all these instances point, – sanctity'. And it is the lack of this in Roman actions, that Newman urges against the Roman Church with words which he later described as 'savage and ungrateful.'

Till we see in them as a Church more straightforwardness, truth and openness, more of severe obedience to God's least commandments, more scrupulousness about means, less of a political, scheming, grasping spirit, less of intrigue, less that looks hollow and superficial, less accommodation to the tastes of the vulgar, less subserviency to the vices of the rich, less humouring of men's morbid and wayward imaginations, less indulgence of their low and carnal superstitions, less intimacy with the revolutionary spirit of the day, we will keep aloof from them as we do. . . . 'By their fruits ye shall know them.' . . . We see it attempting to gain converts among us, by unreal representations of its doctrines, plausible statements, bold assertions, appeals to the weaknesses of human nature, to our fancies, our eccentricities, our fears, our frivolities, our false philosophies. We see its agents smiling and nodding and ducking to attract attention, as gipsies make up to truant boys, holding out tales for the nursery, and pretty pictures, and gold gingerbread, and physic concealed in jam, and sugarplums for good children.

Who can but feel shame when the religion of Ximenes, Borromeo, and Pascal is so overlaid? . . . We Englishmen like manliness, openness, consistency, truth. Rome will never gain on us till she learns these virtues, and uses them. . . . Till she ceases to be what she practically is, a union is impossible between her and England; but if she does reform, . . . then it will be our Church's duty at once to join in communion with the Continental Churches, . . . And though we shall not live to see that day, at least we are bound to pray for it; we are bound to pray for our brethren that they and we may be led together into the pure light of the Gospel, and be one as once we were. . . . It was most touching news to be told, as we were lately, that Christians on the Continent were praying together for the spiritual well-being of England. We are their debtors thereby. May the prayer return abundantly into their own bosom, and while they care for our souls may their own be prospered! May they gain light while they aim at unity, and grow in faith while they manifest their love! We too have our duties to them; not of reviling, not of slandering, not of hating, though political interests require it; but the duty of loving brethren still more abundantly in spirit, whose faces, for our sins and their sins, we are not allowed to see in the flesh. (*Ess.* II, 70–3)

As time went on the argument of sanctity in the Church of England and the supposed lack of it in the Catholic Church assumed greater importance in his search for the Truth. For the moment, however, the view advanced in his article 'kept me quiet for nearly two years, that is, till the Autumn of 1841'. A practical effect, however, was his attempt to give up St Mary's. This he proposed to the College in 1840, wishing to retain Littlemore, but Hawkins the Provost would not hear of the separation.

Meanwhile Wood communicated to Newman his fears about Robert Williams' defecting to Rome. Newman composed a letter to Williams to be given to him if Wood thought fit. It sums up the suggestions he would subsequently use in dissuading persons from converting to Rome. By way of introduction he remarked, 'I really believe I say truly that did I see cause to suspect the Roman Church was in the right, I would try not to be unfaithful to the light given me.' But he would first give two or three years 'as a time of religious preparation towards forming a judgment,' nor would he take such a step 'without having the sanction of one or two persons whom I most looked up to and trusted'. Under ordinary circumstances he felt it an obligation 'to remain where God has placed us. . . . It is surely a much less sin to *remain in*, than to *change to*, a wrong faith.' To Miss Giberne, who related a case of a girl who wanted to change her religion, he wrote, 'our Saviour bids us "count the cost [Luke 14: 28]," which implies taking time before acting.' It was a quotation he would often use in subsequent letters, as he himself noticed when he was going over his correspondence of these years. He added, 'she should act on her convictions, if they are such, but that she should not mistake momentary or accidental feelings for convictions.' (*LD* VII, 180–1, 165)

Two events happened which were a source of embarrassment. John Brande Morris, a Fellow of Exeter College from 1837–46, was known for his extremism and somewhat eccentric ways which earned him the nickname 'Simon Stylites'. A story circulated 'that Morris once at a breakfast table after a long silence turned round to a nice and pretty young lady who was next to him and said with his peculiar smile that he thought it not worse to burn a man for heresy than to hang him for sheepstealing.' (Newman to Thomas Mozley, 21 February, 1843) While Newman was away at the end of September and the beginning of October, the only time he was away from Oxford in a year, his place was taken by J. B. Morris whom Newman described as 'a most simple minded conscientious fellow – but as little possesst of tact or common sense as he is great in other departments,' preached on his favourite topic 'fasting'. 'As the angels feasted on festivals,' it would be a good thing 'to make the brute creation fast on fast days'. Newman commented, 'may he (salvis ossibus suis) have a fasting horse the next time he goes steeple chasing'. The *faux pas* was followed up the next Sunday, when he preached the Roman Catholic doctrine of the Mass and 'added in energetic terms that every one was an unbeliever, carnal, and so forth, who did not hold it.' This was too much for the Vice-Chancellor, who took his family away from St Mary's and Morris was 'had up before him – his sermon officially examined – and he formally admonished'. The Vice-Chancellor then wrote to the Bishop who wrote to Newman, and 'then came a letter (very kind) from the Bishop to Morris, and that *at last* ended the affair.' But since then, Newman added, 'a worse matter has arisen.' (*LD* VII, 176–7, 201)

Newman received a report from William Dodsworth that on a visit to

Dr Rock at Alton Towers, Bloxam, Newman's curate, had attended service at the Romish chapel, in which he bowed down at the elevation of the host. Newman reported this and Bloxam's explanation to the Bishop. Bloxam said that he went into the gallery of the chapel every morning and evening, that after morning service he used to stay some time on his knees, during which time the family came in and had Service, and that he did not take part in the Low Mass on Friday but remained just as on the other days without changing his posture.

The Bishop was irritated at Newman's reporting this to him, as being a matter between his curate and himself. Newman later admitted it was a mistake to have brought it to the attention of the Bishop, 'but this has really been the source of many of my indiscretions, a great impatience of keeping things back and not letting all come out. It was the cause of Number 90'. The correspondence with the Bishop carried on, and the latter administered a somewhat pompously worded admonition, 'and here, My Dear Sir, let me entreat you to exert your own high and influential name among a numerous body of the Clergy, and young men destined for orders who look up to you, – to discourage by every means in your power indiscretions similar to Mr Bloxam's or any little extravagances, the results of youth – harmless perhaps in themselves, but . . . when they occur, and are known, tend to retard the progress of sound and high Church principles which you inculcate.' Newman replied, 'I can assure your Lordship that my efforts neither are nor have been wanting in keeping younger men from the indiscretions to which you allude; but I feel obliged by being reminded of the duty of making them.' The correspondence ended amicably, the Bishop writing, 'Be assured it will always give me pleasure to hear from you, and to have the most unreserved of friendly communication.' (*LD* VII, 184–5, 189–90. 200–1)

CHAPTER SEVENTEEN

The Calm before the Storm

If the Church of England was in schism, as Newman's first doubts suggested, then it followed that it must rejoin the Roman Church. This, however, could not be done without Rome reforming itself. But prayer for unity was both possible and desirable. Even after administering a lashing to the Roman Catholics at the end of his answer to Wiseman, he concluded, 'And though we shall not live to see that day, at least we are bound to pray for it; we are bound to pray for our brethren that they and we may be led together into the pure light of the Gospel, and be one as once we were . . .' (*Ess.* II, 72)

An opportunity to promote unity through prayer was offered by George Spencer, a Catholic priest who visited Oxford at the beginning of January 1840. William Palmer of Magdalen who received him invited Newman to dinner to meet him. Newman declined to dine with him but agreed to see him privately. Newman told Pusey he was impressed.

> He has lately been instrumental in getting Christians in France to pray for the English Church – to whom the Germans are now being added – and he wants in like manner to get the English to pray for the Continental Christians. I suppose he would like nothing better than to have a practice set on foot of praying, e.g. every Thursday, (which is *their* day) for their restoration to the true faith and for the unity of the Church. He urged very strongly that all difficulties would soon vanish if there was real charity on both sides. He is a gentlemanlike, mild, pleasing man, but very smooth. (*LD* VII, 206–7)

Newman was taken with the idea, but Pusey at first was unimpressed, and Manning, quite hostile to it, saying that he could not trust R.C.'s and their duplicity and that 'English Romanism is its most fraudulent aspect.' (*LD* VII, 214–5) Newman, who had expressed concern in a number of letters that there would be a schism in the Church, 'i.e. a split between Peculiars [Evangelicals] and Apostolicals', then proposed to Pusey that instead of prayers for union with the R.C.'s, they have prayers for internal unity. Pusey accepted the idea and tried to get the approval of Bishop Bagot and the Archbishop of Canterbury, but without success. Newman drew up two sets of prayers and printed them for private circulation. (*LD* VII, 296, n. 1 and Appendix)

Despite the favourable impression Spencer made on Newman, the latter having heard that Spencer was puzzled at his not wanting to dine with him, wrote to him what was more like an oration than a letter, one both rude and fierce. It is another instance of Newman not wanting to conceal his real views. It reiterated all he had said at the end of his article on 'The Catholicity of the Anglican Church'. After expressing that he felt touched to learn that a large number of our alienated brethren were praying for us, he could not reciprocate in a manner conformable to his first feelings, because 'your acts are contrary to your words; you invite us to a union of hearts, at the same time you are doing all you can . . . to destroy our Church. . . . You are leagued with our enemies.' After expanding on this theme, he added, 'I cannot meet familiarly any leading persons of the Roman communion, and least of all when they come on a religious mission. Break off, I would say, your alliance with Mr. O'Connell in Ireland and the liberal party in England, or come not to us with overtures for mutual prayers and religious sympathy.' (*LD* VII, 233–5) The harsh tone of this letter is in stark contrast to the gentle and ecumenical spirit pervading the letter of W. G. Ward to Ambrose Phillips in October 1841, a contrast stemming from the divergent attitudes of their respective authors towards Rome. (*W. G. Ward*, pp. 195–9)

Although Newman was pleased that his article on the Catholicity of the English Church 'made a very great impression', he wrote to Bowden saying that he had got into a desponding way about the state of things, and to his sister Jemima he wrote, 'Every thing is miserable. I expect a great attack upon the Bible . . . at the present moment indications of what is coming gather.' These included the Socialists, Carlyle, 'a man of first rate ability, I suppose, and quite fascinating as a writer', Milman's book on the History of Christianity, and the Arnoldian school. 'I begin to have serious apprehensions lest any religious body is strong enough to withstand the league of evil, but the Roman Church. . . . It has [it possesses] *tried* strength. . . . it seems to me as if there were coming on a great encounter between infidelity and Rome, and that we should be smashed between them.' On the other hand he thought it wonderful how good principles have shot up, though he fears defections to Rome. (*LD* VII, 240–2, 244–6)

A good deal of Newman's time was taken up with arranging for articles for the *British Critic* and for dealings with printers. Newman wanted Tom Mozley to take over the brief Notices of Books, but he replied, 'I am convinced that you must keep the notices in your own hands. Besides that nobody but a *chief*, who has his eye on the whole battlefield and is compelled to watch the movements of all parties, can rightly assign to each writer his due portion and sort of notice, – besides this. . . . Your notices are the cream of the number always, and as they say of illustrative engravings, worth the whole 6 shillings.' (*LD* VII, 208, n. 3) Newman's correspondence bears out how *au courant* he was with everything going on whether favourable or unfavourable as regards the Movement, and he passed on a good deal of news to those to whom he wrote. They in turn kept him aware of developments that came to their attention. A good example is a portion of a letter of 21 January 1840 from Frederic Rogers:

I see a popular way of speaking is beginning to be that 'without agreeing with the Oxford people, it must be allowed they have done good *hitherto*' – A young clergyman was saying that in the country people who talked in that way were altering their practice in a way that 'we town people' had no notion of. And spoke of a *foxhunting* style of Clergyman, who, 'without any agreement with the O. Tracts' had been setting up services on Saints days and other days. – He himself, he said, was on the point of taking a curacy of a friend of his, but found to his amazement that he would involve himself in *three daily* services – one at 6 o'clock in the morning – and not liking either to go on with this or to leave it off, receded. (*LD* VII, 223)

PASTORAL INTERLUDE

Bloxam's resignation as Newman's curate for Littlemore in order to tend his seriously ill father gave Newman an ostensible reason for spending Lent there, though his real reason was, as he wrote to his Aunt, to do penance. He did not reveal that penance consisted mainly in stricter fasting in secret, as noted in his private journal.

I have this Lent abstained from fish, fowl, all meat but bacon at dinner; from butter, vegetables of all sorts, fruit, pastry, sugar, tea, wine, and beer and toast. I have never dined out. I have not worn gloves.

I breakfasted on bread & hot milk with an egg; dined on cold bacon, bread, cheese, and water; supped on barley water, bread, and an egg.

On Wednesday and Friday I abstained from all food whatever to 6 p.m. when I added a second egg to my usual supper. I sometimes drank a glass of cold water in the morning for a particular reason. (*AW*, 217)

During the week before Easter he increased the length of his fasting, taking nothing till 6 p.m. On Holy Thursday and Good Friday he restricted his supper to bread and water.

He intended to write what became *Tract 90*, but there was no time for it, as he was preoccupied with the needs of the children and this he enjoyed. In the school that Bloxam had erected he found the children dirty and unkempt, and especially ignorant of religion, not knowing the difference between Adam and Noah. Many who were on the list did not come. The schoolmistress, Mrs Whitman, was 'a dawdle and a do nothing', who 'attempted to be obsequious', and he found out that she drank 'badly'. He wrote to Henry Wilberforce, 'For several days I have been saying to myself, O that Henry would bring his wife to put my school to rights! I see the girls' hair wants combing, but cannot go further in my analysis of the general air of slatterness which prevails.' (*LD* VII, 252)

All of this was a challenge to Newman's activist temperament. By April he was able to tell Jemima, 'I have effected a great reform . . . in the girls' hands and faces – lectured with unblushing effrontery on the necessity of *keeping their work clean*, and set them to knit stockings with all their might. Also, I am going to give them some neat white pinafores for Church use, and am going to contrive to make them make them. I saw some thing of the kind I liked at Bransgore in the Autumn, and have got Mrs H W . . . to send me a pattern with directions . . . about lappets and [pouch] sleeves.' He began to teach the children some new tunes, introduce them to Gregorian chant and rummaged out a violin to lead the children with it on Mondays and Thursdays. He likewise drew up 'a sort of liturgy of School prayers varying with the seasons . . . and mean to have them hung up in the school room and used according to the day'. (*LD* VII, 285)

His greatest success, however, was catechizing the children on Sunday afternoons, which according to a letter of J. B. Mozley to his sister, 'has been a great attraction this Lent, and men have gone out of Oxford every

Sunday to hear it. I heard him last Sunday, and thought it very striking: done with such spirit, and the children so up to it; answering with the greatest alacrity. . . . St Mary's as you may suppose, has been considerably thinned.' (*LD* VII, 282, n. 1)

The practical result of this experience was the desire to get a curate to take St Mary's except for Sundays, and he to live at Littlemore. To Bloxam he confided, '. . . at present I am so drawn to this place . . . that it will be an effort to go back to St Mary's. . . . Every thing is so cold at St Mary's – I have felt it for years. I know no one. I have no sympathy. I have many critics and carpers – If it were not for those poor undergraduates, who are after all *not* my charge, and the Sunday Communions, I should be sorely tempted to pitch my tent here.' (*LD* VII, 261) The early morning communion service had been a great success, the numbers varying between twelve and forty-three, averaging twenty-five. The collections for the year totalled £296.13s.8d. The money Newman gave to the Additional Curates Fund, the Nova Scotia clergy, the Bishop of Toronto, and the Bishop of Australia. (*LD* VII, 193, n. 2) These early morning Sunday communion services were a great joy to Newman, who later fondly recollected them, 'Can I wipe out from my memory, or wish to wipe out, those happy Sunday mornings, light or dark, year after year, when I celebrated your communion-rite, in my own church of St Mary's; and in the pleasantness and joy of it heard nothing of the strife of tongues which surrounded its walls?' (*Diff.* I, 81–2)

As customary, Newman consulted about his proposal, in this instance Pusey, who approved it but thought more time should be spent in Oxford. 'You know how much the presence of a senior fellow helps to form the *ethos* of the body and you have no adequate representative. . . . Then also your Tuesday Evenings certainly have been the means of forming people; so that your occasional residence in Oxford. . . . would have great advantages.' (*LD* VII, 266) Newman also told Pusey of his plan to have a *moné* which might prove a model or type of such institutions. It would train up men for work in the great towns or provide a place where friends might come for a time if they need a retreat. He felt that such a plan would fix him, 'whereas at present I am continually perplexing myself whether I am not called elsewhere, or may not be'. (*LD* VII, 264–5) Perhaps this was what Newman was referring to when, suffering his first doubts, he wrote Rogers, 'if things were to come to the worst, I should turn Brother of Charity in London – an object which, *quite* independently of any such perplexities, is growing on me, and, peradventure, will some day be accomplished, if other things do not impede me. The Capuchin in the

'Promessi Sposi' has struck in my heart like a dart. I have never got over him.' (*LD* VII, 151) As he was determined to erect such a place even if no one else joined him, he later in the year planted trees there.

Newman was delighted with the altar cloth which Jemima and Anne Mozley executed for him for Littlemore, and which he kept for Easter Day. Bloxam was 'quite in extacies about it'. Mrs Barnes took it as a sign of the pains being taken with the parish.[1] Easter Day was a joyous one. Bloxam came up and shared duty with Newman. The chapel was decorated with roses, wallflowers and sweet briar, 'and the Chapel smells as if to remind one of the Holy Sepulchre'. (*LD* VII, 312, 299)

One source of his joy at Littlemore was that upon hearing news from his aunt that his brother Frank was no longer heading a sect, he re-established friendly relations with him, so much so that from 29–30 September he visited Frank in Cheltenham, but on 21 October he received a painful letter which 'to *my* view,' he said, 'is almost a confession of Unitarianism.' On 10 November, in reply to a letter from Frank, he anticipated the argument of the University Sermon, 'The Theory of Developments of Religious Doctrine'. (*LD* II, 300–2, 307–10, 319–20, 412–15, 436–42)

Before the end of the year, Newman had a further reason for joy, in the form of pleasant surprises at the reception of his publishing activity. The second set of volumes of Froude's *Remains*, which appeared in November 1839, did not fulfil his anxieties about a negative reception, nor did the publication of his *Church of the Fathers* which appeared in March 1840. This latter was a collection of a series of letters originally published in the *British Magazine* between 1833 and 1837. Though he published it to *interest* people in the Fathers, he was anxious how it would take, as it contained 'strong meat', especially the views of the Fathers 'about celibacy and miraculous power'. (*LD* VII, 202, 241)

Since his first doubts about the Anglican Church Newman contemplated resigning St Mary's. With a view to this, on 21 October 1840 he wrote to the Provost, asking if the College would be likely to consent to his resigning St Mary's but keeping Littlemore, and on 26 October he consulted Keble. The reasons he gave were that he knew very few of his parishioners, that he had instituted saints' days, daily services, lectures in the de Brome Chapel for them, but they did not come to them. Moreover the authorities, 'the appointed guardians of those who form great part of the attendants on my Sermons, have shown a dislike to my preaching'. Though his sermons were not doctrinal but moral, they tended to lead hearers to the Primitive Church, not to the Church of England. Also whether he willed it or not he was leading them to Rome. Though the *arguments* he published against Rome seemed as cogent as ever, 'men go by their sympathies, not by argument'.

> Nor can I counteract the danger by preaching or writing against Rome. I seem to myself almost to have shot my last arrow in the article on English Catholicity; and I am troubled by doubts, whether, as it is, I have not in what I have published spoken too strongly against Rome; though I think I did it in a kind of faith, being determined to put myself into the English system, and say *all that* our Divines said whether I had fully weighed it or not. (*LD* VII, 416–8)

This point is important to keep in mind when one comes later to understand his Retractations which were the withdrawal not of the arguments but of the abusive language he used.

Keble thought he was not obliged to resign even if Newman believed he was disposing people to Rome. As a result Newman decided he should stay on, and gave the following reasons:

> 1. I do not think that we have yet made a fair trial how much the English Church will bear. I know it is a hazardous experiment, – like proving Cannon. Yet we must not take it for granted the metal will burst in the operation. It has borne at various times, not to say at this time, a great infusion of Catholic Truth without damage. (*LD* VII, 433)

In the *Apologia* Newman commented on this:

> Here I observe, that, what was contemplated was the bursting of the *Catholicity* of the Anglican Church, that is, my *subjective idea* of that Church. Its bursting would not hurt her with the world, but would be a discovery that she was purely and essentially Protestant, and would be really the 'hoisting of the engineer with his own petar.' And this was the result. (*Apo.*, 135)

But it would take the condemnation of *Tract 90* on the part of the bishops, but especially the Jerusalem Bishopric, to convince him of this, as will be seen.

The second reason he gave for not resigning was that he was creating sympathies to Rome no more than Hooker, Taylor, Bull, etc. The third reason was that 'Rationalism is the great evil of the day. May not I consider my post at St Mary's as a place of protest against *it*?' (*LD* VII, 433–4) On 21 October Newman wrote to Tom Mozley, asking him to take over the editorship of the *British Critic* after the spring issue of 1841. (*LD* VII, 411)

In the October 1840 issue of the *British Critic*, Newman reviewed 'Todd's *Discourses on the prophecies relating to Antichrist*'. The latter's position 'that the prophecies concerning Antichrist were as yet unfulfilled and that the predicted enemy of the Church is yet to come', was one with which Newman agreed. He had put aside the view that the Pope was Antichrist which he had absorbed as a boy from reading Newton on the Prophecies. Bishop Samuel Horsly (1733–1806) denied the identification of the Pope as Antichrist and labelled the trends in France as an expression of Antichrist. This was reflected in George Stanley Faber's *The Sacred Calendar of Prophesy: Sympathies to Rome* (1828). It is against this background, and with comparable feelings, that on 15 August 1830 Newman expressed strong abhorrence of events in France to John Marriott, 'in their manifest contempt or hatred of religion. . . . they have been faithful to the character they established 40 years ago'. In Advent 1835 Newman delivered four sermons on the Patristical understanding of Antichrist, which he later published as Tract 83. In it he described the coming of Antichrist as something in the future. Holding the Pope as Antichrist would have been inconsistent with the *Via Media*'s affirmation of apostolical succession, as he had already said in his letter to Faussett. (*VM* II, 219) As he expressed it in the review of Todd, 'If we cannot consistently hold that the Pope is Antichrist, without holding that the principle of establishments, the Christian ministry, and the most sacred Catholic doctrines, are fruits of Antichrist, surely the lengths we must run are a *reductio ad absurdum* of the position with which we start'. (*Ess.* II, 115)

Newman's remark in the *Apologia* that 'my imagination was stained by the effects of this doctrine up to the year 1843; it had been obliterated from my reason and judgment at an earlier date', has not always been properly understood. It is not as though he still imagined the Pope as Antichrist. What then were these 'effects' that stained his imagination up to 1843? They were images of the Church of Rome as corrupt, wily, idolatrous, worshipping the Virgin and the saints, adding to revelation, e.g., its doctrine of purgatory, in short images that repelled him. All of these were described by Newton, especially that of Mary which created in Newman an almost insurmountable obstacle to his conversion. Only in

1843 did he put aside his bias and looked these objections squarely in the face.[2]

THE CAMPAIGN AGAINST LIBERALISM CONTINUES

Two opportunities arose for Newman to continue his campaign against liberalism or rationalism in religion. He undertook a review of Milman's *History of Christianity*. Later in the *Idea of a University* Newman affirmed that each subject matter has its own principles and method of investigation, still it is but a partial view of reality, and that there are relations between subject matters, and to ignore these relations is in some way to distort the truth. In his review of Milman, Newman argues similarly, but on the basis of a patristic distinction.

> The world in which we are placed has its own system of laws and principles, which, as far as our knowledge of it goes, is, when once set in motion, sufficient to account for itself, – as complete and independent as if there was nothing beyond it. . . . Such is confessedly the world in which our Almighty Creator has placed us. . . . it stands to reason that, unless He has simply retired . . . content with having originally imposed on it certain general laws, which will for the most part work out the ends which He contemplates, – He is acting through, with, and beneath those physical, social, and moral laws, of which our experience informs us. . . . this is the one great rule on which the Divine Dispensations with mankind have been and are conducted, that the visible world is the instrument, yet the veil, of the world invisible, – the veil, yet still partially the symbol and index: so that all that exists or happens visibly, conceals and yet suggests, and above all subserves, a system of persons, facts, and events beyond itself. (*Ess.* II, 190–91)

That God had given the world a fillip and then left it to operate on its own laws was the doctrine of the eighteenth century Deists. Milman however was not a deist. He viewed Christianity on its external side, on the side of the world, which is legitimate enough, since it does have this side, but concentrating on externals in so far as they can be separated from their direct religious bearing, he gives the impression, which is not his intention, of '*a denial of what is inside*'. Hence, little as he is aware of it, 'this external contemplation of Christianity necessarily leads a man to write as a Socinian or Unitarian *would* write, whether he will or not'.

Christ's humanity and crucifixion are external facts, forgiveness of sins is not an external fact; but moral improvement is, 'consequently, he will make the message of the Gospel to relate mainly to moral improvement, not to forgiveness of sins'.

Furthermore 'Principles have a life and power independent of their authors, and make their way in spite of them.' Without delineating principles contained in his work 'as they are held by himself personally', he can enunciate 'those principles, which he has adopted indeed, but which are outside of him'. Mr Milman's External Theory seems to manifest itself in the following canon: 'That nothing belongs to the Gospel but what originated in it; and that whatever, professing to belong to it, is found in anterior or collateral systems, may be put out of it as a foreign element.' Now the phenomenon admitted by all is 'that great portion of what is generally received as Christian truth, is in its rudiments or in its separate parts to be found in heathen philosophies and religions. For instance, the doctrine of a Trinity. . . . the ceremony of washing; so is the rite of sacrifice.' From this phenomenon Milman argues ' "these things are in heathenism, therefore they are not Christian;" we, on the contrary, prefer to say, "these things are in Christianity, therefore they are not heathen." ' That is 'from the beginning the Moral Governor of the world has scattered the seeds of truth far and wide over its extent; that these have variously taken root, and grown up as in the wilderness, wild plants indeed but living.'

Newman sums up:

> The distinction between these two theories is broad and obvious. The advocates of the one imply that Revelation was a single, entire, solitary act, or nearly so, introducing a certain message; whereas we, who maintain the other, consider that Divine teaching has been in fact, what the analogy of nature would lead us to expect, 'at sundry times and in divers manners, various, complex, progressive, and supplemental of itself.

Newman concludes. 'What tenet of Christianity will escape proscription, if the principle is once admitted, that a sufficient account is given of an opinion, and a sufficient ground for making light of it, as soon as it is historically referred to some human origin?'

Stylistically the second work against the liberals of the day is a far superior achievement. Whereas the former is slow moving and at times tedious, the latter is fast moving and lively. It consists of seven letters signed 'Catholicus' which Newman wrote at the request of John Walter, the proprietor of *The Times*, urged on by his son who had come under Newman's influence at Oxford. They are a devastating critique of a speech delivered by Sir Robert Peel at the opening of the Tamworth Library and Reading Room, in which he extolled the diffusion of scientific knowledge and literature as a great instrument of moral reform and even a means of drawing the indifferent to a belief in Christianity. Later published as *The Tamworth Reading Room*, it is a brilliant *tour de force*, displaying Newman's considerable powers of biting satire and irony.

Newman argues against Peel that knowledge is not the principle of moral improvement. It is, as Peel presents it, 'the mere lulling of the passions to rest by turning the course of thought; not a change of character, but a mere removal of temptation. . . . When a child cries, the nuserymaid dances it about, or points to the pretty black horses out of the window, or shows how ashamed poll-parrot or poor puss must be of its tantarums [*sic*]. Such is the sort of prescription which Sir Robert Peel offers to the good people of Tamworth.' (*DA*, 264) Knowledge is not a direct means of moral improvement. 'Science, knowledge, and whatever other fine names we use, never healed a wounded heart, nor changed a sinful one; but the Divine Word is with power. . . . It has cleansed man of his moral diseases.'

Peel however goes further than affirming knowledge as a means of moral improvement; he asserts it will lead the indifferent to Christianity. Newman replies:

> Science gives us the grounds or premises from which religious truths are to be inferred; but it does not set about inferring them. . . . This is why Science has so little of a religious tendency; deductions have no power of persuasion. The heart is commonly reached, not through the reason, but through the imagination . . . Persons influence us, voices melt us, looks subdue us, deeds inflame us. Many a man will live and die upon a dogma: no man will be a martyr for a conclusion.
>
> Logic makes but a sorry rhetoric with the multitude; first shoot round corners and you may not despair of converting by syllogism. . . . Life is not long enough for a religion of inferences. . . . Life is for action. If we insist on proofs for everything, we shall never come to action: to act you must first assume, and that assumption is faith. (*DA*, 292–5)

Secular knowledge without personal religion leads not to belief but to unbelief.

The truth is that the system of Nature is just as much connected with Religion, where minds are not religious, as a watch or a steam-carriage. The material world, indeed, is indefinitely more wonderful than any human contrivance; but wonder is not religion, or we should be worshipping our railroads. . . . the system of Nature by itself, detached from the axioms of Religion . . . does not force us to take it for *more* than a system; but why, then, persist in calling the study of it religious, when it can be treated, and is treated, thus atheistically?

Newman summed up his argument by saying 'that intrinsically excellent and noble as are scientific pursuits . . . and fruitful in temporal benefits to the community, still they are not, and cannot be the instrument of an ethical training . . . that apprehension of the unseen is the only known principle capable of subduing moral evil, educating the multitude, and organizing society; and that, whereas man is born for action, action flows not from reasonings, but from Faith', (*DA*, 304)

A NEW CURRENT

By this time a new current had begun to influence the Movement, which would move it in a different direction. First, there were younger members of another generation who were less concerned with doctrine and polemics than with a religious *ethos*. These were attracted to Rome. W. F. D. Hook, a vicar in Leeds, saw this quite clearly, as he wrote to a friend in January 1840:

I think that if the Rulers of the Church of England do not take very good care, we shall have ere long a great defection to Romanism. I do not fear the clergy, but there are young men, the generation below us, who have been educated in a school of transcendental metaphysics mingled with religion, and they require something in their religion which will raise the imagination. For a long period there was a prejudice against everything mysterious in religion; the feeling now is that mystery is *a priori* evidence in favour of a doctrine. These persons see much to admire in Romanism. They admit its doctrinal errors, but they see that many of its practices are superior to our own; that when men are striving for perfection they receive greater encouragement. . . . Men now see that there is good mingled with the evil of Romanism, and that much of what has hitherto been called superstition is a help to devotion. Having got so far as this, there will be many who will consider the doctrinal differences of less importance than they really are. Surely it is important for our rulers . . . to do everything that in them lies . . . to aid men in these their high aspirings after perfection. (*KC*, 30–1)

Those attracted toward Rome included not only young men, as Newman learned from Dodsworth, but also young women, as reported by Manning, Miss Giberne and Pusey. (*LD* VII, 184, 133, 165, 96, n. 2) In response to Manning, Newman wrote:

I feel very anxious about such a case as you mention; from the consciousness that our Church has not the provisions and methods by which Catholic feelings are to be detained, secured, sobered, and trained heavenwards. Our blanket is too small for our bed. . . . I am conscious that we are raising longing and tastes which we are not allowed to supply – and till our Bishops and others give scope to the development of Catholicism externally and visibly, we *do* tend to make impatient minds seek it where it has ever been, *in* Rome. . . . Give us more services – more vestments and decorations in worship – give us monasteries. . . . Till then, you will have continual defections to Rome. (*LD* VII, 133)

The newer members of the Movement regarded Rome in a different way than Newman and the earlier Tractarians. The latter while proposing Catholic doctrines as found in the Church of the Fathers, were at great pains to dissociate themselves from 'Popery'. When persons accused Newman of proposing the latter, he would reply, 'True, we seem to be making straight for it; but go on awhile, and you will come to a deep chasm across the path, which makes real approximation impossible'. (*Apo.*, 55) One of his motives for writing the *Prophetical Office of the Church* was to show how Anglicanism differed from Romanism. The older members of the Movement remained suspicious of Rome. The newcomers took a different view. W. G. Ward is a prime example. Even before he adopted Tractarian principles he was attracted toward Catholic services, which he attended occasionally in London during his early years. 'The systematic discipline of the Church and the simplicity of her logical position were intellectually points in her favour. He had early learnt to dislike the Reformers, . . . and found enough in Milner's writings to lead him to condemn the Reformation . . . He had contemplated the possibility of becoming a Catholic, in his dissatisfaction with the Anglican Church even as interpreted by Arnold.' (*W. G. Ward*, p. 78) We have already mentioned the influence of Froude. Wilfrid Ward points out the difference in view that Ward and his associates brought to the Movement. 'Rome was directly looked on by them as in many respects the practical model; the Reformation was a deadly sin; restoration to the papal communion the ideal – even if unattainable – aim.' (*W. G. Ward*, p. 136)

What distinguished the new school was the love of Rome and of a united Christendom. This was not only a love for ecclesiastical authority but an admiration for the saints of the Roman Church; Froude had sounded the note of sanctity and authority. Those ideals were seen as better realized in the Church of Rome, despite its practical corruptions, than in the Church of the Reformation. This led Ward to study the writings of St Ignatius and the Jesuits. Wilfrid Ward says of his father,

> Both in ascetics and in dogmatics the Jesuits were his favourite reading. The spiritual exercises of St Ignatius with their immediately practical character, their provisions at every turn for testing the reality of spiritual advance, their minute precepts as to the best method of training the will, of uprooting particular faults, of making the unseen world real by practical meditation, of keeping a consistent view of life, and bearing in mind in every action its true supernatural aim and end, – these were adapted with wonderful accuracy to his own special character and needs. (*W. G. Ward*, p. 146)

The newer members of the Movement like Ward and Oakeley were more open and sympathetic to the gestures of Catholics like Ambrose Lisle Phillipps (from 1862 Phillipps de Lisle), Lord Shrewsbury, and Ignatius Spencer in their crusade for union between the Churches. Their attitude differed from Newman's, which eschewed contact with Roman Catholics because he believed any movement toward reunion should be between Church and Church, not between individuals. Meanwhile Newman felt one of his most important tasks was to keep people from defecting to Rome.

PASTORAL COUNSELLING

Persons attracted to Rome began to turn to Newman for spiritual direction, and these he tried to dissuade from acting hastily. Sometimes the correspondence carried on over several years; others, over a shorter time. William C. A. MacLaurin, a clergyman at Elgin, wrote to Newman in June 1840. Newman replied at some length, offering arguments to dissuade him from converting to Rome. First, he thought it dangerous, since, if the Church of Rome were corrupt, one would be taking upon oneself a corrupt creed. Secondly, since an experiment is going on in the English Church, one should wait and see how it progresses. If it is a mere theory, it will not work, but fall apart. (*LD* VII, 256–7)

In a subsequent letter Newman advised him to stop direct inquiry for several years and to devote himself to prayer, fasting, and practical duties. At the end of this time God would enlighten his judgement. Newman then enunciated an important principle, 'I do not think that argument is the mode in which your mind will effectually be relieved.' (*LD* VII, 368–70, 404) Even more explicitly Newman asserted, 'Grace alone surely can guide our argumentative power into truth, and grace is not attained in such anxious and difficult enquiries as those which are in question between us without fasting and prayer.' (*LD* VII, 406–7)

Miss Holmes wrote to Newman at first disguising herself as Z. V. X., giving an account of her conversion three years ago to a spiritual life and recently to apostolical principles. He recommended her not to publish the account, but to concentrate on advancement in her interior life. He recommended a number of devotional books such as à Kempis, Pascal's *Thoughts*, the devotional writings of Bishop Taylor, and using some systematic exercises such as Bishop Cosin's, Bishop Andrewes', or (if she has the slightest knowledge of necessary Latin) the Breviary with such omissions as the English Church requires. Moreover she should set herself deliberately to the task of self-government, unlearning worldly opinions and gaining perfect resignation to God's will. Since there were no religious convents in the Church at present, should she not cultivate a desire for such a life? (*LD* VII, 335–6)

In subsequent letters Miss Holmes plied him with questions about post-baptismal sin, the doctrine of the intercession of the saints, which he answered at length. He gave sound spiritual advice based upon his own experience in living a religious life: not to be discouraged at failures and apparent hopelessness of making progress, but to go steadily on, since one cannot suddenly become what one wishes. He hopes she has not made any vow, but if so, she must keep to it. He closed with 'I am, My dear Madam, Yours truly and with much interest.' (*LD* VII, 360–2)

Undoubtedly encouraged by the interest he was taking in her, she wrote asking for names of books on the saints and the history of the

Church, which he provided. In this and subsequent letters he cautioned against excitement and change of feelings. 'Regularity, whether in business or in devotion, should be your great aim.' (*LD* VII, 376–7) Apparently Miss Holmes spoke of her doubts and asked questions about the Roman Church. Newman's reply is important as showing his attitude to doubt as an Anglican:

> Be assured that I have my doubts and difficulties as other people. Perhaps the more we examine and investigate, the more we have to perplex us. It is the lot of man; the human mind in its present state is unequal to its own powers of apprehension; it embraces more than it can master. I think we ought all to set out on our inquiries, I am sure we shall end them, with this conviction. Were I a member of a Church like the Roman, which claims to be infallible, yet doubts about the *grounds* on which she claims it would be sure to occur to any thinking mind. Absolute certainty then cannot be attained here; we must resign ourselves to doubt as the *trial under* which it is God's will we should do our duty and prepare ourselves for His presence. Our sole question must be, *what* does a Merciful God, who knows whereof we are made, wish *us to do under* our existing ignorance and doubt? (*LD* VII, 407)

As a Catholic, Newman answered this assertion, maintaining that faith and doubt are incompatible. There can be doubt and uncertainty about the grounds and evidence for believing, which makes one seek more *evidence.* 'Faith may *follow* after doubt, and so far is not inconsistent with it; but the two cannot co-exist.' (*VM* I, 87, and notes, cf. *DA*, 391) In what seems like a clear reference to his own first doubts about the Anglican Church and his present state, he writes, 'I think you are in a more excited state than you understand, and I am sure that many persons, who have felt what you now feel, have afterwards felt much more calm and quiet, and have considered that their former state of mind was deficient in these qualities.' He then recommended his own 'Lectures on Romanism' and Butler's *Analogy* (*LD* VII, 407) and sent her a copy of the former, noting that 'by Popery I mean a *spirit in* the Church of Rome, not the system of the Church itself. I wish always to distinguish between the Church, which is holy, and the Spirit which rules it which is earthly.' He adds a remark which shows that he was beginning to suspect he had been too strong in his language against Rome. 'Perhaps in places I have used stronger language against Rome than it is safe to do.' (*LD* VII, 422–3) By this time Newman had developed a view which he felt should be taken to modify the strength of his language against the Church of Rome. He first expressed it in a letter to S. F. Wood (*LD* VI, 112–13), and he mentioned it again in a letter to Miss Giberne on 22 December 1840, in connection with God's providential purposes. 'Places and systems . . . may be carried on by influences short of the simple Truth yet the best under the circumstances. Oxford or the English Church may be carried forward in a certain line which may subserve Providential purposes and tend to perfection without being perfect. With this explanation I think it allowable to speak, as I often do, of the great Chess player, who uses us most wonderfully as his pawns.' Commenting on this letter in 1862 Newman wrote,

True, I thought the Church of Rome possessed, but I thought the Church of England possessed too. I thought that every schism and separation ipso facto fell under the power of a second-best Spirit, not a holy angel, but some imperfect being, the like of which would also rule separate *nations*. The Catholic Church being divided, Latins, Greeks, Anglicans, each body had its own living personal animating, directing intelligence, not a devil but acting in perversion and corruption of what was true; so that what was true in each body was from God, what was bad from this *daimon* [evil spirit] (*LD* VII, 465–6 and n. 3)[3]

CHAPTER EIGHTEEN

Weathering the Storm

From 1831 Newman contemplated writing on the Thirty-nine Articles. (*LD* II, 321) The immediate cause of his doing so in 1841 was, according to his account in the *Apologia*, 'the restlessness, actual and prospective, of those who neither liked the *Via Media*, nor my strong judgment against Rome. I had been enjoined, I think by my Bishop, to keep these men straight, and I wished so to do: but their difficulty was subscription to the Articles. . . . It was thrown in our teeth; "How can you manage to sign the Articles? they are directly against Rome".' (*Apo.*, 78) According to Archbishop Tait: 'Ward worried him into writing Tract 90.' (*W. G. Ward*, 152) It is more likely, however, as Gerard Tracey has suggested, that Newman had a case like Robert Williams in mind.[1]

Newman's concern, therefore, was pastoral, to quiet the consciences of persons who falsely, he thought, considered that the Articles prevented them from holding views found in the Primitive Church. The reason was that the received interpretation of the day was Protestant and exclusive, and a Catholic sense of the Articles, though permitted by their framers and promulgators and implied in the teaching of Andrewes or Beveridge, was never publicly recognized. 'I had in mind', he later wrote in the *Apologia*, 'to remove all such obstacles as lay in the way of all holding the Apostolic and Catholic character of the Anglican teaching; to assert the right of those who chose to say in the face of the day, "Our Church teaches the Primitive Ancient faith".' (*Apo.*, 130–1)

The thesis put forth was in the language of the day 'that the Articles were patient but not ambitious of a Catholic interpretation'. As Newman said in his letter of explanation to Jelf, which partly explains the enormous row the Tract caused, 'The Articles *need* not be so closed as the received method of teaching closes them, and *ought* not to be, for the sake of many persons. If we will close them, we run the risk of subjecting persons, whom we should least like to lose or distress, to the temptation of joining the Church of Rome, or to the necessity of withdrawing from the Church established, or to the misery of subscribing with doubt and hesitation.'

Since he had been urged to keep members of the Church from straggling in the direction of Rome, he thought it would be 'useful to them without hurting any one else'. (*VM* II, 387)[2] There was another reason. 'Keeping silence looks like artifice, and I do not like people to consult or respect me, from thinking differently of my opinions from what I know them to be.' (*Apo.*, 170)

Newman's interpretation of the Articles was based on certain distinctions. When it was said that the Articles were drawn up against Rome, Newman replied,

> What do you mean by 'Rome?'. . . By 'Roman doctrine' might be meant one of three things: 1, the *Catholic teaching* of the early centuries; or 2, the *formal dogmas of Rome* as contained in the later Councils, especially the Council of Trent, and as condensed in the Creed of Pope Pius IV.; 3, the *actual popular beliefs and usages* sanctioned by Rome in the countries in communion with it, over and above the dogmas; and these I called the 'dominant errors'. Now Protestants commonly thought that in all three senses 'Roman doctrine' was condemned in the Articles: I thought that the *Catholic teaching* was not condemned; that the *dominant errors* were; and as to the *formal dogmas*, that some were, some were not, and that the line had to be drawn between them. Thus, 1. The use of Prayers for the dead was a Catholic doctrine, – not condemned in the Articles; 2. The prison of Purgatory was a Roman dogma, – which was condemned in them; but the infallibility of Ecumenical Councils was a Roman dogma, – not condemned; and 3. The fire of Purgatory was an authorized and popular error, not a dogma, – which was condemned.
>
> Further, I considered that the difficulties, felt by the persons whom I have mentioned, mainly lay in their mistaking, 1, Catholic teaching, which was not condemned in the Articles, for Roman dogma which was condemned; and 2, Roman dogma, which was not condemned in the Articles, for dominant error which was . . . .
>
> The main thesis then of my Essay was this: – the Articles do not oppose Catholic teaching; they but partially oppose Roman dogma; they for the most part oppose the dominant errors of Rome. And the problem was, as I have said, to draw the line as to what they allowed and what they condemned. (*Apo.*, 78–9)

Of the elasticity of the Articles there could be no doubt. 'The seventeenth was assumed by one party to be Lutheran, by another

Calvinistic, though the two interpretations were contradictory of each other.' (*Apo.*, 78–9) Moreover the latitudinarians and liberals had allowed for private interpretations as long as the Articles were not publicly opposed. But Newman went beyond this; he asserted that the Articles had been deliberately made unclear in order to keep Catholics within the Elizabethan Church. At the end Newman used an illustration from the political world. 'A French minister, desirous of war, nevertheless, as a matter of policy, draws up his state papers in such moderate language, that his successor who is for peace, can act up to them, without compromising his own principles. . . . The Protestant Confession was drawn up with the purpose of including Catholics; and Catholics now will not be excluded. What was an economy in the Reformers, is a protection to us. What would have been a perplexity to us then, is a perplexity to Protestants now. We could not then have found fault with their words; they cannot now repudiate our meaning.' (*VM* II, 347–8) Pusey disagreed with this view historically and later wanted Newman to leave it out, but Newman declined.

Newman concluded that the Articles are to be studied in the light of certain facts. 1. The Convocation which received and passed them spoke with respect of 'the Catholic Fathers and Ancient Bishops'. They were not therefore intended to be inconsistent with patristic literature. 2. They approved the *Homilies* as containing 'a godly and wholesome doctrine'. It was therefore reasonable to interpret them in light of the *Homilies* and the *Homilies* countenance much Catholic doctrine, indeed some so-called 'Roman' doctrines not found in the Articles. In the *Apologia* Newman listed 26 such theses. (*Apo.*, 82–4) 3. The Articles were published before the decrees of the Council of Trent were promulgated, so that these decrees should not be taken as representing the doctrines which the Articles condemned. What were the Articles aiming at? Newman replied, 'the dominant errors, the popular corruptions, authorized or suffered by the high name of Rome. The eloquent declamation of the *Homilies* finds its matter almost exclusively in the dominant errors. As to Catholic teaching, nay as to Roman dogma, of such theology those *Homilies*, as I have shown, contained no small portion themselves.' (*Apo.*, 84–5)

The Tract was published on 27 February 1841, which Newman listed in his chronological Notes as 'the first day of the No. 90 row'. Like most of its predecessors it was anonymous, but it was pretty well recognized to be Newman's. Newman, who had shown the Tract to Keble, did not expect it would be attacked any more than previous Tracts had been. Ward, however, predicted that it 'would completely electrify the University and the Church'. (*W. G. Ward*, 156, quoting Oakeley) On 27 February, Ward burst excitedly into the room of A. C. Tait, fellow tutor of Balliol, and threw the Tract on Tait's table. 'Here is something worth reading'. When he got to the commentary on the Twenty-second Article, with regard to 'Purgatory, Pardons, Images, Relics, and Invocation of Saints', Tait was outraged. He showed the Tract to 'one person after another; the excitement increased, but still unknown to Newman'. (*LD* VIII, 45, n. 1)

Perhaps more than any single individual Golightly was responsible for the uproar that followed. He was Tait's curate in his parish of Baldon in Oxfordshire and at this time a good deal in and out of Tait's rooms. Golightly and Wynter, the Vice-Chancellor, 'were agreed that rather than reconcile Catholic minded persons to the Church of England, the drift of the Tract seemed rather to reconcile Anglicans to Romanism, or as Golightly expressed it, "so to lessen the distance, by drawing us to them, not them to us: palliating their errors and overshadowing our truths"'.[3]

According to Church, Golightly 'first puffed the Tract all over Oxford as the greatest "curiosity" that had been seen for some time: his diligence and activity were unwearied; he then turned his attention to the country, became a purchaser of No. 90 to such an amount that Parker could hardly supply him, and sent copies to all the Bishops, etc.'. (*LD* VIII, 109) In Oxford there had been a 'smouldering, stern, energetic animosity' against the author of *Tract 90*, Newman asserted in the *Apologia*, especially on the part of the majority of the Heads of Houses, who disliked the Tractarians not least because of their strictness both in living and in preaching. They were not interested in a calm, objective theological analysis of the Tract but saw it as an opportunity to strike a blow. The atmosphere was charged. On 2 March 1841 in the debate in Parliament on the annual grant to Maynooth, Lord Morpeth criticized Oxford divines as 'constantly disclaiming the distinctive Protestant character of the Church, and denouncing what they . . . term the crimes of the Reformation'. Indeed some of their pupils were actually deserting the Church of England and embracing the doctrines of Rome. These remarks raised fears of a possible governmental inquiry. (*LD* VIII, 69, n. 1) *The Times* in an article on 6 March rejected the accusation that it had become Puseyite, and defended its position towards the Tractarians. It did so again in two subsequent articles. (*LD* VIII, 358, n. 1; 108)

But there were other factors as well. It was not only watchful enemies such as the *Record* who were on the look-out for proofs of disingenuousness and bad faith, but numbers of High Churchmen disapproved of Froude's criticism of the Reformation, his Catholic *ethos*, and the impression he gave of being a 'plotter'. Such suspicions were heightened and confirmed by Isaac Williams' Tract 'On Reserve in communicating Religious Knowledge'. Despite its devout and reverential spirit, the word 'Reserve' was enough to arouse suspicions.

> It meant that the Tract-writers avowed the principle of keeping back part of the counsel of God. It meant, further, that the real spirit of the party was disclosed, its love of secret and crooked methods, . . . its disingenuous professions, its deliberate concealments, its holding doctrines and its pursuit of aims which it dared not avow, its *disciplina arcani*, its conspiracies, its Jesuitical spirit. All this kind of abuse was flung plentifully on the party as the controversy became warm, and it mainly justified itself by the Tract on 'Reserve'.[4]

In J. B. Mozley's opinion, 'Those who have always thought the Articles ultra Protestant, and have been accustomed to think so ever since they were born, are naturally horrified at the idea that even their stronghold does not protect them, and that the wolf may come in and devour them any day.' (*LD* VIII, 63, n. 1)

Oakeley added another factor.

> Individual conversions to Rome were at the time so uncommon, involved so serious a step, entailed such costly sacrifices, that ample securities against them were supposed to exist on every side. What, then, was the general amazement on finding that the leader of the movement himself, who must be supposed to know its secrets better than anyone else, actually spoke, in a published document – in an apology too, where he would naturally use peculiar circumspection, – of 'straggling towards Rome' as not merely a possible but a pressing contingency!. . . . 'Secession to Rome' became, from that moment, a practical fear and a popular cry.[5]

Finally, nothing united persons of all parties so much as a common detestation of Rome, of 'Popery', from which the country had liberated itself at the time of the Reformation and again in 1688, and which it regarded as tyrannous, corrupt and unsound in many of its practices. As Newman wrote later,

The whole of England, with its multitude of sects, tolerant for the most part of each other, protests against Rome: its Court, its legislators, its judicial bench, its public press, its literature and science, its populace, forcibly repudiate, view with intense jealousy, any advance, in any quarter, even of a hair's breadth, towards the Roman Church. (*Ess.* II, 103)

Four senior tutors: T. T. Churton, H. B. Wilson, John Griffiths, A. C. Tait and several others met at Wadham College, with Golightly in attendance. (*LD* VIII, 59, n. 2) They drew up a letter dated 8 March to the editor of the Tracts, in which they expressed their apprehension that the Tract had a highly dangerous tendency and they requested the name of its author. It was signed, however, only by the four senior tutors. Unfortunately the grounds of their apprehension betray such a misunderstanding of the nature of the Tract that it has been wondered whether they had carefully read and digested it. For example, the tutors affirmed that the Tract had

a highly dangerous tendency from its suggesting that certain very important errors of the Church of Rome are not condemned by the Articles of the Church of England; for instance, that those Articles do not contain any condemnation of the doctrines, 1, of Purgatory; 2, of Pardons; 3, of the worship and adoration of Images and Relics; 4, of the Invocation of Saints; 5, of the Mass, as they are taught authoritatively by the Church of Rome, but only of certain absurd practices and opinions which intelligent Romanists repudiate as much as we do. (*VM* II, 359)

The tutors requested the name of the author of the Tract. Newman acknowledged reception of the letter the same day.

Golightly, whom Newman called '*the* Tony Fire-the-Faggot of the affair', obtained an interview with the Vice-Chancellor, Philip Wynter, and urged that the Tract be brought to the official notice of the Heads of Houses. This Wynter did at the next meeting of the Hebdomadal Board on 10 March. Decision on what was to be done was postponed to a meeting on 12 March, by which time the members would have had time to read the Tract. 'However they were very fierce against it, and against the Tracts in general, against which they seem to have declared, "war to the knife." (*LD* VIII, 65) When the Board reassembled on Friday, 12 March, they voted to censure the Tract by a majority of nineteen to two.

'A Committee was appointed to draw up the terms of the Censure, which were to be ratified at a final meeting on the following Monday.' (*LD* VIII, xvii) News of the decision got about.

With the speed of execution with which he was capable of exercising in emergencies, Newman composed a letter to Jelf, the Vice-Chancellor. Courteously and humbly, which after twenty-four years Pusey called 'still touching', he acknowledged the tutors' 'zeal for Christian truth and their anxiety for the welfare of our younger members . . . and my very great consciousness that, even though I be right in my principle, I may have advocated truth in a wrong way'. He then clearly explained his statements and motives in publishing the Tract but denied the charge brought against him. 'I consider that the Articles *do* contain a condemnation of the authoritative teaching of the Church of Rome on these points; I only say that, whereas they were written before the decrees of Trent, they were not directed against those decrees.' (*VM* II, 367–686) He concluded his letter with no less humility, expressing his 'great sorrow that I have at all startled or offended those for whom I have nothing but respectful and kind feelings. . . . Still, whatever has been said, or is to be done in consequence, is, I am sure, to be ascribed to the most conscientious feelings; and though it may grieve me, I trust it will not vex me, or make me less contented and peaceful in myself.' (*VM* II, 388) Persons closest to Newman at the time testified to the great calm and peaceful way in which he rode out the storm.

On Sunday 14 March, Newman sent Hawkins a note, which he preserved, indicating that a short explanation was forthcoming on Tuesday or Wednesday next. 'Of course it would be more agreeable to him that it should be in your hands, before any opinion is publicly expressed on the subject by your Board – but he is quite contented to leave it to your judgment.' Hawkins said that he communicated this to the Board, but it went ahead anyway. (*LD* VIII, 72, and n. 1)

On Monday the Board passed its resolution which was promulgated on Tuesday, 16 March. Newman recorded in his diary, 'Hebdomadal act came out early in the morning. My letter to Jelf came out at midday.' On the same day Newman publicly acknowledged himself to be the author of the Tract in a courteous letter to the Vice-Chancellor, in which he said he was sorry for the trouble and anxiety he had given to the Board. 'I beg to return my thanks to them for an act, which, even though founded on misapprehension, may be made as profitable to myself, as it is religiously and charitably intended.' (*VM* II, 363) But there were statements in his letter which were hardly calculated to allay the criticisms of those with a strong anti-Roman and anti-Tractarian bias.

In truth there is at this moment a great progress of the religious mind of our Church to something deeper and truer than satisfied the last century. . . . The age is moving toward something, and most unhappily the one religious communion among us which has of late years been practically in possession of this something, is the Church of Rome. She alone, amid all the errors and evils of her practical system, has given free scope to the feelings of awe, mystery, tenderness, reverence, devotedness, and other feelings which may be especially called Catholic. The question then is, whether we shall give them up to the Roman Church or claim them for ourselves, as we well may, by reverting to that older system, which has of late years indeed been superseded. . . . But if we do give them up, then we must give up the men who cherish them. We must consent either to give up the men, or to admit to their principles. (*VM* II, 386–7)

The resolution or condemnation approved at a meeting of the Vice-Chancellor, Heads of Houses, and Proctors on 15 March 1841 reads as follows:

Considering that it is enjoined in the STATUTES of this University, (Tit. iii. Sect. 2. Tit. ix. Sect. ii. § 3. Sect. v. § 3), that every student shall be instructed and examined in the Thirty-nine Articles, and shall subscribe to them; considering also that a Tract has recently appeared, dated from Oxford, and entitled "Remarks on certain Passages in the Thirty-nine Articles", being No. 90 of the Tracts for the Times, a series of Anonymous Publications purporting to be written by members of the University, but which are in no way sanctioned by the University itself;

RESOLVED, That modes of interpretation such as are suggested in the said Tract, evading rather than explaining the sense of the Thirty-nine Articles, and reconciling subscription to them with the adoption of errors, which they were designed to counteract, defeat the object, and are inconsistent with the due observance of the abovementioned STATUTES.

P. WYNTER,
(Vice-Chancellor)

[Promulgated 16 March 1841.] (*VM* II, 362)

According to Middleton, 'the manner of announcing their condemnation was insulting and was intended to be so. The condemnation was posted up on the buttery hatch of every college in Oxford, to use Newman's own words, "after the manner of discommoned pastry-cooks".'[6] On 16 March 'Newman wrote a short letter to the Vice-Chancellor avowing the authorship, and without giving up the principle of the Tract, taking their sentence with a calm and lofty meekness.' The Heads of Houses were condemned by a great many Fellows and M.A.'s 'for an arbitrary and hasty act, by which they have usurped the powers of Convocation,' Church wrote to Rogers, 21 March. (*LD* VIII, 93, 110) Nevertheless 'evading rather than explaining the sense of the Thirty-nine Articles' echoed throughout the country. As Newman later wrote in the *Apologia*, 'in every part of the country and every class of society, through every organ and opportunity of opinion, in newspapers, in periodicals, at meetings, in pulpits, at dinner-tables, in coffee-rooms, in railway carriages, I was denounced as a traitor who had laid his train and was detected in the very act of firing it against the time-honoured Establishment'. (*Apo.*, 89) In this storm of indignation throughout the country Newman recognized 'much of real religious feeling, much of honest and true principle, much of straightforward ignorant common sense'. (*Apo.*, 88)

Certain criticisms were levelled against the Tract by Newman's friends, Bowden and Pusey, e.g. a certain vagueness, and the use of the expression, 'stammering formularies'. (*LD* VIII, 71, 75) In the second edition of his letter to Jelf, Newman answered or explained his position. He left out 'stammering formularies'. Pusey however wanted Newman to cut out the concluding words of the Tract in the second edition. This Newman declined to do. In 1865 Newman explained the difference between himself and Pusey:

My view was this – 'the Compilers of the Articles intended the words they used to bear several senses, in order that Semi-Catholics, time servers etc etc might avail themselves of them'. This, in the compilers, was dishonest; but *since* it was their intention, I considered we might avail ourselves of it. I used to say frankly, 'Either they are dishonest, or I. If I invent the interpretation, then I shuffle – and if they meant it, they shuffled.' I thought they meant it – and I said, 'This shuffle told for them in their day, for it kept Catholics in the Anglican Church – and now it tells for us, and shall hinder us going out of it.' This view is brought out in the last paragraph of the Tract – and this paragraph Pusey wished me in the second edition to leave it out. 'Why,' I answered, 'it is like playing Hamlet, without the Prince of Denmark;

that paragraph is the key to the whole Tract; for, *if* the compilers were not shuffling, I *am* – and I don't intend to allow this.' His answer would be, 'no, there is no shuffling in Compilers or you – for they actually meant the Catholic sense of the Articles, as you give it in the Tract, as the true sense of their words, and not as a mere trap for waverers.' (*LD* XXII, 78–9; see also XX, 413–5) Manning held the same view as Pusey, and 'coolly' asked Newman to leave the passage out. (*LD* VIII, 149, n. 2)

REACHING AN 'UNDERSTANDING'

Bishop Bagot wrote a letter to Newman, dated 17 March, which was forwarded to him by Pusey, whom the Bishop chose as an intermediary. In it he criticized the Tract as containing much which 'tend both to disunite and endanger the Church', and therefore 'for the peace of the Church,' wished that 'discussions upon the Articles should not be continued in the publications of the "Tracts for the Times"'. Newman promptly replied that there would be no further discussions of the Articles, but assured the Bishop that what was published was not done 'wantonly'. (*LD* VIII, 94–5) The Bishop wrote to thank Newman for his promise, 'though,' he added, 'no more than anticipated from the spirit shown in all our former communications'. Newman replied, 'The kindness of your Lordship's letter of this morning brought tears into my eyes. My single wish . . . is to benefit the Church and to approve myself to your Lordship.' Newman went on to speak of the difficulty of his position. 'Hitherto I have been successful in keeping people together – but that a collision must at some time ensue between members of the Church of opposite opinions < sentiments > I have long been aware. The time and mode have been in the hand of Providence: I do not mean to exclude my own great imperfections in bringing it about, yet I still feel obliged to think the Tract necessary.' (*LD* VIII, 100–1)

Bagot, who was keeping Archbishop Howley informed, received a letter from him, dated 22 March, in which he expressed his opinion it was 'advisable to let things rest,' but 'unadvisable that your Lordship's name should be connected in any way with the discussion on this matter. . . . It seems most desirable that the publication of the Tracts should be discontinued for ever.' (*LD* VIII, 101, n. 1) C. J. Blomfield, Bishop of London, likewise thought the Tracts should be discontinued. In another letter of the following day, 23 March, Blomfield wrote, 'There is no intention of passing any episcopal sentence upon Mr Newman's Tract; that is to say, the Bishops will not do so synodically. What individual Bishops may think fit to say in their charges, or otherwise, I do not know. But if the Tracts go on I doubt if we shall be able to refrain much longer; and therefore I am earnest in wishing that they may be discontinued.' (*LD* VIII, 106, n. 4)

Promptly on 24 March Bishop Bagot invited Pusey to come to his residence 'for a little private conversation on this painful position of things'. The Bishop ratched up his demands, apparently in response to the opinions of Howley and Blomfield. The Bishop proposed: 1. that the Tracts should be discontinued; 2. *Tract 90* should not be reprinted; 3. Newman should make it publicly known that this was done in deference to the Bishop's wishes. Newman agreed to the first and third proposals but expressed reservations about the second, as he explained in a letter to Pusey.

My dear Pusey,

After writing the passage in my projected letter about the Bishop's wish that my Tract should be suppressed, and my submission to it, I have on second thoughts come to the conclusion that I cannot do this, without surrendering *interests* with which I am providentially charged at this moment, and which I have no right to surrender.

However the passage is worded, it will be looked on by the world as the Bishop's concurrence in the act of the Hebdomadal Board, which declares such a mode of interpreting the articles as I adopt, to be evasive and inadmissible. At this moment I am representing not a few, but a vast number all through the country, who more or less agree with me.

I offered the Bishop to withdraw the Tract; but I did not offer to concur, by any act of mine, in his *virtual censure* of it, which is involved in its being suppressed at his bidding.

And I am pained to see that the authorities in London have increased their demands according to my submissiveness. When they thought me obstinate, they spoke only of not writing more in the Tracts about the Articles. When they find me obedient, they add the stopping of the Tracts and the suppression of No. 90.

And they use me against myself. They cannot deliver charges of a sudden, but they use me to convey to the world a prompt and popular condemnation of my own principles.

What too is to be our warrant, that, in addition to this, the Bishops of Chester, Chichester, Winchester etc will not charge against the Tract though suppressed? And what is to stop pamphlets against it?. . . . and the Record and Standard? All this is painful; they exert power over the dutiful; they yield to others.

I feel this so strongly, that I have almost come to the resolution, if the Bishop publicly intimates that I must suppress it, or speaks strongly in his charge against it, to suppress it indeed, but to resign my living also. I could not in conscience act otherwise.

You may show this in any quarter you please. (*LD* VIII, 116–7)

Pusey conveyed Newman's views in a letter to Bishop Bagot in which he included a further clarification which Newman made to him in a brief letter on 25 March, and again in a letter of 26 March. Pusey also said that Newman 'thinks that by your referring to his former correspondence with your Lordship, and his own language in it, and the way in which he had felt and taken your Lordship's communications, he could in a natural way show that your Lordship had exercised a watchful superintendence over those committed to your care'. Newman did this at the beginning of his letter to the Bishop. Pusey also wrote that Newman's bringing the Tracts to a close immediately instead of waiting for the other two in progress to be published would 'fully suffice to prevent your Lordship's "course being misunderstood". . . . It does set a sort of mark upon their close and . . . put some disgrace upon it, that they were brought prematurely and abruptly to a close, in consequence of apprehensions entertained by the Bishop under whom their authors were placed, and in consequence of this desire.'[7]

The withdrawal of *Tract 90*, however, would be an act of condemnation, 'as has not been exercised upon works against which the gravest charges are brought'. Pusey cited as examples Hampden's Bampton Lectures, Milman's book which explains away 'many of the miracles of our Lord in a shocking way', and books 'denying the doctrine of baptismal regeneration, terming the doctrine which our Church teaches a heresy, but no one interferes with or censures them. There is, I believe, no instance of a book being thus withdrawn from free circulation at the desire of a Bishop.' (*LD* VIII, 125–6)

Pusey saw the Bishop again in the same day, 26 March, when the Bishop accepted that Newman would bring the Tracts to an end without any suggestion of 'suppression' of *Tract 90*. It was also agreed that the Bishops would refrain from condemnation of the Tract on the understanding that Newman after his letter to the Bishop would not defend it. Pusey after the publication of the *Apologia* verified this.

> The fact that the Bishops would not, as a body, censure Tract 90, was told me by the late Bishop of Oxford (Bagot). He added, what Dr Newman has already stated in the Apologia . . ., and which I conveyed to him from Bishop Bagot, that perhaps two or three might mention it in their charges. This Bishop Bagot said to me, not as his own opinion, but on authority (although he did not tell me what authority). I suppose that *that* authority had miscalculated. Yet it was a very grave matter; for the non-condemnation of Tract 90 was the inducement held out by him why (with materials for another year at least) we should close the series abruptly.[8]

Newman went ahead with his letter to the Bishop, which was widely felt to be characterized by humility, reverence and obedience. He agreed to stop the Tracts in accordance with the Bishop's wishes, though he took the occasion to defend three of the Tracts: Keble's 'The Mysticism attributed to the Early Fathers of the Church' (No. 89), his own Tract on the Breviary (No. 75), and Isaac Williams' 'Reserve in Communicating Religious Knowledge' (Nos. 80 and 87) from 'the odious charge of scattering firebrands about without caring for or apprehending conse-quences.' (*VM* II. 400)

Newman then explained that he was not leading persons to Romanism or Popery, a system which he always spoke against and which he defined not abstractly, but as 'truth overlaid with corruptions'. On the other hand he considered the Church of England the Catholic Church in this country. Though he wished Rome and the Church of England were one, 'we cannot, without a sin, sacrifice truth to peace; and, in the words of Archbishop Laud, "till Rome be other than it is", we must be estranged from her'. Consequently he was opposed to 'suggestions for considering differences between ourselves and the foreign Churches with a view to their adjustments', by which he meant by way of negotiation, agitation, conferences, etc. But it was more than a question of truth, it was one of holiness. 'Our business is with ourselves – to make ourselves more holy, more self-denying, more primitive . . . .' And till Roman Catholics 'renounce political efforts, and manifest in their public measures the light of holiness and truth, perpetual war is our only prospect'. So while we should be content with the outward circumstances in which Providence has placed us, we must endeavour to raise the moral tone of the Church. 'It is sanctity of heart and conduct which commends us to God ... sanctity is the great Note of the Church.' (*VM* II, 421–2)

Newman did not like having to write again against Rome. In a memorandum of 28 July 1844, in which he spoke of his changed attitude toward Rome, he said that although he was able to commit himself to his remarks about Rome, since his doubts had passed away, he did not like to do so again, 'with the consciousness of the chance of change in prospect, but I did not feel I had any right to put a contingency against a Bishop's command, and to confess I had had doubts while I made it, would have been to scatter firebrands.'[9]

In the final paragraph of his letter Newman resigned his place in the Movement.

And now, my Lord, suffer me to thank your Lordship for your most abundant and extraordinary kindness towards me, in the midst of the exercise of your authority. . . . I have nothing to be sorry for, but everything to rejoice in and be thankful for. I have never taken pleasure in seeming to be able to move a party, and whatever influence I have had has been found not sought after. I have acted because others did not act, and have sacrificed a quiet which I prized. . . . I think I can bear, or at least will try to bear, any personal humiliation, so that I am preserved from betraying sacred interests, which the Lord of grace and power has given into my charge. (*VM* II, 424)

On 2 April the Bishop replied warmly, thanking Newman and praising the spirit in which his letter was written. He further remarked that Newman would 'not have cause to repent having written it'. (*LD* VIII, 144)

CHAPTER NINETEEN

The Aftermath

On 30 March Newman wrote to Jemima, 'I am quite satisfied with the bargain I have got, if this is all, as I suppose it will be.' (*LD* VIII, 145) He had conceded no doctrine or principle nor were any condemned by authority. 'Numbers will be taking advantage silently and quietly of the admission for their benefit. It will soon be *assumed* as a matter of course.' Hence it would be better to let the matter drop. 'We may do any thing if we keep from *disturbance*. . . . We can gain any thing by giving way.' (To Keble, 1 and 10 April, *LD* VIII, 149, 169) He believed this not only because he thought the bishops feared a disturbance, but from a spiritual principle. 'It is a profound gospel principle that victory comes by yielding. . . . We rise by falling.' This however did not mean 'yielding any one point which I hold on conviction – and that the authorities of the Church know full well.' (*LD* VIII, 165)

Pusey wrote to Hope,

> They who have read what Newman has written since on the subject, must be won by his touching simplicity and humility. . . . Every one says how Newman has risen with the occasion. Keble writes to-day: 'I cannot but think that Newman's coming out as he does in this whole business will do the cause a great deal more good, than any fresh stir of which this tract has been made the pretence, is likely to do harm. People quite unconnected write to me as if they were greatly moved by it.'
>
> The pseudo-traditional and vague ultra-Protestant interpretation of the Articles has received a blow from which it will not recover. People will abuse Tract 90, and adopt its main principles. It has been a harassing time for Newman, but all great good is purchased by suffering, and he is wonderfully calm. (*LD* VIII, 178)

The row occurred during Lent when Newman increased his fasting and abstinence. 'I have this Lent abstained, except on Sundays, from flesh (except fish), butter, vegetables except potatoes, wine, tea, toast, pastry, fruit, sugar, and beer; have never dined out, or taken a meal with any one, or gone to wine in Common Room, or worn gloves, or (except now and then) looked at Newspapers . . . On Wednesday and Friday I took no food whatever, except sometimes a glass of water, till 5 or 6 p.m.' (*AW*, 218)

On 21 March Newman preached 'Apostolic Abstinence. A Pattern for Christians', in which he affirmed that the 'great duty of the Gospel is love to God and man; and that this love is quenched and extinguished by self-indulgence'. Without self-denial, Christian love cannot be possessed, but 'love is no common grace in its higher degrees. . . . in any of its higher and maturer stages, it is rare and difficult . . . Happy is it for us, if God's secret grace call us on, as it called St. Paul and Timothy, to a more divine and tranquil life than that of the multitude. It is our duty to war against the flesh as they warred against it, that we may inherit the gift of the Spirit as they inherited them. If Saints are our patterns, this surely means that we must copy them.'

Ever since his first doubts Newman seems to have felt he was called to this higher state. Yet he cautioned his audience that it would be presumptuous to attempt all at once what the Apostles and their associates did, but we can begin. 'Mount up the heavenly ladder step by step.' In contemplating the lives of holy men, we must be on guard 'against attempting just what they did; which might be right indeed in them, and yet may be wrong in us'. It was a warning he had issued in other sermons. So while he regularly advised those who consulted him to be prudent in their fasting, he himself was secretly practising what many a saint did. (*PPS* VI, 3, 26–38)

Although Newman thought the act of the Heads of Houses a 'violent' one, his immediate reaction was a spiritual one. 'I have asserted a great principle, and I ought to suffer for it.' (15 March 1841, *LD* VIII, 77) Nothing said or written during these days reveals his inner attitude so much as the sermon he preached on Good Friday, 'Christ's Cross the Measure of the World', in which he affirmed that

'His cross has put its due value on every thing which we see, upon all fortunes, all advantages, all ranks, all dignities, all pleasures. . . . It has taught us how to live, how to use this world, what to expect, what to desire, what to hope. It is the tune into which all the strains of this world's music are ultimately to be resolved. . . . That Cross will lead us to mourning, repentance, humiliation, prayer, fasting; we shall sorrow for our sins, we shall sorrow with Christ's suffering; but all this sorrow will only issue, nay, will be undergone in a happiness far greater than the enjoyment the world gives. . . . And so, too, as regards this world, with all its enjoyments, yet disappointments. Let us not trust it. . . . They alone are able truly to enjoy this world, who begin with the world unseen. . . . They alone can truly feast, who have first fasted . . . they alone inherit it, who take it as a shadow of the world to come, and for that world to come relinquish it. (*PPS* VI, 7, 83–93)

Newman received many letters of support from friends and strangers during and after the row, though some also frankly expressed reservations about some of his opinions.[1] Before and during the row Ambrose Phillipps was writing letters to Bloxam about corporate reunion. Newman threw a good deal of cold water on these attempts. While Newman's expression of Catholic doctrine in *Tract 90* was encouraging, the reaffirmation in Newman's *Letters* to Jelf and Bishop Bagot of his earlier views critical of Catholic doctrine and practice distressed both Phillipps and Wiseman, who registered their disapproval. The most influential letter came however from another Catholic who was hitherto unknown to Newman, but who in the event 'had, perhaps, more to do with my conversion than any one else'. (*Apo.*, 194)

On Easter Monday, 12 April, Newman received a friendly letter from Dr Russell, then Professor of Humanity at Maynooth College, Dublin. It was written on Holy Thursday after Russell had celebrated the liturgy, and, as he explained, on an impulse that he might do some good in writing to say that the doctrine of transubstantiation was misunderstood and misrepresented in *Tract 90*. To show what Catholics really believe he offered – an offer Newman accepted – to send a copy of Vernon's *Regula Fidei*. Newman replied in a friendly way, and one cannot help contrasting its tone with that of his earlier letter to George Spencer, though some of the same points are made by Newman. After explaining his position in the Tract, he added 'O that you would reform your worship, that you would disown the extreme honors paid to St Mary and other Saints, your traditionary view of Indulgences, and the veneration paid in foreign countries to Images! And as to our own country, O that, abandoning your connexion with a political party, you would, as a body, "lead quiet and peaceable lives in all godliness and honesty".' (*LD* VIII, 172–4)

In his reply Russell thanked Newman for its kind and cordial spirit which verified his estimate of Newman, but he proceeded to assure Newman that a similar scrutiny of other Catholic doctrines would produce the same result, and he referred to the Lutheran scholar, Leibniz, whose *Systema Theologicum* was written during his discussions with Bossuet about reunion. He was sure that if Newman became familiar with Catholic doctrine on Mary and the saints, the views held even by uneducated people on indulgences and use of sacred images, his fears of the so-called Roman 'traditionary system' would disappear. (*LD* VIII, 180–1)

Newman and Russell exchanged several letters, in one of which Newman remarked that even if his position on the traditionary system of Rome were to change, this would not tend to move him from his present position, providentially appointed in the English Church. 'That your communion was unassailable, would not prove that mine was indefensible.' 'We have too great a horror of the principle of private judgment, to trust it in so immense a matter as that of changing from one communion to another. We may be cast out of our communion, or it may decree heresy to be truth . . . but I do not see other conceivable causes of our leaving the Church in which we were baptized.' Nevertheless he admitted that his *sympathies* towards Rome had grown stronger but added that 'my *reasons* for *shunning* her communion have lessened or altered, it will be difficult perhaps to prove, And I wish to go by reason not by feeling.' (5 May 1841; *LD* VIII, 187–8; *Apo.*, 188–9)

Not thinking it opportune to prolong the correspondence Russell had written shortly before expressing the hope, not that individuals would be converted to Rome, but the Church itself would bring itself into communion with ours. 'May He, to use the words of your *Ecclesiastical Almanac* . . . "hasten that union and make us worthy of entering into it".' He concluded, 'I pray daily that you and your friends may be strengthened to dismiss all fears of that secondary and traditionary system among us, which seems to haunt you. Believe me, my dear Sir, it has no existence in fact. . . . I am as confident, as I can be . . . that, had you the same sources . . . of information, you would believe, with me, that your fears are unfounded.' (1 May 1841; *LD* VIII, 186–7) This was one of the obstacles that had to be removed before (with the help of Dr Russell) he would be able to become a Catholic.

In October of the same year Dr Russell returning from Rome thanked Newman for the volume of his *Parochial Sermons*. In return he would send him a copy of Leibniz's *Systema Theologicum*, the original manuscript of which he had examined in Rome and of which he was planning to publish an English translation. He added that he knew 'no work more calculated than it . . . to smooth away the prejudices with which but too many regard the doctrines of the Catholic Church'. (6 October 1841, *BOA*) No further correspondence occurred until 31 October 1842.

Newman published a second edition of *Tract 90* on the same day as the letter to Bagot was published, and this was Newman's last word, but not so others. Wilson, one of the four protesting tutors. published a letter complaining of Newman's ambiguity of expression both in the Tract and in the letter to Jelf. 'This letter, which was hailed with great triumph by Tait and his associates, decided Mr Ward to come forward.' He wrote two pamphlets on the subject, entitled respectively *A Few Words* and *A Few Words More – in defence of Tract 90*. Ward's pamphlet was not only a defence of the Tract, but a clarification, for example, of Newman's meaning of 'authoritative teaching', which Ward said was misunderstood. His criticism of the Reformers was much stronger and more explicit than Newman's. Nor could he conceal his sympathies for the Roman Catholic Church and though acknowledging the 'practical corruptions' of the Church of Rome, at the same time he criticized the corruptions of the Church of England. (*W. G. Ward*, 164–5) Ward knowing that after his second pamphlet it was planned to strip him of his lectureship in Logic and Mathematics at Balliol, resigned.

Neither the situation at Oxford nor the Movement was ever the same after the publication of *Tract 90*. 'An informal inquisition was established, and clerical and academic preferment became dependent on a disavowal of the opinions expressed in the Tracts.' (*W. G. Ward*, 185–6) The newer members of the Movement, such as Ward and Oakeley, became more outspoken in their criticisms of the deficiencies of the Anglican Church and in their sympathies towards Rome. They thought that the principles of the Tract allowed them to hold, 'consistently with subscription . . . all obligatory Roman doctrine'. While Newman kept aloof from contacts with Roman Catholics, Ward through Bloxam made the acquaintance of Ambrose Phillipps and indirectly of Wiseman. On visits to Oscott and St Bernard's Abbey, Ward was deeply impressed, and like Bloxam, he entered into correspondence with the leaders of the Movement for reunion in the Catholic Church. These efforts suffered a blow when Sibthorp, a Fellow of Magdalen College like Bloxam, visited Wiseman at Oscott and suddenly became a Catholic, though he had no intention of doing so when he went there. 'When Sibthorp came back to Oxford,' Bloxam later wrote to Wilfrid Ward, 'Newman called on me, and warned me against monkeys who had lost their tails and wish every one to lose theirs. He always said that Sibthorp went over on Wesleyan principles.' (*W. G. Ward*, 193) This delivered a blow to Bloxam's reunion activities, while Tractarian opponents pointed to it as the fruit of the 'Romish' tendency of the Movement.[2]

Further tension was created by the appearance of the July issue of the *British Critic*, the first under Thomas Mozley's editorship, which marked a change in the tone and spirit of the magazine. Though the articles by Newman, J. W. Bowden, and H. W. Wilberforce escaped criticism, Mozley's articles on 'The Tamworth Reading Room', and 'The Oxford Margaret Professor', and Oakeley's 'Bishop Jewel' stirred indignation. The sarcastic remarks about Peel in the former enraged Establishment-minded readers, while his witty even sarcastic castigation of Dr Faussett, the Lady Professor of Divinity, for his blast against *Tract 90* seemed to Newman to transgress the bounds of charity. Oakeley's attack on Jewel led Pusey to wonder about its author's allegiance to the Church, while Keble termed the spirit of the issue 'beyond the just limits of Christian, and . . . of gentlemanly severity'. Keble wrote to Newman, 'would it not be well to put a drag on T.M's too *Aristophanic* wheels?' Newman replied, 'The B.C. has been, and is a matter of great anxiety to me. The difficulty is how to bring things home to T.M. without dispiriting him. . . . I bargained to see all his articles in proof, but hearing that this was upon Number 90, I thought I was too near a party to see it with propriety, and some one at my elbow whom I asked agreed.' (*LD* VIII, 217–8) Pusey, who apparently had not read the Preface to Froude's *Remains* Part II, which though written by Keble represented Newman's own view of the Reformation, had no suspicion of Newman's attitude toward the Reformation, and he drew from Newman his view 'it requires no deep reading to dislike the Reformation', a view which Pusey did not share. (*LD* VIII, 240–5) Newman briefly and gently brought to Mozley's attention 'a consensus against the Article on Faussett – and we must, I think, banish satire from the Review for a long while', to which Mozley agreed, but the magazine became the organ of the newer school of Tractarians like Ward and Oakeley.

Newman's contribution to the July issue was an important article which stated his position at this time. He began by asserting that serious religious changes have a *prima facie* case against them. Private judgement is an act of individual responsibility. 'A religious man will say to himself, "if I am in error at present, I am in error by a disposition of Providence, which has placed me where I am; if I change into an error, this is my own act. It is much less fearful to be born at disadvantage, than to place myself at disadvantage."'

People in general corroborate these instinctive feelings. On hearing of a conversion they assign all sorts of reasons to explain it. 'If a staunch Protestant's daughter turns Roman, and betakes herself to a convent, why does he not exult in the occurrence? . . . Why is he in this base, disloyal style muttering about priests, and Jesuits, and the horrors of nunneries, in solution of the phenomenon, when he has the fair and ample form of Private Judgment rising before his eyes.' This leads one to suspect that 'private judgment, all private judgment, and nothing but private judgment, – is held by very few persons indeed.' The minority who hold it 'hold, not the right of private judgment, but the private right of judgment; in other words, their own right, and no one's else'. (*Ess.* II, 337–41)

Newman then made a remark that revealed his acute self-knowledge and his recognition of the psychological limitations in one who wishes to search for truth. This self-distrust will be increased with the recurrence of his doubts. 'Who can know ever so little of himself without suspecting all kinds of imperfect and wrong motives in everything he attempts? And then there is the bias of education and of habit; and, added to the difficulties thence resulting, those which arise from weakness of the reasoning faculty, ignorance or imperfect knowledge of the original languages of Scripture, and again, of history and antiquity.' He concluded with the enunciation of a principle which he would assert in letters again and again, 'Divine aid alone can carry any one safely and successfully through an inquiry after religious truth.'

> It is useless, surely, attempting to inquire or judge, unless a Divine command enjoin the work upon us, and a Divine promise sustain us through it. . . . An act of duty must always be right. . . . He can lead us forward by means of our mistakes. . . . . And much more can He shed upon our path supernatural light, if He so will, and give us an insight into the meaning of Scripture, and a hold of the sense of Antiquity, to which our own unaided powers never could have attained.

It is certain that God leads us forward 'in the midst of darkness'. Newman felt a call to institute a religious inquiry, that he did not know where Providence was leading him, but his trust in God was unwavering. Moreover only a call from God would lead him to change his religion.

After examining various conversions mentioned in Scripture Newman affirms that such conversions are brought about through a *teacher*, and not by means of private judgement. Since religion is for practice, it is much easier to form a correct and rapid judgement of persons than of books or of doctrines. The question then is 'Who is God's prophet, and where? Who is to be considered the voice of the Holy Catholic and Apostolic Church?' Even in the apostolic age there were differences between the Apostles, so also today – an analogy which Newman later rejected. If the Church of England 'has certain imperfections', the Church of Rome has 'certain corruptions'. 'The Roman Church practices what looks so very like idolatry, and the English glories in what looks so very like schism.' Since few men have time to scrutinize accurately, there are sufficient notices 'to deter him from joining her'. Newman takes up the objection posed by Augustine's *securus judicat orbis terrarum* and gives the same response as in his article on the Catholicity of the English Church. One difference between the two articles is the absence in the later article of the fierce language Newman used against Rome in the earlier one. In fact he pleaded for a more charitable attitude toward Catholics.

In conclusion Newman saw but one cloud that could darken the horizon. If the Church of England declared itself formally schismatical or owned itself Protestant, 'while foreign communions disclaimed the superstition of which they are too tolerant . . . then doubtless, for a season, Catholic minds among us would be unable to see their way'.

The number of persons attracted to Rome began to increase, some because of the condemnation of *Tract 90* and subsequent events. For these Newman felt concern. To Miss Holmes who was attracted towards Rome he recommended patience and forbearance. 'So great a matter as a change of religion ought not to be thought of without years (I may say) of prayer and preparation. Nor do I think it God's way, generally speaking, for *individuals* to leave one religion for another – it is so much like an exercise of private judgment.' As to the disturbance caused by *Tract 90*, he did not think the cause of Catholic truth would suffer by it. 'It is good for all of us to have reverses and to have our patience tried. Patience and forbearance are great virtues.' (8 April 1841, *LD* VIII, 162–3)

In a letter of 8 August 1841 he showed great sympathy and understanding of her desire to become a Catholic so as to enter a convent. 'That the Church of Rome is possessed of much which your mind naturally looks for and asks, and which the English Church cannot supply, is undeniable – and will be the cause of your conversion, if that takes place.' This motive he had long since predicted to Manning and others. Such conversions he tried to prevent by proposing various reasons. He urged her to wait and pray to discover God's will and to do it.

'Some holy man, I think St Bonaventure, speaking about inward suggestions to a Monastic Life, observes to this effect:- "Never trust a first suggestion – You cannot tell whether the voice is from above or from below – Your rule is, not to attend to it but to go on as usual – At first shrink from it. If it is from God, it will in due time return." And hence to all great changes, a season of thought and preparation is a necessary introduction, if we would know what God's will is.' This was the advice Newman followed when he experienced his first doubts of the Anglican Church in 1839. Other persons who felt like Miss Holmes have remained in the Church of England. To any friend who asked him, he would prescribe a period of three years for thought and prayer. (*LD* VIII, 238–9, and n. 1)

In a much longer letter of 15 August he warned her that if she were in a Roman convent, given her character of mind, she would have as much trial as she now has. 'Let this be your simple and engrossing prayer, to know God's will and to do it. . . . Be the English Church what you fear it is, not a legitimate branch of the True Church, yet surely it is good enough for you; it has gifts . . . which are above you and me. No – the *sole* reason we can have for leaving the Church in which God's Providence has placed us is *a call from God*; not a mere wish on our part to be nearer heaven.' He urged her to remain in the Church and to work for its improvement. (*LD* VIII, 247–8)

In answer to her question 'concerning the primitiveness of the worship of the Blessed Virgin, as at present observed in the Church of Rome', he replied in a lengthy letter of 6 September, that as a historical fact 'that worship was not observed in the primitive Church', and he proceeded to show this at considerable length. The leaders of Rome 'would maintain, if they could, that these additions are not *new* truths, but developments from germs held in primitive times'. This he conceived to be the great difficulty of the Church of Rome, just as our difficulty is separation from the great body of Christians. 'Let us be content with our own. Both we and the Church of Rome must reform. As individuals we can do nothing.' He referred her to his articles on the Catholicity of the English Church and Private Judgment. (*LD* VIII, 261–5)

THREE SUCCESSIVE BLOWS

In July 1841 Newman went to Littlemore, where he took up board and lodging at St George's, which belonged to a well-to-do farming family by the name of Giles. He engaged himself in his translation of St Athanasius. On 8 and again on 14 July he met with Miss Burford about leasing some 'cottages'. The latter were used as a stable for the Oxford–Cambridge coach. They 'consisted of a barn, a stable or two and a few mean cottages, giving on to the yard'.[3] Newman was attracted by the barn as large enough to lodge his library which had outgrown his rooms at Oriel. As he told Pusey, he gave up 'the notion of a monastic body at present, lest a talk should be made. I have got a room where I can put my books, and myself – also I have a number of spare cottages – If any one chooses to come there from London, Oxford, or elsewhere, for any time he may have a retreat, but without any thing of a coenobitium. It is only in fact furnishing him with lodgings.' (*LD* VIII, 238. See also note to Mrs. J. Mozley, 31 October, and note to diary entry, 20 April 1842)

In the *Apologia* Newman recalls that he was working at Littlemore on his translation of St Athanasius, when 'the ghost had come a second time. In the Arian History I found the very same phenomenon, in a far bolder shape, which I had found in the Monophysite. . . . I saw clearly, that in the history of Arianism, the pure Arians were the Protestants, the semi-Arians were the Anglicans, and that Rome now was what it was then. The truth lay, not with the *Via Media*, but with what was called "the extreme party".' (*Apo.*, 139) He did not however enlarge on the subject, but remarks in a letter to Mrs William Froude shed some light on it.

> There was Pope Julius resisting the whole East in defence of St Athanasius; the Eusebians at the great Council of Antioch resisting him, and he appealing to his own authority, (in which historians support him) and declaring that he filled the See of St Peter. . . . There were two parties, a Via Media and an extreme, both heretical, but the Via Media containing pious men, whom St Athanasius and others sympathise in – There were the kings of the earth taking up the heresy against the Church – There was precisely the same appeal to Scripture, which now obtains, and that grounded on a literal interpretation of its text, to which St Athanasius always opposes the 'ecclesiastical sense'. There was the same complaint of introducing novel and unscriptural terms into the Creed of the Church, 'Consubstantial', and 'Transubstantiation' being both of philosophical origin; and, if Trent has opposed some previous Councils, (which I do not recollect) at least the Nicene Council adopted the very term 'Consubstantial' which a celebrated Council of Antioch 60 or 70 years before condemned or discountenanced. (5 April 1844)

Newman did not reveal these doubts to anyone until 26 January 1842, when he felt obliged to tell Robert Wilberforce who elicited a confession from him. His attitude toward Catholics seems to have softened as a result of them. For example, his reply, dated 19 August 1841, to a letter from George Spencer reveals a friendly tone in stark contrast to the hostile belligerent tone of his previous letter to him and to the coldness of his letters to Ambrose Phillipps earlier in the year.

> I have just received your very kind letter, and lose no time to thank you for its inclosure [a variety of papers which Spencer had published in assorted Catholic journals]. . . . Let me express the great satisfaction I have felt at seeing the kind spirit, which many persons of your communion have displayed during the past year towards the English Church. Meekness and sincerity must subdue the most prejudiced among us – and I trust there are already many among us who both rejoice in the show of sympathy which some of yourselves have lately showed us and our Church, and are grateful for the courage and self-sacrifice which is involved, and who earnestly and fervently hope that, it is but the beginning of the exercise of that 'wisdom' towards us which is 'first pure, then peaceable'. [James 3:17] (*LD* VIII, 251)

Notably absent is the previous charge that Catholics were set upon destroying the English Church.

In the *Apologia* Newman speaks of two other blows:

> The Bishops one after another began to charge against me. It was a formal, determinate movement. This was the real 'understanding'; that, on which I had acted on the first appearance of Tract 90, had come to nought. I think the words, which had then been used to me, were, that 'perhaps two or three of them might think it necessary to say something in their charges'; but by this time they had tided over the difficulty of the Tract, and there was no one to enforce the 'understanding'. They went on in this way, directing charges at me, for three whole years. I recognized it as a condemnation; it was the only one that was in their power. (*Apo.*, 139–40)

The third blow came from the politically motivated establishment in October of the Jerusalem Bishopric, allowing Protestants 'to put themselves under an Anglican Bishop, without any renunciation of their errors or regard to their due reception of baptism and confirmation'. (*Apo.*, 142–3) The impetus came from King Frederick William IV of Prussia, who thought his communion incomplete without an episcopal regimen. The plan called for a bishop being established in Jerusalem nominated alternately by the British and Prussian governments. 'Consecrated according to the Anglican rite, the Bishop would be able to ordain Lutherans who accepted the Thirty Nine Articles as well as the Augsburg Confession.' (*LD* VIII, xxii)

In both these instances what distressed Newman were the doctrinal issues. In the former case some of the episcopal charges contained virtual heresy. As he later wrote to Jemima, he and Keble looked on the 'Episcopate as an absolute monarchy – *the right faith* being the constitution, not a presbytery' as Palmer and Hook wanted, '*orthodoxy* being the condition and limit of the Bishop's authority'. (19 April 1844) In the case of the Jerusalem Bishopric, which disturbed him even more, as is evident from the frequency with which he mentioned it in his letters, was the Note of error. The English Church authorities were giving apostolical succession 'to an *heretical* Church, since the recent Prussian amalgam of Lutheranism and Calvinism was effectively that. Moreover in this move he saw the Church acting like the heretics and schismatics in the patristic ages. In the history of the Monophysites, the Donatists, and the Arians, Newman beheld

a constant effort to make alliance with other heresies and schisms, though differing itself from them. Thus the Semiarians attempted the Donatists, and the Arians the Meletians, and the Nestorians (I think) the Pelagians, etc. – Now, I confess, miserable as this Prussian business is to my mind in itself, it is rendered still more startling and unsettling by its apparent fulfilment in this Note of error. . . . This has led me anxiously to look out for the *grounds* of remaining where Providence has placed me – and the most remarkable historical evidence is the case of St Meletius which I have drawn out in an article in the B.C. two years ago. It has also forced me back upon the *internal or personal Notes* of the Church, and with thankfulness I say that I have received great comfort there.

Because he had been 'in a way silenced', he did not think it proper to agitate, though he felt in conscience he had to make a protest against the measure, and this he did by sending an unsigned letter to *The Times*, which was not published. He sent his protest with an accompanying letter to the Bishop of Oxford. A copy of the Protest was also sent to the Archbishop of Canterbury. (*LD* VIII, 327–8; *Apo.*, 144–6)

In Advent 1841 Newman preached four sermons which he subsequently published in *SD* and which developed the argument from internal or personal Notes of the Church. On the one hand he did not want to sugggest doubts to those who did not have them; on the other hand, he thought, as he said to Church at the time he preached the sermons, 'Has not all our misery, as a Church arisen, from people being afraid to look difficulties in the face?' (*LD* VIII, 387) He preached with pastoral concern for those who were likewise distressed without knowing his own state of mind, but 'eager inquisitive sensitive minds have taken alarm, and (though I acted with the greatest anxiety and tried to do what I could to avoid the suspicion) they are beginning to guess that I have not an implicit faith in the validity of the *external* Notes of our Church'. (*LD* VIII, 440–1)

In the first sermon, 'Invisible Presence of Christ', while acknowledging that 'the outward signs of Christ's Presence have well nigh deserted us', and that the 'visible and public notes of His Kingdom among us' have been obscured, nevertheless we are not deprived of 'personal and private' ones. If one is trying to lead a good life, does he not have tokens, 'real and intimate', of Christ's presence especially in the Ordinances. If so, 'pause ere you doubt that we have a divine Presence among us still, and have not to seek it'.

In the third sermon, 'Grounds for Steadfastness in our Religious Profession', he enumerates various reasons, obviously Newman's own, a religious man has for remaining in the Church.

> He ever has experience . . . of a continual conversion; he is ever taking advantage of holy seasons and new providences, and beginning again. . . . Religious men . . . cannot but recollect in the course of years, that they have become very different from what they were. . . . A religious person finds that a mysterious unseen influence has been upon him and has changed him. . . . Again, every religious man may be expected to have experiences more or less of wonderful providences, which he cannot speak about to others, but which make it certain to him that, in spite of his own unworthiness, God is with him.

Newman would subsequently reveal in detail to Keble what those providences were. In addition to having their prayers answered, such persons experience 'the awful sacredness of our Sacraments and other

Ordinances', and find a manifestation of Christ which often attends on deathbeds for the benefit of survivors. Finally, they have 'the evidence of sanctity in the living'. Newman would surely put Pusey and Keble in this number. 'Is it not safe to entrust our souls in their company? is it not dangerous to part company with them in our journey across the trackless wilderness?' He concluded, 'May not we reverently hope, that Almighty God does sometimes vouchsafe to show by-standers then, that our Church, in spite of its manifold disorders, is a safe Church to die in?' A few years later he would judge it was not such a safe place. These passages reveal the reasons for his own strong attachment to the Church; it was the place in which he had found Christ and developed in holiness.

Newman asserted in the *Apologia* that the point of the sermons is brought out in the fourth sermon, 'Elijah the Prophet of latter Days'. The Anglican Church is in the situation of Samaria. 'The Kingdom of Israel was cut off from the Temple; and yet its subjects, neither in a mass, nor as individuals . . . had any command given them, though miracles were displayed before them, to break off from their own people, and to submit themselves to Judah.' Hence 'there was no call at all for an Anglican to leave his Church for Rome, though he did not believe his own to be part of the One Church'. (*Apo.*, 194)

Friends like Keble thought Newman had substituted 'a sort of methodistic self-contemplation . . . for the plain and honest tokens. . . . of a divine mission in the Anglican Church'. Its danger he later admitted was that internal evidence could be equally claimed by Methodists and others outside the Church, and hence could lead to liberalism, that one opinion if sincerely held was as good as another. Nevertheless he also admitted that there was 'a great principle of truth' in the preference of internal evidences to those which are simply outward, but of themselves they are not sufficient to implant convictions and certainty. In the sermons, Newman later wrote, there is a clear admission of doubt, in spite of his reasonings. 'He longed to have faith in the National Church, and he could not. "What *want we*," he exclaims, "*but* faith in our Church? With faith we can do everything; without faith we can do nothing."' (*Diff.* I, 79) Moreover there was a weakness in its controversial value, as the marks of divine presence and life might only be sufficient 'to prove that she was enjoying extraordinary and uncovenanted mercies'. (*Apo.*, 154–5) In *Difficulties of Anglicans* Newman explained the grant of grace on the basis of the dispositions of the recipient, not by reason of the sacrament itself, independently of such dispositions (*ex opere operantis*, not *ex opere operato*). (*Diff.* I, 85–8)

In the course of the first sermon, 'Invisible Presence of Christ', Newman refers to a personal experience. 'If your soul has been, as it were, transfigured within you, when you came to the most Holy Sacrament. . . . O pause ere you doubt that we have a divine Presence among us still, and have not to seek it.' What this experience or experiences were, one has no way of knowing for sure, as Newman was ever reticent about his interior religious life, but he wrote to Miss Holmes on 6 December 1841, 'Without going so far as to speak of miracles, which I do not mean to do, yet really things have happened to me in connexion with the Most Holy Sacrament which quite prove to me it is a reality and not an empty show.' (*LD* VIII, 367)[4]

Since Newman uses the plural, 'things' happening, it would seem that this was not a one-time experience. It may be that a description of one of these was given in a sermon on the Eucharist which Newman did not publish. In it he tells his hearers that by not coming to the Eucharist frequently they 'lose a mysterious entrance to the Court of the Living God . . . the overshadowing presence of Christ your Saviour'.

> Suppose yourself to have your eyes wrapt round and to be carried aloft by Angels to the third heaven and laid at the foot of God's throne – Suppose yourself there to lie unable to rise and look about but with the certain knowledge that there you were – that God was there – and Jesus on His right hand – that He was there sitting glorified but in the same body in which He ascended – with the same flesh and blood, though spiritualized <made immortal and spiritual>, which He had on earth – with the marks of the nails on it and of the spear – and (supposing you were made sensible), though you felt it not, (that) He drew near to you, and placed His hand upon you, sealing you on the forehead with His Father's name, or placing His cross upon your shoulders or on your breast – And supposing (you knew), though still you saw and felt it not, (that) at His touch virtue went from Him and His Spirit entered you, and armed you against all the devices of Satan to which your every day life is exposed – Supposing you knew all this and reflected on all this as you lay, though you had no sensible evidence of it, seeing, hearing, feeling nothing, knowing all – Supposing you knew too that all the while your Lord's praises were being sung though you heard them not, by Angels and Archangels, Cherubim and Seraphim who were there – that Apostles and Prophets were there – that Saints were there – close beside you gathered together at the foot of the throne, lay the souls of the multitude of believers whose bodies

sleep in the dust of the earth, that there they were lying, close and thick[,] silent and motionless, though living – what a thought would all this be to you – such a wonderful entrance into the invisible world, though your mortal senses perceived nothing – and then suppose after a while you were suddenly transported back to where you were before, and sent among men again. Would not this be a privilege so great, that great as the awe of it would be, yet desire of it would overcome fear so far as to make you willing to undergo it? (*Ser.* I, 131–2)

Meanwhile the campaign against the Tractarians touched Keble and more so Isaac Williams, which involved Newman in protracted correspondence in addition to his already heavy load of letter writing at a time when he was beginning to complain of a sore wrist from writing so much. On 8 July Keble's curate, Peter Young, had presented himself at the Bishop of Winchester's residence for examination and ordination to the priesthood, but he was 'sent back *un*ordained'. The anti-Tractarian and Evangelical C. R. Sumner sent him away to 'get clearer views' particularly on the subject of the Eucharist and the Real Presence. Young subsequently managed to obtain a copy of his examination paper. When Newman read his answers, he gave his full approval. In September the Bishop delivered a strong attack on *Tract 90* and continued to hold up Young's ordination. This put Keble in a delicate position, for in his privately printed pamphlet *Letter to Coleridge* in April, he posed the question of a clergyman who found himself under a bishop who did not condone a Catholic interpretation of the Articles. Such a clergyman, Keble had suggested, would either have to appeal to higher authority or resign his living. Newman and Pusey cautioned Keble about any appeal which might bring on some general episcopal statement. After many consultations with Newman, Keble issued a protest which he addressed to the Archbishop of Canterbury on 5 March 1842. (*LD* VIII, 593–5)

Keble was due to retire from the professorship at the end of 1841, having completed the maximum of two five-year terms of office. Isaac Williams was expected by many to succeed him, but news got about that James Garbett was being put forth as an 'anti-Tractarian' candidate, though his literary qualifications were inferior to Williams. Newman who startled his friends by being unhappy at Williams' candidature found himself unwittingly in the midst of a storm centre. He 'had been against his standing throughout, from a dread of Convocation – but considering *I* am the cause of the opposition by Number 90, it would be ungenerous to press my objection'. For four months the contest raged on involving five bishops, Gladstone, and many others. Rumours began to circulate that should Williams lose by a heavy vote a move to suppress Tractarianism by university legislation would result. Hence the drive to capture as many votes as possible. A comparison of pledged votes showed 921 for Garbett against 623 for Williams, who on 20 January 1842 withdrew his candidature, and a week later Garbett became Professor of Poetry.[5]

On 8 February Newman went up to Littlemore for Lent; on the 15th all his books were up, but not the bookcases. These were set in place on the 17th, and the following two days he spent putting in his books, and in so doing managed to injure his thumb from the weight of the books. In response to Henry Wilberforce's concern about the severity of his fasting the previous year, communicated to him by Dr Babington, Newman went to see Dr Wooten who 'said I might have my way'. Though he added milk and butter, still he was stricter in that he took no food between breakfast 8 a.m. and Tea at 6 p.m., and on Wednesdays and Fridays he took no food until 6 p.m. On 6 March he notes in his journal being 'very much exhausted – and from exhaustion have not been regular sometimes in the Breviary Offices.' (*AW*, 220–1)

CHAPTER TWENTY

Life at Littlemore

On 20 April Newman came up to Littlemore in a fly, his library having been moved into the barn part of the row of stables, and Dalgairns joined him on 22nd. Newman's rooms were at the far end of the long arm of the L. On the 25th he began Breviary services. The same day he wrote to Henry Wilberforce about the move, and though he did not know how it would turn out, 'yet a good Providence has so wonderfully guided me on step by step, without my seeing the path before me, that I cannot but think that something will come of it'. On a visit to Littlemore, Harriett described the building in a letter to Jemima on 13 May 1842. 'There are 4 or 5 sets of rooms – sitting and bedroom – all on the ground floor – the door opening into the verandah which runs all along, a length of the diagonal of Oriel quad. The kitchen is in the middle – a pretty little garden before the verandah. At right angles is the library, a large pretty room with a nice roof, the sides covered with books. Inside, another small book room and above a spare bedroom. . . . The new windows were putting up – very old and handsome looking'. (*FL*, 121–7) Fr Dominic later left on record a different impression, perhaps with a touch of Italian exaggeration, which Wilfrid Ward called 'quaint'.

> This unsightly building is divided by a number of walls, so as to form so many little cells; and it is so low that you might touch the roof with your hand. In the interior you will find the most beautiful specimen of patriarchal simplicity and gospel poverty. . . . In the cells nothing is to be seen but poverty and simplicity – bare walls, floors composed of a few rough bricks, without carpet, a straw bed, one or two chairs, and a few books, this comprises the whole furniture !!!. . . . A Capuchin Monastery would appear a great palace when compared with Littlemore.' (*Ward*, I, 106)

Newman wrote to his aunt, 'We shall have some difficulty in keeping the place warm in the winter . . . but a thick sheepskin under the feet will do great things.' (29 August 1842)

The place, however, stirred up gossip. In the *Apologia* he recounted, 'Reports of all kinds were circulated about me. "Imprimis, why did I go up to Littlemore at all? For no good purpose certainly; I dared not tell why." (*Apo.*, 171) As a result of a report in the newspapers that he was building an Anglo-Catholic monastery, his Bishop felt obliged to give him the chance to deny it. This he did, although Newman in letters had spoken of the place as a 'monastery', it really was not. As he told the Bishop, 'I am not attempting a revival of the Monastic Orders, in any thing approaching to the Romanist sense of the term.' Despite this explanation Newman's disavowal has been called 'disingenuous', which simply displays an ignorance of what constitutes a monastery. But that is of little importance. It is, however, that Newman revealed his real intentions. 'For many years, at least thirteen, I have wished to give myself to a life of greater religious regularity than I have hitherto led. . . . and being a resolution of years, and one to which I feel God has called me . . . I should have to answer for it, if I did not pursue it. . . . At the same time, of course, it would be a great comfort to me to know that God had put into the hearts of others to pursue their personal edification in the same way.' He also told the Bishop that he was helping to keep 'a certain class of minds firm in their allegiance to our Church' and he intended to pursue his resolution with or without the 'sympathies of others pursuing a similar course'. Newman further wrote that the parish had been very much neglected, 'and in providing a parsonage-house at Littlemore, as this will be, and will be called, I conceive I am doing a very great benefit to my people'. (*Apo.*, 173–6)

This, however, did not stop the intrusion on his privacy. 'One day when I entered my house, I found a flight of Under-graduates inside. Heads of Houses, as mounted patrols, walked their horses round those poor cottages. Doctors of Divinity dived into the hidden recesses of that private tenement uninvited, and drew domestic conclusions from what they saw there. I had thought that an Englishman's house was his castle, but the newspapers thought otherwise.' (*Apo.*, 172)

Newman was first joined by John Dobrée Dalgairns, a young, intelligent, but perhaps overly self-confident enthusiast who had come up to Exeter at the age of eighteen and took a second in classics in 1839. Born in Guernsey, he was fluent in French. He was much influenced by the principles of the Oxford Movement but like other younger members he was drawn to Rome. He and Ward composed a letter to the French Catholic newspaper *Univers*, Ward supplying most of the content, Dalgairns organizing the ideas and translating them into good French. It bore the signature, 'A young student of the University of Oxford.' (*LD* VIII, 563–7) It applied to French Catholics for sympathy and expressed a strong desire to be united with the Church of Rome. 'We love with unfeigned affection the Apostolic See, which we acknowledge to be the head of Christendom; and the more because the Church of Rome is our mother, which sent from her bosom the blessed St Augustine to bring us her immovable faith.' (*W. G. Ward*, 187–8) The letter caused great excitement both at home and abroad. Though no official notice was taken of it by the authorities in Oxford, Dalgairns was denied testimonials to be ordained.

Dalgairns took an interest in Littlemore before it was set up and hoped to join Newman there. He was probably representative of the younger members of the movement when he wrote in a letter of November 8 1841, 'I am sure that there is very little union *in the party*. Newman is the only man who holds it together. There is a great diversity of opinion between him and Pusey and Isaac Williams, and he holds much more with the younger portion, such as Ward, than with them.'[1] In another letter on 1 December 1841 Dalgairns reiterated his belief in Newman's holding the party together while revealing Newman's appeal to the younger men such as himself.

> You can have no conception of what importance Newman is here; he alone can for a moment hold things together. I attribute less to his wonderful powers of mind, than to his wonderful love for all men. He thinks no human misery beneath him, and seems to love persons the better the wilder and younger they are. I am sure that my most intimate friends have snubbed and scolded me for certain perturbations, which he has taken as if they were his own, and does his very utmost to heal. (1 December 1841)

Shortly after joining Newman at Littlemore, Dalgairns writes on 10 May 1842, describing the place and set-up and remarks, 'Newman declares his object is not to teach people austerities, but only living in a plain, frugal way, so as to get out of the gentleman-parson line.' In another letter he says, 'Newman works for the press, and I am his end; when he has no work in hand he reads theology and so do I. Lockhart, who is our only other regular inmate, does what he pleases, in the way of reading.' Later when Newman had devised the project of the 'Lives of the Saints', which he mentioned for the first time in a letter to Tom Mozley, 18 October 1842, he put Dalgairns on to writing the life of

Stephen Harding, which attracted attention both in England and in France and Germany, where it became known in translation. He also wrote the life of St. Aelred of Rievaulx, being attracted to medieval monasticism and austerity.

Dalgairns was soon joined by William Lockhart, who was at Exeter from 1839 to 1842 when he took his degree. He was deeply influenced by Newman's sermons and in reading the Fathers of the Church was drawn to the Catholic Church. Worried about his past sins, he had recourse to Manning who heard his confession and urged him to continue in his desire to be a clergyman in the Church of England. In July 1842 he joined Newman's community, but becoming unsettled, Newman told him 'You must agree to stay here three years or go at once.' When he hesitated, Newman asked him to see Ward, and after three hours' talk in which Ward emphasized 'the necessity of conscience being clear in order to a right intellectual judgment on religious questions', Lockhart returned to Newman and agreed to promise to stay for three years.[2]

Lockhart described the 'kind of monastic life' they lived at Littlemore:

We spent our time at Littlemore in study, prayer and fasting. . . . We fasted according to the practice recommended in Holy Scripture, and practised in the most austere religious orders of Eastern and Western Christendom. We never broke our fast, except on Sundays and the Great Festivals, before twelve o'clock, and not until five o'clock in the Advent and Lenten seasons.

We regularly practised confession and went to Communion, I think, daily, at the Village Church. At dinner we met together, and after some spiritual reading at table, we enjoyed conversation with Newman. He spoke freely on all subjects that came up, but I think controversial topics were tacitly avoided. He was most scrupulous not to suggest doubts as to the position of the Church of England to those who had them not.

Sometimes, Lockhart recounted, Newman would bring his violin into the library after dinner and entertain us with 'exquisite sonatas of Beethoven'. He would not let his associates treat him as a superior and insisted on their never calling him 'Mr Newman', according to the custom when addressing Fellows and tutors of colleges. He wanted them to call him Newman, though Lockhart doubted they ever did so.[3]

In December 1842 Frederick Bowles joined the community. He had taken his degree at Exeter and was an ordained Anglican priest. In the summer of 1843 came Ambrose St. John. Born in 1815 he took his degree at Christ Church in 1834, and worked under Pusey. He was a good linguist, well versed in Hebrew and Syriac. He was a curate to Henry Wilberforce since 1841, and the latter wanted him to continue when Wilberforce was offered a living in East Farleigh in Kent, but St. John was attracted towards Rome, and Henry did not want to discuss his problems nor did Newman, who welcomed him to come and stay at Littlemore. (*KC*, 240–1) Later he became Newman's closest friend in the Oratory. Bowles later recalled that St. John speaking of his time as Curate to Henry Wilberforce at Walmer, 'used to tell us of the Duke of Wellington going to sleep during his (St. John's) Sermons, and of the manly soldierly way in which he used to join.'[4]

Newman laid out the order of the day and the rules in a memorandum:[5]

MEMORANDUM. ORDER OF THE DAY AT LITTLEMORE

[i]

at 5 Matins etc.
at 8 breakfast begins
　11 Morning prayers
at 1 breakfast ends
　　2 speaking begins
　　3 Chapel
　　6 Supper
　　7 vespers
　　8 compline

Rules

1. every one to rise at 6 <5?>
2. every one to make his own bed
3. breakfast to be taken in one place but separately and not sitting down – at any hour between 8 and 1. at the discretion of each person – or in like manner a breakfast and luncheon too
4. No one to speak, unless spoken to, except between 2 and 8; except to avoid an inconvenience greater than breaking the rule
5. festivals an exception to rules 3 and 4
6. every new comer or guest is to be put under a resident to teach him the ways of the place

[ii]

5 a.m. Matins, Lauds, Prime

6 or 7 bedmaking – servant comes and lights fire and prepares and lays out breakfast, then cleans knives, blacks shoes. goes away. the day begins

11. Morning Prayers in Church – meanwhile the servant takes water to the bedrooms and sweeps etc.

p.m.

1. Servant removes breakfast things and washes up
2. Speaking begins
3. Afternoon Prayers at Chapel <Church>
6. Servant puts out tea – meal of the day – all together sometimes meat hot and pudding
7. Vespers
8. speaking ends
9. compline in English – if a servant present, or others who do not understand Latin. then

---

Servant prepares and lays out breakfast, cleans knives and shoes any time before *8*

dusts rooms and takes water *at 11*

removes breakfast things *at 1*

lays tea etc. *at 6*

Bowles recalled that as there was no regular servant, 'it was the rule for each one to take it in turn to answer the bell'.

The word 'retirement' when used to describe Newman's move to Littlemore must not be interpreted to mean that he became a hermit or a recluse there. True he was no longer in his rooms in Oriel surrounded by younger fellows and students, but he came into Oxford on Saturday for the services at St Mary's on Sunday, and he invariably dined with others. He generally came into Oxford once during the week on business and again he met with others. And of course he came in whenever there was College business to attend to. The Buttery Books at Oriel confirm Newman's frequent dining with guests. 'During the period between April 1842 and September 1843 (at which later date he resigned his post as vicar) charges in the Buttery Books appear on nearly a hundred weekdays, other than Saturdays, on ten Saturdays, and sixty Sundays. . . . Among the hundred weekdays above mentioned, there are three periods of continuous residence of ten to twelve days, two of which were clearly in connection with the College half-yearly meeting in October 1842 and April 1843. He also attended the gaudies. Even after he resigned St Mary's he continued to come to Oriel on Sundays, showing that it was not simply a matter of convenience with regard to St Mary's.[6] Newman's diary confirms that his visits to Oriel were not occasional, as biographers have asserted, since they include days not mentioned in the Buttery Books. It was not until the summer of 1844 that his occasional visits to Oriel almost entirely ceased. Moreover Newman was in constant communication with others by letter. His diaries show that he received many letters, which he promptly answered usually at night. Sometimes these amounted to six in one day, but unfortunately only twenty to thirty per cent of the total are known to be extant.

There were many visitors who came for a day or longer. To Miss Giberne, who asked for news of Littlemore, he replied on 12 August that it was full at the moment but 'men come and go'. Among these were Anthony Froude, Hurrell's younger brother, and Mark Pattison, Rector of Lincoln College, who at that time was a devoted follower of Newman but later, like the former, no longer believed in Christianity. In later years he left an account of a fortnight's stay at Littlemore. In what Middleton called 'rather superior tones' he remarked that even in those days Newman did not find his own intellectual equals in the young men around him. 'Indeed it was a general wonder how Newman himself could be content with the society of men like Bowles, Coffin, Dalgairns, St. John, Lockhart and others.'[7]

Wilfrid Ward later wrote that Newman would often take his disciples for a walk.

Then he was his old fascinating self. While walking so fast that his companions could hardly keep pace with him, he conversed on all subjects – except the one which was most anxiously pressing on him. . . . In public his conversation was of current politics, of literature, and still more of early Oxford memories, of Keble, Hawkins, Blanco White. Whately was a favourite theme. He and other old friends, whose intimacy belonged to the past, were held in the affectionate grasp of that clinging memory. (*Ward I*, 85)

TORRES VEDRAS

In the *Apologia* Newman recorded that he 'called Littlemore my Torres Vedras, and thought that some day we might advance again within the Anglican Church, as we had been forced to retire,' (*Apo.*, 148), a reference to Wellington's tactics in Portugal. Newman was happy and contented at Littlemore. His first task was to finish the essay on miracles which was a preface to the translation of Fleury's *Ecclesiastical History*, published separately in 1843 as *An Essay on the Miracles Recorded in the Ecclesiastical History of the Early Ages*. Newman argued by analogy that if one accepts the miracles of Scripture one ought to accept those of subsequent ages. The section giving examples from ecclesiastical history took the longest time to compose, and was anathema to sceptics and Protestants alike. Newman defended his views against Kingsley in Note B of the *Apologia*. Did the miracle actually occur, what is wrong in accepting it, granted of course the possibility and likelihood that such an event occurred, which a religious mind would have no problem in accepting.

To Miss Giberne he wrote, 'Had I my will, I really think I should write nothing more – for what I do, is misinterpreted, not only by enemies, which I can bear, but by friends.' (12 August 1842) There were reports that he was 'rearing at Littlemore a "nest of Papists"', and 'actively in the service of the enemy,' when in truth he was keeping men from defecting to Rome. To Pusey he confided, 'What I *was* hurt about, was . . . that persons should think me capable of *holding an office* in the Church, and yet countenancing and living familiarly with those who were seceding from it. I do not see how this could be without treachery. The very fact that I hold a living ought to show people that I am necessarily in the *service* of the English Church. (24 August 1842)

To a theological question posed in a letter by Cecil Wynter, What and where is the Church? Newman compared the present situation of the Church to the breakup of the Ottoman Empire.

Our Lord founded a kingdom, it spread over the earth and then broke up – Our difficulties in faith and obedience are just those which a subject in a decaying Empire has in matters of allegiance. We sometimes do not know what is of authority and what is not – who has credentials and who has not – when local authorities are exceeding their power and when they are not; how far old precedents must be modified in existing circumstances, how far not. . . . When we are asked 'Where is the Church?' I can but answer where it *was*. . . . It is under an eclipse or in deliquium now. . . . we can but do what we think will best *please* the Lord . . . we obey those that are set over us first because they *are* set over us – next because at least the apostolical succession is preserved . . ., further because they are the nearest representatives we can find of the whole Church, and are to a very great extent her instruments. We consider the local Church the type and deputy of the whole. (16 July 1842)

He did not try to cover up the difficulties in the current situation of the Church. To his old friend of Trinity days, S. L. Pope, he writes, 'I feel quite what you say and assent to it with all my heart. . . . The laity say, *Whom* are we to believe. . . . How can that be practically a church, how can it *teach*, which speaks half a dozen things in the same breath?' Newman put his finger on the problem which has lingered until the present day and accounted for the large number of recent conversions to the Catholic Church – the English Church has no unified teaching authority. At the time, Newman still believed what he had said in the article on the state of religious parties in the Church. In twenty years 'the old Protestant generation will be extinct. . . . But if not, if either zealots force matters on to a collision, or the old party does not disappear in time, our church must inevitably go to pieces. For this reason I am very much against the meeting of Convocation . . . fearing it would bring on a crisis. The Protestant party would do all in their power to eject their opponents from the church.' (4 September 1842)

In August, Newman wrote to Miss Holmes, who was following a controversy between Wiseman and Palmer, that her faith should not depend upon a point of controversy.

It seems a more simple view to ask, 'what is my *duty*'? It does not seem to me that a *proof* that the English Church was in a false position, or wrong in its controversy with Rome, or in a quasi-schismatical state, could it be framed, would at once make it the duty of a member of that Church to quit it for Rome. . . . most persons seem to think that *truth as it approves itself to their reason* is their sufficient warrant for acting – I cannot see this. . . . 'Lord, what *wilt Thou* have me to *do*?' seems the true question. (1 August 1842)

In November Miss Holmes had the opportunity of meeting Newman in Oxford, and she was somewhat disappointed that he turned out not to be the venerable old person she had imagined him to be. Being as frank as he she mentioned it in a letter, to which Newman replied, 'You are not the first person who has been disappointed in me. Romantic people always will be. I am, in all my ways of going on, a very ordinary person – However, ordinary or not, I shall not cease, if you will suffer me, to speak from time to time when I think a word may be useful – for though I am not an old man, as you expected, I suppose I am almost double your age, and have a right to advise.' (20 November 1842)

In his next letter he sympathized with the 'inconveniences' of her situation but said all places including a convent, to which she like other young Tractarian ladies were attracted, have their temptations, and one's task is to overcome one's infirmities which last all one's life, and he recommended a morning meditation of half an hour after placing oneself in the presence of God with great reverence, and then he added,

> As to myself, be quite sure that if you saw me again, you would quite [?] feel as you did when you saw me before – I am *not* venerable, and nothing can make me so. I am what I am. I am very much like other people, and I do not think it is necessary to abstain from the feelings and thoughts, not intrinsically sinful, which other people have. I cannot speak words of wisdom; to some it comes naturally. Do not suffer any illusive notion about me to spring up in your mind. No one ever treats me with deference and respect who knows me – and from my heart I trust and pray that no one ever may. I never have been in office or station; people have never bowed to me – and I could not endure it. I tell you frankly, my infirmity, I believe is, always to be rude to persons who are deferential in manner to me. I really do fear it is. (27 December 1842)

In a later letter in January he assured her she had not offended him, as perhaps she might have thought, and he urged her, given her emotional nature, to learn self-control in patient expectation of some good work she could perform for the Church. (24 January 1843)

In a letter to Miss Giberne, Newman described the anniversary ceremonies at Littlemore. The days coming in Ember Week made him feel it less pleasant 'as requiring too great an effort'. No doubt he felt the effects of his fasting during these days. In the procession they began this year to sing the 24th psalm from the school room. Between sixty and seventy persons stayed for Holy Communion, the largest number so far, consisting of Littlemore people, partly St Mary's, partly Oxford men and ladies from

Oxford. 'There was a vulgar riotous stranger there, making a noise, all through the service, crying popish etc. If I had heard him, I should have had him turned out for brawling . . . . Then he would have said "What persecution already! I thought the wily Puseyites would have kept the cloven foot out of sight a little longer." '

They did not get out until near three o'clock when they had 'a cold collation for some ladies (the first and last of the kind) in the library of the Parsonage.' It may have been on this occasion that Emily Bowles, sister of Frederick, first met Newman. She later became a lifelong friend.[8] The young girl was quite overcome when Newman asked her, 'Will you have some cold chicken?' She remembered the 'kind smile as he bent down with his singular chivalrous courtesy, mingled with an indescribable reserve to all women', and her mother had to reply for her.

In September, Tom Mozley's Bishop issued a criticism of the *British Critic* for speaking well of Rome, and preferring the Catholic body to the English branch. Since some time would elapse before the charge was printed, Tom should consider what course he should adopt. Newman suggested four possibilities, two of them extreme: 1) resign your living; 2) resign editorship of the magazine; 3) change the tone of the magazine, keeping out offending articles of Ward and Oakeley (the solution Newman preferred); 4) that there are questions in which the Bishop's voice is not law and this is one of them, 'that the line he would have you take is contrary to your duty to the Holy Catholic Church as imposed upon you as a Christian. . . . to cultivate Christian relations with all parts of the Church – it is a duty to prefer the general Church to your own branch of it'. (26 September 1842)

When Mozley told him he was going to ignore his Bishop's charge, Newman urged him not to do so. 'He wishes you to steer clear of certain subjects or views in the Review. . . . You either mean to obey him or not – if not, people *will* ask, Why not?' He could use the Notice of Books to give a diplomatic answer. 'As for myself, I do really think . . . that when a Bishop speak ex cathedra about his Presbyter, that Presbyter is bound to consult his wishes.' (30 October 1842) Mozley followed his advice.

This did not mean that Newman disagreed with Ward and Oakeley; he thought they were doing a good work by removing prejudices. To Pusey he explained,

As to my being entirely with Oakeley and Ward, I think my sympathies *are* entirely with them; but really I cannot determine whether my opinions are. I do not know the limits of my own opinions. If Ward says this or that is a development from what I have said, I cannot say yes or no – It is plausible; it *may* be true,. . . . I cannot assert it is not true. . . . It is a nuisance to me to be *forced* beyond what I can fairly go.

I have intended ever since the Bishop of Salisbury's charge to take the first public opportunity which occurred, of saying that I agreed with the substance of Ward's and Oakeley's articles.

I think either the whole of this or nothing should be told to Oakeley. (*Apo.*, 171, *KC*, 199)

Not only does this show a desire to be open with others, but it enunciates a distinction which it is important to keep in mind with regard to Newman's attitude towards Rome. On a number of occasions going back to 1833 he said his sympathies were with Rome, but his reason was against her. As he put it in the *Apologia*, 'Thus I learned to have tender feelings towards her; but still my reason was not affected.' (*Apo.*, 54)

On 31 October 1842, a year after his former letter, Dr Russell of Maynooth sent Newman a copy of the translated sermons of St Alphonsus Liguori, founder of the Redemptorists and writer on moral and spiritual subjects. Being strongly devoted to Our Lady, Alphonsus would be a likely one to manifest excesses of devotion to Our Lady if such existed among ordinary Italians. In his reply of 22 November Newman thanked Russell and said, 'I only wish that your Church were more known among us by such writings. . . . It is not by learned discussions . . . or reports of miracles, that the heart of England can be gained. It is by men "approving themselves," like the Apostle, "ministers of Christ." '[9]

Nevertheless, before he could answer Russell's question whether the volume is not calculated 'to remove my apprehensions that another gospel is substituted for the true one in your practical instructions', he would have to know how far the sermons are selected from a number, or whether they are the whole, or such as the whole of the author's. He assured Russell that 'if it is ever clearly brought home to me that I have been wrong in what I have said on this subject, my public avowal of that conviction will only be a question of time with me'. This, however, would have no necessary tendency, which Russell seems to expect, to draw a person from the Church of England to that of Rome. 'There is a divine life among us, clearly manifested, in spite of all our disorders, which is as great a note of the Church as any can be. Why should we seek our Lord's presence elsewhere, when He vouchsafes it to us where we are? What *call* have we to change our communion?' (*Apo.*, 193)

Russell replied promptly that the sermons were essentially unaltered, but the translator (in order not to give unnecessary offence to non-Catholics) had omitted the name of Queen Elizabeth and a couple of quotations about Mary which, though capable of a correct interpretation, were open to misunderstanding. In the *Apologia* Newman commented on this. 'This omission, in the case of a book intended for Catholics, at least showed that such passages as are found in the works of Italian Authors were not acceptable to every part of the Catholic world.' (*Apo.*, 195) To Newman's invitation to visit him at Oriel he had to decline, as he had been appointed Vicar Apostolic of Ceylon and, since the Pope did not accept his withdrawal, he had to go to Rome.

Newman in a letter of 10 December thanked Russell for his 'kind and satisfactory answer' to his questions, but said he was sorry about the omissions as they were likely to be discovered and give offence. He added that it 'was a disappointment to me to find there was so little chance of your coming to Oxford'. One must not read too much into Newman's reception of St. Alphonsus's sermons, for he said in the *Apologia* 'it was still a long time before I got over my difficulty, on the score of the devotions paid to the Saints; perhaps, as I judge from a letter I have turned up, it was some way into 1844 before I could be said fully to have got over it.' (*Apo.*, 196) Nor was Russell's gift necessarily connected with his Retractations of Statements against Rome, a draft of which he sent to R. W. Church on 29 November. 'If I could get it into an *American* Paper first, it would not be so much flying in people's faces here; and again I should not be so much bound to answer any attacks at home.'

Newman disapproved of the attempts of some Catholics to make individual converts from Anglicanism.[10] At this time Lord Shrewsbury, a zealous, well-meaning Catholic, but not a theologian, published a second edition of his pamphlet dealing with the reported ecstatics of the south Tyrol, both of whom exhibited the stigmata, *Letter from the Earl of Shrewsbury to Ambrose Lisle Phillipps, Esq. descriptive of the Ecstática of Caldaro and the Addolorata of Capriana. Being a second edition, revised and enlarged to which is added the relation of three successive visits to the Ecstática of Monte Sansavino, in May 1842.* Shrewsbury considered the phenomenon miraculous, but he used it as an argument for the Roman Church and he attacked the Tractarian doctrine of the Eucharist, especially as enunciated by Pusey, and its denial of transubstantiation and the propitiatory sacrifice of the Mass. It is curious that in a footnote Shrewsbury criticizes Pusey in a way that Newman did when he became a Catholic. 'Dr. Pusey always appears to write as if he trusted to his own individual inspiration from God, both as to the doctrines he should teach, and the fittest seasons for proposing them, and this in the very teeth of his deference to authority, and his solicitude to be guided by the tenets of primitive authority.'[11]

Having forsworn public controversy but concerned about the possible effect the pamphlet might have on unsettled persons whom he was trying to keep from converting to Rome, Newman cleverly handled his response by quoting from Père Bouhours' *Life of Loyola*, in which the saint discussed with Fr Ribadeneyra his view of a similar ecstatic woman in Bologna.[12]

The Father replied that God's way was to act upon the soul, and to pour upon it the unction of His spirit; that He did this sometimes in such abundance, that the fulness of the grace, which filled the soul, overflowed upon the body; but that that happened but seldom, and only in the case of persons very dear to God. He added that *the evil spirit*, who could not act upon the depth of the soul, *was accustomed to counterfeit outwardly the divine operations*, by way of imposing on it by these appearances. Ribadeneyra understood from this discourse, *that the nun might perhaps be deceived with her raptures and her stigmata*, and, in fact, *it was discovered that all her sanctity was but the subtle illusion of the evil spirit.*

Newman simply added to this quotation the following observation:

Though we make this extract, we must not be supposed to express any definite judgment for or against the case of a similar kind to which Lord Shrewsbury has directed public attention. We are concerned with him, not with them. Even if they are real miracles, they may not be intended for the purpose to which he has put them.[13]

When the Notice appeared, Robert Williams complained of it as did Oakeley, who wrote to Mozley, the editor, 'I confess that I am peculiarly sorry for any thing which tends to distress and perplex those who are tempted to leave us.' Newman dismissed Williams' 'figetting.' 'He wants us to join Rome – and therefore quarrels with *any* thing whatever it is, without regard to principles, which I don't think in these minutiae he sees clearly – though I have long thought he has had a sharper sight for certain greater things than most of us.' He wrote to Oakeley, taking full responsibility, 'and if necessary, blame,' for the article. 'You may be sure

I would not have gone out of my way to send it, unless I had felt strongly that it was not right (according to the constant judgment of the Catholic Church) to rest such important matters as Lord Sh. writes about on manifestations of that kind. I never intended to imply any irreverence towards the manifestation alleged itself, and am very sorry if I have appeared to do so.' (13 January 1843)

Newman's attitude toward the ritualist movement was one of reserve. 'All true attention to rites must be founded . . . on deep inward convictions, and this makes me dread the fine arts when disjoined from what is practical and personal. All about the country people are taking up architecture. I rejoice at it, *if* they take the severer side of Religion as well as the imaginative and beautiful – but no good can come of all sunshine and no shade. Jonah's gourd will be the type of our religion in that case.' (To J. Russell, 29 December 1842)

If Newman preached a stricter religion, he was practising it during Advent. On Monday of the first week the group rose at 2 a.m. for Matins, then to bed until 6 a.m. Nones were at ½ past 3 p.m., Vespers at 6 and Compline at 8. The following day, however, the time was changed to 3 a.m., 'some returning to bed, others not'. This time order was followed for the rest of Advent, except on the Feast of St Thomas and on Sundays. Newman, and probably the others, fasted till 5 p.m. on 29 and 30 November, and in December, not only on the Ember Days: 14, 16, and 17, but also on 2, 7, 9, 20, 21, 23, 24. On the 25th they stopped rising at 3 a.m., and returned to 6 o'clock rising. (Daily Memorandum in *Ecclesiastical Almanac*)

CHAPTER TWENTY-ONE

Turning in the Direction of Rome

A HUMBLE GESTURE

In a letter to the editor of the *Conservative Journal*, dated 12 December 1842, Newman, goaded on by his conscience, retracted the fiercest of his anti-Catholic statements. The document was published in the *Conservative Journal* in February preceded by the statement, 'The following letter has been forwarded to us for publication: It is without signature; but we dare say some of our Oxford readers will find no difficulty in fixing upon the name of the writer. For ourselves we give it without note or comment.'

As Fr Bacchus has pointed out, 'Newman had intended, for the sake of his friends, that his retractation should steal upon the world unobserved, without creating a sensation, and only become generally known by the time it was ancient history'. (*KC*, 203) As he told Hope, 'I had intended it for a time of peace, the beginning of December, but against my will and power the operation has been delayed, and now unluckily falls upon the state of irritation and suspicion which Bernard Smith's step has occasioned. I had committed myself when all was quiet.' (Moz. II, 406) The reference is to Smith's conversion to Rome.

Newman did *not* retract his arguments against Rome nor those in favour of the Anglican Church, but passages 'which read like "declamations".' He quoted passages from his works since 1833 to 1837 but without identifying the work. He likewise listed examples of rebukes addressed to him by 'an intimate friend', i.e., Hurrell Froude, 'in order,' according to Fr Bacchus, 'to make his confession more humiliating'. How could he come to use such language against Rome? He replied, 'I said to myself, "I am not speaking my own words, I am but following almost a *consensus* of the divines of my Church. They have ever used the strongest language against Rome . . . I wished to throw myself into their system. While I say what they say, I am safe. Such views, too, are necessary for our position".' But with great honesty he acknowledged other motives as well, which could have been uncovered only from a deep analysis of himself. 'Yet I have reason to fear still, that such language is to be ascribed, in no small measure, to an impetuous temper, a hope of approving myself to persons I respect, and a wish to repel the charge of Romanism.' (*VM II*, 428–33)

In the *Apologia* Newman expanded on these statements. With regard to the Anglican Divines he was angry with them. 'I thought they had taken me in; I had read the Fathers with their eyes. I had sometimes trusted their quotations or their reasonings; and from reliance on them, I had used words or made statements, which by right I ought rigidly to have examined myself. . . . I had exercised more faith than criticism in the matter. . . . it implied carelessness in matters of detail. And this of course was a fault.' (*Apo.*, 203) This statement has been misunderstood.[1] Newman was not saying that he always read the Fathers through the eyes of the Anglican Divines, but on this particular issue. As he wrote to Mrs William Froude, as a result of his reading the Monophysite and Arian controversies with new eyes, 'I had got a *key*, which interpreted large passages of history which had been locked up from me. I found every where one and the same picture prophetic of our present state, – the Church in communion with Rome decreeing, and heretics resisting. Especially as regards the Arian controversy, how could I be so blind before! except that I looked at things bit by bit, instead of putting them together.' (5 April 1844)

Newman stated in letters to his friends his motive in making the retractations. He did not want to be thought what he was not. 'I am not aware that I have any great motive for this paper beyond this, setting myself right, and wishing to be seen in my proper colours, and not unwilling to do such penance for wrong words as lies in the necessary criticism which such a retractation will involve on the part of friends and enemies.' (To Hope, 3 February 1843) As he explained to Pusey, '. . . intimate friends have made it a reproach against me that I use words in my writings which are formally true in *my* sense but which in *their* *effect* are far more Antiroman; "keeping the word of promise to the ear" but "breaking it to the hope".' (6 February 1843)[2] As Fr Bacchus summed it up, 'he was intent upon performing, in obedience to the dictates of his conscience, a solemn act of reparation and self-humiliation'. (*KC*, 204)

Newman's words in explanation of his having used violent and abusive language against Rome were twisted and cited again and again against him as though it were a confession that, 'when in the Anglican Church, I said things against Rome which I did not really believe'. (*Apo.*, 201) He was branded a hypocrite, liar, a shuffler, a mole in the Anglican Church doing the work of a hostile enemy. Golightly attacked him in the *Oxford Herald* for 'economizing', and elicited from Edward Copleston, Bishop of Llandaff, the statement that Newman 'seems fast approaching the crisis long expected – and in my opinion the sooner he reaches it the better – his influence being now much more pernicious than it will be when he is an avowed instead of a disguised Romanist'. The learned Joseph Mendham of Sutton Coldfield considered Newman essentially Jesuitical 'sly and scheming'.[3]

Newman sounded out David Lewis whether he could get the whole passage about the economy from his *Arians* into the *Oxford Herald*, having, he felt, some claim from the *Herald*'s 'having repeatedly put in the slander and if it were shortened, it would be said to be garbled etc.'. As he said to Lewis, he was afraid that people whom he might influence would think he patronized lying, and he suspected people high in the Church really 'do think I am partial to lying'. (10 March 1843) Some one wrote to Newman on 31 January, asking him to deny the statement which he had seen twice in one week in the *Record* that 'it is lawful to support truth by "falsehood" and "lies".'

It was with a feeling of heaviness oppressing him which arose 'from the sense of the base calumnies' thrown on him on all sides, that he sought consolation in the history of those servants of the Church in history who had suffered the same accusations, though innocent of them. This was the frame of mind in which he preached in February the sermon 'Wisdom and Innocence', which brought the criticism of 'fraud and cunning', 'craftiness and deceitfulness', 'double-dealing', 'priestcraft', of being 'mysterious, dark and subtle, designing' – charges resurrected many years later by Kingsley, which led to Newman's writing the *Apologia*.[4] What Newman affirmed in the sermon was that the world recognized only force or guile as the causes of success. Since Christians should not use force, they were sometimes credited with having used guile.

Newman defined innocence as 'simplicity in act, purity in motive, honesty in aim; acting conscientiously and religiously, according to the matter in hand, without caring for consequences or appearances; doing what appears one's duty, . . . and leaving the event to God'. Was not this precisely what Newman was doing in issuing his Retractations and in his resignation from St Mary's, which he had by this time decided upon but would not do before consulting Keble? '*Do* what your present state of opinion requires in the light of duty, and let that *doing* tell: speak by *acts*.' (*Apo.*, 216)

One would have to be pretty thick-skinned not to feel the sting of such attacks. Of all those made on him the one he felt most, he told Keble, a year and a half later, was 'the charge of dishonesty. Really no one but O'Connell is called so distinctly and so ordinarily a liar, as I am. I think nothing tends to hurt my spirits but this.' (*KC*, 349–50) Well might it do so, since he was conscious of his unwillingness to conceal from people what he thought and how he felt, by reason of which he was often getting into hot water or as he sometimes described it, 'scrapes'. As he said to Henry Wilberforce at this time, 'I wish to be out of hot water, and something or other is always sousing me again in it.' (3 February 1843)

Newman was now being soused by a widespread rumour that he had urged Bernard Smith after his conversion to Rome to retain his living in the Anglican Church. As Newman had written some letters to Smith, he could not deny any contact with him, but he denied advising him to continue in his parish with the purpose of making converts to Rome. (Editor of the *English Churchman*, 23 and 27 February 1843; to John Kaye, Bishop of Lincoln and Smith's bishop, 2 and 7 March 1843) As to whether a person holding Roman Catholic opinions could in honesty remain in the Church of England, Newman told the Bishop, 'I see nothing wrong in such a person's continuing in communion with us, provided he holds no preferment or office, abstains from the management of ecclesiastical affairs, and is bound by no subscription or oath to our doctrines.'

On the other hand, Newman's inner feelings were troubled in a different way. As he confided to Henry Wilberforce, he felt unsettled and had a bad conscience because he was having 'more sympathy and regard shown me, and more kind words said of me, than at any other time; now, that is, when I cannot take them to myself or enjoy them and feel I have no right to them. . . . and when I say I have a guilty conscience, I mean to express my deep feeling that people do not know me, and that I am a Roman in my heart when they think me an Anglican. I am sure I have no wish to take people in, yet, having outgrown former faith by present convictions, I have managed effectually to do so.' (3 February 1843) So also he wrote to Samuel Rickards, 'I prize most highly the good opinion of friends, perhaps too highly – but an evil conscience always is haunting me, that they place more confidence in me than I deserve.' (7 March 1843) And to Pusey he wrote, 'One thing I am sure of – that you in your great kindness have far more "confidence" in me than I deserve. For years I have been eager that people should not have confidence in me because I have not confidence in myself.' (4 February 1843)

Newman also received appreciative letters from Catholics because of his Retractations, e.g., from Thomas Doyle of St George's Chapel in

London (15 February 1843). and Ambrose Phillipps. Newman's reply of 5 February was written in a kinder and more gracious tone than his previous letters to Catholics.

PILGRIMS ON EARTH

Newman continued to answer Miss Holmes' letters though in February he had taken the initiative to issue some warnings. One was to be on her guard for the approaching visit of Dr Wiseman to Mr Leigh by whom she was employed, as it could be a temptation 'of acting, not on *judgment* but on *feeling* – Your feelings are in favour of Rome, so are mine. Yet I would not trust my self among R Catholics without recollecting how apt feeling is to get the better of judgment.' (8 February 1843) And a few days later he wrote that Mr Leigh's friends are alarmed about his continuance in our Church, and he urged her not to speak, (more than she could help), '*against our existing system. . . .* lest by any expressions against the sad unreality and disorders, which too truly exist on all sides of us, (as I should be the last to deny) you increase that leaning [towards the Church of Rome].' (11 February 1843)

In March he wrote a long reply to the many questions posed by Miss Holmes: It reveals not only Newman's mind at this time but also his prudence in exercising spiritual direction.

1) 'As to the alleged miracles in the Tyrol, I think I should wish to follow the example of St Ignatius, as quoted in the Notices of Books in the last British Critic. I would not deny, but I would suspend my judgment.'

2) Praises Isaac Williams' book on the passion of Christ as 'unlike any thing else in our ecclesiastical literature'. The great benefit of Roman books of devotion 'is their great and business-like practicalness. . . . They do for one what one wants, as being the writings of persons who *knew* the wants of people.' Roman Catholics, however, cannot write English and hence are driven to foreign writers, they write English like foreigners. 'As to supplying our great deficiency in devotional works, it is a matter of time.'

3) As to the Council of Trent, the problem is that one can't reconcile the Council's holding transubstantiation with the Thirty-nine Articles. The gist of *Tract 90* was not to reconcile the Articles with Tridentine decrees.

4) Does not think it safe for her to use the Invocations to Mary and

Saints in the Breviary or in Roman Catholic books of devotion. 'There is nothing presumptuous or irreverent towards Rome or the Saints in your doing so – you are simply obeying your Church.' With regard to the apparent influence of addresses to the saints over her conduct, 'such influence does not prove the propriety of the practice, but only that *you* are *such* as to be influenced in that way. And again it is just a case, in which our Enemy may disguise himself as an Angel of light,' and he quotes the passage from Ignatius he used in his notice of Lord Shrewsbury's pamphlet on the alleged miracles in the south Tyrol. As to her uncertainty of salvation, the Roman Church could not give her certainty. She must be patient and wait for the eye of the soul to be formed in her. 'Religious truth is reached, not by reasoning, but by an inward perception. Any one can reason; only disciplined, educated, formed minds can perceive. Nothing is more important to you than habits of self command. . . . You are overflowing with feeling and impulse – all these must be restrained, ruled, brought under, converted into principles and habits, or elements of character. Consider that you have this great work to do – to change yourself.'

5) He urged her to study and live upon such works as 'The Spiritual Combat,' and Thomas à Kempis, being careful not to put aside Scripture reading. 'If you give yourself in good measure to interior religion, you may let your faith on such points as you have mentioned, take its chance.' This was the direction he also gave to others who were in a similar state.

6) Supposes all at Littlemore use the Prayers for Unity, but not together. It would be a temptation for persons enough inclined towards Rome without stimulating this longing. 'As to leaving the English Church *now*, considering what Divine Providence is doing for it, it seems leaving God's manifested Presence. Shall we leave it, before He does?'

7) 'Mohler's works are, I believe, very interesting – e.g., – his Symbolique – (of course it is theological) – Essay on Unity – Athanasius. And Hurder's (or some such name) Life of Innocent the Third.'

On 29 April he wrote, 'I have no doubt you often feel forlorn – but recollect that it is the fate, not only of yourself, but of all, however circumstanced, who wish to live a life to God and religion – they are pilgrims on earth, and have no business here – and seem in the way to other people.'

TOWARD A PHILOSOPHY OF RELIGION

In February 1843 Newman published *Fifteen Sermons preached before the University of Oxford*, frequently called the *Oxford University Sermons*. Newman told his sister Jemima, 'they are not theological or ecclesiastical, though they bear immediately upon the most intimate and practical religious questions'. (*Moz. II*, 406) In 1872 he added a preface to the third edition, in which he clarified the meaning of certain passages especially those dealing with the meaning of 'Reason'.

The first nine have already been examined. Sermon X, 'Faith and Reason, as contrasted as Habits of Mind', is a phenomenological analysis, an example of the method long before it was developed in twentieth-century philosophy, and one to which no summary can do entire justice. Faith as revealed in the Scriptures is 'the chosen instrument connecting heaven and earth, as a novel principle of action'. Newman denies that it is a rational conviction dependent on evidence, that it is the result of Reason exercising itself explicitly on *a posteriori* evidential methods. It is however conformable to Reason. It does not demand evidence so strong as is necessary for what is commonly considered a rational conviction, or belief on the ground of Reason, 'because it is mainly swayed by antecedent considerations. In this way it is, that the two principles are opposed to one another: faith is influenced by previous notices, prepossessions, and (in a good sense of the word) prejudices; but Reason, by direct and definite proof.' Faith being 'a principle for the multitude and for conduct, is influenced . . . less by evidence, more by previously-entertained principles, views, and wishes.' This is true of all faith, not merely religious faith, as Newman demonstrates. Newman does not disparage proofs for Christianity, the so-called Evidences; they may be of service to persons in particular frames of mind.

> I would only maintain that proof need not be the subject of analysis, or take a methodical form or be complete . . . in the believing mind; and that probability is its life. I do but say that it is antecedent probability that gives meaning to those arguments from facts which are commonly called the Evidences of Revelation; that, whereas mere probability proves nothing, mere facts persuade no one; that probability is to fact, as the soul to the body; that mere presumptions may have no force, but that mere facts have no warmth. A mutilated and defective evidence suffices for persuasion where the heart is alive; but dead evidences, however perfect, can but create a dead faith.

In Sermon XI, 'The Nature of Faith in Relation to Reason', Newman defines Reason as 'the faculty of proceeding from things that are perceived to things which are not'. Faith is an exercise of Reason, but the world considers it an exercise of weak, bad or insufficient Reason because it relies on antecedent probabilities, 'on presumption more, and on evidence less'. Yet in all reasoning 'there must ever be something assumed ultimately which is incapable of proof, and without which our conclusion will be as illogical as Faith is apt to seem to men of the world'. For example, there is such a strong antecedent probability that our senses are faithful, even though at times they deceive us, that we dispense with proof.

> And in an analogous way, Faith is a process of the Reason, in which so much of the grounds of inference cannot be exhibited, so much lies in the character of the mind itself, in its general view of things, its estimate of the probable and the improbable, its impressions concerning God's will, and its anticipations derived from its own inbred wishes, that it will ever seem to the world irrational and despicable; – till, that is, the event confirms it. The act of mind, for instance, by which an unlearned person savingly believes the Gospel, on the word of his teacher, may be analogous to the exercise of sagacity in a great statesman or general, supernatural grace doing for the uncultivated reason what genius does for them. (*US*, 218)

In Sermon XII, 'Love, the Safeguard of Faith against Superstition', Newman distinguishes true from false faith, 'It is holiness, or dutifulness, or the new creation, or the spiritual mind, however we word it, which is the quickening and illuminating principle of true faith, giving it eyes, hands, and feet. . . . in scholastic language, justifying Faith, whether in Pagan, Jew, or Christian, is *fides formata charitate*.' 'The divinely-enlightened mind sees in Christ the very Object whom it desires to love and worship, – the Object correlative of its own affections; and it trusts Him, or believes from loving Him'. Newman develops this from Scripture, and distinguishes faith as an 'act of Reason, viz., a reasoning upon presumptions', and right faith as 'a reasoning upon holy, devout, and enlightened presumptions'.

> The grounds of Faith, when animated by the spirit of love and purity, are such as these:- that a Revelation is very needful for man; that it is

earnestly to be hoped for from a merciful God; that it is to be expected; nay, that of the two it is more probable that what professes to be a Revelation should be or should contain a Revelation, than that there should be no Revelation at all, that, if Almighty God interposes in human affairs, His interposition will not be in opposition to His known attributes, or to His dealings in the world, or to certain previous revelations of His will.

This argument is developed more fully in Newman's treatment of natural religion in the *Grammar of Assent*.

Newman then argues, not entirely convincingly, that right faith is protected from excesses of superstition, credulity or fanaticism by the 'spirit of wisdom and understanding, of counsel and ghostly strength, of knowledge and true godliness, and holy fear', not by 'processes of investigation, discrimination, discussion, argument, and inference'. Faith acts, because it is faith; 'but the direction, firmness, consistency, and precision of its acts, it gains from Love.'

By exploring reason and faith in the individual Newman opposed the narrowness of the rationalists who confined the activity of reasoning to logic and systematic reasoning and so his well-known distinction in Sermon XIII, 'Implicit and Explicit Reason'.

The mind ranges to and fro, and spreads out, and advances forward with a quickness which has become a proverb, and a subtlety and versatility which baffle investigation. It passes on from point to point, gaining one by some indication; another on a probability; then availing itself of an association; then falling back on some received law; next seizing on testimony; then committing itself to some popular impression, or some inward instinct, or some obscure memory; and thus it makes progress not unlike a clamberer on a steep cliff, who, by quick eye, prompt hand, and firm foot, ascends how he knows not himself, by personal endowments and by practice, rather than by rule, leaving no track behind him, and unable to teach another. It is not too much to say that the stepping by which great geniuses scale the mountains of truth is as unsafe and precarious to men in general, as the ascent of a skilful mountaineer up a literal crag. It is a way which they alone can take; and its justification lies in their success. And such mainly is the way in which all men, gifted or not gifted, commonly reason, – not by rule, but by an inward faculty.

'Reasoning, then, or the exercise of reason,' Newman concludes, 'is a living spontaneous energy within us, not an art.' When however the mind attempts to analyse various processes which take place during it and the principles on which it operates, it comes up with the science of logic, and various terms to designate particular methods of reasoning and particular states of mind that influence its reasoning, such as analogy, parallel cases, testimony, and circumstantial evidence; and such states of mind as prejudice, deference to authority, party spirit, attachment to such and such principles, and the like. Contrary to the opinion of Samuel Johnson, 'some men's reason becomes genius in particular subjects, and is less than ordinary in others'. All men reason, but not all men reflect upon their reasoning. Uneducated men therefore can have good reasons for their believing though they cannot enunciate them nor is it necessary that they digest the so-called evidences. In these latter, nothing properly can be assumed but what men in general will grant as true; that is, nothing but what is on a level with all minds, good and bad, rude and refined. Moreover 'conviction for the most part follows, not upon any one great and decisive proof . . . but upon a number of very minute circumstances together, which the mind is quite unable to count up and methodize in an argumentative form'. 'All reasons formally adduced in moral inquiries, are rather specimens and symbols of the real grounds, than those grounds themselves. They do but approximate to a representation of the general character of the proof which the writer wishes to convey to another's mind.'

Newman concludes that 'the reasonings and opinions which are involved in the act of Faith are latent and implicit; that the mind reflecting on itself is able to bring them out into some definite and methodical form; that Faith, however, is complete without this reflective faculty, which in matter of fact, often does interfere with it, and must be used cautiously.'

Sermon XIV, 'Wisdom, as contrasted with Faith and with Bigotry' is important for its definition and description of wisdom, which is also called philosophy or enlargement of mind. Knowledge, though a condition of the mind's enlargement, is not identical with it.

It is not the mere addition to our knowledge which is the enlargement, but . . . the movement onwards, of that moral centre, to which what we know and what we have been acquiring, the whole mass of our knowledge, as it were, gravitates. And therefore a philosophical cast of thought, or a comprehensive mind, or wisdom in conduct or policy, implies a connected view of the old with the new, an insight into the bearing and influence of each part upon every other; without which there is no whole, and could be no centre. It is the knowledge, not only of things, but of their mutual relations. It is organized, and therefore living knowledge. (*US*, 286–7)

After giving examples of mental growth on the natural level Newman enquires 'into the nature of Christian Wisdom as a habit or faculty of mind distinct from Faith, the mature fruit of Reason, and nearly answering to what is meant by Philosophy'. He is not denying its spiritual nature or its divine origin. 'Almighty God influences us and works in us, through our minds.' We gain Truth by reasoning whether implicit or explicit, in a state of nature: we gain it in the same way in a state of grace. Both faith and wisdom, are intellectual: the former the elementary, the latter, the perfecting gift of the Holy Spirit. 'Wisdom is the last gift of the Spirit, and Faith the first.'

Religion, therefore, 'has its own enlargement'. Uneducated persons turning to God and studying the inspired Word, 'seem to become, in point of intellect, different beings from what they were before', and those used only to divinity of non-conformity or latitudinarianism, upon introduction 'to the theology of the early Church, will often have a vivid sense of an enlargement, and will feel they have gained something, as becoming aware of the existence of doctrines, opinions, trains of thought, principles, aims, to which hitherto they have been strangers'.

Faith therefore can take discursive views, though not systematic. It has not the gift of tracing out and connecting one thing with another as wisdom has, and bigotry professes to have. Faith 'forms its judgment under a sense of duty and responsibility, with a view to personal conduct, according to revealed directions, with a confession of ignorance . . . in a teachable and humble spirit, yet upon a range of subjects, which Philosophy itself cannot surpass. In all these respects it is contrasted with Bigotry'.

Men of narrow minds, far from confessing ignorance and maintaining Truth mainly as a duty, profess . . . to understand the subjects which they take up and the principles which they apply to them. They do not see difficulties. They consider that they hold their doctrines . . . at least as much upon Reason as upon Faith; and they expect to be able to argue others into a belief of them, and are impatient when they cannot. . . . They conceive that they profess just *the* truth which makes all things easy.

Narrow minds have no power of throwing themselves into the minds of others. They have stiffened in one position. . . . They think that any one truth excludes another which is distinct from it, and that every opinion is contrary to their own opinions which is not included in them. They cannot separate words from their own ideas, and ideas from their own associations.

Though faith and bigotry as habits of mind are entirely distinct from each other, 'They may and do exist together in the same person. No one so imbued with a loving Faith but has somewhat, perhaps, of Bigotry to unlearn; no one so narrow-minded, and full of self, but is influenced, it is to be hoped, in his degree, by the spirit of Faith.'

The concluding sermon in the volume, No. XV, 'The Theory of Developments in Religious Doctrine', was hastily composed and delivered on 2 February 1843. He tells Manning that it was 'a subject intended for years. And I think its view *quite* necessary in justification of the Athanasian Creed.' (*KC*, 277) Newman takes Mary as the 'pattern of Faith, both in the reception and in the study of Divine Truth. She does not think it enough to accept, she dwells upon it . . . not enough to assent, she developes [*sic*] it. . . . Thus she symbolizes to us, not only the faith of the unlearned, but of the doctors of the Church also, who have to investigate, and weigh, and define, as well as to profess the Gospel; to draw the line between truth and heresy.' Newman then proposes to show the use of reason investigating the doctrines of faith, not in the history of development, which he would do later, but in the principle itself.

Developments in dogma have their ultimate source in an intuition of faith. The latter, an effect of illuminating grace, arises through the action of the concrete intelligence contemplating the realities of faith through the various media of revelation. Therein Christ is confronted in a living personal relationship. Subsequently another act of the mind ('notional' as distinguished from 'real') attempts to formulate in abstract propositions and systematic categories the reality thus perceived. Dogmas and theological statements therefore express in explicit terms that which was implicitly known in the original 'real' apprehension of faith. This reflective delineation of the intuition is not essential to its genuineness, as a 'peasant may have such a true impression, yet unable to give any intelligible account of it'. The individual moreover may not be conscious of the idea which possesses it. Nor is the absence of or the incompleteness of dogmatic statements a proof that there is an absence of impressions in the mind of the Church. Centuries may pass before it gives formal expression to them.

Newman is mainly concerned, however, with the difficulties posed against this view of development by the modernists who denied any real correspondence between the interior vision of faith and the formulas of doctrine. Theological science, in their view, varies according to time, place, and accident, whereas faith alone is unchanging. Newman prefaces his reply with the remark that science and philosophy face the same problem: to find formulas so accurate that they will correspond exactly with the reality being expressed. All subject-matters admit of true and false theories, and the false are no prejudice to the true. The principles of these subject-matters likewise admit of implicit reception and explicit statement. There should be no a priori objection therefore to the possibility of a real and exact correspondence in the area of theological knowledge. Moreover, a positive argument for correspondence between dogmatic formula and religious faith can be constructed. Since God is identical with Himself, the inward impression of Himself given in relevation must share in this identity. And in so far as human nature operates according to fixed laws, the formulation of theological statements will be found to correspond with the vision of faith itself. Such statements, although frequently representing only one aspect of the Divine reality which is being contemplated by faith, nevertheless have their life and meaning in the implicit reception of the reality itself.

There are difficulties, however, against this argument by analogy with nature. How are *natural* words and concepts to express and to transmit *supernatural* realities? Newman's reply to the question is based on the 'economical' character of all language and concepts. Language is but a limited vehicle of communication between men, and human concepts are never fully adequate to represent the total reality which the mind perceives. *A fortiori*, then, theological statements will be 'economical' and inadequate, although valid and accurate within the boundaries of their intrinsic limitations. Any feeling of anxiety or of scepticism arising from the acknowledgement of such human inadequacy will be dispelled upon a consideration of the mercy and providence of God. God is the ground of all truth and in His providence has determined that through such human limitations He will lead man to Himself. It is man's duty, therefore, to submit to the human condition, even in the supernatural order, and to place his trust in the providence of God.

Newman thought this volume the best he had published, though imperfect, – imperfect because there was more to develop in it. In fact, he did develop some of the ideas, e.g., his several statements that grace provides a light to the mind in one's path to faith, he expanded in Discourse IX, 'Illuminating Grace', in *Discourses addressed to Mixed Congregations*. The pages on wisdom are used almost verbatim in the *Idea of a University*, where it is said to be the immediate end of a university. Explicit and implicit reason became formal and informal reason, and the ability to reason well in a particular subject matter was explored in the 'Illative Sense', in the *Grammar of Assent*. Other ideas from these sermons are likewise developed in this later work. Newman also made a brilliant use of the argument from antecedent probability in chapter II, 'The Antecedent Argument in behalf of Developments in Christian Doctrine,' in *An Essay on the Development of Christian Doctrine*.

It is understandable then that he felt he had made a breakthrough in his notion of antecedent probability. Later in Rome he wrote, 'The chief thing which I think is original is one which I have worked on a great deal . . . that antecedent probability is the great instrument of conviction in religious (nay in all) matters. Here [i.e. Rome] persons at first misunderstood me, and because I talked of 'probable arguments', they thought I meant that we could not get beyond a probable conclusion in opposition to a moral certainty; which is a condemned proposition. . . . I use probable as opposed to demonstrative, not to certainty.'[5] In another letter he wrote at the same time, he explained further that 'moral certainty is a *state of mind*, in all cases however produced by probable arguments which admit of more or less – the measure of probability necessary for certainty varying with the individual mind'. (*LD* XI, 293, 289)

Without an understanding of Newman's philosophy of religion as revealed in these sermons, it is difficult to comprehend fully the final stages of his intellectual and spiritual journey to the Catholic Church. That he thought the Catholic Church the true Church and the Anglican Church external to it, did not mean that he was certain and that he should therefore take such a step. Time is an essential condition for the growth of a real conviction or certitude, as he explained to Mrs William Froude,

> Time alone can show whether a view will hold. . . . Time alone can turn a view into a conviction – It is most unsatisfactory to be acting on a syllogism, or a solitary, naked, external, logical process. But surely it is possible in process of time to have a proposition so wrought into the mind, both ethically and by numberless fine conspiring and ever-recurring considerations as to become part of our mind, to be insepar-

able from us, and to command our obedience. And then the greater the sacrifice, the more cogent the testimony shall we have to its authority, for to overcome impediments is a token of power.

And time alone can show whether what forces itself upon us, influences others also. It seems impossible, humanly speaking, that we should be moved, and others not moved.[6] (9 December 1843)

In light of this, one understands the significance of his remarks on logic in the *Apologia*:

I had a great dislike of paper logic. For myself, it was not logic that carried me on; as well might one say that the quicksilver in the barometer changes the weather. It is the concrete being that reasons; pass a number of years, and I find my mind in a new place; how? the whole man moves; paper logic is but the record of it. All the logic in the world would not have made me move faster towards Rome than I did; as well might you say that I have arrived at the end of my journey, because I see the village church before me, as venture to assert that the miles, over which my soul had to pass before it got to Rome, could be annihilated, even though I had been in possession of some far clearer view than I then had, that Rome was my ultimate destination. Great acts take time. (*Apo.*, 169)

Newman had to become certain that the contemporary Catholic Church was identical with the Church of the Fathers. The objection to this was stated by one of the disputants in 'Home Thoughts from Abroad', The present Roman Church is not like St Augustine's Catholic Church; it has departed from primitive Christianity, viz., 'the practical idolatry, the virtual worship of the Virgin and Saints, which is the offence of the Latin Church, and the degradation of moral truth and duty, which follows from these'. (*DA*, 17) The key to answering these objections was the development of doctrine, and to the examination of this question he gave greater and greater attention starting in 1843, as revealed in the number of questions and comments regarding this he entered in his private diary.

The entries made in March and April 1843 deal with possible answers to the objections against Rome. Three touch on the question of development as the latter is treated in the Oxford University sermon, whereas the entries in 1844 deal almost exclusively with historical questions of development.

2. What are the Roman doctrines of the Invocation of Saints etc but

vivid realizations of truths which we profess to believe as well as R Catholics? Is it possible to realize that God is 'the God of' St Paul, or St Stephen, without believing that those saints live and are present? March 18/1843.

4. Are not the doctrines of purgatory, saint-worship etc but the realizations, or vivid representations, of the feelings and ideas which the primitive principles involve? does any other system contain, secure those ideas and feelings? April 7/43.

Two other entries reveal the movement of his mind in the direction of Rome:

5. Is not the RC. system the nearest far to the primitive?. . . .

7. In my letter to the Bishop I said that we ought to wait for a union with Rome, till Rome was holier. What has affected my feelings very much lately is to find the holiness of the Roman saints *since* our separation – which seems a sufficient answer to my demand; especially the Jesuits, whose Exercises I have been lately studying. April 12/43.

There was another barrier – a spiritual one – to his leaving the Anglican Church. As he said in one of the Oxford sermons, 'the divinely-enlightened mind finds in Christ the very Object whom it desires to love and worship'. (XII, 236) Christ he had found in the Anglican Church. As he had written to Fr Russell, 'Why should we seek our Lord's presence elsewhere, when He vouchsafes it to us where we are? What *call* have we to change our communion?' (*Apo.*, 193) As he later wrote to Henry Wilberforce, in so doing 'I fled back to one's inward experiences. . . . But in time this would not stand, it was no sure footing – and would lead to the veriest liberalism.' (30 November 1848, *LD* XII, 357)

Moreover like Scott, his first spiritual guide, he had to follow Truth wherever it led.

CHAPTER TWENTY-TWO

Treading the Path of Sanctification

Following the advice he gave to others, Newman determined to cultivate what he called interior religion or sanctification. Accordingly he increased his fasting during the Lent of 1843, not taking food before 5 p.m. with the exception of Sundays and the Feast of the Annunciation, when breakfast was as on feast days. He abstained from all flesh meat, even on Sundays. The three holy days at the end of Passion Week he and his companions took only bread and tea. He slept less, sometimes only four or five hours. (*AW*, 221–2)

During Passion Week he and his companions made an Ignatian retreat, for which he prepared himself for some time. Writing to Miss Giberne on 28 February 1843, he remarked, 'I wish to master St Ignatius's Spiritual Exercises, if "master" is not a presumptuous word. They are in Latin, very celebrated, and very instructive.' The edition he used, extant at the Oratory, his name inscribed, was *Exercitia Spiritualia S. P. Ignatii cum sensu eorundem Explanatio et Directorium additis tribus appendicibus.* Auctore P. Ignatio Diertins S.I., 1838. The Directorium was one of the many going back to Ignatius's time which explain how the Exercises should be given and what they are intended to achieve, and how they can be adapted to different persons and different situations. Newman made detailed notes from the Exercises, the Directorium and Rosmini's Manual. When Fr Gentili, head of the Rosminians in England, visited Oxford, Newman asked him to instruct him on the way to give retreats, and Gentili sent him Rosmini's *Manual for Retreats*. The notes are dated 15 March 1843.

The Exercises of St Ignatius are divided into four weeks, preceded by the 'Purpose of the Exercises', and 'the Principle and Foundation'. The first week is devoted to meditations on sin and repentance; the second, on the life of Christ, the third, on the passion of Christ; the fourth on the glorious mysteries of Christ's life, ending with a meditation for obtaining love. The length of each week varies according to the needs of the individual and sometimes only the first week is made. The purpose of the

Exercises is to help one make a decision 'free from inordinate attachment', as to one's state of life, or if that is fixed, how to regulate and orientate to sanctity and perfection the life one is living.

Newman drew up a summary of the first week and the 'Additional Directives', which conclude the first week. Between the two he inserted a number of remarks based on the Directorium and Rosmini's Manual. One remark in reference to the Director should be noticed, as he takes it up in the *Apologia*. 'The person under exercises should surrender himself wholly to his Maker's will. No one may interfere between him [the exercitant] and his Maker; God must deal with His creature; and he with God.' In the *Apologia*, Newman remarked,

> In the intercourse between God and the soul, during a season of recollection, of repentance, of good resolution, of inquiry into vocation, – the soul was 'sola cum solo;' there was no cloud interposed between the creature and the Object of his faith and love. The command practically enforced was, 'My son, give Me thy heart.'

Newman then applied this to devotion to angels and saints, the Catholic doctrine concerning them having been a stumbling block in his road to Rome. So he concludes,

> The devotions then to Angels and Saints as little interfered with the incommunicable glory of the Eternal, as the love we bear our friends and relations, our tender human sympathies, are inconsistent with that supreme homage of the heart to the Unseen, which really does but sanctify and exalt, not jealously destroy, what is of earth. (*Apo.*, 196)

This study was in preparation for the making of the Exercises from 8 April to 14 April, the night of Good Friday. He was joined by Bowles, Bridges, Lockhart, and John Morris. To accustom themselves to meditation, from the beginning of Lent for the first four weeks they had an hour's meditation together in the morning before Matins, using the Dialogues in the *Paradisus Animae*. This was a popular work of devotion by James Merlo Horstius (1597–1644), a parish priest of Cologne. The first chapter of each section of the work is a conversation between Christ and man, e.g. Section III, ch. 1. A Conversation on the mode of doing penance. During the 5th week, they used a translation of an early seventeenth-century work by a Spanish Jesuit, F. Francis Salazar, called

The Sinner's Conversion reduced to Principles to which was added an English translation of the Exercises themselves. The development of the meditations is long, and Newman in places put square brackets around some portions. He also put the same around portions which were not in accord with Anglican theology, e.g., colloquies with Our Lady, or in the meditation on death where the exercitant is imagining his death bed and hears the priest administering the Sacrament of Extreme Unction. For the week of retreat the exercitants used a work by a recently deceased Jesuit, the Very Revd Father Stone, from Stonyhurst College, Lancashire, *Meditations and Considerations for a Spiritual Retreat of Eight Days*, which bears the publisher's date of 1843.[1] The meditations are considerably shorter, more concise, more sober and less emotional, than those in Salazar. Moreover the brevity of the 'points' for meditation is more in accord with the directions of St Ignatius. One important element of an Ignatian retreat was lacking, that of a director, '*because*,' as Newman later told Hope, 'we did not know where to go for one'. (*KC*, 310)

In accordance with these directives Newman was careful after each meditation to examine how he fared in the meditation and to record what 'lights' he got during it. (*AW*, 222–8) The first meditation went quickly. The thought that struck him most was that 'I have acted hardly ever for God's glory, that my motive in all my exertions during the last 10 years, has been the pleasure of energizing intellectually. . . . that it is fearful to think how little I have used my gifts in God's service; that I have used them for myself. . . . e.g. vanity, desire of the good opinion of friends, etc. have been my motive.' This realization must have remained with him, for he remarked later to Keble on 20 August 1843, 'My great fault is doing things in a mere literary way from the love of the work, without the thought of God's glory.' (*KC*, 245) At the end of the meditation he solemnly gave himself up to God 'to make me what He would'.

In the second meditation at ½ past 1 p.m., 'on the motives that oblige us to tend to our last end', he was sleepy and had wandering thoughts and ran out of matter. He fidgeted waiting for the clock to strike, and hence in accordance with St Ignatius's directive, he prolonged the meditation some minutes beyond the hour 'to conquer myself'. With great honesty he records various great trials which he might have to endure and would do so, if it were God's will:

1. the having to make a General Confession to some one in our Church, I not having full faith that our Church has the power of

Absolution. 2. having to join the Church of Rome. 3. Having to give up my Library. 4. bodily pains and hardship. I considered what God is used to accept offers, but I trust He will not exact such.

In the second exercise on Monday, he found the going slow. 'Though the subject was so full of topics ("my sins") yet I seemed unable to interest or engage my mind. . . . Various miserable feelings came over me, and I found I dared not go through some of my sins. One reason of my want of spirit, as on Saturday, may be the want of *novelty* in the subject; yet these are just the circumstances under which St Ignatius says that the affections ought to have most exercise.' This is true, but it is also true that if St Ignatius were directing the retreat, he would not have allowed Newman to spend so much time on the meditations on sin since Newman was already living a most religious, indeed a holy life, but would have had him advance more quickly to the second week. 'I suspect I do not proceed in the way of Colloquy enough, though I do not know how to do it. My prayers are very short, and the same things repeated, and with very little realization of God's presence.' He resolved to read Scripture for a quarter of an hour each day, 'i.e., ordinarily'. It seems probable that when he took up reading the Breviary every day, he was content with the readings in Scripture which it provided in addition to that read in the daily service in the church.

Again in the exercise on venial sins, he felt the want of matter, 'I could but repeat my own prayers for light, pardon, and strength in case of such sins. I put before me, as very frequent ones in my case, distraction in prayer, self complacency, inaccuracy or lying, greediness, and want of self control in little things. And I resolved at once to confess to L[ockhart] that I just now, in excuse for omitting to read out loud something from Stone, said that I thought it came after Compline, whereas in fact I forgot it.'

Newman does not seem to have changed his youthful view that prayer should not be delayed to evening when one would be sleepy. In the reflection on the meditation on Death and Judgment, he was provoked at having overslept because 'my morning exercise seems the best'. He prayed that he might always look at his actions, as he would wish on his death bed. He gave as an example how he ought to behave towards Rogers, who had written to Newman that he could no longer be on intimate terms with him.

The exercise on Tepidity he considered 'more impressive than any of the foregoing'. He noted that for almost nine years since he established daily service at St Mary's 'I have not attended perhaps to one daily service'. 2. Except for isolated good actions his efforts for the movement were not done with a pure intention, and hence their 'availableness at the Last Day, is *lost*'. Then with an oblique reference to his call to a higher state of perfection, 3. 'that there are persons, who, being destined by Providence to a high path, have no medium between it and hell; so that, if I do not pursue the former, I may be falling into the latter'.

In the third exercise he felt an improvement on the previous evenings, and he considered and prayed against the present great aversion to the very name of penance. The 4th day, 'On the Incarnation, Kingdom, and Obedience of Christ', the only thought worth recording was that it was an absurdity to praise someone for humility, 'since the Word's condescension; it is unmeaning. Humility is the very *condition* of *being* a Christian; it comes into the idea of it, and is nothing superadded.' Newman seems to have been interested in the subject matter of the Two Standards (Christ and Satan), but the only reflection set down was, 'I seem unwilling to say, "Give me utter obscurity"; partly from a hankering after posthumous fame, partly from a dislike that others should do the work of God in the world, and not I.'

On Good Friday on the Passion of Christ he was struck 'how much I hurt my *faith* (and hence my power of realizing and feeling grateful for our Lord's passion) by *entering into* infidel thoughts, views, arguments, etc. E.g. principally of the Pantheist, and those who treat the gospels as myths'.

Newman must have been satisfied with the experience of the retreat, for without specifically mentioning it he wrote to Keble a letter dated Easter Monday,

I have for some time past been studying Loyola's Spiritual Exercises and I may say in a certain sense making use of the hints they contain – and I must own my great admiration of them, or rather sense of their extreme utility. He, and his followers after him, seem to have reduced the business of self discipline to a science – and since our Enemy's warfare upon us proceeds doubtless on system, every one, I suppose, must make a counter system for himself, or take one which experience has warranted. (Easter Eve, 15 April 1843, but at the end Newman gives Easter Monday)

And to Henry Wilberforce he confided, 'Do you know, though you need not say it, that I have taken to liking the Jesuits? You see I am determined to shock you.' (9 June 1843)

Given the widespread condemnation of *Tract 90* and the uproar about his Retractation, it is perhaps not surprising that not all would want to be closely associated any longer with Newman. One such was Rogers who wrote 3 April 'how improbable, perhaps impossible – a recurrence to our former terms is'. He went on to express his gratitude to Newman for all he had received from Newman's friendship. Newman replied at once,

> I have just received your kind letter and I must not let you go on supposing what I have before now attempted to explain to you. You have not pained me by differing from me in opinion. I never have assumed you acted on the notion that you *agreed* with me. On the contrary, I have not been slow, whenever asked by others, to declare that I did not know what your opinions were, nay, on almost *any* subject. You never have told me your opinions. What did more than pain me was, first and chiefly your deliberately refusing me that advice which I had a right to ask as a friend, whether he agreed with me or not – and next your refusing to receive my confidence. I hope you will not refuse to continue to me the benefit of your prayers. (draft, 5 April 1843)

This elicited a reply from Rogers which put a different light on Rogers's motives:

> You have been in the habit of asking for my opinion not only in matters merely personal, but as the conductor of a great movement in the English Church. And I fancy that . . . I have been of use to you as habitually showing you in my own person what ordinary men would think of this or that course of conduct, and enabling you to adapt your course to their notions. I cannot feel myself at liberty to occupy this place in a movement which, *I* feel, is tending to a secession from England to Rome. I think it would, *in me*, be treachery to the English Church, to which I belong, and to which I feel more and more contented to belong.

Newman set this aside to the end of the retreat when on Easter Eve, the same day he wrote such a warm and grateful letter to a true friend, Keble, he jotted down at the end of Rogers's letter, 'NB. He is wrong in saying I USED him as a *specimen* of others. I have gone *by his advice*. I have not done, or have modified, by his *judgment* what I should have done by my own. No one has so much restrained me as he. But it is not worth while to write him to explain. JHN' Nevertheless he did draft a letter in which in conscience he repudiated the idea he had used Rogers, but he never sent it. The draft ended, 'May you find others as *reverential* in their feelings towards you as I have been.' Rogers publicly defended Newman's character in 1845, but their friendship was not restored until 1863 when Rogers suddenly appeared in Birmingham to visit Newman at the Oratory. Newman told Fr Neville that there was no one, not even Froude, with whom he had been more intimate. This may have been overlooked, as most of their communication was oral, occupying as they did rooms at Oriel. The loss of Rogers's friendship must have been a severe blow, and it could hardly have not made him realize the price he would have to pay if he continued on the road to Rome. It was shortly afterwards that he had another blow in the death of his 'great friend', Samuel Wood. He later called it 'one of my first great losses'. To Miss Giberne he wrote that Wood was 'more of what the RCs call an interior man, than most even high Anglo Catholics. Indeed of course, in the present miserable state of things, to try to cultivate personal holiness, is all that is left us.' (11 May 1843) In announcing the death to Jemima, he remarked, 'but really I ought to be very thankful, or rather I cannot be thankful as I ought to be, for the wonderful way in which God makes to me new friends when I lose old. To be sure they are younger, which is a drawback, as making me feel so very antique; but there are compensations even there. My dear Jemima, my life is done, before it seems well begun.' (30 April 1843) In confidence he said, 'I think, he considered the Church of Rome the true Church, but thought God had placed him where he was.' Newman later maintained that he would have entered the Catholic Church with him. In the same letter Newman asked Jemima to write a line to Mrs Tonks, a Littlemore parishioner, who lost her husband and 'is now very forlorn'.

A CRISIS OF CONSCIENCE

Newman was no longer repressing his doubts about the Anglican Church, but only three persons were aware of the original doubts: Rogers, Henry and Robert Wilberforce. The latter two were not in Oxford, and Rogers was more and more in London. It would have been possible for Newman to continue as he had been, but his conscience was perplexed, so on 14 March 1843 he consulted Keble once again about resigning from St Mary's. 'It seems to me as if Lent were a fitting time, when one has more

hope than at ordinary seasons of being guided amid perplexity. . . . I am
so bewildered that I don't know right from wrong, and have no confidence
of being real in any thing I think or say.'

The reasons he gave for resigning, not immediately, but as a hypothesis, were: 1) he is influencing the undergraduates who are not his
parishioners; 2) willing or not, he is influencing persons towards doctrines
and practices not sanctioned by the Anglican Church, and he can no
longer counterbalance this by statements against Rome, as he has done in
the past; 3) condemnation by almost all the bishops of *Tract 90* without
specifying *what* they condemn in it. 'This gives an opening to every
reader who agrees with it on the whole, to escape the force of their
censure. I alone cannot escape it. . . . Now there *are* cases when a
consciousness of being in the right suffices to outweigh the censure even
of authority; but in this instance I cannot deny, first, that my interpretation has never been drawn out . . . before . . . and next . . . I am not . . .
promoting the Anglican system of doctrine, but one very much more
resembling in matter of fact, the doctrine of the Roman Church'; 4) if he
can keep Littlemore, even as a curate, he is not losing influence since
more work of a pastoral kind is available to him in directing consciences.
(*KC*, 210–3)

Newman told Keble he did not expect a quick answer to his letter. In
his letter of Easter Eve Newman asked him if he would contribute a life
of Venerable Bede to the Lives of the Saints which he hoped to publish
the following January. In his reply of 3 May Keble said he saw no reason
why Newman should not resign, if he felt he should do so, especially if
he could keep Littlemore, but at the same time he was not sure he should
not himself resign, 'committed as I am to the very same principles; only
that I do not think so much of Bishops' words in their Charges as you do,
and as I did myself, now that I have found out how they might act on
them and do not, thereby proving themselves not in earnest.' (*KC*, 216–7)

The subsequent correspondence between Newman and Keble is characterized by humility, sincerity, mutual respect and affection. Newman
replied to Keble telling him that his last expedient for keeping Littlemore
had fallen through. This circumstance plus the very kind tone of Keble's
letter 'has strongly urged me to tell you something which has at last been
forced upon my full consciousness'. (*KC*, 218)

There is something about myself, which is no longer a secret to me . . .
I have enough consciousness in me of insincerity and double dealing,
which I know you abhor, to doubt about the correctness of what I shall

tell you of myself. . . . Some thoughts are like hideous dreams, and we wake from them, and think they will never return; and though they do return, we cannot be sure still that they are more than vague fancies; and till one is so sure they are not, as to be afraid of concealing within what is at variance with one's professions, one does not like, or rather it is wrong, to mention them to another. . . . Any how, you will be undergoing a most dreadful suffering at my hands, if you read the other paper.

I do not feel distress at putting on you the *necessity of advising* ; . . . but what shall I say for the *pain* I shall be causing you?

This other paper is prefaced by a touching appeal for sympathy and understanding. 'Oh forgive me, my dear Keble, and be merciful to me in a matter, in which, if I have not your compassion, my faith is so weak and I have so little sense of my own uprightness, that I shall have no refuge in the testimony of my conscience, such as St Paul felt, and shall be unable to appeal from you to a higher judgment seat. But if you do on deliberation accuse me of insincerity, still tell me, for I shall deserve to bear it, and your reproof will be profitable.' Keble, as was to be expected, rejected this outright at the beginning of his reply. 'Believe me, my very dear Newman, that any thought of wilful insincerity in you can find no place in my mind. You have been and are in a most difficult position . . . I have no thought but of love and esteem and regard and gratitude for you in this as in everything.'

Newman reviewed the beginning of his doubts and how he strove to conquer them, but the original impression had become on the whole stronger and deeper.

At present, I fear, as far as I can realize my own convictions, I consider the Roman Catholic Communion the Church of the Apostles, and that what grace is among us (which, through God's mercy, is not little,) is extraordinary, and from the overflowings of His Dispensation.

I am very far *more* sure that England is in schism, than that the Roman additions to the Primitive Creed may not be developments, arising out of a keen and vivid realizing of the Divine Depositum of faith . . .

You will now understand what gives edge to the Bishop's charges, without undue sensitiveness on my part. They distress me in two ways; 1. as being in some sense protests and witnesses to my conscience against my secret unfaithfulness to the English Church; and 2. next, as being average samples of her teaching and tokens how very far she is from aspiring to Catholicity.

This of course is one element in the answer to those critics who said Newman left the Church of England because of his treatment at the hands of the bishops.

He added that within the last month Rogers told him why for the last two years he would not give him advice one way or other on Church matters was because 'it would be treachery in him to the English Church, to assist one who is conducting a movement, tending to carry over her members to Rome'.

In the light of his significant contribution to Littlemore parish, Newman showed remarkable humility in his willingness not only to serve as curate but to Eden, whose dictatorial ways and pomposity were widely known. This arrangement, however, was declined by Eden who said that 'were he Vicar of St. Mary's, he would not engage even to let me read daily prayers at Littlemore, though he did not provide any one else'. (*KC*, 226)

Keble in his reply inclined against resignation for the following reasons: 1) withdrawing from ministry would be perilous as exposing him to the temptation of going over to Rome; 2) we are not responsible for the faults in the place where God's providence has set us, but we are for what may be wrong in the position we choose for ourselves; 3) this difference of responsibility should outweigh evidence on behalf of Rome, especially, 4) since Newman's impression is based on historical evidence, which does not overpower him; 5) should not one be patient with the Anglican Church, expecting more tolerance from the bishops; 6) Keble admits his ignorance of those portions of history on which Newman bases his evidence, but does it add up to moral certainty, and if not, would not a small probability on the other side weigh against it practically? Keble admits that his deep feeling against Newman's remove from the ministry has to do with its consequences (by which he meant secession), and he feels unequal to the task Newman is placing on him, and hopes Newman will put no sort of implicit faith in him, but take up whatever seems reasonable and helpful. 'I still cling to the hope you taught me to entertain, that, in the present distress, where the Succession and the Creeds are, there is the Covenant, even without visible intercommunion.'

It is important to have listed these reasons as they show where Newman and Keble diverged from now on. Keble was willing to be patient and look forward to greater tolerance of Catholic views in the future Anglican

Church. Keble seems to have accepted Butler's axiom, 'probability is the guide of life', which Newman had difficulty in embracing fully, as he explained in the *Apologia*. When F. Coleridge asked Newman whether in this passage in the *Apologia*, pp. 18–20, Newman had in mind Keble's view as expressed in the Preface to his Sermons, Newman replied, he was alluding rather to Keble's conversation and he explained Keble's view:

> He considered religious truth came to us as from the mouth of Our Lord – and what would be called doubt was an imperfect hearing as if one heard from a distance. And, as we were at this time of the world at a distance from Him, of course we heard indistinctly – and faith was not a clear and confident knowledge or certainty, but a sort of loving guess. This after all is little more than *practical* certainty – and Bishop Butler seems to encourage it – then my own theory, (which I have since found is pretty much the same as Amort's) was intended to show how we could be *certain* on probabilities. (*LD* XXI, 129 and n. 2)

Speculative in contrast to practical certitude is certitude that this or that is *true*. (*LD* XV, 460–1) It is incompatible with doubt; not so, practical certitude. (Keble to Newman, 12 June 1844, *KC*, 320)

Moreover Keble had not the historical knowledge of the Fathers which Newman would explore more and more especially in relation to the development of doctrine, which would lead him, not to a 'practical certitude' but a 'speculative certitude' that the present Roman Church was identical with the Church of the Fathers. Hence he could not longer accept the catholicity of the Anglican Church without visible intercommunion. As he explained to Keble in his reply, he meant by 'hideous dream', 'to begin to suspect oneself external to the Catholic Church, having publicly, earnestly frequently, insisted on the ordinary necessity of being within it'.

It must have been an enormous relief to have unburdened himself and to have found a compassionate reception.

> I feel it to be almost ungenerous to entangle you in my troubles. . . . to whom can I go . . . but to you who have been an instrument of good to so many, myself inclusive?. . . . to whom would Hurrell go, or wish me to go but to you? And doubt not that, if such is the will of Providence, you will in the main be able to do what is put on you – I feel no doubt that in consulting you I am doing God's will . . . the alternative lies between selfwill and consulting you.' (*KC*, 225)

After answering some of Keble's suggestions, Newman made the point 'persons are keen-sighted enough to make out what I think on certain points, and then they infer that such opinions are compatible with holding situations of trust in the Church . . . A number of younger men take the validity of their interpretation of the Articles etc. from me *on faith*. Is not my present position a cruelty to them, as well as a treachery towards the Church?'

Newman then explained how he had started the Series of the Lives of the English Saints to employ 'the minds of persons . . . bringing them from doctrine to history, from speculation to fact . . . giving them an interest in the . . . English Church, and keeping them from seeking sympathy in Rome as she is; and further, as tending to promote the spread of right views.' Since the plan was taken up with great interest, to abandon it would cause 'much surprise and talk'. He asked Keble if the project was incompatible with his holding St Mary's though it might be in addition to his Fellowship and editorship of the 'Library of the Fathers' a 'sort of guarantee' of his remaining in the Church of England, while giving up St Mary's.[2]

Meanwhile Newman wrote telling Henry Wilberforce that he was consulting Keble. 'It was *necessary* to tell him in honesty and propriety – and I shall in all things go implicitly by his advice. But it is impossible to act in any way without laying oneself open on one side or other to the greatest misrepresentations of enemies – but they are not my Judge. . . . Everything external to my consciousness is most flourishing . . . openings occurring continually – lines of influence offerd me – etc. Could I trust myself [[if I did not fear my growing convictions]] I have a clear path.' (16 May 1843)

In a letter of 30 May, Keble rendered his judgement 'that on the whole my leaning is towards your retiring as quietly as you can'. Since Keble thought he could continue with the Lives of the Saints, as it might serve to keep Newman in the Anglican Church, Newman proceeded with the project, publishing in September a prospectus and drawing up a long calender of the saints on which he spent a good deal of time.

Having disposed of Newman, the enemies of the Movement in Oxford targeted Pusey. On 24 May, Pusey preached a sermon on the Eucharist as a comfort to the penitent. Dr Faussett, the Margaret Professor of Divinity, delated the sermon to the Vice-Chancellor as teaching heresy. Pusey was condemned without trial or hearing, without being told who his accuser was, forbidden to preach for two years, and bound to absolute silence. These disgraceful proceedings aroused a storm of protest. A memorial signed by Gladstone, Justice Coleridge and others was sent back to London in the hands of the bedel by the Vice-Chancellor who lost his temper. Newman who was afraid of the effect on Pusey's health nevertheless urged him to publish the sermon and supported the idea of a protest in his favour. 'If one thing after another is done against the holders of Catholic doctrine, without protest from any quarter, the imaginations of certain persons will be gradually affected with the notion that the Church of England does not hold them, and is not their place.' (*KC*, 233) Newman confided to Ambrose St John, who was about to join the group at Littlemore, 'Things are very serious here. . . . The Authorities find that by the Statutes they have more than military power – and the general impression seems to be that they intend to exert it and put down Catholicism at any risk.' (*KC*, 236–7) Protests followed, pamphlets published to no avail. Dean Church, who has given a thorough account of the proceedings, described the disastrous effect on the atmosphere of the university. 'Difficulties arose between Heads of Colleges and their tutors. Candidates for fellowships were closely examined as to their opinions and their associates. Men applying for testimonials were cross-questioned on No. 90, as to the infallibility of general councils, purgatory, the worship of images, the *Ora pro nobis*, and the intercession of the saints . . . .'[3]

With the decision taken to resign from St Mary's and the continued opposition of the bishops to Tractarianism, Newman must have felt that his mission to the Church of England was nearing its end. To Jemima he writes on 22 July, 'I am not in the best spirits though I do not show it. This general move of the governing body of the Church against us is a very serious matter. From the first I only proposed and wished to help them; of course hoping to carry them forward too to measures which otherwise they would not have undertaken – but when they resist and reject, one's occupation is gone.' These low spirits continued, as noted in his journal.

Keble suggested that Newman might put himself unreservedly in 'some *really worthy* confessor'. (*KC*, 243) In obedience to this suggestion Newman immediately started to keep a minute journal of himself, 1–9 August, which he might show to a confessor. Only the chief headings are given in the *Autobiographical Writings*. The journal follows the normal order of the day at Littlemore, beginning at 5 a.m. or shortly after, except when he went into Oxford, for example to see Fr Russell of Maynooth. During this time also he spent 3 3/4 of an hour with Bowden who came up on his way to the Continent to cure a bad cold. Newman was working on editing Atkinson's *Athanasius* and the translation of Fleury's *Ecclesias-*

tical History. Part of the time he seemed in low physical and emotional spirits. August 2, he notes in parentheses 'at various times very tired, languid, drowsy, sleepy all through these days.'

> Aug. 4. Perceval's Sermons. Palmer's pamphlet. (they felt for Pusey, not for *me* – this was *just*, I know – so I am put aside! this fussed me.)
> Aug. 5 rose with a headache
> Aug. 6   1. a bad night. Languid and irritable in head and nerves.
>   2. lay down some time before the 11 o'clock service.
>   6. afternoon Service at St Mary's – preached. Perhaps some people will be sorry that they never heard me, when I shall have given up St Mary's.
> Aug. 8   1. Up at ¼ past 5 –
>   2. Six o'clock – office – dreamy
>   12. at Athanasius, till I could not keep awake. 'Twas not mere sleepiness – but a sort of collapse of the whole of me – my head falling down etc (*AW*, 242–5)

Why did Newman discontinue the journal? He could think of no one but Keble to show the journal to, but after keeping the journal he received a letter from Keble, which made him feel Keble 'had enough of anxiety already without my increasing it. It also struck me that after all it would not assist any one in advising me – but of that perhaps I am no judge.' Nevertheless he was willing to send him the journal if Keble thought it best, but Keble declined. (*KC*, 245–6, 248) Though Keble did not exercise the role of confessor with power to command without giving reasons, he really acted as a spiritual counsellor, and Newman continued to ask for his advice, e.g., whether he should publish his volume of *Sermons on Subjects of the Day*, containing the four Advent sermons on the safety of continuance in the Anglican Communion.

He thought even if later he should change his mind about the Anglican Church, his publishing would be a sort of guarantee of his not leaving the Church soon, and also he felt that people should not rush to Rome without a period of thought. This was the argument he used with persons like F. W. Faber who was tempted to become a Roman Catholic:

> One thing . . . I feel very strongly – that a very great experiment . . . is going on in our Church – going on, not over. Let us see it out. Is it not our happiness to follow God's Hand? . . . if he is trying and testing the English Church, if He is proving whether it admits or not of being

Catholicized, let us not anticipate His decision; let us not be impatient, but look on and follow. . . . Ought not, moreover, a certain term of probation to be given to oneself, before so awful a change as that I am alluding to? (*KC*, 253)

This was not wishful thinking on Newman's part. As he wrote to Dalgairns, Mr Skinner, a Durham man, 'says that throughout the North, wherever he knows the country, the younger men are uniformly taking the high church line. Such news as this shows how wrong it is to be impatient. It is quite impossible such persons can stop where they are . . .' ([26 April] 1843)

Keble approved his publishing the volume of sermons, but with a footnote warning readers, which Newman accordingly added before sermons XXI–XXIV.

Despite his depression he was able to compose a humorous letter to his aunt giving the story of the Devonshire farmer who having heard Pusey very much abused, believed and joined in the abuse, but being undeceived relieved his remorseful feeling by naming the bull he was sending up to Derby to stand for the prize, Dr Pusey.

You see how Puseyism is spreading. It has reached our very cattle. Here is the first Puseyite bull. Our domestic animals will be the next victims. Homer talks of the plague falling first on mules and dogs, then on man. This has observed a reverse order; except that I think Heads of Houses will catch it last. We shall have Puseyite lapdogs and kittens – butcher's meat and grocery will come next – till at last we shall be unable to pay a morning call, or put our candle out at night without Puseyism,' (To Elizabeth Newman, 28 July 1843)

CHAPTER TWENTY-THREE

The Parting of Friends

Although Newman intended to wait until October to resign from St Mary's, Lockhart's defection to Rome offered him the opportunity of doing so before then. Lockhart had gone away from Littlemore for three weeks. He parted from his mother apparently without any intention of taking the step, but when he visited Dr Gentili he asked to go into retreat and then to be received into the Church. Gentili did not urge him to change his religion. Lockhart joined the Order of Charity, also called the Rosminians, of which Gentili was the head in England.

In announcing his decision to resign, Newman was met by a chorus of protests from relatives and friends, including Keble, Jemima, Anne and James Mozley and Henry Wilberforce. For Anne and James Mozley it was a sense of abandonment by their leader and champion. Anne, who was representative of persons at a distance from Oxford, wrote to Jemima

> He has been the means under Providence of making them what they are. . . . To them his voluntary resignation of ministerial duties will be a severe blow. . . . There is something sad enough and discouraging enough in being shunned and eyed with distrust by neighbours, friends, and clergy, but while we have had some one to confide in, to receive instruction from, this has been borne easily. . . . Such *was* our guide, but he has left us to seek our own path; our champion has deserted us – our watchman, whose cry used to cheer us, is heard no more. (*Moz.* II, 420–1)[1]

Henry Wilberforce, arguing against the condemnation of the bishops as not the decision of the *body* of the bishops, since the condemnation was not in synod, thought Newman would allow the Bishops to put a false interpretation on his resigning. (30 August 1843)

Jemima while regretting the decision, was the most sympathetic, 'Yes, dear John, . . . whichever way you decide it will be a noble and true part, and not taken up from any impulse, or caprice, or pique, but on true and right principles that will carry a blessing with them.' (*Moz.* II, 419) In reply Newman told her he had the approval of Keble and Rogers, that 'no time is "the" time. . . . The question is, Ought it to be done?. . . Every thing that one does honestly, sincerely, with prayer, with advice, must turn to good. . . . Most religious . . . is it to take into account such considerations as A. M. [Anne Mozley] mentions . . . but if this be a case of duty . . . I must leave the consequences to Him who makes it a duty.' (31 August; text in *Moz.* is not complete)

As Keble did not see how the resignation would smooth matters, Newman was ready to keep St Mary's if Keble thought best, but he capitulated. 'You can do but what seems right for the time, taking care not to act from mere impulse, and there is Another to be trusted with the results.' (*KC*, 255)

Before he could send his letter of resignation to the Bishop, he was interrupted by a letter from Tom Mozley, in which he said he had to join the Catholic Church at once. Tom had taken his wife Harriett and the baby Grace to France for a holiday, as she was suffering from insomnia. While there they encountered Catholics, and Tom was so overwhelmed that, using the excuse of the *British Critic*, of which he was editor, he returned to England and wrote to Newman of his need to convert at once. Newman hurried off to Cholderton, walked in the countryside with Tom, told him of his own doubts, and tried to persuade Tom to wait, though Tom would not promise to do so. He then rushed back to Oxford and completed his letter of resignation, 7 September. Meanwhile Tom had written to his wife still in France. The news, as she wrote to Jemima, 'came upon me like a thunderclap. . . . He never gave me the slightest idea of what was passing in his mind.' She was angry both with Tom and John.

Newman was more concerned about the pain Tom was causing to all at Derby than to Harriett and he wrote both to Jemima and Tom on 21 September: to the former that they mistake Tom's manner; to the latter that he had not acted very kindly, that 'a deep, hopeless, bitter prejudice will sink into the minds of your whole family, as well as into H's. . . . Do undo this, and as quick as ever you can.' He suggested Tom go over at once to Harriett in France. Tom had told Derby of Newman's own doubts which he revealed when he saw Tom. To Harriett he tried to explain Tom's action and his own position.

I am much pained at Tom's great indiscretion . . . but I am sure that he meant everything that was kind, and he thought (most erroneously) that he gave the least pain by being frank and open. I think his abruptness arose from awkwardness how to tell you what he felt must be told.

Only see what a position we are in, and how difficult to please you. Tom you blame for telling you a thing – me for not telling. Tom is cruel; and I am disingenuous.

However, I am only concerned with myself. First, I will say that [Tom] had no right to tell what he told you about me, and I shall write to him to beg him not to do the like to others. Next Jemima has not understood me, certainly has not quoted my words.

I do so despair of the Church of England, I am so evidently cast off by her, and on the other hand, I am so drawn to the Church of Rome, that I think it *safer*, as a matter of honesty, not to keep my living.

This is a very different thing from having any *intention* of joining the Church of Rome. However to avow generally as much as I have said, would be wrong for ten thousand reasons, which I have not time to enter upon here, and I hardly think you will consider necessary. People cannot understand a state of doubt, of misgiving, of being unequal to responsibilities, etc – but they *will* conclude that you have a clear view one way or the other. All I know is, that I could not without hypocrisy profess myself any longer a teacher in and a champion of our Church.

Very few persons know this – hardly one person, (only one I think) in Oxford, [[viz. James Mozley.]] – not any one in Oxford at present. I think it would be most cruel, most unkind, most unsettling to tell them. I could not help telling Tom the other day at Cholderton. (*FL*, 142–3; *Moz.* II, 425–6)

This is perhaps the clearest explanation that he gave of his state of mind at this time. After his resignation he would confess his doubts to friends who asked him. His letter to Harriett continued:

As to Tom he surprised me by writing me word that he thought he must go over at once to the Church of Rome. I never had a dream that he was unsettled. I set off for Cholderton the next hour; and though I could not get any promise from him, I succeeded 1st in restraining him from any immediate step. 2nd from giving up Cholderton at once – but 3rd I acquiesced readily in his relinquishment of the British Critic. It is a step I had twice formally recommended to him in the last two years. As to his state of excitement it is very great, but if you knew what the feeling is for it to break upon a man that he is out of the Church, – that in the Church only is salvation, you would excuse any thing in him. (To Harriett 29 September 1843, *BOA*. Texts given in *FL*, 142–3; *Moz*. II, 425–6 vary somewhat from *BOA*.)

He had a week earlier tried to explain to Jemima how Tom was so suddenly overcome. 'You cannot estimate what so many (alas!) feel at present, the strange effect produced on the mind when the conviction flashes, or rather pours, in upon it that Rome is the true Church. Of course it is a most revolutionary, and therefore a most exciting tumultuous conviction. For this reason persons should not act under it, for it is impossible in such a state of emotion that they can tell whether their conviction is well founded or not. They cannot judge calmly.' (*Moz*. II, 424) Although Tom did not convert, Harriett blamed John, and her feelings toward him were never the same again, while her repugnance to the Catholic Church increased.

On 24 September Newman preached the last time in St Mary's and on 25th, the anniversary of the dedication of Littlemore, he preached his farewell sermon, 'The Parting of Friends' (*SD*), having selected the same text he used for his first sermon, 'Man goeth forth to his work and to his labour: until the evening,' taken from Ps. 104. 23. An eye witness said, 'Dr. Pusey, Morris of Exeter and some others sobbed aloud, and the sound of their weeping resounded throughout the church.'[2] The best account was given by Edward Bellasis, a barrister who became a lifelong friend of Newman. He wrote to his wife the following day:

The service was at eleven, and, as usual, the chapel was decorated, with flowers upon the altar, in the windows above, over Mrs. Newman's tomb, and on every seat on both sides of the middle aisle, chiefly dahlias, Passion flowers, and fuschias [*sic*], and they were most beautiful as well as elegantly arranged, the service commenced with a procession of the clergy and school-children from the schools to the chapel, chanting a psalm as they walked; the officiating clergy were Newman (for the last time), Pusey, Copeland, and Bowles. There was a Communion, and Newman preached his farewell sermon. It is easy enough to tell you these simple facts, but it would be no easy thing to convey to you any adequate impression of the whole scene, the crowd of friends from all parts, the half-mournful greetings, the extreme silence of the chapel, though crowded till chairs were obliged to be set in the churchyard, the children with their new frocks and bonnets (Newman's parting gift). I did not see Newman himself speak to any one before service, the offertory was stated to be intended to be applied to completing the re-seating of the chapel, and the communicants were one hundred and forty in number. But the sermon I can never forget, the faltering voice, the long pauses, the perceptible and hardly successful efforts at restraining himself, together with the deep interest of the subject, were almost overpowering; Newman's voice was low, but distinct and clear, and his subject was a half-veiled complaint and remonstrance at the treatment which drove him away. We had a contrast drawn between the conduct of Ruth and Orpah towards their mother-in-law, Orpah kissed and left her, but Ruth clave unto her, and the conduct of Ruth recommended to our imitation. Then we had the story of David and Jonathan, the scene of their separation, when David quitted the Court of Saul, leaving his friend behind him, with an address almost personal to Dr. Pusey who sat by, and an application of the story to themselves. Then fancy such a passage as the following, addressed to the English Church: 'O my Mother! my Mother! how is it that those who would have died for thee fall neglected from thy bosom? how is it that whatever is keen in intellect, or patient in investigation, or energetic in action, or ardent in devotion, or enthusiastic in affection, remains unused by thee? why are they forced to stand idle in the market-place, whilst with ready hands and eager hearts they are eager to toil for thee? How is it thou hast no words of kindness, no sign of encouragement for them, but that thou suspectest, or slightest, or scornest, or fearest them, or at best dost but endure them?' Or fancy his allusion to his own mother's laying the first stone of the building, and to the many happy anniversaries of the consecration, of which that was probably the last, 'these have been happy days, we met with cheerful hearts, and kept festival after our fashion, now we eat our feast with our staff in our hands, sorrowing most of all that thus at least we shall meet no more.' And then his conclusion: 'And now, my friends, my dear friends (*here a long pause*), if you should be acquainted with any one who by his teaching, or by his writings, or by his sympathy has helped you, or has seemed to understand you, or feel with you, &c. Oh! my friends (*here a long pause*), remember such a one and pray for him.'[3]

After the sermon Newman descended from the pulpit, took off his hood and threw it over the altar rail, a symbolic gesture, if ever there was one. Pusey 'consecrated the elements in tears, and once or twice became entirely overcome and stopped altogether'. Principal Shairp recalled his feelings when Newman's voice was no longer heard nor would be heard again in Oxford. 'It was as when, to one kneeling by night, in the silence of some vast cathedral, the great bell tolling solemnly overhead has suddenly gone still. . . . Since then many voices of powerful teachers have been heard, but none that ever penetrated the soul like his.'[4]

Rumours which proved to be premature flew about that Newman was about to secede from the Church. Stanley wrote, 'it would be impossible to exaggerate the effect produced by this rumour'.

> It really reminded me of that one grand scene that I saw in the 'Medea', when the murder takes place within the palace, and the terrifed slaves fly backwards and forwards between the Chorus and the closed gates, and the Chorus mounts the steps of the altar and invokes the sun to hide its rays, and darkness rapidly falls over the stage. No one asked about it in public, but everyone rushed to and fro to ask in private, and recalled the last time that Newman had been seen walking in the streets, how he looked, and what he had said. At last some reassurance was brought by the news that he was, at any rate, still at Littlemore, and it does not appear that there is any ground for anticipating an immediate move. Still, the shock has been given, and I think the public mind is prepared for it. My impression from the kind of sensation produced by this rumour is, that the effect would be very great; deep, but within a narrow circle, at first, and then gradually widening, till a great crash came. To any one who has been accustomed to look upon Arnold and Newman as *the* two great men of the Church of England, the death of one and the secession of the other could not but look ominous, like the rattle of departing chariots that was heard on the eve of the downfall of the Temple of Jerusalem.'[5]

In reply to a letter from Henry Woodgate about W's pamphlet in defence of Pusey's sermon on the Eucharist and about Newman's resignation of St Mary's, Newman wrote, 'we are all coming to pieces. . . . The fact is our system is rotten and won't hold together.' When Woodgate asked what he meant 'by going to pieces,' Newman replied,

> Indeed I do not doubt that the Articles were drawn up by persons either heretics or heretical (in loco haereticorum). I do not believe that the compilers acknowledged any Catholic sense. This has been reserved for those who came after – e.g. those who received and subscribed and promulgated the Articles in 1571 and 1662. But leave the Articles in

their *intended* meaning and they are Protestant. Well – the Bishops and the body of the Church at this day have decided on taking them in their Protestant sense – and the question is whether they have not as much right to do so, as the Convocations of 1571 and 1662 to take them in their Catholic sense. This is one of the things I had in view when I called our system rotten. We have no system over and above the administered one. The administered gives sense to the theoretical system, which is either vague or self-contradictory.

I cannot keep people from seeing this, do what I will, – and that a distrust in our system is growing. The Church as a body is ruling or has ruled that it is not *Catholic*, i.e. that it does not hold Catholic doctrine, This is what people feel. You have no notion how (1) the condemnation of Number 90 (2) the Jerusalem Bishoprick (3) the 2 Societies' dealings with the Nestorians etc (4) the condemnation of Pusey, are unsettling men. They are all acts one way. (13 October 1843)

Charles Seager, Hebrew and Oriental scholar and one-time resident of Newman's 'house for young writers', converted to Rome and asked Newman to tell his wife. In his diary for 16 October, Newman recorded, 'went up at once to Mrs Seager to break to her the news – saw her once or twice.'

On 8 October, Manning wrote to Newman that he had intended to come to Littlemore the day before but was unable, indicating in a diplomatic and tactful way that there were undoubtedly 'differences of view and feeling, and I have always a desire to understand yours more clearly, and to be understood by you in turn'. At the same time he was fishing for reasons why Newman resigned. In reply Newman indicated his reason for resigning St Mary's.

The nearest approach I can give to a general account of them is to say that it has been caused by the general repudiation of the view contained in No. 90 on the part of the Church. I could not stand against such an unanimous expression of opinion from the Bishops, supported as it has been by the concurrence, or at least silence, of all classes in the Church lay and clerical. If there ever was a cause in which an individual teacher has been put aside, and virtually put away by a community, mine is one. No decency has been observed in the attacks upon me from authority: no protests have appeared against them. It is felt, I am far from denying, justly felt, that I am a foreign material – and cannot assimilate with the *Church* of England. Even my own Bishop has said that my very mode of interpreting the Articles makes them mean anything or nothing. When I heard this delivered I did not believe my ears. . . . This astonished me the more, because I published that letter to him (how unwillingly you know) on the understanding that *I* was to deliver his judgment on No. 90 *instead* of him. A year elapses, a second and heavier judgment came forth. I did not bargain for this. Nor did he, but the tide was too strong for him. I fear I must confess that in proportion as I think the English Church is showing herself intrinsically and radically alien from Catholic principles, so do I feel the difficulties in defending her claims to be a branch of the Catholic Church. It seems a dream to call a communion Catholic, when one can neither appeal to any clear statement of Catholic doctrine in its formularies, nor interpret ambiguous formularies by the received and living sense past or present. Men of Catholic views are too truly but a party in our Church,. . . . I do not say all this to everybody, as you may suppose – but I do not like to make a secret of it to you.' (*BL*, 270–3)

Manning wrote a sympathetic letter developing his assertion, 'Surely you cannot feel that the Church of England regards you as a foreign element.' He praised what Newman had done for the Church in the last ten years, the full effect of which would only be realized in the future. He disagreed that men of Catholic views were but a party in the Church. In reply to this 'most kind' letter Newman said 'you are engaged in a most dangerous correspondence', and went on to assert that 'it was from no disappointment, irritation, or impatience, that I have . . . resigned St. Mary's, but because I think the Church of Rome the Catholic Church, and ours not a part of the Catholic Church, because not in communion with Rome, and I felt I could not honestly be a teacher in it any longer'. He then traced the origin of his doubt and his efforts to dispel it, and concluded, 'This I am sure of, that such interposition as yours *kind as it is, only does what you* would consider harm. It makes me realize my views to myself, it makes me see their consistency, it assures me of my own deliberateness – it suggests to me the traces of a Providential Hand. It takes away the pain of disclosures, it relieves me of a heavy secret.' (*KC*, 276–8)

Manning sent this and Newman's previous letter to Gladstone who was utterly stunned, but, according to Fr Bacchus, jumped to the erroneous conclusion that when Newman had spoken, in his Letter to the

Bishop of Oxford about *Tract 90*, 'he had *committed himself for a second time*, he was practically avowing that he said things [i.e. against Rome] which he did not believe'. Gladstone thought that if Newman's letters to Manning were divulged, Newman would be a disgraced man, and the cause which he had advocated would be hopelessly discredited. (*KC*, 278)

Gladstone sent Newman's letters to Pusey, but the latter replied he did not think Newman's 'portentous expressions' had any necessary bearing 'upon certain steps of outward conduct'. Manning was influenced by Gladstone who held strong anti-Roman feelings because his sister, a drug addict, joined the Catholic Church the previous year and was still coping with her problem. He wrote to Pusey a strong letter in which he said he was 'reduced to the painful, saddening, sickening necessity of saying what he felt about Rome.' (*KC* 280, and n. 1) This he did on Guy Fawkes' Day, November 5, when he preached a No-Popery sermon in St Mary's. Newman and other Tractarians were accustomed to omit it. Although Manning was more anti-Roman in his feelings than Newman, the vehemence of Manning's sermon suggests not only the influence of Gladstone but his own desire to disassociate himself publicly from the disgraced portion of the Movement. On the next day Manning went to Littlemore, as indicated by the entry in Newman's diary, 'Manning came.' Anthony Froude later was reported to have said Newman told him to go to the door and tell Manning he would not see him. Late in his life when the issue came up, Newman could not remember and hence could not confirm or deny its accuracy, but he was extremely doubtful that it was true.[6]

Meanwhile life went on at Littlemore. Eden allowed Copeland to stay on as curate there. When the Provost tried to deny Eden testimonials for St Mary's unless he repudiated *Tract 90*, Eden though not a Tractarian had refused, and the Provost gave way. Newman did not like his pomposity. He invited Newman to preach at 'our Littlemore Commemoration' on the anniversary day. 'Independently of the benefit to be derived to my people at Littlemore I confess I have a selfish feeling on the occasion; I shall be truly glad that there should be exhibited to them such a mark of friendly confidence on your part to your (tho' unworthy) successor.' Newman politely declined. Underlining 'our' and 'my', Newman on 7 May 1878 wrote on the letter, 'Wonderful! considering what he owed to me, that he should thus repeatedly dig it into me that I was no longer to be looked upon as having any place in St Mary's and Littlemore. That I had to resign my charge into *his* hands, was one of the various trials which came upon me.' (10 September 1844)

Eden's eccentricities were not unobserved in Oxford.

His manner in church was quaint. . . . He could not stand coughers: 'If worshippers cannot restrain their coughs, they would better go out,' he used to say in eager, snapping tones. . . . He had a theory that the letter of the Bible carried sacramental efficacy, that merely to read it to a worldling or a reprobate would drive out devils and sow germinating-seeds. He tried it on poor old Miss Horseman, who was in his parish and supposed to be near her end. She told me that he walked into her drawing-room, said no word, took down and opened her big Bible, read it to her for half an hour, and again without farewell departed. He, of course, succeeded only in alarming and disturbing her; to a chapter of the Bible she had no objection, but her formal, old-fashioned breeding was outraged by his unceremonious aggression. When he left St Mary's for the College living of Aberford, a large congregation came to hear his farewell sermon, prepared for an affecting and *larmoyant* valediction. He preached on some ordinary topic: then shut up his sermon case with a snap: 'The volume – of the book – of my ministry among you – is closed. It is sealed up – and will be opened at the Judgment Day.'[7]

In December Newman was perplexed whether to continue with the Lives of the Saints, as a result of Pusey's view that they would create a sensation. Newman had expended a fair amount of time and energy to the project which was not without its own intrinsic complexities. Newman hoped that the series would combine devotion with history, but in using the available hagiographic sources the problem was how to satisfy the claims of historical criticism while handling the legends which were mixed with the accounts. There was no way of separating the facts inextricably linked with the fiction. Legends were used by the hagiographers to bring out the action of some principle, point of character or the like, and this was its religious purpose. The only thing to do then was to accept what had survived and been handed down as symbolical of the unknown, and use it for a religious purpose in a religious way.[8] In the Prospectus, Newman presented the series as a 'compensation of the disorders and perplexities of these latter times of the Church', when we are witnessing 'a disorganization of the City of God'. 'The wonders of His grace in the soul of man, its creative power, its inexhaustible resources, its manifold operation' as manifested in the saints provide a 'solace and recompense of our peculiar trials'. Now it seemed that people would not see the Lives as a consolation but as a further manifestation of Popery. ('Note D,' *Apo.*, 323–4)

As usual Newman saw all sides of the question which he discussed with Hope, who consulted Gladstone who also thought publication would cause a row. All in all there were about 30 persons involved in the project. One of the problems was that 'men have written, hoping for a fair emolument, and putting aside other means of gaining a livelihood. It seems very unfair to disappoint them. I know myself, when I was much younger, how very annoying such a disappointment is; the more so, because it cannot be, or is not, hinted at.' (*KC*, 284) Moreover when Newman examined the Life to which Pusey objected on the grounds that it brought in the Pope's supremacy, he found this not to be true and he agreed with Hope that if the Pope's supremacy were brought in, it should be *argumentatively*. Finally Newman decided not to stop the publication of the Lives but to stop them as a series, for the reasons he set down in a Memorandum of 11 December: 1. On Pusey's and Gladstone's misgivings. 2. because a publisher may not be found, or if found may draw back on a clamour. [Rivington the original publisher withdrew] 3. Because the Bishops may interfere as in Tracts for Times – and then I should be in a false position.

Newman decided to bring out separately such Lives as were in type, or written, and 'let them grow into a series, *if so be*'. Consequently in the following year, Newman withdrew as editor and announced that each author was responsible for the life he published. But he did not conceal from Hope 'to find that the English Church cannot bear the Lives of her Saints . . . does not tend to increase my faith and confidence in her'. (*KC*, 287; *Apo.*, 211–3) This did not mean that he was knocking under, for the *British Critic* having ceased publication, Newman also told Hope, 'I have serious thoughts of giving in to the idea which some people have, of setting up a review or some thing of the kind, and supporting it as well as I can. And I should not be loth to discuss in *it* such questions as the Pope's supremacy.' (*KC* 287–8) He did not tell Hope another reason for starting the review which he set down in his memorandum 'it is necessary to do something to gain money for certain persons'.

During the latter days of Advent, from 19 to 23 December inclusive, Newman, St John, Bowles, Bridges, and Dalgairns made a retreat, using the meditations from the 'Journal of Meditations' for November and December except for the meditation on the Two Standards which was taken from Stone. Newman's knowledge of Scripture is evident in his notes in which he mentions various texts that struck him during the meditations. Most of the meditations followed the order of the Spiritual Exercises of St Ignatius. (*AW*, 228–33)

In the meditation on the End of Man, Newman offered to give up to Christ, 'if for His greater glory, my fellowship, my Library, the respect of friends, my health, my talent, my reason – but added "Lord, be merciful".' This was a total renunciation of all that was most dear to him.

The call to perfection echoed in his mind in the next meditation which was on venial sins.

The thought which principally struck me was this, the duty, the absolute necessity of avoiding little sins, if we would be real Christians. If our sole end is to live to God, not to the world, or (as the Meditation spoke) to be soldiers of Christ fighting against the world, we are engaged in ridding ourselves of the shadows of this world, emancipating ourselves from the meshes of time and sense – that is resisting the daily little compliances with them in which consists our slavery. I thought of my three sins, and prayed to be able to get rid of them, indulgence of the appetite, self conceited thoughts, and wanderings in prayer.

Newman had a fine sense of taste: it was said that he was appointed to choose the wines for Oriel, – but given his rigorous fasting the entry comes as a surprise, though it should not if we recall how the saints considered themselves the worst sinners. Newman could not be unaware of his own enormous talents and abilities, which could result in self-complacency, unless checked. With so active a mind, wanderings in prayer would not be unexpected. Even with persons advanced in the spiritual life, these occur.

To these sins he added in his reflections in a subsequent meditation on venial sins: impatience, impetuosity, rudeness, inaccuracies in speech sometimes approaching lying. These latter seem to be the excesses of his active mind, enormous energy and drive to action, as well as his rudeness to those who paid deference to him – a deference he could not stand. His sensitivity to inaccuracy in speech was allied to his view of style as expressing one's thoughts as exactly as possible. One man's temptations are not another's. Temptations to venial sins frequently stem, as it seems in Newman's case as well, from one's physical, mental, psychological and emotional make-up.

In the meditation on the sin of the angels and one's own sins, Newman was impressed with the thought 'that "I have been all but damned" – just as when you saw a man fall from a horse, you might say that he had been all but killed, and had a very narrow escape indeed.' Then his imagination began to work on what might serve as a composition of place:

> 'Suppose their footing giving way, when persons were on some high ground, and they rolled down with the swiftness of lightning down, down, a steep descent towards a chasm; let them fall in it, and let one be caught by a projecting rock. That was I, but this was not all. I clamber up a little, but the sides are slippery, whether with snow or other cause – and the footing scarcely possible, and the greatest care necessary to hinder destruction after all – that is I now.'

Sleepiness and a notation about aching limbs from the frost so 'that I could hardly kneel, and was obliged to keep more or less in motion' provide an insight into the ascetic type of life he was leading at Littlemore. That the friar in Manzoni's novel, *I Promessi Sposi* was still stuck in his heart like a dart, emerges from his wondering 'whether I ought not to resolve, having now got free from the Lives of the Saints, not to engage in any *new* work, i.e. undertaking; so as to keep myself open for any new thing, – e.g. office of charity or the like'. On the last day of the retreat in meditating on the Two Standards, Newman opted for the side of the saints:

> Are we on the side of the Saints or not? There are not many parties to judge between, but two only. 2. I felt I ought to renounce and abjure Satan, yet how it would anger him, and how sure he would be to turn on me, and how able and certain to destroy me, if I were by myself – therefore how mad to do it except as a simple act of obedience to Christ and a reliance on His power and grace to bring me through.

In December Newman's new volume *Sermons on Subjects of the Day* containing his farewell sermon appeared. Whether by reason of his sensitivity to public criticism or from guilty feelings Manning thought Newman referred to him in his mention of Orpah, the daughter-in-law of Naomi, who in contrast to Ruth, kissed her but left.

> I felt it bitterly from the thought you might think my words the smooth words of one who would leave you for the world. I will use no professions of attachment to you, or of my own intentions and desires for myself. I had rather submit to any thoughts in your heart, or in others. You have a hard life and an empty home before you, and so

have I, and I trust we shall walk together long enough to trust the singleness of each other's eye and to love each other as friends.

It is not easy to interpret the following paragraph, but Manning seems to be saying that he can not take the route of doubt as to the Church, which Newman has, for it would undermine everything to which he has devoted all his energies, namely, strengthening the Church, but he wishes nevertheless to be friends.

> My dear Newman, do not suspect me as an empty pretender if I say that the only thing that has kept me up in the last six years and more of trial [the death of his wife], and the only thing I look for until death is to save the Church in which I was born again. Doubtful thoughts about it are dreadful – and seem to take all things from me.
>
> I could not help writing this to you, for it has been in my mind day after day: and yet I have shrunk from doing it, until I read your words about Orpah. And after all I feel that all this may seem to you no better than her kiss. (*KC*, 290–1)

On Christmas Eve, fresh from his retreat, Newman sent a humble and gentle reply: 'What can have led you to entertain the thought that I could ever be crossed by the idea which you consider may have been suggested to me by the name of Orpah? Really, unless it were so sad a matter, I should smile.' Newman went on to speak of himself. He felt no blame in having tried to defend the Church

> on that basis which our divines have ever built and on which alone they can pretend to build [i.e. the Fathers of the Church]. And how could I foresee that when I examined that basis I should feel it to require a system different from hers and that the Fathers to which she had led me would lead me from her?. . . . yet it would be strange if I had heart to blame others who are honest in maintaining what I am abandoning.
>
> Surely I will remain where I am as long as ever I can. . . . If my misgivings are from above, I shall be carried on in spite of my resistance. . . . And believe me the circumstance of such men as yourself being contented to remain is the strongest argument in favour of my own remaining. It is my constant prayer, that if others are right I may be drawn back – that nothing may part us. (*KC*, 292–3, corrected)

This letter when shown to Gladstone evoked a sympathetic response. 'Cords of silk should one by one be thrown over him to bind him to the Church. Every manifestation of sympathy and confidence in him, as a man, must have some small effect.' (*KC*, 293 and n. 1)

CHAPTER TWENTY-FOUR

Cheerfulness amid Dreariness and Pain

In January 1844 Keble wrote a kind letter to Newman, in which he gave a gentle warning against the effort of the Evil One to ruin a good work once begun, by getting a hold of tendencies in its agents to entice them from the English Church.

> Such tendencies one can imagine in your case; among the rest a certain restlessness, a longing after something more, something analogous to a very exquisite ear in music, which would keep you ... in spite of yourself, intellectually and morally dissatisfied wherever you were. . . . May it not be your duty ... to suppress your misgivings ... as you would any other bad thoughts, making up your mind that the conclusion is undutiful, and therefore there must be some delusion in the premisses.

Keble issued a second warning: the confusion and shock of *thousands* were their guide and comforter to forsake them all at once, 'making them sceptical about everything and everybody'. Keble also remarked that if the medieval system is really the intended development of Primitive Catholicity, 'is it not the most natural way for the English Church to recover it *through* Primitive Catholicity, instead of being urged directly to it?' (*KC*, 297–9)

In his reply Newman told Keble he felt no call to do anything but remain as he was. He took up the last point of Keble. It was in the very line of reading in the Fathers and 'no other, which has led me Romeward', though he had not read them with this view. He wished to resist and thought it a duty, but 'was it undutifulness to the Mosaic Law, to be led on to the Gospel? was not the Law from God? How could a Jew, formerly or now, ever become a Christian, if he must at all hazards resist convictions and for ever?' Newman assured Keble he was not mentioning these things by way of argument, but to reveal the state of his mind. He also stated he had at times the uncomfortable feeling he would not like to die in the English Church, 'did He cut short one's hours of grace, this would be a call to make up one's mind on what seemed most probable', i.e., on the basis of a practical, not a speculative certitude. Newman did not say anything about the possibility of being under a delusion, yet in a short while this would become a question in his mind.

To Pusey he revealed that he was not in any perplexity or anxiety. 'I fear that I must say that for four years and a half I have had a conviction, weaker or stronger, but on the whole constantly growing, and at present very strong, that we are not part of the Catholic Church. I am too much accustomed to this idea to feel pain at it. I could only feel pain, if I found it led me to action. At present I do not feel any such call. Such feelings are not hastily to be called convictions, though this seems to me to be such. Did I ever arrive at a full persuasion that it was such, then I should be anxious and much perplexed.' (19 February 1844) He had moreover to assure Pusey he was mistaken in attributing his manner to sensitiveness, or sharp feeling, though 'I have no doubt there is fault in me, which has made you so write.' (23 February 1844) Pusey later attributed his defection from the Church to sensitivity. Newman's reply was that had he been sensitive to the way he was treated, he would have left the Church long before he did.

On 21 February at 10:30 in the morning he wrote to Bowden, whose birthday was also on the 21st,

> I am just up, having a bad cold; the like necessity has not happened to me (except in January) in my memory, but this winter has been very trying here. . . . I could not come to see you, there were so many difficulties in the way – and I (though I shall pain you by my saying so) I am not worthy of friends. With my opinions, to the full of which I dare not confess, I feel like a guilty person with others – though I trust I am not so. People kindly think that I have much to bear externally – disappointment, slander, etc., No, I have nothing to bear but the anxiety which I feel for my friends' anxiety for me and their perplexity.' (21 February 1844, *Apo.*, 226. N added 'their' for clarity sake)

There were all sorts of reports about him going about: one that he had written to Ambrose Phillipps 'There are many of us in Oxford who are quite ready to join you; but we think that we are serving your cause much more effectually by remaining where we are at present.' This he repudiated in a letter to the Rev. C. J. Myers, 'To remain in the English Church from a motive of expediency seems to me altogether unjustifiable both in a theological and a religious point of view.' (25 February 1844) He had likewise to deny a report in Manchester that he was forced to leave the Church of Rome.

On his return from his successful visit to Rome, Dr Russell of Maynooth visited Newman in Oxford, on 1 August the previous year, but apparently there was no discussion of theological topics. In the *Apologia* Newman wrote, 'he had, perhaps, more to do with my conversion than anyone else. . . . He was always gentle, mild, unobstrusive, uncontroversial. He let me alone.' To Fr Matthew Russell, S. J., Russell's nephew, Newman later remarked that his uncle 'struck me before I was a Catholic as no other Catholic did. He made a great impression on me – so much so that in my Apologia I said I had seen him more than once, whereas he assures me this was not the case.' (*LD* XXVII, 51. *Apo.*, 194–6: 389–90)

In early 1844 Russell sent Newman 'a large bundle of penny or half-penny books of devotion, of all sorts, as they are found in the booksellers' shops at Rome; and, on looking over them, I was quite astonished to find how different they were from what I had fancied, how little there was in them to which I could really object'. (*Apo.*, 196) This was the last communication until October 1845 when Newman wrote him a short note announcing his intention of becoming a Catholic.[1]

That Newman withdrew from the editorship of the Lives of the Saints did not mean that he washed his hands of the project. He was not annoyed that Rivington rejected it, 'but that they should cast all the expense on me *so cavalierly*. They might just as well have sent in the bills to me of an edition of my Sermons instead of paying me sundry pounds they had promised.' (To Mrs John Mozley, 21 January 1844) He engaged James Toovey to publish the works, Pugin to make designs for them, and Oakeley to become editor. The first Life, that of Stephen Harding by Dalgairns, went into a second edition very quickly. Responses were varied: some favourable, others seeing in it Popery, others asking questions that arose from reading it.

Fourteen volumes appeared in 1844–5, Newman being editor of the first two volumes. He himself wrote *A Legend of St. Gundleus, hermit in Wales, about A.D. 500*; *A Legend of St. Edelwald, hermit in Farne, A.D. 700*; and *A Legend of St. Bettelin, hermit, and patron of Stafford, towards*

A.D. 800 (Prose by N; verse by J. D. Dalgairns). Gladstone was pleased with what Newman did, but the latter told Hope that Gladstone should be made aware that

> a series of thwartings such as I have experienced, (I do not mean, creates, which logically they cannot do) but realizes, verifies, substantiates, a *phantasia* of the English Church very unfavourable to her Catholicity. If a person is deeply convinced in his *reason* that her claims to Catholicity are untenable, but fears to trust his reason, such events, when they come upon him again and again, seem to do just what is wanting, corroborate his reason experimentally. They force upon his imagination and familiarize his moral perception with the conclusions of his intellect. Presumptions become facts. (*KC*, 310–1)

The Lenten fasting was lighter than the previous year, possibly because the strict fasting in Advent had taken its toll on Newman's health. The first meal was at 12, and their full meal at five in the afternoon, though there was no restriction on tea at any hour. They ate no flesh meat, Sundays or weekdays. (*AW*, 234–5) Though Newman recorded in his journal 'I am told I do not look ill,' Dr Babington in a stern warning to him later in September mentioned specifically, 'When I last saw you – about the close of Lent, I believe, I was much struck with your appearance, which was shrunk and debilitated; and it is impossible to avoid the suspicion, that, partly by overwork, and partly by deficient nutriment, you are rendering yourself unfit for exertion and reducing yourself to the state of a helpless and almost useless invalid.' (copied by Newman, from letter of Babington dated 26 September 1844) (*Moz.* II, 439) Newman, however, did not attribute his poor health to fasting, but rather to the loss of friends, actual and prospective. 'The separation from friends was the one thing which weighed on me for two years before I became a Catholic – and it affected my health most seriously.' (R. I. Wilberforce, 1 September 1854, *LD*, XVI, 242)

From the beginning of April to July Newman wrote to Mrs William Froude a series of letters which constitute the fullest personal account of his change of views. He was motivated to do this by his fear that the revelation of his doubts had disturbed her faith and in William's case had resulted in scepticism as to the objectivity of truth. He began by recounting how the Anglican Church had a theory which he admired and felt was a duty to maintain. In looking into the Fathers, he saw portions of it such as the supremacy of Scripture confirmed. He also saw there was a risk of Anglican principles running into Roman. Despite his admiration of much of the Roman system he felt a repulsion 'arising from *particular doctrines* of the Church of Rome'. The only way to resist it was to speak violently against it. In so doing, he was not acting on private judgement, but at the command of all the Anglican Divines. His only reservation was that the Anglican position might be a mere theory unrealized in fact. In the course of reading the Fathers, 'which I had hitherto read with the eyes of our Divines', it flashed on him 'that (not only was it a theory never realized,) but a theory unproved, or rather disproved, by antiquity'. (3 April 1844)

Nor should such a change of view militate against the objectivity of truth. 'Surely the *continuance* of a person who wishes to go right in a wrong system, and not his giving it up, would be that which militated against the objectiveness of Truth – leading to the suspicion, that one thing and another were equally pleasing to our Maker, where men were sincere.' This latter was of course the position of the liberals. He was not sorry that he defended the system in which he found himself. 'For is it not one's duty . . . to throw oneself generously into that form of religion which is providentially put before one? . . . . May we not, on the other hand, look for a blessing *through* obedience even to an erroneous system, and a guidance by means of it out of it? . . . . Certainly, I have always contended that obedience even to an erring conscience was the way to gain light, and that it mattered not where a man began, so that he began on what came to hand and in faith; that any thing might become a divine method of Truth, that to the pure all things are pure and have a self-correcting virtue and a power of germinating.' Nevertheless he has very little claim to feel confidence; he is right, 'This of course is what keeps me back.' (4 April 1844)

The following day on Good Friday evening (Newman usually answered letters at night) he continued his account of his first doubts in reading the Fathers in 1839. His reactions and steps he took were recounted at length in a subsequent letter on 9 April but apparently not sent until later in the month or even as late as June. Excerpts from the letter of 9 April have been given already. (See Chapter Sixteen) The probable reason was that he wanted assurances from the Froudes whether it was good to continue, as he asked in a letter of 12 April.

In a long letter of 19 May he told why he had difficulty with the Anglican theory of the unity of the Church, which based it on succession. Each bishop is independent and claims obedience without claiming to be a depository and transmitter of true doctrine. Each bishop is joined to others only in so far as 'the civil power or his own choice happens to unite him'. Since there is but one bishop and Church in each place, therefore the Roman succession and Church are intruders here. But this is unreal, for 'who can deny that the true difference between us and Rome is one of *doctrine and practice*? yet such an explanation sinks that difference altogether, and reduces our quarrel with Rome to one of ecclesiastical arrangement. Do members of our Church on going abroad communicate with the Roman Church in places where that Church has possession? If they do not, we are *not* one Church with Rome. The Anglican theory then cannot be acted upon – it is a mere set of words – facts confute it.'

Newman continued this letter on 28 May in which he discussed at length the Anglican theory of episcopacy and the development of Roman supremacy. Perhaps confining his views to paper helped him to clarify them, for he wrote to Jemima on 21 May that his views were 'very much clearer and stronger than they were even a year ago', but he could not calculate how soon they might affect his will and become practical. He assured her, 'Unless any thing happened which I considered a divine call, and beyond all calculation, I never should take any one by surprise.' On 3 June he wrote to her again, saying that she should not be surprised 'if I should determine on giving up my Fellowship, but at present I have no plan formed'. He also told her he did not put on cheerfulness because people do not find out he had cares. 'The truth is (thank God) I *am* cheerful. . . . having sound sleep at night and quiet days and trying to serve Him without aims of this world, however imperfectly, how can I be but cheerful, as I am?' He trusts in God's help to bear whatever pain he or others have to bear, but adds, 'Of course the pain of my friends is what cuts me and I do not know how I shall bear it – but He gives us strength according to our day.'

This may seem remarkable in light of the agonizing letter he wrote to Keble a few days later, in which revealing all the instances of God's personal providence over him, starting with his first conversion leading up to the stricter life he was attempting to lead in the last few years, he asked if God had deserted him because of some secret fault or sins so that he was under a delusion. God had answered his prayers for improvement, 'why should Providence have granted my prayers in these respects, and not when I have prayed for light and guidance?' There are inducements not to move, not only loss of friends, esteem, but 'the disturbance of mind which a change on my part would cause, . . . the temptation to which many would be exposed of scepticism, indifference, and even infidelity'. He confesses he sometimes has an uncomfortable feeling about himself: 'a sceptical, unrealizing temper is far from unnatural to me – and I may be suffered to relapse into it as a judgment'. And so he ends as he began:

> Am I in a delusion, given over to believe a lie? Am I deceiving myself and thinking myself convinced when I am not? Does any subtle feeling or temptation, which I cannot detect, govern me, and bias my judgment? But is it possible that Divine Mercy should not wish me, if so, to discover and escape it? Has He led me thus far to destroy me in the wilderness? (8 June 1844; *KC*, 313–8)

Keble was sympathetic as usual. He did not think that Newman should assume that 'if after all you should be allowed to be erroneous in this your judgment, it is equivalent to judicial blindness or something of that sort'. 'If your present view is right, Pusey's I suppose is wrong: should one therefore infer that his prayers for light and guidance are not heard?' Keble further remarked that he fancied Newman was over sanguine 'in making things square, and did not quite allow enough for Bishop Butler's notion of doubt and intellectual difficulty being some men's intended element and appropriate trial'. That Newman's painful position did not disturb his cheerfulness, as he told Jemima, emerges again in his remark to Keble, 'I hope it is not wrong to be cheerful, for I cannot help being so. . . . Do not lament that you do not lose your sleep. I think sleep is the greatest of our ordinary blessings. Nothing goes well with the mind without it; it heals all trouble.' (*KC*, 313–21)

Whether it was by reason of Keble's warning, Newman became increasingly concerned about taking people by surprise; should he in time convert to the Roman Church. Accordingly he began to prepare people for it little by little. He told Mrs Froude, 'I do not mind it being said, as an historical fact, whenever you care to do so and have opportunity, that you have reason to know that I was very much unsettled on the subject of Rome in the year 1839' without mentioning anything about his present state of mind or how she got her information. ([28 May 1844]) He made the same request of Henry Wilberforce, who does not seem to have taken kindly to the idea, and urged him not to take any hasty step. Newman in reply reiterated that it was cruel to take people by surprise. 'That friends should know a *fact*, and a fact five years old, seems an easy way of leading them to conjecture what my present state of mind is.' But he went on to mention that of late he has had at times 'fears of the lawfulness of my remaining where I am, of the responsibility of knowing without acting, which I never have had before and if these were to increase, it is plain what the consequence would be.' In deference to Henry's feelings he withdrew the request. (8 June and 17 July 1844)

On 9 June Newman continued the history of his change of views in a letter to Mrs Froude.

> two considerations . . . kept me from having any fear of Rome – the one that we had the Apostolical succession. . . . I have been forced from this ground . . . by the question of Schism, which suspends the grace of that succession, even where the succession is found. The second point was my conviction that certain definite doctrines of Rome were not to be found in Antiquity – and this objection has been removed from my mind by a consideration of the principle of *development*, which I implied . . . in what I said in my last about the growth of the Papal power.

Newman then cited doctrines or practices such as honours to Mary, purgatory, which were not in place in the early Church, and thus differ from Rome at present. Were these then '*corruptions*' of Christianity, as originally given? Newman answers *no*; they are developments. Newman then mentions how he had held development in some points of theology in various works, especially those on Romanism, e.g., the *Prophetical Office of the Church*. His present view is contained in the last of the University Sermons, which differs, not in principle but in two respects from the Prophetical Office:

1. In considering that developments may be made at any time, for the Church is always under the guidance of Divine Grace . . . .
2. that developments are not only *explanations* of the sense of the Creed, but further doctrines involved in and arising from its articles. (9 June 1844)[2]

In a letter of 14 July Newman summed up his conclusions with regard to the development of doctrine:

1. I am far more certain (according to the Fathers) that we *are* in a state of culpable separation *than* that developments do *not* exist under the gospel, and that the Roman developments are *not* true ones.
2. I am far more certain that *our* (modern) doctrines are wrong, *than* that the *Roman* (modern) doctrines are wrong.

3. Granting that the Roman (special) doctrines are not found drawn out in the early Church, yet I think there is sufficient trace of them in it, to recommend and prove them, *on the hypothesis* of the Church having a divine guidance, though not sufficient to prove them by itself. So that the question simply turns on the nature of the promise of the Spirit made to the Church.

4. The proof of the *Roman* (modern) <special> doctrines is as strong <(or stronger)> in Antiquity, as that of certain doctrines which *both we and the Romans hold*. E.g. there is more evidence in Antiquity for the necessity of Unity than for that of the Apostolical Succession – for the supremacy of the See of Rome than for the Presence in the Eucharist – for the practice of Invocation than for certain books in the present Canon of Scripture etc. etc.

5. The Analogy of the Old Testament and the New leads to acknowledgment of doctrinal developments.

TO BE OR NOT TO BE

In February Newman had received word from Miss Holmes that she felt called to the Catholic Church. She was at the time governess to the children of Mr Leigh, a friend of Oakeley, who was becoming a Catholic. Miss Holmes was being urged to convert at Easter, but she could not bear to be separated from her 'idol'. 'You keep me in the Church by a spell I cannot comprehend or break.' As a result of his advice not to act on feeling but only on a deliberate resolution made and written down six months before, she put off her reception until the autumn. Meanwhile she was becoming almost hysterical. 'You are made of marble. Those cold words of yours fell on my heart like an iceberg. . . . O what would I give to find a Roman Catholic priest like you in mind and manner.' He replied that what she was seeking, a relation of father and daughter, she would not find in the Catholic Church. Unlike Miss Giberne who never revealed to Newman her austerities including beating herself with the cords of her trunk as a penance, Miss Holmes told Newman she was using the discipline as a result of reading St Stephen Harding. He told her she should not have done so, without asking advice to mode and degree and where to use it.

Somewhat like Ambrose St John whose unsettlement when he came to Littlemore was owing to his belief in transubstantiation and invocation of the saints, Miss Holmes had to force herself and laboured in vain to believe in the real presence in the Protestant Sacrament. She likewise got great consolation from praying to the saints, a practice which Newman did not approve of. At Easter time she attended the Vespers and Compline service with the Leighs. At the Benediction service tears of joy burst forth at feeling Christ present. She also went with the Leighs family to the Catholic chapel to attend a marriage ceremony performed by Dr Wiseman. At Mass she was much affected. 'When the Saving Victim was raised, I felt as if I dared not refuse to go to my Saviour. I made my resolution unalterably then.' (20 April 1844) Newman for his part told her that he had too much experience of Christ present 'in an extraordinary way in our rite' to doubt it. She told Wiseman that she would wait six months, at least until the Feast of St Teresa, 15 October. Newman gently told her he could not see how she could continue under his guidance, after having made, in her words 'an unalterable resolution' to join the Roman Church. 'In its *nature* it would be the same sort of impropriety as saying mass or dressing in Pontifical vestments'. He then humbly asked pardon. 'In all the various imperfections in my mode of dealing with you – whatever was harsh, inconsiderate, or unkind. . . . I pray that He [God] would bless you every day, and guide you continually, and enable you ever to discern between His voice and your own feelings.' Then he added feelingly, 'In losing you, I lose what I can seldom expect to meet with – an affectionate heart. All along I have seemed to be throwing away from me what is so rare, so costly – and in doing so, I have often seemed unmindful of your feelings and ungrateful to you.' (22 April 1844) Miss Holmes responded that she thought she had almost broken the bondage to him when she wrote, but as a result of his kind letter she felt 'as if the chain were rivetted again. Oh how galling it is! but I love it, as I love the discipline.'

Numerous letters were exchanged during May and June. She hoped he would not refuse to give her help a little while longer, as it would take a year for another director to get to know her as he does. Moreover, 'Not all the Bishops in Christendom would have power to make me break this resolution.' Also 'it is my nature to take a long time to gain courage for any thing painful. When I have time, I can go through any thing.' The drama played on, Bishop Wiseman urging her to take instructions at once and she resisting. She told Mrs Leigh she wanted to leave in July so as not to be troubled by being surrounded by Roman Catholics urging her on, as Mr Leigh was doing, especially to put herself under a Roman Catholic director. A sensible Catholic lady related several instances of Wiseman's erring with regard to young people, such as hurrying people into a vocation. This convinced Miss Holmes that one may acknowledge Rome to be an infallible Church, yet distrust one of her bishops as being a fallible man. This strengthened her against yielding to Wiseman's pressure upon her. She was however racked with doubt and among other things defended her practice of invoking the saints. (13 June 1844)

Newman was unwilling to argue with her, but calmly and quietly reiterated his position that he would not dissuade her from joining the Church of Rome, if he thought she had a steady conviction that Rome was the true Church, but she kept acting under impulse. She should not think herself under his guidance when she has not obeyed what he advised, for example, not invoking the saints, which she was both doing and defending by arguments. (19 June 1844) This elicited several desperate and highly emotionally charged letters, in which she defended herself against the charge of disobedience, and pleaded with him, 'Oh my dearest Mr Newman, can you refuse to take me back? I never thought you would mind my arguing with you. . . . I will never argue again, I assure you. I make no terms.' (21–22 June 1844) 'You look and speak as if you were mildness and gentleness itself; but you can *act* so sternly. . . . Can you be so stern, my dear, my very dear Mr. Newman, as to lead me to guide myself?' (23 June 1844) He had answered that he had offered advice, not guidance. He is willing, however, to continue to give advice, but not direction. His advice is to go into Somersetshire and remain quiet there, leaving off every practice which is not Anglican and pray continuously 'that God would bring you into the Truth, and make you worthy of it. This I earnestly recommend, as a true friend, who takes a great interest in you.' This made Miss Holmes happy. 'You are not so hard hearted as I thought; and yet you will not be weakly indulgent.' She seems to have calmed down. 'I will not now ask you to accept any thing like obedience. I feel very thankful for any thing you give me; advice or guidance, or what you please, as little or as much as you think good for me.' (25 June 1844)

Miss Holmes resisted the pressure of Wiseman to see her in August, and she left the Leighs and went into the country, as Newman had suggested. There she struggled with her indecision, but finally she entered the Catholic Church in November. Newman evidently wrote her a kind letter, to which she replied, 'Forgive me all the pain and perplexity I must have caused you. You are so generous and unselfish, that I am sure you will think it reward enough for all you have suffered on my account, to hear that I am more happy than I ever dared to hope or conceive I could be.' (30 November 1844) With the zeal of a recent convert she began to lecture him, 'Oh my dear Mr Newman, what are you losing! my only grief is that I did not join three years ago.' (4 December 1844) But her question, 'Could St Thomas of Canterbury, St Anselm and Venerable Bede rise from their graves, can you doubt an instant which side they would take?' is curiously similar to the passage in the Essay on the Development about St Athanasius and St Ambrose coming to Oxford. (*Dev*, 98; 1st. ed, 138; cf. *LD* XIII, 78)

On 30 January and 4 February 1845 Newman wrote to Miss Holmes that their relationship had been a religious one, but she had ended it by becoming a Catholic. He omitted from the second letter of which he gives only the substance, a remark, 'When you joined the Church of Rome, it was as if you died. No unkindness, no want of interest and good will, is connected with our thoughts of the dead, though henceforth we are separated from them. For those particular purposes, on account of which you first made me know you, you are plainly dead to me.' When Newman transcribed the correspondence, he added an NB. 'My friends have treated me in this way, since I have become a Catholic; and I should never dream of complaining of them, while they acted *on principle*. But I doubt much whether many of them would avow that it was as *a simple duty* that they ignored me as they have done.' He continued, 'Nor should you, religiously, to complain or think it strange. No such great act as you have made, should be without sacrifices. And the special sacrifice, connected by our Lord Himself with the change of religion is the loss of houses, brethren, parents, and friends.' He omitted however the following reference to himself: 'I am not teaching what I do not experience. Mine own especial trial is the distress and the loss of friends, some who live, and some who die. It is my portion.'

Newman did not end the correspondence entirely, as there are entries in the diary of subsequent letters to her. In a letter of 31 May 1845 to Miss Holmes he remarked

> You know I have wished to break off our correspondence, except on matters in which I thought (with your director's leave) I could serve you, from the time you joined the Church of Rome.
>
> After your recent letters, I have come to the resolution of breaking it off altogether. . . . It is useless to attempt to alter my resolution.

He sent a copy the same day to Miss Holmes' director, mentioning in his letter that 'she lately has been hurt at two notes of mine'. This however did not stop Miss Holmes writing to him, and Newman transcribed portions of her letters until 21 April 1846, the last reading, 'I have found your kind letter. . . . I *will* try to "act like a rational person", as you say; but is it *irrational* to love you very much?'

As a Catholic Miss Holmes wandered from job to job and from place to place, never being able to settle, but she kept in contact with Newman, who tried to help her, writing frequently until her death in 1876. In 1862, a particularly low period for Newman as a Catholic, when his Anglican friends had not yet renewed contact with him, he thanked her for 'a beautiful little book'. 'In this world of change, it is a great thing to have unchanging friends – and you are one of those who have been most faithful to me amid all vicissitudes. It is not every Saint even, who can persevere.' (*LD* XX, 180)

The following year Newman transcribed the bulk of the correspondence entitling the collection, 'A History of a Conversion to the Catholic Faith, in the years 1840–1844 exhibited in a Series of Letters.' The correspondence portrays the psychological and emotional trauma that could precede a conversion in the last century, and the price that had to be paid in terms of social relations. It also reveals Newman's kindness, his patience, and self-control, his refusal to be caught up in a mere worldly, human relationship, sticking rather to his role as spiritual adviser.[3]

NEARING THE KING'S HIGHWAY

During the summer of 1844 Newman went to London frequently to visit Bowden and to bring him the Sacrament. In between he sat for his portrait by Richmond, arranged by Henry Wilberforce. On the vigil of St James, 24 July, after having walked from Littlemore to Oxford Station with his luggage, and walking and riding 2½ hours in London, he set off on foot for Roehampton, in heat of 86 degrees in the shade. He stopped by Fulham to get a glimpse of his grandmother's house, but the chemist who occupied the ground floor did not take his hints. He plied the chemist with questions which show his remarkable visual memory for details including the long coach in which he left when about five years old. To his aunt he mused;

How little did the little child whom you used to fondle, think of what *he* thinks now! He had no thoughts. There is a poem of mine in the Lyra, ('Did we but see, When life first opened, how our journey lay' etc) which applies to one at any two periods – but how strangely does it apply to me then and now! I know not now of course what is before me, before my end comes – still more strange may be the contrast – but it is very touching and subduing as it is. . . . I really do think I love peace, yet I am destined to be 'a man of strife'. ([25 July] 1844)

On 15 September Bowden died. 'His end,' Newman wrote to Harriett, 'was as peaceful and beautiful as became such a blameless life; so cheerful, so playful, so tender, smiling through his tears, and in nothing great or small wishing any thing whatever but what Supreme Love and Wisdom thought best for him.' (19 September 1844) Newman stayed till after the funeral. In a subsequent letter to Harriett on 22 September he gave a more detailed account of Bowden's last days, concluding, 'One always thinks the time is too soon. I wished to have said many things to him but I rather ought to be thankful that I had seen so much of him.' He did not reveal what he put in a note of May 20 1862, 'I sobbed bitterly over his coffin, to think that he had left me [while I was] still dark to what the way of truth was, and what I ought to do in order to please God and fulfil His will.' – an indication of the connection in his mind between the quest for truth and holiness.

Newman continued to visit Mrs Bowden, when he went in October to London to see Dr Babington, who 'has been firing a gun over my head with such noise and fury. . . . He threatens to make me as idle as the day is long, to go the whole hog in eating, and to sleep like a top.' (To St John, 3 October 1844) After one such visit, he got into the carriage when it was dark. There were three persons in the parallel carriage talking quite loudly in the dark. ' "I know the soundest divine in the Church – the soundest divine is Mr Stanley Faber of Durham, and he said to me, Depend on it, Newman, Newman, (very loud) is a jesuit, a jesuit." Somehow I could not help interfering. . . . So I put my head through the cross window which separates the carriages and said (in the dark) "Gentlemen, please don't speak so loud, for persons are here whom you would not like to speak before." ' (To Mrs Bowden, 8 October 1844)

Newman felt obliged to reveal the state of his mind to Mrs Bowden, to whom he writes, 'You cannot tell what relief it is to me that you know what I am. Till then I feel to people like a hypocrite. . . . I seem taking people in.' (15 October 1844) It had, however, upset her, as she wrote, 'What you told me of your mind made me very unhappy – I hardly think I ever felt so thoroughly desolate as that night – for I had always persuaded myself it was not so . . . it seemed to throw me more upon myself, to find you differing from John – yet I had much rather now *know* than be in doubt – and your talking with me afterwards made me happier.' She enclosed £100 with a message from John, copied from a memorandum which he had dictated 'with tears in his eyes'. (16 October 1844) It affected Newman emotionally. 'I have had many bitter sighs since I read your note. Yet what could I do?'

> Dear John has been kind enough to call my friendship for him 'true'. I do sincerely wish to be true to you and yours. O, that I may be able and yet here I begin with what seems to be the most unfriendly of acts, as if I would deny you such service as he asks of me. Unless my heart is very self deceived, I most profoundly wish to be a servant to you. O do suffer me to be such, and take me for what I am, though I cannot be all you might have thought and could wish. (21 October 1844)

Indeed Newman did become such a servant, visiting and helping her in any way he could.

In November a realization of the pain he would inflict on friends and on the many unknown persons he had influenced grew in intensity. A report in the 'Standard' and 'Herald' claimed that he had written to Isaac Williams a letter in which he asserted he could no longer remain in the Anglican Church. Perhaps this gave Newman the idea of writing, in the form of a letter, an anonymous pamphlet in which he would reveal the state of his mind and how he arrived at it. Only a draft of a letter to Keble exists, dated 30 October 1844, but whether it was ever completed and sent is not known. Although Williams issued a denial, Newman was inundated with letters, pleading with him not to leave the Church, or at least to pause before doing so. Take for example the letter of Charles Crawley living in Littlemore and a benefactor of the Church there.

> Here at home in our own Communion, what confusion to our Friends – what triumph to our Enemies! and to Rome what an argument to confirm her in all her errors and abuses!
>
> What hope, humanly speaking, can remain to our poor humbled Church after such a blow? and now that she is beginning to show signs of life and raise her drooping head, to find herself all at once despaired of and deserted by her best champion; one who under Providence has been the chief instrument in raising her from her degraded state, and as it were breathing into her afresh the breath of life! surely the bare

thought of this is enough to make the whole head sick and the whole heart faint. – But I cannot I will not yet believe such a fearful calamity is in store for us. . . .

I am encouraged too by the apprehension you expressed that your present doubts might arise from some delusion (21 November 1844)

By the time he received this letter he was already in great pain. 'The unsettling so many peaceable innocent minds is a most overpowering thought, and at this moment my heart literally aches and has for some days. I am conscious of no motive but that of obeying an urgent imperative call of duty.' Yet his spirits have not yet given way. 'But what with this long continued inward secret trial, and the unwearied violence of the attacks on me, most cruel, though they mean it not so, at a time when I most need peace, I am just now in straits.' (To Mrs Froude, 12 November 1844) The same day he told Gladstone that he was affected by the attacks, which 'is an unusual thing with me, and I trust will pass away'.

To Manning he revealed, 'my trust only is that every day of pain is so much from the necessary draught which must be exhausted'. Of the two sources of pain, the 'perplexity, unsettlement, alarm, scepticism which I am causing to so many – and the loss of kind feeling and good opinion on the part of so many, known and unknown, who have wished me well', the former was the 'constant, urgent, unmitigated one. I had for days a literal pain about my heart, and from time to time all the complaints of the Psalmist seemed to belong to me'. In store for him were 'sacrifices irreparable, not only from my age, when people hate changing, but from my especial love of old associations and the pleasures of memory'. (16 November 1844)

By 24 November these pains had not gone, as revealed in a letter to Jemima:

It is astonishing what little feeling certain people have, Golightly and the Newspapers would think it very wrong to put out a statement on doubtful authority to the effect that I had broken my leg – yet they have no remorse in circulating what is adapted to shock friends indefinitely more. But the said G. is a man literally without bowels. I doubt whether he has any inside, or is more than a walking and talking piece of mechanism.

I have gone through a great deal of pain, and have been very much cut up. The one predominant distress upon me has been the unsettlement of mind I am causing. This is a thing that has haunted me day by day – and for some days I had a literal pain in and about my heart, which I suppose at any moment I could bring on again. I have been overworked lately – the translation of St Athanasius is, I am glad to say, just coming to an end, and I shall (so be it) relax – I suppose I need it. This has been a trying year.

Newman further remarked that he was not conscious of 'any motive but a sense of indefinite risk to my own soul in remaining where I am', and that he was 'not conscious of any resentment, disgust, or the like to repel me from my present position', but he did not contemplate any early step even now. He cannot but think, though he can no more realize it 'than being made Dean of Christ Church or Bishop of Durham, that some day it will be and at a definite distance of time'. At present he is in a state of mind which divines call 'indifferentia', 'inculcating it as a duty, to be set upon nothing but be willing to take whatever Providence wills'. It is his full intention to give up his Fellowship 'some time before any thing happens'. (24 November 1844)

Not all the letters he received were sympathetic. A father wanted Newman to plead with his daughter who broke off her engagement and wanted to become a nun, which he attributed to one of Newman's sermons. To a letter from an officious person who thought he had the right and duty to lecture him on his supposed moral faults, even though he did not know him personally, Newman could deliver a deserved *tu quoque*:

I have no call to correspond with a gentleman, who professing for me 'love, respect and affection' speaks of my 'absurd hobbies'. I have no power of corresponding with him when he accuses me of a 'want of straightforward honesty', and suspects that I am one of those described by the Apostle in reprobation 'who having put away a good conscience, concerning faith have made shipwreck'.

I am sure, My dear Sir, and I say it with every kind feeling, that you will find you have to tend to your own advancement in gentleness, tenderness, sympathy, modesty and delicacy rather than to criticise another.' (draft, 27 November 1844)

Of the attacks on him in the press, the ones which hurt the most were those accusing him of dishonesty, of being a traitor, not only believing in Romanism but actually in the pay of the Pope. How could he explain that he would not leave the Church, not only because he was not certain of his view of the Roman Church and might be deluded, but also for spiritual motives, one of which was touched upon by Dalgairns, who wrote, 'A good deal of the misunderstanding which exists about him and *some* of the charges of dishonesty arise from his guiding himself by circumstances, i.e., by Providence, and so not being able to say what he will do.' (15 November 1844)

The report that he was about to leave the Church brought home to Newman two things: 'that every one is prepared for such an event, next that every one expects it of me', but he felt no call at present to do so. He admitted, however, that the widespread negative opinion of him 'has great force', but this could not move him to act. 'I have a great dread of going merely by my own feelings, lest they should mislead me. By one's sense of duty one must go, but external facts support one in doing so.' (To Miss Giberne, 7 November 1844)

As was natural, not only enemies but friends speculated about possible secret motives which would explain his conduct, Edward Coleridge thought it was a preference for the Roman Catholic Church to his own. But he knew only its external aspects which were so unattractive.

> In the 'Tablet' and 'Dublin Review,' in radical combinations and liberal meetings, this is how I know them. My habits, tastes, feelings are so different as can well be conceived from theirs, as they show outwardly.
>
> No – as far as I know myself the one single over-powering feeling is that our Church is in schism, and that there is no salvation in it *for one who is convinced of this.* . . . I have waited not because my conviction was not clear, but because I doubted whether it was a duty to trust this. I am still waiting on that consideration.' (*KC*, 345–8; also to Manning, 16 November 1844; to Keble, *KC*, 351)

Newman had likewise a difficult time convincing friends that it was not the treatment he was receiving that was influencing him. Judge Coleridge wanted to get up a private address which would assure Newman of 'gratitude, admiration, and love'. In reporting this, Keble wrote, 'Therefore, my dear Newman, do not in any case imagine, that you have not hundreds, not to say thousands, sympathizing with you and feeling indeed that they owe their very selves to you.' Keble added his own tribute, 'Your sermons put me in the way, and your healing ministration helped me beyond measure,' but also that of others, 'Wherever I go, there is some one to whom you have been a channel of untold blessing.' (*KC*,

347–9) Though grateful for the gesture, Newman declined not out of modesty but on spiritual grounds. 'If there is a cross which is blessed from those who have borne it from our Lord's own time, it is this – and it is safest to be content with it.' (*KC*, 349–50)

It is probable that Newman forwent or at least mitigated his fasting during Advent as a result of Babington's advice, for he was unwell. 'I had no fever, no cold or cough – but a wonderful pain in my head and limbs, and prostration of strength – so that I could hardly lift myself from my bed – and even at the end of a week could hardly walk,' he told Mrs Bowden. (27 December 1844) Upon recovery he went off to London to attend Robert Williams who was seriously ill, and stayed until it was safe to leave.

To Jemima, with whom he wanted to be completely open, since 'there can be no exercise of love between persons without this openness', and 'it is most repugnant to my nature to conceal things', he confided that over a long period he could not detect any secret *bad* motive which would indicate blindness in his belief. 'If God gives me certain light, supposing it to be such, this is a reason for *me* to act – yet in so doing I am not condemning those who do not so act. There *is* one truth, yet it may not please Almighty God to show every one in the same degree or way what and where it is.' (22 December 1844)

Perhaps it was to this period that Maria Poole, later a Dominican nun, referred:

> In a singularly graphic, amusing vision of pilgrims, who were making their way across a bleak common in great discomfort. . . . continually nearing, 'the king's highway', on the right, she says, 'All my fears and disquiets were speedily renewed by seeing the most daring of our leaders, (the same who had first forced his way through the palisade and in whose courage and sagacity we all put implicit trust), suddenly stop short, and declare that he would go on no further. He did not, however, take the leap at once, but quietly sat down on the top of the fence with his feet hanging towards the road, as if he meant to take his time about it, and let himself down easily.' (*Apo.*, 218–9)

Newman began to realize that he could not straddle the fence forever. The danger of not moving was falling back into scepticism. Given Newman's ability to enter into so many various opinions and to see many sides of a question, this danger was not illusory. The oft-quoted statement of Thomas Huxley, namely that 'a Primer of Infidelity' could be compiled from Newman's writings, contained an element of truth. To Manning he wrote, 'this most serious feeling is growing on me; viz that the reasons for which I believe as much as our system teaches, *must* lead me to believe more – and not to believe more, is to fall back into scepticism'. (*Apo.*, 229) Moreover, as he wrote to Robert Wilberforce, 'Nothing but the feeling that I should forfeit God's favour by not acting can be a warrant for my acting. Nothing but the feeling that I am not safe in remaining where I am, can warrant my not remaining.' (16 November 1844)

'To be certain is to know that one knows; what inward test had I, that I should not change again after I had become a Catholic?' Newman wrote in the *Apologia*. 'However, some limit ought to be put to these vague misgivings; I must do my best and then leave it to a higher Power to prosper it. So, at the end of 1844, I came to the resolution of writing an Essay on Doctrinal Development; and then, if, at the end of it, my convictions in favour of the Roman Church were not weaker, of taking the necessary steps for admission into her fold.' (*Apo.*, 228) Although exhausted from just having finished the second volume of his St Athanasius and having looked forward to a period of rest, he thus embarked on the monumental task of writing the Essay. That he almost completed a work of vast patristic erudition in eight months can only be regarded as a triumph of intellectual genius and perseverance.

Meanwhile he would not adopt 'Roman practices such as direct and habitual invocations', as he told Frederick W. Faber. 'Really I have a great repugnance at mixing religions or worships together, it is like sowing the field with mingled seed. . . . I do not like decanting Rome into England; the bottles may break . . . Private judgment comes in, and eclecticism. There is an absence of submission to religion as a rule.' ([1 December] 1844)

CHAPTER TWENTY-FIVE

Heading into Port

The previous Long Vacation saw the publication of Ward's massive volume of 600 pages, *Ideal of a Christian Church*, an amplification of articles that had appeared in the *British Critic*. If their eulogies of things Roman and disparagement of the English Church disturbed and irritated many, his book enraged even more. In the words of Dean Church, 'starting with an "ideal" of what the Christian Church may be expected to be in its various relations to men, it assumes that the Roman Church, and only the Roman Church, satisfies the conditions of what a Church ought to be, and it argues in detail that the English Church, in spite of its professions, utterly and absolutely fails to fulfil them'. Though its philosophy of religion had much that was worthy of calm philosophic debate, what overshadowed this and caused a sensation was its assertion that one could hold all Roman doctrines while remaining in the English Church. Moreover Ward affirmed, 'Three years have passed since I said plainly that in subscribing the Articles I renounce no Roman doctrine; yet I retain my fellowship . . . and have received no ecclesiastical censure in any shape.'[1]

The attempt of some of the Tractarians to challenge in Convocation the nomination of Dr Symonds, Warden of Wadham and their opponent, to succeed Dr Wynter according to the normal method of succession only added fuel to the fires of anger. The Tractarians were roundly defeated in this attempt. 'The heads of houses,' in the words of Dalgairns, 'are going to try to crush Catholicism once and for all.'

They are going to propose to Convocation to degrade Ward – that is, to deprive him of all his degrees. And next they bring in a statute empowering the Vice-Chancellor to send for any suspected individual that he pleases, and to propose to him as a test, a declaration that he signs the articles, as the unhesitating sign or exponent of his opinions, and in the sense in which they were first framed, and in which the University now imposes them.[2]

Newman did not agree with Ward's thesis; in fact he thought no one besides Ward himself and Oakeley did. He felt, however, it was unjust 'that, considering the atrocious heresies which have just been published without censure on the other side, he must be visited so severely for being over-catholic'. (To J. B. Mozley, 5 January 1845) 'There are however great hopes of its not passing,' Dalgairns wrote, 'for everybody seems disgusted at the notion of such an inquisitorial power set up in the 19th century.' Newman called it the 'reign of Golightlyism'. As Wilfrid Ward pointed out, 'it was a two-edged sword, and would certainly affect the subscription of such men as Dr Hampden and Dr Whately quite as much as that of the Puseyites'. (*W. G. Ward*, 327) Ward for his part published a challenge in an address to Convocation, 'in which he enlarged on the difficulties attending the test, and drew out more fully his challenge to all parties in the English Church to show that they were able to subscribe all the Anglican formularies in a natural sense'. None of the parties wanted such a test, and it was withdrawn; 'and thus all attempt at meeting Mr Ward's challenge as to the *principle* of his condemnation was abandoned.' (*W. G. Ward*, 327, 333) Had it not been withdrawn it would have endangered the votes against Ward. In announcing on 23 January that the condemnation of Ward was to take place on 13 February, the Vice-Chancellor also announced that the third proposal as to the test was withdrawn.

The next step was the petition by 474 members of Convocation that *Tract 90* should be censured by Convocation as well as Ward's book, on the grounds that the book is 'a legitimate development of the principles of *Tract 90*, and a practical exhibition of the pernicious effects which must necessarily result from their adoption'. (*W. G. Ward*, 334) Charles Marriott, Dean of Oriel, who a short time before wrote Newman a warm letter of personal gratitude, came to Newman's defence as did Rogers. The former ended his protest with the observation, 'It is impossible not to observe that the idea of censuring Mr Newman was not mentioned until the defeat of the recently proposed New Test, and its abandonment by the Board. It was then put forward with all the appearance of being an expedient for balancing that defeat, and as a measure of party retaliation.'[3] The protest was signed by several members of Convocation. Hook, Palmer and others who supported Newman by personal letters at the time of the original condemnation of *Tract 90* had long since abandoned him.

Ward showed the skeleton of his proposed speech before Convocation to Newman, who approved it. 'He was in the highest spirits, and talked very agreeably. . . . He is supremely indifferent as to the fate of this new move about himself.' (*W. G. Ward*, 335) Ward's statement is confirmed by Newman's own words in several letters. 'I have ills which Heads of Houses can neither augment nor cure. Real inward pain makes one insensible to such shadows.' (To Manning, 9 February 1845) He had hinted at this interior pain in letters to Jemima. 'You don't know how poor a creature I am just now, though I should not and do not show it to others.' (23 January 1845) He was anxious about the outcome of a censure of *Tract 90*, only in so far as it created a kindly and compassionate feeling towards him which, while a satisfaction, was also distressful, because his subsequent actions would seem ungrateful and disappointing.

Part of his pain was the lack of divine enlightenment. 'O that in the course I am pursuing, I might see more clearly than [that] I am following God's Hand, and not judicially deluded for past sins!' (10 February 1845) Waiting when prolonged is generally tedious. It was now at least eight months since he revealed to Keble that he wondered whether he was under a delusion and why God did not answer his prayers for guidance. Continuance in such a state would tend to confirm that indeed he was in a state of judicial blindness. One is tempted to compare Newman's interior trial to the dark night of the mystics, but only experts in the phenomenon of mysticism would be able to say whether there is sufficient evidence to justify such a comparison. Nevertheless, Newman himself did speak of his state as one of darkness. 'How dreadful it is,' he wrote to Henry Wilberforce, 'to have to act on great matters so much in the dark – yet I, who have preached so much on the duty of following in the night whenever God may call, am the last person who have a right to complain.' (27 April 1845) By that time, however, he had decided he would act. Part of the pain too, especially with regard to others, was the inability to share the real state of his mind and how it had developed. To Miss Giberne he wrote, 'I know perfectly well, I ought to let you know more of my feelings and state of mind than you do – but how is that possible in a few words? Any thing I say must be abrupt – nothing can I say which will not leave a bewildering feeling, as needing so much to explain it, and being isolated and, as it were, unlocated, and not having any thing to show its bearing upon other subjects.' (8 January 1845) In a comment on this letter, 3 September 1862, Newman remarked, 'This is the best description of my feelings about others during these years, my habitual feelings. "How miserable! you are kept inspired by the thoughts suggested by my words in former years, and rest in them, and remain where you are. None but those who are close to me can comprehend or share the body of thought in me with all its ramifications which has gradually developed and changed, and places me in an altogether different position of mind." '

He still believed that the state of Roman Catholics was unsatisfactory, though the first hand experiences of them which Miss Holmes sent him suggested otherwise. Only a dictate of conscience could justify one's leaving the Church of England,

> No preference for another Church, no delight in its services, no hope of greater religious advancement in it, no indignation, no disgust at the persons and things among which we find ourselves in the Church of England. The simple question is, can *I* (it is personal, not whether another, but can *I*,) be saved in the English Church? am I in safety, were I to die tonight? is it a mortal sin in me, not joining another Communion? (To Miss Giberne, 8 January 1845)

On the other hand the action of Convocation could have a confirmatory effect. He told Pusey, 'I shall be glad, selfishly speaking, if this decree passes. Long indeed have I been looking for external circumstances to determine my course – and I do not wish this daylight to be withdrawn.' (6 February 1845)

Convocation met on 13 February and condemned Ward's book, and stripped him of his degrees. When the censure of *Tract 90* came up, all hell broke loose, people shouting for and against. In the midst of this the two Proctors, Guillemard and Church, Newman's friend and later Dean of St Paul's, arose and over the din Guillemard's *nobis Procuratoribus non-placet* was heard like a trumpet and cheered enormously.' This stopped the proceedings and the Vice-Chancellor hurried from the theatre. 'Mr. Ward was cheered by the undergraduates as he left the theatre, and the Vice-Chancellor was saluted by hisses and snowballs from the same quarter.' (*W. G. Ward*, 343)

Ward shortly after married, to the derision of his enemies as he had extolled celibacy, and then converted. Oakeley holding the same views as Ward felt obliged in conscience to resign his post at St Margaret's Chapel in London and then converted in October. Dalgairns seems to have been affected. At the request of Dalgairns, who suggested the topics to be discussed, Newman wrote to Dalgairns' father a lengthy letter. It is a revealing one in many ways. First Newman confesses that he can no longer suggest keeping his son back from the step he is contemplating and the reasons why. Dalgairns has developed and matured and his act will not be considered that of 'a rash headstrong young man', as it would have been had he done so three years ago. He is wasting his talents at present. 'He will have a place to fill, and a duty to discharge.' Newman then revealed how his own thinking had evolved. 'It really does seem to me . . . that a movement is beginning or has begun, which will take in many persons besides himself. How many it is impossible to say, or in what a period of time, but whether many or few, whether at once or one after another, I think a number quite large enough to be a gratification to him, even in the eyes of those most anxious for his wellbeing.' (18 February 1845) In March Dalgairns 'was writing as though his mind was quite made up. But he hesitates still to take the step, showing a reluctance like that of Newman to leave Littlemore and go out into the open sea.'[4]

As for Newman himself, he saw a providential direction in the events that had taken place. Thanking Pusey for his sympathetic note about *Tract 90*, he told him,

> My dear P, please do not disguise the fact from yourself, that, as far as such outward matters go, I am as much gone over as if I *were already gone*. It is a matter of time only. I'm waiting, if so be, that if I am under a delusion, it may be revealed to me though I am quite unworthy of it – but outward events have never been the *causes* of my actions, or in themselves touched *feelings*. They have had a *confirmatory, aggravating* effect often. (25 February 1845)[5]

It is doubtful that Newman ever did convince Pusey of this.

Why he was not moving sooner Newman revealed to Miss Giberne, saying that he was revealing more than anyone else knows, except two friends later identified as St John and Dalgairns. First, although his convictions were as strong as he supposed they ever can become, 'it is so difficult to know whether it is a call of *reason* or of *conscience*. I cannot make out if I am impelled by what seems to me *clear*, or by a sense of *duty*. You can understand how painful this doubt is.' As has been seen, only a call in conscience could justify the step. Hence he has waited hoping for light – using the words of the Psalmist 'Show some token upon me etc.' Secondly, he is waiting because friends are asking for guidance for him. Thirdly, delay serves the purpose of preparing men's minds. He can't avoid giving incalculable pain to friends, but he wants to lessen it. 'So if I had my will I should like to wait till the summer of 1846, which would be a full seven years from the time that my convictions first began to fall on me. But I don't think I shall last so long.' He intends to publish something so that people will know why as well as what he is doing. (30 March 1845) He had already started to tell others including Henry Wilberforce and Mrs Bowden of his intentions. He would soon tell Mrs William Froude.

Perhaps the conversion of George Tickell and George Bridges encouraged him. Certainly he was cheered by a letter of Lockhart's mother to Dalgairns which he quoted in at least two letters. '. . . all his own natural cheerfulness is restored, and he is as merry as a boy; not at all like the melancholy notion gained from novels and tales of a gloomy monk, and more interested in us and our doings than he has been for years, and loving us better than he ever did. I wish your Mother could see him, and many more who are dreading, with so much misery and so little faith, all I dreaded this time two years ago. He has never been so much to me in life before.' (To Mrs Bowden, 7 April, and to Mrs William Froude, 20 April 1845)

COUNTING THE COST

In March a painful correspondence between Jemima and her brother took place, apparently occasioned by his telling her he intended 'to resign his fellowship in October, with a view to a subsequent step'. (*Moz.* II, 457)

> O dear John, can you have thought long enough before deciding on a step which . . . must plunge so many into confusion and dismay? I know what you will answer – that nothing but the risk of personal salvation would lead you to it. . . . But think what must be our feelings who cannot entertain your view, but can only deplore it as a grievous mistake!

This elicited a poignant reply which reveals how well he knew the price he would pay for his proposed act. (15 March 1845)

> I have just received your very painful letter, and wish I saw any way of making things easier to you or to myself. . . .
>
> If I am right to move at all, surely it is high time not to delay about it longer. Let me give my strength to the work, not my weakness – years in which I can profit His cause who calls me, not the dregs of life. . . .
>
> As to my convictions, I can but say what I have told you already,

that I cannot make out *why* I should determine on moving except as thinking I should offend God by not doing so . . . I am giving up a maintenance, involving no duties, and adequate to all my wants; what in the world am I doing this for, (I ask *myself* this) except that I think I am called to do so? . . . I have a good name with many – I am deliberately sacrificing it. I have a bad name with more – I am fulfilling all their worst wishes and giving them their most coveted triumph – I am distressing all I love, unsettling all I have instructed or aided – I am going to those whom I do not know and of whom I expect very little – I am making myself an outcast, and that at my age – Oh what can it be but a stern necessity which causes this?

Pity me, my dear Jemima – what have I done thus to be deserted, thus to be left to take a wrong course, if it be wrong. I began by defending my own Church with all my might when others would not defend her. I went through obloquy in defending her. I in a fair measure succeed – at the very time of this success, before any reverse, in the course of my reading, it breaks upon me that I am in a schismatical Church. I oppose myself to that notion – I write against it – Year after year I write against it – and I do my utmost to keep others in the Church – From the time my doubts come upon me, I begin to live more strictly – and really from that time to this, I have done more towards my inward improvement, as far as I can judge, than in any time of my life. Of course I have all through had many imperfections, and might have done every single thing I have done, much better than I have done it – Make all deductions on this score – still after all, may I not humbly trust that I have not so acted as to forfeit God's gracious guidance? And how is it that I have improved in other points, if in respect of this most momentous matter I am so fearfully blinded?

Suppose I were suddenly dying – one may deceive oneself as to what one should do – but I think I should directly send for a Priest. Is not this a test of one's state of mind? Ought I to live where I could not bear to die? . . .[6]

Meanwhile may not I, may not you and all of us, humbly take comfort in the thought that so many persons are considerately praying for me? Of course the human heart is most mysterious. I may have some deep evil in me which I cannot fathom – I may have done some irreparable thing which demands punishment – but may not one humbly trust that the earnest prayers of many good people will be heard for me? . . . Let us not doubt, may we never have cause to doubt, that He is with us. Continually do I pray that He would discover to me, if I am under a delusion – what can I do more? what hope have I but in Him?

Newman finished the letter on Palm Sunday when he felt in better spirits, reflected in the changed tone. 'Have I not a right to ask you not to say, as you have said in your letter, that I shall be *wrong*? What right have you to judge me?. . . . who has a right to judge me but my Judge? who has taken such pains to know *my* duty (poor as they have been) as myself? who is more likely than I to know what I ought to do? I may be wrong, but He that judgeth me is the Lord, and judge nothing before the time.' He concluded, 'Let us do our best, and leave the event to Him. He will give us strength to bear all that is to come upon [us] – whatever others have to bear, surely I have to bear most; and if I do not shrink from bearing it, others must not shrink'.

Jemima answered affectionately and sympathetically but did not alter her view. Though having no bias against Rome, 'I am afraid of paining you by saying she does not approve herself to me . . . far from it. She appears to me to contain un-Christian elements, which as long as she cherishes them seem an absolute barrier to her converting the world.' (*Moz.* II, 457–63)

In thanking James Mozley for his kind article in the *Christian Remembrancer* for April, Newman remarked 'how difficult it is for minds to keep pace with each other which walk apart. You may fancy how all this oppresses me. All that is dear to me is being taken from me. My days are gone like a shadow, and I am withered like grass.' (2 April 1845) In writing about the article to Church, he said he never had even a temptation to regret leaving St Mary's. 'How could I be responsible for souls . . . with the . . . persuasion which I had upon me? It is indeed a dreadful responsibility to act as I am doing – and I feel His hand heavy on me, without intermission, who is all Wisdom and Love, so that my mind and heart are tired out, just as the limbs might be from a load on one's back; that sort of dull aching pain is mine.' (3 April 1845)

The decision to resign his Fellowship brought some relief from the pain he was feeling because he was unsettling others. 'In proportion as one feels confident that a change is right, in the same proportion one wishes others to change too . . . it cannot pain me that they should take my change as a sort of warning, or call to consider where the Truth lies.' In this same letter to Pusey of 14 March, he traced how he had attempted in three separate steps to overcome his new convictions occasioned by his study of the Monophysite controversy and Wiseman's article on the

Donatists. 'I have retreated and kept fighting.' In his articles on Catholicity of the Anglican Church, on Private Judgment, and in the four sermons
he had argued for unity of the Church of England and the Church of
Rome, on the basis of apostolical succession and the presence of grace in
the sacraments. But now he could not see how the Church of England
and the Church of Rome were one, no more than the United States are
one kingdom with England. 'A common *descent* is not a unity of polity.'
As for graces our Lord imparts in our sacramental rites, which we humbly
and surely believe, this proves 'nothing beyond the *fact that He does so in
those instances.* Whether it is an ordinary or extraordinary grant is not
proved thereby. Multitudes of people flocked to the Holy Robe of Trèves
just now – and cures were wrought – Faith might thus be rewarded, even
though the Robe was not a genuine relic.'

'Again it has pressed most strongly upon me that we pick and choose
our doctrines. There is more, I suspect, in the first four centuries, or as
much, for the Pope's Supremacy, than for the Real Presence, or the
authenticity of certain books of Scripture.' This in turn has led him to
see the necessity of the development of doctrine. Certain doctrines grew
up in the course of centuries. 'One age corrects the expressions and
statements of even the Saints of the foregoing. Why should I believe the
most sacred and fundamental doctrines of our faith, if you cut off from
me the ground of development? But if that ground is given me, I must go
further. I cannot hold precisely what the English Church holds and
nothing more – I must go forward or backward – *else* I sink into a dead
scepticism, a heartless acedia, into which too many in Oxford, I fear, are
sinking.' He thanks God that 'He has shielded me morally from what
intellectually might easily come on me, general scepticism.' He assured
Albany Christie, who wrote to him about a report that he was a sceptic,
'I never have felt the temptation for an instant from within.' True he
'thought the English system was so inconsistent, that a careful thinker
would find himself obliged to believe more than it contains or less; and
that if on perceiving this he did not go forward, he might as a judgment
be left to fall behind'. (8 April 1845) He told Pusey that as far as he could
see, he would resign his Fellowship by November.

NO MEDIUM

The 'dreadful feelings' that not to go forward might mean being allowed
to fall into scepticism as a punishment were heightened by the publication

of Blanco White's autobiography. He called it 'the most dismal horrible work I ever saw.'

> He dies a Pantheist, denying that there is an ultra-mundane God . . . doubting, to say the least, the personal immortality of the soul . . . and considering that St Paul's epistles are taken from the Stoic philosophy . . . and rejects the gospels as historical documents . . . gives up *religion* (by name) altogether. He says that Christianity is not a religion . . . it is remarkable he should run into Pantheism, which I have said in the 'Arians' is the legitimate consequence of giving up our Lord's Divinity. . . . For years I have an increasing intellectual conviction that there is no medium between Pantheism and the Church of Rome. (To H. W. Wilberforce, 27 April 1845)

The narrative of Blanco White's intellectual journey from Catholicism to Anglicanism to Unitarianism ending in Pantheism sheds light on Newman's statement in the *Apologia* about the 'concatenation of argument by which the mind ascends from its first to its final religious idea; and I came to the conclusion that there was no medium, in true philosophy, between Atheism and Catholicity, and that a perfectly consistent mind, under those circumstances in which it finds itself here below, must embrace either the one or the other.' (*Apo.*, 198–9) Newman there speaks of the ascent; in Blanco White he saw the reverse process: the descent. Newman agreed with Gladstone, who was doing an article on White, 'that Bl. W. had no *proposition* before his mind – but I thought he *acted out* a position, the same arguments which brought him down one step forcing him down the next. It was "If I give up a, I must give up b; but if I give up b, I must give up c, and so on."' (To Gladstone, 17 June 1845) To Gladstone, he also affirmed, that White's course seems to exemplify, 'There is no medium between the Church of Rome and Infidelity.' Newman thought 'one of the most influential and abiding feelings in B W's mind was a hatred against the Church of Rome such as a man might feel towards one who has injured him. . . . The Church of Rome had, he considered, been the bane of his life – she was his enemy – he never forgave her.' Despite this, Newman confessed, 'his image haunts me more than the dearest friends whom I have lost.' (To Gladstone, 12 June 1845)

There were other considerations which distressed Newman in reading White. The latter like Arnold is 'sincere and honest' in his search for truth, 'or rather for liberty of thought'. Newman could put his finger on faults in their characters, which would explain their views, but *they* could not see them. 'How can I be sure I have not committed sins which bring this unsettled state of mind on me as a judgment?' One wonders if anyone of Newman's contemporaries besides perhaps Froude ever examined his motives and his conscience so deeply and assiduously as Newman.

White spoke of Newman with affection, but 'of what is gone and over – it hardly seems I that he speaks of – I, this old dry chip who am worthless, but of a past I.' This lighted up in Newman's mind by contrast the conduct of others toward him.

My friends who have had means of knowing me have spoken against me. Whately and Hawkins have both used opprobious language about me, till I began to think myself really deceitful and double dealing. Golightly has known me only to lift up his hand against me and to accuse me of many things of which I am guiltless. Eden who has come near enough me to know me has shown no tenderness, no real respect, no gratitude. Others have kept silent in my greatest troubles. The mass of men in Oxford who know me a little, have shown me a coldness and suspicion which I did not deserve. In the affair of number 90 few indeed showed me any sympathy, or gave me reason to believe that I was at all in their hearts. I have not thought of all this, *indeed* – it comes to me now as a *new* thought by the contrast of what B W says of me, which is like light showing the previous darkness. I say to myself, 'Is it possible, was I this?'

These feelings were succeeded by another set. 'My spring, my summer, are over – and what has come of it?. . . . Heads of houses whom I knew have been unkind to me, and have set the fashion; and now my prime of life is past, and I am nothing.' He wonders what might have been if he had been allowed to continue in the tutorship for which his talents were especially suited, but 'now it is all gone and over, and there is no redress, no retrieving – and I say with Job, "O that it were with me as in years past, when the candle of the Lord shone on me." And yet, charissime, I don't think any thing of ambition or longing is mixed with these feelings as far as I can tell. . . . Rather I think of it in the way of *justice* – and with a sort of tenderness towards my former self, now no more.' (To H. W. Wilberforce, 27 April 1845) Henry Wilberforce was probably the only friend to whom he could pour out such feelings and emotions.

Meanwhile Dalgairns and St John had begun planning for the future. Dalgairns was intent on going to France, but Newman thought he should not stay there permanently. 'I do seriously think *your line* is reading and writing, not (primarily) labour. On the other hand I think St John's *is* labour, sorrowful indeed as is to me the prospect of parting with him; which I think he will make up his mind to. I think your letter for the moment has somewhat unsettled him, as throwing him out of his St Sulpice plan.' (To Dalgairns, 9 May 1845) Subsequently he thought Oscott, where Spencer was director, or the Jesuits would be the more suitable choice and more agreeable to his father. (To Dalgairns, 28 May 1845) Various rumours began to circulate about Newman, that he was planning to become a Catholic, that he had already done so, that he had joined the Jesuits. This brought numerous letters of enquiry, of appeals not to take the step. Burgon, the later author of *Twelve Good Men*, wrote a preachy letter (27 June 1845) which he followed up by a visit to Littlemore to reinforce it. It reveals the high esteem in which the undergraduates still held Newman. Other letters testify to the enormous impact Newman had had on the Church, 'the happy change in our church,' as one lady put it, 'which you have been the chief instrument of resuscitating, and restoring from one end of the Kingdom to the other'. She asked him to declare his intentions, not only for herself, 'but for the thousands who have gladly followed you to the heights of true scriptural doctrine, but cannot go beyond it'. Like so many others she mentioned the 'errors' of Rome, worship of the Virgin and saints, etc. (Harriet Jones, 15 June 1845)

Although he continued to feel sorrow at the pain and unsettlement he was causing others, which he described as 'a sword through me', he was getting better, and 'almost think the crisis over'. There was a growing confidence that he was not deceiving himself, and 'if not, how should it be but right in acting on so very long a conviction as that which obliges me to acknowledge that Christ's home is elsewhere and that I must seek him there?' (To Edward Coleridge, 3 July 1845)

Although Newman told a few friends of the pains he suffered by receiving these letters, he apparently never showed this on the outside in his contact with others. 'I have many letters which necessarily pain me, as expressing painful feelings, and that though I do not show it openly, my mind is quite in a raw state.' (To Crawley, 14 July 1845) Given Newman's temptation to impetuosity and speaking his mind, this demonstrates the remarkable self-control he had acquired by internal discipline. To impertinent letters such as an Irishman wanting to engage him in controversy, Newman gave short shrift. 'As you say in your letter which I have just received that you have borrowed for me the work you send, though I did not ask you for it, and I have books enough to read without it, and say also that you wish it back, I lose no time, with thanks for your kind intention, in returning it to you. (To Tresham Gregg, 17 July 1845)

Barter actually came to Littlemore to tell him that there was madness in his family 'or at least great oddity and liability to twists – and this ought to be an intimation to me not to leave the Church of England'. Tickell who came three times and dined twice, 'began converting me the first day for two minutes,' Newman wrote to Dalgairns, 'but did not get on and has since been quiet. I have kept my gun loaded and cocked, intending to discharge upon him, if he made a second attempt.' (9 May 1845)

Newman finally convinced Pusey that he was really going to leave the Church. He is one of those, Newman wrote to Mrs Bowden, 'who is determined not to look at trouble in the face and now that at last he believes what is to be, he is trying to smooth it over – as if it involved no great separation necessarily.' (25 June 1845) Upon Newman's conversion Pusey said that he was moved to another part of the vineyard, at which Coffin laughed when he heard that Pusey was keeping people back from converting and taking the responsibility upon his own conscience. (*LD* XI, 128, 135) Some friends communicated through Pusey their wish that Newman would join abroad, but he felt 'that seems disguising my real ground, misrepresenting myself, giving countenance to wrong notions for such a step, and laying a foundation for future inconsistency and disappointment. If the Church of England is the lawful authority here, why leave it? if not, why go abroad?' (To Mrs Bowden, 25 June 1845)

Newman was extremely busy, writing letters and meeting people, in between composing the Essay on Development, 'the sort of work which tires my body as much as my mind.' He had consumed several months in the spring 'in working upon it in ways which will not turn to any direct account. I have had to remodel my plan'. (To Mrs W. Froude, 1 June 1845) The fact was that he was exhausted, 'suffering from fatigue of mind, partly from former distress, partly from other causes'. The previous winter he had had several illnesses and was not well even now. As his time was divided, he could devote only six or seven hours a day to the book. 'Never has anything cost me . . . so much hard thought and anxiety, though when I got to the end of my Arians thirteen years ago, I had no sleep for a week, and was fainting away or something like it day after day.' Besides re-writing it, 'every part has to be worked out and defined as in moulding a statue. I get on, as a person walks with a lame ankle, who does get on and gets to his journey's end.' (To Mrs W. Froude, 10 June 1845)

Later he wrote to Henry Wilberforce, 'if that book is asked, why does its author join the Catholic Church? The answer is, because it is the Church of St Athanasius and St Ambrose. Vid. the passage about St Ath. and St Ambr. coming from Trèves to Oxford.'⁷ (*LD* XIII, 78) This was the argument Dr Wiseman had used and which Newman attempted to answer in his article on the Catholicity of the English Church. (*LD* VII, 241) The difficulty in Newman's mind was that the Roman Church seemed to have added doctrines and this difficulty he answered by the hypothesis of development. The doctrines of the creeds had been developed; why stop there. As he put it to Westmacott, 'I think the Church of Rome in every respect the continuation of the early Church. . . . They differ in doctrine and discipline as child and grown man differ, not otherwise. I do not see any medium between disowning Christianity, and taking the Church of Rome. . . . I cannot believe only just as much as our Reformers out of their own heads have chosen we should believe – I must believe less or more. If Christianity is one and the same at all times, then I must believe, not what the Reformers have carved out of it, but what the Catholic Church holds.' (11 July 1845)

The definitions of the Church are not mere accidents, the results of sheer human decisions of men coming together in councils and simply determining arbitrarily, as it were, what interpretations, among various possible ones, it wants to adopt and by force or politics, imposing them on the rest of the Church. 'This process of doctrinal development . . . is not of an accidental or random character; it is conducted upon laws.' And so he wrote to Charles Russell of Maynooth, his *Essay* 'is an attempt to give the *laws* under which implicit faith becomes explicit – this is the very subject of the book.' (20 February 1848, *LD* XII, 171)

Though the Essay is an answer to a difficulty, it is also 'a positive argument' in favour of the Roman Church, 'for the immutability and uninterrupted action of the laws in question throughout the course of Church history is a plain note of identity between the Catholic Church of the first ages and that which now goes by that name.' (*Diff.* I, 395–96)⁸ Moreover the variations in teaching being 'found . . . to proceed on a law, and with a harmony and a definite drift . . . actually constitute an argument in their favour, as witnessing to a superintending Providence and a great Design in the mode and in the circumstances of their occurrence.' (*Dev.* vii–viii)

CHAPTER TWENTY-SIX

An End and a Beginning

As usual Newman was extremely busy not only in composing the Essay on Development but in preparing a preface to a posthumous work of Bowden. There were letters to be answered, visitors to be entertained. Mrs Bowden had come with her little girls. Then Jemima and Herbert her son. Together with John they visited people in the village. On 22 July Elizabeth Lendall died. She was the only parishioner that he regularly visited after he resigned as Vicar, and his 'last link with St Mary's'. The last time he was in St Mary's was for her funeral there.

Richard Stanton, who joined the community in June, remembered many years later, that 'in the afternoon it was usual to take a walk, and sometimes Mr Newman accompanied us, and kept up a most delightful conversation; but I may be allowed to say that he walked along the road and over the commons at such a pace, as to keep his younger companions on the trot, and almost breathless'.[1] Sometimes he went to London, to see Mrs Bowden, for example, before she left for the north country and to sit for Ross, who was doing his portrait. To Pusey who continued to consult him about persons who were unsettled, Newman answered that 'in proportion to the increase on one's conviction, does one shorten the time of probation for another'. (26 July 1845) In replying to his brother Frank's enquiry, he wrote he had no desire to leave the English Church, that his reason for going to Rome was that he thought the faith of the Roman Church the only true religion, and that there is no salvation outside of it. He added what became his habitual view as a Catholic. 'This of course does not interfere with my thinking an exception is made for those who are in involuntary ignorance; for myself, when I am once certainly convinced on the point [[of the claims of the Roman Church]], and I have given myself a long trial of my conviction, I am no longer in such ignorance.' (August 1845)

He wrote to Jemima that his book was not yet done. 'I was fagged when I began, and now am very much tired – but I must go on till it is finished. Whatever literary work may be to such as Walter Scott, it has never been any thing but a work of labour and pain to me – and this is one's comfort, considering that one's line has been in talking more than in acting.' (17 August 1845) To Mrs Bowden he wrote he was writing it again and again. (31 August 1845)

To a lady who wrote to him about the case of Honorius and Meletius, he replied, 'No truth, no conclusion about what is true, is without its difficulties. You must give up faith, if you will not believe till all objections are first solved. Don't you believe that God is most good and can do what He wills? yet you cannot account for the existence of evil in His Work.' This was an anticipation of his famous remark in the last chapter of the *Apologia*, 'Ten thousand difficulties do not make one doubt.' (*Apo.*, 239)

Dalgairns expecting his parents in Oxford on 1st of October thought it best that he should become a Catholic first. So on 25 September he left for Stone to be received into the Catholic Church on the feast of St Michael, 29 September, by Fr Dominic, the Passionist who had founded the first Passionist house in England. On the same day St John gave up his Studentship at Christ Church and left the following day to be received at Prior Park on 2 October, Feast of the Guardian Angels. On 2 October Dalgairns returned to Littlemore telling Newman that Fr Dominic had asked his leave to stop by Littlemore *en route* to Belgium. 'If you saw how happy, and how altered Dalgairns is, you would wonder,' Newman wrote to Mrs Bowden the following day in announcing to her that he had just written to the Provost to resign his Fellowship. He also wrote to Pusey, Wilson, Christie, Mrs William Froude, Mr Phillips, Jemima, and Henry Wilberforce. After acknowledging the reception of Newman's resignation, Hawkins the Provost concluded:

> And yet I cannot forbear expressing the most earnest hope (in all sincerity and with feelings of real kindness), that whatever course you may have resolved upon, you may still at least be saved from some of the worst errors of the Church of Rome, such as praying to human Mediators or falling down before images – because in you, with all the great advantages with which God has blessed and tried you, I must believe such errors to be most deeply sinful. But may He protect you! (*KC*, 388)

On 4 October Newman also wrote to Stanton, in reply to his letter that he was seeking admission into the Catholic Church and was thinking of going to Stonyhurst, the Jesuit College, for that purpose. He invited

Stanton to be received with him, when he intended to ask Fr Dominic, who was stopping by Littlemore. If he could not come, he approved his plan of Stonyhurst; otherwise he recommended Prior Park, where St John had been received, rather than Oscott. The same day Dalgairns wrote to Mrs Bowden telling her he felt 'a tremendous load off my breast'. He added, 'I cannot think or speak enough about dear Newman's considerateness and kindness to me in all this trying time. I owe him a debt of gratitude which I can never repay.'

Newman refers to Fr Dominic's coming as 'an accident', but it was one of those small seeming accidents in which he saw a providential hand. What took place was the sudden realization not only that he was reflexively certain of objective Truth but he had a call in conscience to act at once, the response which he had preached all calls demand. Accordingly he left the Essay unfinished. Interestingly enough he was writing of a not infrequent theme in his writing – the resilience of the Church reviving after being 'thrown into what was almost a state of deliquium; but her wonderful revivals, while the world was triumphing over her, is a further evidence of the absence of corruption in the system of doctrine and worship into which she has developed'. It is a reaffirmation of what he had not infrequently taught, especially in the magnificent ending of the *Prophetical Office of the Church*, but with a new twist.[2] Did Newman have some of his old friends in mind when in the short warning he added:

And now, dear Reader, time is short, eternity is long. Put not from you what you have here found; regard it not as mere matter of present controversy; set not out resolved to refute it, and looking about for the best way of doing so; seduce not yourself with the imagination that it comes of disappointment, or disgust, or restlessness, or wounded feeling, or undue sensibility, or other weakness. Wrap not yourself round in the associations of years past; nor determine that to be truth which you wish to be so, nor make an idol of cherished anticipations. Time is short, eternity is long.

NUNC DIMITTIS SERVUM TUUM; DOMINE,
SECUNDUM VERBUM TUUM IN PACE:
QUIA VIDERUNT OCULI MEI SALUTARE TUUM.

It was late when Dominic arrived in Oxford, the coach having been delayed because of the weather. Dalgairns and he took a chaise out to

Littlemore, Dominic thoroughly soaked from five hours on the top of the coach. It was eleven o'clock; Stanton had already gone to bed. 'I took up my position by the fire to dry myself', Dominic later wrote to his superior. 'The door opened – and what a spectacle it was for me to see at my feet, John Henry Newman begging me to hear his confession and admit him into the bosom of the Catholic Church! And there by the fire he began his general confession with extraordinary humility and devotion.' It had to be finished the next day.

According to Stanton the next day Fr Dominic, accompanied by St John went to the Catholic chapel to say Mass and they returned, bringing with them an altar stone, a chalice, and the requisites for celebrating Mass at Littlemore, where a temporary altar was constructed in the Oratory. In the afternoon Fr Dominic heard the confessions of Bowles and Stanton, and the evening was appointed for the reception of the three into the Catholic Church. They made their profession of faith and received conditional baptism, 'if you have not been baptized before'. The next morning Fr Dominic said Mass in the chapel, using a writing desk of Henry Wilberforce as an altar, and administered Holy Communion. He then went to see the Woodmasons and received husband and wife and two daughters, the rest of the family joining later.

Fr Dominic had to leave on Saturday, the 12th, after Mass. On October 7 Newman had begun writing letters, thirty in all, in which he announced his conversion to his friends, but they were "not to go till all was over".[3] Of these the following became Catholics, either shortly after or later: T. W. Allies, William Anderdon, Edward Badeley, Robert Belaney, Mrs Bowden, Henry Bowden, William Dodsworth, F. W. Faber, Mrs William Froude, Miss Giberne, Henry Manning, M. Watts Russell, Henry Wilberforce, and Mrs Wood and her daughter. (*LD* XI, 3–15, 309–10) John Moore Capes had already converted, and Charles Russell of course was Catholic. Only after many years did Newman reveal that in becoming a Catholic his greatest suffering was the loss of friends in the Anglican Church. (To Isaac Williams, 21 October 1861; W. J. Copeland, 23 January 1863; Charles Robbins, 30 May 1863; *LD* XI, 59–60, 400, 449) Newman was sustained in this, as in other trials in his life as a Catholic, e.g., the death of Ambrose St John, by the presence of Christ in the Blessed Sacrament, to whom he had constant recourse.[4] In the present ecumenical atmosphere it is difficult for persons to realize the painful severance from family and friends that took place when one joined what was considered a despised, corrupt minority.

Newman described this in his *Lectures on the Present Position of Catholics in England,*

> ... friends fight shy of him; gradually they drop him, if they do not disown him at once. There used to be pleasant houses open to him, and a circle of acquaintance. People were glad to see him, and he felt himself, though solitary, not lonely. .... It is now all at an end; he gets no more invitations; he is not a welcome guest. He at length finds himself in *Coventry*. (*Prepos.* 191–2) At his death the *Birmingham Daily Post* was not alone in affirming 'his character was the chief instrument in destroying the bigoted hatred of Roman Catholicism which had almost become an English tradition. So changed was the atmosphere that Fr Williams in a sermon preached in the back street church of St Peter's in Birmingham had to ask his audience 'to realize what the sacrifice to God of that giant intellect meant; it was a degree of heroism surpassing, in a sense, the sacrifice of the martyrs of God (*Birmingham Gazette*, 18 August 1890)

In the preface to the *Apologia* Newman refers to himself as one 'who has given up much that he loved and prized and could have retained, but that he loved honesty better than name, and truth better than dear friends.' (*Apo.*, XV) If the loss of friends continued to pain him as a Catholic, the pain he had felt at disappointing friends and well-wishers ceased after his conversion. When Christopher Churchill Bartholomew speculated in 1868 what Newman 'would or might have done or prevented if matters had been otherwise than they are', Newman replied to Rogers who conveyed the view, 'it is pleasant, while it is painful to me, to have left a lasting regret in the minds of such as him – yet I have reciprocated it, though my own deep wound was *before* I left them, and *in* leaving them; and it was healed, when the deed was done, as far as it was personal, and not from the reflection of their sorrow. To-day is the 20th anniversary of my setting up the Oratory in England, and every year I have more to thank God for, and more cause to rejoice that he helped me over so great a crisis.' And what seems an answer to those critics who triumphantly announced that Newman was not better treated by ecclesiastical authorities in the Catholic Church than he was by those in the Church of England, he added,

> I have found in the Catholic Church abundance of courtesy, but very little sympathy, among persons in high place, except a few – but there

is a depth and a power in the Catholic religion, a fulness of satisfaction in its creed, its theology, its rites, its sacraments, its discipline, a freedom yet a support also, before which the neglect or the misapprehension about oneself on the part of individual living persons, however exalted, is as so much dust, when weighed in the balance. (*LD* XXIV, 24–5)

From the time of his first doubts about the Anglican Church it had taken him six years to ascertain God's will; so now he would not be rushed in his search for it as regards the future. As he wrote to Jemima, who fearful of his influence did not want him to remain at Littlemore, 'I feel it very doubtful what is best to be done, and what is God's will. I have always looked at Littlemore as under the special protection of St Mary, and so many providential circumstances have brought me and fixed me here where I am, that I fear to move.' (*LD* XI, 17) He had, however, to think also of his companions who wanted to keep together. When Dr Wiseman offered them Old Oscott to be simply Littlemore continued, a novena was begun which lasted till 20 December, when a final decision was made. Making a novena at the end of a period of deliberation from now on became a standard procedure with Newman.

While engaged in packing at Littlemore, thoughts of passed happiness there crowded in upon him, as he wrote to Mrs William Froude,

Part of us are gone – part going – I shall, I suppose remain the last, as I came in first. A happy time indeed have I had here, happy to look back on, though suspense and waiting are dreary in themselves; – happy, because it is the only place perhaps I ever lived in, which I can look back on, without an evil conscience. In Oxford indeed, where I have been near 30 years from first to last, I trust I have all along served God from the day I went there – but in those many years, amid the waywardness and weakness of youth and the turmoil of business, of course many things must have occurred to leave sad thoughts on the memory. . . . Doubtless if my life here for these last years were placed in the light of God's countenance, it would be like a room when a sunbeam comes into it, full of hidden unknown impurities – but still I look back to it as a very soothing happy period. I came into this house by myself, and for nights was the sole person here, except Almighty God Himself, my Judge; and St Francis's 'Deus meus et omnia', was ever and spontaneously on my lips. And now, so be it, I shall go out of it by myself, having found rest. (*LD* XI, 113)

Moreover he was 'in perfect peace and contentment', and never thereafter had one doubt. 'I was not conscious to myself, on my conversion, of any change, intellectual or moral, wrought in my mind. I was not conscious of firmer faith in the fundamental truths of Revelation, or of more self-command; I had not more fervour; but it was like coming into port after a rough sea; and my happiness on that score remains to this day without interruption.' (*Apo.*, 238) Since all of life is considered by Christians as a pilgrimage and a journey to eternal life, Newman had to set sail again. As he put it to St John, 'You may think how lonely I am. Obliviscere populum tuum et domum patris tui has been in my ears for the last 12 hours. I realize more that we are leaving Littlemore, and it is like going on the open sea.' (19 January 1846, *LD* XI, 95)

EX UMBRIS ET IMAGINIBUS IN VERITATEM

Appendix

Note: The following prayers are contained in a notebook marked 'Most private and personal Memoranda in two books (parts) 1805 to 1828' (A.10.4) Of these pages Newman later copied out a portion intending to have the notebooks destroyed at his death, but this was later revoked. Nevertheless he did destroy pages 7–12 and an appendix of prayers. Of the pages later transcribed, the style was improved (verbal changes), and the lengthy paragraphs were broken into shorter ones. The re-copied versions are printed in darker type.

GROUP ONE

April 1817 [I]
Lord of heaven and earth, creator of all things, who knowest our necessities before we ask and our ignorance in asking, and who hast graciously allowed poor humble sinful mortals to address thee, the Almighty, and to call thee by the endearing name of father, help me for thy dear son's sake in offering up my morning <evening> sacrifice of praise and thanksgiving, in confessing my sins and acknowledging my manifold and grievous offences, in praying for thy Holy Spirit, the Lord and giver of life, the Comforter, in asking of thee all things necessary for my soul and body, and in beseeching thee in behalf of my relatives, friends, in behalf of all mankind, conscious at the same time of the inefficacy of my weak devotions, unless offered in the name and through the mediation of thy Son, God our Saviour, who has purchased me with his blood; hear me, O Lord God, for his sake, O hearken unto the supplication that I make before thee!

[II]
O! Who can tell the number of offences? who can relate in colours strong enough my repeated, my daring [space in MS] my transgressions? who can

show forth worthily the innumerable mercies of God, or the multitude of benefits which he continued to shower upon me, while I remained still in hardened obstinacy; till at last, O incomprehensible goodness, he deigned to turn me from the error of my ways, to open my eyes and to guide me into the right path, to give me his Holy Spirit, and make me fall down before him! O God most merciful, enable me for Jesus Christ's sake to try to imitate thee in thy forbearance, thy long-suffering, and great goodness, let me praise Thy name always, and remain in stedfast faith, believing in thee, till I shall have run my race, finishing my [?] course with joy. Save me, Lord, make me whole. I have sinned against thee, and sin daily, but for Jesus Christ's sake, have mercy upon me; make me stedfast in faith, joyful with hope, rooted in charity; give me true repentance, let me persevere to the end, one of thy elect, deaf to the contempt of the infidel, and the derision of the thoughtless, unmoved by the persecution of the cruel and the temptations of the crafty man; let me by thy Holy Spirit surmount every temptation, and be purified and refined by them, as gold is by the furnace; yea, Lord, such is my desire. For our Saviour's sake send me thy grace to keep me in the right way, to stedfast my weak and wavering faith, and to show forth the fruits of it in an holy and religious life and in good works – Lord I ask, I seek, I knock, give me for Jesus' sake!

O who can tell the number and the heinousness of my sins! who can show forth worthily the innumerable mercies of God or the benefits He continued to shower upon me, while I remained nevertheless in hardened obstinacy, till at last, O incomprehensible goodness! He deigned to turn me about from the error of my ways, to open my eyes and to guide me into the right path, to give me His Holy Spirit, and to make me fall down before Him.

O God, most merciful, enable me for Jesus Christ's sake to desire and try to imitate Thee in Thy forbearance, long suffering and great goodness. Let me praise Thy Name always, and remain stedfast in faith till I shall have run my race, finishing my course with joy. Give me true repentance, and let me persevere to the end, one of Thy elect.

[III]
Praised be thy name to me O Lord, evermore; for the manifold temporal blessings which I enjoy; for thy so often granting the petitions of thy servant; for so often having turned my heaviness into joy, and in the midst of uneasiness, brought on by sins, relieved my oppressed spirit.

Lord! how am I better than the poor I behold hungry, and cold and wretched in the streets, that I should be so much better than they? Praised be the infinite goodness, for having bestowed upon me a home, and the comforts of home, affluence, health, and the numerous other benefits I enjoy! For having given me a kind and affectionate Father and Mother, and very [sic] other dear relations and friends! For having kept me from sickness, from the disorders that distract many other persons, for having given me the use of my limbs and preserved me from any deformity of body! For having given me some abilities, and provided me with excellent Tutors who have encouraged them! Praised be thy Name O! Lord, for all my blessings, for my Creation, Redemption, and Preservation, if I have any abilities, if I ever did a good action, to thee be ascribed the glory! Not unto me, O Lord! not unto me but unto thy Name, be the Praise, let me show forth thy praise always, not only with my lips but in my life, by giving up myself to thy service and by doing the thing that is right always – Our Father etc. I believe etc.

Praised be Thy Name for the manifold temporal blessings which I enjoy, for Thy having so often granted my petitions, for having so often turned my heaviness into joy. Lord, how am I better than the cold and hungry, and wretched creatures I see in the streets, that I should be better circumstanced than they? Praised be Thy infinite goodness to me for having given me a home and its comforts, affluence, health, and other benefits – kind and affectionate parents and other dear relations; for having kept me from sickness and disorders, for having given me the use of my limbs and preserved me from any deformity; for having given me abilities and excellent Tutors to encourage them. Praised be Thy Name, O Lord, for all these blessings, for my creation, redemption, and preservation, if I have any abilities, if I ever did a good action, to Thee be the glory.

[IV]
Lord! I praise thee for Jesus Christ's sake, continue to me thy benefits, encrease [sic] thy spiritual benefits and continue the temporal. Bless me O Lord Jesus! Bless my parents! Shower down thy choicest gifts spiritual and temporal upon them! Bless the whole family! Make us all good by thy spirit. Bless etc. – Bless the King of this country and all in power. Bless my native land! Lord! show thyself to the whole world, and turn all to thy truth! Sacred Trinity in Unity hear my prayer!

[V] (*For the Morning*)
God Almighty! Keep me through this day! Let me grow in grace! Thou, O God! hast graciously brought me to the beginning of this day, defend me in the same by thy mighty power! Grant, O Lord! that as I now rise this morning, after sleep, fresh, healthful and rejoicing, so my body after the sleep of death may rise, spiritualised and blessed to dwell with thee for evermore!

[VI] (*For the Evening*)
Lord I thank thee, that thou hast safely brought me to the end of this day. Protect me from the perils and dangers of the night. Let me rest in peace. Let me lay myself down piously and gratefully as if in death, knowing my spirit may this night be required of me; give me grace that whenever that time comes I may be prepared for it and that when my soul parts from this body, it may hear the grateful words 'Well done, thou good and faithful servant, enter thou into the joy of the Lord'.

[VII]
These prayers and praises I humbly offer up to thy Divine Majesty, in the Name and through the mediation of our Lord and Saviour Jesus Christ. Since I, in human frailty, must have omitted much, grant O God all things necessary for my soul and body. Since also in human [?] blindness I must have asked much prejudicial to myself, grant me all good and refuse me all evil, and whatsoever thou givest me let me always esteem it as the best, and bless thy name for ever and ever! Therefore with Angels and Archangels I praise and magnify thy Holy name, saying, Holy, Holy, Holy, Lord God of Sabaoth! The earth is full of this majesty! O God the Father of Heaven! O God the Son, redeemer of the world! O God the Holy Ghost proceeding from the Father and the Son. O holy, blessed and glorious Trinity, three persons and one God, evermore will I praise thee the Father of an infinite Majesty, thine Honorable, true and only Son; thee, the king of Glory O Christ! and thee, O Holy Ghost, the Comforter, *again* joining in the Heavenly chorus and saying, Holy, Holy, Holy, Lord God of Hosts, heaven and earth are full of thy glory; glory be to thee, O Lord, most high! We praise thee, we bless thee, we worship thee, we glorify thee, we give thanks to thee for thy great glory, O Lord God, heavenly King, God the Father Almighty! O Lord, the only begotten Son, Jesus Christ, O Lord God, Lamb of God, Son of the Father, Thou who takest away the sins of the world, and sittest at the right hand of God, the Father. O blessed, glorious and eternal Spirit, for

thou only art holy, thou only art the Lord! Thou only, O Christ, with the Holy Ghost are most high in the glory of God the Father, for thine, O Lord, is the Kingdom and the power and the glory for ever and ever, Amen.

GROUP TWO

J. H. Newman. November 17th 1817. Morning prayers –

[I]
O God, the strength of all them that put their trust in thee, mercifully accept my prayers, for our blessed Saviour's sake; and because, through the weakness of my mortal nature, I can do no good thing without thee, grant me the help of thy grace, that in keeping thy commandments, I may please thee both in will and deed, and more especially enable me at the time present to offer up my humble and hearty thanks for the innumerable blessings that thou daily showerest down upon me, and also to beseech thee to forgive my manifold offences, to give me thy Holy Spirit, to continue thy temporal mercies towards me and to bless my relations, friends and all mankind; prefacing these my prayers by that most perfect form of words thy blessed Son vouchsafed to give his disciples, Our Father etc.

[II]
Lord I am unworthy of the least of all thy favours and yet thou art continually good to me; I daily provoke thee with my sins, and yet thou stretchest not forth thy right hand in wrath, but causest thy face to shine upon me, and warmest me with the beams of thy mercy. Without thee I am nothing; in thee I live, I move, I have my being; thou gavest me life, and hast added to life its blessings; and yet I transgress thy law and my heart is continually wandering from thee, the fountain of all happiness and joy. Oh God most merciful from whom all holy desires, all good counsels, and all just works do proceed, direct me in the way I should go by the inspiration of the Holy Spirit, forgive me all my sins and strengthen me against the allurements of the world the flesh and the devil, so that I may fight the good fight to faith, under the banners of my crucified Master in whose most holy name and through whose infinite merits I dare now offer up my supplications to the throne of grace.

[III]

Praised be the Lord from the rising up of the sun to the going down of the same! Thou art my God and I will praise Thee; Thou art my God and I will thank Thee; Thou hast made me after Thine own image; Thou daily preservest and providest for me; Thou hast redeemed me by the precious blood of Thy dear Son; Thou hast given me Thy Holy Word for my direction and promised Thy Holy Spirit for my assistance; Thou hast raised up for me friends and benefactors who have taken care of my education and instruction; Thou hast kept me from the evils of poverty and blessed me with an ignorance of misfortune; Thou hast raised me from sleep this morning to endeavour to adorn the doctrine of God our Saviour by holiness and pureness of living; For these and all Thy favours, spiritual and temporal, my soul doth bless and magnify thy Holy Name, humbly beseeching thee to accept this imperfect sacrifice of praise and thanksgiving, through Jesus Christ our Lord ------- (*Here temporary petitions for separate blessings.*)
I believe in God etc.

[IV]

Blessed Lord! I have to praise thee for thy infinite loving kindness and mercy in calling me to the light of thy Gospel. And first for my birth in a country where thy true religion flourishes, and then for thy goodness in enlightening my soul with the knowledge of thy Truth; that whereas I was proud, self-righteous, impure, abominable, and altogether corrupt in my sinful imaginations, thou was pleased to turn me to thee from such a state of darkness and irreligion by a mercy which is too wonderful for me; and to make me fall down humbled and abased before thy foot-stool. Oh! merciful Saviour continue thy grace, and let me so run the race that is set before me, that I may lay hold of everlasting life; let me be a faithful soldier, zealous for thy cause, and armed with that spiritual armour which will foil the devices of the wicked one; let me not be of them that fall away, but let me, (with the example of so many illustrious Saints before my eyes, who are now, either with thee at this moment enjoying a blessed anticipation of the exceeding weight of glory which is prepared for them, or still journeying on here below in patient continuance of well-doing,) follow their good example, and especially make thee, O holy Jesus, the guide and pattern of my pilgrimage here, that thou mayest be the portion of my soul to all eternity.

Par. IV Lord, I praise Thee for calling me to the light of Thy Gospel – for my birth in a country where Thy true religion is

found, and for Thy goodness in enlightening my soul with the knowledge of Thy truth, that, whereas I was proud, self-righteous, impure, abominable, Thou wast pleased to turn me from such a state of darkness and irreligion, by a mercy which is too wonderful for me, and make me fall down humbled and abased before Thy footstool. O let me so run the race that is set before me that I may lay hold of everlasting life, and especially let me make Thee, O Holy Jesus, my pattern in my pilgrimage here, that Thou mayst be the portion of my soul to all eternity.

[V]
I also pray thee, O Lord, by the precious blood of our Redeemer, to continue thy temporal blessings to me, and let me fulfil the duties of my station to the honour and praise of thy name and the benefit of my own soul. Let me attend and apply to my studies but let me have thy glory in view as the end of all my pursuits. Bless, O almighty Father, my parents, relations, friends, and all mankind, enlighten all by thy Holy Spirit; turning all Jews, Musselmen [*sic*], and Pagans to thee; converting all Atheists and Infidels, whether so in principle or practice; recovering all Heretics from the error of their ways, and restoring all Schismatics to thy Holy Church; that there may be one fold, and one Shepherd, and sin with all its attendant misery may be banished from the earth.

[VI]
Lord, I thank thee that thou hast brought me to the beginning of this day, defend me in the same by thy mighty power, and grant as I now rise after sleep, fresh, healthy and rejoicing, so my body after the sleep of death may rise spiritualized and blessed to dwell with thee for ever.

[VII]
Keep me, Lord of all power and might, from the perils and dangers of this day; let me fall into no sin, neither run into any kind of danger, but let all my doings be ordered by thy governance, to do always that is righteous in thy sight, through Jesus Christ our Saviour.

[VIII]
These prayers and praises I humbly offer up unto thy divine majesty, in the name and through the mediation of our Lord and Saviour Jesus Christ.

[IX]

Now unto him that rideth on the heaven of heavens, to the King eternal, immortal, invisible, the only wise God, be adoration paid for ever; Unto him who is the blessed only Potentate, the King of Kings and Lord of Lords, who only hath immortality, dwelling in the light which no man can approach unto, whom no man hath seen, nor can see, who loved us and washed us from our sins in his own blood, and hath made us kings and priests unto God and his Father to him be honour and glory everlasting; Unto him who cleanseth the thoughts of our hearts, who maketh our bodies the temples of God, the blessed, holy and eternal Spirit to him be worship and blessing for ever and ever; Yea, unto the incomprehensible Triune God who created, redeemed, and sanctifieth us to him alone, as is most fit, be ascribed all glory, praise, might, majesty, and dominion both now and ever. I will love thee, O Lord my strength; the Lord is my rock, and my fortress, my Saviour, my God and my strength; in whom I will trust, my buckler, the horn also of my salvation, and my refuge. Thy throne, O God, is for ever and ever, the sceptre of thy Kingdom is a right sceptre. Thou Lord in the beginning hast laid the foundation of the earth, and the heavens are the work of thy hands. They shall perish, but thou shalt endure; yea, all of them shall wax old as doth a garment, but thou art the same and *thy* years shall not fail. My heart is fixed, O God, my heart is fixed; I will sing and give praise; Awake up my glory, awake lute and harp. I myself will awake up early; I will praise thee, O Lord among the people; Be thou exalted O God above the heavens; let thy glory be above all the earth; for thou, O Lord, art a shield for me; thou art my glory and the lifter up of my head, I cried unto the Lord with my voice, and he heard me out of his holy hill. I laid me down and slept; I awaked for the Lord sustained me. Thy mercy, O Lord, is in the heavens and thy faithfulness reacheth unto the clouds. Thy righteousness is like the great mountains; Thy judgments are a great deep; O Lord thou preservest man and beast. How excellent is thy loving kindness, O Lord! The Lord is gracious and full of compassion; slow to anger and of great mercy. The Lord is righteous in all his ways and holy in all his works. The Lord is nigh unto all them that call upon him, yea unto all that call upon him faithfully. Thou visitest the earth and waterest it; thou greatly enrichest it with the river of God which is full of water; thou makest it soft with showers, thou blessest the springing thereof. Thou crownest the year [with] thy goodness, and thy clouds drop fatness. They drop upon the pastures of the wilderness, and the little hills rejoice on every side. The pastures are clothed with flocks, the valleys are also covered over with corn. O God thou art my God, early will I seek thee; my soul thirsteth for thee; my flesh longeth for thee in a dry and thirsty land where no water is. Thou hast ascended on high, thou hast led captivity captive, thou hast received gifts for men; yea, for the rebellious also, that the Lord God might dwell among them. One day in thy courts is better than a thousand. I had rather be a door-keeper in the house of my God, than to dwell in the tents of ungodliness. For the Lord is a [illegible] shield, the Lord will give grace and glory; no good then will he withhold from them that walk uprightly. My voice shalt thou hear betimes, O Lord; early in the morning will I direct my prayer unto thee and will look up. I will bless the Lord at all times; his praise shall continually be in my mouth. My soul shall make her boast in the Lord; the humble shall hear thereof, and be glad. The Angel of the Lord encampeth round about them that fear him, and delivereth them. In God have I put my trust; I will not be afraid what man can do unto me: thou hast delivered my soul [?] from death; thou will preserve my feet from falling, that I may walk before thee in the light of the living; My soul wait thou upon God alone; for my expectation is from him; O Lord, let me not trust in oppression, nor, become vain in robbery. If riches increase, let me never set my heart upon them. Keep me as the apple of an [*sic*] eye, hide me under the shadow of thy wings. So teach me to number my days, that I may apply my heart unto wisdom. Show me the path of life, for in thy presence is fulness of joy and at thy right hand there are pleasures for evermore.

NOTE: Written on the first page crosswise, but seems to belong to the end of the prayers of November 17, 1817.

[X]

Turn to me, O Lord God of Hosts; show the light of Thy countenance, and I shall be whole. Let all those that seek thee, rejoice and be glad in Thee! Let such as love thy salvation say always: The Lord be praised. But as for me, I am poor and needy, yet the Lord regardeth me; thou art my helper and deliverer, make no long tarrying, O my God! Thou God art my Saviour for ever and ever, Thou wilt be my guide even unto death. Thou shalt guide me with thy counsel and afterwards receive me to glory. Whom have I in heaven but thee? And whom upon earth that I desire besides thee? My flesh and my heart faileth, but God is the strength of my heart and my portion forever!

GROUP THREE

Evening Prayer. September 20th 1818 – J. H. Newman

God be merciful unto us, and bless us, and cause his face to shine upon us, that His way may be known upon earth, His saving health [?] among all nations. Thine we are, by Thee we are created, at Thy will we yield our breath and die; therefore let all the world praise Thee O Lord! Let all the people praise Thee. With Thee the darkness is no darkness, but day and night are both alike; angels and the spirits of just men made perfect are chanting praises before Thy everlasting throne; Thou sittest encompassed with glory, the fountain of excellence and happiness, the heaven of heavens cannot contain Thee, for Thou inhabitest eternity; how then shall I a wretched sinful creature presume to offer up these prayers to Thee except in the name and through the mediation of Jesus Christ the righteous! Father of Mercies assist me with Thy Holy Spirit and let seriousness and attention and devotion accompany my supplications; Oh make me reflect on thy infinite goodness and my own lowliness!
                              Our Father etc.

Oh Lord, the great and terrible God, keeping the covenant and mercy [?] to them that love Thee and to them that keepeth Thy commandments. I have sinned and committed iniquity and have done wickedly and have rebelled even by departing from Thy precepts and from Thy judgments. Oh Lord, righteousness belongeth unto Thee, but unto me confusion of face – Unto Thee, O Lord, belong mercies and forgiveness, though I have rebelled against Thee; wherefore, O my God, incline Thine ear and hear; open Thine eyes and behold our misery; for I do not present my petitions before Thee for my righteousness, but for Thy great mercies. My sins are red as scarlet but make Thou them as white as snow; purify me thoroughly from my wickedness, Oh Lord, who can tell how oft he offendeth! cleanse thou me from my secret faults; let the blood of Christ cleanse me from all sins; purify me from envy hatred and malice; intemperance, love of the world, love of the flesh, take from me lying lips and a deceitful tongue and the mouth that speaketh proud things; Give me, Oh Lord, true repentance and a lively faith producing the blessed fruits of everlasting life; make me fear Thy name always and adore Thee for Thy infinite loving kindness and mercy, and love Thee with all my heart, with all my mind, with all my soul and with all my strength. Make me humble, meek, forgiving, charitable; and holy in all my thoughts, words, and actions. Let me cast off the works of darkness, and put on the armour of light; looking upon Jesus and bearing his reproach; hear me, Lord God almighty, for our blessed Saviour's sake, our only Mediator and Advocate.

Lord! Thou art a terrible God; if Thou be severe to mark what is done amiss, who shall abide Thee? Lo! the very heavens are not pure in Thy sight and Thy angels Thou chargest with folly! But, praised be Thy name, Thou hast revealed thyself as the God of mercies, in the Gospel of Thy Son, as the Father of Mankind, reconciling in Christ the world unto Thyself, and not as the terrible judge of all the earth punishing us according, 'to our deserts'.

Blessed is the man that putteth his trust in Thee, O God Almighty, for Thou art faithful and wilt remember the righteous in the day of tribulation – Praised be Thy name for Thy tender mercies; for the blessings Thou showerest upon the Sons of Men; Thou createdst us and breathedst into us the breath of life, Thou preservest us and surroundest us with plenty, Thou hast redeemed us and hast promised us the Spirit of Truth to sanctify our breasts; Oh Heavenly Father give me that Spirit that through his assistance I may walk uprightly in the present evil world and in the end triumph over sin and death through the merits of thy blessed Son Jesus Christ our Saviour.

It is now night and I am going to lie myself down to sleep, and I may wake in an eternal world and I may be obliged to appear before the judgment – seat of Christ. That night may come in which no man can work. Am I prepared? and ready? Could I leave the vanities of this world without regret, and stand before my judge without despair? Oh God assist me in preparing myself for that awful hour! May to me to die be gain and the entrance to everlasting felicity! Oh may I often reflect on that last, that terrific scene! For who can tell the day of Thy coming? Even now the archangels' trump may sound and our doom may be unchangeably fixed for ever! Lord! give us grace, sanctify us all, my parents, relations, friends and all mankind, that at Thy second coming to judge the world in righteousness we may be found an acceptable people in Thy sight and live with Thee for ever!

These prayers I offer up unto Thee, O Lord God, not for any merit of mine that I am better than others, but in the name of Christ our Saviour. Blessed be Thy name, O God, the Creator, the Redeemer, the Sanctifier! Oh Heavenly King, Oh holy Lord Almighty! I will rejoice in Thy name, exceedingly glad will I be of Thy salvation! I will lay me down in peace and take my rest, for Thou only, Oh Lord, makest me close my eyes in safety! Thy angels shall protect me while I sleep; Thy Kingdom come, O Lord; Thy Kingdom of Glory come, as Thy Kingdom of grace now is! Come, Lord God, come to rule over us! – The Lord hath said, 'Behold I come quickly, and my reward is with Me!' – Even so, Come Lord Jesus!

The Grace of our <the> Lord Jesus Christ, and the love of God, and the communion of the Holy Ghost be with me now and for ever. Amen.

GROUP FOUR

NOTE: Later dated as: '1824?'

Sunday – Intercession for the extension of Christ's Kingdom

Morning
Isaiah 62. 6 & 7. Revelation 11, 15–7 – collect for 3rd Sunday in Advent – prayer in Friendly Visitor – vol. 3, p. 7. – Lord's Prayer – Psalm 68. 31–5.

Evening
Psalm 67 – Revelation 19. 6–9 – 2nd & 3rd Collects – Good Friday – 1 Chronicles 29. 10–12 – Revelation 5. 12 & 13–2 Corinthians 13. 14.

MONDAY – prayer for faith, holiness etc.

Morning
Psalm 139, 23 & 24 – Psalm 63, 1–7, Psalm 51. 10–14 Trinity – 6 Epiphany – 1 Lent – 7th Trinity – 4th Easter – 1 Timothy 1. 17.

Evening
Psalm 65. 1–4 – Psalm 84. 4–12 – Easter Eve – 1st Easter – Ascension – 6th Trinity – Jude 24, 25.

TUESDAY – prayer for good works, usefulness etc.

Morning
Psalm 119, 133. 35–40 – Isaiah 26. 13 & 14 – Easter Day – Quinquages-
ima – 9 Trinity – 11th Trinity – 4th Communion service – Psalm 73.
24–26 – 2 Corinthians 13. 14.

Evening
1 Corinthians 16. 13 – Deuteronomy 31. 3 & 6 – Psalm 31. 2 Easter –
13 Trinity – 25 Trinity – All Saints – Romans 16. 25–27.

WEDNESDAY – intercession for Christ's Church, particularly his
ministers

Morning
Psalm 122: 6–9 – 1 Peter 2. 9 & 10 – Deuteronomy 33. 26–29 –
16 Trinity – 22 Trinity – 18th Trinity – 3rd Easter – Psalm 80 –
Psalm 79. 13 – *Gloria Patri* etc.

Evening
1 Peter 5. 1–4 – 2 Timothy 4. 5–8 – Psalm 32. 9 – St Peter – St Matthias
– 2nd Ember – St Simon & St Jude – Lord's Prayer.

THURSDAY – prayer for heavenly wisdom –

Morning
James 1. 5–3. 13–18 – Proverbs 8. 32–36 – Whitsunday – St Barnabas –
8th Communion Service – Ephesians 3. 16–21 or Psalm 68. 18–20.

Evening
Psalm 19. 7–11 – Psalm 119. 97, 103–5, 111, 113, – 2nd Advent –
St Mark – St John the Evangelist – Psalm 1. 1–3 – Daniel 2. 20–24 –
Gloria Patri etc.

FRIDAY – prayer for deliverance from sin, for pardon and peace

Morning
Psalm 51. 1–4 – Psalm 40. 11–13 – Psalm 103. 8–13 – 4 Advent –
Confession in Commination Service – Collect immediately preceding –

24 Trinity – Ash Wednesday – O God whose nature etc. – Psalm 65. 1–4
– Psalm 97. 9–12.

Evening
Psalm 51. 7–12 – Psalm 90. 14–17 – 1 after Ascension – 21 Trinity –
12 Trinity – O Lord look down from heaven etc. – Visitation of Sick
– Lord's Prayer – Psalm 103. 1–5 [2 illegible references] – Gloria Patri
etc.

SATURDAY – prayer for strength and ready help.

Morning
Man that is born etc – Psalm 90. 1–6 – Psalm 125. 1–2 – 1 Trinity –
4 Epiphany – 2 Lent – 15 Trinity – 1st Communion Service –
Exodus 15. 2, 11, 13, 17, 18 – Psalm 140. 6–7 – Gloria Patri etc.

Evening
Psalm 144. 1–4 – Psalm 121 – Psalm 16. 8–11 – 2 Trinity – 3 Trinity –
20 Trinity – 4 Trinity – 2 Communion – Almighty Lord etc. – Visitation
of Sick.

NOTE: later transcription of the above omitting references to Scripture
and the Book of Common Prayer

1824
Sunday – intercession for the extension of Christ's Kingdom
Monday – prayers for faith, holiness etc
Tuesday – prayers for good works, usefulness etc
Wednesday – intercession for Christ's Church, particularly for His
    ministers
Thursday – prayers for heavenly wisdom
Friday – for deliverance from sin, for pardon and peace
Saturday – for strength and ready help

GROUP FIVE

NOTE: There are two versions. The original Newman later dated as
'1824 or 25. JHN.' On the later transcription he first wrote '1824–25?'

but subsequently crossed out '25?' and put in square brackets 'N.B. between June and September'. As the changes are mostly verbal, the later version is given with omissions added from the earlier version.

Sunday –   For spirituality

      fervency in prayer
         faith, submission, resignation
      trust – hope
         a realizing view of the unseen
      concern for the ungodly
         indwelling of Christ and fellowship of the Spirit
         heavenlymindedness
      indifference to the world
      disinterestedness
         soberness and gravity of behaviour

against hardness of heart, frivolity, etc

Intercede for

Universal Church – our and other Churches, nominal Christians; heretics, schismatics, ['papists' omitted] Jews, Mohammedans and heathen – For Missionaries and all Propa-gation societies – for converts – for the diffusion of Christ's Spirit and the coming of His Kingdom.

    for my Parents and each member of our family – ['Mr Mayers' omitted]

Monday   For humility

      lowliness
      poorness of spirit
      meekness
      gentleness
      long suffering
      patience
         forgiveness of injuries
         preferring others to myself
      modesty

against pride, haughtiness, vanity, self-conceit, arrogance, self-sufficiency, rashness.

Intercede for

Oriel, Provost and fellows individually – Trinity – the two Universities – all professions – England, British Isles, dominions – all nations – my benefactors.

Tuesday   for love towards man

> kindness
>> affection towards all
>> love of the brethren
>
> tender mercy
>> charitableness
>
> thinking no evil
>> sweetness of temper

against anger, harsh words, etc etc.

Intercede for

St Clement's flock, churchmen, dissenters ['Romanists' omitted] etc. those without a religion – pious and worldly – rector, church wardens, etc, sick ['old' omitted] young, labouring with child, rich and poor.

    for a blessing on my work – that the church may be rebuilt and well – for unity – for the growth of godliness

Wednesday   for purity

> sobriety,
> chastity,
>> temperance
>> self denial,
>
> simplicity,
> sincerity,
> truthfulness.
> openness
> candour

against excess in eating, uncleanness in thought, word or deed, worldlimindedness, lying, hollowness.

Intercede for

friends, pupils, relations, etc. [omitted: 'Bowden – Pegus – Thresher – Westmacott – Pope – Smalley – Dear – Scott and serious men of Oxford – Dr Nicholas – Foudriniers']

Thursday   for wisdom and knowledge

      judgment,
      discretion,
      tact,
      coolness
      caution
        presence of mind
      decision
        penetration,
        discerning of spirits
        resourcefulness
        gift of conversation,
      moderation
        full assurance of understanding
      memory
        power of applying and illustrating
        gift of preaching, both as to accuracy of thought and
in expression

against nervousness, cowardice, absence of mind, confusion etc

Intercede for

Bishops, priests and deacons – all ministers of God's word.

Friday   for zeal

      activity,
      diligence
        perseverance,

   unweariedness,
   undauntedness,
   resoluteness,
  firmness

against indolence, lukewarmness, fear of man

NOTE: the following omitted in later transcription:
Pray for
in church – Singleness of heart – 1 Corinthians x, 31. 2 Corinthians iii, 5. Galatians vi, 14. Philippians iv, 13 – a view to God's glory – simple dependence on the grace of Christ – regarding myself as an *instrument*.

for liveliness and fervency of prayer – for a deep sense of the awful nature of my sacred office – regarding myself as the voice of the people to God, and of God to the people.

for the spirit of devotion, affection towards my people – love, faith, fear, confidence, towards God.

for strength of body, nerves, voice, breath etc earnestness of manner – distinctness of delivery

SATURDAY   **for usefulness**

   opportunities of serving the poor
   of obliging the more wealthy
   of edifying all
   success in preaching,
    in visiting teaching, catechizing

     ———

also for singleness of heart, aiming at God's glory, dependence on Him, sense of my ministerial responsibilities – strength of body, voice, breath etc distinctness of delivery –
 for humility, mercy, forbearance, wisdom, a word in season, in dealing with dissenters.

NOTE: The following was omitted in later transcription

Pray for

In the parish – vigilance – alertness, unweariedness, presence of mind – *meekness* of *wisdom* – simplicity – quickness – power of reply – love – humility – discerning of spirits.

In visiting sick – lowliness, mercy, dependence on Christ, judgment, knowledge, firmness, candour.

in catechizing etc. – patience, gentleness, kindness, cheerfulness, clearness in teaching, wisdom.

Towards dissenters – humility, charity, mercy, forbearance, wisdom, a word in season.

GROUP SIX

NOTE: this group of prayers has two versions. The first was transcribed from rough copy on 3 December 1851, when Newman was praying to find witnesses for the Achilli Trial. He dated it as 'about 1830 (or perhaps 1829),' but these dates he crossed out after he completed the transcription, when he wrote, 'I am almost certain this was in 1828'. He also listed in square brackets, '*Evening?*' and '*Against Sin.*'

The second version contains the usual 'verbal,' changes, but in one instance the change involves a difference in the theological understanding of original sin. The later version is printed here.

Oxford   **1828**   **Evening**

[O Almighty and most merciful God and Father]

O God, give me grace at this time duly to confess my sins before Thee, and truly to repent of them, as I review them.

O Lord, I am not in myself fit to lift up my face to Thee. I acknowledge my utter unworthiness in Thy sight, the perverseness of my heart, my wilful ignorance and blindness, and my habitual sinfulness. Thou gavest me a sense of right and wrong, and a moral nature, and the aid of Thy Holy Spirit; but I have dishonoured Thy gifts and rebelled against Thee. I have no plea for pardon but Thy mercy offered to us all in Thy Son, Jesus Christ.

Blot out of Thy book, O gracious Lord God, all my manifold acts
of sin committed against Thee in former years, remembered or
forgotten, every impulse of anger, jealousy, hatred, pride, ill-
temper, uncleanness, covetousness, self-conceit; every unkind,
deceitful, quarrelsome, intemperate, irreverent, or corrupting
word, which has passed my lips; and every deed of cowardice,
malice, injustice, cruelty, meanness, sullenness, obstinacy, glut-
tony, lewdness, and self indulgence, which I ever committed –
Impute them not unto me for my Saviour's sake. Forgive me,
Lord, every act of ingratitude towards Thee, and unwillingness to
think of Thee, and to do Thy will, every disobedience to my loving
parents and to my superiors, every rudeness and want of humility
and of considerate love in my dealings with my friends or with
the world. Forgive me all my wanderings in prayer, my unbelief,
my sins of omission, my deliberate and repeated sins against
conscience and conviction.

O Lord, I need deliverance also from my sinful heart, as well
as from its actual bad fruits – As in baptism Thou forgavest me
Adam's sin ['the principle and taint of sin inherent in nature'] so now
pardon all of evil habit that Thou seest in me, since my new birth;
– pride, self esteem, blameful error, selfishness, sloth, hardness of
heart, fear of man, love of the world, and all other marks of evil
in me such as are hid from my own view.

And, O Holy Lord, while Thou savest me from the imputation
of sin, save me also from its power within me. Give me eyes to
see what is right, and a heart to follow it, and strength to perform
it; and grant that I may in all things press forward in the work of
sanctification and ever do Thy will, and at length through Thy
mercy attain to the glories of Thy everlasting Kingdom through
Jesus Christ our Lord.

———

Oxford   1828   morning

O Almighty God and Father of our Lord Jesus Christ, who day
by day renewest Thy mercies to sinful man, accept, I pray Thee,
this morning sacrifice of praise and thanksgiving, and give me
grace to offer it reverently, and in humble faith, and with a
willing mind.

I praise Thee for my birth from kind and anxious parents, and in a Christian land; for the gifts of health and reason; for sound body and perfect senses; for Thy continued care of me, for my baptism into Thy Holy Church, and the early knowledge given me of Thee, my Creator and Redeemer, through the affection of dear relatives; for all the prayers offered for me, and every measure of Thy grace granted to me from my youth up; for the blessing of a good education; for the gifts of mind Thou hast entrusted to me, and the means of their cultivation; for all known and unknown escapes, vouchsafed to me, from bodily and spiritual evil; for Thy gracious forgiveness of all my aggravated sins, and for the victory Thou gavest me in my youth over my rebellious passions and misguided reason. I thank Thee for Thy bountiful providence in opening on me prospects of life beyond my birthright, and for the temper of mind and principles of conduct with which I came to this place; for the friends Thou hast given me here, and for the success with which, amid many trials, Thou hast blest my toil; for Thy great condescension and abundant mercy in putting me into the ministry of Thy church, and setting me up on high, and fitting me in a measure for my office, and giving me opportunities in various ways of being useful to Thy redeemed people. Also I praise and magnify Thy name for every affliction and anxiety Thou hast laid, or now layest, upon me, and I acknowledge thankfully that hitherto all has worked for good.

Lord, I am abashed before Thee, and abhor myself in Thy sight. I am not worthy of the least of all Thy mercies; Thou hast given me good gifts, and I have dishonoured them by my neglect or corrupt use of them. I sinned before Thou gavest them, and I have sinned since Thou gavest. Yet Thou renewst Thy goodness to me every morning. Praise the Lord, O my soul, and all that is within me praise His holy name.

GROUP SEVEN

NOTE: The following set of prayers exists in three versions. Version C must have been written after the death of King William IV in 1837, as it substitutes 'Queen' for 'King'.

VERSION A

In pencil: [beginning of 1835]

    For
The Church Catholic
Its Branches –
    internally, and as regards its extension.

The Reformed Churches
    The Churches of these isles
Bishops, Priests and Deacons
    Bishop of Oxford and other ecclesiastical authorities.

St Mary the Virgin's

The Universities – Oxford, Oriel, Trinity, St Alban Hall
    The Provost and Fellows etc. late fellows – servants.

The King and Royal family.
The Legislature
All who are in authority
All the King's subjects – the nation – all who are sick, or tempted.

VERSION B   1836?

    For
The Church Catholic
    in all its branches

internally, in unity, purity, and peace –
externally – in strength and increase

    The Churches of these islands
Bishops, Priests, and Deacons
    enlighten their hearts and strengthen their hands
    let them know their duty and do it.

Raise up labourers into Thy vineyard.
    Rd. Thy Servant our Bishop and all in authority under him
    Archdeacons Rural Deans Chancellors.

St Mary the Virgin
   in Oxford and Littlemore
Bless it, and me in and for it.

The Universities as Schools of the Church
Oxford – Trinity, Alban Hall, Oriel –
The Chancellor, The Provost, Fellows, Bible Clerks, Commoners,
              Servants,
Late fellows, incumbents
Visitor.

The King, the Queen, the Royal family
   enlighten them and make them Thine

The King's Ministers
   Bless them in all good works, turn them to Thee and
   overrule all they do for good,

Duke of Wellington – Sir R[obert] Peel, and their friends,
   enlighten them and make them Thine.

The Legislature.
The Magistrates and all in authority.
All the King's subjects – the nation – the British Empire.

All heathen nations – Mahometans – Jews – Turks – infidels – and
          heretics –
Cause Thy light to shine on them.

All conditions of men –
All who are sick, tried, or tempted.

VERSION C

   The Church Catholic in all its branches
      internally – unity, purity, peace –
      externally – strength and increase.
   The Church in these islands
      Bishops, Priests and Deacons – enlighten their hearts and
      strengthen their hands – let them know their duty and do it.

Raise up Labourers.
Prosper endeavours, fulfill beginnings
Reverend our Bishop and all committed to him.
Archdeacons, Rural Deans, Chancellor,
Dean of Chapter
St Mary the Virgin in Oxford and Littlemore.
Bless it, and me in it and for it.

The Universities as schools of the Church.
Oxford – Chancellor, Vice-Chancellor, etc.
Trinity, Alban Hall, Oriel.
The Provost, Fellows, Bible Clerks, Scholars, Commoners,
Servants.
Late fellows, incumbents.

The Queen, the Court, make them serious.
Ministers – bless what they do well, overrule what they will
do ill.
The Conservative Party and their leaders –
Let what is good in them have strength to expel what is bad.

The Legislature – the Magistracy – all the population – the nation
– the Empire.

All heathen nations – all nations in which the Church is.
Jews, Turks, Infidels, Heretics.

All conditions of men,
All who are sick, tried, or tempted.

GROUP EIGHT

NOTE: In a letter to Henry Wilberforce on 25 March 1837, Newman remarked, 'Another characteristic of the Breviary services is the shortness of the prayers they contain.' It is probable that they served as a model for the following prayers composed in medieval or Church Latin. Newman transcribed the first thirteen probably in 1875 with a few verbal changes. This version is given with the earlier version put in square brackets. Newman's first prayers in Latin were composed in 1816. See *AW*, 151, and *LD* I, 29. Other Latin prayers are contained in *AW*, 215, 233–4.

July 10. 1837

1. Ecclesiam electorum tuorum, Omnipotens Deus, ne obliviscaris in finem; sed, quam pretioso sanguine tuo redemisti, illam in coelesti gloriâ constituere digneris, qui vivis etc.

2. Da quaesumus, Domine, Ecclesiae tuae in terrâ militanti, ut unitate et sanâ fide intus coalita, augeatur foras et undique dilatetur. Per Dominum.

3. Deus, qui nobis in Unigenito tuo aeternuam sacerdotium contulisti [condidisti] miserere omnium quotquot eidem [illi] alicubi deserviunt, ut illuminata sint illorum corda, confirmatae manus; sciant quae agenda sint et agant quae sciverint, Per Dominum.

4. Visita Ecclesias nostras, Domine Jesu Christe, praesentiore gratiâ, ut oriantur passim qui te glorificent, praedicent verbum tuum, [et] praeparent tibi populum tui dignum, qui vivis etc.

5. Respice, clementissime Deus, in opera illorum quotquot antiquam et veram religionem tuam, in his locis jacentem, erigere et stabilire conamur <conantur>, ut te duce prosperè procedamus <procedant>, et ipsi ad vitam aeternam tandem perveniamus <perveniant>. Per Dominum.

6. Dirige, Deus, in viam rectam omnes qui haesitant in plenâ confessione sanctissimi Evangelii tui, praesertim – Per Dominum.

7. Benefac, misericors Deus, servo tuo R. episcopo etc. [nostro, C. Archidiacono ejus, Cancellario, Decano, et Capitulo aedis Christi, Decanis in rura degentibus, et caeteris Ecclesiae Oxoniensis ministris; ut in fide et sanctitate vivent, et se invicem suscipiant et ament per Dominum.]

8. Benigne respice, Domine, paroeciam meam et ecclesias meas, et me, populum [populos] et comministros meos; ut quae pastores fecerimus fideliter, ea grex amabiliter valeant accipere. Per Dominum. [et quae pastores fecerimus fideliter, fac gregem amabiliter ea accipere per Dominum.]

9. Clementer suscipe, omnipotens Deus, omnes quotquot baptizavimus, catechizavimus, admonuimus, edocuimus, absolvimus, santâ coenâ cibavimus, in matrimonio conjunximus [benediximus] in morbis curavimus, in sepulturam commendavimus. Per Dominum.

10. Deus, qui nos peccatores ad oves tuos pascendos gratiâ tuâ vocasti, humiliter te rogamus, ut quos moribundos curavimus, iis quidquid [quicquid] deliquimus, id tu [ipse] suppleas et nobis delinquentibus parcas. Per Dominum.

11. Custodi, Domine, in die malâ Universitatem nostram et scholas et sodalitia <collegia> ejus, praesertim Collegia SS Trinitatis et Beatae Mariae Virginis de Oriel, et Aulam S. Albani, ut unusquisque in loco suo vigilet, sobrius sit, in te confidat, te expectet, tibi serviat. Per Dominum.

12. Deus, veniae largitor et humanae salutis amator, quaesumus clementiam tuam, ut nostri Collegii fundatores, etc. [et benefactores, et qui ex hoc saeculo transciere [?], fratres cum omnibus Sanctis tuis ad perpetuae beatitudinis consortium pervenire concedas per Dominum.]

13. Memineris, clementissime Deus, Victoriae Reginae nostrae, et fac ut inimici ejus confrigantur et decidant subditi ad poenitentiam et bona opera convertantur, concilia, magistratus, sodalitia, municipia urbes, <omnes ordines et [?]> gloriam tuam quaerant et promoveant. Per Dominum.

14. Deus, qui nos patrem et matrem honorare praecepisti, miserere clementer animabus patris et matris meae, eorumque peccata dimitte; meque eos in aeternae claritatis gaudio fac videre per Dominum.

15. Inclina, Domine, aurem tuam ad preces meas quibus misericordiam tuam supplex deprecor ut animam famulae tuae, clarissimae aviae meae N., et aliorum avorum et aviae, quos numquam vidi, animas, quas de hoc saeculo migrare jussisti in pace ac lucis regione constituas, et Sanctorum tuorum jubeas esse consortes per Dominum.

16. Absolve, Domine, animam famuli tui Gualteri M[ayers], cui multum debeo, ut defunctus saeculo tibi vivat, et quae per fragilitatem carnis humanâ conversatione commisit, tu veniâ misericordissimae pietatis absterge per Dominum.

17. Fidelium defunctorum Deus, amplectere pietate tuâ animas dulcissime sororis Mariae Sophiae, et plusquam fratris in Domino Ricardi Hurrell, ut quos è mundi contagione eripuisi, in Angelorum puritate in dies proficiant, et Diem judicii tuâ virtute susteneri mereantur per Dominum.

18. Benignitate tuâ fovere et edocere digneris, clementissime Deus, ami–tam meam Elizabetham Goode, et in viâ veritatis secure et fideeliter incedens, ad te Deum suum in dies appropinquet per Dominum.

19. Custodi sapienter et suaviter, misericors Deus, fratres et sorores meas, T[homam] et H[arriett] M[ozley], J[oannem], et J[emimam] M[ozley], ut singuli cum singulis religiosi et feliciter viventes, te unicè Deum suum, se invicem in te diligant, et dilectionis suae fructum in longitudine dierum videant, foveant, et perficiant per Dominum.

20. Suscipe clementia tuâ, piissime Deus, fratrem meam C[arolem] R[obertum], aliquando lapsum nunc tuâ gratiâ revententem ad te, ut verae poenitentiae in illo gignantur fructus, sincera fides, et sanctitatis renovatae rudimenta per Dominum.

21. Memineris, Domine, fratris et sororis meae F[rancisci] et M[ariae] N[ewman] et in viam rectam eos clementissime redige per Dominum.

22. Obsecro te, parvulorum et lactentium Deus, dulcis et suavis es [se] fratribus illis puerulis, quos in sacro baptimate suscepi, ut per vitae hujus pericula ad vitam tandem perveniant sempiternam per Dominum.

23. Memineris omnium propinquorum meorum praesertim

24. Memineris omnium amicorum meorum praesertim

25. Memineris omnium qui aegrotant aut aliter exercentur, praesertim

26. Memineris omnium defunctorum in Domino praesertim

Notes

CHAPTER ONE: EARLY YEARS

1. Newman was referring to his prose style; his Latin verses he said were 'without any assistance whether from book or master or English'. *LD* I, 23.
2. See Richard Liddy, 'Spirituality and the Dogmatic Principle'. *The Priest*, 43 (June 1987), pp. 41–5.
3. Scott, Essay XVI: 'On the Believer's Warfare and Experience'. *Essays on the Most Important Subjects in Religion.* Edinburgh, 1829, pp. 240–55.
4. One is reminded of the passage in St Peter of Alcantara, 'Let a man return into his own self, and there in the centre of his soul, let him wait upon God, as one who listens to another speaking from a high tower, as though he had God in his heart, as though in the whole creation there was only God and his soul.' Quoted in Juan Mascaro's book, *Lamp of Fire.* London, 1961.
5. *Apo*, 7; Louis Bouyer, *Newman: His Life and Spirituality.* London, 1958, p. 8.
6. The full title is *Private Thoughts. In Two Parts Complete. Part i. Upon Religion digested into Twelve Articles: with Practical Resolutions formed Thereupon. Part II. Upon a Christian Life; or Necessary Directions for its beginning and Progress upon Earth, in order to its Final Perfection in the Beatific Vision.* 24th Edition includes 'The Life and Character of the Author'. London, 1812.
7. 'J.H.N. 14 Oct. 1874' (*LD* I, 30, n.1). It seems that Newman first wrote 'ever', but changed it to 'even'. Not all Newman's memoranda are written in Beveridge's style, which is easier to read than that of Scott.
8. *British Critic* XIX (October 1836), pp. 389–91.

CHAPTER TWO: SNAPDRAGON AND GLITTERING PRIZES

1. 'A grave feeling, with something of sadness and even awe in it at the prospect before him, increased as the year 1820 opened and the months moved on.' (*AW*, p. 45)
2. G. J. Davie, who witnessed the event and was prepared to intervene, if necessary, recounted the incident later in a letter to Newman, 8 March 1864. (*BOA*).

3. Louis Bouyer, *Newman: His Life and Spirituality*, London, 1958 (French edition, 1951).

CHAPTER THREE: INNER WARFARE: CONQUERING SELF

1. Thomas L. Sheridan, *Newman on Justification*, New York, 1967, p. 57.
2. For these questions see *Ibid*, p. 50.
3. *Ibid*, pp. 48–9.
4. 'The form of social prayer' is probably the 'Prayer for all Conditions of Men' in the Book of Common Prayer.
5. Presumably this date is when he thought of standing for the Oriel Fellowship, but the diary gives 15 November.
6. Sheridan, p. 59.
7. *Ibid*, pp. 59–62.
8. *Ibid*, pp. 64–5 (*BOA*, A. 9.1).
9. Ibid, pp. 65–6.

CHAPTER FOUR: TURNING POINT

1. Culler's remark that Newman's development of the theme 'Know thyself' in the Oriel examination 'is simply an analysis of his own difficulties during the previous two years', may be correct, but it does not really elucidate the "shuddering at his own weaknesses," which Newman called an habitual principle of five years standing'. A. Dwight Culler, *The Imperial Intellect*, New Haven, 1955, p. 33.
2. Vincent Ferrer Blehl, 'John Henry Newman on Latin Prose Style: A Critical Edition of his *Hints on Latin Composition*,' *Classical Folio*, XV (1961), pp. 1–12.
3. For the previous letter to the *Christian Observer* see *LD* I, pp. 102–5, and for the remark of his father, see *AW*, p. 179.
4. *Memoir of the Rev. Henry Martyn, B.D.*, London 1819.

CHAPTER SEVEN: BEHIND THE VEIL: AN INVISIBLE WORLD

1. Sheridan, p. 149. Since Froude's journal later on had a spiritual effect on Newman, it could be that he was also referring to this.
2. For the meaning of *ethos* see Geoffrey Rowell, 'John Keble – *A Speaking Life*, ed. Charles R. Henery, Leominster 1995.
3. For a full treatment of Newman on universal revelation, see Francis McGrath, F. M. S., *John Henry Newman: Universal Revelation*, Tunbridge Wells, Kent 1997.

CHAPTER EIGHT: LOSS AND GAIN

1. R. D. Middleton, *Newman at Oxford: His Religious Development*, Oxford 1950, p. 169.
2. An excellent treatment of reserve is given in Robin C. Selby, *The Principle of Reserve in the Writings of John Henry Cardinal Newman*, Oxford 1975.
3. St Augustine, *A Letter to Proba*, (English translation in the *Liturgy of the Hours*, New York 1975–6, IV, pp. 407–9, 412–13). St John Chrysostom, (*Liturgy*, II, 68–70).
4. *Ari*, 35–58. Mark Pattison, *Memoirs*, London 1885, p. 79; *Ess* I, Essay II.
5. Roderick Strange, *Newman and the Gospel of Christ* (Oxford 1981). Newman's statements about the Holy Spirit prior to his sermons on the Indwelling can be interpreted as the action of the Holy Spirit from *without*.
6. These sermons seem to have been prompted by the passage of the Reform Bill. Newman wrote to his aunt on 24 August, 'What a miserable state the Country is in! the ministry now show themselves to be, what they have always been . . . deeply infected with the cold-hearted indifferent spirit of liberalism. . . . May I be kept from having any thing to do with those who are "neither hot nor cold – ".' (*LD* III, p. 81)
7. For Newman's view of preaching and catechetics see *LD* V, pp. 44–8.

CHAPTER NINE: A LONG DAY'S JOURNEY INTO LIGHT

1. Ps. 121: 'I raise my eyes toward the mountains. /From where will my help come?/ My help comes from the Lord.'
2. 'St Paul's Gift of Sympathy'. *OS*, 8, pp. 106–20. St Paul was often in his mind during this trip, more so than indicated by the Index to volume III of the *Letters* and *Diaries*.
3. Froude to Christie, April 1833, *Remains* I, pp. 306–8.

CHAPTER TEN: SETTING SAIL

1. R. W. Church, *The Oxford Movement: Twelve Years 1833–1845*, London and New York 1900, pp. 129–30.
2. Thomas William Allies, *A Life's Decision*, London 1880, pp. 41–2.
3. Church, *op cit.*, p. 302.
4. For the letters exchanged see Louis Allen, *John Henry Newman and the Abbé Jager: A Controversy on Scripture and Tradition (1834–1836)*, London 1975.
5. See the discussions of the first principles in *Prepos*, pp. 283–4 and *GA*, 60ff.
6. Since Newman habitually believed that morning was a better time for prayer than evening, no doubt these early morning periods were devoted to prayer and reading Scripture.

7. *West Oxford: Historical Notes and Pictures concerning the Parish of St. Thomas the Martyr, in Oxford.* Ed. Thomas W. Squires, London, pp. 124–5.
8. George Anthony Denison, *Notes of My Life 1805–1878*, London and New York 1878, p. 61.

CHAPTER ELEVEN: AN UNDIVIDED HEART

1. As time went on, Newman received fresh evidence of the spread of apostolic principles, e.g. in a letter from Mrs William Wilberforce who had been in Italy for well over a year, writing on 3 August 1835, 'I cannot tell you the daily amazement I am in, on finding the immense progress those apostolic opinions have made, held, when I left England, by so small a circle. Now I find a large body speaking out, and taking the high ground I longed to see them take – with all my heart I wish them God speed.' (*LD* V, p. 115, n. 3) Surprised how well his volumes of sermons were selling, he remarked to Froude, 'I do verily believe a spirit is abroad at present, and we are but blind tools, not knowing whither we are going. I mean a flame seems arising in so many places, as to show that no one mortal incendiary is at work – though this man or that may have more influence in shaping the course or [modifying] the nature of the flame.' (*LD* V, p. 99) In this sense then perhaps one should understand Hutton's remark. 'The truth was that he really did feel to the bottom of his heart that he was doing a work of which he himself knew neither the scope nor the goal. . . . He believed that it was given to him to open to the Church of England a new career, to raise it up as a new power to witness against the sins and whims and false ideals of the day and the various idolatries of the *Zeitgeist*.' Richard Holt Hutton, 'Cardinal Newman', *Essays on Some of the Modern Guides of English Thought in Matters of Faith*, London 1887.
2. See Pierre Gauthier, 'Richard Hurrell Froude's Influence on Newman and the Oxford Movement,' *From Oxford to the People*, ed. Paul Vaiss, Leominster 1996, pp. 259–60.
3. John Oldcastle, *Cardinal Newman: A Monograph*, London and New York 1990, p. 50.
4. Sabellianism was 'the denial of the distinction of Persons in the Divine Nature,' a sort of Unitarianism. (*Ari*, pp. 117–18) Socianism refers to the tenets of Faustus Socinus, an Italian theologian (1539–1604) who denied the Trinity and divinity of Christ and gave rationalistic explanations of sin, salvation and the like. Newman thought Socinianism may be hid from a man's own consciousness, as he believed was so with Mr Abbott. See *Ess.* I, p. 79.

CHAPTER TWELVE: A LOST COMRADE

1. Froude developed his ideas on the Eucharist in his 'Essay on Rationalism' (1834), which was later published in his *Remains*.
2. Günter Biemer, *Newman on Tradition*, Freiburg and London 1967, p. 47.
3. Gauthier, *op. cit.*, pp. 263–65.
4. *Autobiography of Isaac Williams*, ed. George Prevost, London 1892, p. 107.
5. Originally in the *British Critic*, but quoted by R. W. Church, *The Oxford Movement Twelve Years 1833–1845*, London 1900, p. 40.
6. *Ibid*, pp. 48–9.
7. Frederick Oakeley, *Historical Notes on the Tractarian Movement 1833–1845*, London 1865, pp. 5–6.
8. A number of studies are devoted to Froude, including Louise Imogen Guiney, *Hurrell Froude, Memoranda and Comments*, London 1904. Piers Brendon, *Hurrell Froude and the Oxford Movement*, London 1974; Pierre Gauthier, *La pensée religieuse de R. H. Froude (1803–1836)*, Paris 1977.

CHAPTER THIRTEEN: THE EMERGING LEADER

1. Donald A. Withey, *John Henry Newman: the Liturgy and the Breviary*, London 1992, p. 87.
2. Rose's letter is published in John William Burgon, *Lives of Twelve Good Men*, 2 vols., London 1888, I. pp. 209–23. Newman's letter to Rose of 23 May 1836 is confusing without a knowledge of Rose's letter, to which it is a detailed reply.
3. Wilfrid Ward, *William George Ward and the Oxford Movement*, 2nd ed., London and New York 1890, p. 83. Gerard Tracey, editor of the *Letters and Diaries*, thinks it more likely that this incident took place during the lectures given in 1838, which won Ward over to the Movement.
4. R. W. Greaves, 'Golightly and Newman, 1824–1845', *Journal of Ecclesiastical History*, XIX (1958), p. 217. The best account is given by Maisie Ward, *Your young Mr. Newman*, London 1952, p. 328 and n. 1.
5. William Tuckwell, *Reminiscences Of Oxford*, London, 1900, pp. 182–83.
6. R. D. Middleton, *Newman & Bloxam: An Oxford Friendship*, Oxford 1947, pp. 35–8.
7. 'Rise, Progress, and Results of Puseyism', *Rambler* VI (December 1850), p. 526.
8. Middleton, *Newman & Bloxam*, pp. 96–100, and John William Burgon, *Lives of Twelve Good Men*, 2 vols., London 1888, I, p. 58.

CHAPTER FOURTEEN: SPIRITUAL GROWTH

1. Jeremy Taylor, *The Golden Grove. A Choice Manual, containing what is to be believed, practiced, and desired or prayed for.*Oxford, 1836, pp. 103–21, and *The Private Devotions of Lancelot Andrewes, Bishop of Winchester.* London 1830, pp. 282–92.
2. Donald A. Withey, *John Henry Newman: the Liturgy and the Breviary*, London 1992, pp. 114–23.
3. William Knight, *Principal Shairp and His Friends.* London 1888, quoting from Shairp's essay on Keble, p. 59. William Lockhart, *Cardinal Newman. Reminiscences of 50 Years by One of His Oldest Living Disciples.* London 1891, p. 24.
4. Williams, *Autobiography*, pp. 80–1.
5. *Ibid*, pp. 106–7.
6. E. G. Sandford, *Frederick Temple: An Appreciation*, London and New York 1907, pp. 42–3.
7. Newman developed these ideas in a sermon preached shortly before, on 7 May, 'Christ Manifested in Remembrance', *PPS* IV, 17, pp. 262–4.
8. *Comfort in Sorrow*, ed. James Tolhurst, Leominster 1996.
9. For a more detailed account of Newman's views of sin and forgiveness while he was an Anglican, see Vincent Ferrer Blehl, *The White Stone: the Spiritual Theology of John Henry Newman*, Petersham, Mass., 1992.
10. *Primate Alexander Archbishop of Armagh.* A memoir edited by Eleanor Alexander, London 1913, pp. 93–5.

CHAPTER FIFTEEN: THEOLOGIAN AND EDITOR

1. Henri Bremond, *The Mystery of Newman*, trans. H. C. Corrance, London 1907, p. 133.
2. Wilfrid Ward, *William George Ward and the Oxford Movement*, 2nd ed., London and New York 1890, p. 83.
3. The project of translating the Breviary was taken up again in 1841 by Robert Williams, assisted by Woods and Oakeley, but was again beset with problems. Newman opposed it, but, as he told Keble, 'men *will* be doing something'. (N. to Keble, 23 July 1841, *LD* VIII, p. 277) A third attempt was made in 1843 with the initiative coming from Pusey, but the work was not published. See Withey, pp. 50–66.
4. Frederick Oakeley, *Historical Notes on the Tractarian Movement (1833–1845)*, London 1865, pp. 78–9.

CHAPTER SIXTEEN: INFLUENCE AND SHOCK

1. *Primate Alexander Archbishop of Armagh, A Memoir*, ed. Eleanor Alexander, London 1913, pp. 70–1.
2. *Life and Correspondence of John Duke Lord Coleridge, Lord Chief Justice of England*, written and edited by Ernest Hartley Coleridge, 2 vols., London 1904, I, pp. 58–9.
3. William Lockhart, *Cardinal Newman: Reminiscences of Fifty Years Since*, by one of his oldest living disciples, London 1891, p. 23.
4. *Memorials of William Charles Lake, Dean of Durham 1869–94*, ed. Katharine Lake, London 1901, p. 50.
5. James Anthony Froude, 'Oxford Counter Reformation, Letter III,' *Short Studies on Great Subjects*, Vol. V, London 1907, pp. 196–7.
6. Frederick Oakeley, *Historical Notes on the Tractarian Movement (A.D. 1833–45)*, London 1865, pp. 50–51.
7. Principal Shairp, 'Keble.' *Studies in Poetry and Philosophy*, quoted in Knight, p. 59. William Knight, *Principal Shairp and his Friends*, London 1888, p. 59.
8. Principal Shairp, *Studies in Poetry and Philosophy*, 3rd. ed., Edinburgh 1876, pp. 244–5.
9. I. Williams, *Autobiography*, pp. 101–3.
10. Lockhart, *op. cit.* p. 26.
11. 'F. Newman's Oxford Parochial Sermons,' *Dublin Review*, new series, XII (April 1869), p. 326.
12. Froude, *op. cit.* pp. 199–201.
13. Lake, *op. cit.* pp. 40–1.
14. Shairp, *op. cit.* p. 249.
15. Lockhart, *op. cit.* pp. 25–6.
16. J. M. Capes, 'Rise, Progress, and Results of Puseyism', *Rambler*, VI (December 1850), pp. 52–5.
17. *Recollections of Aubrey de Vere*, New York and London 1897, pp. 256–7.
18. *Ibid.*, pp. 278–81.
19. Charles Whibley, *Lord John Manners and his Friends*, London 1925, I. p. 72.
20. Oakeley, *op. cit.*, p. 110.
21. Richard Whittington (d. 1423) as a youth ran away from his master because he was ill-treated. Resting at Holloway, he fancied he heard Bow Bells ringing:

> Turn again, Whittington,
> Lord Mayor of London.

He returned to his master's house to become eventually three times Mayor of London.

In his *Confessions*, Bk. VII, ch.12. St Augustine narrates that when weeping for his sins and asking God's help, he heard a child's voice saying,

'Take and read, take and read.' He opened the Bible and the passage he found (Rom. 13. 13) led to his conversion.

22. Since Newman's letters to Rogers exist only in extracts made by Copeland, it is possible that Newman expressed this alarm in his letter to Rogers of 15 September, for Rogers replied the next day, 'What do you mean by "things coming to the worst" – ? Ejectment from Oriel and St Mary's or – ' Here Rogers made a small drawing of the papal triple tiara.

23. 'F. Newman's Oxford Parochial Sermons,' *Dublin Review, new series*, XII (April 1869), pp. 327–8.

CHAPTER SEVENTEEN: THE CALM BEFORE THE STORM

1. For a description of the cloth see *LD* VII, 300, n. 1.

2. Maisie Ward provided a correct interpretation of Newman's statement in the *Apologia*. (*Young Mr. Newman*, London 1952, pp. 26–30). Gilley's otherwise acceptable summary of Newman's review of Todd's work is somewhat clouded by his failure to understand completely Newman's assertion. Knockles's statement, 'As Sheridan Gilley has demonstrated, it was eschatology as much as ecclesiology that provided the essential ingredient in Newman's conversion', does not seem to represent accurately Gilley's view and the assertion of 'eschatology as an essential ingredient in Newman's conversion', is hardly borne out by the evidence. Peter B. Knockles, *The Oxford Movement in Context*, Cambridge 1994, p. 177.

3. This idea was suggested to Newman by the doctrine of the Fathers of the Church with regard to the fallen angels, as he explained in a letter to Woods, (*LD* VI, p. 112).

CHAPTER EIGHTEEN: WEATHERING THE STORM

1. *LD* VII, xxiii and *LD* VIII, 58, n. 1. Though Ward, when ordained a deacon, subscribed to the Articles in the Arnoldian sense, he subscribed to them in a Catholic sense when ordained priest, a sense he called non-natural. Moreover, Ward at this time had no urge to leave the Church of England. Williams, on the other hand, was troubled by the Thirty-nine Articles. In addition to the letter Newman wrote him urging him not to leave the Church (*LD* VII, pp. 180–1) Newman wrote to Pusey, 'R. W. [Williams] is stationary at present – but what is to be done with a man who begins with assuming, as a first principle which is incontroversibly borne in upon his mind, that the Roman is the Catholic Church, that therefore the Tridentine Decrees are eternal truth, that to oppose them is heresy, that all who sign the 39 articles do oppose them, and that it is a sin to be in common with heretics?' (*LD* VII, pp. 371–2)

2. This motivation is confirmed by Newman's remark to Thomas Mozley, 7

March 1841, 'The Tract was necessary to keep our young friends etc from stumbling at the Articles and going to Rome.' (*LD* VIII, p. 58)

3. Greaves, *op. cit.*, 220ff.

4. Church, *op. cit.*, pp. 264–5.

5. Oakeley, *op. cit.*, p. 43.

6. Middleton, *Newman at Oxford*, pp. 186–7.

7. This seems to have represented a change. At the meeting of Pusey and the bishop, 23 March, according to Liddon, 'the whole series should cease after the publication of two more tracts which were already prepared'. (*LD* VIII, p. 115, n. 2)

8. *Tract XC . . . with a Historical Preface by the Rev. E. B. Pusey . . . Revised Edition of the Preface.* Oxford 1866, p. xxvii. See *Apo.*, pp. 139–40, 90) Contrary to those critics and commentators who claimed that Newman misrepresented or even invented historical evidence, there can be little doubt that there was an 'understanding'. In addition to Pusey's testimony, Newman wrote to Miss Giberne, 9 May 1841, 'The Bishops are very desirous of hushing the matter up – and I certainly have done my utmost to co-operate with them, on the understanding that the Tract is not to be withdrawn or condemned.' (*LD* VIII, pp. 189–90) Newman annotated this letter, 2 September 1862, before the publication of the *Apologia*. 'N. B. I have always thought I was unfairly used here especially by the Archbishop (Howley). His party was in a stew lest I should not submit, and there was a talk of a *Declaration* on my side from the Clergy. Jelf came to me, and said "If so, there will be a counter-declaration" and wanted me to co-operate with the Archbishop's party in keeping things quiet. I *did* do so.' (*LD* VIII, pp. 190, n. 1) It is to this Newman seems later to refer after the publication of the *Apologia*. 'I had been condemned by ecclesiastical authority, without a word said in my favour, though Jelf came to me, on the beginning of the row about it, from Archbishop Howley to say that, if my friends would consent not to move, nothing should be done on the other side.' (*LD* XXIV, p. 96)

Newman continued his annotation of the 9 May 1841 letter to Miss Giberne, 'Also, *I* have letters, I think, from Dr Bagot, Bishop of Oxford, (unless they were, probably, addressed to Pusey) to the effect that if *I* did nothing, no one in authority would do any thing against me; for they knew, I suppose, that I cared not a rap for the Hebdomadal Board, but, from my published and avowed *principles*, dreaded a censure from the Bishops. I had at once written my letter to Dr Jelf – why should I write any more in the way of Apology? I think my second letter, viz. to the Bishop of Oxford . . . was written *on condition* that, if I wrote it, the Bishops would not pronounce against me. Certainly, (as the text of my letter to Miss Giberne shows, and as *I well recollect*) it was promised to me, that the Bishops should be silent about Tract 90. Well, the Long Vacation of 1841 came and . . . one after another, as thick as hail, came out Episcopal Charges against me.' (*LD* VIII, p. 190, n. 1)

In the *Apologia* Newman did not think it necessary to name who told him, which J. D. Coleridge wondered about, especially who could have spoken for Coleridge's own bishop, Phillpotts of Exeter. Newman replied, 'I cannot conceive why it is necessary to say who told me. I am willing to be considered credulous and dull – though I don't think I was – I think I had the best reason for believing what I believed; but whether I had sufficientreason or not, believe it I did, and that belief accounts for my silence. As to the objection you offer about your own Bishop, the words on which I relied expressly said "That perhaps *one* or two Bishops would charge, but that would be all – it would not be a general charging". The Bishops contemplated I conceive to be John B. Sumner [Bishop of Chester at the time] and H. Phillpotts.'

In the previous paragraph of this letter Newman wrote, 'I never defended Number 90, though I didn't withdraw it. This seemed mysterious. People could not make out whether I thought it untenable or not. The open frank way is, to say out what you have to say, to show fight or to give in. Again, my *friends* defended it, and they gave opposite interpretations. Pusey almost said that the Catholic interpretation of the Articles was the only true interpretation. Ward said that it was a non-natural interpretation. I kept silence; till now, I have never given the reason why I kept silence; now I have given it. It was part of an understanding between myself, and one who had a right to know what the Bishops meant to do or wished, and to speak for them. "If I kept silence, they would not condemn it". This was a compromise; and, in the belief of saving it from condemnation, I did keep silence. All that is necessary for the appositeness of the explanation is the fact that I did so understand what was said to me from authority – and this the contemporary letters of mine which I have published sufficiently show.' (*LD* XXI, p. 262)

9. Newman always maintained this. 'I spoke, what I internally felt, and what I was called by my Bishop to say, but what (from my love of the Roman Church) I would not have said *then*, (though I had said worse things in years past,) unless it had been extorted from me by what I held to be then competent authority. . . . I recollect saying to Dr. Manning at the time, "I can't help it – the Bishop asks me – *I* don't wish to speak against the Church of Rome – but it is a fact I think this and that of her, and I *must* tell out my opinions on the subject".' (*LD* XVIII, pp. 101–2)

CHAPTER NINETEEN: THE AFTERMATH

1. A fair number of these letters have been printed in Volume VIII of *LD*; many more are in the archives of the Birmingham Oratory.
2. For details of these efforts at reunion, see *W. G. Ward*, 191ff., and Middleton, *Newman & Bloxam*, ch. 5: 'Letters on Reunion,' pp. 101–62.

3. Bernard Basset, *Newman at Littlemore*, Warley [1983], p. 32.

4. He also wrote to Samuel Wood who was unsettled about the catholicity of the English Church, 'If it is not presumptuous to say, I trust I have been favoured with a much more definite view of the (promised) inward evidence of the Presence of Christ with us in the Sacraments, now that the outward notes of it are being removed. And I am content to be with Moses in the desert – or with Elijah excommunicated from the Temple.' (13 December 1841, *LD* VIII, p. 375)

5. The successive stages of the controversy are given in the Introductory Note to vol. VIII of *LD*.

CHAPTER TWENTY: LIFE AT LITTLEMORE

1. This and subsequent letters of Dalgairns appeared in 'Letters From Oxford and Littlemore: An Unpublished Correspondence on the Oxford Movement,' ed. by E. Hermitage Day, D.D., *The Treasury*, July-October 1911. Oakeley wrote, 'Of all popular errors on the subject of the Oxford controversy, none is more palpable than that which supposes a kind of confederacy, or premeditated union among those who ultimately ended in becoming Catholics. . . . On many important questions, we were found on different sides . . . and when the various persons who are popularly identified with Oxford opinions met together in company, there was an uncertainty of sympathy, and a dread of collision . . .' Quoted in *KC*, p. 239.

2. Lockhart, *op. cit*, pp. 13–4. When at Exeter Lockhart once asked William Sewell, Professor of Moral Philosophy, to hear his confession because he felt he had had too much to drink the previous evening at a Scottish dinner and was in mortal sin. 'What a preposterous demand!. . . .' said Sewell; 'but – I recommend you to go into my bedroom and take a dose of Epsom salts: you will find a box on my dressing-table . . .' Lockhart commented, 'I asked my father for bread, and he gave me a stone.' Claude Letham, *Luigi Gentili: A Source for the Second Spring*, London 1965, p. 172.

3. Lockhart, pp. 10–12.

4. Middleton, *Newman & Bloxam*, pp. 90–1.

5. This differs slightly from the memorandum given in *KC*, p. 295, because the hours were changed in winter and summer.

6. Cecil S. Emden, *Oriel Papers*, Oxford 1948, pp. 130–71.

7. Middleton, *Newman & Bloxam*, p. 89.

8. Emily in her memoir gave the date as 1840 but refers to the 'monastery'.

9. In mentioning 'reports of miracles' Newman probably had in mind Lord Shrewsbury's pamphlet on the ecstatics of the south Tyrol. See below.

10. See letters quoted in *Apo.*, pp. 187–92, and letters of Newman to Bloxam and Phillipps, June 1841. In Middleton, *op. cit.*, pp. 148–51.

11. Shrewsbury, pp. 102–3. Newman later wrote to Catherine Ward, '. . . he

[Dr. Pusey] cannot name the individual for 1800 years who has ever held his circle of doctrines; he cannot first put down his own creed, and then refer it to doctor, or school before him . . . he witnesses for his own opinions. . . . Since he refers us to his Church and considers that he puts forth its doctrine not his own, I want to know what single individual that ever belonged to the Anglican Church does he follow.' (*LD XII*, pp. 273–4).

12. Dominique Bouhours (1632–1702), *Vie de S. Ignace* (Paris 1679). A new English translation appeared in 1840.

13. 'Notices of Books,' *British Critic*, XXXIII (January 1843).

CHAPTER TWENTY-ONE: TURNING IN THE DIRECTION OF ROME

1. Ignoring the context of this remark as well as Newman's other statements on how he read the Fathers at various times, Knockles even goes so far as to endorse Jacob Abbott's judgement that this was one of Newman's 'self-deceptions.' *op. cit.* p. 112.

2. The reference is to Macbeth's words when he discovered the double meaning of the witches' prophecy. One of the intimate friends was most probably, if not certainly, Rogers. See next chapter.

3. Greaves, *op. cit.* pp. 227–8.

4. 'Answer in Detail to Mr Kingsley's Accusations,' No. 2: 'My sermon on "Wisdom and Innocence", being the 20th of "Sermons on Subjects of the Day".' *Apo.*, 1st ed.

5. Newman used the word 'probable' in the sense defined by Dugald Stewart, in *Elements of the Philosophy of Mind*, Part II, ch. 5, sec. 14. See *LD* XI, p. 289, n. 4.

6. For the importance of time in Newman's thought and life, see Vincent Ferrer Blehl, 'En el tiempo de Dios', Salmanticensis XL. Fasc. 1 (Enero-Abril 1993), pp. 77–83.

CHAPTER TWENTY-TWO: TREADING THE PATH OF SANCTIFICATION

1. *Meditations and Considerations for a Spiritual Retreat of Eight Days.* Useful not only for Ecclesiastical Seminaries and Religious Communities, but also for the Devout Laity who wish to accomplish the Apostle's advice – 'This is the will of God, your Sanctification.' 1 Thess. 4.3. By the Very Rev. Father Stone, S. J., late of Stonyhurst College, Lancashire, Dublin 1843.

2. Gilley, whose sympathies are more with Keble than with Newman, in reviewing the correspondence affirms, 'Keble had to weigh to a nicety all these nuanced doubts; to separate out the many fine threads of an intellect and sensibility raised to a fine pitch of morbid oversensitivity by an intolerable position.' Is this not an indication that the myth of the hyper-sensitive Newman or what Fr Bacchus called the 'hyper-sensitive Newman

of fiction' is still alive? Sheridan Gilley, *Newman and His Age*, London 1990, p. 217. Newman, as so often, was simply looking at all sides of an issue.

3. Church, *Oxford Movement*, pp. 327–34.

CHAPTER TWENTY-THREE: THE PARTING OF FRIENDS

1. The lady, despite Anne's disclaimer, was actually she. See autograph of letter of Newman to Jemima, 31 August 1843.

2. *Autobiography of Robert Gregory*, ed. W. H. Hutton, London 1912, p. 28, as quoted by Middleton, *Newman at Oxford*, p. 215.

3. Edward Bellasis, *Memorials of Mr. Serjeant Bellasis* (1800–1873), London 1893, pp. 52–4.

4. Shairp, *Studies in Poetry and Philosophy*, p. 255, as quoted in *Moz.* II, p. 424, n. 1.

5. R. E. Prothero, *Life and Correspondence of Arthur Penrhyn Stanley*, London 1893, pp. 332–3.

6. A fuller draft of Newman's memorandum on this matter was discovered in the Ushaw archives after the shorter version was published in *LD* XXX, pp. 437–8. It reads:

'I have no recollection of this incident, and cannot affirm or deny its accuracy. But there are difficulties [?] in the narrative, which hinder me from receiving it. It was not likely that the contents of a sermon preached on the 5th should be known so exactly at Littlemore on the 6th that anticipating Archd. Manning, I should have acted upon the information so promptly as to have openly given orders to a much younger man [?] to tell him I would not see him. Nor was it my way to talk on serious and private matters with younger men. For instance in a few days before in a confidential letter written to Manning, speaking of my own religious unsettlement I had said: "No one in Oxf[ford] knows or here (Littlemore) but one near friend whom I felt I could not help telling the other day." Is it in keeping with his character that he should "show his grief" to a stranger. Farther I find I have entered in my journal "Manning called". This in itself tells neither for or against the story, but I will observe that I generally added a few words, e.g. I find recorded in the same weeks.'

Newman checked with Church, and in answer to his letter which spoke of Froude's version Newman added a P.S.: 'I should be very much surprised to find J. A. F. ever once slept in our house or even that he ever was in it except for a call. I half recollect his once coming to see me at Oriel or my going to him to talk over his own matter.' (*LD* XXX, p. 449, and XXXVI, pp. 4–5 and notes.)

7. Tuckwell, *op.cit.*, pp. 191–3.

8. See the two excellent articles of J. Derek Holmes, 'Newman's Reputation and *The Lives of the English Saints*', *The Catholic Historical Review*, 51

(January 1966), pp. 528–38; and 'John Henry Newman's Attitude towards History and Hagiography', *Downside Review*, 92 (1974), pp. 86–106.

CHAPTER TWENTY-FOUR: CHEERFULNESS AMID DREARINESS AND PAIN

1. For detailed accounts, see Henry Tristram, 'Dr. Russell and Newman's Conversion,' *Irish Ecclesiastical Record* no. 933 (September 1945), pp. 189–200 and Ambrose Macaulay, *Dr. Russell of Maynooth*, London 1983.
2. As Günter Biemer has pointed out, 'Thus Newman found in the process of development the key to the integration of the prophetic and episcopal tradition.' *Newman on Tradition*, Freiburg and London 1967, p. 53.
3. For the relationship of Newman and Miss Holmes as Catholics, see Joyce Sugg, *Ever Yours Affly: John Henry Newman and His Female Circle*, Leominster 1996, *passim*.

CHAPTER TWENTY-FIVE: HEADING INTO PORT

1. Church, *op. cit.*, pp. 373–4.
2. Dalgairns, *loc. cit.*, p. 121. It seems that Whately set them going 'by a letter in which he threatened to ordain no more Oxonians unless they did something'. Keble to Woodgate, 28 January 1843.
3. Marriott's letter is quoted in *Apo.*, pp. 233–4; his protest, in *Moz.* II, p. 454. Rogers' *Short Appeal to Members of Convocation on the proposed Censure on No. 90* is quoted in Church, *op. cit.*, pp. 383–4.
4. Dalgairns, *loc. cit.*, p. 121.
5. Newman had written Jemima to the same effect: 'I *do* wish people to agree with me in turning Romeward; but, as I do not wish them so to feel because *I* am so feeling, so do I deprecate their so feeling from mere disgust with what is happening among ourselves. Disgust makes no good converts; change of opinion is, commonly speaking, the work of a long time. People who are disgusted one way, may be disgusted the other.' (11 February 1845)
6. Anne Mozley left this out of her transcription.
7. 'Did St Athanasius or St Ambrose come suddenly to life, it cannot be doubted what communion he would take to be his own . . . were those same Saints, who once sojourned, one in exile, one on embassy, at Trèves, to come more northward still, and to travel until they reached another fair city, seated among groves, green meadows, and calm streams, the holy brothers would turn from many a high aisle and solemn cloister which they found there, and ask the way to some small chapel where a mass was said in the populous alley or forlorn suburb?' *Dev.* pp. 97–8; 1st ed. p. 138.
8. For further discussion of the *Essay*, see V. F. Blehl, 'John Henry Newman on the Development of Doctrine,' *Euntes Docentes* (Commentaria Urbaniana), Bd. 36 (1983), pp. 267–82. For Newman's Roman Catholic Writings on

Development, see *Roman Catholic Writings on Doctrinal Development by John Henry Newman*, ed. with translation and commentary by James Gaffney, Kansas City 1997; and Ian T. Ker, 'Newman's Theory – Development or Continuing Revelation?' *Newman and Gladstone Centennial Essays*, ed. James D. Bastable, Dublin 1978, pp. 145–59.

CHAPTER TWENTY-SIX: AN END AND A BEGINNING

1. Richard Stanton, 'Some Reminiscences of the Early Days of Cardinal Newman's Catholic Life,' *Dublin Review* XXIV – No II (Third Series), pp. 403–4.
2. 'But in truth the whole course of Christianity from the first . . . is but one series of troubles and disorders. Every century is like every other, and to those who live in it seems worse than all times before it. The Church is ever ailing, and lingers on in weakness. . . . Religion seems ever expiring, schisms dominant, the light of Truth dim, its adherents scattered. . . .' (*VM* I, pp. 354–5)
3. The extant letters are printed in *LD* XI; an Appendix, pp. 309–10, identifies the others. Isaac Williams seems to have been the only one of his Anglican friends who kept up some contact with him. Just before Newman visited him in 1865, he wrote on 31 March, 'I don't forget, but remember with much gratitude, how for twenty years you are perhaps the only one of my old friends who has never lost sight of me – but by letters, or messages, or inquiries, have ever kept up the memory of past and happy days.' (*LD* XXI, p. 441)
4. Loyalty of Cardinal Newman,' *The Month*, LXX (November 1890), pp. 306–7.

Index